THE KNUTH FAMILY

THE KNUTH FAMILY

TEACHINGS AND COMMENTARIES

on the

NEW TESTAMENT

TEACHINGS AND COMMENTARIES

on the

NEW TESTAMENT

ED J. PINEGAR *and* RICHARD J. ALLEN

Covenant Communications, Inc.

Cover painting *Sermon on the Mount* by Carl Heinrich Bloch. Courtesy of Det Nationalhistoriske Museum på Frederiksborg, Hillerød, Denmark
Cover and book design © 2006 by Covenant Communications, Inc.

Published by Covenant Communications, Inc.
American Fork, Utah

Printed in Canada
First Printing: October 2006

11 10 09 08 07 06   10 9 8 7 6 5 4 3 2 1

ISBN 1-59811-080-2

PREFACE

The record of the Savior's mortal ministry of mercy and Atonement is sacred evidence of the scope and power of His infinite love and redemption. This priceless chronicle reinforces and strengthens our personal commitment to truly honor our covenants. The greatest story ever told did not emerge without roots or context. It was the fulfillment of a divine plan originating in the premortal realm before the foundations of the world. "Here am I, send me" (Abr. 3:27) were the words that inaugurated the mission of salvation for all mankind. From the moment that God the Father approved and activated this holy commission for His First Begotten, "full of grace and truth" (John 1:14), to bring about the eternal plan of happiness, the pathway toward the ultimate triumph of light over darkness, good over evil, life over death, was established with irreversible momentum and infinite power. The Beloved Son of God was to become the "author of eternal salvation unto all them that obey Him" (Heb. 5:9). He was to ensure the perpetuity of life beyond death. He was to be "the life and the light of the world" (Alma 38:9; D&C 10:70; 11:28). That is the message of the New Testament.

With the voice of prophecy, Isaiah declared, "For unto us a child is born, unto us a son is given" (Isa. 9:6). This child, born of Mary in the stable, was Jehovah of the Old Testament, signifying "the Unchangeable One," "The Eternal I Am." He was the Son of God—the only Begotten Son of God in the flesh. This little child born beneath the light of a new star was the Messiah or (in the Greek formulation) the Christ, meaning, the "Anointed"—the one divinely commissioned, authorized, and foreordained to complete the mission of the Atonement. This little child, who "grew, and waxed strong in spirit, filled with wisdom," having the "grace of God . . . upon him" (Luke 2:40), was the Great Creator, the Word of God, the Giver of Life, the Light of the World. This young child grew into manhood and immersed Himself in the ministry of salvation. He was Emmanuel (or Immanuel), "God among us," with a mortal mission of divine sanctification as the Messenger of the Covenant who condescended to come among us as the Good Shepherd, fearing neither betrayal nor death. This Son of God, "full of grace and truth" (2 Ne. 2:6; D&C 66:12; 93:11; Moses 1:6, 32; 5:7; 6:52; 7:11) was Jesus, "God is help," even the Redeemer, the one chosen to bring about the infinite sacrifice and Atonement on behalf of mankind—the Lamb of God, the Bread of Life. Passing through the crucifixion and resurrection, according to the will of the Father, He became the Life of the World, even the great King, Judge, Mediator, Advocate, and Bridegroom—the same who is to come again in glory to inaugurate the millennial reign and serve as our Law Giver, the Prince of Peace, and the Covenant Father of all who shall believe on Him and overcome in faith and righteousness.

The New Testament tells this story of salvation and hope through the mouths of personal witnesses who labored with Jesus in the ministry, suffered with Him as He wrought the infinite Atonement, gloried with Him in the resurrection, obeyed His commandment to take the message of the gospel unto all the world (Matt. 28:19–20), and in many cases sealed their testimony with their lives. The "New Testament" means, in effect, the "New Covenant," or the covenant between God and His children that binds them to Him with sacred promises to be fulfilled on the basis of everlasting principles and powers inherent in God's design to "bring to pass the immortality and eternal life of man" (Moses 1:39). This covenant or testament was ordained of God and foretold by His prophets:

> Behold, the days come, saith the Lord, that I will make a new covenant with the house of Israel, and with the house of Judah:
>
> Not according to the covenant that I made with their fathers in the day that I took them by the hand to bring them out of the land of Egypt; which my covenant they brake, although I was an husband unto them, saith the Lord:
>
> But this shall be the covenant that I will make with the house of Israel; After those days, saith the Lord, I will put my law in their inward parts, and write it in their hearts; and will be their God, and they shall be my people. (Jer. 31:31–33)

Can we write the message of the New Testament in our hearts and become the "children of the prophets" and the "children of the covenant" (3 Ne. 20:25–26)? Can we follow in the footsteps of the Savior and become, as He commanded, "even as I am" (3 Ne. 27:27)? The answer given by the New Testament and confirmed by the resurrected Savior to the ancient American Saints is a resounding "Yes"—if we will but honor our covenants and mold our daily lives in the spirit of meekness and righteousness after the patterns set by our Lord and Master. In this current volume, the authors have attempted to present the patterns, principles, and precepts of salvation that are formulated in the New Testament as the record given of Christ's ministry of hope and life, confirmed by all the holy scriptures. We are told that "the government shall be upon his shoulder: and his name shall be called Wonderful, Counsellor, The mighty God, The everlasting Father, The Prince of Peace" (Isa. 9:6). We are assured "that there shall be no other name given nor any other way nor means whereby salvation can come unto the children of men, only in and through the name of Christ, the Lord Omnipotent" (Mosiah 3:17). In that spirit, the authors hope that this volume will help the reader to understand and apply the scriptures prayerfully and invite the Spirit to confirm these truths and sustain every noble effort to come unto Christ and follow in His footsteps.

The approach we have used is thematic, each major theme in the reading selection being addressed in a consistent pattern of study that includes relevant scriptural passages; an introduction; a "moment of truth," giving the historical context of pertinent sections from the New Testament; selected statements from modern-day prophets; an enrichment section, where appropriate; one or more illustrations and scriptural applications for our time; and a concluding summary. We encourage you to "liken the scriptures" unto yourselves, as Nephi counseled, "that ye may have hope" (1 Ne. 19: 23, 24).

The authors wish to express appreciation for the undeviating support of the staff members of Covenant Communications and their devoted interest in this project.

Special thanks go to Pat Pinegar, wife of Ed Pinegar, and to Carol Lynn Allen, wife of Richard Allen, for their support and encouragement as this work progressed to its completion.

Ed J. Pinegar
Richard J. Allen

ABBREVIATIONS

AGQ   Joseph Fielding Smith. *Answers to Gospel Questions.* 5 vols. Salt Lake City: Deseret Book, 1957–66.

CR   Conference Report. Salt Lake City: The Church of Jesus Christ of Latter-day Saints.

Discourses   John A. Widtsoe, sel. *Discourses of Brigham Young.* Salt Lake City: Deseret Book, 1954.

DNTC   Bruce R. McConkie. *Doctrinal New Testament Commentary,* 3 vols. Salt Lake City: Bookcraft, 1965–73.

DS   Joseph Fielding Smith. *Doctrines of Salvation.* Ed. Bruce R. McConkie. 3 vols. Salt Lake City: Bookcraft, 1954–56.

Encyclopedia Daniel H. Ludlow, ed. *Encyclopedia of Mormonism,* 4 vols. New York: Macmillan, 1992.

HC   Joseph Smith. *History of the Church of Jesus Christ of Latter-day Saints.* Ed. B. H. Roberts. 7 vols. Salt Lake City: The Church of Jesus Christ of Latter-day Saints, 1932–51.

JC   James E. Talmage. *Jesus the Christ: A Study of the Messiah and His Mission According to Holy Scriptures Both Ancient and Modern.* Salt Lake City: Deseret Book, 1983.

JD   Brigham Young and others. *Journal of Discourses.* 26 vols. Liverpool: George Q. Cannon, 1855–86.

MD   Bruce R. McConkie. *Mormon Doctrine.* 2nd ed. Salt Lake City: Bookcraft, 1966.

TETB   Ezra Taft Benson. *The Teachings of Ezra Taft Benson.* Salt Lake City: Bookcraft, 1988.

TGBH   Gordon B. Hinckley. *Teachings of Gordon B. Hinckley.* Salt Lake City: Deseret Book, 1997.

THBL   Harold B. Lee. *The Teachings of Harold B. Lee.* Ed. Clyde J. Williams. Salt Lake City: Bookcraft, 1996.

THWH   Howard W. Hunter. *The Teachings of Howard W. Hunter.* Ed. Clyde J. Williams. Salt Lake City: Bookcraft, 1997.

TPJS   Joseph Smith. *Teachings of the Prophet Joseph Smith.* Comp. Joseph Fielding Smith. Salt Lake City: Deseret Book, 1976.

TSWK   Spencer W. Kimball. *The Teachings of Spencer W. Kimball.* Ed. Edward L. Kimball. Salt Lake City: Bookcraft, 1982.

TABLE OF CONTENTS

CHAPTER 1

JESUS IS *the* CHRIST—
THE PROMISED MESSIAH

Reading Assignment: Isaiah 61:1–3; JST, Luke 3:4–11; John 1:1–14; 20:31.

Additional Reading: Luke 4:16–21; Mosiah 3:5–10; Abraham 3:22–27.

> *"God anointed Jesus of Nazareth with the Holy Ghost and with power" (Acts 10:38). Jesus was the Anointed One. Because of this fact, He was accorded two specific titles. One was the Messiah, which in Hebrew means "the anointed." The other was the Christ, which comes from the Greek word that also means "the anointed." Thus, "Jesus is spoken of as the Christ and the Messiah, which means he is the one anointed of the Father to be his personal representative in all things pertaining to the salvation of mankind" (BD, "Anointed One," 609). Scriptures declare that Christ is the only name under heaven whereby salvation comes (see 2 Ne. 25:20). So one may add either of these titles to signify adoration for Jesus: the Christ or the Messiah, both signifying an anointing by God for that supernal responsibility."*

—Russell M. Nelson, "Jesus the Christ: Our Master and More," *Ensign*, Apr. 2000, 11.

THEMES *for* LIVING

1. Search and Ponder the Prophecies of the Savior's Mission
2. Witness and Testify that Jesus Is the Christ—The Life and Light of the World

INTRODUCTION

All scriptures testify and witness that Jesus was and is the promised Messiah, the Anointed One, even Jesus the Christ, the Savior and Redeemer of the world. His mission was to do the will of the Father. The Savior describes His mission in terms of His gospel. He said:

> Behold I have given unto you my gospel, and this is the gospel which I have given unto you—that I came into the world to do the will of my Father, because my Father sent me.
>
> And my Father sent me that I might be lifted up upon the cross; and after that I had been lifted up upon the cross, that I might draw all men unto me, that as I have been lifted up by men even so should men be lifted up by the Father, to stand before me, to be judged of their works, whether they be good or whether they be evil—
>
> And for this cause have I been lifted up; therefore, according to the power of the Father I will draw all men unto me, that they may be judged according to their works.
>
> And it shall come to pass, that whoso repenteth and is baptized in my name shall be filled; and if he endureth to the end, behold, him will I hold guiltless before my Father at that day when I shall stand to judge the world. (3 Ne. 27:13–16)

Old Testament and Book of Mormon prophets prophesied of the coming of Jesus Christ and His mission as the Savior and Redeemer of the world. Nephi records, "He doeth not anything save it be for the benefit of the world; for he loveth the world, even that he layeth down his own life that he may draw all men unto him. Wherefore, he commandeth none that they shall not partake of his salvation" (2 Ne. 26:24).

Our testimonies of Christ will deepen as we come to realize and remember His goodness and our total dependence upon Him and His grace through our Heavenly Father's plan. He is our personal Savior and nurtures us in all things as described by Alma:

> And he shall go forth, suffering pains and afflictions and temptations of every kind; and this that the word might be fulfilled which saith he will take upon him the pains and the sicknesses of his people.
>
> And he will take upon him death, that he may loose the bands of death which bind his people; and he will take upon him their infirmities, that his bowels may be filled with mercy, according to the flesh, that he may know according to the flesh how to succor his people according to their infirmities. (Alma 7:11–12)

We are commanded to seek our Savior and come to know Him: "And this is life eternal, that they might know thee the only true God, and Jesus Christ, whom thou hast sent" (John 17:3). As our knowledge and testimony of Christ increase, we will seek to become like Him and take upon ourselves His divine nature (see 2 Pet. 1:3–12).

1. SEARCH AND PONDER THE PROPHECIES OF THE SAVIOR'S MISSION

THEME: The prophets foretold the mission of the Savior Jesus Christ. Isaiah spoke of His preaching to the meek, blessing the brokenhearted, proclaiming liberty to the captives, and comforting those who mourn (see Isa. 61:1–2). Luke described the Savior's mission as one of bringing salvation to mankind, gathering the lost sheep, providing a way for our sins to be forgiven, and shining forth as the light of the world. Jesus brought to pass the blessing of the resurrection and would administer justice so as to convince the ungodly of their wickedness (see JST, Luke 3:4–9).

MOMENT OF TRUTH

I really like this quote – put it in the front of my N.T.

To open the pages of the New Testament is to cross over the threshold of spiritual discovery and enter into sacred precincts. Because this sacred account was preserved through the blessings of heaven, we can retrace the footsteps of the Master as He embarks upon His mortal ministry and consummates His divine mission of Atonement and redemption. John provides the compass for our scriptural journey when he states with profound simplicity: "In the beginning was the Word, and the Word was with God, and the Word was God. The same was in the beginning with God. All things were made by him; and without him was not any thing made that was made. In him was life; and the life was the light of men. And the light shineth in darkness; and the darkness comprehended it not" (John 1:1–5).

It is the Word who provides for us the illumination to comprehend and internalize the truths of the New Testament. Our moment of truth is the realization, through the Spirit, that the mission of the Word is for *us*—undertaken and completed on *our* behalf. He is our personal Savior. He is our personal Advocate with the Father. He is the perfected "author of eternal salvation unto all them that obey him" (Heb. 5:9). As we study and ponder the principles and truths of the New Testament—confirmed and enriched through the other scriptures of the holy canon—we find our true identity. We discover that we are indeed the "seed" of the Master, as Isaiah proclaimed:

> He was taken from prison and from judgment: and who shall declare his generation? for he was cut off out of the land of the living: for the transgression of my people was he stricken.
>
> And he made his grave with the wicked, and with the rich in his death; because he had done no violence, neither was any deceit in his mouth.

Yet it pleased the Lord to bruise him; he hath put him to grief: when thou shalt make his soul an offering for sin, he shall see his seed, he shall prolong his days, and the pleasure of the Lord shall prosper in his hand. (Isa. 53:8–10; compare the words of Abinadi in Mosiah 15:10–11)

MODERN PROPHETS SPEAK

Bruce R. McConkie:

As part of the great mission of our Lord was the command, "To open the blind eyes, to *bring out the prisoners from the prison,* and them that sit in darkness out of the prison house" (Isa. 42:7; Ps. 142:7; 146:7). He was sent, "to bind up the broken-hearted, *to proclaim liberty to the captives, and the opening of the prison to them that are bound*" (Isa. 61:1–3; Luke 4:16–21). And as Peter taught, while our Lord's body lay in the tomb, his Spirit "went and preached unto *the spirits in prison*" (1 Pet. 3: 18–22; 4:6; D&C 76:73–74; *Gospel Doctrine,* 5th ed., 472–76; *DS,* 129–180). "Let the dead speak forth anthems of eternal praise to the King Immanuel, who hath ordained, before the world was, that which would enable us to redeem them out of their prison; for *the prisoners shall go free*" (D&C 128:22). (*MD,* 601–602)

ILLUSTRATIONS FOR OUR TIMES

A Universal Witness for the Savior

All things testify of Christ, as Alma explained to the dissident Korihor: "The scriptures are laid before thee, yea, and all things denote there is a God; yea, even the earth, and all things that are upon the face of it, yea, and its motion, yea, and also all the planets which move in their regular form do witness that there is a Supreme Creator" (Alma 30:44). M. Russell Ballard expands on this thought:

The Book of Mormon is an interesting mix of Old and New Testament styles and forms. . . . The Book of Mormon is a compilation of fifteen books, or scriptural accounts, written by men with names like Nephi, Alma, Helaman, Mosiah, and Ether. It includes narrative, faith-promoting stories and experiences, historical accounts of the rise and fall of entire civilizations, doctrinal essays, testimonies of the divine mission of the resurrected Lord Jesus Christ, and prophecy regarding the days in which we live. The centerpiece of the record is a moving account of the appearance of the Lord Jesus Christ to a group of His "other sheep" (John 10:16) on the American continent soon after His death and resurrection in Jerusalem. (*Our Search for Happiness: An Invitation to Understand The Church of Jesus Christ of the Latter-day Saints,* 45)

It is interesting to note that in the 6,607 verses of the Book of Mormon, there are 3,925 references concerning Jesus Christ and His mission—using over 100 titles or descriptions of the Lord Jesus Christ. Is it any wonder that the Book of Mormon is subtitled Another Testament of Jesus Christ? Moroni's title page reads: "And also to the convincing of the Jew and gentile that JESUS is the CHRIST, the ETERNAL GOD, manifesting himself unto all nations."

As we search the scriptures, hearken to our living prophets, and feast upon the word of God, we will strengthen our testimony of the Lord Jesus Christ. This will deepen our conversion, and we will seek to become like Him and take upon ourselves His divine nature. [Pinegar] *Strengthening testimony requires us to work take active part in keeping it strong.*

"Come, Follow Me"

Many years ago, when I was a young boy, my father took several of us on a fishing trip to a remote lake in the Canadian Rockies. We hiked over a towering summit and down into the lake area, otherwise accessible only by a narrow goat trail leading across and up a dangerous cliff at the end of a box canyon. Unfortunately, the inbound hike took much longer than expected, leaving us with the unpleasant choice between spending the night in the wilds without overnight equipment or braving the treacherous trip down the cliff located a short distance beyond the edge of the lake. Just looking over the edge at the valley floor thousands of feet below was enough to instill terror in our hearts. What to do?

Just at the moment of our greatest panic, we were surprised to hear laughter and whistling resounding through the evergreen trees. Presently, two men appeared from nowhere, carrying their fishing gear and wearing broad smiles. They must have sensed our forlorn spirits, for they joked and teased us with their banter. One of them, named Slim, pronounced the magic words: "We can take you down the cliff. Come follow us. And don't look down." With that, we inched our way behind them along the goat trail, in some parts only an inch or two wide, clutching the rock face above us for balance. After following our expert guides each step of the way for what seemed like an eternity, we completed the transit and moved gratefully into safer territory.

Since then, I have often thought of the words of those guides: "Come follow us." They knew the trail. They knew the dangers. They had cultivated the techniques and the attitude of success. And they knew how to lead the inexperienced to safety.

On the cliffs of life there are dangers lurking. There is an abyss of spiritual emptiness that yawns upward to the lonely traveler. But then the words of the Savior echo in our hearts: "Come, follow me" (Luke 18:22), and we know that the Shepherd is near, guiding us into pathways of security and joy. "My sheep hear my voice," He said, "and I know them, and they follow me" (John 10:27). The word of the Lord is the iron rod across the cliffs of life. It is the anchor to the fearful heart. It is the comfort to the wary and the balance to the unsteady.

The Savior's condescension in taking upon Himself mortality marked the fulfillment of millennia of prophetic proclamations concerning His atoning ministry. The consummate summary of His message to us is the simple phrase, "Come, follow me" (Luke 18:22). He is our only sure guide, our only channel of grace and redemption. [Allen]

LIKENING THE SCRIPTURES TO OUR LIVES

John 20:31 But these are written, that ye might believe that Jesus is the Christ, the Son of God; and that believing ye might have life through his name.

Application: All scriptures have the underlying foundation and purpose to show that Jesus is the Christ and Savior of the world. As we search the scriptures, we can learn to recognize His goodness and love toward us in all things.

2. WITNESS AND TESTIFY THAT JESUS IS THE CHRIST—THE LIGHT AND LIFE OF THE WORLD

THEME: We have been commanded to stand as a witness of God at all times and in all places (see Mosiah 18:9) and to testify of Christ (see Matt. 16:13–20; 1 Cor. 1:6; Rev. 19:10; Alma 7:13; Moro. 7:44; 10:7; D&C 76:22–24).

MOMENT OF TRUTH

The Savior was explicit during His earthly ministry in bearing personal testimony of His true identity:

> Then said Jesus unto them [the Pharisees], When ye have lifted up the Son of man, then shall ye know that I am he, and that I do nothing of myself; but as my Father hath taught me, I speak these things.
>
> And he that sent me is with me: the Father hath not left me alone; for I do always those things that please him.
>
> As he spake these words, many believed on him.
>
> Then said Jesus to those Jews which believed on him, If ye continue in my word, then are ye my disciples indeed;
>
> And ye shall know the truth, and the truth shall make you free. (John 8:28–32; cf. John 9:9; 13:19; 18:5–6, 8)

Our moment of truth in the wake of such testimony is to seek the confirmation of the Spirit, so that we might also stand as witnesses of the divinity of the Savior and His mission. Each time we articulate before others our heartfelt conviction of the truth of the gospel of Jesus Christ, we add a thread of strength and courage to the magnificent tapestry depicting the history of God's dealings with His children within the framework of the plan of salvation.

MODERN PROPHETS SPEAK

Gordon B. Hinckley:

> Absolutely basic to our faith is our testimony of Jesus Christ as the Son of God, who under a divine plan was born in Bethlehem of Judea. . . . In the course of his brief earthly ministry, he walked the dusty roads of Palestine healing the sick, causing the blind to see, raising the dead, teaching doctrines both transcendent and beautiful. . . . He "went about doing good," and was hated for it (Acts 10:38). His enemies came against him. He was seized, tried on spurious charges, convicted to satisfy the cries of the mob, and condemned to die on Calvary's cross.
>
> The nails pierced his hands and feet, and he hung in agony and pain, giving himself a ransom for the sins of all men. He died crying, "Father, forgive them; for they know not what they do" (Luke 23:34).
>
> He was buried in a borrowed tomb and on the third day rose from the grave. He came forth triumphant, in a victory over death, the first fruits of all that slept. With his resurrection came the promise to all men that life is everlasting, that even as in Adam all die, in Christ all are made alive (see 1 Cor. 15:20-22). Nothing in all of human history equals the wonder, the splendor, the magnitude, or the fruits of the matchless life of the Son of God, who died for each of us. He is our Savior. He is our Redeemer. . . .
>
> He is the chief cornerstone of the church which bears his name, The Church of Jesus Christ of Latter-day Saints. There is no other name given among men whereby we can be saved (see Acts 4:12). He is the author of our salvation, the giver of eternal life (see Heb. 5:9). There is none to equal him. There never has been. There never will be. Thanks be to God for the gift of his Beloved Son, who gave his life that we might live, and who is the chief, immovable cornerstone of our faith and his church. ("The Cornerstones of Our Faith," *Ensign,* Nov. 1984, 51–52)

ILLUSTRATIONS FOR OUR TIMES

The Power of Testimony

Paul taught that "no man can say that Jesus is the Lord, but by the Holy Ghost" (1 Cor. 12:3). Once that revelatory confirmation has been given to an individual through the love and grace of the Lord, it is incumbent upon him or her to bear witness of the Savior, as Alma the Elder said, "at all times and in all things, and in all places that ye may be in, even until death, that ye may be redeemed of God, and be numbered with those of the first resurrection, that ye may have eternal life" (Mosiah 18:9). The expression of one's testimony often takes courage—whether in the life of a plucky youngster at the podium on testimony Sunday, in the confirmation of standards by brave teens being coaxed by peers to deviate from principle, or in the fearless and spirited pronouncements of missionaries among strangers. Not infrequently, such a moment of courage comes in unexpected ways into the lives of those who have been blessed with a testimony of the Savior and His mission. Will we be prepared to act with faith and valor?

From the scriptures we learn how those with a resolute will stood up to the enemies of truth, displaying devotion and uncompromising courage. Thus the Prophet Abinadi, facing the tribunal of the evil King Noah, encountered his moment of courage when he was commanded to recant his witness of the Savior, or face death:

> Now Abinadi said unto him: I say unto you, I will not recall the words which I have spoken unto you concerning this people, for they are true; and that ye may know of their surety I have suffered myself that I have fallen into your hands.
>
> Yea, and I will suffer even until death, and I will not recall my words, and they shall stand as a testimony against you. And if ye slay me ye will shed innocent blood, and this shall also stand as a testimony against you at the last day. (Mosiah 17:9–10)

With similar courage, the imprisoned Prophet Jeremiah, when confronted by King Zedekiah of Judah, confirmed unflinchingly what the Spirit had already communicated through him, i.e., that Jerusalem was about to fall because of the wickedness of the people: "Then Zedekiah the king sent, and took him out: and the king asked him secretly in his house, and said, Is there any word from the Lord? And Jeremiah said, There is: for, said he, thou shalt be delivered into the hand of the king of Babylon" (Jer. 37:17). In the same spirit, Lehi and Nephi, the sons of Helaman, did not recoil from the threat of their detractors in bearing powerful testimony of the Savior—even from within a prison of fire (Hel. 5). Nor did the Prophet Samuel shrink—even at the peril of his life—from the commission of calling a perverse nation to repentance (Hel. 13–14). Similarly, the Prophet Moroni, when pursued relentlessly by his enemies who killed all who would not deny the Christ, stood firmly in his witness: "And I, Moroni, will not deny the Christ; wherefore, I wander whithersoever I can for the safety of mine own life" (Moro. 1: 3). As a result of his stalwart service in preserving the sacred records, we have the Book of Mormon, which serves as "Another Testament of Jesus Christ."

The Savior warned: "But whosoever shall deny me before men, him will I also deny before my Father which is in heaven" (Matt. 10: 33). The young Joseph Smith, benefactor of the extraordinary First Vision, instinctively understood that verity and knew that he had to withstand the local ministers who reviled against him for his testimony:

> However, it was nevertheless a fact that I had beheld a vision. I have thought since, that I felt much like Paul, when he made his defense before King Agrippa, and related the account of the vision he had when he saw a light, and heard a voice; but still there were but few who believed him; some said he was dishonest, others said he was mad; and he was ridiculed and reviled. But all this did not destroy the reality of his vision. He had seen a vision, he knew he had, and all the persecution under heaven could not make it otherwise; and though they should persecute him unto death, yet he knew, and would know to his latest breath, that he had both seen a light and heard a voice speaking unto him, and all the world could not make him think or believe otherwise.
>
> So it was with me. I had actually seen a light, and in the midst of that light I saw two Personages, and they did in reality speak to me; and though I was hated and persecuted for saying that I had seen a vision, yet it was true; and while they were persecuting me, reviling me, and speaking all manner of evil against me falsely for so saying, I was led to say in my heart: Why persecute me for telling the truth? I have actually seen a vision; and who am I that I can withstand God, or why does the world think to make me deny what I have actually seen? For I had seen a vision; I knew it, and I knew that God knew it, and I could not deny it, neither dared I do it; at least I knew that by so doing I would offend God, and come under condemnation. (JS—H 1:24–25)

And so it is with us all. The glorious witness of the Spirit is not imparted to the faithful only to remain confined within the heart, but it demands expression so that others may be blessed by our testimony of the Savior and His plan of salvation and come to "believe that Jesus is the Christ" (John 20:31). [Allen]

LIKENING THE SCRIPTURES TO OUR LIVES

Matthew 16:16–17 And Simon Peter answered and said, Thou art the Christ, the Son of the living God. And Jesus answered and said unto him, Blessed art thou, Simon Bar-jona: for flesh and blood hath not revealed it unto thee, but my Father which is in heaven.

Application: We can come to know that Jesus is the Christ in the same manner—by revelation. It is the only way. It is central to the gospel plan that we receive a witness by the power of the Holy Ghost that Jesus is the Christ. This comes as we study, pray, and live His doctrine, knowing that He was indeed sent from God the Father to be the Savior of the world (see John 7:17–18).

SUMMARY

From the account of the premortal council in heaven, we know that the Savior was chosen of the Father to accomplish the work and glory of the plan of redemption: "And the Lord said: Whom shall I send? And one answered like unto the Son of Man: Here am I, send me" (Abr. 3:27). Jesus was indeed sent. He accomplished His divine mission, as He confirmed to the ancient American Saints: "Behold, I am Jesus Christ, whom the prophets testified shall come into the world. And behold, I am the light and the life of the world; and I have drunk out of that bitter cup which the Father hath given me, and have glorified the Father in taking upon me the sins of the world, in the which I have suffered the will of the Father in all things from the beginning" (3 Ne. 11:10–11).

As we search and ponder the prophecies of the Savior's mission and read and reread the account of His mortal ministry, we will come to know through the Spirit that He is indeed the Word, the very Son of God. Thus we will be enabled to witness and testify that Jesus is the Christ—the Life and Light of the world. Gordon B. Hinckley has shown us the pattern:

> I believe in the Lord Jesus Christ, the Son of the eternal, living God. I believe in Him as the Firstborn of the Father and the Only Begotten of the Father in the flesh. I believe in Him as an individual, separate and distinct from His Father. . . .
>
> I believe that in His mortal life He was the one perfect man to walk the earth. I believe that in His words are to be found that light and truth which, if observed, would save the world and bring exaltation to mankind. I believe that in His priesthood rests divine authority—the power to bless, the power to heal, the power to govern in the earthly affairs of God, the power to bind in the heavens that which is bound upon the earth. ("Words of the Prophet: My Testimony of Christ," *New Era*, Apr. 2001, 4)

CHAPTER 2

INCREASING OUR FAITH *in the* LORD JESUS CHRIST THROUGH *the* RIGHTEOUSNESS *of* OTHERS

Reading Assignment: Luke 1; Matthew 1.

Additional Reading: Isaiah 40:3; 1 Nephi 10:7–10.

I shall never forget him. He is poor in the things of the world. But he is educated—a teacher by profession. I know little of his circumstances. But this I know—when we talked with him, the fire of faith burned in his heart, and our own faith was quickened also.

As we traveled from that scene and there was time to meditate, I wished that faith of his kind was found more widely, both among us and among others. His example has provided a text for me. It is found in the fifth verse of the seventeenth chapter of Luke. Jesus had been teaching his disciples by precept and parable. "And the apostles said unto the Lord, Increase our faith." This is my prayer for all of us—"Lord, Increase our faith." . . . Increase our faith to bridge the chasms of uncertainty and doubt.

—GORDON B. HINCKLEY, "LORD, INCREASE OUR FAITH," *ENSIGN,* NOV. 1987, 52.

THEMES *for* LIVING
1. The Role of Forerunner of Christ—John the Baptist, an Elias
2. Mary the Mother of the Son of God—An Example of Righteousness

INTRODUCTION

We all seek to increase our faith in the Lord Jesus Christ. Faith is the foundation of all righteousness. It is required if one is to please God (see Heb. 11:6). It is the power by which all things are done (see Ether 12). Faith has three degrees: (1) that of hope and belief, (2) the moving cause of our actions, and (3) the power to do the will of the Lord. It is the first principle of the gospel of Jesus Christ and leads us to repent, keep sacred covenants, receive the blessing of the Holy Ghost from our Heavenly Father, and endure to the end. We increase our faith as we hear the word of God (see Rom. 10:17), as we fast and pray with all our hearts (see Hel. 3:35), and as we witness the lives of righteous Saints. Such is the case as we study the lives of Elisabeth, Zacharias, John the Baptist, Mary, and Joseph. We can be empowered by their examples of goodness and righteousness.

1. THE ROLE OF FORERUNNER OF CHRIST— JOHN THE BAPTIST, AN ELIAS

THEME: It is vital that we heed the promptings of the Lord and honor our God-given commissions to help prepare the way for the unfolding of His eternal purposes.

MOMENT OF TRUTH

Certain commissions in the great design of our Father in Heaven are so fundamentally important that they are attended by angelic ministrations. Such was the case in regard to the coming mission of John the Baptist, chosen and sent to prepare the way in mortality for the very Son of God. An angelic messenger, Gabriel, announced the birth and mission of John the Baptist to his future parents, Zacharias and Elisabeth. They proved to be faithful in their stewardship of sustaining and supporting the work of an Elias—even the one who was to anticipate the coming of the Savior and open the pathways for His foreordained mission of redemption.

MODERN PROPHETS SPEAK

Bruce R. McConkie:

> Jesus' companions knew that John the Baptist—whose spirit body they had seen on the holy mount—as Gabriel promised, had come before the Lord "in the spirit and power of Elias, to turn the hearts of the fathers to the children, and the disobedient to the wisdom of the just; to make ready a people prepared for the Lord" (Luke 1:17). They knew that when the Jews sent priests and Levites from Jerusalem to ask

John, "Who art thou? . . . Art thou Elias?" the Son of Zacharias had said "he was Elias," but that he was "not that Elias who was to restore all things." They knew that John, speaking of Christ, had then testified: "He is that prophet, even Elias, who, coming after me, is preferred before me, whose shoe's latchet I am not worthy to unloose, or whose place I am not able to fill" (JST, John 1:20–28). They also knew that when John, imprisoned by Antipas in Machaerus, had sent messengers to Jesus, that they might learn for themselves of his divine Sonship, Jesus had said of John: "If ye will receive it, this is Elias, which was for to come" (Matt. 11:14). (*The Mortal Messiah: From Bethlehem to Calvary,* 4 vols., 3:65)

ILLUSTRATIONS FOR OUR TIME

Bruce R. McConkie:

Joseph Smith taught that a preparatory work, one that lays a foundation for a greater work, one that goes before to prepare the way for a greater which is to come, is a work performed by the *spirit of Elias.* This principle is called the *doctrine of Elias.* The Prophet explained that *the spirit and doctrine of Elias pertain to the Aaronic Priesthood only.* He used himself as an example, saying that he worked by the spirit of Elias from the time he received the Aaronic Priesthood (which is a preparatory priesthood) until the Melchizedek Priesthood was restored. In the same way John the Baptist, he explained, served in the spirit and power of Elias; that is, as our Lord's forerunner, serving in the lesser priesthood, he prepared the way for a greater work.

Work done by authority of the Melchizedek Priesthood is not performed in accordance with the spirit of Elias. To distinguish between the spirit of Elias and a higher power, the Prophet said that a man could be baptized by the spirit of Elias, but he could not receive the Holy Ghost by that power, and "any man that comes, having the spirit and power of Elias, he will not transcend his bounds" (*Teachings,* 335–41). . . .

No better illustration is found in the revelations of one who acted in the spirit and power of Elias—and yet who expressly disavowed any claim to being the Elias who was to restore all things—than that seen in the ministry of John the Baptist. Gabriel foretold that John would go before the Lord "in the spirit and power of Elias" (Luke 1:17); and the skeptical and unbelieving Jews—knowing that *Elijah* was to come again and that *Elias* was to restore all things—made pointed inquiry of John to determine if he claimed to fulfil ancient predictions in this field.

"And this is the record of John, when the Jews sent priests and Levites from Jerusalem, to ask him: Who art thou? *And he confessed, and denied not that he was Elias;* but confessed, saying: I am not the Christ. And they asked him, saying: *How then art thou Elias? And he said, I am not that Elias who was to restore all things.* And they asked him, saying, Art thou that prophet? And he answered, No. . . . And they asked him, and said unto him: Why baptizest thou then, if thou be not the Christ, nor Elias who was to restore all things, neither that prophet? John answered them, saying: I baptize with water, but there standeth one among you, whom ye know not; He it is of whom I bear record. *He is that prophet, even Elias, who, coming after me, is preferred before me,* whose shoe's latchet I am not worthy to unloose, or whose place I am not able to fill; for he shall baptize, not only with water, but with fire, and with the Holy Ghost" (*Inspired Version,* John 1:21–28).

After Moses and Elijah (Elias) had appeared on the Mount of Transfiguration our Lord's "disciples asked him, saying, Why then say the scribes that Elias must *first* come?" That is, the scribes knew that Elias (Elijah) was to precede the coming of the Lord, and yet here Peter, James, and John had seen the heavenly visitant come *after* the Lord had been manifest among the people.

"And Jesus answered and said unto them, Elias truly shall first come, and restore all things, as the prophets have written. And again I say unto you that Elias has come already, concerning whom it is written, Behold, I will send my messenger, and he shall prepare the way before me; and they knew him not, and have done unto him, whatsoever they listed. Likewise shall also the Son of Man suffer of them. But I say unto you, Who is Elias? Behold, this is Elias, whom I send to prepare the way before me. Then the disciples understood *that he spake unto them of John the Baptist, and also of another who should come and restore all things, as it is written by the prophets*" (*Inspired Version,* Matt. 17:9–14; *DS,* 2:108–12). (*MD,* 220–22)

LIKENING THE SCRIPTURES TO OUR LIVES

John 1:7–9 The same came for a witness, to bear witness of the Light, that all men through him might believe. He was not that Light, but was sent to bear witness of that Light. That was the true Light, which lighteth every man that cometh into the world.

Application: We are to be witnesses of Christ at all times (see Mosiah 18:9). We are to be a light, even the light emanating from Christ (see 3 Ne. 18:24) unto all the world that all might come unto Him (see 3 Ne. 12:14–16; 15:12; D&C 103:9–10).

2. MARY THE MOTHER OF THE SON OF GOD— AN EXAMPLE OF RIGHTEOUSNESS

THEME: The mother of our Lord Jesus Christ was a paragon of virtue, obedience, and rectitude. Similarly, righteous mothers through all generations of time have set the standard for enduring sacrifice and love, fulfilling their eternal commission to bring into the world the sons and daughters of God. As such, they participate in the work

— Why I don't need to hear the Priesthood

~~and glory of God~~ "to bring to pass the immortality and eternal life of man" (Moses 1:39) ~~and merit our everlasting gratitude and honor.~~

MOMENT OF TRUTH

"And behold, he shall be born of Mary, at Jerusalem which is the land of our fore-fathers, she being a virgin, a precious and chosen vessel, who shall be overshadowed and conceive by the power of the Holy Ghost, and bring forth a son, yea, even the Son of God" (Alma 7:10). The moment in time when Mary learned that she would serve as the mother of Jesus is a sacred moment, for it announced and confirmed the impending fulfillment of the will of God to provide a Lamb of Life on behalf of His children, hungering as they did (and ever do) for spiritual sustenance and the substance of hoped-for salvation. Through the family gateway that was to be provided by Mary and Joseph, the young Lord would enter into the realm of His mortal ministry and grow in stature and wisdom unto the measure of the Redeemer, being blessed and empowered by a gracious Father in Heaven and nurtured by a loving mother chosen from before the foundations of the world for this very commission. When Gabriel announced to Mary her endowed role as the mother of the Savior, she replied with simple humility: "Behold the handmaid of the Lord; be it unto me according to thy word" (Luke 1:38), and later (while visiting Elisabeth), she declared the celebrated words: "My soul doth magnify the Lord, And my spirit hath rejoiced in God my Saviour" (Luke 1:46–47). Not many births are announced like this by an angelic emissary, but many are announced through the promises and pronouncements of the patriarchs of the Church, who envision under inspiration the coming forth of the sons and daughters of God as blessings and gifts to mortal mothers and fathers—parents who aspire to fulfill the righteous purposes of our Father in Heaven.

MODERN PROPHETS SPEAK

James E. Talmage:

> His message delivered, Gabriel departed, leaving the chosen Virgin of Nazareth to ponder over her wondrous experience. Mary's promised Son was to be "The Only Begotten" of the Father in the flesh; so it had been both positively and abundantly predicted. True, the event was unprecedented; true also it has never been paralleled; but that the virgin birth would be unique was as truly essential to the fulfillment of prophecy as that it should occur at all. That Child to be born of Mary was begotten of Elohim, the Eternal Father, not in violation of natural law but in accordance with a higher manifestation thereof; and, the offspring from that association of supreme

sanctity, celestial Sireship, and pure though mortal maternity, was of right to be called the "Son of the Highest." In His nature would be combined the powers of Godhood with the capacity and possibilities of mortality; and this through the ordinary operation of the fundamental law of heredity, declared of God, demonstrated by science, and admitted by philosophy, that living beings shall propagate—after their kind. The Child Jesus was to inherit the physical, mental, and spiritual traits, tendencies, and powers that characterized His parents—one immortal and glorified—God, the other human—woman. (*JC*, 77)

ILLUSTRATIONS FOR OUR TIME

Mary, Mother of Jesus

Centuries before her birth, Book of Mormon prophets referred to Mary by name in prophecies of her vital mission (Mosiah 3:8). Describing her as "most beautiful and fair above all other virgins" (1 Ne. 11:13–20) and a "precious and chosen vessel" (Alma 7:10), they prophesied that Mary would bear the Son of God and was therefore blessed above all other women. "We cannot but think that the Father would choose the greatest female spirit to be the mother of his Son, even as he chose the male spirit like unto him to be the Savior." (McConkie, *The Mortal Messiah*, 327)

Mary's willingness to submit to the will of the Father was noted in the biblical account. When Gabriel announced that she would be the mother of the Savior, Mary was perplexed; yet she did not waiver in her humble OBEDIENCE and FAITH in God. Her response was unadorned: "Behold the handmaid of the Lord; be it unto me according to thy word" (Luke 1:38).

Had Judah been a free nation, Mary could have been recognized as a "princess of royal blood through descent from David." Being of that earthly lineage, Jesus was correctly called a descendant of David. (*see* JESUS CHRIST IN THE SCRIPTURES: THE BIBLE)

As a faithful Jewish woman, she followed the customs of her day. At least forty-one days after giving birth to her first son, Mary went to the Court of the Women, where she became ceremonially clean in the purification rite, offering two turtle-doves or two pigeons at the temple as a sacrifice (Luke 2:22–24). In the years that followed, Mary bore additional children by her earthly husband Joseph (Matt. 1:25; 13:55–56; Mark 6:3). One of them, "James the Lord's brother" (Gal. 1:19), became a Christian leader in Jerusalem.

In the New Testament, Mary is mentioned in conjunction with the accounts of the youthful Jesus teaching in the temple (Luke 2:41–51), his turning the water to wine at Cana (John 2:2–5), his crucifixion (John 19:25–26), and as mourning with the apostles after Jesus' ascension (Acts 1:14).

Doctrinally, Latter-day Saints do not view Mary as the intercessor with her son in behalf of those who pray and they do not pray to her. They affirm the VIRGIN

Not everyone agrees w/ this, but its true

BIRTH but reject the traditions of the IMMACULATE CONCEPTION, of Mary's perpetual virginity, and of her "assumption." Mary, like all mortals, returns to the Father only through the atonement of her son Jesus Christ. (Camille Fronk, in *Encyclopedia*, 863–64)

LIKENING THE SCRIPTURES TO OUR LIVES

Luke 1:47 And my spirit hath rejoiced in God my Saviour.

Application: Rejoicing in the Lord can bring us a sense of inner fulfillment and peace, knowing the source of our strength, power, and blessings. Gratitude will fill our very souls. This can motivate us to receive the goodness of God in our lives by being obedient to His will.

SUMMARY

Our Heavenly Father is the consummate Master of preparing the way for His children. In the case of His Only Begotten, He prepared the way through the ministry of John the Baptist, an Elias of first rank. It was the same John who held the keys of restoring the Aaronic Priesthood in our day in order to empower all worthy young priesthood brethren to fulfill their missions as "preparers of the way," as leaders-in-training who are aspiring to receive and honor the higher or Melchizedek Priesthood. Upon the faith of their mothers, they can build their future of service in the kingdom of God, much as Helaman's stripling warriors remained ever anchored in the example of love and conviction provided by their mothers (see Alma 56:47–48). In the same context, the righteous example of Mary the Mother of the Son of God remains an eternal beacon of love and humility to illuminate the pathway for all mankind.

It's interesting to think that in fulfilling my role as a mother, I participate with God in the plan of salvation and need to have faith strong enough for Dougie to draw on as he prepares to hold the Melchizedek Priesthood and lead in the church.

CHAPTER 3

JOY *to the* WORLD— CHRIST *the* LORD IS BORN

Reading Assignment: Luke 2; Matthew 2.

Additional Reading: Isaiah 9:6; 1 Nephi 11:13–21; Helaman 14:1–8; 3 Nephi 27:13–16.

As we open scriptural pages to read of the plan for life on earth, we see that our Father in Heaven made known to the prophets of the Old Testament that the Savior, His Only Begotten Son, would come to earth. Isaiah the prophet said that "a virgin shall conceive, and bear a son" (Isa. 7:14), and "the government shall be upon his shoulder "(Isa. 9:6), and later said that "the Lord, the Creator of the ends of the earth" (Isa. 40:28) was the "Holy One of Israel" (Isa. 43:3), even the "redeemer that maketh all things" (Isa. 44:24; see Isa. 40–45). Jeremiah, Zechariah, Job, Moses, and others of the prophets had revealed to them the Christ and that He would come to provide the way for all of us to return to our Father in Heaven. These prophets left their witnesses for us to study and to pray about and to receive our own testimony of the "looked for Savior" of the Old Testament.

—JAMES M. PARAMORE, "THE MANY WITNESSES OF JESUS CHRIST AND HIS WORK," *ENSIGN,* NOV. 1990, 62.

THEMES *for* LIVING

1. Remember with Reverence the Birth of the Lord Jesus Christ
2. Rejoice in the Lord Jesus Christ as the Promised Messiah
3. Prepare to Serve—The Lord's Early Preparations for His Ministry

INTRODUCTION

The most transcendent event in all of history was the coming of the Son of God to the earth to complete His mission of redemption and Atonement. He was to be the Only Begotten Son of God in the flesh, to be born of the virgin Mary, to deliver the doctrines, laws, and ordinances concerning eternal life, to bestow the power to act in the name of God, to perform the infinite and eternal Atonement, and, by the power of the resurrection, to make it possible that through Him all mankind might return unto the Father—if they would but come unto the Lord and keep the commandments. When we come to understand and appreciate this marvelous plan of exaltation made possible by the goodness of God the Father and the sacrifice of our Lord and Savior, we should in pure devotion and enduring gratitude rejoice in the coming of our Lord and Savior Jesus Christ.

1. REMEMBER WITH REVERENCE THE BIRTH OF THE LORD JESUS CHRIST

THEME: Let us learn to appreciate the condescension and graciousness of our Lord to suffer the will of the Father and be born in humble circumstances that He might fulfill the measure of His mission as Savior and Redeemer of the world.

MOMENT OF TRUTH

It was a humble birth; the Creator and Lord to the earth was placed by his young mother in a manger in the city of David, called Bethlehem. The shepherds in the fields served in the region as the able communicators of the extraordinary event, because they had been favored to hear and view the proclamation by the angelic messengers praising God and saying: "Glory to God in the highest, and on earth peace, good will toward men" (Luke 2:14) and because they had witnessed the manger scene in person. "But Mary kept all these things, and pondered them in her heart" (Luke 2:19). Soon thereafter, according to the account of Luke, the parents brought the child to Jerusalem so that they could offer sacrifices of thanksgiving in the temple. It was there that the devout and inspired priest Simeon blessed the child and uttered prophetic confirmation of the coming mission of the Savior. The aged prophetess Anna likewise recognized the divine mission of this coming Redeemer. In no less measure should we recognize, through the confirming witness of the Holy Spirit, that the birth of Emmanuel was real, was foreordained from before the foundation of the earth, and inaugurated the ministry of redemption foretold by all the prophets up to that time.

MODERN PROPHETS SPEAK

Gordon B. Hinckley:

> Believe in His Divine Son, His firstborn, His Only Begotten in the flesh, Jesus the Christ, who condescended to leave His Father on high to be born in a manger under the most humble of circumstances among people in a vassal state, who walked the dusty road of Palestine doing good, healing the sick, blessing and teaching and uplifting and giving strength and hope and faith to those who would listen. Then, in the greatest act of human history, He allowed His quivering flesh to be nailed to the cross and lifted up in an act of Atonement for each of us. We cannot comprehend it in all of its meaning, but it is marvelously wonderful. . . . Thanks be to God for the gift of His Son and thanks be to the Lord Jesus Christ for the gift of His life, which makes possible for each of us the blessing of eternal life. Nothing, nothing is of greater significance in all the history of the world than that atoning sacrifice of the Son of God. He was the Son of God. (*TGBH,* 283)

ILLUSTRATIONS FOR OUR TIME

When we come to understand the "Condescension of God" and its indispensable role in the magnificent gospel plan, we gain a sense of how deep and abiding must be the love that our Heavenly Father and His Son have for each of us as a child of God. This doctrine was explained beautifully by Byron B. Merrill. He wrote:

> The Book of Mormon prophet Nephi 1 (c. 600 B.C) was asked by an angel, "Knowest thou the condescension of God?" (1 Ne. 11:16). Nephi was then shown in a vision a virgin who was to become "the mother of the Son of God, after the manner of the flesh" (11:18). He next beheld the virgin with a child whom the angel identified as "the Lamb of God, yea, even the Son of the Eternal Father" (11:21). Then Nephi understood that the condescension of God is the ultimate manifestation of God's love through Jesus Christ (11:20–22). Such condescension denotes, first, the love of GOD THE FATHER, who deigned to sire a son, born of a mortal woman, and then allow this Son to suffer temptations and pain (Mosiah 3:5–7), "be judged of the world," and be "slain for the sins of the world" (1 Ne. 11:32–33). Second, it signifies the love and willingness of God the Son (Jesus Christ) to die for mankind.
>
> The word "condescension" implies "voluntary descent," "submission," and "performing acts which strict justice does not require." This definition is particularly applicable to Jesus in the portrayal of him by prophets who lived before his birth and who affirmed: "God himself shall come down" to make an Atonement (Mosiah 15:1); "the God of Abraham, and of Isaac, and the God of Jacob, yieldeth himself into the hands

of wicked men" (1 Ne. 19:10); "the great Creator suffereth himself to become subject unto man in the flesh" (2 Ne. 9:5); and "he offereth himself a sacrifice for sin" (2 Ne. 2:7). "The Lord Omnipotent," said King Benjamin, "shall come down from heaven among the children of men, and shall dwell in a tabernacle of clay" (Mosiah 3:5).

In fulfillment of these prophecies, Jesus descended from the realms of glory for the purposes of experiencing mortal infirmities that he might have mercy and compassion according to the flesh and of taking upon himself the sins, transgressions, pains, and sicknesses of men in order to satisfy the demands of justice and gain victory over death, thereby redeeming his people (Mosiah 15:8–9; Alma 7:11–13). Christ's selfless sacrifice merits profound gratitude and endearing love from all who are recipients of his supernal offering. (*Encyclopedia,* 305; compare Bruce R. McConkie, "Behold the Condescension of God," *New Era,* Dec. 1984, 34–39)

LIKENING THE SCRIPTURES TO OUR LIVES

1 Nephi 11:16–18 And he said unto me: Knowest thou the condescension of God? And I said unto him: I know that he loveth his children; nevertheless, I do not know the meaning of all things. And he said unto me: Behold, the virgin whom thou seest is the mother of the Son of God, after the manner of the flesh.

Application: If the Savior can condescend to come to the earth to do the will of the Father that He might draw all men unto Him (see 3 Ne. 27:13–14), then surely we should humble ourselves and submit our will to the Father that we might keep the commandments and seek to bless our fellowmen by inviting all to come unto Christ.

2. REJOICE IN THE LORD JESUS CHRIST AS THE PROMISED MESSIAH

THEME: Recognizing the blessings of the Lord Jesus Christ in our lives will cause us to be filled with joy and rejoicing and strengthen our feelings of love and reverence for our Savior Jesus Christ.

MOMENT OF TRUTH

We can scarcely imagine the motherly joy Mary experienced in fulfilling the promise of the annunciation of Gabriel by bringing the Savior into the world—a healthy and radiant child whose mission was to ensure the vitality and well-being of all mankind. The angel who appeared in glory to the shepherds guarding their flocks on that occasion set the tone for the appropriate response: "Fear not: for, behold, I bring you good tidings of great joy, which shall be to all people. For unto you is born this day in the city of David a Saviour, which is Christ the Lord" (Luke 2:10–11). In far-off America, on the eve of that glorious event, the prophet Nephi was engaged in mighty prayer on behalf of his people. Their lives were threatened by the enemies of the Church should the sign not appear that was promised by Samuel, confirming the birth of the Redeemer. Then these comforting words were heard by the prophet:

> Lift up your head and be of good cheer; for behold, the time is at hand, and on this night shall the sign be given, and on the morrow come I into the world, to show unto the world that I will fulfil all that which I have caused to be spoken by the mouth of my holy prophets.
>
> Behold, I come unto my own, to fulfil all things which I have made known unto the children of men from the foundation of the world, and to do the will, both of the Father and of the Son—of the Father because of me, and of the Son because of my flesh. And behold, the time is at hand, and this night shall the sign be given. (3 Ne. 1:13–14)

Soon thereafter the sign was given: celestial light miraculously filled that entire night and a new star appeared in the sky (3 Ne. 1:21), perhaps the same star of joy that guided the wise men from the east to the Holy Child. Through this unprecedented birth, the spiritual light of the Only Begotten burst upon the world to nurture the joy of all believers.

Yet there were some who believed only in their own self-serving way—belief mixed with fear. Herod was one of those. He was not overjoyed at the news of a King being born in his realm. When the wise men failed to report back details of the birth to him (they having been warned by God in a dream not to return to the royal court), the king took drastic measures to protect his hegemony against the perceived interloper and mercilessly ordered the death of all infants in Bethlehem and its vicinity who were two years old and younger (Matt. 2:16). Following the death of Herod, an angel appeared to Joseph (who had been forewarned by an angel to flee with his wife and child) in Egypt and beckoned him to return to his homeland (Matt. 2:20–21) where the unfolding history of the newborn Savior could proceed. Thus, after millennia of prophetic anticipation, the curtains were parted and the light of redeeming joy dawned over the world as it hungered for spiritual cheer and salvation.

MODERN PROPHETS SPEAK

Neal A. Maxwell:
> We can, in fact, become "alive in Christ because of our faith" (2 Ne. 25:25). No wonder those who respond to the invitation to "come unto Christ" (D&C 20:59)

"talk of Christ . . . rejoice in Christ . . . and preach of Christ . . . that their children may know to what source they may look" (2 Ne. 25:28). They know the Lord will "comfort their soul in Christ" and help them to "endure it well" (Alma 31:31–32). It is fitting that when those who were once lost manage to come home they are rightfully and enthusiastically described as being "alive again" (Luke 15:32).

When so engaged in these various forms of service, will we still have cares? Oh, yes! However, we have the invitation "cast all your care upon Him" (1 Pet. 5:7). Only He can carry all our cares, anyway. No wonder we are to talk, preach, and rejoice in Christ, ever knowing to whom to look (2 Ne. 25:26). (*If Thou Endure It Well* [Salt Lake City: Bookcraft, 1996], 117)

ILLUSTRATIONS FOR OUR TIME

Quentin L. Cook has taught us well about rejoicing. He said:

The chorus of one of my favorite hymns entreats, "Lift up your heart! Lift up your voice! Rejoice, again I say, rejoice!" ("Rejoice, the Lord Is King!" *Hymns,* 66). The text of the hymn is taken from Paul's writings to the Philippians: "Rejoice in the Lord alway: and again I say, Rejoice" (Philip. 4:4). The dictionary defines *rejoice* as "to feel joy or great delight." . . .

That having been said, the Resurrection and Atonement wrought by the Savior and the promise of eternal life with our loved ones are of such overwhelming significance that to not rejoice would demonstrate a lack of understanding of the Savior's gift.

Joy comes when we have the Spirit in our lives (see Alma 22:15). When we have the Spirit, we rejoice in what the Savior has done for us.

What do we need to do to have this kind of joy? In addition to attaining saving ordinances and following the living prophet, we need to live in accordance with certain fundamental spiritual principles, such as prayer, scripture study, righteous living, and service to others. . . .

If we truly want to have the Spirit of the Lord and experience joy and happiness, we should rejoice in our blessings and be grateful. We should especially rejoice in the blessings that are available through the temple." . . .

Let the hearts of your brethren rejoice, and let the hearts of all my people rejoice, who have, with their might, built this house to my name." Let us rejoice in the promise that is ours through the Atonement of the Savior and through Christlike living adhere to the counsel of the Psalmist: "This is the day which the Lord hath made; we will rejoice and be glad in it" (Ps. 118:24). That each of us may do this is my prayer. (Quentin L. Cook, "Rejoice!" *Ensign,* Nov. 1996, 28–31)

LIKENING THE SCRIPTURES TO OUR LIVES

2 Nephi 25:26 And we talk of Christ, we rejoice in Christ, we preach of Christ, we prophesy of Christ, and we write according to our prophecies, that our children may know to what source they may look for a remission of their sins.

Application: When we make Christ the center of our very being, we can begin to emulate Him in our everyday lives. We will rejoice in our blessings from our Savior and we will look to Him in all things, remembering how we receive a remission of our sins (see Mosiah 4:11).

3. PREPARE TO SERVE—THE LORD'S EARLY PREPARATIONS FOR HIS MINISTRY

THEME: Preparation precedes power. In all things there is a time of preparation that we might better serve the Lord.

MOMENT OF TRUTH

As the account in the Joseph Smith translation of Luke reads: "And the child grew, and waxed strong in spirit, being filled with wisdom, and the grace of God was upon him" (JST, Luke 2:40). Not many years hence, the foundational preparation of the mortal Messiah was consummated in the atoning sacrifice:

> For behold, I, God, have suffered these things for all, that they might not suffer if they would repent;
> > But if they would not repent they must suffer even as I;
> > Which suffering caused myself, even God, the greatest of all, to tremble because of pain, and to bleed at every pore, and to suffer both body and spirit—and would that I might not drink the bitter cup, and shrink—
> > Nevertheless, glory be to the Father, and I partook and finished my preparations unto the children of men.
> > Wherefore, I command you again to repent. (D&C 19:16–20)

What transpired between the Savior's adolescent youth and His crowning achievement as Redeemer was a sequence of proactive developments that included the young Savior's dialogue in the temple to inaugurate His engagement in His "Father's business" (Luke 2:49); His consistent growth and maturation whereby He "increased in wisdom and stature, and in favour with God and man" (Luke 2:52); His baptism at the hands of John the Baptist (Matt. 3:13–17); and all the rest of the miraculous happenings leading to the unfolding of His three-year mission to become the perfected "author of eternal salvation unto all them that obey him" (Heb. 5:9). In all of this, He gave us the heavenly pattern of preparation and fulfillment that should be emulated in the lives of all those who aspire to be His disciples.

MODERN PROPHETS SPEAK

Thomas S. Monson:

> It's wonderful that you are willing and prepared to serve wherever the Spirit of the Lord directs. This alone is a modern miracle, considering the times in which we live. As missionaries, you also can share in this sweet feeling of realizing that Heavenly Father knows each of His children. He will permit you to help rescue those who are spiritually drowning, to see and to share in His divine power to save.
>
> Missionary work is hard work. Missionary service is demanding and requires long hours of study and preparation so that the missionary himself might match the divine message he proclaims. It is a labor of love but also of sacrifice and devotion to duty. ("Save Her! Save Her!" *New Era,* May 1997, 4:6)

ILLUSTRATIONS FOR OUR TIME

Thomas S. Monson has taught clearly about the need for preparation in all things:

> When we contemplate the eternal nature of our choices, preparation is a vital factor in our lives. The day will come when we will look back upon our period of preparation and be grateful that we properly applied ourselves. . . .
>
> Preparation precedes power. To obtain the knowledge and skill we require need not be an insurmountable task if we adopt for our pattern the experience of the sons of Mosiah. Alma was journeying from the land of Gideon southward, away to the land of Manti, when he met the sons of Mosiah journeying toward the land of Zarahemla. Alma rejoiced "exceedingly to see his brethren; and what added more to his joy, they were still his brethren in the Lord; yea, and they had waxed strong in the knowledge of the truth; for they were men of a sound understanding and had searched the scriptures diligently that they might know the word of God. But this is not all; they had given themselves to much prayer, and fasting; therefore, they had the spirit of prophecy, and the spirit of revelation, and when they taught, they taught with power and authority of God" (see Alma 17:1–3). (*Pathways to Perfection,* 276–277)

LIKENING THE SCRIPTURES TO OUR LIVES

Luke 2:52 And Jesus increased in wisdom and stature, and in favour with God and man.

Application: We should remember that growth is a process and that it takes time. We must work as well as ask for help in our daily efforts (see D&C 9:7–8). The Lord will make us equal to the task as we work diligently, exercise our faith, and ask for His help.

SUMMARY

As we remember with reverence the birth of our Lord Jesus Christ and rejoice in His mission as the promised Messiah, we can show our gratitude by following His matchless example in all that we do, especially in preparing ourselves more fully to serve in building up His Kingdom. Our preparations commenced long before we came to this earth, as Joseph F. Smith confirmed, concerning those in the premortal spirit realm awaiting their transition to mortality: "Even before they were born, they, with many others, received their first lessons in the world of spirits and were prepared to come forth in the due time of the Lord to labor in his vineyard for the salvation of the souls of men" (D&C 138:56). Once introduced into this mortal sphere, we then continued our preparations within the framework of truth given in the scriptures and the words of the living prophets. The Apostle Paul characterized such preparations as the process of taking upon ourselves the spiritual armor of God:

> Stand therefore, having your loins girt about with truth, and having on the breastplate of righteousness;
>
> And your feet shod with the preparation of the gospel of peace;
>
> Above all, taking the shield of faith, wherewith ye shall be able to quench all the fiery darts of the wicked.
>
> And take the helmet of salvation, and the sword of the Spirit, which is the word of God:
>
> Praying always with all prayer and supplication in the Spirit, and watching thereunto with all perseverance and supplication for all saints. (Eph. 6:14–18; compare D&C 27:15–18).

CHAPTER 4

"PREPARE YE THE WAY *of the* LORD"

Reading Assignment: Matthew 3–4; John 1:35–51.

Additional Reading: Luke 15:3–10; 2 Corinthians 7:9–10; 1 John 1:8–9; Alma 34:15–17, 31–34; D&C 19:15; 58:42–43.

> *In partaking of the sacrament, we can renew the effects of our baptism. When we desire a remission of our sins through the Atonement of our Savior, we are commanded to repent and come to him with a broken heart and a contrite spirit (see 3 Ne. 9:20; 3 Ne. 12:19; Moro. 6:2; D&C 20:37). In the waters of baptism we witness to the Lord that we have repented of our sins and are willing to take his name upon us and serve him to the end (see D&C 20:37). The effects are described by Nephi: "For the gate by which ye should enter is repentance and baptism by water; and then cometh a remission of your sins by fire and by the Holy Ghost" (2 Ne. 31:17; see also Moro. 6:4). That last promise is fulfilled as a result of our receiving the gift of the Holy Ghost.*
>
> *The renewal of our covenants by partaking of the sacrament should also be preceded by repentance, so we come to that sacred ordinance with a broken heart and a contrite spirit (see 2 Ne. 2:7; 3 Ne. 12:19; D&C 59:8). Then, as we renew our baptismal covenants and affirm that we will always remember him (D&C 20:77), the Lord will renew the promised remission of our sins, under the conditions and at the time he chooses. One of the primary purposes and effects of this renewal of covenants and cleansing from sin is that [we] may always have his Spirit to be with [us] (D&C 20:77).*

—DALLIN H. OAKS, "ALWAYS HAVE HIS SPIRIT," *ENSIGN*, NOV. 1996, 61.

THEMES *for* LIVING

1. Prepare the Way of the Lord
2. Follow the Savior's Example by Being Baptized
3. Withstand and Overcome the Temptations of the Devil
4. Follow Christ Faithfully

INTRODUCTION

The Lord has given us the invitation: "Come unto Me." The only way to come to the Lord is by exercising faith unto repentance, taking upon us His name through the ordinance of baptism, keeping the commandments, and receiving the gift and cleansing power of the Holy Ghost—that we might in the strength of the Lord overcome temptation and endure to the end. This is the way of the Lord. He and His prophets have counseled us repeatedly to repent and be baptized (see Matt.4:17; Mark 1:4; Luke 3:8; Acts 2:38; Mosiah 4:10; Alma 9:12; 3 Ne. 11:32; D&C 11:9; 19:4; 20:29; Moses 6:57). Upon the foundation of the fundamental principles and ordinances of the gospel, the sons and daughters of God can build their lives in righteousness in accordance with the example of the Savior: they can put on the "whole armour of God" (Eph. 6:13–18; D&C 27:15–18) to fortify themselves against evil; they can selflessly help prepare the way for others to join the flock of God; and they can take up their cross (3 Ne. 12:30; D&C 23:6; 112:14) and endure resolutely to the end in faith and devotion.

1. PREPARE THE WAY OF THE LORD

THEME: In the universal sense, all Saints of God are called upon with the commandment: "Prepare ye the way of the Lord" (Matt. 3:3; Isa. 40:3; and see also Mark 1:3; Luke 3:4; 1 Ne. 10:8; Alma 7:9; D&C 45:9; D&C 65:1, 3). To prepare the way of the Lord is to do all in our power to facilitate and uphold the three-fold mission of the Church in proclaiming the gospel, perfecting the Saints, and completing family history and vicarious temple work for the purpose of redeeming the dead. All of these contributions help illuminate the pathway that leads us—in company with our "fellowcitizens" (Eph. 2:19)—closer to the Savior and His perfect way of life. They prepare us for the Second Coming when the Messiah will return in power and glory. John the Baptist (with his specific calling as an Elias, or forerunner of the Savior) set the example for us to follow.

MOMENT OF TRUTH

Imagine the refreshing and enlightened atmosphere associated with the discourses of John the Baptist as he drew followers from the grand cities of Judea and into the countryside, far from the trappings and entanglements of ossified and lifeless traditions that had become the staple of ecclesiastic leadership in his day. Imagine the excitement as the people were fed pure doctrine about the coming mission of the Messiah. John wore homely clothing fit for the wilderness, but he dressed his language in power and authority from God fit for effecting change with eternal consequences. He baptized those who confessed their sins and desired to make a vow of obedience to the Lord. He reviled against the "generation of vipers" (Matt. 3:7), those among the Pharisees and Sadducees who purported to be followers of Abraham but understood little about using the Spirit to soften hearts and change lives for the better. And John proclaimed the coming era of the Spirit that would be inaugurated with the ministry of Jesus Christ: "he that cometh after me is mightier than I, . . . he shall baptize you with the Holy Ghost, and with fire" (Matt. 3:11).

MODERN PROPHETS SPEAK

Joseph Fielding Smith:

> Is it not rather a remarkable thing that in every revelation given to Joseph Smith he has been found absolutely in harmony with the scriptures? The Lord, as I have stated, declared through one of his prophets that before his second coming a messenger should be sent to prepare the way and make it straight. You may apply this to John if you will, and it is true. John, the messenger who came to prepare the way before the Lord in the former dispensation, also came in this dispensation as a messenger to Joseph Smith, so it applies, if you wish to apply it so, to John who came as a messenger to prepare the way before the Lord. But I go further and maintain that Joseph Smith was the messenger whom the Lord sent to prepare the way before him. He came and under direction of holy messengers laid the foundation for the kingdom of God and of this marvelous work and a wonder that the world might be prepared for the coming of the Lord. (CR, April 1920, 107)

ILLUSTRATIONS FOR OUR TIME

Preaching Repentance

There is no greater example for preparing the way of the Lord than preaching repentance. Alma did it with great success:

> I know that which the Lord hath commanded me, and I glory in it. I do not glory of myself, but I glory in that which the Lord hath commanded me; yea, and this is my glory, that perhaps I may be an instrument in the hands of God to bring some soul to repentance; and this is my joy.

> And behold, when I see many of my brethren truly penitent, and coming to the Lord their God, then is my soul filled with joy; then do I remember what the Lord has done for me, yea, even that he hath heard my prayer; yea, then do I remember his merciful arm which he extended towards me. (Alma 29:9–10)

> Yea, and from that time even until now, I have labored without ceasing, that I might bring souls unto repentance; that I might bring them to taste of the exceeding joy of which I did taste; that they might also be born of God, and be filled with the Holy Ghost. (Alma 36:24)

The Sons of Mosiah preached repentance, just as Alma did: "And they had been teaching the word of God for the space of fourteen years among the Lamanites, having had much success in bringing many to the knowledge of the truth; yea, by the power of their words many were brought before the altar of God, to call on his name and confess their sins before him" (Alma 17:4). The Whitmer brothers were encouraged to preach repentance: "And now, behold, I say unto you, that the thing which will be of the most worth unto you will be to declare repentance unto this people, that you may bring souls unto me, that you may rest with them in the kingdom of my Father" (D&C 15:6). Throughout every dispensation of time, God's anointed have pleaded for repentance: "Then Peter said unto them, Repent, and be baptized every one of you in the name of Jesus Christ for the remission of sins, and ye shall receive the gift of the Holy Ghost" (Acts 2:38). And so it is today, with thousands and thousands of missionaries throughout the world preaching the gospel of Jesus Christ and inviting all to repent and come unto Christ. This is our duty—our joy and glory—in this, the dispensation of the fullness of times. This is the last time the vineyard will be pruned (see Jacob 5:70–77; D&C138:56). This is the last gathering before the Second Coming. [Pinegar]

We Can All Assist in Preparing the Way
In our neighborhood, there resides a noble and devoted high priest of senior age, with a long history of service in the kingdom of God. Despite severe and crippling medical challenges, he is constantly reaching out to express concern for others and help them in any way possible.

Recently, his name came up on the schedule of those appointed to take their turn cleaning the chapel. He insisted on participating, even though his condition made it difficult to walk, let alone operate one of the vacuum cleaners. "What can I do to help?" was his inquiry. The captain of the cleaning team thought a moment and then suggested that he might want to try using one of the dusting wands to clean the picture frames that hung along the hallways of the building. He smiled and cheerfully went about his duties—slowly though devotedly—not ceasing until every picture was restored to its optimum cleanliness.

We watched him throughout the cleaning period, dragging his lame foot along as he reached up and attended to his duties. His demeanor reminded us of the scripture: "Wherefore, now let every man learn his duty, and to act in the office in which he is appointed, in all diligence" (D&C 107:99). If our duty of the moment is to dust pictures in the chapel, then we can do so with valor and dedication and feel the pride of accomplishment and service.

Does that kind of activity constitute helping to prepare the way for the Savior? Of course! If the Savior were to visit our chapels, would we not want Him to find everything in pristine condition? If the Savior were to visit our homes, would we not want Him to find our circumstances reflecting cleanliness and order? If the Savior were to visit us in person, would we not want Him to find that our hearts were cleansed and our minds purified through righteous living? Whatever we can do to set things in order and prepare for the coming of our Lord is part of our ongoing responsibility. We are counseled: "Organize yourselves; prepare every needful thing; and establish a house, even a house of prayer, a house of fasting, a house of faith, a house of learning, a house of glory, a house of order, a house of God" (D&C 88:119).

Sometimes we are called upon to serve in leadership offices; sometimes we are called upon to teach and counsel; sometimes we are called upon to go to the house of the Lord and offer up our oblations and sacraments to the Most High (D&C 59:12); and sometimes we are called upon to dust the chapel. All of this is part of the Lord's work when done willingly and with an eye single to the glory of God. Our elderly friend was not aware that we on the cleaning team were watching him and being edified by his example of faithfulness. Similarly, we ourselves may not be aware that others are learning from our performance and that our Father in Heaven is watching us, mindful of our service in the Kingdom—across a full spectrum of duties and assignments. Over all such servants the angels rejoice, we are told in the scriptures (D&C 62:3; 88:2; 90:34).

As John H. Vandenberg noted many years ago:

> The Lord has decreed that "the Church hath need of every member" (see D&C 84:110). This implies development of its members by participation in the programmed activities of children and youth, filling the numerous teaching opportunities, administration assignments, fulfillment of member duties, the fulfillment of priesthood duties, not forgetting to visit the homes of members (which, until this day, has not been attended to as the Lord directed), searching out the records of ancestors, and temple participation, all of which are only part of the never-ending list of activities with which to fill our leisure hours.
>
> The individual power is attested to in this scripture: "Verily I say, men should be anxiously engaged in a good cause, and do many things of their own free will, and bring to pass much righteousness; For the power is in them, wherein they are

agents unto themselves. And inasmuch as men do good they shall in nowise lose their reward" (D&C 58:27–28). ("Becoming a Somebody," *Ensign,* Jan. 1973, 39)

Let us therefore examine our internal motivation and attitude and ensure that we are truly aligned with the spirit of preparing the way of the Lord (Matt. 3:3; Isa. 40:3). [Allen]

LIKENING THE SCRIPTURES TO OUR LIVES

Alma 7:9 But behold, the Spirit hath said this much unto me, saying: Cry unto this people, saying—Repent ye, and prepare the way of the Lord, and walk in his paths, which are straight; for behold, the kingdom of heaven is at hand, and the Son of God cometh upon the face of the earth.

Application: We are to warn the world and preach faith unto repentance to help fulfill and magnify the sacrifice and life of our Savior. If we do so, then "His way" can be efficacious for all mankind.

2. FOLLOW THE SAVIOR'S EXAMPLE BY BEING BAPTIZED

THEME: We should become worthy and follow the example of our Savior and be baptized.

MOMENT OF TRUTH

What John the Baptist did was truly revolutionary in his time: he revived ancient ordinances on behalf of his followers and reactivated the doctrine of faith, repentance, and baptism as a covenant of purification and preparation for higher blessings. What the Savior did was yet more revolutionary, for He, as a Being of perfection, submitted Himself to divine practice by entering into the covenant of baptism as a model for all to follow: "Then cometh Jesus from Galilee to Jordan unto John, to be baptized of him. But John forbad him, saying, I have need to be baptized of thee, and comest thou to me? And Jesus answering said unto him, Suffer it to be so now: for thus it becometh us to fulfil all righteousness. Then he suffered him" (Matt. 3:13–15). So important was this milestone that the Spirit of God descended upon Jesus immediately thereafter "like a dove" (Matt. 3:16) and the voice of the Father Himself—as on very few other occasions—bore witness of the Savior's divine identity: "This is my beloved Son, in whom I am well pleased" (Matt. 3:17). In this manner, the promised era of the Holy Ghost was opened once again for the faithful in the dispensation of the meridian of time.

MODERN PROPHETS SPEAK

Bruce R. McConkie:

> In the covenant of baptism, among other things, men promise: 1. To remember the death, burial, and resurrection of their Lord—the very ordinance itself being so ordained as to symbolize these things; 2. "To take upon them the name of Jesus Christ"; and 3. To "serve him and keep his commandments." In return, the Lord on his part promises: 1. That he will "pour out his Spirit more abundantly" upon such persons; and 2. That they shall "have eternal life" (Mosiah 18:8–10; D&C 20:37). (*MD*, 296–297)

ILLUSTRATIONS FOR OUR TIME

The Joy of Baptisms

> In 1964, while serving as a missionary in the New Zealand South Mission, I experienced the blessings of being fervently in touch with the Spirit.
>
> One day, my companion, Elder Ken Adams, and I decided to travel to an outlying area called Bridge Pa. In our prayers before leaving we asked the Lord that we would be able to find certain people and that a woman who had been taught for some time would consent to be baptized. . . .
>
> Upon arriving at her home, we reaffirmed our desires to the Lord in a prayer in our car and then approached the door. As we had done many times before, we told her that we had a baptism scheduled for next Wednesday, and asked if she would like to be baptized.
>
> "No, Elders, not at this time. How about Thursday?" was her response.
>
> Her baptism the following Thursday was wonderful, with just us, her husband and one of her children present—as per her wishes.
>
> Almost 30 years later, I heard that a Maori missionary was serving in our Fairfield California Stake. I invited him and his companion over for dinner.
>
> As we talked about the different areas where I had served while in New Zealand, we discovered that he was the grandson of the woman we had baptized. What joy it gave me to relate the story of this special sister's baptism to this elder who had not heard it before! (David Child, "Missionary Moments: What Joy!" *LDS Church News,* 14 Oct. 1995, 16)

LIKENING THE SCRIPTURES TO OUR LIVES

D&C 20:37 *And again, by way of commandment to the church concerning the manner of baptism*—All those who humble themselves before God, and desire to be baptized, and come forth with broken hearts and contrite spirits, and witness before the church that they have truly repented of all their sins, and are willing to take upon them the name of Jesus Christ, having a determination to serve him to the end, and truly manifest by their works that they have received of the Spirit of Christ unto the remission of their sins, shall be received by baptism into his church.

Application: Each time we partake of the sacrament, we should inquire of ourselves to determine if we would be qualified at that moment to be baptized and receive a remission of our sins. Partaking of the sacrament is a renewing of all our covenants with the Lord and is a most sacred ordinance. It is important that we prepare ourselves for this weekly ordinance so that we might be worthy to have His Spirit to be with us always.

3. WITHSTAND AND OVERCOME THE TEMPTATIONS OF THE DEVIL

THEME: It is requisite to the efficacy of this probationary mortal period that we experience opposition in all things (see 2 Ne. 2:11) and that we be tempted as a trial of our faith (see D&C 29:39). Our goal is to learn how to withstand and overcome temptation.

MOMENT OF TRUTH

On the eve of His ministry, the Savior endured a self-imposed, forty-day fast and then afterward submitted Himself to the temptations of Satan (Matt. 3:1–11). Searching in vain for a chink in the Lord's armor, Satan appealed to Him, in a sequence of sinister overtures, to do such things as relieve His hunger miraculously, exercise His power in a superficial way, and subscribe to the pride and glory of worldly things. In each case, the Savior demurred and countered with scriptural references that neutralized and enervated the devil's already shaky position. At the bottom of the tempter's ploy was a desire to get the Lord to worship him. But it could not succeed, for the Lord had committed Himself from before the foundations of the earth to honor the Father and submit Himself in every respect to the Father's will (Abr. 3:27–28; Moses 4:2). The result of this extraordinary encounter was simply this: "Then the devil leaveth him" (Matt. 4:11).

The general contours of this instructive story remain the same in the Joseph Smith Translation of the passage; however, some of the details adjusted by the Prophet render a more accurate accounting of the details. The following chart shows the changes:

King James Version of Matthew 4

1 Then was Jesus led up of the Spirit into the wilderness to be tempted of the devil.

2 And when he had fasted forty days and forty nights, he was afterward an hungered.

3 And when the tempter came to him, he said, If thou be the Son of God, command that these stones be made bread.

4 But he answered and said, It is written, Man shall not live by bread alone, but by every word that proceedeth out of the mouth of God.

5 Then the devil taketh him up into the holy city, and setteth him on a pinnacle of the temple,

6 And saith unto him, If thou be the Son of God, cast thyself down: for it is written, He shall give his angels charge concerning thee: and in *their* hands they shall bear thee up, lest at any time thou dash thy foot against a stone.

7 Jesus said unto him, It is written again, Thou shalt not tempt the Lord thy God.

8 Again, the devil taketh him up into an exceeding high mountain, and sheweth him all the kingdoms of the world, and the glory of them;

9 And saith unto him, All these things will I give thee, if thou wilt fall down and worship me.

10 Then saith Jesus unto him, Get thee hence, Satan: for it is written, Thou shalt worship the Lord thy God, and him only shalt thou serve.

11 Then the devil leaveth him, and, behold, angels came and ministered unto him.—

12 ¶ Now when Jesus had heard that John was cast into prison, he departed into Galilee;

Joseph Smith Translation (with substantive changes in italics)

1 Then Jesus was led up of the Spirit, into the wilderness, *to be with God.*

2 And when he had fasted forty days and forty nights, *and had communed with God,* he was afterwards an hungered, and *was left to be tempted of the devil.*

3 And when the tempter came to him, he said, If thou be the Son of God, command that these stones be made bread.

4 But Jesus answered and said, It is written, Man shall not live by bread alone, but by every word that proceedeth out of the mouth of God.

5 *Then Jesus was taken up into the holy city, and the Spirit* setteth him on the pinnacle of the temple.

6 *Then the devil came unto him and said,* If thou be the Son of God, cast thyself down, for it is written, He shall give his angels charge concerning thee, and in their hands they shall bear thee up, lest at any time thou dash thy foot against a stone.

7 Jesus said unto him, It is written again, Thou shalt not tempt the Lord thy God.

8 And again, *Jesus was in the Spirit, and it taketh him* up into an exceeding high mountain, and showeth him all the kingdoms of the world and the glory of them.

9 *And the devil came unto him again, and said,* All these things will I give unto thee, if thou wilt fall down and worship me.

10 Then said Jesus unto him, Get thee hence, Satan; for it is written, Thou shalt worship the Lord thy God, and him only shalt thou serve. Then the devil leaveth him.

11 *And now Jesus knew that John was cast into prison, and he sent angels, and, behold, they came and ministered unto him [i.e., John].*

12 And Jesus departed into Galilee . . .

MODERN PROPHETS SPEAK

N. Eldon Tanner:

> We are aware that there has always been a conflict between right and wrong, right-
> eousness and evil, good and bad. We must prepare ourselves to meet these conflicts
> and teach our children and help others to choose the right and make the decisions
> that will keep them from yielding to temptation. Someone asked me the other day
> why we have all these temptations, and why the Lord has given us the desires such
> as appetites and passions, and why we have to be tempted and tested.
>
> One reason is to help us develop and grow through the schooling we receive in
> the experiences we encounter in mortal life. Brigham Young said: "I am happy . . . for
> the privilege of having temptations" (*JD,* 3:195). Temptations are necessary for our
> advancement and our development. "When temptations come to you, be humble and
> prayerful, and determined that you will overcome, and you will receive a deliverance
> and continue faithful, having the promise of receiving blessings" (*JD,* 16:164).
>
> All of these temptations—these appetites and passions—are for our good and
> enjoyment if we will but let wisdom's voice control. Temptations come to all, but
> long before we are faced with them, we and our children must have determined what
> our course will be. It is too late if we wait until the moment of temptation before
> making our decision. If we have been taught and determined always to choose the
> right and resist evil, we will have the strength to overcome.
>
> We must remember that Satan is always on the job, determined to destroy the
> work of the Lord and to destroy mankind, and as soon as we deviate from the path
> of righteousness, we are in great danger of being destroyed. The scriptures and his-
> tory give us many examples of men in high places who, when they turned from and
> despised the teachings of the Lord, or in any way deviated from the path of right-
> eousness, suffered much sorrow, loss of position, loss of friends and even family.
> ("Where Art Thou," *Ensign,* Dec. 1971, 34)

ILLUSTRATIONS FOR OUR TIME

President Hinckley has given us prophetic advice in regard to temptation. He has
counseled us on various occasions in the following manner:

> We cannot afford to be tainted by moral sin. We live in a world where temptation
> is constantly being thrown at us, particularly at you young people. It is on televi-
> sion. It is in magazines. It is in books. It is on videos which are readily available.
> Stay away from these things. They will only hurt you. When it comes to the moral
> law, you know what is expected of you. If you find yourself slipping under the

pressure of circumstances, discipline yourself. Stop before it is too late. You will be forever grateful that you did. (*TGBH,* 642)

If you are tempted in any direction, remember that somewhere, someone's on his or her knees praying for the missionaries. That's true. That's absolutely true. Never forget it. You live where there is temptation. You live where there is a great let-down in morals. Rise above it. Stand tall. Be clean. Be pure. Be faithful. Be true. (*TGBH,* 643)

To you young people who face temptation, my plea to you is to be clean, to be pure, to be chaste. I make you a promise that if you will do so the time will come when you will thank the Lord with all your heart that you have chosen to behave your-selves. (*TGBH,* 643)

LIKENING THE SCRIPTURES TO OUR LIVES

D&C 29:39 And it must needs be that the devil should tempt the children of men, or they could not be agents unto themselves; for if they never should have bitter they could not know the sweet.

Application: Temptation is a necessary part in the test of mortality (see Abr. 3:25). As we learn to overcome and avoid temptation, we can know the joy and peace of right-eousness and be led by the Spirit in all things (see 2 Ne. 32:5; D&C 11:12–13).

4. FOLLOW CHRIST FAITHFULLY

THEME: The Savior has entreated us to come and follow Him. Let us forsake the things of the world that we might partake of the gospel of Jesus Christ and become joint heirs with Christ.

MOMENT OF TRUTH

Christ's injunction to His disciples was simple and direct: "Follow me." That pattern began when He first encountered Peter and Andrew: "And Jesus, walking by the sea of Galilee, saw two brethren, Simon called Peter, and Andrew his brother, casting a net into the sea: for they were fishers. And he saith unto them, Follow me, and I will make you fishers of men. And they straightway left their nets, and followed him" (Matt. 4:18–20). In similar encounters, the Savior issued the same action command to follow Him (see Matt. 8:22; 9:9; 16:24; 19:21; Mark 2:14; 8:34; 10:21; Luke 5:27; 9:23, 59; 18:22; John 1:43; 10:27; 12:26; 13:36; 21:19). Perhaps the most memorable articulation of this formula is this: "My sheep hear my voice, and I know them, and they follow me: And I give unto them eternal life (John 10:27–28). The most urgent moment of truth in this context is when each individual comes to terms with the fact that Christ's invitation is extended personally to him or to her and that action of a positive and obedient nature is then required. Such action results in extraordinary blessings of an immediate as well as an eternal nature (see Alma 34:31).

MODERN PROPHETS SPEAK

Bruce R. McConkie:

> This is the sum and substance of the whole matter. Salvation, eternal life, rewards in all their degrees and varieties—all come by obedience to the laws and ordinances of the gospel. Salvation must be won; it is not a free gift. "Let us hear the conclusion of the whole matter: Fear God, and keep his commandments: for this is the whole duty of man" (Eccl. 12:13). But what of grace? Grace is the love, mercy, and condescension of God in making salvation available to men. "It is by grace that we are saved, after all we can do" (2 Ne.25:23). Eternal life is freely available; salvation is free in that all may drink of the waters of life; all may come and partake; but none gains so high a reward as eternal life until he is tried and tested and found worthy, as were the ancients. . . .
>
> Eternal life can come to those only who put first in their lives the things of God's kingdom; who love the riches of eternity more than a handful of mortal pelf; who are willing to forsake all and follow Christ. Where a man's treasure is, there will his heart be also. (*The Mortal Messiah,* 3:302–04)

ILLUSTRATIONS FOR OUR TIME

Following are three modern-day exhortations on how we can more faithfully follow Christ:

Nephi Revisited

> Thus Nephi presents a complete parallelism between the baptisms of Christ and of the believer. In this sermon, Christ was immersed to prove his obedience through baptism, but also as a pledge of future loyalty "that he would be obedient." The believer's baptism also indicates "that ye are willing to keep my commandments." "To be willing" is mainly future: it is the language of personal covenant in Book of Mormon religious contexts. Indeed, Nephi's sermon stresses the lifetime commitment to righteousness one makes through baptism (2 Ne. 31:15–21). Nephi's overall point is that the believer should follow Christ both in baptism and also in keeping the

personal promises made then. Immersion is a means of forgiveness, but covenant baptism is also preventive medicine. It is a solemn promise not to sin—a promise even shared by Christ. He entered that baptismal covenant and lived up to it perfectly, so Nephi finally calls on everyone baptized to "endure to the end, in following the example of the Son of the living God" (2 Ne. 31:16). (*By Study and Also by Faith: Essays in Honor of Hugh W. Nibley on the Occasion of His Eightieth Birthday, 27 March 1990*, 2 vols., ed. John M. Lundquist and Stephen D. Ricks [Salt Lake City and Provo: Deseret Book, Foundation for Ancient Research and Mormon Studies, 1990], 2:13)

Grace and Determination

However, through the Atonement of Jesus Christ, when men, women, or children have faith in Jesus, are truly penitent, call upon his name, and are baptized, they become eligible for the redeeming grace extended through Jesus Christ. In this sense they become justified. This is given as a gift by grace, since fallen man must rely "alone upon the merits of Christ" (Moro. 6:4; 1 Ne. 10:6). The faith by which one receives this grace manifests itself in an active determination to follow Christ in all things. It is demonstrated by obedience to the commandments to repent and be baptized, followed by a life of submission, obedience, and service to God and others (2 Ne. 31:16–20; Moro. 8:25–26; see Gospel of Jesus Christ). (Richard L. Anderson, in *Encyclopedia*, 776)

A Timeless Formula

The gospel message today is the same as it has always been: love God, follow Christ, serve one another, develop self-mastery and spiritual power, keep the commandments with the assurance that thereby God will be pleased and you will obtain eternal joy, never give up in well doing, continue faithful to the end. (Camilla Eyring Kimball, *The Writings of Camilla Eyring Kimball*, ed. Edward L. Kimball [Salt Lake City: Deseret Book, 1988], 81)

LIKENING THE SCRIPTURES TO OUR LIVES

Luke 18:22 Now when Jesus heard these things, he said unto him, Yet lackest thou one thing: sell all that thou hast, and distribute unto the poor, and thou shalt have treasure in heaven: and come, follow me.

Application: We are to forsake the world and its so-called treasures, for they have no exalting power. We are instead to build up treasures in Heaven by accepting the infinite Atonement and demonstrating our faithfulness through our good works (see Matt. 6:20; 2 Ne. 25:23).

SUMMARY

After Jesus had commissioned Phillip with the words "Follow me" (John 1:43), Phillip went and found Nathanael and shared with him the good news concerning the Messiah. "And Nathanael said unto him, Can there any good thing come out of Nazareth? Philip saith unto him, Come and see" (John 1:46). Therein lies a failsafe strategy, for we are all invited to "come and see" the glory and abundance of the Savior's plan and then invite others to "come and see" the same thing with an open heart and a willing mind. Those who accept Jesus in faith and humility become engaged in the ongoing process of preparing the way of the Lord. They willingly follow the Savior's example by being baptized for the remission of their sins in anticipation of receiving the gift of the Holy Ghost. They learn how to withstand and overcome the temptations of the devil as they proceed onward toward the goal of eternal life, following Christ faithfully in all they do.

CHAPTER 5

BORN AGAIN—THE MIGHTY CHANGE

Reading Assignment: John 3–4.

Additional Reading: 1 Nephi 11:25; Mosiah 5:1–7; 27:25–26; Alma 5:14–16; 22:15–18; D&C 63:23; Moses 6:59.

> *So, my beloved brothers and sisters, as we seek to qualify to be members of Christ's Church—members in the sense in which He uses the term, members who have repented and come unto Him—let us remember these six principles. First, the gospel is the Lord's plan of happiness, and repentance is designed to bring us joy. Second, true repentance is based on and flows from faith in the Lord Jesus Christ. There is no other way. Third, true repentance involves a change of heart and not just a change of behavior. Fourth, part of this mighty change of heart is to feel godly sorrow for our sins. This is what is meant by a broken heart and a contrite spirit. Fifth, God's gifts are sufficient to help us overcome every sin and weakness if we will but turn to Him for help. Finally, we must remember that most repentance does not involve sensational or dramatic changes, but rather is a step-by-step, steady, and consistent movement toward godliness.*

—EZRA TAFT BENSON, "A MIGHTY CHANGE OF HEART," *ENSIGN,* OCT. 1989, 5.

THEMES *for* LIVING

1. Being Born of the Water and of the Spirit
2. Partake of the "Living Water"
3. Invite Others—The Field Is White Already to Harvest

INTRODUCTION

Born of God or "born again" refers to the personal spiritual experience in which repentant individuals receive a forgiveness of sins and a witness from God that if they continue to live the COMMANDMENTS and endure to the end, they will inherit ETERNAL LIFE. The scriptures teach that just as each individual is "born into the world by water, and blood, and the spirit," so must one be "born again" of water and the Spirit and be cleansed by the blood of Christ (John 3:5; Moses 6:59). To be born of God implies a sanctifying process by which the old or NATURAL MAN is supplanted by the new spiritual man who enjoys the companionship of the Holy Ghost and hence is no longer disposed to commit sin (Col. 3:9–10; Mosiah 3:19; *TPJS,* 51). When individuals are born again they are spiritually begotten sons and daughters of God and more specifically of Jesus Christ (Mosiah 5:7; 27:25). The Book of Mormon prophet ALMA calls this inner transformation a "mighty change in your hearts" (Alma 5:14).

LDS scripture and literature contain numerous examples of individuals who have undergone this process of spiritual rebirth. Enos relates that after "mighty prayer and supplication" the Lord declared that his sins had been forgiven (Enos 1:1–8). After King Benjamin's discourse, the people said that the Spirit had "wrought a mighty change in us, or in our hearts," and that they had "no more disposition to do evil, but to do good continually" (Mosiah 5:2). Of his conversion experience, Alma the Younger says, "Nevertheless, after wading through much tribulation, repenting nigh unto death, the Lord in mercy hath seen fit to snatch me out of an everlasting burning, and I am born of God" (Mosiah 27:28). Similar experiences are recounted about King Lamoni and his father (Alma 19, 22). In an account written in 1832, the Prophet Joseph Smith describes his FIRST VISION as being significant not only for opening a new DISPENSATION of the gospel, but also for his personal conversion. He writes, "The Lord opened the heavens upon me and I saw the Lord and he spake unto me saying Joseph my son thy sins are forgiven thee. And my soul was filled with love and for many days I could rejoice with great joy and the Lord was with me" (*TPJS* 1:6–7).

MORMON explains the "mighty change" that must occur if one is to be born of God. The first fruit of repentance is the BAPTISM of water and fire, which baptism "cometh by faith unto the fulfilling of the commandments." Then comes A REMISSION OF SINS that brings a meekness and lowliness of heart. Such a transformation results in one's becoming worthy of the companionship of the Holy Ghost, who "filleth with hope and perfect love, which love endureth by diligence unto prayer" (Moro. 8:25–26).

LDS scriptures teach that spiritual rebirth comes by the GRACE of God to those who adhere to the principles and ordinances of the gospel of Jesus Christ, namely, faith, repentance, baptism, and reception of the GIFT OF THE HOLY GHOST. For the process to be genuine, however, one must be diligently engaged in good works, for as James says, "faith without works is dead; . . . by works is faith made perfect" (James 2:20, 22). A mere confession of change, or receiving baptism or another ordinance, does not necessarily mean that one has been born of God.

Other Christian faiths also emphasize the importance of being "born again." Unlike many of these, Latter-day Saints do not believe this experience alone is sufficient for SALVATION. Instead, the process of spiritual rebirth signals to Latter-day Saints the beginning of a new life abounding with faith, grace, and good works. Only by ENDURING TO THE END may the individual return to the presence of God. Those who receive the ordinance of baptism and are faithful in keeping the commandments may enjoy the constant presence of the Holy Ghost who, like fire, will act as a sanctifier, and will witness to the hearts of the righteous that their sins are forgiven, imparting hope for eternal life.

Persons who have experienced this mighty change manifest attitudinal and behavioral changes. Feeling their hearts riveted to the Lord, their obedience extends beyond performance of duty. Harold B. Lee taught, "Conversion must mean more than just being a 'card-carrying' member of the Church with a tithing receipt, a membership card, a temple recommend, etc. It means to overcome the tendencies to criticize and to strive continually to improve inward weaknesses and not merely the outward appearances" (*Ensign,* June 1971, 8). Latter-day Saints believe that individuals who are truly born of God gladly give a life of service to their fellow beings—they share the gospel message, sacrifice their own time, energy, and resources for the benefit of others, and in general hold high the Light of Christ, being faithful to all the commandments. (Ed J. Pinegar, in *Encyclopedia,* 218)

1. BEING BORN OF THE WATER AND OF THE SPIRIT

THEME: It is the doctrine of Christ that one must be born again in order to enter the kingdom of God.

MOMENT OF TRUTH

The setting is extraordinary: a contemplative and reasonable ruler among the Jews and a leading Pharisee by rank engages in a dialogue about ultimate things with the Creator of the world and Author of eternal salvation for all mankind. Nicodemus has come to Jesus by night, no doubt to avoid detection by his ultra-conservative colleagues, and confesses to the Savior that he believes He is "a teacher come from God" (John 3:2), whereupon the Savior makes the mind-stopping statement: "Verily, verily, I say unto thee, Except a man be born again, he cannot see the kingdom of God" (John 3:3). There then ensues a remarkable exchange of ideas at two separate but related levels: the everyday level of physical reality and the higher level of spiritual truth—birth in the mortal sense and renewal in the spiritual sense, logic in the cognitive sense and illumination in the heavenly sense. A second birth—"How can these things be?" (John 3:9), Nicodemus wants to know.

Then the Savior chides him (and his school of thought) for failing to comprehend the simple truth of spiritual matters. Just as Moses lifted up a brass serpent in the wilderness as an emblem of the Redeemer, the Preserver of Life (Num. 21:8–9), so must the Savior be lifted up on the cross to bring about the atoning sacrifice on behalf of all who have faith in Him. And that is the key to rebirth: *faith*.

The Savior then makes the timeless statement: "For God so loved the world, that he gave his only begotten Son, that whosoever believeth in him should not perish, but have everlasting life" (John 3:16). The lesson—which embraces the foundational imperatives for baptism, or spiritual rebirth—ends when Jesus gives Nicodemus the secret for understanding the doctrine being taught: *action*. "But he that doeth truth cometh to the light, that his deeds may be made manifest, that they are wrought in God" (John 3:21)—a statement anticipating the well-known formula that Christ would later pronounce: "If any man will do his will, he shall know of the doctrine, whether it be of God, or whether I speak of myself" (John 7:17).

MODERN PROPHETS SPEAK

James E. Faust:

> A rebirth out of spiritual adversity causes us to become new creatures. From Mosiah we learn that all mankind must be born again—born of God, changed, redeemed, and uplifted—to become sons and daughters of God (Mosiah 27:24–27). Marion G. Romney, speaking for the Lord, has stated of this marvelous power: "The effect upon each person's life is likewise similar. No person whose soul is illuminated by the burning Spirit of God can in this world of sin and dense darkness remain passive. He is driven by an irresistible urge to fit himself to be an active agent of God in furthering righteousness and in freeing the lives and minds of men from the bondage of sin." (*To Reach Even unto You* [Salt Lake City: Deseret Book, 1980], 99)

ILLUSTRATIONS FOR OUR TIME

True Conversion Means Being Born Again Through the Mighty Change
Being born again and experiencing the mighty change of heart constitutes true conversion and has a lasting effect upon the soul. Once you have been through this spiritual

transition, you have an overwhelming desire to bless others by helping them come unto Christ. Howard W. Hunter explained this process during a Mission Presidents Seminar, as reported in the *LDS Church News* of July 1, 1989:

> President Hunter affirmed that "no man or woman can receive eternal life without the Atonement of Jesus Christ being fully efficacious in one's life."
>
> He cited the pattern of conversion in the Book of Mormon following King Benjamin's sermon in Mosiah 4. The effect of the message, President Hunter observed, was that the people viewed themselves in their worldly state, and they next cried to the Lord for mercy, forgiveness and purification. Ultimately the Spirit of the Lord rested upon them and filled them with joy.
>
> "That pattern of conversion applies to every member of the Church today," President Hunter said.
>
> Posing the question of what the Atonement has to do with missionary work, President Hunter said, "Any time we experience the blessings of the Atonement in our lives, we cannot help but have a concern for the welfare of others." . . .
>
> "Those of us who have partaken of the Atonement are under obligation to bear faithful testimony of our Lord and Savior," he declared. ("Baptism Is Gateway to Eternal Life," *LDS Church News,* 1989, 1 Jul. 1989, 5)

LIKENING THE SCRIPTURES TO OUR LIVES

Mosiah 27:25 And the Lord said unto me: Marvel not that all mankind, yea, men and women, all nations, kindreds, tongues and people, must be born again; yea, born of God, changed from their carnal and fallen state, to a state of righteousness, being redeemed of God, becoming his sons and daughters.

Application: The commandment is clear. We must be born again and experience this mighty change (see Alma 5:14). We are to strive to become like Him so that when He appears we will indeed be like Him (see Moro. 7:48). This is the purpose for our life on earth—to keep the Lord's commandments as we ply the pathway leading to life eternal.

2. PARTAKE OF THE "LIVING WATER"

THEME: Christ is the "Living Water." This living water encompasses the knowledge, doctrines, principles, covenants, and ordinances of the gospel of Jesus Christ that lead to eternal and everlasting life.

MOMENT OF TRUTH

Close to the main road from Judaea to Galilee, near the ancient city of Shechem (now Nablus) where Jacob lived for several years after his return from serving Laban (Gen. 33:18; 37:12) was a well called Jacob's well. It was at the site of this well that Jesus encountered a woman of Samaria and had a far-reaching discussion with her, the implications of which still resonate in the hearts of all those who are seekers of truth (see John 4:1–42). The Samaritans were an ancient people of mixed heritage, deriving partly from foreign colonists who occupied central and northern Israel after the captivity by the Assyrians (2 Kgs. 17:5–6) and later by the Babylonians, and deriving partly from Israelites who escaped at the times of the captivity. Between the Samaritans and the Jews there smoldered an enduring antagonism, stemming partly from the exclusion of the former from the temple-building enterprise during the ministry of Ezra and Nehemiah (mid-fifth century B.C.).

But for the Savior there was no such antagonism. He knew that the message of truth would soon be preached among the Samaritans and other non-Jewish peoples by His emissaries. For Him, this woman of Samaria was a daughter of God—and He could read her heart and know full well of her history and disposition. He therefore presently made the prophetic statement: "Whosoever drinketh of this water shall thirst again: But whosoever drinketh of the water that I shall give him shall never thirst; but the water that I shall give him shall be in him a well of water springing up into everlasting life" (John 4:13–14). In this manner, the Savior spoke symbolically on two different but harmonizing levels: everyday reality and eternal verity. The water of which He spoke is the water of salvation, imparted to those who "worship the Father in spirit and in truth" (John 4:24), regardless of their heritage and descent. Because the Savior had been able to reflect back to this woman of Samaria the facts of her life—things that a stranger could not have known—she believed on His divine nature: "Sir, I perceive that thou art a prophet" (John 4:19). The Savior then identified Himself as the promised Messiah, which news the woman subsequently delivered to her compatriots, many of whom received Jesus with open and believing hearts.

MODERN PROPHETS SPEAK

Harold B. Lee:

> The rod of iron as seen in the vision interpreted was the word of God, or the gospel of Jesus Christ, which led to the tree of life that the Master explained to the woman at the well in Samaria was as "a well of [living] water springing up into everlasting life" (John 4:14). (*Stand Ye in Holy Places,* 351)

ILLUSTRATIONS FOR OUR TIME

Dallin H. Oaks explains beautifully the story of the woman at Jacob's well and the essence of the "living water." He said:

> A final contrast between the ways of the Lord and the ways of the world—symbolic of all of the others—appears in an incident recorded in the Gospel of John. During his journey across Samaria, Jesus rested at Jacob's well. A Samaritan woman came to draw water, and he asked her for a drink. When she marveled that a Jew would speak to a Samaritan, he told her that if she knew who he was, she would ask him for living water. Seeing that he had no implement to draw water from the deep well, she asked him how he could obtain any water to give her. . . .
>
> In answer to the question how he could give the Samaritan woman living water without any way to draw it from the well, Jesus answered: "Whosoever drinketh of this water shall thirst again: but whosoever drinketh of the water that I shall give him shall never thirst; but the water that I shall give him shall be in him a well of water springing up into everlasting life" (John 4:13–14). . . .
>
> Jesus taught us how to obtain the living water. The teaching he gave the Samaritan woman reminds us, even as we are involved in acquiring the worldly skills and knowledge and methods to draw water from earthly wells, that what we obtain from Jacob's well gives only temporary relief. The water of Jacob's well, however significant in satisfying temporary earthly desires, is insignificant in value beside what we can obtain from Jesus' words and from his atoning sacrifice. And when we seek to obtain or share that living water, we must do it in the Lord's way. (*The Lord's Way* [Salt Lake City: Deseret Book, 1991], 13–15)

LIKENING THE SCRIPTURES TO OUR LIVES

D&C 63:23 But unto him that keepeth my commandments I will give the mysteries of my kingdom, and the same shall be in him a well of living water, springing up unto everlasting life.

Application: It is one thing to know about the living water and all its accompanying blessings, and it is another to continually drink from the eternal spring of living water unto everlasting life. To drink enduringly of the living water means that we will keep the commandments of God faithfully and render ongoing service in building His Kingdom. In this manner, we will be blessed with an understanding of the principles and doctrines of the gospel of Jesus Christ.

3. INVITE OTHERS—THE FIELD IS WHITE ALREADY TO HARVEST

THEME: There are people ready to hear the gospel, but they are kept from truth "because they know not where to find it" (D&C 123:12). It thus behooves us to reach out and find the honest in heart so that they might embrace the truth and come into the fold. Harvest time is quickly coming to an end. Let us therefore thrust in our sickles with our might and help people come unto Christ (see D&C 4; 31:5).

MOMENT OF TRUTH

About the time the Savior had His conversation with the woman of Samaria concerning the "living water" (John 4:10–14), He taught a powerful lesson to His disciples about the process of doing effective missionary work. When His disciples encouraged Him to eat a portion of meat, He invoked once again His emblematic language that operated simultaneously on two different levels of understanding:

> But he said unto them, I have meat to eat that ye know not of.
>
> Therefore said the disciples one to another, Hath any man brought him ought to eat?
>
> Jesus saith unto them, My meat is to do the will of him that sent me, and to finish his work.
>
> Say not ye, There are yet four months, and then cometh harvest? behold, I say unto you, Lift up your eyes, and look on the fields; for they are white already to harvest.
>
> And he that reapeth receiveth wages, and gathereth fruit unto life eternal: that both he that soweth and he that reapeth may rejoice together. (John 4:32–36)

In this manner, the Savior imparted to these disciples the commandment to carry the gospel message to others, for the harvest He referred to is tied neither to the domestic calendar nor to the seasons of earth life but is the immediate and urgent harvest of bringing souls unto God. Those with spiritual eyes perceive the opportunity at hand for such a spiritual harvest: "look on the fields; for they are white already to harvest" (v. 35). The laborers are the missionaries of the Lord; the yield consists of individuals who experience the "mighty change" of heart that King Benjamin spoke of (Mosiah 5:2–7; compare Alma 5:14); the outcome for the penitent and believing consists of salvation and eternal life; the blessings for both learner and teacher consist of enlightenment and eternal joy (see D&C 50:22–24).

MODERN PROPHETS SPEAK

Richard G. Scott:

> There are few things in life that bring as much joy as the joy that comes from assisting another improve his or her life. That joy is increased when those efforts help someone understand the teachings of the Savior and that person decides to obey them, is converted, and joins His Church. There follows great happiness as that new convert is strengthened during the transition to a new life, is solidly grounded in truth, and obtains all of the ordinances of the temple with the promise of all the blessings of eternal life. President McKay showed us how to obtain such joy with his profound clarification of our responsibility to share the gospel: Every member a missionary. I know many more would follow that charge were they to realize that there are many different ways to fulfill that responsibility. I will describe some of them. But first, why has each of us been asked to be a missionary?
>
> The Savior emphasized the vital importance of sharing the gospel when He said to His disciples: "Go ye into all the world, and preach the gospel to every creature. He that *believeth and is baptized shall be saved; but he that believeth not shall be damned*" (Mark 15:15–16). He charged His servants to seek not the things of this world but "seek ye first to *build up the kingdom of God*" (Matt. 6:38). ("Why Every Member a Missionary?" *Ensign,* Nov. 1997, 35)

ILLUSTRATIONS FOR OUR TIME

Why Are You Here?

In a recent presentation as part of the Young Missionary Training Program that my wife and I direct in our stake, Brother Mel Gourdin, former Mission President of the California San Bernardino Mission, explained to the assembled group that he would always ask newly arriving missionaries the question: "Why are you here?" The answers varied. Some missionaries were following in the footsteps of their fathers; some were there out of duty; some did not know. For those who seemed uncertain, President Gourdin had this follow-up question: "Have you asked the Lord? Have you been on your knees to ask Him if the gospel is true?"

He explained that many missionaries who came into the mission field had indeed been on their knees and knew precisely why they were there. They had a clear focus about their calling. They were to participate in the spiritual harvest that the Lord spoke about (see John 4:31–38; compare D&C 4). One such missionary from a very large family arrived virtually penniless. "Why are you here?" asked the mission president in his kindly way. The young elder said: "I have followed what the Prophet Joseph Smith did. I prayed about it and know it's true. And I want to share this message with the world." This young elder had a light in his eyes and a firm testimony in his heart, but he had no financial support for his labors. President Gourdin said to him, "We will pray and see what the Lord wants."

The very next day, a family from the area called the mission home to say, "We have been greatly blessed in our business and we want to support a missionary. Do you have someone who needs help?" That was the answer to the prayer. As a result of the kindness and charity of the family, the young missionary received the support he needed to carry on his missionary labors. He was an extraordinarily devoted and successful emissary for the Lord, always acting in the strength of the Lord with complete faith.

The message for all missionaries and for people everywhere is clear, said President Gourdin, referring to the well-known scripture: "I, the Lord, am bound when ye do what I say; but when ye do not what I say, ye have no promise" (D&C 82:10). President Gourdin then cited the following scripture for all who are preparing to enter missionary service: "Search diligently, pray always, and be believing, and all things shall work together for your good, if ye walk uprightly and remember the covenant wherewith ye have covenanted one with another" (D&C 90:24). [Allen]

There Is No Joy Like the Joy of Helping Someone Repent
The Lord said, "Remember the worth of souls is great in the sight of God . . . And how great is his joy in the soul that repenteth!" (D&C 18:10, 13). The Lord's purpose is to invite all to come unto Him that they might have everlasting life. The purpose of the work of Heavenly Father and our Savior is our immortality and eternal life (see Moses 1:39). As members of the Church, this should be our goal as well. How do we thrust in our sickles? How do we warn our neighbors? How do we share the gospel? How do we assist the missionary effort?

Here are some ideas:

- Pray for all those who know not God (see Alma 6:6).
- Warn your neighbor by example and with loving service (see D&C 88:81).
- Open your mouth and it will be filled (see D&C 33:8–11).
- Give out passalong cards when you travel or to acquaintances in your neighborhood.
- Prayerfully place a copy of the Book of Mormon with a promise of blessings to those who read it.
- Prayerfully set a date to have someone ready to receive the missionaries.
- Pray for the missionaries.

- Invite people to a ward activity or to a family home evening.
- Pray to be led to someone who is seeking the truth.
- Make missionary work part of your family home evening lessons and activities.
- Prepare your children to serve missions.
- Make plans in your later years to serve as senior missionaries (they are really needed).

Remember that we are missionaries at all times by example and precept. We are to stand as witnesses of Christ at all times. [Pinegar]

LIKENING THE SCRIPTURES TO OUR LIVES

John 4:35–36 Say not ye, There are yet four months, and then cometh harvest? behold, I say unto you, Lift up your eyes, and look on the fields; for they are white already to harvest. And he that reapeth receiveth wages, and gathereth fruit unto life eternal: that both he that soweth and he that reapeth may rejoice together.

Application: The time to reap the harvest is now. The Lord reminds us "For behold the field is white already to harvest; and lo, he that thrusteth in his sickle with his might, the same layeth up in store that he perisheth not, but bringeth salvation to his soul" (D&C 4:4). Let us make our plans to be instruments in the hand of the Lord to assist in this great work, that we may bring souls unto Him (see D&C 15:6).

SUMMARY

From the beginning of His ministry, the Savior lifted the spirits of His hearers toward a higher level of truth and enlightened their minds with the edifying hope of fulfilling their destiny as sons and daughters of God. He taught that the pathway to eternal life requires being born again of the water and of the Spirit, just as He Himself had demonstrated in the waters of the Jordan. He taught that we are to partake of the living water and quench forever our spiritual thirst. He taught that those who ply this appointed pathway are to reach out and bring others along with them. As He said to the ancient American Saints: "And behold, I am the light and the life of the world; and I have drunk out of that bitter cup which the Father hath given me, and have glorified the Father in taking upon me the sins of the world, in the which I have suffered the will of the Father in all things from the beginning" (3 Ne. 11:11). Let us faithfully pursue our course, availing ourselves of the saving doctrines and ordinances of the gospel of Jesus Christ—the "living water" that sustains our journey toward eternal life.

Let us experience the mighty change of heart and then endure to the end with courage and dignity.

CHAPTER 6

"THEY STRAIGHTWAY LEFT THEIR NETS"—THE CALLING *of the* TWELVE APOSTLES

Reading Assignment: Luke 4:14–32; 5; 6:12–16; Matthew 10.

Additional Reading: Ephesians 4:11–15; D&C 107:23–24, 33, 35; 112:14, 19–22; 124:128.

> *The Twelve Apostles hold "the keys to open up the authority of my (God's) kingdom upon the four corners of the earth" (D&C 124:128). It is their duty, also, "to ordain and set in order all other officers of the Church (D&C 107:58). "The Twelve are a Traveling Presiding High Council, to officiate in the name of the Lord, under the direction of the Presidency of the Church, agreeable to the institution of heaven; to build up the Church, and regulate all the affairs of the same in all nations, first unto the Gentiles, and secondly unto the Jews" (D&C 107:33). They are "special witnesses of the name of Christ in all the world; and they form a quorum, equal in authority and power" to the First Presidency (D&C 107:23–24). The Twelve Apostles have full authority to perform any and all ordinances in the Church, under the direction of the First Presidency (D&C 18:27–29; 20:38–44; 107:35; 124:127–128).*
>
> *By direction of the First Presidency, the Council of the Twelve have general supervision of the quorums of the Melchizedek Priesthood throughout the Church. From this Council will proceed plans of work, forms of reports and suggestions for the betterment of the work, and to this council also, the summarized reports of quorum activity will be sent.*

—JOHN A. WIDTSOE, PRIESTHOOD AND CHURCH GOVERNMENT [SALT LAKE CITY, DESERET BOOK, 1939], 128-29.

THEMES *for* LIVING

1. Jesus Declares That He Is the Promised Messiah
2. Jesus Calls, Ordains, and Instructs the Twelve Apostles
3. Sustaining Our Prophets, Seers, and Revelators

INTRODUCTION

From the Holy Scriptures, we can be edified by the account of how Jesus proclaimed His role as the Promised Messiah and began to set up His Kingdom upon the earth. He called His Apostles and prophets after spending the night on a mountain in prayer to His Father (see Luke 6:12). Thus the Lord's Apostles were called by revelation—and it is even so today. We learn from the fifth Article of Faith the following: "We believe that a man must be called of God, by prophecy, and by the laying on of hands by those who are in authority, to preach the Gospel and administer in the ordinances thereof." We show our respect and love for our Heavenly Father as we sustain His leaders with all our heart. Heavenly Father loves and respects us as we participate in the law of common consent—the act whereby we show our love and devotion to God by accepting and sustaining our leaders. We too are called of God in our various capacities of service in His Kingdom. This doctrine of being called of God through revelation should bring joy to our souls, knowing as we do that Heavenly Father cares about each of us. By sustaining those in authority over us we are in fact showing reverence to God. Similarly, we show our reverence and gratitude by accepting our own calls to serve faithfully and willingly.

1. JESUS DECLARES THAT HE IS THE PROMISED MESSIAH

THEME: The Savior was called to His atoning office from before the foundations of the world. He quotes prophetic scripture concerning the promised Messiah and declares that in fact He is the Promised Messiah. In a similar way, let us have the courage to present ourselves with courage as representatives of His Church and Kingdom and bear solemn witness that the gospel is true.

MOMENT OF TRUTH

The miracles wrought by the Savior in His early travels soon generated wonderment and excitement throughout the region. They came from all over to listen to Him preach and observe His blessing and healing of the infirm and sick. It was therefore as a celebrity of considerable reputation that He made His appearance one day in the synagogue at Nazareth, where He had been raised. Having been presented with a copy of the book of Isaiah, the Lord found a place of His choosing and read these words: "The Spirit of the Lord is upon me, because he hath anointed me to preach the gospel to the poor; he hath sent me to heal the brokenhearted, to preach deliverance to the captives, and recovering of sight to the blind, to set at liberty them that are bruised, To preach the acceptable year of the Lord" (Luke 4:18–19: compare Isa. 61:1–2). He then returned the book to the rabbi and sat down as all eyes were riveted to him and all ears were opened to what He might say. To the amazement of the audience, He pronounced these words of solemn witness: "This day is this scripture fulfilled in your ears" (Luke 4:21). The Lord's testimony of His own divine calling, which He declared frequently and consistently (see, for example, John 4:26; 8:28; 13:9), demonstrates His courage in the face of incredulity and ridicule on the part of dissenters and clergy and reveals His bold strategy of permitting His enemies to be emboldened in the wake of His telling them the truth. It was in this manner that the framework for the crucifixion was being established even from the beginning of His ministry.

MODERN PROPHETS SPEAK

Bruce R. McConkie:

> A number of Messianic passages speak of "the Lord, and . . . his anointed" (Ps. 2:2), signifying that the Chosen One was consecrated and set apart for the ministry and mission that was his. Jesus applied these passages to himself by quoting Isaiah's prophecy, "The Lord hath anointed me to preach good tidings unto the meek" (Isa. 61:1), and then saying: "This day is this scripture fulfilled in your ears" (Luke 4:21). Peter made the same application by speaking of "thy holy child Jesus, whom thou hast anointed" (Acts 4:27), and by telling "how God anointed Jesus of Nazareth with the Holy Ghost and with power" (Acts 10:38). In a revealed prayer, given in our day, we find this petition: "Wilt thou turn away thy wrath when thou lookest upon the face of thine Anointed" (D&C 109:53). (*The Promised Messiah: The First Coming of Christ,* 182-183)

ILLUSTRATIONS FOR OUR TIME

Noted scholar Robert L. Millet reminds us of the Promised Messiah. He said:

> Jesus Christ is the Promised Messiah, our Savior and Redeemer, and because of what he has done and is doing for us, we need not fear. The Gods of heaven have restored the everlasting gospel to earth in these last days through the instrumentality of a modern prophet, Joseph Smith, and all the powers and knowledge needed to exalt

us in the highest heaven are vested in The Church of Jesus Christ of Latter-day Saints. Further, living apostles and prophets preside over this, the 'only true and living church' on the face of the earth (D&C 1:30). Let us each choose to come unto Christ, partake of his healing and regenerating powers, and find joy and peace in this world and eternal life in the world to come. God grant that we may be true and faithful—true to who we are and faithful to Him whose we are. (*Selected Writings of Robert L. Millet: Gospel Scholars Series* [Salt Lake City: Deseret Book, 2000], 497)

Notice what Brother Millet has taught us in the previous paragraph. Because Jehovah came as the Promised Messiah and suffered and sacrificed and was resurrected, He became the Savior and Redeemer, even Jesus the Christ. When we understand and appreciate this truth, we will have no need to fear, since the restoration of the gospel brings with it the true Church and the power to exalt, if we are but righteous. We have Apostles and prophets as special witnesses of Christ to lead us, and we can choose to come unto Christ and partake of His healing and regenerating powers. [Pinegar]

LIKENING THE SCRIPTURES TO OUR LIVES

Luke 4:21 And he began to say unto them, This day is this scripture fulfilled in your ears.

Application: We are to accept Jesus as the promised Messiah, as prophesied in the scriptures, and recognize and appreciate that He indeed is the Lord and Savior of all mankind. As we search the scriptures, they will testify that He is the Christ and we can know this by the power of the Holy Ghost.

2. JESUS CALLS, ORDAINS, AND INSTRUCTS THE TWELVE APOSTLES.

THEME: The Lord calls and delegates to His chosen Twelve the power to act for God, to be His special witnesses, and to build up the kingdom of God on the earth. Knowing that this same authority has been passed on to our current Apostles—prophets, seers, and revelators—should give us comfort and conviction in the face of life's challenges.

MOMENT OF TRUTH

The Sea of Galilee (also known as the Sea of Chinneroth or the Lake of Gennesaret) is some 12.5 miles long and 7.5 miles wide at its widest point. The Gennesaret area to the north and west of the Sea of Galilee was very fertile, supporting considerable commerce, including fishing. It was in this area where the Savior was preaching when, so pressing was the throng, He retired to a fishing boat that happened to be owned by Simon Peter and asked that the boat be positioned offshore so that He could continue His discourse. Following the preaching, the Savior instructed Simon Peter to move the boat into deeper waters and cast forth the fishing net. "And Simon answering said unto him, Master, we have toiled all the night, and have taken nothing: nevertheless at thy word I will let down the net" (Luke 4:5). To the amazement of this stalwart fisherman, his net became so full of catch that it started to break, and he had to appeal to his partners, James and John, the sons of Zebedee, to come with haste and help with the recovery of caught fish. Having established this teaching moment, the Savior said, "Fear not; from henceforth thou shalt catch men. And when they had brought their ships to land, they forsook all, and followed him" (Luke 5:10–11).

Soon thereafter, He consolidated His selection of the Twelve from among His disciples: "And when it was day, he called unto him his disciples: and of them he chose twelve, whom also he named apostles; Simon, (whom he also named Peter,) and Andrew his brother, James and John, Philip and Bartholomew, Matthew and Thomas, James the son of Alphaeus, and Simon called Zelotes, And Judas the brother of James, and Judas Iscariot, which also was the traitor" (Luke 6:13–16). He then instructed His Apostles how to proceed with their calling, teaching them, among other things, to be "wise as serpents, and harmless as doves" (Matt. 10:16; compare Alma 18:22), to follow the promptings of the Spirit in what they should say before the people under all circumstances (Matt. 10:19–20), to understand that they were priceless to the Father, who knew of them personally and valued them (Matt. 10:29–31), to rejoice in persecution, for the Father was reserving for them a heavenly reward (Luke 6:23), and to return love for hate, cultivate humility, and build upon the foundation of truth (see Luke 6:27–49).

MODERN PROPHETS SPEAK

M. Russell Ballard:

> When faith and faithfulness are added to priesthood authority, marvelous things can happen in the lives of men, women, and families. We learn in the scriptures that after the Lord "called unto him his twelve disciples, he gave them power against unclean spirits, to cast them out, and to heal all manner of sickness and all manner of disease" (Matt. 10:1; see also Mark 3:14; Mark 6:7; and Luke 9:1). It was that same priesthood authority that Peter employed when he healed the lame beggar outside the temple in Jerusalem soon after the day of Pentecost. (*Our Search for Happiness: An Invitation to Understand The Church of Jesus Christ of the Latter-day Saints*, 60–61)

ILLUSTRATIONS FOR OUR TIME

The Calling of the Twelve and Their Duties

In this same revelation [D&C 18], it is stated that there are to be Twelve Apostles, whose calling is to "declare my gospel, both unto Gentile and unto Jew" (18:26). These brethren are to receive their appointment because they sincerely desire to take upon them the name of the Lord (18:26–28). Oliver Cowdery and David Whitmer were called to search out the Twelve who are to be known by "their desires and their works" (18:37–38; also Chapter 10). In fulfillment of this revelation, the Prophet later said that the Lord had revealed that the Three Witnesses were to select the Twelve. . . .

The duties of the Twelve, as given in Section 18, are to ordain men to Priesthood offices, declare the gospel, baptize, and to testify of the truth as revealed (D&C 18:31–36).

In concluding Section 18, dealing with the worth of the human soul and the calling of the Twelve, it is declared that a marvelous work will be performed by the Lord through his servants in this dispensation "unto the convincing of many of their sins, that they may come unto repentance, and that they may come unto the kingdom of my Father" (18:44). (Roy W. Doxey, *The Doctrine and Covenants Speaks* [Salt Lake City: Deseret Book, 1964], 1:95–96; compare the further duties of the Twelve as outlined in D&C 107:23, 33)

The Precious Fold

When the Savior called His Twelve to be special representatives of the gospel to the world, He instructed them in the principles of leadership and the doctrines of the Kingdom (see Matt. 10 and Luke 6). Among other important truths, He emphasized how priceless they were before the Father. This lesson in leadership from the Savior should be an inspiration to every individual in the Church charged with the responsibility to mobilize workers in Zion with enthusiasm and conviction, and to every parent with the duty to draw children onward in the process of spiritual development. The first lesson in leadership is to let others know that you love them unconditionally, just as the Father and His Son do.

It was in that spirit, after reading early one morning these choice passages concerning the training of the new Apostles by the Savior, that I was considering how much I loved my own children and how much I yearned to know the joy that John had in mind when he stated: "I have no greater joy than to hear that my children walk in truth" (3 Jn. 1:4). I felt the inspiration to communicate this love to my children and therefore responded to the prompting by immediately sending each of them an e-mail message with this manner of wording: "Sometimes when I get an insight in my writing, there is no one to share it with at that moment. Your mom is still asleep, having spent much time last evening pondering and planning on behalf of our children, every one. So maybe I could share this thought with you in the wee hours of the morning. I have just been reviewing those passages from the New Testament concerning the calling of the Twelve Apostles by Jesus. He is teaching His Apostles how valuable they are and says to them, 'Are not two sparrows sold for a farthing? and one of them shall not fall on the ground without your Father. But the very hairs of your head are all numbered. Fear ye not therefore, ye are of more value than many sparrows' (Matt. 10:29–31). If the Father is aware of each sparrow ('not one of them is forgotten before God'—Luke 12:6), how much more is He aware of each of His sons and daughters in His eternal loving-kindness! So my thought is this: You are valuable before God, just as your siblings are valuable before Him and just as our precious grandchildren are valuable before Him. He loves you and cares for you—just as we, your parents, do. And that is my thought for the day. Love, Dad."

Unbeknownst to me, one of our daughters had just experienced a devastating humiliation at work, having been unjustly blamed by a colleague for poor results in a company project. By coincidence, my e-mail of support arrived just at the precise moment where her spirit needed to be buoyed and hope engendered. As she reported to us the next day, she was able to transcend the challenge through much prayer and faith. The corporate leadership came to her support and exonerated her fully, assuring her that they had full confidence in her service. In a similar way, we can build on our faith and prayers to look forward to the redeeming support of our Savior, who is the Advocate with the Father. Let us all remember and practice more fully the lesson that the Savior taught His Apostles during His ministry: that all of His children are valuable before the Father, who loves His precious fold. [Allen]

LIKENING THE SCRIPTURES TO OUR LIVES

D&C 107:30–31 The decisions of these quorums, or either of them, are to be made in all righteousness, in holiness, and lowliness of heart, meekness and long suffering, and in faith, and virtue, and knowledge, temperance, patience, godliness, brotherly kindness and charity; Because the promise is, if these things abound in them they shall not be unfruitful in the knowledge of the Lord.

Application: We should love and sustain our prophets and the governing councils and quorums of the Church. The method whereby they make their decisions should be our method, even with the divine nature of Jesus Christ—the pure love of Christ—charity.

3. SUSTAINING OUR PROPHETS, SEERS, AND REVELATORS

THEME: We should sustain the leaders in the Church—from our local leaders to our prophets, seers, and revelators—with all our heart, might, mind, and strength.

MOMENT OF TRUTH

In a celebrated passage, the Apostle Paul recalls the extraordinary blessings bestowed upon mankind through the divine structure of God's Kingdom on earth:

> And he gave some, apostles; and some, prophets; and some, evangelists; and some, pastors and teachers;
>
> For the perfecting of the saints, for the work of the ministry, for the edifying of the body of Christ:
>
> Till we all come in the unity of the faith, and of the knowledge of the Son of God, unto a perfect man, unto the measure of the stature of the fulness of Christ:
>
> That we henceforth be no more children, tossed to and fro, and carried about with every wind of doctrine, by the sleight of men, and cunning craftiness, whereby they lie in wait to deceive;
>
> But speaking the truth in love, may grow up into him in all things, which is the head, even Christ. (Eph. 4:11–15)

The lesson is clear: By accepting and participating in the inspired governance structure of the Church—including the sustaining of our leaders—we become the recipients of wonderful blessings, including unity among the community of Saints, the security of following enduring principles in a world of transitoriness and whim, greater understanding of the truth, and becoming more perfect in the measure of Christ's perfection. By firmly establishing His ecclesiastical leadership patterns during His ministry, including the calling of choice and faithful disciples to positions of authority, the Savior prepared the way for the flow of heavenly blessings to His fold.

MODERN PROPHETS SPEAK

James E. Faust:
> Each of the apostles called since then has been sustained as a prophet, seer, and revelator, but those succeeding Joseph as president of the Church have been those apostles in whom *all* of the keys of Christ's earthly kingdom have been active and functioning.

I do not believe members of the Church can be in full harmony with the Savior without sustaining his living prophet on the earth, the president of the Church. If we do not sustain the living prophet, whoever he may be, we die spiritually. Ironically, some have died spiritually by exclusively following prophets who have long been dead. Others equivocate in their support of living prophets, trying to lift themselves up by putting down the living prophets, however subtly. (*Reach Up for the Light* [Salt Lake City: Deseret Book, 1990], 110–11)

ILLUSTRATIONS FOR OUR TIME

Sustaining Our Living Prophets

As you think of the word *sustaining,* ask yourself this question: Is sustaining the living prophets different from having a testimony that we have prophets? When we sustain, it means we *do* something about our belief. Our testimony of the prophet turns into action when we sustain him. My faith in a living prophet began in Primary and continued with me into my growing-up years. I had a testimony that we have prophets, but I hadn't thought about what it meant to sustain the prophets. . . .

Surely we are standing as witnesses of God when we sustain his living prophets, especially when we know what it means to sustain. We will abide by the direction and counsel of the prophets. We indeed become witnesses when we make this solemn covenant. . . .

As each of us listens to the prophet and responds to his message, if we are in tune we can carry his message with us. Others will feel the prophet's message because of the way we act. In this way the message doesn't end tonight—it just begins. Isn't that exciting to think about? We can make his message be a force for good in our own lives, but also in our homes, in our neighborhoods, and at school. . . .

In general conference next week, as we young women and leaders raise our hands to sustain the living prophets, we understand that we are making a solemn covenant. We know as we follow the counsel and direction of the living prophets, we will be better prepared to "make and keep sacred covenants, receive the ordinances of the temple, and enjoy the blessings of exaltation" (*Personal Progress,* 6).

It is my prayer that we will show by our behavior that we are a covenant people, that we sustain the living prophets. (Janette Hales Beckham, "Sustaining the Living Prophets," *Ensign,* May 1996, 84–85)

LIKENING THE SCRIPTURES TO OUR LIVES

D&C 26:2 And all things shall be done by common consent in the church, by much prayer and faith, for all things you shall receive by faith. Amen.

Application: Charles W. Penrose has given us valuable counsel concerning the doctrine of common consent:

> It may seem rather a dry and formal matter to some of the people to come together and lift up their hands to sustain the authorities of the Church, but it is a necessary duty and if we look at it properly, we shall take pleasure therein. It may seem a little monotonous, but as I have said, it is necessary, for it was designed by the Almighty in the organization of this Church, that the voice of the people should respond to the voice of the Lord. It is the voice of the Lord and the voice of the people together in this Church that sanctions all things therein. In the rise of the Church the Lord gave a revelation which said that "all things shall be done by common consent." And the Lord designs that every individual member shall take upon him or her the spirit of the Church, and be an active living member of the body. (Roy W. Doxey, comp., *Latter-day Prophets and the Doctrine and Covenants* [Salt Lake City: Deseret Book, 1978], 1:283)

SUMMARY

The Savior knew who He was: "I AM THAT I AM" (Ex. 3:14), and declared the truth of His divine ministry with boldness and courage, knowing full well that such declarations before His enemies would eventually lead to His crucifixion. He called, ordained, and instructed the Twelve Apostles in the doctrines of the Kingdom and empowered them to build up His Church and gather together the true believers. Many followers sustained these early Church leaders in humility and faith, but most of the people did not. Hence the Savior prepared His disciples to face persecution, vilification, and even death. Let us place our lot with those who sustain the prophets and Apostles. Let us stand up and declare our confidence in the Lord's anointed. As David B. Haight confirmed: "it takes the sustaining of the people to give the leaders of the Church the authority that the Lord has designated by revelation that is necessary" ("Sustaining the Prophets," *Ensign,* Nov. 1998, 36).

CHAPTER 7

JESUS TEACHES FAITH *and* PERFORMS MIRACLES

Reading Assignment: Mark 1–2; 4:35–41; 5; Luke 7:11–17.

Additional Reading: Matthew 9:30; 2 Nephi 27:23; 3 Nephi 17:5–10; Ether 12:12; Mormon 9:15–21.

Jesus is the Christ, the Eternal God; . . . he manifesteth himself unto all those who believe in him, . . . working mighty miracles, signs, and wonders, among the children of men according to their faith (2 Ne. 26:12–13)."It is by faith that miracles are wrought; . . . if these things have ceased, then has faith ceased also" (Moro. 7:37–38). "If there be no faith among the children of men God can do no miracle among them" (Ether 12:12). . . .

Miracles are the fruit of faith. Signs follow those who believe. If there is faith, there will be miracles; if there are no miracles, there is no faith. The two are inseparably inter- twined with each other; they cannot be separated, and there cannot be one without the other. Faith and miracles go together, always and everlastingly. And faith precedes the miracle.

Faith is power, the power of God, the power by which the worlds were made. Where there is faith there is power, and where a people do not have power to heal the sick and perform miracles, they have no faith. . . .

In this connection, be it also noted that among the gifts of the Spirit—where healings are involved—there are two gifts: one is faith to heal, the other, faith to be healed. Manifestly Jesus had faith to perform miracles under any and all circumstances and for whomsoever he chose; that his acts always conformed to holy and just principles is implicit in the very nature of things. We are aware that at times he performed miracles on his own motion and for his own purposes, as in the casting out of the legion of devils from the Gadarene demoniac and in the stilling of the storm on the lake of Gennesaret. But as we are about to see, except in special and unusual circumstances—and these were numerous in the life of Jesus—healing miracles are and should be performed as a result of the faith of the one receiving the divine blessing.

—Bruce R. McConkie, *The Mortal Messiah: From Bethlehem to Calvary*, 4 vols. [Salt Lake City: Deseret Book, 1979–1981], 2:286-87.

THEMES *for* LIVING

1. Faith Precedes Miracles: The Savior Teaches Faith and Performs Miracles
2. Forgiveness Is Central to the Gospel: The Savior Can Forgive Sins

INTRODUCTION

In the gardens of spiritual living, sweet and priceless miracles spring up as a natural outgrowth of faith and godly power, sustained by the light of heavenly compassion and the warmth of heavenly love. Miracles are a blessing from God and are wrought by the power of God (John 3:5). It is at the hands of the righteous that miracles take place (3 Ne. 8:1). Miracles are performed by the power of faith (Ether 12:16). There can be no miracles performed save it be in the name of Jesus Christ (4 Ne. 1:15). Miracles can occur according to the will of God as we exercise our faith (Ether 12:18). Miracles happen every day as lives are changed through spiritual transformation. Miracles happen through prayer and are performed by the power of the priesthood. If we have eyes to see and hearts to feel, we can and will see everyday miracles, for God is a God of miracles and "God is the same yesterday, today, and forever, and in him there is no variableness neither shadow of changing" (Morm. 9:9) He loves us now just as He loved the Saints of yesterday. He seeks to bless us—and He will and does bless on a daily basis. Miracles never cease to occur in the household of faith.

1. FAITH PRECEDES MIRACLES: THE SAVIOR TEACHES FAITH AND PERFORMS MIRACLES

Theme: The Savior taught His gospel among the people and performed great miracles as a blessing to those with faith.

MOMENT OF TRUTH

What a marvelous scene: the Creator of the world, even the Only Begotten of the Father, moving from city to city and countryside to countryside, dispensing truth to the gathering multitudes, expanding their vision to a higher grasp of eternal possibilities, cultivating their hope in a better quality of life, discerning the manifestation of faith among them, performing mighty miracles of healing, and restoring life where their faith was sufficiently strong. "We never saw it on this fashion" (Mark 2:12) is how the people responded to the miraculous experiences with which He endowed them. And truly their world was being transformed through the Master's hand, for they saw with their own eyes and experienced with their very being the touch of the Savior—and felt, perhaps for the first time in their lives, the power of faith that simmered inwardly, awaiting the turning of the key by priesthood authority from a divine source to open the doorway of blessings to them and their families. The ancient American prophet Mormon perceived the universal reality: "God has not ceased to be a God of miracles" (Morm. 9:15). Just as in former times, God blesses us with miracles as a natural product of our faith and devotion.

MODERN PROPHETS SPEAK

Spencer W. Kimball:

> We do have miracles today—beyond imagination! If all the miracles of our own lifetime were recorded, it would take many library shelves to hold the books which would contain them.
>
> What kinds of miracles do we have? All kinds—revelations, visions, tongues, healings, special guidance and direction, evil spirits cast out. Where are they recorded? In the records of the Church, in journals, in news and magazine articles and in the minds and memories of many people. (*TSWK,* 499)

ILLUSTRATIONS FOR OUR TIME

Gordon B. Hinckley enumerates the multiplicity of miracles attending the daily lives of the faithful:

> I have seen miracles in my time, my brothers and sisters. The greatest miracle of all, I believe, is the transformation that comes into the life of a man or a woman who accepts the restored gospel of Jesus Christ and tries to live it in his or her life. (*TGBH,* 340)

This is a work of miracles. Miracles are performed in the lives of the missionaries. . . . The history of this Church is replete with miracles of healing. I know that. I am confident of that. I recall once when I arrived in Hong Kong I was asked if I would visit a woman in the hospital whose doctors had told her she was going blind and would lose her sight within a week. She asked if we would administer to her and we did so, and she states that she was miraculously healed. I have a painting in my home that she gave me which says on the back of it, "To Gordon B. Hinckley in grateful appreciation for the miracle of saving my sight." I said to her, "I didn't save your sight. Of course, the Lord saved your sight. Thank Him and be grateful to Him." (*TGBH,* 343)

Virtue—The Spirit of Life

Those who labor diligently in the Kingdom know the exhilarating feeling of serving the Lord with all their "heart, might, mind and strength" (D&C 4:2). There is solace in the bliss of exhaustion from an uncompromising investment of energy on the Lord's errand. Where can one's energy be better spent than in service?

When the Savior was passing through a throng of people, en route to help the twelve-year-old daughter of Jairus, a ruler of the synagogue, a woman emerged from the crowd and discreetly touched the border of His garment with the hope of obtaining relief from a malady that had plagued her for many years. "And Jesus said, Who touched me? When all denied, Peter and they that were with him said, Master, the multitude throng thee and press thee, and sayest thou, Who touched me? And Jesus said, Somebody hath touched me: for I perceive that virtue is gone out of me" (Luke 8:45–46). Then the woman confessed that she had touched him, resulting in her being healed. "And he said unto her, Daughter, be of good comfort: thy faith hath made thee whole; go in peace" (Luke 8:48). The Savior then proceeded onward in His quest to bless lives, and restored the young daughter of Jairus to life.

On March 14, 1843, Jedediah M. Grant inquired of Joseph Smith why the latter had turned pale and lost strength while blessing 19 of 27 children at a meeting the previous evening. The Prophet's answer is instructive: "I saw that Lucifer would exert his influence to destroy the children that I was blessing, and I strove with all the faith and spirit that I had to seal upon them a blessing that would secure their lives upon the earth; and so much virtue went out of me into the children, that I became weak, from which I have not yet recovered." Referring to the case of the woman touching the garment of Jesus (Luke 8), he continues, "The virtue here referred to is the spirit of life; and a man who exercises great faith in administering to the sick, blessing little children, or confirming, is liable to become weakened" (*HC* 5:303). Thus, whether nurturing or being nurtured, we can all look to the Lord as the source of all vitality.

The lesson is clear: We need to exercise faith and virtue to bless the lives of those under our care and be for them a source of the "spirit of life." As the Prophet said: "I strove with all the faith and spirit that I had to seal upon them a blessing." May we similarly invest our all to bring about good and help to build the Kingdom. The energy that we expend will surely be returned to us in manifold ways by the Lord. [Allen]

LIKENING THE SCRIPTURES TO OUR LIVES

Ether 12:12 For if there be no faith among the children of men God can do no miracle among them; wherefore, he showed not himself until after their faith.

Application: Until we increase in our faith (through the word and fasting and prayer) and exercise it with all our hearts, we cannot enjoy the blessings of miracles in our lives. They work according to our faith (see Ether 12:13–22).

2. FORGIVENESS IS CENTRAL TO THE GOSPEL: THE SAVIOR CAN FORGIVE SINS

THEME: The Lord Jesus Christ has power to forgive sins. He is our judge and advocate with the Father.

MOMENT OF TRUTH

On one occasion, the Savior came to Capernaum, a city on the northwestern shore of the Sea of Galilee, preaching and blessing lives. The throng was so pressing and large that a man suffering from palsy had to be lowered by his attendants through a hole in the roof of the house where the Savior was located so that the Savior might address his needs. "When Jesus saw their faith, he said unto the sick of the palsy, Son, thy sins be forgiven thee" (Mark 2:5). But the scribes among the audience were offended by His action and reasoned "who can forgive sins but God only?" (Mark 2:7). What the Savior then did has become memorialized as one of His most instructive acts of authority and kindness:

> And immediately when Jesus perceived in his spirit that they so reasoned within themselves, he said unto them, Why reason ye these things in your hearts?
>
> Whether is it easier to say to the sick of the palsy, Thy sins be forgiven thee; or to say, Arise, and take up thy bed, and walk?
>
> But that ye may know that the Son of man hath power on earth to forgive sins, (he saith to the sick of the palsy,)
>
> I say unto thee, Arise, and take up thy bed, and go thy way into thine house.
>
> And immediately he arose, took up the bed, and went forth before them all; insomuch that they were all amazed, and glorified God, saying, We never saw it on this fashion. (Mark 2:8–12)

In this manner, the Savior taught a lesson about the power of faith and about the nurturing and redeeming nature of His own commission, for He does indeed have the power to heal—both physically and spiritually—and to forgive sins for those who are penitent and come to Him with a broken heart and contrite spirit.

MODERN PROPHETS SPEAK

Marion G. Romney:

> Real joy and happiness consists of being healed spiritually. It comes from inside. If you will read in the Book of Mormon the first four verses in the fourth chapter of Mosiah, you will learn of a multitude of people, to whom King Benjamin had been speaking, who were brought by the power of the Spirit to a realization of their transgressions. So concerned were they about their sins that they cried out unto the Lord:
>
> "O have mercy, and apply the atoning blood of Christ that we may receive forgiveness of our sins, and our hearts may be purified; for we believe in Jesus Christ, the Son of God . . ." (Mosiah 4:2).
>
> They then received forgiveness because of their faith in Christ and their repentance: their hearts were filled with joy because their sins were forgiven, and they had peace of mind because they were spiritually healed. Jesus Christ, our Savior, has the power to heal our spirits. Every person's spirit is ill when it is burdened with sin. No son or daughter of God is ever completely happy until his spirit is healed by the power of the Spirit of God. When one receives forgiveness, his spirit is healed and he has peace of conscience. ("Joy and Happiness," *Ensign,* Sept. 1973, 2)

ILLUSTRATIONS FOR OUR TIME

Robert J. Matthews expands on the story of the healing of the palsied man and explains with clarity the miracle of forgiveness of sins. He wrote:

> Jesus used the miracle of curing a man of palsy as a teaching device (Mark 2:1–12; Matt. 9:1–8). The man, lying on a bed, was let down through the roof of a house into the midst of a crowd of people. Although it was evident that the man was suffering from a physical ailment and was unable to walk, Jesus' first words to him were, "Son, thy sins be forgiven thee." This greatly agitated the scribes who were sitting there, and they reasoned in their hearts: "Why doth this man [Jesus] thus speak blasphemies? who can forgive sins but God only?" Jesus then said to them, "Is it not easier to say, Thy sins be forgiven thee, than to say, Arise and walk?" (JST, Matt. 9:5; see also JST, Mark 2:7). It is as if he had said to them, "You cannot determine through mortal sight whether his sins are forgiven, but you can perceive whether he gets up

and walks." Then Jesus made this clarifying statement as to his purpose: "But that ye may know that the Son of man hath power on earth to forgive sins, (he saith to the sick of the palsy,) I say unto thee, Arise, and take up thy bed, and go thy way into thine house." It is very clear from the way this miracle is reported, particularly in the JST, that Jesus used the healing of the man's body, which they who were witnesses could perceive with their eyes, to illustrate His ability to heal a soul, which they could not see. This miracle was a teaching device. It surely worked well, for the people were all amazed and said, "We never saw it on this fashion." I suppose you could say it was a case of moving from the known to the unknown, from the visible to the invisible, from the physical to the spiritual dimension. (*A Bible! A Bible!* [Salt Lake City: Bookcraft, 1990], 224)

LIKENING THE SCRIPTURES TO OUR LIVES

Mark 2:5 When Jesus saw their faith, he said unto the sick of the palsy, Son, thy sins be forgiven thee.

Application: Through the goodness of God and the magnificent and infinite Atonement, we can be forgiven of our sins if we repent. Our guilt can be swept away (Enos 1:6) and the Lord will remember them no more (D&C 58:42–43). Let us always retain a remembrance of the goodness of God and how we have been forgiven of our sins (Mosiah 4:11–12).

SUMMARY

From the scriptural passages assigned for this chapter, we learn that faith precedes miracles. The Savior was the Eternal Exemplar of this process, for He taught the true doctrine of the Father and performed many miraculous deeds in blessing people of faith and showing forth the power of God to heal. In this regard, we note that the healing process of repentance and forgiveness is central to the Gospel of Jesus Christ. The Savior can forgive sins. He can make us whole, if we come forth and demonstrate the fruits of contrition, faith, and repentance. "For behold, I am God; and I am a God of miracles; and I will show unto the world that I am the same yesterday, today, and forever; and I work not among the children of men save it be according to their faith" (2 Ne. 27:23; compare D&C 35:8).

CHAPTER 8

THE SERMON *on the* MOUNT—THE HIGHER LAW

Reading Assignment: Matthew 5.

Additional Reading: Ether 12:27; Moroni 10:32–33; D&C 76:68–70.

> *In His Sermon on the Mount the Master has given us somewhat of a revelation of His own character, which was perfect, or what might be said to be "an autobiography, every syllable of which He had written down in deeds," and in so doing has given us a blueprint for our own lives. Anyone clearly understanding the true import of His words comes to the realization that an unworthy member of the Church, although he might be in the kingdom of God, yet would not be of the kingdom because of his unworthiness.*

—HAROLD B. LEE, *THBL*, 13.

THEMES *for* LIVING

1. The Beatitudes: The Lord's Agenda for Blessing His People
2. The Salt of the Earth and the Light of This People
3. Living the Higher Law
4. The Nature of True Discipleship

INTRODUCTION

The Lord Jesus Christ, the Savior of the world, delivers the higher law to the people in the Sermon on the Mount. This is the law of celestial living, the law which, when honored and kept, leads to eternal life. It is the pattern of life for the disciples of the Lord Jesus Christ—the law that will make us free. When we learn to love His law and follow it, it will become our way of living, and we will become even as He is.

1. THE BEATITUDES: THE LORD'S AGENDA FOR BLESSING HIS PEOPLE

THEME: The Savior teaches the doctrine of happiness through the magnificent pronouncement known as the Beatitudes. The word "blessed" as used in these sayings refers to "enjoying spiritual happiness and the favor of God; enjoying heavenly felicity" (An American Dictionary of the English Language, Noah Webster, 1828).

> Blessed are ye if ye shall give heed unto the words of these twelve whom I have chosen. . . . Blessed are ye if ye shall believe in me and be baptized. . . .
>
> More blessed are they who shall believe in your words. . . .
>
> Yea, blessed are the poor in spirit who come unto me, for theirs is the kingdom of heaven.
>
> And again, blessed are all they that mourn, for they shall be comforted.
>
> And blessed are the meek, for they shall inherit the earth.
>
> And blessed are all they who do hunger and thirst after righteousness, for they shall be filled with the Holy Ghost.
>
> And blessed are the merciful, for they shall obtain mercy.
>
> And blessed are all the pure in heart, for they shall see God.
>
> And blessed are all the peacemakers, for they shall be called the children of God.
>
> And blessed are all they who are persecuted for my name's sake, for theirs is the kingdom of heaven.
>
> And blessed are ye when men shall revile you and persecute, and shall say all manner of evil against you falsely, for my sake;
>
> For ye shall have great joy and be exceedingly glad, for great shall be your reward in heaven; for so persecuted they the prophets who were before you. (3 Ne. 12:1–12 see also Matt. 5:3–12)

MOMENT OF TRUTH

The Savior teaches the multitude and reveals the agenda by which He will bless the faithful. This sequence of illuminating sayings known as the Beatitudes is given as a gift of heavenly doctrine to the people. It is a wondrous endowment of truth and divine love that outlines the resplendent array of blessings held in store by the Lord to bless His followers.

MODERN PROPHETS SPEAK

Blessed are ye if ye shall give heed unto the words of these twelve whom I have chosen. (3 Ne. 12:1)

Boyd K. Packer:

> Follow the Brethren. Three words. There is nothing in your life that will destroy you if you will follow the Brethren. (*Things of the Soul* [Salt Lake City: Bookcraft, 1996], 79–80)

Yea, blessed are the poor in spirit who come unto me for theirs is the kingdom of heaven. (3 Ne. 12:3; compare Matt. 5:3)

Bruce R. McConkie:

> The poor in spirit! If they come unto Christ, salvation is theirs; and it is so often easier for those who are not encumbered with the cares and burdens and riches of the world to cast off worldliness and set their hearts on the riches of eternity than it is for those who have an abundance of this world's goods. (*The Mortal Messiah: From Bethlehem to Calvary,* 4 vols. [Salt Lake City: Deseret Book, 1979–1981], 2:121)

And again, blessed are all they that mourn, for they shall be comforted. (3 Ne. 12:4; compare Matt. 5:4)

Harold B. Lee:

> We are here to help lift the eyes of those who mourn from the valley of despair to the light upon the mountain peaks of hope, to endeavor to answer questions about war, to bring peace to troubled souls, not as the world giveth, but only that which comes from the Prince of Peace. We are here to lift all of us out of the shadows into life and light. (*Ye Are the Light of the World: Selected Sermons and Writings of Harold B. Lee* [Salt Lake City: Deseret Book, 1974], 251–52)

And blessed are the meek, for they shall inherit the earth. (3 Ne. 12:5; compare Matt. 5:5)

Gordon B. Hinckley:

> The Lord has said that the meek shall inherit the earth (Matt. 5:5). I cannot escape the interpretation that meekness implies a spirit of gratitude as opposed to an attitude of

self-sufficiency, an acknowledgment of a greater power beyond oneself, a recognition of God, and an acceptance of his commandments. This is the beginning of wisdom. Walk with gratitude before him who is the giver of life and every good gift. (*Faith: The Essence of True Religion* [Salt Lake City: Deseret Book, 1989], 82)

And blessed are all they who do hunger and thirst after righteousness, for they shall be filled with the Holy Ghost. (3 Ne. 12:6; compare Matt. 5:6)

Neal A. Maxwell:

There is too the significant blessing of personal momentum that always comes when we practice decision making in which we both *reject wrong* and *choose the good*. We thus avoid what one prophet called the in-betweenness of the "sorrowing of the damned" (Morm. 2:13). It is not enough to reach a bland behavioral point when we no longer take pleasure in sin; we must hunger and thirst for righteousness. (*Notwithstanding My Weakness* [Salt Lake City: Deseret Book, 1981], 104)

And blessed are the merciful, for they shall obtain mercy. (3 Ne. 12:7; compare Matt. 5:7)

Bruce R. McConkie:

Mercy is for the merciful; mercy is reserved for the righteous; mercy comes to those who keep the commandments. And the Old Testament prophets had similar insight. Hosea said: "Sow to yourselves in righteousness, reap in mercy; break up your fallow ground: for it is time to seek the Lord, till he come and rain righteousness upon you" (Hosea 10:12). (*The Promised Messiah: The First Coming of Christ* [Salt Lake City: Deseret Book, 1978], 246)

And blessed are all the pure in heart, for they shall see God. (3 Ne. 12:8; compare Matt. 5:8)

Harold B. Lee:

If you would see God, you must be pure. . . . Only the righteous saw him as the Son of God. Only if you are the pure in heart will you see God, and also in a lesser degree will you be able to see the "God" or good in man and love him because of the goodness you see in him. Mark well that person who criticizes and maligns the man of God or the Lord's anointed leaders in his Church. Such a one speaks from an impure heart. (*Decisions for Successful Living* [Salt Lake City: Deseret Book, 1973], 59)

And blessed are all the peacemakers, for they shall be called the children of God. (3 Ne. 12:9; compare Matt. 5:9)

Theodore M. Burton:

> Thus, from the beginning of creation, God planned to have leaders available in the last days holding the power of the holy priesthood. With this power we can help bring peace to the world by practicing peace. It must begin in our homes, in our quorums, in our auxiliaries, and within every single Church unit. People are so hungry for peace today that if we truly demonstrate peace among ourselves and to others, they will flock to the Church in great numbers. The greatest missionary tool we have is that of demonstrating friendliness, brotherly kindness, harmony, love, and peace in our homes and in all our Church meetings. If we follow the example of Jesus Christ and become true peacemakers, that flood of love will cover the earth as with a blanket. The only way Satan can ever be bound will be through the love of man for God and for one another. ("Blessed Are the Peacemakers," *Ensign,* Nov. 1974, 56)

And blessed are all they who are persecuted for my name's sake, for theirs is the kingdom of heaven. (3 Ne. 12:10; compare Matt. 5:10)

O. Leslie Stone:

> Today members of the Church do not often face persecution in the form of physical violence or harm, but perhaps some application can be made to the pressures we may feel from society, particularly the peer group pressures that our young people feel when they live up to the standards of dress and morality set by our present-day leaders. If these young people are prayerful and live the commandments, they will feel good about these high standards and will be able to stand up to criticism.
>
> Our youth should always remember that when they were baptized they took upon themselves the name of Jesus Christ; they can be proud to stand up for his principles and those of our present-day leaders. By so doing they will receive rich rewards in this life and in the eternities to come, for theirs is the kingdom of heaven.
>
> Whenever we live up to the best that is in us, we live up to the principles and the ideals the Savior gave us. To follow him brings peace to the soul. ("The Beatitudes," *Ensign,* Nov. 1974, 31)

ILLUSTRATIONS FOR OUR TIMES

A Simple Lesson

He was the meekest of elders, a humble farmboy called as a servant of the Lord among a distant people. His speech was homely, his social skills basic, his only polish the weather-tanned skin of a man of the soil. But when he opened his mouth to bear fervent testimony of the truth of the gospel and the sacredness of the Book of Mormon, there was something special there, something that resonated with simple grandeur. He spoke the words that were in his heart as conveyed by the Holy Spirit. We, his missionary colleagues, noticed the radiance shining from his frontier countenance and learned from him. So did the families he taught.

The lesson is simple: It is not the learning of the world or cultural sophistication that changes hearts; rather, it is the word of God, spoken by His humble servants, and confirmed by the Spirit, that touches lives and opens the soul for gospel illumination. "And blessed are the meek, for they shall inherit the earth" was the promise of the Savior to his listeners in Jerusalem (Matt. 5:5) as well as in America (3 Ne. 12:5). This young elder was doubtless just the type of person who shall indeed inherit the earth. [Allen]

LIKENING THE SCRIPTURES TO OUR LIVES

The Beatitudes (Matt. 5:3–12; Ne. 12:1–11): The Lord teaches us the celestial way of living: how to live happily. How blessed (how happy) are those who do these things.

Application: The way to happiness is to give heed to the word, believe in Christ, be baptized both by water and fire, and endure to the end. Those who do so will be comforted in mourning. They will be meek, will hunger and thirst after righteousness, will be merciful, will be pure in heart, will be peacemakers, and will have the privilege of discipleship—even though they may be persecuted for His name's sake.

2. THE SALT OF THE EARTH AND THE LIGHT OF THIS PEOPLE

THEME: Being part of the fold of Christ brings great blessings but also great responsibilities to glorify God through righteous living.

> Verily, verily, I say unto you, I give unto you to be the salt of the earth; but if the salt shall lose its savor wherewith shall the earth be salted? The salt shall be thenceforth good for nothing, but to be cast out and to be trodden under foot of men. Verily, verily, I say unto you, I give unto you to be the light of this people. A city that is set on a hill cannot be hid. Behold, do men light a candle and put it under a bushel? Nay, but on a candlestick, and it giveth light to all that are in the house; Therefore let your light so shine before this people, that they may see your good works and glorify your Father who is in heaven. (3 Ne. 12:13–16; see also Matt. 5:13–16)

MOMENT OF TRUTH

The Savior, having outlined the blessings awaiting those who follow in His footsteps, now explains that His disciples are to be "the salt of the earth" and "the light of this people" (Matt. 5:13–16; 3 Ne. 12:13,14). With that opportunity and privilege comes great responsibility, for participating in the Abrahamic covenant entails becoming servants of the Most High who carry the gospel message to the world.

MODERN PROPHETS SPEAK

Joseph F. Smith:

> Christ, teaching his disciples, called attention to the importance of their position and place in the world. Though poor and despised of men, yet he told them they were the salt of the earth, the light of the world.
>
> Then he encouraged them to effort and achievement by showing them that their exalted position would avail them little, unless they made proper use of their high callings. . . .
>
> One fault to be avoided by the Saints, young and old, is the tendency to live on borrowed light, with their own hidden under a bushel; to permit the savor of their salt of knowledge to be lost; and the light within them to be reflected, rather than original.
>
> Every Saint should not only have the light within himself, through the inspiration of the Holy Spirit, but his light should so shine that it may be clearly perceived by others.
>
> Men and women should become settled in the truth, and founded in the knowledge of the gospel, depending upon no person for borrowed or reflected light, but trusting only upon the Holy Spirit, who is ever the same, shining forever and testifying to the individual and the priesthood, who live in harmony with the laws of the gospel, of the glory and the will of the Father. They will then have light everlasting which cannot be obscured. By its shining in their lives, they shall cause others to glorify God; and by their well-doing put to silence the ignorance of foolish men, and show forth the praises of him who hath called them out of darkness into his marvelous light. (*Gospel Doctrine: Selections from the Sermons and Writings of Joseph F. Smith,* comp. John A. Widtsoe [Salt Lake City: Deseret Book, 1919], 87–88)

ILLUSTRATIONS FOR OUR TIMES

Some Questions and Answers
We are to be the salt of the earth. What does this mean?

Hoyt W. Brewster, Jr.:

> Those who are the true "salt of the earth" bring out the wholesome "savor of men" (D&C 101:39–40; 103:10; Matt. 5:13; 3 Ne. 12:13). Webster defines *savor* as a verb meaning "to have a specified taste or quality; a special flavor or quality." Faithful members of the Church, the true "salt of the earth," should provide a special quality in whatever social situation they find themselves. Their presence should be edifyingly *savory*, bringing out the best in others and adding to the righteous pleasure of all. (*Doctrine and Covenants Encyclopedia* [Salt Lake City: Bookcraft, 1988], 492–93)

We are to be the light of the world. To whom does this apply and what do we do in regard to this light?

> As defined by the Lord, the "light to the world" is the everlasting covenant, or, in other words, the fulness of the gospel of Jesus Christ as revealed through his church (D&C 45:9, 28). Isaiah wrote of a "standard" that was to be set up to the people of this world (Isa. 49:22; 1 Ne. 21:22). Marion G. Romney identified the Church as that standard of which Isaiah spoke (CR, Apr. 1961, 119).
>
> To the Church the Lord declared: "Arise and shine forth, that thy light may be a standard for the nations" (D&C 115:5). The charge to the Saints in all ages has been to dispel darkness with the light of the gospel (Matt. 5:14–16; 3 Ne. 12:14–16; D&C 115:42–5). For example, Paul declared that his mission was to open the eyes of the people and "to turn them from darkness to light, and from the power of Satan unto God" (Acts 26:18). (*Doctrine and Covenants Encyclopedia* [Salt Lake City: Bookcraft, 1988], 325)

The Spectrum of Heavenly Light

In the Sermon on the Mount, delivered both in Jerusalem as well as in Bountiful, the Savior commissioned His followers to be "the salt of the earth" (Matt. 5:13; 3 Ne. 12:23) and to be "the light of the world" (Matt. 5:14; 3 Ne. 12:14). Both tasks imply the same responsibility: to fulfill with honor the provisions of the Abrahamic covenant by carrying the gospel message—in word and by example—to the four quarters of the world. The latter symbolic image, to be "the light of the world," resonates harmoniously with the revelation given through the Prophet Joseph Smith at Kirtland, Ohio, on December 27, 1832, and designated in the heading as "the olive leaf . . . plucked from the Tree of Paradise, the Lord's message of peace to us."

In the opening passages of this revelation, the Lord recognizes the prayers of the Saints sent up to Him on high and imparts the promise of sending another Comforter to them, "even the Holy Spirit of promise . . . the promise which I give unto you of eternal life, even the glory of the celestial kingdom; Which glory is that of the church of the Firstborn, even of God, the holiest of all, through Jesus Christ his Son—" (D&C 88:3–5).

Then in the next verses of the "olive leaf" the Savior gives us a portrait of Himself as the Master of light—"the light of truth, Which truth shineth. This is the light of Christ" (D&C 88:6–7). This light of truth or light of Christ is then traced by the Savior across a spectrum of additional manifestations (in addition to the gift of the Holy Ghost), including the light by which celestial bodies (sun, moon, stars, earth) operate and were created (v. 7–10), the light of reasoning for the inhabitants of the earth ("And the light which shineth, which giveth you light, is through him who enlighteneth your eyes, which is the same light that quickeneth your understanding"— v. 11), the light by which the earth is sustained in its life-generating vitality (v. 13), and the light and glory by means of which the entire Creation is governed—"even the power of God who setteth upon his throne, who is in the bosom of eternity, who is in the midst of all things" (v. 13).

If one adds to this panoramic spectrum the references to the "light of Christ" as the operant principle of discerning between right and wrong (the light of conscience), then an even fuller picture of the concept of light emerges: "For behold, the Spirit of Christ is given to every man, that he may know good from evil; wherefore, I show unto you the way to judge; for every thing which inviteth to do good, and to persuade to believe in Christ, is sent forth by the power and gift of Christ; wherefore ye may know with a perfect knowledge it is of God" (Moro. 7:16).

If one looks at this system of light in its various manifestations, a hierarchy of principles emerges to illuminate more fully the commission to be "the light of the world":

Spectrum of the Light of Truth or Heavenly Light:

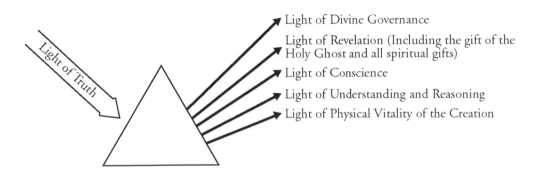

The Savior said to the people: "Verily, verily, I say unto you, I give unto you to be the light of this people. A city that is set on a hill cannot be hid. Behold, do men light a candle and put it under a bushel? Nay, but on a candlestick, and it giveth light to all that are in the house; Therefore let your light so shine before this people, that they may see your good works and glorify your Father who is in heaven" (3 Ne. 12:14–16).

By following these steps upward across the spectrum of heavenly light, the student of the gospel can then take his or her place in the fold of the Lord, savor the blessings of the kingdom of God as governed and nurtured by the power of God, and, by enduring to the end in righteousness, look forward to the transcendent blessing of entering into God's rest, "which rest is the fulness of his glory" (D&C 84:24). When the Savior commanded that we should be the light of the world, He opened up an opportunity of consummate scope which permits us, as emissaries of the Lord, to help bring people into the light of the gospel of Jesus Christ in all of its glorious manifestations. [Allen]

LIKENING THE SCRIPTURES TO OUR LIVES

Matt. 5:13–16; 3 Ne.12:13–16 These are the instructions of the Savior to be the "salt of the earth" and the "light of the world."

Application: As members of the Church, we are reminded by the Lord to honor our covenants. We are the salt of the earth, and if we lose our savor, we are good for nothing. The Lord also indicates that we are to be a light unto the world and to do good works that we might glorify our Heavenly Father.

3. LIVING THE HIGHER LAW

THEME: The gospel is structured to help us progress to ever higher levels of spirituality in ever more perfect compliance with the patterns of heaven. The law of Moses was a schoolmaster that was intended to help the people look forward to Christ. The Lord, as Jehovah of the Old Testament, gave the law of Moses and now proceeds to give the higher law.

> Think not that I am come to destroy the law, or the prophets: I am not come to destroy, but to fulfil. For verily I say unto you, Till heaven and earth pass, one jot or one tittle shall in no wise pass from the law, till all be fulfilled. (Matt 5:17–18)

> Marvel not that I said unto you that old things had passed away, and that all things had become new. Behold, I say unto you that the law is fulfilled that was given unto

Moses. Behold, I am he that gave the law, and I am he who covenanted with my people Israel; therefore, the law in me is fulfilled, for I have come to fulfil the law; therefore it hath an end. (3 Ne. 15:3–5)

MOMENT OF TRUTH

The Lord had already announced a new and illuminating doctrine to the people. Now, continuing His Sermon on the Mount, the Lord expounds on this remarkable new form of sacrifice by unfolding to the people the transition from the old patterns of external ordinances under the law of Moses to the new patterns of devotion and spirituality characteristic of the higher law. He makes it clear that the Law of Moses was fulfilled in Him. At the same time, He declares that all prophetic utterance applying to a later date was still in force and valid and that the sacred covenant between the Lord and His people was still in effect. The old law was centered in codes and regulations of an outward nature, all pointing to Christ; the new law is centered in the Savior Himself: "Behold, I am the law, and the light. Look unto me, and endure to the end, and ye shall live; for unto him that endureth to the end will I give eternal life" (3 Ne. 15:9).

MODERN PROPHETS SPEAK

Jeffrey R. Holland:

> Thus it is crucial to understand that the law of Moses was overlaid upon, and thereby included, many basic parts of the gospel of Jesus Christ, which had existed before it. It was never intended to be something apart or separated from, and certainly not something antagonistic to, the gospel of Jesus Christ. It was more elementary than the full gospel—thus its schoolmaster's role in bringing people to the gospel—but its purpose was never to have been different from the higher law. Both were to bring people to Christ. (*Christ and the New Covenant: The Messianic Message of the Book of Mormon* [Salt Lake City: Deseret Book, 1997], 147)

ILLUSTRATIONS FOR OUR TIME

A Preparatory Gospel

The law of Moses was a preparatory gospel. It was a schoolmaster to help people not only look forward to Christ but prepare for Christ. In life, there are many preparatory experiences that prepare us for greater blessings. It is line upon line, precept upon precept, here a little and there a little—such is the process of growth. Tithing is an example of a lesser law preparing for the law of consecration.

Joseph Fielding Smith:

> This was, in fact, the inauguration of the law of tithing, the lesser law, to be a school-master for the members of the Church, like the Law of Moses was to Israel, to prepare them for the higher law which had been taken away because of disobedience. (*Church History and Modern Revelation,* 4 vols. [Salt Lake City: The Church of Jesus Christ of Latter-day Saints, 1946–1949], 3:45)

LIKENING THE SCRIPTURES TO OUR LIVES

3 Nephi 12:17–48 The Lord explains in this passage that the law of Moses is fulfilled in Him. The higher law is now given for us to live by.

Application: The higher law is a law for celestial living. It is a law of the heart and soul. It is not a schoolmaster of specific behaviors, but a law of living a Christlike life, that we might become perfect. This is the charge: to become as He is—and we can (see 3 Ne. 27:27; Moro. 7:48).

4. THE NATURE OF TRUE DISCIPLESHIP

THEME: We are to be perfect, even as the Father and the Son are perfect. This process of perfection comes by living the Lord's word—both inwardly, through a broken heart and a contrite spirit, and outwardly, through a godly walk and conversation.

MOMENT OF TRUTH

The Savior imparts to His followers on the mount the teachings that the true disciples of our Savior embrace, internalize, and practice in order to become more like Him. The Savior fulfills the commandment of the Father by teaching the Saints. He admonishes us to be perfect (Matt. 5:48; 3 Ne. 12:48).

MODERN PROPHETS SPEAK

Ezra Taft Benson:

> To walk in the steps of Jesus is to emulate His life and to look unto Him as our source of truth and example. Each of us would do well to periodically review His teachings in the Sermon on the Mount so that we are totally familiar with His way. In that sermon, one of the greatest of all sermons, we are told to be a light to others, to control our anger, to reconcile bad feelings with others before bringing gifts to the Lord, to love our enemy, to refrain from unholy and unvirtuous practices, to not

allow lust to conceive in our hearts. We are further instructed how to pray, how to fast, and how to regulate our priorities. When these teachings are applied, Jesus said, we are like the wise man who built his house on a firm, solid foundation.

We, His disciples, must follow the way of the Master. He is our guide to happiness here and eternal life hereafter. Our success in life will be determined by how closely we learn to walk in His steps. (*Come unto Christ* [Salt Lake City: Deseret Book, 1983], 37)

ILLUSTRATIONS FOR OUR TIME

A disciple of Jesus Christ is one who believes, follows, and attempts to live as the Savior lived. One need not have a special title or calling but rather be converted to the gospel of Jesus Christ and truly attempt to be even as He is. Everyone can be a pure disciple of Jesus Christ if he or she chooses to follow and represent Him in righteousness. Such is an example of a sweet sister missionary as told by Elray L. Christiansen:

> Last spring I attended the quarterly conference in one of the stakes in southern Idaho. Among the missionaries who reported was Sister Santana, a young woman of Mexican nationality. She had come to that stake to report her mission to those who had sent her. One of the families there had provided the funds for her mission, and it was reported that this Mexican girl had been instrumental in bringing into the Church more than fifty people during her time in the mission field. Among other things, she said through an interpreter: "My testimony is the brightest gem in my possession. It is of more worth to me than is my life. I hope to bear it in good deeds." And she added, to those who had helped her, "*Muchas gracias.*" It touched our hearts to see her with this priceless combination of treasures—a testimony and a desire to bear it in good deeds.
>
> Any individual who has a testimony that is borne in clean living and in good works can expect to feel in that testimony a tremendous motivating power. It will help to direct him in his life, to guide him, to prompt him, to warn him. It becomes a formidable weapon against evil itself. (Elray L. Christiansen, CR, Oct. 1952, 54)

LIKENING THE SCRIPTURES TO OUR LIVES

3 Ne. 14:21–23 Not every one that saith unto me, Lord, Lord, shall enter into the kingdom of heaven; but he that doeth the will of my Father who is in heaven. Many will say to me in that day: Lord, Lord, have we not prophesied in thy name, and in thy name have we cast out devils, and in thy name done many wonderful works? And then will I profess unto them: I never knew you; depart from me, ye that work iniquity.

Application: The Lord teaches us that it is essential to come to know Him in order to gain eternal life. We need to be motivated by love in our quest to know Him. We will know of the truth of His doctrine as we live it (see John 7:17) with an eye single to His glory (see D&C 88:67). As we do these things, we will know God and Jesus Christ, and they will know us.

SUMMARY

The message of the Savior to the saints in the Sermon on the Mount is universal and timeless. In the Beatitudes, He revealed His agenda for blessing them and all covenant peoples of every generation. He taught them that they were "the salt of the earth" and "a light to this people" (Matt. 5:13–16). With the law of Moses fulfilled in Him, He taught them how to live the higher law of perfection, including the practices that characterize the nature of true discipleship.

In Matthew 5, the Lord Jesus Christ gives to us His law for living. No cursory lesson can possibly do justice to these celestial and transcendent truths. What He taught should serve as the basis for a lifetime of study and application. He instructs us later in His discourse that we need to ponder and meditate over these teachings. These are words to live by. These are our standards and values for living. They become our strength in the hour of need. They are the principles of light to illuminate our souls with the saving truths of the gospel of Jesus Christ. They come as principles with a promise, even happiness and eventual eternal life.

CHAPTER 9

"SEEK YE FIRST *to* BUILD UP *the* KINGDOM *of* GOD"

Reading Assignment: Matthew 6–7.

Additional Reading: JST, Matthew 6; Matthew 16:24–25; John 8:31; 13:35; 2 Nephi 31:10–13; Moroni 7:48.

> *It is our duty to be active and diligent in doing everything we can to sustain ourselves, to build up His Kingdom, to defend ourselves against our enemies, to lay our plans wisely, and to prosecute every method that can be devised to establish the kingdom of God on the earth, and to sanctify and prepare ourselves to dwell in His presence.*
>
> —BRIGHAM YOUNG, *DISCOURSES*, 294–295.

THEMES *for* LIVING

1. True Disciples Do the Right Thing for the Right Reason—Motive Makes the Difference
2. True Disciples Follow the Savior's Example of Prayer
3. True Disciples Are Charitable
4. True Disciples Serve God and Do His Will

INTRODUCTION

The Sermon on the Mount is the Lord's personal training in the discipleship of charity and godliness. As disciples of the Lord Jesus Christ, we have taken upon us His name. Our attitude and behavior as His disciples change as we are filled with gratitude for His word, His doctrines, His principles, His covenants, and His ordinances—even to the point that we can become like Him (Moro. 7:48). Above all things, we offer as a sacrifice a broken heart and a contrite spirit (3 Ne. 9:20; 12:19; D&C 59:8); we submit our will to His will and serve Him with all our heart, might, mind, and strength. We become true disciples of the Lord Jesus Christ, full of love for all mankind (see John 13:34–35).

1. TRUE DISCIPLES DO THE RIGHT THING FOR THE RIGHT REASON—MOTIVE MAKES THE DIFFERENCE

THEME: Our motive determines whether our acts are acceptable to the Lord (see Moro. 7:6–14). Our eye is ever to be single to the glory of God (see D&C 88:67).

MOMENT OF TRUTH

In the Sermon on the Mount, the Savior commences His discourse with an unfolding of inner qualities or blessed states we have come to designate as the Beatitudes (see the detailed discussion in Chapter 8). It is instructive that He establishes first a foundation of spiritual attitudes for the people to follow, for it is upon such a foundation that spiritual actions can be generated. The outer behaviors of life flow from the inner storehouse of thoughts, desires, and motivations that define a person's nature and being.

He then goes on to enumerate and explain the patterns of living that constitute discipleship of the kind that would bless the world as well as the disciples acting in His name. They are to do and teach the commandments of the Lord (Matt. 5:19). They are to live and demonstrate the higher law in all aspects of their lives.

The Savior then chooses to shed instructive light on a practice that the "hypocrites" had mastered—how to give their alms in such a manner that they could accumulate maximum recognition and praise for their supposed generosity. In contrast to this, the Savior teaches a higher strategy: When giving alms, His disciples are to act from a godly motivation, seeking only the glory of God rather than a desire to gain stature in the eyes of men (Matt. 6:1–5). How can one ensure that the motivation is right? By giving in secret: "thy Father which seeth in secret himself shall reward thee openly" (Matt. 6:4).

MODERN PROPHETS SPEAK

Dallin H. Oaks:

> We must not only *do* what is right. We must act for the right reasons. The modern term is *good motive.* The scriptures often signify this appropriate mental attitude with the words *full purpose of heart or real intent.*
>
> The scriptures make clear that God understands our motives and will judge our actions accordingly. If we do not act for the right reasons, our acts will not be counted for righteousness. . . .
>
> Just as it is the spirit that identifies and gives life to the ministry, so it is the motive that gives life and legitimacy to the acts of the believer. . . .
>
> Priestcraft is the sin committed by the combination of a good act—such as preaching or teaching the gospel—and a bad motive. The act may be good and visible, but the sin is in the motive. On earth, the wrong motive may be known only to the actor, but in heaven it is always known to God. (*Pure in Heart* [Salt Lake City: Bookcraft, 1988], 15–16)

ILLUSTRATIONS FOR OUR TIMES

The Wind Beneath Your Wings

> Through your personal righteousness the Spirit of God will guide you to learn to control yourself, to enhance your attitude, to increase your spiritual altitude, and to find and trust the true source of divine power. . . . [M]any things are required to make an airplane fly and fly safely, but the most important thing, as I used to call it, is the "wind beneath your wings." Without it, there is no lift, no climb, no flight into the wild blue yonder or to faraway, beautiful destinations.
>
> The Holy Ghost will be the wind beneath your wings, placing in your heart the firm conviction of the divinity of the Lord Jesus Christ and His place in the eternal plan of God your Eternal Father. Through the Holy Ghost you will know your place in this plan and your divine eternal destination. You will be converted to the Lord, His gospel, and His Church, and you will never fall away. (Dieter F. Uchtdorf, "On the Wings of Eagles," *Ensign,* July 2006, 10)

LIKENING THE SCRIPTURES TO OUR LIVES

Psalm 24:4–5 He that hath clean hands, and a pure heart; who hath not lifted up his soul unto vanity, nor sworn deceitfully. He shall receive the blessing from the Lord, and righteousness from the God of his salvation.

Application: Surely the Lord knows the desires of our hearts—the reasons and motives for all our actions. As we seek to purify our hearts and have an eye single to the glory of God, our motives will be pure, and we will thus be filled with the pure love of Christ.

2. TRUE DISCIPLES FOLLOW THE SAVIOR'S EXAMPLE OF PRAYER

THEME: In all things, we should seek to follow the example of our Savior. The pattern for prayer is simple and direct. At the heart of it all is that the will of the Father might be done.

MOMENT OF TRUTH

Continuing with His Sermon on the Mount, the Savior instructs His followers concerning the appropriate manner for praying to the Father. Just as with almsgiving, praying is to be conducted in a private, reverential, and sincere manner—not for the purpose of attracting praise from others or putting on a display of oratory with "vain repetitions" (Matt. 6:6). The purpose is not so much to disclose to the Father your needs—"for your Father knoweth what things ye have need of, before ye ask him" (Matt. 6:8)—but rather to bring before the Father your needs in faith and humility, seeking to follow His will in all things. As an example of a prayer, the Savior then gives to the people what has come to be called the "Lord's Prayer" (Matt. 6:9–13), including the supplication for the Father to "forgive our debts, as we forgive our debtors" (Matt. 6:12). Associated with praying is the practice of fasting, which the Lord admonishes the people to carry out in a sincere manner as part of one's genuine worship before the Father, not as the "hypocrites" do it—for recognition and display (Matt. 6:16). All of this counsel from the Savior belongs to His doctrine of serving God in such a way as to lay up for oneself eternal treasures in heaven rather than putting one's trust in earthly treasures that expire: "For where your treasure is, there will your heart be also" (Matt. 6:21).

MODERN PROPHETS SPEAK

Russell M. Nelson:

> Jesus taught us how [to pray]. We pray to our Heavenly Father, in the name of Jesus Christ, by the power of the Holy Ghost. This is the true order of prayer, in contrast to vain repetitions or recitations given to be seen of men.
>
> Jesus revealed that we pray to a wise Father who knows what things we have need of, before we ask Him. . . .

Prayers can be offered even in silence. One can think a prayer, especially when words would interfere. We often kneel to pray; we may stand or be seated. Physical position is less important than is spiritual submission to God.

We close our prayer in the name of Jesus Christ, amen. When we hear another's prayer, we audibly add our amen, meaning, That is my prayer, too. ("Sweet Power of Prayer," *Ensign,* May 2003, 7)

LIKENING THE SCRIPTURES TO OUR LIVES

D&C 19:28 And again, I command thee that thou shalt pray vocally as well as in thy heart; yea, before the world as well as in secret, in public as well as in private.

Application: We are to pray always and for all things (see Alma 34:17–18). We should always carry a prayer in our hearts (see 3 Ne. 20:1).

Matthew 6:10 Thy kingdom come. Thy will be done in earth, as it is in heaven.

Application: In the Lord's Prayer and in Gethsemane, the ever-submissive Savior always sought that the will of His Father in Heaven be fulfilled. Such submissiveness demonstrates whether we have learned to become easily entreated and willing to submit to all things that He sees fit to inflict upon us, that we might grow and become like Him (see Mosiah 3:19).

3. TRUE DISCIPLES ARE CHARITABLE

Theme: True disciples seek to be full of charity, abounding in good works and demonstrating Christlike love to everyone—showing forgiveness and brotherly kindness.

MOMENT OF TRUTH

The Sermon on the Mount is, ultimately, a discourse about charity. The Savior uses the occasion to teach the people that a person of charity focuses on the process of self-cleansing through repentance and godly practice. The person of charity gives to others freely out of love and compassion—just as parents willingly and lovingly serve the interests of their children. The epitome of charity is the Father, for we can approach the Father with full faith in His ability and desire to bless our lives: "Ask, and it shall be given you; seek, and ye shall find; knock, and it shall be opened unto you: For every one that asketh receiveth; and he that seeketh findeth; and to him that knocketh it shall be opened" (Matt. 7:7–8). How disposed are we to emulate the Father in how we practice charity in our lives? The Savior gives the key, which has come to be known as the "Golden Rule": "Therefore all things whatsoever ye would that men should do to you, do ye even so to them: for this is the law and the prophets" (Matt. 7:12).

MODERN PROPHETS SPEAK

Howard W. Hunter:

> The world in which we live would benefit greatly if men and women everywhere would exercise the pure love of Christ, which is kind, meek, and lowly. It is without envy or pride. It is selfless because it seeks nothing in return. It does not countenance evil or ill will, nor rejoice in iniquity; it has no place for bigotry, hatred, or violence. It refuses to condone ridicule, vulgarity, abuse, or ostracism. It encourages diverse people to live together in Christian love regardless of religious belief, race, nationality, financial standing, education, or culture.
>
> The Savior has commanded us to love one another as he has loved us; to clothe ourselves "with the bond of charity" (D&C 88:125), as he so clothed himself. We are called upon to purify our inner feelings, to change our hearts, to make our outward actions and appearance conform to what we say we believe and feel inside. We are to be true disciples of Christ. (*THWH,* 99)

ILLUSTRATIONS FOR OUR TIME

The Handyman

Many years ago, when I was just a very young boy growing up in a small western town, one of the townspeople taught me a grand lesson about charity and faith. He was a quiet and self-effacing man who made his living repairing appliances during the day and serving as the projectionist for the local movie theater in the evenings and on Saturdays. He had the reputation of being able to fix anything that needed to be repaired—washing machines, radios, phonographs, and refrigerators.

But as a four- or five-year-old, my mind was not focused on anything so practical in nature. What I valued above all else were my toys. The sun rose and set on those toys—the little English metal cars, the wind-up trains with spring-tension motors, the pistols that looked real and fired caps with a loud noise. As long as those toys worked, the world was in order. But when one of them broke, the world fell out of joint. And when that happened, there was only one thing to do: Go to the handyman.

His position in the community was lowly. He wasn't on the same level as the mayor or the school principal or the physician or the chief of police. He was just a handyman. But to kids like me, he was a hero. He had a gift of magic where it really counted. With his collection of tools and boxes filled with miscellaneous nuts and bolts and spare parts of all kinds, he could give life to dead toys and renew the spirit of little boys. It didn't seem to matter if toy parts were broken or rusty or lost. He could improvise and put things miraculously back together again and make them work.

I believed that he could literally fix anything. If anyone at the time had wanted to explain the concept of "faith" or "charity" to me, they would only have had to refer to my confidence in the handyman and his kindness, and I would have understood.

When I went to visit him with a broken toy he never turned me away. He never seemed to be too busy. And he never charged me anything. It was as if the arrangement was just between him and me, and he understood that I had nothing to give— so that was the price of his service.

I have thought about the handyman off and on for all these years. His image keeps coming back again and again—not in the form of a person whose countenance is clear in all of its details, but rather in the form of a symbol or a parable for the spirit of service and charity. It's difficult to describe the fix-up spirit adequately except in terms of what it does: restores, heals, puts in order, refreshes, revives, renews. It's one thing to fix toys; it is quite another to fix hearts. In a world that is predominantly thing-oriented, we put great emphasis on keeping our machines and tools working well. When our computers and cars break down, the world is suddenly thrust off center. It is as if our values were in peril—so important have our modern "toys" become to us.

But there are other things, more important things that can break—hearts, hope, confidence in self and others, spirits, faith. How do you go about fixing a broken or confused heart? How would you restore a downcast or wandering spirit? How do you build faith when the supply is depleted or when there is uncertainty about who it is to have faith in? How do you repair confidence when it fades? How do you replenish hope when it dims? And how do you make life worth living?

The handyman of my youth was a type and shadow of the kind of handyman we seek. Like the handyman of my childhood, the One we seek is also without worldly stature. As Isaiah described him: "He hath no form nor comeliness; and when we shall see him, there is no beauty that we should desire him. He is despised and rejected of men." (Isa. 53:2–3). He whom we seek partakes of the spirit of simplicity and meekness: "And God hath chosen the weak things of the world to confound the things which are mighty" (1 Cor 1:27). "And out of small things proceedeth that which is great" (D&C 64:33). The Handyman we seek, like the handyman of my childhood, is accessible to all. With clarity we hear His words of welcome and acceptance: "Ask, and it shall be given you; seek, and ye shall find; knock, and it shall be opened unto you" (Matt 7:7). What He gives, He gives freely and without charge. Neither are His services purchased with the currency of the world, as Jacob confirmed: "Come, my brethren, every one that thirsteth, come ye to the waters; and he that hath no money, come buy and eat; yea, come buy wine and milk without money and without price" (2 Ne. 9:50). This priceless commodity has eternal implications: "But whosoever drinketh of the water that I shall give him shall never thirst; but the water that

I shall give him shall be in him a well of water springing up into everlasting life" (John 4:14).

The handyman of my childhood put playthings in order and lifted the burdens of disappointment and concern. But this higher Handyman performs miracles of another magnitude. As the Psalmist proclaimed: "My help cometh from the Lord" (Ps. 121:2). "Cast thy burden upon the Lord, and he shall sustain thee" (Ps. 55:22). And He to whom we now refer said to the ancient American Saints: "Will ye not now return unto me, and repent of your sins, and be converted, that I may heal you?" (3 Ne. 9:13).

In his own simple way, the handyman of my childhood was a person of light, for he kindled hope in a childish heart set upon the simple playthings of the world. But this higher Handyman is a light that "shineth in the darkness" (John 1:5). He said: "Behold I am the light; I have set an example for you" (3 Ne. 18:16). And again: "I am the light of the world: he that followeth me shall not walk in darkness, but shall have the light of life" (John 8:12).

The handyman of my childhood taught me an early lesson about faith and charity. But this higher Handyman teaches that there is a faith strong enough to heal the soul and charity encompassing enough to reach out to all humankind.

No doubt I would have survived my childhood without a handyman to fix my toys. But the celestial Handyman is essential to life and indispensable to the restoration of the soul. As King Benjamin declared in Mosiah 3:17: "And moreover, I say unto you, that there shall be no other name given nor any other way nor means whereby salvation can come unto the children of men, only in and through the name of Jesus Christ, the Lord Omnipotent" (Mosiah 3:17). [Allen]

LIKENING THE SCRIPTURES TO OUR LIVES

John 13:34–35 A new commandment I give unto you, That ye love one another; as I have loved you, that ye also love one another. By this shall all men know that ye are my disciples, if ye have love one to another.

Application: As disciples of Christ, we should seek to show our love to God, our Savior, and our fellowmen (see Matt. 22:36–40)—this truly fulfills all the law. The love that our Savior was attempting to teach Peter (see John 21:15–17) is a Godlike, perfect, and unconditional love that never fails. Indeed, it is the pure love of Christ.

4. TRUE DISCIPLES SERVE GOD AND DO HIS WILL

THEME: The test of a true disciple is in serving God and submitting to His will in all things (see Matt. 7:13–14; 21; 26:39).

MOMENT OF TRUTH

The Savior concludes His Sermon on the Mount by admonishing the people to enter in through the correct gate, then follow the correct path leading to eternal life—both gate and pathway being narrow, rather than wide (Matt. 7:13–14). The Savior ends His sermon with a parable that encapsulates all of what He has taught the people: Those who follow His sayings are like the man who wisely builds his house upon the rock so that the winds and tempest will have no power to bring it down. By contrast, those who do not follow His sayings are like the man who foolishly builds his house upon the sand, where there is no security and no longevity (see Matt. 7:24–28). What was the response of the people to the Savior's Sermon on the Mount? "And it came to pass, when Jesus had ended these sayings, the people were astonished at his doctrine: For he taught them as one having authority, and not as the scribes" (Matt. 7:28–29).

MODERN PROPHETS SPEAK

Thomas S. Monson:

> To those who humbly seek, there is no need to stumble or falter along the pathway leading to truth. It is well marked by our Heavenly Father. We must first have a desire to know for ourselves. We must study; we must pray. We must do the will of the Father. And then we will know the truth and the truth shall make us free. Divine favor will attend those who humbly seek it. (*Pathways to Perfection* [Salt Lake City: Deseret Book, 1973], 34–35)

ILLUSTRATIONS FOR OUR TIME

True Test of Discipleship

King Benjamin taught us a great truth regarding discipleship. He said: "And behold, I tell you these things that ye may learn wisdom; that ye may learn that when ye are in the service of your fellow beings ye are only in the service of your God" (Mosiah 2:17). The characteristics of true discipleship of Jesus Christ embody believing His words, following His example, keeping His commandments, and entering into His covenants. Within this framework of action it comes down to our living as we know we should. The Lord said: "Verily I say unto you, Inasmuch as ye have done it unto one of the least of these my brethren, ye have done it unto me" (Matt. 25:40). Therefore, after the pattern given us by Christ—who served His God and His fellowman—we can apply these teachings as a true test of discipleship.

How do we serve? Dallin H. Oaks has taught us concerning our daily activities to follow Christ and serve our fellowmen:

He calls us to take time from our daily activities to follow him and serve our fellowman. Even the greatest among us should be the servant of all. Those who always remember him will straightway assume and faithfully fulfill the responsibilities to which they are called by his servants. . . .

As we always remember him, we should strive to assure that we and our family members and, indeed, all the sons and daughters of God everywhere follow our Savior into the waters of baptism. This reminds each of us of our duties to proclaim the gospel, perfect the Saints, and redeem the dead. . . .

We should always remember how the Savior taught us to love and do good to one another. Loving and serving one another can solve so many problems! (*Ensign,* May 1988, 30–31) [Pinegar]

LIKENING THE SCRIPTURES TO OUR LIVES

Matthew 7:7–8 Ask, and it shall be given you; seek, and ye shall find; knock, and it shall be opened unto you: For every one that asketh receiveth; and he that seeketh findeth; and to him that knocketh it shall be opened.

Application: As we ask, let us take care not to ask amiss (see D&C 88:53–65). Let us pray with real intent, filled with the desire to be charitable, being submissive to the Father in all things, and exercising our faith (see Moro. 7:9).

SUMMARY

If we are following the Savior's admonitions as laid out for us in the Sermon on the Mount—the greatest of all gospel sermons—then we will find ourselves leading the lives of true disciples of Christ. We will act out of pure motivation, doing the right things for the right reason. We will follow the Savior's example by praying and fasting with sincere purpose, submitting our own will to the will of the Father in all things. We will exercise charity, compassion, and forgiveness in our dealings with others. And we will serve God, building our house upon the solid foundation of eternal principles and saving doctrines. The spirit of this supreme counsel is well summarized by the prophet Alma:

And now I would that ye should be humble, and be submissive and gentle; easy to be entreated; full of patience and long-suffering; being temperate in all things; being diligent in keeping the commandments of God at all times; asking for whatsoever things ye stand in need, both spiritual and temporal; always returning thanks unto God for whatsoever things ye do receive.

And see that ye have faith, hope, and charity, and then ye will always abound in good works.

And may the Lord bless you, and keep your garments spotless, that ye may at last be brought to sit down with Abraham, Isaac, and Jacob, and the holy prophets who have been ever since the world began, having your garments spotless even as their garments are spotless, in the kingdom of heaven to go no more out. (Alma 7:23–25)

CHAPTER 10

"TAKE MY YOKE UPON YOU, *and* LEARN *of* ME"

Reading Assignment: Matthew 11:28–30; 12:1–13; Luke 7:36–50; 13:10–17.

Additional Reading: Mosiah 24:8–15; Alma 12:33–35; D&C 19:23; 54:10; 59:23.

God has repeatedly said He would structure mortality to be a proving and testing experience (see Abr. 3:25; Mosiah 23:21). Hence our fiery trials, said Peter, should not be thought of as "some strange thing" (1 Pet. 4:12). Still some of us approach our experience in this mortal school as if it were to be mostly relaxing recesses with only the occasional irritant of summoning bells. In fact, any recesses are merely for renewal and for catching one's breath; and these are not to become a prolonged sigh of relief that introduces protracted leisure or languor.

By taking Jesus' yoke upon us we learn most deeply of Him, and especially how to be like Him. This includes emulating His power to endure (see Matt. 11:29). Even though our experiences are micro compared to His, the process is the same. True enduring, therefore, represents not merely the passage of time but also the passage of the soul—not merely going from A to B, but the "mighty change"—all the way from A to Z.

—NEAL A. MAXWELL, *IF THOU ENDURE IT WELL* [SALT LAKE CITY: DESERET BOOK, 2006], 123.

THEMES *for* LIVING

1. His Yoke Is Easy and His Burden Light
2. Jesus Is Lord of the Sabbath
3. The Joy of Forgiveness

INTRODUCTION

As the Lord continued His ministry, He expanded His reach among the people and imparted additional truth, as the scripture says: "line upon line, precept upon precept, here a little and there a little; and blessed are those who hearken unto my precepts, and lend an ear unto my counsel, for they shall learn wisdom; for unto him that receiveth I will give more; and from them that shall say, We have enough, from them shall be taken away even that which they have" (2 Ne. 28:30; compare Isa. 28:10, 13; D&C 98:12; 128:21).

The Savior's disciples savored His teachings and were hungry for more light and guidance, but the more part of the ecclesiastical leaders, jealous of His authoritative delivery and miraculous power to heal, steadily increased their closed-mindedness and bitterness. Consequently, they failed to comprehend that they were dealing with the Creator, even Jehovah of the Old Testament, whom they studied with meticulous focus and impassioned zeal. Lacking the spirit of understanding, they missed the mark (see Jacob 4:14–15).

With the faithful among the Savior's followers it was different. He was able to teach them how to take upon them His yoke of redeeming glory and how to learn that His burden is light and His blessings abundant. The gospel of Jesus Christ is the pathway of rebirth (John 3:3–5) and the source of "living water" (John 4:10) that brings peace, comfort, hope, and salvation.

1. HIS YOKE IS EASY AND HIS BURDEN LIGHT

THEME: We can gain peace by taking the yoke of Christ upon us.

MOMENT OF TRUTH

The Savior often spoke in the form of a paradox. How can one find one's life by losing it? How can heavy burdens be light at the same time? How can a troubled soul find rest? Through the Gospel of Jesus Christ. When we take upon ourselves the yoke of the Lord—namely by embracing the principles and ordinances of the Gospel—we receive of His strength. The Lord has said, "Come unto me, all ye that labour and are heavy laden, and I will give you rest. Take my yoke upon you, and learn of me; for I am meek and lowly in heart: and ye shall find rest unto your souls. For my yoke is easy, and my burden is light" (Matt 11:28–30). The unique truth of this apparent dichotomy is that when we are troubled and overwhelmed with our burdens and we take upon us the Savior's yoke and do His will, we become strengthened in the Lord. In this process we find joy, solace, and peace for our souls. The Lord also said this in another way: "Learn of me, and listen to my words; walk in the meekness of my Spirit, and you shall have peace in me" (D&C 19:23). This peace is freedom from guilt and sin. Our conscience is free and at peace with God.

MODERN PROPHETS SPEAK

Neal A. Maxwell:

> If we enlist and take the Savior's yoke upon us we "shall find rest unto [our] souls" (Matt. 11:29). If we are only part-time soldiers, though, partially yoked, we experience quite the opposite: frustration, irritation, and the absence of His full grace and spiritual rest. . . . The meek and fully yoked, on the other hand, find God's reassuring grace and see their weakness yielding to strength (see Ether 12:27).
>
> Strange as it seems, a few of the partially yoked, undeservedly wearing the colors of the kingdom, are just close enough to the prescribed path and process to be able to observe in others some of the visible costs of discipleship. Sobered by that observation, they want victory without battle and expect campaign ribbons merely for watching; but there is no witness until after the trial of their faith (see Ether 12:6).
>
> These same Church members know just enough about the doctrines to converse superficially on them, but their scant knowledge about the deep doctrines is inadequate for deep discipleship (see 1 Cor. 2:10). Thus uninformed about the deep doctrines, they make no deep change in their lives. They lack the faith to "give place" (Alma 32:27) consistently for real discipleship . . . King Benjamin described. "For how knoweth a man the master whom he has not served, and who is a stranger unto him, and is far from the thoughts and intents of his heart?" (Mosiah 5:13)—these people are not drawing closer either. (*Men and Women of Christ* [Salt Lake City: Bookcraft, 1991], 2–3)

ILLUSTRATIONS FOR OUR TIME

A Higher Peace

We were living in England and our son Cory had returned home to America for school. He was living with our son Steve and his family. Cory was full of life. He was good. He was sensitive, and he was a tough outside linebacker on the football team. The Provo High School Bulldogs had just beaten their cross-town rival Timpview Thunderbirds. Cory had sacked the quarterback, blocked a punt, and in general had an awe-inspiring game.

Following the game, Cory had a date with his girlfriend. It was dark as they were driving along, and the road was not well lit. All of a sudden, the road curved. Cory overcorrected and the car rolled over, throwing him from the car. The ambulance came and took them to the hospital. The girl was bruised, but had no major injuries and was okay, but Cory had suffered a concussion, and the doctors didn't give him any hope for survival. We were contacted in London and returned home immediately.

I can still remember looking down at my son, his eyes closed and his body still. The machines breathed for him and helped his body function, but his brain waves were flat. We prayed and pleaded, but the answer was no. Cory was to die. I felt as if my insides had been ripped from my body. I hurt. My sweetheart and children cried—our beloved son and brother was dead. As those who have experienced this pain know, at that moment you wonder if you can make it because the hurt is so deep.

Something happened as we turned it over to the Lord. It was miraculous. Our hearts began to heal. Life was bearable, and a power came into our lives that transcended life itself. This was a power greater than mortals can exhibit. It was a power from on high. Peace filled my soul. I could go on. We will all live again through the miracle of the Atonement and the resurrection. This peace filled me with hope, and life was not only livable, but became wonderful.

We still remember Cory. In fact, we celebrate his life on his birthday every year with the family. My sweetheart prepares Cory's favorite dinner, and then we all talk about Cory and his wonderful life. Our family is at peace. There is a peace that transcends our earthly trials and tribulations and our heartaches and heartbreaks, and the reason is clear through the words of the Savior: "Peace I leave with you, my peace I give unto you: not as the world giveth, give I unto you. Let not your heart be troubled, neither let it be afraid" (John 14:27). [Pinegar]

LIKENING THE SCRIPTURES TO OUR LIVES

John 14:27 Peace I leave with you, my peace I give unto you: not as the world giveth, give I unto you. Let not your heart be troubled, neither let it be afraid.

Application: One of the ultimate purposes of life is to find that "peace of God, which passeth all understanding" (Philip. 4:7). We should seek peace in righteous living and sow peace in our conscience (see Ps. 34:14). Peace of mind and heart should be one of our main goals as we seek happiness here and in the hereafter.

2. JESUS IS LORD OF THE SABBATH

THEME: The Lord's Sabbath is a day to worship God and bless others.

MOMENT OF TRUTH

On one occasion the Savior was passing through the cornfields of the countryside with His followers. Because His disciples were hungry, they plucked ears of corn to eat. Such behavior caused concern among the Pharisees, who judged it to be a violation of the law, which provided stringent rules for keeping the Sabbath holy. The Savior responded by referring them to instances in the scriptures where apparent violations of the Sabbath day by leaders took place with impunity. Then the Savior stated the truth of the matter: "For the Son of man is Lord even of the sabbath day" (Matt. 12:8).

Somewhat later, the Savior healed the withered hand of a man on the Sabbath, reminding the concerned priests who sought to find a cause against Him: "What man shall there be among you, that shall have one sheep, and if it fall into a pit on the sabbath day, will he not lay hold on it, and lift it out? How much then is a man better than a sheep? Wherefore it is lawful to do well on the sabbath days" (Matt. 12:11–12).

On another occasion the Lord healed a woman of a serious infirmity on the Sabbath day, much to the indignation of the ruler of the synagogue. The Savior responded: "Thou hypocrite, doth not each one of you on the sabbath loose his ox or his ass from the stall, and lead him away to watering? And ought not this woman, being a daughter of Abraham, whom Satan hath bound, lo, these eighteen years, be loosed from this bond on the sabbath day? And when he had said these things, all his adversaries were ashamed: and all the people rejoiced for all the glorious things that were done by him" (Luke 13:15–17).

MODERN PROPHETS SPEAK

Spencer W. Kimball:

> The Sabbath is a holy day in which to do worthy and holy things. Abstinence from work and recreation is important, but insufficient. The Sabbath calls for constructive thoughts and acts, and if one merely lounges about doing nothing on the Sabbath, he is breaking it. To observe it, one will be on his knees in prayer, preparing lessons, studying the gospel, meditating, visiting the ill and distressed, writing letters to missionaries, taking a nap, reading wholesome material, and attending all the meetings of that day at which he is expected. ("The Sabbath—A Delight," *Ensign,* Jan. 1978, 4)

> [The Sabbath is] a day to visit the sick, a day to preach the gospel, a day to prose-lyte, a day to visit quietly with the family and get acquainted with our children, a day for proper courting, a day to do good. (*TSWK,* 216)

ILLUSTRATIONS FOR OUR TIME

Victor Ludlow summarizes in a succinct way the practice of keeping the Sabbath day holy. He said:

In all respects, the Sabbath day should be a day that is different from others during the week. . . .

If we allow our selfish and materialistic concerns to govern our Sundays, we become like a battery with a weakened seam that allows the chemicals to seep out. Such a battery not only loses its power, but it corrodes whatever it touches. If we corrupt the Sabbath, we not only lose our own spiritual powers, but we also weaken the resolve and ability of others to have a proper Sabbath experience. For example, if we insist on shopping on Sunday, we encourage employers to keep their businesses open on the Sabbath, requiring employees to work on what should be a day of rest and worship. Or if we disturb the Sabbath spirit in our families with inappropriate activities, especially those that take us away from Church, we dilute the spiritual energy that should be coming into our family members.

On the other hand, as we set this day apart from the rest of the week and treat it with a special spirit of reverence, we will be physically refreshed, emotionally strengthened, and spiritually renewed. The Lord promises us—as he did ancient Israel—that as we keep the Sabbath holy, we will both inherit special spiritual blessings and be provided with basic physical needs: "Inasmuch as ye do this, the fulness of the earth is yours, the beasts of the field and the fowls of the air, and that which climbeth upon the trees and walketh upon the earth; yea, and the herb, and the good things which come of the earth, whether for food or for raiment, or for houses, or for barns, or for orchards, or for gardens, or for vineyards. . . . And it pleaseth God that he hath given all these things unto man; for unto this end were they made to be used, with judgment, not to excess, neither by extortion. . . . But learn that he who doeth the works of righteousness shall receive his reward, even peace in this world, and eternal life in the world to come" (D&C 59:16–17, 20, 23). (Victor L. Ludlow, *Principles and Practices of the Restored Gospel* [Salt Lake City: Deseret Book, 1992], 411–12)

The Home Game

He was a bright young man, pleasant and articulate, with a charming wife and growing family—just the kind of brother you would want to have as one of your ward clerks. When the Spirit whispered a quiet confirmation, I went to visit him with the invitation. He was honored by the calling but somewhat reserved in his response. "Bishop," he said, "I want to be of help. But you know, there is something I need to explain."

Oh, oh, I thought to myself, preparing to hear a confession.

"Ever since I joined the Church a few years ago," he continued, "I have tried to do my duty and attend my meetings, but I have always had season tickets to see the Baltimore Colts play on Sundays. That's why you don't see me at the meetings sometimes."

I thought about his situation for a few seconds, then felt impressed to offer him a special arrangement. The Lord wanted him to be a part of our team. Therefore, he would complete his Church assignment to the best of his ability and we would work around his schedule. When the team was in town with a home game, he would be away, and we would understand. He accepted the assignment, but I could see that he had a struggle going on inside—and that is just as it should be when one is learning.

For the next few months, every time my wife and I drove past Memorial Stadium on the way to our Church meetings, I thought of this young man's struggle. One Sunday when there was a home game, I was surprised when this young man showed up at my office. He was energized, with a kind of glow about him and a sparkle in the eyes. "Bishop," he said, "I have decided to give up my season tickets. The gospel is more important. I will always be here on the Sabbath." I put my arm around his shoulder and bore witness to the strength and courage of his correct decision, and I thanked the Lord in my heart for the patient way the Spirit often works. The words of the Savior came to my mind: "If any man will do his will, he shall know of the doctrine, whether it be of God, or whether I speak of myself" (John 7:17). Then I thought: There is always a home game. It takes place within the heart of every individual as he or she engages in the choices of life, the choices that go to define character and honor and devotion to the cause of building up the kingdom of God. [Allen]

LIKENING THE SCRIPTURES TO OUR LIVES

Mark 2:27–28 And he said unto them, The sabbath was made for man, and not man for the sabbath: Therefore the Son of man is Lord also of the sabbath.

Application: The Sabbath was made that we might rest from our labors, worship God, and seek to serve Him by blessing the lives of our fellowmen.

3. THE JOY OF FORGIVENESS

THEME: When we feel godly sorrow for sin, we can begin to feel exquisite joy from repentance and forgiveness through the Atonement of Jesus Christ.

MOMENT OF TRUTH

The Savior was invited on one occasion to dine at the home of Simon the Pharisee. Hearing of the Savior's presence, a woman of the city came and washed His feet with her tears, dried them with her hair, and anointed them with ointment while He sat at supper. The Pharisee reasoned within himself that Jesus, were He a prophet, would have recognized the woman as a sinner. In truth, the Savior had discerned the woman's circumstances. He responded to the Pharisee—whose capacity for charity was manifestly minute—by presenting him with a parable: "There was a certain creditor which had two debtors: the one owed five hundred pence, and the other fifty. And when they had nothing to pay, he frankly forgave them both. Tell me therefore, which of them will love him most?" (Luke 7:41–42). When Simon surmised that the debtor who owed the creditor most would therefore love him most, the Savior confirmed his judgment, then turned this logic in defense of the sinful woman. She had expressed her love for the Savior in genuine ways of faith and contrition—things that Simon had not thought to do: "Wherefore I say unto thee, Her sins, which are many, are forgiven; for she loved much: but to whom little is forgiven, the same loveth little. And he said unto her, Thy sins are forgiven. . . . Thy faith hath saved thee; go in peace" (Luke 7:47–50).

MODERN PROPHETS SPEAK

Neal A. Maxwell:

> Repentance is a joy-producing process. In fact, it is impossible to find genuine happiness without it, because it is integral to that quality. Alma explained this to his son Corianton: "Men . . . have gone contrary to the nature of God; therefore, they are in a state contrary to the nature of happiness" (Alma 41:11). And in his impassioned speech to the unrepentant Nephites, the Lamanite prophet Samuel stressed the same theme: "Ye have sought all the days of your lives for that which ye could not obtain; . . . happiness in doing iniquity, which thing is contrary to the nature of that righteousness which is in our great and Eternal Head" (Helaman 13:38).
>
> It follows that iniquity is perspective-shrinking, since it increasingly diminishes one's perception of redemptive reality. "If ye have no hope," Moroni wrote, "ye must needs be in despair; and despair cometh because of iniquity" (Moro. 10:22). (*A Wonderful Flood of Light* [Salt Lake City: Bookcraft, 1992], 8)

ILLUSTRATIONS FOR OUR TIME

The Joy of Deliverance from Sin
The depth of one's feelings for sorrow and sin is best illustrated by the great prophet Alma the Younger when he described his feelings in this process of suffering sorrow for sin and subsequently the joy in being relieved of sin. He said:

> But I was racked with eternal torment, for my soul was harrowed up to the greatest degree and racked with all my sins.

Yea, I did remember all my sins and iniquities, for which I was tormented with the pains of hell; yea, I saw that I had rebelled against my God, and that I had not kept his holy commandments. . . .

And now, for three days and for three nights was I racked, even with the pains of a damned soul.

And it came to pass that as I was thus racked with torment, while I was harrowed up by the memory of my many sins, behold, I remembered also to have heard my father prophesy unto the people concerning the coming of one Jesus Christ, a Son of God, to atone for the sins of the world.

Now, as my mind caught hold upon this thought, I cried within my heart: O Jesus, thou Son of God, have mercy on me, who am in the gall of bitterness, and am encircled about by the everlasting chains of death.

And now, behold, when I thought this, I could remember my pains no more; yea, I was harrowed up by the memory of my sins no more.

And oh, what joy, and what marvelous light I did behold; yea, my soul was filled with joy as exceeding as was my pain! . . .

Yea, and from that time even until now, I have labored without ceasing, that I might bring souls unto repentance; that I might bring them to taste of the exceeding joy of which I did taste; that they might also be born of God, and be filled with the Holy Ghost.

Yea, and now behold, O my son, the Lord doth give me exceedingly great joy in the fruit of my labors. (Alma 36:12–13, 16–20, 24–25)

The test of true repentance and forgiveness is always found as one seeks to keep the commandments and serve God by building up His Kingdom through serving one's fellowmen and inviting all to come unto Christ. [Pinegar]

LIKENING THE SCRIPTURES TO OUR LIVES

Luke 7:47 Wherefore I say unto thee, Her sins, which are many, are forgiven; for she loved much: but to whom little is forgiven, the same loveth little.

Application: Our joy is magnified according to the depth of sorrow and sin we have experienced. We can come to realize the goodness of God and why our Savior rejoices over those who repent (see D&C 18:13).

SUMMARY

We learn from these sacred scriptures and accounts that the Savior's yoke is easy and His burden light, that He is the Lord of the Sabbath, and that there is profound joy in repenting and being forgiven of sins. All of these aspects of the plan of salvation fit together seamlessly. When we come unto the Lord and accept in faith and devotion His invitation to become one of His disciples in thought, word, and deed, we find the burden of sin lifted from us, replaced with the buoyancy and bliss of heavenly forgiveness. We can experience the joy and happiness that righteous living brings to us and to our families. As the Apostle Paul taught: "For godly sorrow worketh repentance to salvation not to be repented of: but the sorrow of the world worketh death" (2 Cor. 7:10). Through the Atonement, we gain passage to cross over from that which is worldly and dead, to that which is celestial and alive—even immortality and eternal life.

CHAPTER 11

PARABLES *of* JESUS

Reading Assignment: Matthew 13.

Additional Reading: Mark 4:1–34; Luke 8:4–18; 13:18–21; D&C 86:1–7; Mosiah 2:9; Alma 10:2–6; 12:9–11; Bible Dictionary, "Gospels, Harmony of," 689; "Parables," 740–41; and "Kingdom of Heaven or Kingdom of God," 721.

> *When Jesus of Nazareth taught and ministered among men, he spoke not as did the scribes and scholars of the day but rather in language understood by all. Jesus taught through parables. His teachings moved men and motivated them to a newness of life. The shepherd on the hillside, the sower in the field, the fisherman at his net—all became subjects whereby the Master taught eternal truths.*
>
> —THOMAS S. MONSON, "HANDS," *ENSIGN,* AUG. 1990, 2.

THEMES *for* LIVING
1. Jesus Teaches in Parables
2. Parable of the Sower
3. Parables Concerning the Kingdom of God on the Earth

INTRODUCTION

Robert J. Matthews provides insightful commentary on the use of parables in the Gospels:

The word *parable* is Greek in origin and means a "setting side-by-side" or a "comparison." The popular use of the word parable is very broad, and is often not correct because it is used to refer to all sorts of symbolic language, including similitudes, allegories, and even proverbs.

Jesus used many figurative expressions to communicate. But true parables are longer stories, and he used them to conceal the central meaning. (Robert J. Matthews, *Behold the Messiah* [Salt Lake City: Bookcraft, 1994], 169)

1. JESUS TEACHES IN PARABLES

THEME: The Lord desires to add truth to those who willingly accept His truth. He withdraws truth from those who reject His truth. In keeping with this principle, Jesus taught in parables so that those who were His disciples might understand the mysteries of the Kingdom and those who were antagonistic and not of the Spirit could not (see Matt. 13:10–11).

MOMENT OF TRUTH

The Savior consistently taught in parables: "All these things spake Jesus unto the multitude in parables; and without a parable spake he not unto them." (Matt. 13:34). The impact of His discourse was dramatic: "And when he was come into his own country, he taught them in their synagogue, insomuch that they were astonished, and said, Whence hath this man this wisdom, and these mighty works?" (Matt. 13:54). (For a succinct summary of the parables used in the New Testament, refer to "Parables" in the Bible Dictionary, pp. 740–41.)

MODERN PROPHETS SPEAK

James E. Talmage:

"Perhaps no other mode of teaching was so common among the Jews as that by parables. Only in their case, they were almost entirely illustrations of what had been said or taught; while in the case of Christ, they served as the foundation for His teaching. . . . In the one case it was intended to make spiritual teaching appear Jewish and national, in the other to convey spiritual teaching in a form adapted to the stand-point of the hearers. This distinction will be found to hold true, even in instances where there seems the closest parallelism between a Rabbinic and an Evangelic parable. . . . It need scarcely be said that comparison between such parables, as regards their spirit, is scarcely possible, except by way of contrast" (Edersheim, 1, 580–81). Geikie tersely says: "Others have uttered parables, but Jesus so far transcends them, that He may justly be called the creator of this mode of instruction" (2, 145). (*JC,* 282)

ILLUSTRATIONS FOR OUR TIME

Parables—Keys to Doctrine and Daily Life

Parables are used to teach us eternal truths. Some of these truths are of the doctrines of the gospel and kingdom of God here upon the earth, but others are of how to live—a new way of thinking and behaving. They unfold the mysteries of the gospel. When we learn to liken the parables to our lives, these particular scriptures will become part of our lives.

Gerald N. Lund has said:

> The Lord told his disciples that he taught in parables so that those who are spiritually sensitive might receive the message of his teachings, but the message would be missed by those who "seeing see not; and hearing they hear not" (Matt. 13:13). Elder McConkie said of the Lord's use of parables: "His purpose . . . was not to present the truths of his gospel in plainness so that all his hearers would understand. Rather it was so to phrase and hide the doctrine involved that only the spiritually literate would understand." In other words, the Lord used a form of spiritual esoteric language to simultaneously reveal and conceal the meaning, depending on his listeners' gospel readiness. (*Selected Writings of Gerald N. Lund:* Gospel Scholars Series, 66)

Bruce R. McConkie has taught clearly concerning the additional light and knowledge that a parable can unfold to us. He said:

> We now, as a prelude to our study of the parables as such, have considered their nature and character. We have reminded ourselves that the Lord gives to men only that portion of his word which they are prepared, spiritually, to receive, and we have seen how parables hide the doctrines of salvation from those whose eyes are not open to spiritual realities. We have also set forth how these wondrously phrased and perfectly presented parabolic utterances of Jesus do in fact reveal great spiritual truths to those whose hearts are open and whose souls hunger and thirst for the things of the Spirit, and we have even come to know that inspired parables are types and shadows of heavenly things, and that by them the light of heaven is cast earthward for the eternal betterment and blessing of all those upon whom its rays shine. And we have noted that it is an act of divine mercy to withhold from shriveled and spiritually sick souls the full light of heaven, lest its assured rejection further condemn the unreceptive and disbelieving among men.
>
> There remains for us one added verity to consider, and it is, perhaps, the greatest and most important use to which parables are put. Jesus came to preach the gospel and bear the sins of all those who would believe his words and live his laws. He came

to proclaim the acceptable year of the Lord, to bring good tidings to the meek, to open the prison doors of darkness and unbelief, and to let the light of heaven dwell in the hearts of men on earth. He came to give every man as much of the truth of heaven as each man's earthbound soul would permit him to receive. (*The Mortal Messiah: From Bethlehem to Calvary*, 4 vols. [Salt Lake City: Deseret Book, 1979–1981], 2:243–44) [Pinegar]

The Greater Honor

On one occasion several years ago, an associate with whom I was sharing the gospel came to me with an anti-Mormon pamphlet that a colleague had given to him—ostensibly as a means of dissuading him from accepting the truths of the Restoration. I read the pamphlet carefully and prepared a scripture-based response to correct the misconceptions and untruths it reflected. It saddened me to observe that yet another detractor was degrading the glory and dignity of the plan of salvation and attempting to deprive an honest seeker after truth of the happiness that comes from embracing the principles and ordinances of the gospel of Jesus Christ. I felt impressed to pen a little parable to convey to my friend my perspective on the situation:

> A certain man had a garden which he cultivated with care from sunrise to sunset. Every day, this man gave thanks to God for the bounteous and delicious harvest and for the sunshine, rain, and good seed that made it possible. With the fruit of the garden, he nourished his family, generously remembered his neighbors in need, and laid up the surplus against the winter season.
>
> However, a certain neighbor took offense at the garden and noised about that the fruit thereof was of no worth. Then, by night, he crept into the garden and trampled it underfoot so that the owner had to start afresh. Which of these two now is of greater honor before God and His angels? What say ye?

My friend received this little parable with a smile and a twinkle in his eye. He understood the principle and continued with his study of the gospel—the pearl of great price—undeterred by the voices of hostility and dissent that so often ricochet off the solid defenses that protect the honest at heart. As the Savior said: "Again, the kingdom of heaven is like unto a merchant man, seeking goodly pearls: Who, when he had found one pearl of great price, went and sold all that he had, and bought it" (Matt. 13:45–46). [Allen]

LIKENING THE SCRIPTURES TO OUR LIVES

Matt 13:10–13 And the disciples came, and said unto him, Why speakest thou unto them in parables? He answered and said unto them, Because it is given unto you to know the mysteries of the kingdom of heaven, but to them it is not given. For whosoever hath, to him shall be given, and he shall have more abundance: but whosoever hath not, from him shall be taken away even that he hath. Therefore speak I to them in parables: because they seeing see not; and hearing they hear not, neither do they understand. (Matt 13:10–13)

Application: If we live by the Spirit and seek to understand by that same Spirit, the magnificent truths of the parables will be unfolded to us. The doctrine will distill upon our souls as the dews from heaven (D&C 121:45), and we will change for the better.

2. PARABLE OF THE SOWER

THEME: The essence of the life of enduring happiness is to receive the word of God and make it the governing principle of one's life. The essence of the life of temporality and woe is to receive the word of God and reject it as a thing of naught. The Savior gave us the parable of the sower to make clear this distinction. This parable speaks of planting seeds in different venues—by the wayside, in stony places, in thorny places, and in good ground—and then gives the results of the harvest in each case. The ground is our heart. The seed is the word of God. The question is: Are our hearts prepared to receive the word of God and cultivate a way of life in keeping with the commandments of God?

MOMENT OF TRUTH

Why did the Savior have such an immense following, with throngs of people listening to Him wherever He went in conducting His ministry? Naturally, the sequence of miracles and healings that He performed created a great demand among those with personal infirmities or with family members needing special help. But His eloquence and power of speech had a profound effect as well, "For he taught them as one having authority, and not as the scribes" (Matt. 7:29). One particularly transfixing element of His delivery was the use of parables to project His message. Parables include a theatrical/visual dimension, presenting to the mind, as they do, an unfolding story—sometimes short and sometimes extended, but always involving an action into which the listener is carried on the wings of his or her imagination. Virtually everyone likes a story and delights in tracing the development of circumstances and characters from beginning to end. Similarly, everyone is essentially constrained to detect how the parabolic story might relate to his or her life. When the Savior related the parable of the sower, with its four-fold action tracks, the listeners were no doubt captivated with the challenge of seeing with which track they were most closely aligned. Those of faith would comprehend that the Savior was speaking about receiving and cultivating the seed of truth, symbolizing the gospel of redemption; those with clouded spiritual vision would be left to plumb for the mysterious and elusive interpretation. That was the whole intention behind the use of parables:

> And now Alma began to expound these things unto him, saying: It is given unto many to know the mysteries of God; nevertheless they are laid under a strict command that they shall not impart only according to the portion of his word which he doth grant unto the children of men, according to the heed and diligence which they give unto him.
>
> And therefore, he that will harden his heart, the same receiveth the lesser portion of the word; and he that will not harden his heart, to him is given the greater portion of the word, until it is given unto him to know the mysteries of God until he know them in full.
>
> And they that will harden their hearts, to them is given the lesser portion of the word until they know nothing concerning his mysteries; and then they are taken captive by the devil, and led by his will down to destruction. Now this is what is meant by the chains of hell. (Alma 12:9–11)

MODERN PROPHETS SPEAK

Joseph Smith:

> But listen to the explanation of the parable of the Sower: "When any one heareth the word of the Kingdom, and understandeth it not, then cometh the wicked one, and catcheth away that which was sown in his heart." Now mark the expression—that which was sown in his heart. This is he which receiveth seed by the way side. Men who have no principle of righteousness in themselves, and whose hearts are full of iniquity, and have no desire for the principles of truth, do not understand the word of truth when they hear it. The devil taketh away the word of truth out of their hearts, because there is no desire for righteousness in them. "But he that receiveth seed in stony places, the same is he that heareth the word, and anon, with joy receiveth it; yet hath he not root in himself, but dureth for a while: for when tribulation or persecution ariseth because of the word, by and by, he is offended. He also that receiveth seed among the thorns, is he that heareth the word; and the care of this world, and the deceitfulness of riches choke the word, and he becometh unfruitful. But he that received seed into the good ground is he that heareth the word, and understandeth it, which also beareth fruit, and bringeth forth, some an hundred fold, some sixty, some thirty." Thus the Savior Himself explains unto His disciples the parable which He put forth, and left no mystery or darkness upon the minds of those who firmly believe on His words. (*HC*, 2:266–67)

ILLUSTRATIONS FOR OUR TIME

James E. Talmage illustrates beautifully the parable of the sower when he comments:

> Further exposition may appear superfluous; some suggestion as to the individual application of the contained lessons may be in place, however. Observe that the prominent feature of the story is that of the prepared or unprepared condition of the soil. The seed was the same, whether it fell on good ground or bad, on mellow mold or among stones and thistles. The primitive method of sowing, still followed in many countries, consisted in the sower throwing the grain by handfuls against the wind, thus securing a widespread scattering. . . .
>
> Even according to literary canons, and as judged by the recognized standards of rhetorical construction and logical arrangement of its parts, this parable holds first place among productions of its class. Though commonly known to us as the Parable of the Sower, the story could be expressively designated as the Parable of the Four Kinds of Soil. It is the ground upon which the seed is cast, to which the story most strongly directs our attention, and which so aptly is made to symbolize the softened or the hardened heart, the clean or the thorn-infested soil. Observe the grades of soil, given in the increasing order of their fertility: (1) the compacted highway, the wayside path, on which, save by a combination of fortuitous circumstances practically amounting to a miracle, no seed can possibly strike root or grow; (2) the thin layer of soil covering an impenetrable bed-rock, wherein seed may sprout yet can never mature; (3) the weed-encumbered field, capable of producing a rich crop but for the jungle of thistles and thorns; and (4) the clean rich mold receptive and fertile. Yet even soils classed as good are of varying degrees of productiveness, yielding an increase of thirty, sixty, or even a hundred fold, with many inter-gradations. . . . In the parable we are considering, the Teacher depicted the varied grades of spiritual receptivity existing among men, and characterized with incisive brevity each of the specified grades. He neither said nor intimated that the hard-baked soil of the wayside might not be plowed, harrowed, fertilized, and so be rendered productive; nor that the stony impediment to growth might not be broken up and removed, or an increase of good soil be made by actual addition; nor that the thorns could never be uprooted, and their former habitat be rendered fit to support good plants. The parable is to be studied in the spirit of its purpose; and strained inferences or extensions are unwarranted. A strong metaphor, a striking simile, or any other expressive figure of speech, is of service only when rationally applied; if carried beyond the bounds of reasonable intent, the best of such may become meaningless or even absurd. (*JC,* 264–66)

As we read this wonderful explanation by Elder Talmage, there are questions we need to ask ourselves: Are we humble and easily entreated (see Alma 7:23)? Are we offering as a sacrifice a broken heart and contrite spirit (see 3 Ne. 9:20)? Are we yielding our hearts unto God (see Hel. 3:35)? We need to recognize that those who harden their hearts against the word dwindle in unbelief and fail to repent (see Mosiah 11:29). Yes, the one gift that we can present to the Lord that will give us the greatest joy and happiness is our hearts—His word will swell within our breasts and we can partake of the precious fruit as we nurture it with faith, diligence, and patience (see Alma 32:40–43). [Pinegar]

LIKENING THE SCRIPTURES TO OUR LIVES

Alma 32:27–31, 41–43 But behold, if ye will awake and arouse your faculties, even to an experiment upon my words, and exercise a particle of faith, yea, even if ye can no more than desire to believe, let this desire work in you, even until ye believe in a manner that ye can give place for a portion of my words. Now, we will compare the word unto a seed. Now, if ye give place, that a seed may be planted in your heart, behold, if it be a true seed, or a good seed, if ye do not cast it out by your unbelief, that ye will resist the Spirit of the Lord, behold, it will begin to swell within your breasts; and when you feel these swelling motions, ye will begin to say within your-selves—It must needs be that this is a good seed, or that the word is good, for it beginneth to enlarge my soul; yea, it beginneth to enlighten my understanding, yea, it beginneth to be delicious to me. Now behold, would not this increase your faith? I say unto you, Yea; nevertheless it hath not grown up to a perfect knowledge. But behold, as the seed swelleth, and sprouteth, and beginneth to grow, then you must needs say that the seed is good; for behold it swelleth, and sprouteth, and beginneth to grow. And now, behold, will not this strengthen your faith? Yea, it will strengthen your faith: for ye will say I know that this is a good seed; for behold it sprouteth and beginneth to grow. And now, behold, are ye sure that this is a good seed? I say unto you, Yea; for every seed bringeth forth unto its own likeness. . . . But if ye will nour-ish the word, yea, nourish the tree as it beginneth to grow, by your faith with great diligence, and with patience, looking forward to the fruit thereof, it shall take root; and behold it shall be a tree springing up unto everlasting life. And because of your diligence and your faith and your patience with the word in nourishing it, that it may take root in you, behold, by and by ye shall pluck the fruit thereof, which is most pre-cious, which is sweet above all that is sweet, and which is white above all that is white, yea, and pure above all that is pure; and ye shall feast upon this fruit even until ye are filled, that ye hunger not, neither shall ye thirst. Then, my brethren, ye shall reap the rewards of your faith, and your diligence, and patience, and long-suffering, waiting for the tree to bring forth fruit unto you.

Application: These verses convey the essence of the parable of the sower, for those who have prepared their hearts (the soil) receive and act upon the word of God (the seed). This is the key to holding fast to the iron rod and partaking of the fruit of the tree of life—even the love of God.

3. PARABLES CONCERNING THE KINGDOM OF GOD ON THE EARTH

THEME: This life is a probationary period in which we have the opportunity to receive a mortal body and apply our agency in obeying the Lord and keeping His commandments in all things. Through devotion in adhering to the principles and ordinances of the gospel and helping to build His Kingdom through service to others, we show ourselves worthy of immortality and eternal life. Hence the importance of our understanding what is expected of us in relation to the kingdom of God. The parables of the wheat and the tares, the mustard seed, the treasure, the pearl of great price, and casting the net into the sea all have to do with the kingdom of God.

MOMENT OF TRUTH

The Messiah who stood before the people and disseminated stimulating parables about the kingdom of God on the earth was the same exalted Being who, as the premortal Jehovah, instructed Moses concerning the purpose for all Creation: "For behold, this is my work and my glory—to bring to pass the immortality and eternal life of man" (Moses 1:39). This was the same supernal Being who inspired the prophet Daniel to interpret the King's dream about a coming kingdom of magnificence—that a "stone was cut out without hands, . . . and became a great mountain, and filled the whole earth" (Dan. 2:34–35). This was the same perfect Being who declared to the Prophet Joseph Smith: "Therefore, thou art blessed from henceforth that bear the keys of the kingdom given unto you; which kingdom is coming forth for the last time" (D&C 90:2). The kingdom of God is the fold of the Good Shepherd in all its glory. The parables concerning the kingdom of God are keys for detecting one's true motivation in being a disciple of Christ within the community of Saints.

MODERN PROPHETS SPEAK

Joseph Smith:
> Kingdom of Heaven and the Leaven
> "Another parable spake he unto them; The kingdom of heaven is like unto leaven, which a woman took, and hid in three measures of meal, till the whole was leavened." It may be understood that the Church of the Latter-day Saints has taken

its rise from a little leaven that was put into three witnesses. Behold, how much this is like the parable! It is fast leavening the lump, and will soon leaven the whole. But let us pass on.

Explanation of Tares of the Field

"All these things spake Jesus unto the multitude in parables; and without a parable spake he not unto them: that it might be fulfilled which was spoken by the prophet, saying, I will open my mouth in parables; I will utter things which have been kept secret from the foundation of the world. Then Jesus sent the multitude away, and went into the house: and his disciples came unto him, saying, Declare unto us the parable of the tares of the field. He answered and said unto them, he that soweth the good seed is the Son of Man; the field is the world; the good seed are the children of the kingdom; but the tares are the children of the wicked one." Now let our readers mark the expression—"the field is the world, the tares are the children of the wicked one, the enemy that sowed them is the devil, the harvest is the end of the world, [let them carefully mark this expression *the end* of the world,] and the reapers are the angels."

Now men cannot have any possible grounds to say that this is figurative, or that it does not mean what it says; for he is now explaining what he has previously spoken in parables; and according to this language, the end of the world is the destruction of the wicked, the harvest and the end of the world have an allusion directly to the human family in the last days, instead of the earth, as many have imagined; and that which shall precede the coming of the Son of Man, and the restitution of all things spoken of by the mouth of all the holy prophets since the world began; and the angels are to have something to do in this great work, for they are the reapers. As, therefore, the tares are gathered and burned in the fire, so shall it be in the end of the world; that is, as the servants of God go forth warning the nations, both priests and people, and as they harden their hearts and reject the light of truth, these first being delivered over to the buffetings of Satan, and the law and the testimony being closed up, as it was in the case of the Jews, they are left in darkness, and delivered over unto the day of burning; thus being bound up by their creeds, and their bands being made strong by their priests, are prepared for the fulfillment of the saying of the Savior—"The Son of man shall send forth his angels, and gather out of his kingdom all things that offend, and them which do iniquity, and shall cast them into a furnace of fire, there shall be wailing and gnashing of teeth." We understand that the work of gathering together of the wheat into barns, or garners, is to take place while the tares are being bound over, and preparing for the day of burning; that after the day of burnings, the righteous shall shine forth like the sun, in the Kingdom of their Father. Who hath ears to hear, let him hear.

Kingdom of Heaven and a Treasure Hid in a Field

But to illustrate more clearly this gathering: We have another parable—"Again, the kingdom of heaven is like a treasure hid in a field, the which, when a man hath found, he hideth, and for joy thereof, goeth and selleth all that he hath, and buyeth that field!" The Saints work after this pattern. See the Church of the Latter-day Saints, selling all that they have, and gathering themselves together unto a place that they may purchase for an inheritance, that they may be together and bear each other's afflictions in the day of calamity.

Kingdom of Heaven and the Pearl of Great Price

"Again, the kingdom of heaven is like unto a merchantman seeking goodly pearls, who, when he had found one pearl of great price, went and sold all that he had, and bought it." The Saints again work after this example. See men traveling to find places for Zion and her stakes or remnants, who, when they find the place for Zion, or the pearl of great price, straightway sell that they have, and buy it.

Kingdom of Heaven and the Net Cast into the Sea

"Again, the kingdom of heaven is like unto a net that was cast into the sea, and gathered of every kind, which when it was full they drew to shore, and sat down, and gathered the good into vessels, but cast the bad away." For the work of this pattern, behold the seed of Joseph, spreading forth the Gospel net upon the face of the earth, gathering of every kind, that the good may be saved in vessels prepared for that purpose, and the angels will take care of the bad. So shall it be at the end of the world—the angels shall come forth and sever the wicked from among the just, and cast them into the furnace of fire, and there shall be wailing and gnashing of teeth.

"Jesus saith unto them, Have you understood all these things? They say unto him, Yea, Lord." And we say, yea, Lord; and well might they say, yea, Lord; for these things are so plain and so glorious that every Saint in the last days must respond with a hearty Amen to them.

Kingdom of Heaven and the Householder

"Then said he unto them, therefore every scribe which is instructed in the kingdom of heaven, is like unto a man that is an householder, which bringeth forth out of his treasure things that are new and old."

For the works of this example, see the Book of Mormon coming forth out of the treasure of the heart. Also the covenants given to the Latter-day Saints, also the translation of the Bible—thus bringing forth out of the heart things new and old, thus answering to three measures of meal undergoing the purifying touch by a revelation of Jesus Christ, and the ministering of angels, who have already commenced this work in the last days, which will answer to the leaven which leavened the whole lump. Amen. (*HC,* 2:264–72)

Kingdom of Heaven and the Marriage Supper

In the 22nd chapter of Luke's [Matthew's] account of the Messiah, we find the kingdom of heaven likened unto a king who made a marriage for his son. That this son was the Messiah will not be disputed, since it was the kingdom of heaven that was represented in the parable; and that the Saints, or those who are found faithful to the Lord, are the individuals who will be found worthy to inherit a seat at the marriage supper, is evident from the sayings of John in the Revelation where he represents the sound which he heard in heaven to be like a great multitude, or like the voice of mighty thunderings, saying, the Lord God Omnipotent reigneth. Let us be glad and rejoice, and give honor to him; for the marriage of the Lamb is come, and his wife hath made herself ready. And to her was granted that she should be arrayed in fine linen, clean and white: For the fine linen is the righteous of Saints (Rev. 19). (*Discourses of the Prophet Joseph Smith,* compiled by Alma P. Burton [Salt Lake City: Deseret Book, 1977], 263)

ILLUSTRATIONS FOR OUR TIME

Robert J. Matthews conveys with clarity how the parables of Jesus, and the related commentary of the Prophet Joseph Smith, relate to our latter-day circumstances:

The parables of the sower, the tares, the mustard seed, leaven, pearl of great price, hidden treasure, and gospel net all have to do with preaching the gospel, gathering converts into the Church, the sacrifice that must be made to secure one's salvation beyond mere membership, and the final judgment, for the gospel net has collected all kinds. The Prophet Joseph discussed each one of these in his article (see *TPJS,* 94–102). In his explanation the Prophet sees these parables as having application to missionary work, the Book of Mormon, the Three Witnesses, the Church in the latter days, the JST, and the covenants the Lord has made with the Latter-day Saints. (*Behold the Messiah* [Salt Lake City: Bookcraft, 1994], 180–81)

LIKENING THE SCRIPTURES TO OUR LIVES

Matthew 13:31–32 Another parable put he forth unto them, saying, The kingdom of heaven is like to a grain of mustard seed, which a man took, and sowed in his field: Which indeed is the least of all seeds: but when it is grown, it is the greatest among herbs, and becometh a tree, so that the birds of the air come and lodge in the branches thereof.

Application: We are part of this great miracle of building up the kingdom of God here upon the earth. We are the weak and simple things that, in the hands of the Lord, will bring about His great work.

SUMMARY

Nephi gave us the key to applying the scriptures for productive results: "For I did liken all scriptures unto us, that it might be for our profit and learning" (1 Ne. 19:23). If we are to follow this advice in relation to the parables of Jesus, then we should be willing to do a little role-playing by projecting ourselves into the persona of the leading characters of the parables and seeing if the role fits our current modus operandi in desirable ways or if we need to change our manner of living to bring ourselves into alignment with the teachings of the gospel of Jesus Christ. The parable of the sower, the parables concerning the kingdom of God, and all other parables of the Savior are gateways into a state of mind where we can test our allegiance to the Master and discern the truth about our degree of faithfulness and devotion to eternal principles. "Take heed therefore how ye hear: for whosoever hath, to him shall be given; and whosoever hath not, from him shall be taken even that which he seemeth to have" (Luke 8:18).

CHAPTER 12

"I AM THE BREAD of LIFE"

Reading Assignment: John 5–6; Mark 6:30–44; Matthew 14:22–33.

Additional Reading: Matthew 14:1–21; 26:26–28; Mark 6:1–29, 45–52; Luke 9:10–17; John 20:31; Acts 18:28; 2 Nephi 25:26; Alma 5:33–35; D&C 20:77.

> *That none might misunderstand he said: "I am the bread of life: he that cometh to me shall never hunger; and he that believeth on me shall never thirst. . . . He that believeth on me hath everlasting life. I am the bread of life. Your fathers did eat manna in the wilderness, and are dead. This is the bread which cometh down from heaven, that a man may eat thereof, and not die. I am the living bread which came down from heaven: if any man eat of this bread, he shall live for ever. . . . As the living Father hath sent me, and I live by the Father: so he that eateth me, even he shall live by me. This is the bread which came down from heaven: not as your fathers did eat manna, and are dead: he that eateth of this bread shall live for ever" (John 6:1–58).*

—BRUCE R. MCCONKIE, *THE PROMISED MESSIAH: THE FIRST COMING OF CHRIST* [SALT LAKE CITY: DESERET BOOK, 1978], 399.

THEMES for LIVING

1. Jesus Bears Witness That He Is the Son of God
2. The Miracle of Feeding the Five Thousand
3. Faith to Follow the Savior upon the Waters of Life
4. Jesus Is "the Bread of Life"

INTRODUCTION

Jesus is the Son of God. He came to do the will of His Father. He is the light and life of the world. He, through the infinite and eternal Atonement, literally became the "bread of life." Only in and through Him can mankind be saved. As all must have sustenance to live, the metaphor of the bread of life is clear: we cannot live happily here on earth or eternally with our Father in Heaven save we partake of the "bread of life."

1. JESUS BEARS WITNESS THAT HE IS THE SON OF GOD

THEME: With irrefutable authority and unshakable certainty, the Savior declares His identity as the Son of God and bears witness of His divine commission to do the will of the Father. In this manner, He shows us the way to uphold the truth and proclaim the sovereignty of eternal principles. We can follow His example by remembering and declaring who we are: the sons and daughters of God with a calling to keep the covenants and bear witness of God at all times and in all places (Mosiah 18:9).

MOMENT OF TRUTH

It was at the Pool of Bethesda near the sheep market in Jerusalem that individuals with diverse infirmities would congregate in the hope of being cured. This pool was equipped with five porches or "cloisters." Apparently a spring flowing into the pool would cause a bubbling phenomenon from time to time. According to popular opinion, the pool had medicinal or healing properties, some people believing that the waters were subject to "troubling" by an angel (John 5:4). On this occasion, the "angel" who visited the pool was the Savior Himself. He observed a man waiting by the pool who had been suffering from a crippling malady for 38 years. The man explained that he had no one to carry him into the waters and that others would always go in before him. The Savior then asked a question of universal implication: "Wilt thou be made whole?" (John 5:6). When the man confirmed this desire, the Savior proclaimed: "Rise, take up thy bed, and walk" (John 5:8). Immediately the man was cured.

Because this miracle occurred on the Sabbath, the Jewish leaders were offended and inquired of the man about the circumstances with the mysterious man who performed the miracle. When the healed man later determined in the temple that Jesus was his benefactor, he reported this to the authorities, who then sought to kill the Master. Against this backdrop, the Savior took the opportunity to bear bold witness of His divine provenance and commission: "Then answered Jesus and said unto them,

Verily, verily, I say unto you, The Son can do nothing of himself, but what he seeth the Father do: for what things soever he doeth, these also doeth the Son likewise. . . . Verily, verily, I say unto you, He that heareth my word, and believeth on him that sent me, hath everlasting life, and shall not come into condemnation; but is passed from death unto life. . . . I can of mine own self do nothing: as I hear, I judge: and my judgment is just; because I seek not mine own will, but the will of the Father which hath sent me" (John 5:19, 24, 30). Then, alluding to John the Baptist, who had prepared the way for the Savior and testified of His divine office, Jesus said, "But I have greater witness than that of John: for the works which the Father hath given me to finish, the same works that I do, bear witness of me, that the Father hath sent me. And the Father himself, which hath sent me, hath borne witness of me. Ye have neither heard his voice at any time, nor seen his shape. . . . Search the scriptures; for in them ye think ye have eternal life: and they are they which testify of me" (John 5:36–37, 39).

MODERN PROPHETS SPEAK

Ezra Taft Benson:

> We declare the divinity of Jesus Christ. We look to Him as the only source of our salvation. We strive to live His teachings, and we look forward to the time that He shall come again on this earth to rule and reign as King of Kings and Lord of Lords. In the words of a Book of Mormon prophet, we say to men today, "There [is] no other name given nor any other way nor means whereby salvation can come unto the children of men, only in and through the name of Christ, the Lord Omnipotent" (Mosiah 3:17). (*TETB*, 10)

ILLUSTRATIONS FOR OUR TIME

Marvin J. Ashton explains how we must look to God and Christ in all things. He taught:

> How often have we ourselves said or have we heard others exclaim in times of crisis or trouble, "I just don't know where to turn"?
>
> If we will just use it, a gift is available to all of us—the gift of looking to God for direction. Here is an avenue of strength, comfort, and guidance. The scriptures promise us: "Behold, I am the law, and the light. Look unto me, and endure to the end, and ye shall live; for unto him that endureth to the end will I give eternal life" (3 Ne. 15:9). "Look to God and live" (Alma 37:47). . . .
>
> What a spiritual comfort and blessing it is to know that if we look to our Savior Jesus Christ and endure to the end, eternal life and exaltation can be ours. Our capacity to see and comprehend is increased only in proportion to our willingness

to look. God becomes more approachable as we look to him. Looking to God teaches us to serve and live without compulsion. Being a leader in the Church should never diminish our looking-to-God time. (Marvin J. Ashton, *The Measure of Our Hearts* [Salt Lake City: Deseret Book, 1991], 18)

LIKENING THE SCRIPTURES TO OUR LIVES

John 5:39 Search the scriptures; for in them ye think ye have eternal life: and they are they which testify of me.

Application: In the scriptures, we will come to know that Jesus is the Christ. The scriptures testify and witness that He is indeed the promised Messiah, the Savior and Redeemer of the world, and that through Him and through obedience to His word we can gain eternal life.

2. THE MIRACLE OF FEEDING THE FIVE THOUSAND

THEME: The Savior is the Lord of abundance, the Master of magnifying souls before the Father. The magnifying of the gift of the young boy with his five loaves and two fishes shows that the Lord could feed five thousand—and so likewise will He magnify our gifts, that we might assist in His work of feeding His sheep.

MOMENT OF TRUTH

On one occasion, an endless throng of people followed after the Savior, who went up into the mountain with His disciples. When the multitude came up to Him, He tested Phillip by asking him, "Whence shall we buy bread, that these may eat?" (John 6:5). Phillip, not discerning the dual meaning of these words, wondered how they could afford to go and purchase the needed food, but Andrew, brother of Simon Peter, took note of a young lad nearby who had five barley loaves and two small fish to spare. From these, the Savior compounded the provisions miraculously to feed some five thousand people. Following the repast, the Savior said, "Gather up the fragments that remain, that nothing be lost" (John 6:12). Twelve baskets of surplus remained. Similarly, these same disciples would in the future be sent forth to gather up the remnants of the Lord's people through the vast missionary work of the Kingdom, so that none of faith would be lost.

MODERN PROPHETS SPEAK

James E. Talmage:

> Jesus, realizing that the people were hungry, asked Philip, one of the Twelve, "Whence shall we buy bread, that these may eat?" The purpose of the question was to test the apostle's faith; for the Lord had already determined as to what was to be done. . . .
>
> Jesus gave command, and the people seated themselves on the grass in orderly array; they were grouped in fifties and hundreds; and it was found that the multitude numbered about five thousand men, beside women and children. Taking the loaves and the fishes, Jesus looked toward heaven and pronounced a blessing upon the food. . . . The substance of both fish and bread increased under the Master's touch; and the multitude feasted there in the desert, until all were satisfied. To the disciples Jesus said: "Gather up the fragments that remain, that nothing be lost"; and twelve baskets were filled with the surplus.
>
> As to the miracle itself, human knowledge is powerless to explain. . . . The broken but unused portion exceeded in bulk and weight the whole of the original little store. Our Lord's direction to gather up the fragments was an impressive object-lesson against waste; and it may have been to afford such lesson that an excess was supplied. The fare was simple, yet nourishing, wholesome and satisfying. Barley bread and fish constituted the usual food of the poorer classes of the region. (*JC*, 310–311)

ILLUSTRATIONS FOR OUR TIME

James E. Faust explains the miracle of the five loaves and two fishes as it can relate to our lives in seeking to magnify our callings by giving our all. He relates:

> In our time, we seem to have forgotten the miracle of the five loaves and the two fishes in favor of the miracles wrought by the mind and hand of men. I refer to the marvels of modern transportation and the increasing sophistication of all scientific knowledge, including the new electronic highway. We have forgotten that this amazing knowledge comes to mankind only as God chooses to reveal it, and it should be used for purposes nobler and wiser than mere entertainment. This knowledge permits the words of the prophets of God to be bounced off satellites hovering over the earth so it is possible for much of mankind to hear their messages. . . .
>
> A miracle even greater than that of the loaves and the fishes was the vision of the Prophet Joseph Smith, who saw the Father and the Son in the Sacred Grove near Palmyra, New York. Subsequently the keys, the priesthood, and the saving ordinances were restored in their fulness, and Christ's church was reestablished in our time. Thus God has again fed us and filled our baskets to overflowing.

It has been said that this church does not necessarily attract great people but more often makes ordinary people great. Many people with little-known names and with gifts equal only to five loaves and two small fishes magnify their callings and serve without attention or recognition, feeding literally thousands. In large measure, they make possible the fulfillment of Nebuchadnezzar's dream that the latter-day gospel of Christ would be like a stone cut out of the mountain without hands, rolling forth until it fills the whole earth (see Dan. 2:34–35; D&C 65:2). . . .

A major reason this church has grown from its humble beginnings to its current strength is the faithfulness and devotion of millions of humble people who have only five loaves and two small fishes to offer in the service of the Master. They have largely surrendered their own interests and in so doing have found "the peace of God, which passeth all understanding" (Philip. 4:7). I wish only to be one of those who experience this supernal inner peace. (James E. Faust, *Finding Light in a Dark World* [Salt Lake City: Deseret Book, 1995], 44–45, 47)

LIKENING THE SCRIPTURES TO OUR LIVES

Ether 3:4 And I know, O Lord, that thou hast all power, and can do whatsoever thou wilt for the benefit of man.

Application: Let us never forget that the Lord has all power. He can do all things. We can do all things according to His will and in the strength of the Lord (see Alma 26:11–12). Remember that our finite minds cannot comprehend His ways or His thoughts (see Isa. 55:8–9).

3. FAITH TO FOLLOW THE SAVIOR UPON THE WATERS OF LIFE

THEME: Jesus demonstrated on many occasions His power over the elements—including His miraculous walk upon the sea (Matt. 14:25–26). As we exercise faith, we too can bring about miracles, controlling the elements according to the will of God (see Ether 12) and serving as instruments in the hands of God to bring about His marvelous purposes on behalf of His children.

MOMENT OF TRUTH

James E. Talmage explains the powerful event in the lives of the Apostles when they witnessed their Master walking upon the stormy sea. He recorded:

Though they had labored through the night they had progressed less than four miles on their course; to turn and run before the wind would have been to invite disastrous wreck; their sole hope lay in their holding the vessel to the wind by sheer power of muscle. Jesus, in His place of solitary retirement, was aware of their sad plight, and along in the fourth watch, that is, between three and six o'clock in the morning, He came to their assistance, walking upon the storm-tossed water as though treading solid ground. When the voyagers caught sight of Him as He approached the ship in the faint light of the near-spent night, they were overcome by superstitious fears, and cried out in terror, thinking that they saw a ghostly apparition. "But straightway Jesus spake unto them, saying, Be of good cheer; it is I; be not afraid."

Relieved by these assuring words, Peter, impetuous and impulsive as usual, cried out: "Lord, if it be thou, bid me come unto thee on the water" (Matt. 14:28). Jesus assenting, Peter descended from the ship and walked toward his Master; but as the wind smote him and the waves rose about him, his confidence wavered and he began to sink. Strong swimmer though he was, he gave way to fright, and cried, "Lord, save me." Jesus caught him by the hand, saying: "O thou of little faith, wherefore didst thou doubt?"

From Peter's remarkable experience, we learn that the power by which Christ was able to walk the waves could be made operative in others, provided only their faith was enduring. . . . His attempt, though attended by partial failure, was a demonstration of the efficacy of faith in the Lord, such as no verbal teaching could ever have conveyed. Jesus and Peter entered the vessel; immediately the wind ceased, and the boat soon reached the shore. The amazement of the apostles, at this latest manifestation of the Lord's control over the forces of nature, would have been more akin to worship and less like terrified consternation had they remembered the earlier wonders they had witnessed; but they had forgotten even the miracle of the loaves, and their hearts had hardened. Marveling at the power of One to whom the wind-lashed sea was a sustaining floor, the apostles bowed before the Lord in reverent worship, saying: "Of a truth thou art the Son of God." (*JC*, 312–13)

MODERN PROPHETS SPEAK

Neal A. Maxwell:

In that episode on Galilee when Jesus walked on the water, remember that Peter first asked Jesus to beckon him to come? Jesus did. Then Peter walked on water, however briefly. He is the only mortal to have done so, as far as we know. However, Peter did it not for display, but in order "to go to Jesus." (Matt. 14:29) . . . It was only when he saw the "wind boisterous" that he became afraid and began to sink. Even though Peter no longer walked on water, he had not lost his faith in Jesus' power to save Him. He cried out to Jesus, "Save me," fearing he would drown. Jesus then extended His hand to Peter, both catching him and reproving him because Peter had doubted. (Matt. 14:30–31) . . . How loving yet tutoring! Perhaps it was Peter's failure to keep his eye fixed on Jesus? Like the not fully committed plowman? Instead of looking straight ahead at Jesus, Peter looked around, computed the odds, and was terrified. As any of us would be! How does one ignore wind-whipped whitecaps? . . . But if we are willing to proceed with our eye upon Jesus Christ instead of upon all that might go wrong, or upon the waves pounding and swirling about us, if we "go to Jesus" directly, knowing that He can save us, we will not be forsaken either. Even if we seem to be sinking, we are still to reach out to Him. (*We Talk of Christ, We Rejoice in Christ* [Salt Lake City: Deseret Book, 1984], 17–18; Note: Written as a conversation between people. Ellipses marks signify deletion of names.)

ILLUSTRATIONS FOR OUR TIME

An illustration made by Bruce A. Van Orden and Brent L. Top brings additional insight to this remarkable event of walking on the water and coming unto Christ. They said:

When Christ appeared near the ship, Peter wanted to go to the Savior by walking on the water. Christ invited him to do so. "And when Peter was come down out of the ship, he walked on the water, to go to Jesus" (Matt. 14:29). . . .

Yet, when Peter walked toward the Son of God, he began to sink. Had he not seen the Savior and believed in him? Was he not coming to Christ? Why then did he sink? Matthew explains it this way: "When he saw the wind boisterous, he was afraid" (Matt. 14:30). Peter became distracted by the boisterous wind. His eyes were no longer single to (or focused on) the glory of God, and he wavered.

The Apostle James said, "He that wavereth is like a wave of the sea driven with the wind and tossed" (James 1:6). And, like all those who waver, Peter began to sink into the tempestuous sea. As we hear Peter cry out, "Lord, save me" (Matt. 14:30), we simultaneously hear Alma the Younger crying out, "O Jesus, thou Son of God, have mercy on me, who am in the gall of bitterness, and am encircled about by the everlasting chains of death" (Alma 36:18). That is the cry of all those who awaken to the realization that they are "without God in the world" (Alma 41:11). (*The Lord of the Gospels: The 1990 Sperry Symposium on the New Testament* [Salt Lake City: Deseret Book, 1991], 109–10)

LIKENING THE SCRIPTURES TO OUR LIVES

Moroni 10:32 Yea, come unto Christ, and be perfected in him, and deny yourselves of all ungodliness; and if ye shall deny yourselves of all ungodliness, and love God with all your might, mind and strength, then is his grace sufficient for you, that by his grace ye may be perfect in Christ; and if by the grace of God ye are perfect in Christ, ye can in nowise deny the power of God.

Application: In life, our only hope is to come unto Christ. He can perfect us through the grace of God if we but overcome all ungodliness and love God and thus keep His commandments (see John 14:15).

4. JESUS IS "THE BREAD OF LIFE"

THEME: Jesus, the Savior and Redeemer, is the Bread of Life. His infinite Atonement, His gospel, His example, His priesthood, His doctrine, and His kingdom—even The Church of Jesus Christ of Latter-day Saints—provide the way to immortality and eternal life.

MOMENT OF TRUTH

The day following the miracle of feeding the five thousand with the loaves and fishes, the multitude sought out the Savior, who discerned their character: "Jesus answered them and said, Verily, verily, I say unto you, Ye seek me, not because ye saw the miracles, but because ye did eat of the loaves, and were filled. Labour not for the meat which perisheth, but for that meat which endureth unto everlasting life, which the Son of man shall give unto you: for him hath God the Father sealed. Then said they unto him, What shall we do, that we might work the works of God?" (John 6:26–28). The Savior fed them the meat of the gospel, not just the bread, by telling them point blank what their spiritual diet must consist of thereafter, namely, His flesh and His blood—meaning the fruits of the Atonement, savored and enjoyed by those with a broken heart and a contrite spirit.

He continued His exposition of the eternal truth: "I am the living bread which came down from heaven: if any man eat of this bread, he shall live for ever: and the bread that I will give is my flesh, which I will give for the life of the world. . . . Verily, verily, I say unto you, Except ye eat the flesh of the Son of man, and drink his blood, ye have no life in you. . . . This is that bread which came down from heaven: not as your fathers did eat manna, and are dead: he that eateth of this bread shall live for ever" (John 6:51, 53, 58). The response of some of the listeners to this teaching is instructive: "Many therefore of his disciples, when they had heard this, said, This is an hard saying; who can hear it?" (John 6:60). Who, indeed, can hear the penetrating news of the justice of God and the mercy of the Atonement—with all the attendant requirements that are incumbent upon those who would profess to be the disciples of Christ—and still remain faithful and valiant? That is the question we all face. Will we stay with the Savior, or do as many of His disciples did that day, who were offended, and "went back, and walked no more with him" (John 6:66)?

MODERN PROPHETS SPEAK

Harold B. Lee:

> Some years ago at a stake conference, the late President J. Reuben Clark, Jr., made a significant statement to teachers and a promise to youth: "Youth of the Church are hungry for the words of the Lord. Teachers, be sure you are prepared to feed them the 'bread of life'—which is the teachings of Jesus Christ. If they, the youth, will live up to His teachings, they will have more happiness than they ever dreamed of." (*Ye Are the Light of the World: Selected Sermons and Writings of Harold B. Lee* [Salt Lake City: Deseret Book, 1974], 129)

ILLUSTRATIONS FOR OUR TIME

The Doctrine of the Bread of Life
Bruce R. McConkie:

> To eat the flesh and drink the blood of the Son of God is, first, to accept him in the most literal and full sense, with no reservation whatever, as the personal offspring in the flesh of the Eternal Father; and, secondly, it is to keep the commandments of the Son by accepting his gospel, joining his Church, and enduring in obedience and righteousness unto the end. Those who by this course eat his flesh and drink his blood shall have eternal life, meaning exaltation in the highest heaven of the celestial world. Speaking of ancient Israel, for instance, Paul says: *They 'did all eat the same spiritual meat; And did all drink the same spiritual drink: for they drank of that spiritual Rock that followed them: and that Rock was Christ'* (1 Cor. 10:3–4).
>
> In the waters of baptism the saints take upon themselves the name of Christ (that is, they accept him fully and completely as the Son of God and the Savior of men), and they then covenant to keep his commandments and obey his laws (Mosiah 18:7–10). To keep his saints in constant remembrance of their obligation to accept and obey him—or in other words, to eat his flesh and drink his blood— the Lord has given them the sacramental ordinance. This ordinance, performed in remembrance of his broken flesh and spilled blood, is the means provided for men,

formally and repeatedly, to assert their belief in the divinity of Christ, and to affirm their determination to serve him and keep his commandments; or, in other words, in this ordinance—in a spiritual, but not a literal sense—men eat his flesh and drink his blood. . . .

The message is now delivered to the Jews and to us. The meaning is clear; the doctrine is strong; the effects of the teaching—either belief or disbelief; obedience or disobedience; eternal life or eternal death—such are now in the hands of those who have heard the message. And that the message may live anew in our hearts, we are commanded to go to the house of prayer on the Lord's day and there partake of the sacramental emblems, offered to us in similitude of the spilt blood and broken flesh of Him whose blood we must drink and whose flesh we must eat, if we are to be his and have life with him as he has life with his Father. (*The Mortal Messiah: From Bethlehem to Calvary,* 4 vols. [Salt Lake City: Deseret Book, 1979–1981], 2:379–80)

LIKENING THE SCRIPTURES TO OUR LIVES

John 6:35 And Jesus said unto them, I am the bread of life: he that cometh to me shall never hunger; and he that believeth on me shall never thirst.

Application: To live, we need sustenance. This scripture makes it crystal clear that the only power that can give us the food of eternal life is the Lord Jesus Christ. When we come unto Christ, He blesses us and strengthens us in all things.

SUMMARY

In keeping with the venerable law of witnesses (Deut. 19:15; compare Matt. 18:16; 2 Cor. 13:1; D&C 6:28), the Savior boldly and fearlessly declared to the people precisely who He was: the Son of God, the Redeemer of the world—He told the truth as it was, and many were offended by His assertions because they were troubling to their comfort and threatening to their supposed authority. But in the face of such disbelief, the Savior continued with His practice of showing forth miracles and teaching by the power of God. He magnified the gift of a small boy by compounding five loaves and two fishes into a feast for five thousand. He walked upon the stormy sea and calmed the elements. He presented Himself as the Bread of Life through which spiritual hunger could be sated forever. He opened the pathway for His followers to come unto Him in faith and righteousness.

If we will but follow Him and partake of the bread of life, we will become in His hands a miracle of transformation, a wonder of conversion, a marvel of edification. In all our amazement at His unsurpassed deeds and words, let us not forget that the greatest miracle of all is the mighty change of heart that each of us can experience through obedience to the principles and ordinances that He has provided for our eternal blessing. "Wilt thou be made whole?" asked the Savior of the man at the Pool of Bethesda. If asked the same question, would we not also have the faith to respond affirmatively, and merit the choice response: "Rise, take up thy bed, and walk" (John 5:8)?

CHAPTER 13

THE MOUNT of TRANSFIGURATION—
THE PRIESTHOOD KEYS RESTORED

Reading Assignment: Matthew 15:21–17:9.

Additional Reading: Mark 7:24–9:10; Luke 9:18–36; 12:54–57; Proverbs 29:18; Amos 3:7; 1 Corinthians 2:9–12; Galatians 1:11–12; 2 Peter 1:20–21; Alma 5:46; Moroni 10:5; Bible Dictionary, "Revelation," 762; "Transfiguration, Mount of," 786.

> *During the years of my life, I have gone to my knees with a humble spirit to the only place I could for help. I often went in agony of spirit, earnestly pleading with God to sustain me in the work I have come to appreciate more than life itself. . . .*
>
> *It has been as though I have struggled up an almost real Mount of Transfiguration and upon occasion felt great strength and power in the presence of the Divine. A special, sacred feeling has been a sustaining influence and often a close companion.*
>
> *It is my testimony that we are facing difficult times. We must be courageously obedient. My witness is that we will be called upon to prove our spiritual stamina, for the days ahead will be filled with affliction and difficulty. But with the assuring comfort of a personal relationship with God, we will be given a calming courage. From the Divine so near we will receive the quiet assurance: "My son, peace be unto thy soul; thine adversity and thine afflictions shall be but a small moment;*
>
> *"And then, if thou endure it well, God shall exalt thee on high; thou shalt triumph over all thy foes" (D&C 121:7–8).*
>
> —JAMES E. FAUST, "THAT WE MIGHT KNOW THEE," *ENSIGN*, JAN. 1999, 4–5.

THEMES *for* LIVING

1. The Healing and Nurturing Spirit of Christ
2. The Testimony of Christ Through Revelation
3. The Keys of the Kingdom

INTRODUCTION

As we strengthen our testimony of Jesus Christ by pondering and studying, by praying that we might receive revelation, by living the principles of the gospel, and by bearing witness of its verities, our conversion deepens and the lives of the people we associate with will be blessed. There is surely power in bearing pure testimony (see Alma 4:19). The Lord in His goodness wanted to ensure that His beloved disciples had the power to act in the name of God; thus He bestowed the keys of the Holy Priesthood upon His Apostles. The chief Apostle, the president of the Church, holds the authority to exercise all the keys and authorizes and delegates to other Apostles and servants of the Lord the commission to utilize them under his direction.

1. THE HEALING AND NURTURING SPIRIT OF CHRIST

THEME: The goodness and compassion of our Savior Jesus Christ are ever evident as He heals the sick and blesses the lives of God's children.

MOMENT OF TRUTH

The gospels of the New Testament are a precious and abundant source of evidence that the Lord is compassionate and ever loving toward God's children. We recall His kindness toward the Samaritan woman at the well (John 4:5–42), even though she was of a lineage despised of the Jews. In a similar episode, a woman of Canaan (a person of Greek/"Syrophenician" extraction—Mark 7:26) came to the Lord, seeking relief for her troubled daughter. At first, He declined, saying, "I am not sent but unto the lost sheep of the house of Israel" (Matt. 24). But after she had displayed deep humility and faith, He brought about the healing she so desired: "O woman, great is thy faith: be it unto thee even as thou wilt. And her daughter was made whole from that very hour" (Matt. 15:28; compare Mark 7:24–30). Thereafter, Jesus went over by the Sea of Galilee and retired to a mountain location with His disciples. As so often was the case, an enormous throng of people followed after Him, seeking His blessings of healing for their family members. He felt "compassion" for them (Matt. 15:32) because they had been underway with Him for three days and were hungry. When the

Savior was reluctant to send them away without feeding them, His disciples (evidently forgetting how the Savior had just recently fed five thousand people on five loaves and two fishes) inquired how they should acquire supplies adequate for this crowd of some four thousand people. At this, the Savior took of the supplies they had—seven loaves and a few fish—and miraculously accomplished the service (see Matt. 15:34–39; compare Mark 8:1–9).

MODERN PROPHETS SPEAK

Neal A. Maxwell:

> In this respect, Jesus gave us a needed lesson about timing. Did He not send forth the Twelve instructing them not to go "into the way of the Gentiles, and into any city of the Samaritans"? Why? Because they were rather to go "to the lost sheep of the house of Israel." Did not Jesus for a moment withhold a healing from the daughter of a woman of Canaan? Though He enunciated that He had been sent only to the lost sheep of the house of Israel, He made an exception in the case of this woman because of her faith, and her daughter was "made whole from that very hour."
>
> Just how long it was from the time of divine constraint regarding sharing the gospel with the Gentiles until Peter and others received the marvelous divine instructions to take the gospel to them, we do not know precisely. But it did involve some time.
>
> The issue for us is trusting God enough to trust also His timing. If we can truly believe He has our welfare at heart, may we not let His plans unfold as He thinks best? The same is true with the second coming and with all those matters wherein our faith needs to include faith in the Lord's timing for us personally, not just in His overall plans and purposes. (*Even As I Am* [Salt Lake City: Deseret Book, 1982], 93)

ILLUSTRATIONS FOR OUR TIME

Power of God

There are few who cannot, with pondering and prayerful recollection, recall times in their lives where the power of God was made manifest to them. It might have been a moment of illumination by the Holy Spirit, confirming the divine commission of the Savior—since "no man can say that Jesus is the Lord, but by the Holy Ghost" (1 Cor. 12:3). It might have been an occasion where the Lord provided guidance to ensure safety and prevent sorrow. It might have been revelatory insights conveyed through an inspired patriarchal blessing. It might have been a miraculous blessing of healing at the hands of the priesthood of God.

One such occasion is recorded in the historical record of the restoration of the Church in the latter days. It happened on July 22, 1839, a day coined by Wilford

Woodruff as "a day of God's power" (*Church History in the Fulness of Times,* 218). The Saints had responded to Joseph Smith's call to settle in the new gathering place of Nauvoo on the banks of the Mississippi River. Thousands were arriving there, unaware of the dangers posed by the malaria-bearing mosquitoes that flourished in the as yet undrained swamplands nearby.

That summer, hundreds contracted the disease, including the Prophet, who took many into his own house so that he and Emma could nurse them. Many of the victims at the settlement and in nearby Quincy were dying. On July 22, the Prophet, moved by the Spirit, rose up from his sick bed and went out to begin administering to the ill in Nauvoo and in Montrose, Iowa, across the river, healing many in a marvelous manifestation of the power of God (see *HC,* 4:3–5). Wilford Woodruff characterizes this extraordinary event as the "greatest day for the manifestation of the power of God through the gift of healing since the organization of the Church" (*Leaves from My Journal,* 65, as cited in *Church History in the Fulness of Times,* 219).

In one especially poignant incident, a nonmember traveler from the West who had witnessed the miraculous events of the day beckoned the Prophet to come and heal his stricken three-month-old twins. The Prophet was unable to go back the two miles to the bedside of the children, so he took from his pocket a silk bandanna handkerchief and gave it to Wilford Woodruff with the instructions to take it and wipe the faces of the children, promising that they would be healed: "As long as you keep that handkerchief it shall remain a league between you and me" (*HC,* 4:5). Elder Woodruff obeyed, and the twins were healed.

Such events recall the numerous compassionate blessings of restoration and healing rendered by the mortal Savior during His ministry as well as in His post-resurrection visit to the Saints in ancient America. We are reminded by evidence of this kind that "He giveth power to the faint; and to them that have no might he increaseth strength" (Isa. 40:29). It would be well for all of us to look into our own lives and discern the nurturing hand of God at work on our behalf. It would be an act of gratitude for each of us to memorialize and testify of those times in our lives when we have experienced or witnessed the manifestation of God's power. [Allen]

LIKENING THE SCRIPTURES TO OUR LIVES

Matt 15:28 Then Jesus answered and said unto her, O woman, great is thy faith: be it unto thee even as thou wilt. And her daughter was made whole from that very hour.

Application: The Lord has compassion on all His children, whether Jew or Gentile, and seeks to bless them by their faith. As we exercise our faith in the Lord Jesus Christ, the blessings of Heaven can be ours.

2. THE TESTIMONY OF CHRIST THROUGH REVELATION

THEME: In His intercessory prayer, the Savior uttered these words: "And this is life eternal, that they might know thee the only true God, and Jesus Christ, whom thou hast sent" (John 17:3). It is essential that we come to know our Father in Heaven and His Son—to know that Jesus is the Christ, the Savior and Redeemer of the world. The only way to know this is through revelation by the power of the Holy Ghost.

MOMENT OF TRUTH

On one very special occasion, the Savior taught His disciples an unforgettable lesson on the subject of how to gain a testimony based on the rock-solid foundation of revelation. As He came to the coasts of Caesarea Phillipi (a town near the source of the Jordan River, at the foot of Mount Herman, being the northernmost point of the travels of Jesus), He asked His disciples to tell Him who the people were saying that He, the Son of man, was. Their responses provided the framework for the Master's lesson:

> And they said, Some say that thou art John the Baptist: some, Elias; and others, Jeremias, or one of the prophets.
>
> He saith unto them, But whom say ye that I am?
>
> And Simon Peter answered and said, Thou art the Christ, the Son of the living God.
>
> And Jesus answered and said unto him, Blessed art thou, Simon Bar-jona: for flesh and blood hath not revealed it unto thee, but my Father which is in heaven.
>
> And I say also unto thee, That thou art Peter, and upon this rock I will build my church; and the gates of hell shall not prevail against it.
>
> And I will give unto thee the keys of the kingdom of heaven: and whatsoever thou shalt bind on earth shall be bound in heaven: and whatsoever thou shalt loose on earth shall be loosed in heaven. (Matt. 16:14–19)

In this manner the Lord confirmed that knowledge of spiritual things comes through revelation from the Holy Ghost—providing a foundation for the operation of priesthood leadership in the kingdom of God. In Greek, the word "petra" refers to bedrock, but the closely associated word "petros" refers to a small stone, which is the code name that Christ gave to His chief Apostle (see John 1:42). Thus Peter is linguistically incorporated into the theme of the moment—not as the foundation of the Church, but as a critically important element of its structure. What is the foundation? It is the system of revelation that ensures eternal integrity and everlasting consistency of the Kingdom. What is the rock and chief cornerstone thereof? Christ Himself is the Stone of Israel (see Acts 4:10–12; 1 Cor. 3:10–12; 10:4; Eph. 2:20; D&C 50:44; 128:10).

MODERN PROPHETS SPEAK

Joseph F. Smith:

> Some have held that *revelation* alone was the "Rock" referred to. This could not be, because without Christ, revelation would not avail. Some have held it was "Christ alone" that was meant as the "Rock"; but this could not be, because without revelation, not even Simon Bar-jona could *know* that Jesus was "The Christ, the Son of the Living God," for "flesh and blood" not only *did not,* but absolutely cannot reveal Christ unto man. The revelation must come from God. Therefore, it may be summed up, that "The Christ," and "Revelation from God" constitute the "Rock" on which Christ built and will build His Church. . . . I know that both Christ and revelation are essential to the salvation of man, and indispensible to the building up of the Church. Both go together; they are inseparable, and one without the other would not avail. (*From Prophet to Son: Advice of Joseph F. Smith to His Missionary Sons,* comp. Hyrum M. Smith III and Scott G. Kenney [Salt Lake City: Deseret Book, 1981], 87–88)

ILLUSTRATIONS FOR OUR TIME

Understanding the Use of the Term "Rock"
Joseph Fielding Smith:

> The expression "the rock" is used in the scriptures with different meanings that must be interpreted according to the context. There are times when it refers to Christ and times when it refers to the gospel and other times when the reference is to revelation and again to the Church. (*AGQ,* 1:94)

Gordon B. Hinckley:

> This rock of revelation is the source of knowledge concerning the things of God. It is the witness of the Holy Spirit that testifies of eternal truth, and the gates of hell shall not prevail against any man who seeks it, who accepts it, who cultivates it, and who lives by it. (*Be Thou an Example* [Salt Lake City: Deseret Book, 1981], 9)

LIKENING THE SCRIPTURES TO OUR LIVES

Matthew 16:16–18 And Simon Peter answered and said, Thou art the Christ, the Son of the living God. And Jesus answered and said unto him, Blessed art thou, Simon Barjona: for flesh and blood hath not revealed it unto thee, but my Father which is in heaven. And I say also unto thee, That thou art Peter, and upon this rock I will build my church; and the gates of hell shall not prevail against it.

Application: The Rock of our Salvation is the Lord Jesus Christ (see 2 Sam. 22:47; Ps. 62:2, 6; 95:1; 1 Ne. 13:36; 2 Ne. 4:30; 9:45; Jacob 7:25; Hel. 5:12; D&C 18:17). He is the chief cornerstone with which we build our foundation. We can only come to know this by revelation.

3. THE KEYS OF THE KINGDOM

THEME: The blessings of the Lord and His gospel are administered through the power and keys of the priesthood.

MOMENT OF TRUTH

When the Savior taught His disciples concerning the rock of revelation, He also alluded to the sealing powers of the priesthood that He would soon bestow upon them: "And I will give unto thee the keys of the kingdom of heaven: and whatsoever thou shalt bind on earth shall be bound in heaven: and whatsoever thou shalt loose on earth shall be loosed in heaven" (Matt. 16:19). From that moment on, the Savior began to prepare His flock for the hour of the crucifixion and divine Atonement (Matt. 16:21–23). Some six days hence, He took Peter, James, and John into a high mountain where He was transfigured before them—"and his face did shine as the sun, and his raiment was white as the light" (Matt. 17:2). On that supremely sacred occasion, Moses and Elias (Elijah) appeared and conversed with the Lord concerning His coming sacrifice (see Luke 9:31). The voice of Elohim was heard from the covering of a cloud, proclaiming: "This is my beloved Son, in whom I am well pleased; hear ye him" (Matt. 17:5; compare the accounts in Mark 9:2–13 and Luke 9:28–36). On the Mount of Transfiguration, Jesus, Moses, and Elijah bestowed upon the three presiding apostles the promised keys of the priesthood, as the Prophet Joseph Smith confirmed in his reference to "The Nature of the Priesthood":

> The Priesthood is everlasting. The Savior, Moses, and Elias, gave the keys to Peter, James, and John, on the mount, when they were transfigured before him. The Priesthood is everlasting—without beginning of days or end of years; without father, mother, etc. If there is no change of ordinances, there is no change of Priesthood. Wherever the ordinances of the Gospel are administered, there is the Priesthood. (*HC,* 3:387)

In a subsequent discussion of this awe-inspiring event, the disciples asked the Savior, "Why then say the scribes that Elias must first come?" (Matt. 17:10). In answer, the

Savior confirmed that "Elias [that is, Elijah, with the keys of the sealing power] truly shall first come, and restore all things" (Matt. 17:11)—but that Elias (that is, the forerunner) had already come. The disciples then understood that He was referring in this latter sense to John the Baptist, while at the same time also alluding to a future day when Elijah would come again as part of the restoration of the gospel. Here is the precise rendition of this passage as reported in the Joseph Smith Translation: "Then the disciples understood that he spake unto them of John the Baptist, and also of another who should come and restore all things, as it is written by the prophets" (JST, Matt. 17:14). Moses, Elias, and Elijah did indeed return to convey their respective keys upon Joseph Smith and Oliver Cowdery on April 3, 1836, at the Kirtland Temple (see D&C 110:11–16).

MODERN PROPHETS SPEAK

Bruce R. McConkie:

> The keys of the priesthood are the right and power of presidency. They are the directing, controlling, and governing power. Those who hold them are empowered to direct the manner in which others use their priesthood. Every ministerial act performed by a priesthood holder must be done at the proper time and place and in the proper way. The power of directing these labors constitutes the keys of the priesthood. Every elder, for instance, has the power to baptize, but no elder can use this power unless he is authorized to do so by someone holding the keys.
>
> The keys of the kingdom are the power, right, and authority to preside over the kingdom of God on earth, which is the Church, and to direct all of its affairs. The keys of any particular ministerial service authorize the use of the priesthood for that purpose. Thus, the restoration by Moses of the keys of the gathering of Israel and the leading of the Ten Tribes from the land of the north opened the door so the priesthood could be used to gather Israel, the Ten Tribes included, into the true fold of their ancient Shepherd. (*A New Witness for the Articles of Faith* [Salt Lake City: Deseret Book, 1985], 309–10)

ILLUSTRATIONS FOR OUR TIME

The Keys Restored in the Dispensation of the Fullness of Times

On April 3, 1836, Joseph Smith and Oliver Cowdery were privileged to participate in an extraordinary visionary experience in which the Savior appeared unto them and presided over the process of their receiving the keys of the priesthood to carry out the work of the Restoration, with all its attendant blessings to God's children:

> After this vision closed [the appearance of the Savior], the heavens were again opened unto us; and Moses appeared before us, and committed unto us the keys of

the gathering of Israel from the four parts of the earth, and the leading of the ten tribes from the land of the north.

After this, Elias appeared, and committed the dispensation of the gospel of Abraham, saying that in us and our seed all generations after us should be blessed.

After this vision had closed, another great and glorious vision burst upon us; for Elijah the prophet, who was taken to heaven without tasting death, stood before us, and said:

Behold, the time has fully come, which was spoken of by the mouth of Malachi—testifying that he [Elijah] should be sent, before the great and dreadful day of the Lord come—

To turn the hearts of the fathers to the children, and the children to the fathers, lest the whole earth be smitten with a curse—

Therefore, the keys of this dispensation are committed into your hands; and by this ye may know that the great and dreadful day of the Lord is near, even at the doors. (D&C 110:11–16)

Keys of Gathering from Moses
Harold B. Lee:

> Six years after the Church was organized, the keys of gathering were committed to Joseph Smith and Oliver Cowdery in the Kirtland Temple. . . . The spirit of gathering has been with the Church from the days of that restoration. Those who are of the blood of Israel, have a righteous desire after they are baptized, to gather together with the body of the Saints at the designated place. This, we have come to recognize, is but the breath of God upon those who are converted, turning them to the promises made to their fathers. (Roy W. Doxey, comp., *Latter-day Prophets and the Doctrine and Covenants* [Salt Lake City: Deseret Book, 1978], 4:103)

Keys of the Dispensation of the Gospel of Abraham from Elias
Joseph Fielding Smith:

> Elias came, after Moses had conferred his keys, and brought the gospel of the dispensation in which Abraham lived. *Everything that pertains to that dispensation, the blessings that were conferred upon Abraham, the promises* that were given to his posterity, all had to be restored [Abr. 2:8–11], and Elias, who held the keys of that dispensation, came. (*Latter-day Prophets and the Doctrine and Covenants*, 4:109)

Keys of Sealing from Elijah
Joseph Smith:

> The Bible says, "I will send you Elijah the Prophet before the coming of the great and dreadful day of the Lord; and he shall turn the heart of the fathers to the children, and the heart of the children to the fathers, lest I come and smite the earth with a curse."

Now, the word *turn* here should be translated *bind,* or seal. But what is the object of this important mission? Or how is it to be fulfilled? The keys are to be delivered, the spirit of Elijah is to come, the Gospel to be established, the Saints of God gathered, Zion built up, and the Saints to come up as saviors on Mount Zion. (*Latter-day Prophets and the Doctrine and Covenants,* 4:109)

The Windows of Heaven Can Be Opened unto Us

As Moses recorded, "But now mine own eyes have beheld God; but not my natural, but my spiritual eyes, for my natural eyes could not have beheld; for I should have withered and died in his presence; but his glory was upon me; and I beheld his face, for I was transfigured before him" (Moses 1:11). The challenge and promise is for all of us to know God and Jesus Christ (see John 17:3). The question is how? The Lord instructed the Prophet Joseph in this process when He said, "And again, verily I say unto you that it is your privilege, and a promise I give unto you that have been ordained unto this ministry, that inasmuch as you strip yourselves from jealousies and fears, and humble yourselves before me, for ye are not sufficiently humble, the veil shall be rent and you shall see me and know that I am—not with the carnal neither natural mind, but with the spiritual" (D&C 67:10). Like Moses, we too can see God, not by the natural or carnal but only by the spiritual. This can only happen as we strip ourselves of our jealousy by being full of the love of Christ, overcome our fears through love (1 Jn. 4:18), strengthen our faith (Rom. 10:17; Hel. 3:35), prepare ourselves (see D&C 38:30), increase our knowledge (see John 5:39), and gain experience by doing His will. As we offer our sacrifice of a broken heart and contrite spirit to God, the windows of Heaven are opened to us and the blessings of our Heavenly Father can come upon us. [Pinegar]

LIKENING THE SCRIPTURES TO OUR LIVES

D&C 128:15 And now, my dearly beloved brethren and sisters, let me assure you that these are principles in relation to the dead and the living that cannot be lightly passed over, as pertaining to our salvation. For their salvation is necessary and essential to our salvation, as Paul says concerning the fathers—that they without us cannot be made perfect—neither can we without our dead be made perfect.

Application: As saviors on Mount Zion (see Obad. 1:21) we are to seek out our dead and do the vicarious work on their behalf in the temples of God, that we, with them, might be made perfect.

Luke 9:28 And it came to pass about an eight days after these sayings, he took Peter and John and James, and went up into a mountain to pray.

Application: The pattern of prayer is exemplified by our Savior—in calling the Twelve, in preparation for the transfiguration on the mount, and in the prelude to His suffering and sacrifice. Let us, too, call upon our Father at all times and in all things for strength and direction to do His will.

SUMMARY

From the scriptural account in the New Testament we can be strengthened in our conviction that the Savior is the source of healing and nurturing—unto our personal salvation and exaltation—if we will but exercise faith, repent, receive the ordinances of the gospel, and endure to the end. Through the Holy Spirit we can, just as Peter, receive revelation concerning the truth of these matters. We can have the assurance that the priesthood keys of the kingdom of God have been restored in these latter days and that all the rights, privileges, powers, and authorities pertaining to the operation of the kingdom of God are at work in our time to bring about the designs of heaven in this, the last dispensation. We can know that prophets of God lead His work today for our happiness and security, because "Where there is no vision, the people perish: but he that keepeth the law, happy is he" (Prov. 29:18). And we can know of the grand blessings that await the faithful: "But as it is written, Eye hath not seen, nor ear heard, neither have entered into the heart of man, the things which God hath prepared for them that love him. But God hath revealed them unto us by his Spirit: for the Spirit searcheth all things, yea, the deep things of God" (1 Cor. 2:9–10). Our commission, therefore, is to take up our cross and follow Him (Matt. 16:24) in all diligence and love.

CHAPTER 14

"WHO IS MY NEIGHBOUR?"

Reading Assignment: Matthew 18; Luke 10.

Additional Reading: Leviticus 19:18; Matthew 22:35–40; John 13:34–35; Mark 9:33–50; Mosiah 2:17–21; 4:16–19, 26; D&C 38:24–25.

Jesus was once asked a provocative question by a lawyer: "Who is my neighbour?" (Luke 10:29). Indeed, that is a question we all should ask—"Who is my neighbor?"

The Savior provided a penetrating, unexpected answer to the lawyer. He taught him with a parable—the parable of the Good Samaritan. . . .

A more perfect parable could not have been conceived to teach the eternal truth that God is the Father of us all and therefore we are brothers one to another.

My neighbor—my brother! Such is the teaching of our Lord and Savior. We are to esteem every man as our brother, our neighbor as ourselves (see D&C 38:24).

This truth is the fundamental basis for our inspired missionary effort throughout the world—to share the glorious truths of the restored gospel with our neighbors, who are our brothers and sisters.

—David B. Haight, "My Neighbor—My Brother!" *Ensign*, May 1987, 59.

THEMES *for* LIVING

1. Be Converted and Become as a Little Child
2. Forgiveness—The Divine Attribute
3. Charity—The Parable of the Good Samaritan

INTRODUCTION

Only when we humble ourselves and become truly converted will we seek to take upon us the divine nature of Christ (2 Pet. 1:4–8), become as a little child (innocent before the Lord through repentance), and begin the process of possessing charity. Charity "never faileth" (Moro. 7:46) because Christ never fails. When we have this love—this charity—we will love our fellowmen. This is the love that Christ spoke of to Peter as He trained him on how to feed His sheep (see John 21:15–17). Love as a function of reciprocal devotion, though good, was not enough. It had to be godlike love—perfect and unconditional. With such love, we will love everyone and truly be the Lord's disciples (see John 13:34–35).

1. BE CONVERTED AND BECOME AS A LITTLE CHILD

THEME: True conversion requires a saintliness that embodies the humble qualities of a little child.

MOMENT OF TRUTH

The disciples came to Jesus one day and wanted to know "Who is the greatest in the kingdom of heaven?" The Savior used the teaching moment to demonstrate the path to follow: "And Jesus called a little child unto him, and set him in the midst of them, And said, Verily I say unto you, Except ye be converted, and become as little children, ye shall not enter into the kingdom of heaven. Whosoever therefore shall humble himself as this little child, the same is greatest in the kingdom of heaven. And whoso shall receive one such little child in my name receiveth me" (Matt. 18:2–5; compare Mark 9:33–37). A close examination of this doctrine shows that the childlike innocence to which we should aspire includes conversion to gospel principles, humility, and charity toward others (since all are children before God). King Benjamin explained the process of spiritual transformation in these terms:

> For the natural man is an enemy to God, and has been from the fall of Adam, and will be, forever and ever, unless he yields to the enticings of the Holy Spirit, and putteth off the natural man and becometh a saint through the Atonement of Christ the Lord, and becometh as a child, submissive, meek, humble, patient, full of love, willing to submit to all things which the Lord seeth fit to inflict upon him, even as a child doth submit to his father. (Mosiah 3:19)

MODERN PROPHETS SPEAK

Neal A. Maxwell:

> In order to enter the kingdom of heaven we must be childlike. This term describes a particular manner of men and women (see Matt. 18:3; 2 Pet. 1:4–7; 3:11). But what do those requirements mean? King Benjamin spells out the angel's message in his marvelous sermon, describing how, through Jesus' Atonement, one can "[become] a saint . . . as a child, submissive, meek, humble, patient, full of love, willing to submit to all things which the Lord seeth fit to inflict upon him, even as a child doth submit to his father" (Mosiah 3:19).
>
> Striving to incorporate these cardinal qualities makes us more saintly and helps us immeasurably to endure it well. Significantly, submissiveness, that reverent expression of enduring, is mentioned twice. Giving enduring extra emphasis is capped by directing that we "submit to" and endure "all things which the Lord seeth fit to inflict upon [us], even as a child doth submit to his father" (Mosiah 3:19). Much of enduring well requires this reverent submissiveness. The living Church greatly facilitates living discipleship in which opportunities and reminders of the needed virtues are all about us.
>
> Developing these saintly qualities is every bit as essential as receiving the ordinances of the gospel. Even the gifts of God are not of full use if one has not, for instance, developed the quality of charity. (*If Thou Endure It Well*, 33)

ILLUSTRATIONS FOR OUR TIME

A State of Innocence

The key to becoming as a little child is to return to a state of innocence. This is a state of being free from guilt—the same state that Enos was in after he prayed for forgiveness and his guilt was swept away because of his exceeding faith in Jesus Christ (Enos 1:8). The Lord has revealed that "Every spirit of man was innocent in the beginning; and God having redeemed man from the fall, men became again, in their infant state, innocent before God."(D&C 93:38).

Being free from guilt becomes our quest as we confess and forsake our sins. We want to share the joy of being free from sin as was Alma, when he said, "Yea, and from that time even until now, I have labored without ceasing, that I might bring souls unto repentance; that I might bring them to taste of the exceeding joy of which I did taste; that they might also be born of God, and be filled with the Holy Ghost" (Alma 36:24).

As I look upon little children, I see the innocence, goodness, and radiating holiness that they possess. My heart sometimes cries out that they might be protected from all the wickedness that is about them. Then my heart melts with gratitude for our beloved Savior, who invites us all to come unto Him so that He may heal us. He will be our advocate as we repent, and He will take us home to our Heavenly Father. [Pinegar]

LIKENING THE SCRIPTURES TO OUR LIVES

Matt 18:3–4 Verily I say unto you, Except ye be converted, and become as little children, ye shall not enter into the kingdom of heaven. Whosoever therefore shall humble himself as this little child, the same is greatest in the kingdom of heaven.

Application: Humility is the beginning of goodness and righteousness. Conversion begins with humility, which opens the gateway to acquiring the saintly qualities of Christ.

2. FORGIVENESS—THE DIVINE ATTRIBUTE

THEME: Forgiving others is the key to be forgiven of our Father in Heaven.

MOMENT OF TRUTH

Peter came one day to the Lord and asked Him a question of great significance: "Lord, how oft shall my brother sin against me, and I forgive him? till seven times? Jesus saith unto him, I say not unto thee, Until seven times: but, Until seventy times seven" (Matt. 18:21–22). Forgiveness is an enduring commandment—we are to forgive as often as people will repent. In modern times, the Lord said: "I, the Lord, will forgive whom I will forgive, but of you it is required to forgive all men" (D&C 64:10). To confirm this truth, the Savior presented to Peter a parable of central relevance to the plan of salvation: the parable of the unmerciful servant. The servant owed a very large sum to the king. Unable to pay his debt, the servant found that he and his family members were to be sold in order to raise the revenue for the compensation. But the man begged for mercy, and the king, having compassion, forgave him the debt. In turn, the man came against a debtor of his own who owed him but a small amount, and when the debtor could not pay, the man caused him to be thrown into prison until he could pay the debt. Hearing of this, the king summoned the first man and proclaimed: "O thou wicked servant, I forgave thee all that debt, because thou desiredst me: Shouldest not thou also have had compassion on thy fellowservant, even as I had pity on thee? And his lord was wroth, and delivered him to the tormentors, till he should pay all that was due unto him" (Matt. 18:32–34). The Savior then concluded the parable with the interpretation: "So likewise shall my heavenly Father do also unto you, if ye from your hearts forgive not every one his brother their trespasses" (Matt. 18:35).

MODERN PROPHETS SPEAK

Gordon B. Hinckley:

> Now, as we draw the curtain on 150 years of our history, it becomes us as a grateful people to reach out with a spirit of forgiveness and an attitude of love and compassion toward those we have felt may have wronged us.
>
> We have need of this. The whole world has need of it. It is of the very essence of the gospel of Jesus Christ. He taught it. He exemplified it as none other has exemplified it. In the time of his agony on the cross of Calvary, with vile and hateful accusers before him, they who had brought him to this terrible crucifixion, he cried out, "Father, forgive them; for they know not what they do" (Luke 23:34).
>
> None of us is called on to forgive so generously, but each of us is under a divinely spoken obligation to reach out with pardon and mercy. The Lord has declared in words of revelation: "My disciples, in days of old, sought occasion against one another and forgave not one another in their hearts; and for this evil they were afflicted and sorely chastened.
>
> "Wherefore, I say unto you, that ye ought to forgive one another; for he that forgiveth not his brother his trespasses standeth condemned before the Lord; for there remaineth in him the greater sin.
>
> "I, the Lord, will forgive whom I will forgive, but of you it is required to forgive all men.
>
> "And ye ought to say in your hearts—let God judge between me and thee, and reward thee according to thy deeds" (D&C 64:8–11). (*Be Thou an Example* [Salt Lake City: Deseret Book, 1981], 47–48)

ILLUSTRATIONS FOR OUR TIME

John K. Carmack explains beautifully the principle and power of forgiveness. He said:

> The doctrine of forgiveness is pervasive in the New Testament. It is a foundational doctrine of Christ (see Matt. 6:12, 14–15; 18:15, 21–22). We also find it forcefully and clearly expressed in modern revelation. The essence of the teaching in the Doctrine and Covenants is that only the Lord has enough knowledge and authority to judge who is eligible for divine forgiveness. His judgment will be just because he will know all the facts and laws that govern. We, however, having imperfect knowledge, must forgive all others. The Lord explains that the failure to forgive leaves the

greater sin with the embittered one who refuses to forgive. (See D&C 64:7–10) The Lord also suggests a proper attitude of mind. When we are victimized, we should say in our hearts, "Let God judge between me and thee, and reward thee according to thy deeds" (D&C 64:11). . . .

Elder David O. McKay quoted this practical advice given by a discerning writer: "In the very depths of your soul dig a grave; let it be as some forgotten spot to which no path leads; and there, in the eternal silence bury the wrongs which you have suffered. Your heart will feel as if a load had fallen from it and a divine peace come to abide with you." . . .

Tolerant humans are slow to anger and quick to forgive. Whether or not their antagonist forgives them in turn, they freely forgive, leaving judgment to God. They know that not all problems can be solved and are willing to walk away from situations without bitterness or recrimination. This does not mean that they lack intelligence, judgment, or backbone, or that they handle their affairs loosely and without regard to their families' well-being, but rather that their action results from a Christlike character trait." (*Tolerance: Principles, Practices, Obstacles, Limits,* 48–50)

Forgiving Is Key to Enduring

What does it mean to endure to the end? Hartman Rector Jr., had this counsel:

> Then after baptism by the water and the Spirit, it appears that all the Father requires of us is that we endure to the end. What does that mean? I believe it means basically three things.
>
> One: We must continue to repent for the rest of our lives because we will still make mistakes, and we must go home clean or we can't dwell with the Father and the Son (see D&C 84:74).
>
> Two: We must continue to forgive others. If we do not forgive others, we cannot obtain forgiveness ourselves (see D&C 64:9–10). And three: Yes, we must be nice. If we're not nice, I don't think we're going to make it. In other words, we must have charity, which is really love plus sacrifice. ("Endure to the End in Charity," *Ensign,* Nov. 1994, 26)

Recently my wife and I attended a funeral of a friend and relative where one of the speakers referred to this talk. He had heard Elder Rector explain that enduring to the end means continually repenting, forgiving, and rendering charity. Within this framework, the funeral speaker was extolling the character of his 81-year-old father-in-law, who had just passed away after a 35-year-long battle against cancer. This gracious and exemplary family man had ever been patient and willing to endure to the end in faith. He had always been stalwart in keeping his covenants, forgiving others, and being charitable to everyone.

As an illustration of the importance of forgiveness, the funeral eulogist told a personal story about one of his own uncles, who had been involved in a family business that failed because of the misguided performance of another relative, a younger man of questionable character. As a result, the uncle found it difficult to be forgiving—even right up to the moment where a health emergency rendered him comatose. The attending physician announced the sad news that the uncle would not recover. His family, heartbroken, prepared to bid him farewell. But miraculously, after a few days, the uncle regained consciousness and requested that all family members be summoned to his bedside, including the young man who had given offense. When all were assembled, the uncle announced, "I have been on the other side. And I had to come back to forgive [the young man]." Then, addressing the young man, the uncle said, "I forgive you. Will you forgive me for holding a grudge against you?" To this, the young man readily assented, and then the uncle went to his reward. [Allen]

LIKENING THE SCRIPTURES TO OUR LIVES

Matt 18:21–22 Then came Peter to him, and said, Lord, how oft shall my brother sin against me, and I forgive him? till seven times? Jesus saith unto him, I say not unto thee, Until seven times: but, Until seventy times seven.

Application: Our direction from the Lord is to forgive everyone (D&C 64:10). Remember that we are forgiven as we forgive. After all is said and done, it is essential that we repent and forgive, that we might gain eternal life.

3. CHARITY—THE PARABLE OF THE GOOD SAMARITAN

THEME: Everyone is our neighbor. We should treat everyone with compassion and charity.

MOMENT OF TRUTH

On one occasion, a lawyer, thinking to tempt the Savior, asked Him the question, "What shall I do to inherit eternal life?" (Luke 10:25). Discerning the devious thoughts and motives of the lawyer, the Savior asked him: "What is written in the law? how readest thou? And he answering said, Thou shalt love the Lord thy God with all thy heart, and with all thy soul, and with all thy strength, and with all thy mind; and thy neighbour as thyself. And he said unto him, Thou hast answered right: this do, and thou shalt live" (Luke 10:26–28).

But the lawyer was not satisfied with truth and divine counsel. So he posed a second question: "And who is my neighbour?" (Luke 10:29). To this, the Savior responded by reciting one of His most celebrated parables, that of the Good Samaritan. A man had been robbed, beaten, and left for dead along the road from Jerusalem to Jericho. In turn, he was ignored by a priest traveling along the same road and then by a Levite. But a Samaritan came to his rescue in compassion and charity.

When He had finished the parable, the Savior asked the lawyer, "Which now of these three, thinkest thou, was neighbour unto him that fell among the thieves? And he said, He that shewed mercy on him. Then said Jesus unto him, Go, and do thou likewise" (Luke 10:36–37). To this, the lawyer had no response.

MODERN PROPHETS SPEAK

Howard W. Hunter:

> An old axiom states that a man "all wrapped up in himself makes a small bundle." Love has a certain way of making a small bundle large. The key is to love our neighbor, including the neighbor that is difficult to love. We need to remember that though we make our friends, God has made our neighbors—everywhere. Love should have no boundary; we should have no narrow loyalties. Christ said, "For if ye love them which love you, what reward have ye? do not even the publicans the same?" (Matt. 5:46). (*THWH,* 95)

> To love one's neighbor is noble and inspiring, whether the neighbor is one who lives close by, or in a broader sense, a fellow being of the human race. It stimulates the desire to promote happiness, comfort, interest, and the welfare of others. It creates understanding. The ills of the world would be cured by understanding. Wars would cease and crime disappear. The scientific knowledge now being wasted in the world because of the distrust of men and nations could be diverted to bless mankind. (*THWH,* 95)

ILLUSTRATIONS FOR OUR TIME

"I'm a People Too"

All people deserve respect and consideration in regard to their individuality and particular needs. Since everyone is so different, all must be treated appropriately and in special ways, according to each situation.

The story is told of two men sitting at a table following dinner. One of the men had his boy with him, about four years old. The two men were conversing back and forth. Every once in a while, the little boy would try to say something to his father, but his father would respond with words such as this: "Can't you see we adults are talking?" "Don't interrupt when others are talking." " Wait just a minute." " Be quiet."

This went on for several minutes, until finally the little toddler got off his chair and came over and pulled on his daddy's shirt and said, " I'm a people too." The father sat stunned. He had ignored his beloved little child.

Situations may vary, and it is not the purpose of this story to be judgmental of that father, but rather to draw attention to the need for showing compassion and concern. Would not any adult understand something like, "Excuse me, Bill, my little boy has got something important to say to his dad." This would show respect and, above all, let the child know that you love him, that he matters to you, and that the things he has to say are important to you. Children are precious—and they, too, are our neighbors. Let us treat them in a way that we as adults would like to be treated, and surely they will grow up treating others in a loving and Christlike manner. [Pinegar]

LIKENING THE SCRIPTURES TO OUR LIVES

Matt 25:40 And the King shall answer and say unto them, Verily I say unto you, Inasmuch as ye have done it unto one of the least of these my brethren, ye have done it unto me.

Application: Remember, however we choose to treat others, it is as though we have treated the Savior that very way. This should be a reality check on our actions and reactions to every living soul with whom we come in contact.

SUMMARY

The Savior counseled that we should become converted and manifest the qualities of humility and innocence as exhibited by little children. He called upon us to adopt the divine attributes of forgiveness and charity as a pattern for our lives. What better summation of this doctrine is there than the answer the Savior gave to the lawyer who wanted to know "Which is the great commandment in the law?" (Matt. 22: 36). The Savior responded: "Thou shalt love the Lord thy God with all thy heart, and with all thy soul, and with all thy mind. This is the first and great commandment. And the second is like unto it, Thou shalt love thy neighbour as thyself" (Matt. 22:37–39). Amplifying this latter commandment, He also said: "A new commandment I give unto you, That ye love one another; as I have loved you, that ye also love one another. By this shall all men know that ye are my disciples, if ye have love one to another" (John 13:34–35; compare Mosiah 2:17; D&C 38:24–25).

CHAPTER 15

"I AM THE LIGHT *of the* WORLD"

Reading Assignment: John 7–8.

Additional Reading: Psalm 27:1; Isaiah 2:5; Alma 38:9; 3 Nephi 15:9; 18:24; D&C 88:6–13.

> *How vastly different, therefore, is fully witnessing to the world that Jesus Christ is "the light, and the life, and the truth of the world."*
>
> *When we think of Jesus Christ as the Light of the World, not only does His light illuminate the only pathway of life, but His light, in the dusk of civilization's decadence, also reminds us what true light really is. . . .*
>
> *His church and its faithful people strive to follow the counsel of the resurrected Savior, who said, "Therefore, hold up your light that it may shine unto the world. Behold I am the light which ye shall hold up—that which ye have seen me do."*
>
> *Since some of Jesus' noblest deeds predate His unique Palestinian ministry, we ought to "hold up" that which He did before His mortal ministry—as well as that which He will yet do.*
>
> —Neal A. Maxwell, *Even as I Am* [Salt Lake City, Deseret Book, 1982], 113–14.

THEMES *for* LIVING

1. Faithful Obedience Builds Testimony
2. Overcoming Grievous Sin
3. Jesus Is the Light of the World

INTRODUCTION

The teachings of Christ are the doctrines of our Heavenly Father. Our Father sent our Elder Brother Jesus Christ to do His will. Our Savior was not only to atone for our sins, but also to show us the way back to our Heavenly Father's presence. The doctrine of Christ with all of its associated truths encompasses all the principles, covenants, and ordinances pertaining to eternal life.

1. FAITHFUL OBEDIENCE BUILDS TESTIMONY

THEME: We can know that the doctrines taught by our Savior are true if we live them.

MOMENT OF TRUTH

The time for the Feast of Tabernacles had arrived, and some of Jesus' colleagues encouraged Him to go to Jerusalem to participate and show forth His works. But Jesus declined, saying that His time had not yet come (John 7:6). Nevertheless, He went up somewhat later, discreetly rather than openly. The joyful Feast of Tabernacles—which memorialized the sojourn of the children of Israel in the wilderness and the harvesting of the crops for the year—was celebrated on the 15th to 21st days of the seventh month, with an added eighth day as a holy convocation. In the midst of the celebration, Jesus went to the temple and began to teach. As they had done so often before, the listeners marveled at His discourse. "How knoweth this man letters, having never learned?" (John 7:15). The Savior deflected any credit away from Himself by replying with a statement that has come to be recognized as a governing principle of testimony building: "My doctrine is not mine, but his that sent me. If any man will do his will, he shall know of the doctrine, whether it be of God, or whether I speak of myself. He that speaketh of himself seeketh his own glory: but he that seeketh his glory that sent him, the same is true, and no unrighteousness is in him" (John 7:16–18). The Savior was teaching eternal principles while at the same time calling His listeners to repentance, for they purported to believe the law of Moses but did not keep it. How could they know of divine things without living the divine patterns of conduct that had been given them by a prophet of God? Then, referring to their indictment of His healing on the Sabbath, He adjured the Jewish leaders to judge righteously, not by the appearance of things.

Many were impressed with His bold delivery and said: "Do the rulers know indeed that this is the very Christ?" (John 7:26). Yet they still vacillated, since they knew of this man's local origins and whence He came, whereas they expected the authentic Christ to come of mysterious origins: "but when Christ cometh, no man knoweth whence he is" (John 7:27). Their blindness invoked in the Master a declaration that indeed they both knew Him and knew whence He came, for He came from the Father, "whom ye know not" (John 7:28). At this the leaders were sorely offended, and they took steps to seize Him. His response was sharp and incisive: "Ye shall seek me, and shall not find me: and where I am, thither ye cannot come" (John 7:34). Not understanding that He spoke of ultimate consequences, they continued to debate the meaning of His words until, on the eighth and final day of the Feast of Tabernacles, the Savior provided the key: "If any man thirst, let him come unto me, and drink" (John 7:37). In this, He had reference to the coming blessings of the Holy Ghost, which would be poured out as a confirming witness upon those who believe (v. 38). But the people were divided as to their opinions about the Savior, some doubting, others persuaded that He was a prophet or the promised Christ. Even the officers charged with the task of arresting Jesus were perplexed and in awe: "Never man spake like this man" (John 7:46). Nevertheless, despite the cautioning of Nicodemus among his peers to reserve judgment until a fair hearing could take place, the Jewish leaders were incurably possessed in their hearts of the spirit of retribution and vengeance against this man who claimed to be the Christ.

MODERN PROPHETS SPEAK

Bruce R. McConkie:

> Any accountable person can gain a testimony of the gospel by obedience to that law upon which the receipt of such knowledge is predicated. This is the formula: 1. He must *desire* to know the truth of the gospel, of the Book of Mormon, of the Church, or of whatever is involved. 2. He must *study* and learn the basic facts relative to the matter involved. "Search the scriptures" (John 5:39). "Search these commandments" (D&C 1:37). 3. He must *practice* the principles and truths learned, conforming his life to them. "My doctrine is not mine, but his that sent me. If any man will do his will, he shall know of the doctrine, whether it be of God, or whether I speak of myself" (John 7:16–17). 4. He must *pray* to the Father in the name of Christ, *in faith,* and the truth will then be made manifest by revelation "by the power of the Holy Ghost. And by the power of the Holy Ghost ye may know the truth of all things" (Moro. 10:3–5; 1 Cor. 2). (*MD,* 786–87)

ILLUSTRATIONS FOR OUR TIME

When You Live the Doctrine, You Will Know

For the inquiring mind—one who seeks eternal verities—the Lord's challenge to do the will of the Father is a fair test. One can know of the truthfulness of His doctrine.

Too many people simply love sin and the pleasures of the world. Some are afraid to try, simply because it is hard and requires them to get out of their comfort zone. Such is life. The greatest feeling of joy comes from the blessings of the Holy Spirit (see D&C 11:13; Gal. 5:22). The joy experienced as one applies the Atonement through faith unto repentance has been described by many (see Alma 36:24; D&C 18:10–16). This is doing the will of the Father, living the doctrine, and coming to know that that doctrine is true. This happens when one reads the Book of Mormon and comes to know that it is true. This happens in every convert's life as he or she experiences the mighty change. This happens when you do good and you feel the witness of the Spirit.

I recall a story told to me of a father who had organized a family home evening with his family to clean up the yard of an elderly widow in their neighborhood. She was sweet and kind but unable to rake her leaves and do the tasks required to keep her yard clean. The family arrived with several children, and all joined in to do the work. The work was easy for them, and it wasn't long before the task was completed. The sweet widow invited them in for cookies and punch. The little children were excited, and her gesture made them feel appreciated for what they had done. The widow expressed her gratitude to each child and thanked them sincerely, and then they departed for home. When they got home, the wise father asked the children how they felt. The little eight-year-old girl responded, "Daddy, that was wonderful. She was so grateful it made me want to do more. I felt so good inside because we really helped her. She couldn't have done it by herself."

Then the father said, "Isn't it wonderful to help others. It is like helping our Savior, and that is why you feel that joy inside your heart."

All the children smiled; the lesson was learned. When you do good the Spirit will cause you to *feel* good. When you live the doctrine of the Lord you will know the truthfulness of it. [Pinegar]

You Know the Gospel Is True When You . . .

In His discourse at the temple during the Feast of Tabernacles (John 7), the Savior disclosed to the sinister and plotting leaders among the clergy an infallible key for establishing the truth of the doctrine of salvation that He was preaching: "If any man will do his will, he shall know of the doctrine, whether it be of God, or whether I speak of myself" (John 7:17). Long before the Savior's mortal ministry, King Benjamin had invoked the same counsel of action: "And again, believe that ye must repent of your sins and forsake them, and humble yourselves before God; and ask in sincerity of heart that he would forgive you; and now if you believe all these things see that ye do them" (Mosiah 4:10). Alma, too, had encouraged the people to subscribe to an active experiment with the word of truth so that it could spring up in them as a living tree, in the measure of the fullness of knowledge, and bear precious fruit (Alma 32).

Prophets down through the ages of time have made it clear that the gospel of Jesus Christ is an action plan with a built-in dimension of verification, substantiation, and authentication. Doctrine plus sincere application yields certainty; concept plus devoted action yields revealed testimony; do it and you will know that it is true. [Allen]

LIKENING THE SCRIPTURES TO OUR LIVES

John 7:24 Judge not according to the appearance, but judge righteous judgment.

Application: Let us remember that we are forgiven as we forgive. We receive mercy as we are merciful. "Judge not, that ye be not judged" (Matt. 7:1). Or as the Joseph Smith Translation reads: "Judge not unrighteously, that ye be not judged: but judge righteous judgment" (JST, Matt. 7:1). Let us remember, too, that the Lord looks upon the heart in rendering judgment.

2. OVERCOMING GRIEVOUS SIN

THEME: The depth of godly sorrow increases in the process of repentance in alignment with the nature of the sin. The greater the sin, the more intense will be our godly sorrow. The Lord is forgiving if we but confess and forsake.

MOMENT OF TRUTH

Early one morning, the Savior came to the temple to teach. The scribes and Pharisees, who were plotting against Him, brought to Him a woman taken in adultery, and, referring to the provision in the law of Moses requiring capital punishment for such an offense (Lev. 20:10), asked the Lord how He would handle the matter. The Savior responded by stooping down to write something on the ground, and then spoke the riveting words: "He that is without sin among you, let him first cast a stone at her" (John 8:7). As He stooped down again to write something on the ground, the accusers departed one by one until the Savior and the woman were left alone. "When Jesus had lifted up himself, and saw none but the woman, he said unto her, Woman, where are those thine accusers? hath no man condemned thee? She said, No man, Lord. And Jesus said unto her, Neither do I condemn thee: go, and sin no more" (John 8:10–11).

MODERN PROPHETS SPEAK

Bruce R. McConkie:

> In ancient Israel, death by stoning was the penalty imposed upon betrothed or
> married persons found guilty of sex immorality. The official witnesses, two or more,

upon whose testimony the conviction rested, were obligated to cast the first stone (Ex. 20:14; Lev. 20:10; Deut. 13:9–10; 17:2–7; 22:13–21; Ezek. 16:35–43).

By the time of Jesus, however, it was no longer the practice to impose the death penalty for adultery. Indeed, no penalty of death could be imposed without the sanction and approval of the Roman overlords, and in case of adultery the law of Rome did not prescribe death.

In bringing this adulteress to Jesus, the scribes and Pharisees were laying this trap for the Master: (1) If he *agreed* with Moses that she should be stoned, he would both (a) arouse the ire of the people generally by seeming to advocate the reinstitution of a penalty which did not have popular support, and (b) run counter to the prevailing civil law by prescribing what Rome proscribed. (2) If he *disagreed* with Moses and advocated anything less than death by stoning, he would be accused of perverting the law, and of advocating disrespect of and departure from the hallowed practices of the past.

John 8:7 He that is without sin No man is without sin in the sense of having completely avoided the commission of evil acts (1 Jn. 1:5–10). All men are sinners to some degree. Yet these very sinners, who themselves stood as the witnesses against convicted adulterers in ancient Israel, were obligated to cast the first stone when the death penalty was imposed by the judges. Jesus, therefore, could not have meant that penalties are to be imposed only by persons who are themselves wholly free from sin. Rather, he was here dealing with men who themselves were guilty, either actually or in their sin-laden hearts, of the *same* offense charged against the woman; that is, they were in effect adulterers worthy of death according to the terms of the very law they now sought to invoke against the woman (Matt. 5:28).

Neither do I condemn thee This is not in any sense a pardon, nor is our Lord condoning an adulterous act. He does not say, 'Go in peace, thy sins are forgiven thee.' He merely declines to act as a magistrate, judge, witness, or participant of any kind in a case that legally and properly should come before an official tribunal of which he is not a member.

Go, and sin no more Could this woman gain forgiveness of so gross a crime as adultery? Certainly. Through faith, repentance, baptism, and continued obedience, it was within her power to become clean and spotless before the Lord and a worthy candidate for his celestial presence. Repentant persons have power to cleanse themselves even from so evil a thing as sex immorality (1 Cor. 6:9–11; 3 Ne. 30). That such seemingly was the course taken by this woman is inferred from the Inspired Version statement that she believed in Christ and glorified God from that very hour. (*DNTC*, 1:450–51)

ILLUSTRATIONS FOR OUR TIME

The Light of the Gospel

Here was a delightful young couple preparing for marriage—bright, faithful in Church participation, eager to do the right thing. But now there was a problem—a compromising of values and propriety. They were embarrassed and heartbroken as they sat across from me, wondering what to do. We counseled. We sorrowed together. We pondered the consequences. But we also took comfort together in the process of repentance empowered by the Atonement. Yes, there needed to be change. There needed to be prayerful godly sorrow and faithful commitment to a better lifestyle (2 Cor. 7:10). But they had caught themselves at the edge of the precipice, and they had recoiled under the strength of conscience and now wanted to do right before the Lord. They were good young people with the desire for righteousness. The Lord loved them and wanted them to have the fulness of His blessings. There needed to be some regular appointments for a few weeks to give momentum to the new commitments. But things went very well, so we came up with a plan—a code just between the bishop and these two. When we crossed paths each week thereafter at the meetings, it took only a nod of the head and a twinkle in the eye as an indication that all was well. You can't disguise the light of the gospel in the eye. It is a sure sign that the Spirit is at work. And it was at work for them. They prospered. They rebounded. They rose to new heights, and once more, the age-old story of the gospel transforming lives was repeated in a real-life setting. Thank heaven for the principles of the gospel. Thank heaven for the Atonement of Jesus Christ. "And how great is his joy in the soul that repenteth!" (D&C 18:13). [Allen]

The Lord Gives Us Hope

The Lord has promised forgiveness if we but repent, save in the case of the sin against the Holy Ghost. The Lord said, "I, the Lord, forgive sins unto those who confess their sins before me and ask forgiveness, who have not sinned unto death" (D&C 64:7). Satan would destroy our hope in Christ. Christ is our only hope—we must never forget this great truth. When hopelessness is our feeling or attitude, sin stands at the door knocking. Apathy becomes the devil's tool, which is fed by hopelessness. We, as the children of God, must never forget our divine heritage. Knowing who we are can help us in the time of deep sorrow for grievous sins and will drive hopelessness and despair from our souls.

I will never forget the look in the eye of a person who had committed a grievous sexual sin when that person came to realize that there was hope and that through our Savior Jesus Christ, forgiveness was possible. The Lord gave this hope when He said, "Behold, he who has repented of his sins, the same is forgiven, and I, the Lord, remember them no more. By this ye may know if a man repenteth of his sins—behold, he will confess them and forsake them" (D&C 58:42–43). [Pinegar]

LIKENING THE SCRIPTURES TO OUR LIVES

JST, John 8:11 She said, No man, Lord. And Jesus said unto her, Neither do I condemn thee; go, and sin no more. And the woman glorified God from that hour, and believed on his name.

Application: The Lord did not condemn her and neither can we. It is given that all can repent if they come unto the Lord through repentance. Let us pray that all might repent.

3. JESUS IS THE LIGHT OF THE WORLD

THEME: All who seek the illumination of divine guidance can know through the Spirit that Jesus is the light and life of the World and that His atoning sacrifice opens up the way for all to return to God.

MOMENT OF TRUTH

Continuing His discourse in the temple, the Savior declared: "I am the light of the world: he that followeth me shall not walk in darkness, but shall have the light of life" (John 8:12). The Pharisees responded by saying that the Savior's witness of Himself was untrue, but He challenged them, saying: "It is also written in your law, that the testimony of two men is true. I am one that bear witness of myself, and the Father that sent me beareth witness of me" (John 8:17–18). To this, they could venture only the weak response, "Where is thy Father?" (John 8:19). The Savior then spoke words that must have penetrated them to the heart: "Ye neither know me, nor my Father: if ye had known me, ye should have known my Father also" (John 8:19). As He concluded His words, the Savior confirmed with power and authority that He was indeed the Christ, as He had declared from the beginning (John 8:25). Some believed in His witness, and to these He had the following uplifting counsel and promise, which has echoed forcefully down through the ages, "If ye continue in my word, then are ye my disciples indeed; And ye shall know the truth, and the truth shall make you free" (John 8:32).

MODERN PROPHETS SPEAK

Jeffrey R. Holland:

> Of all the messages that could come from the scroll of eternity, what was the declaration he brought? The Nephite faithful listened as he spoke: "I am the light and the life of the world; and I have drunk out of that bitter cup which the Father hath given me, and have glorified the Father in taking upon me the sins of the world, in the

which I have suffered the will of the Father in all things from the beginning." [3 Ne. 11:11.] Fifty-six words. The essence of his earthly mission. Obedience and loyalty to the will of the Father, however bitter the cup or painful the price. That is a lesson he would teach these Nephites again and again during the three days he would be with them. By obedience and sacrifice, by humility and purity, by unflagging determination to glorify the Father, Christ was himself glorified. In complete devotion to the Father's will, Christ had become the light and the life of the world. "And . . . when Jesus had spoken these words the whole multitude fell to the earth." (*Christ and the New Covenant: The Messianic Message of the Book of Mormon* [Salt Lake City: Deseret Book, 1997], 251)

ILLUSTRATIONS FOR OUR TIME

Disciples and Ambassadors of Christ

As missionaries and missionary leaders, we talk of Christ, we preach of Christ, we testify of Christ. All of us who are serving the Lord in the mission field are disciples, hoping to be pure ambassadors of our Savior, Jesus Christ.

As ambassadors of Christ, we must remember that everything connected with God's plan exists through and by his beloved Son, Jesus Christ. The foundation of the Church is his gospel, and central to the gospel is the Atonement of Christ. When we live the gospel of Jesus Christ, when we believe in the principles and ordinances of faith, repentance, covenant making and the gift of the Holy Ghost, we believe in those things because of Jesus Christ. We are his disciples and ambassadors. The light that we hold (see 3 Ne. 18:24) is the Lord Jesus Christ. . . .

We cannot bear testimony of this Church and this kingdom without knowing Jesus Christ, the Savior of the world. When we know Christ, we can hold up his light; he is the light and the life of the world (see John 8:12). And when we hold up that light, then we truly become his disciples.

In 3 Nephi 15:12, Jesus Christ tells his disciples that "ye are a light unto this people," and he explains that they will bless all of Heavenly Father's children. Earlier, Christ had instructed the Nephites not to put their light under a bushel, but to put it "on a candlestick, and it giveth light to all that are in the house" (3 Ne. 12:15). That same instruction applies to each of us: when we possess the light of Jesus Christ, we must not put it under a bushel. That light must be held up, and then—and only then—will we be true and worthy representatives of our Savior, Jesus Christ.

We must not be manipulative salespeople. We must be disciples of Christ. All the knowledge and skills we learn must be magnified by the power of God, by the attributes of Christ, by the Spirit of the Lord, by the mind and will of the Lord. (Ed J. Pinegar, *Especially for Missionaries,* 4 vols. [American Fork, UT.: Covenant Communications, 1997], 4:1–2)

LIKENING THE SCRIPTURES TO OUR LIVES

John 8:12 Then spake Jesus again unto them, saying, I am the light of the world: he that followeth me shall not walk in darkness, but shall have the light of life.

Application: The following scriptures emphasize that Christ is the Light and Life of the World and our only hope is to come unto Him and partake of His goodness and grace.

> And now, my son, I have told you this that ye may learn wisdom, that ye may learn of me that there is no other way or means whereby man can be saved, only in and through Christ. Behold, he is the life and the light of the world. Behold, he is the word of truth and righteousness. (Alma 38:9)

> He is the light and the life of the world; yea, a light that is endless, that can never be darkened; yea, and also a life which is endless, that there can be no more death. (Mosiah 16:9)

> And behold, I am the light and the life of the world; and I have drunk out of that bitter cup which the Father hath given me, and have glorified the Father in taking upon me the sins of the world, in the which I have suffered the will of the Father in all things from the beginning. (3 Ne. 11:11)

SUMMARY

From the vivid New Testament account of the Savior's ministry, we can imagine Him walking our own streets and blessing the lives of our own families and neighbors. He taught comforting truths: faithful obedience builds testimony; we can overcome sin—even grievous sin—through sincere repentance and the power of the Atonement; and we can depend upon His light to guide us securely through the obscurity of life's highways and byways. With the Psalmist we can sing: "The Lord is my light and my salvation; whom shall I fear? the Lord is the strength of my life; of whom shall I be afraid?" (Ps. 27:1). With Isaiah we can declare: "O house of Jacob, come ye, and let us walk in the light of the Lord" (Isa. 2:5). And we can rejoice in the promise of the Savior: "Behold, I am the law, and the light. Look unto me, and endure to the end, and ye shall live; for unto him that endureth to the end will I give eternal life" (3 Ne. 15:9; compare D&C 88:6–13).

CHAPTER 16

CHRIST *the* GOOD SHEPHERD

Reading Assignment: John 9–10.

Additional Reading: Alma 5:37–42, 60; Psalm 23:1–6; Isaiah 40:11; Ezekiel 34:11–12; Mosiah 26:21; TG, Shepherd.

Our Lord's likening Himself to a shepherd and His followers to sheep has been an inspiration to poets, preachers, artists, and devout souls generally throughout the centuries of our era. While all His discourses are fraught with a significance that increases with repeated readings, some of His utterances are of outstanding interest because of their universal application and personal appeal. The sermon of the Good Shepherd is prominent in this class. Read John 10. . . .

Our literature contains no more striking differentiation of devoted service from money-loving effort than that presented in this brief, terse, yet comprehensive discourse.

—JAMES E. TALMAGE, *THE VITALITY OF MORMONISM* [BOSTON: GORHAM PRESS, 1919], 154–55.

THEMES *for* LIVING

1. Power and Goodness of Jesus
2. Jesus Is the Good Shepherd
3. Our Role as Shepherds for the Lord

INTRODUCTION

The New Testament is filled with descriptions of the Savior's miraculous powers. In all things, He seeks to lift and bless others, whether it be temporally or spiritually. Milton R. Hunter describes the Savior in His role as the Good Shepherd:

> When Christ was upon the earth teaching the gospel in the Holy Land, he called himself the Good Shepherd, just as the ancient prophets of Israel had referred to him in the Old Testament times. Perhaps the outstanding discourse given by the Master on this subject was recorded by John. Jesus pointed out clearly that the shepherd and the sheep will enter into the door, but thieves and robbers attempt to climb into the sheepfold by some other method. He described the tender care given the sheep by the shepherd who owned the flock, saying: "he goeth before them, and the sheep follow him: for they know his voice"; (John 10:4) and a little later in his discourse, Jesus said:
>
> I am the good shepherd: the good shepherd giveth his life for the sheep. But he that is an hireling, and not the shepherd, whose own the sheep are not, seeth the wolf coming, and leaveth the sheep, and fleeth: and the wolf catcheth them, and scattereth the sheep.
>
> The hireling fleeth, because he is an hireling, and careth not for the sheep (John 10:11–13). (*Christ in Ancient America* [Salt Lake City: Deseret Book, 1959], 93–94)

1. POWER AND GOODNESS OF JESUS

THEME: Just as Jesus gave sight to the man born blind, He can also give spiritual sight to all who follow Him in faith, believing that He is the Son of God, the Redeemer.

MOMENT OF TRUTH

As Jesus passed by the way on the Sabbath day, He saw a man who had been blind from birth. The disciples asked the Savior whose fault this was—the man's or the man's parents. "Jesus answered, Neither hath this man sinned, nor his parents: but that the works of God should be made manifest in him" (John 9:3), whereupon He anointed the man's eyes with clay made of spittle and dirt and commanded him to wash in the Pool of Siloam. This the man obediently did and received his sight. The miracle caused much turmoil among the Jewish leaders, who were determined to establish Jesus as a sinner and deceiver. They collected the testimony of the man, then his parents (who withheld information out of fear of retribution by the authorities), then the man again, who told them, with irrefutable logic: "Whether he be a sinner or no, I know not: one thing I know, that, whereas I was blind, now I see. . . . If this man were not of God, he could do nothing" (John 9:25, 33). Nevertheless, the Pharisees cast the man out. Later the Savior came to him and gave witness that He, the Savior, was indeed the Christ. Then the man replied: "Lord, I believe. And he worshipped him" (John 9:38). Against the backdrop of this miracle to restore sight in the midst of those who were blinded to the truth, the Savior declared: "For judgment I am come into this world, that they which see not might see; and that they which see might be made blind" (John 9:39).

MODERN PROPHETS SPEAK

Bruce R. McConkie:

> Both the logic and the testimony here presented by Jesus are perfect. He has just performed, openly and boldly, a miracle which all but the most spiritually darkened viewers must acknowledge could be done only by the power of God (3 Ne. 8:1). Then having shown himself to be the agent of Deity through the use of divine power, he says plainly: "I am the Son of God." Accordingly, his hearers are faced with this problem: Either he is the Son of God, as he says, or he is a blasphemous sinner worthy of death. If he is a blasphemer, how could he work a miracle that requires the approval and power of God?
>
> "I am come into the world to sit in judgment upon all men, to divide them into two camps by their acceptance or rejection of my word. Those who are spiritually blind have their eyes opened through obedience to my gospel and shall see the things of the Spirit. Those who think they can see in the spiritual realm, but who do not accept me and my gospel shall remain in darkness and be made blind to the true spiritual realities." (*DNTC,* 1:481–82)

ILLUSTRATIONS FOR OUR TIME

The Miracle of Sight

As a young boy, I enjoyed astronomy, spending hours outdoors during the evening observing the stars and planets with my modest though effective 100-power telescope. What a thrill it was to admire the rings of Saturn and the moons of Jupiter with this tool that made the invisible miraculously visible to the eye. What an inspiration it was to explore the craters of the moon many decades before the advent of Apollo and the era of firsthand lunar discovery.

From those early years, I cultivated an appreciation of the scriptures about God's majestic creation: "The earth rolls upon her wings, and the sun giveth his light by day, and the moon giveth her light by night, and the stars also give their light, as they roll upon their wings in their glory, in the midst of the power of God. Unto what shall I liken these kingdoms, that ye may understand? Behold, all these are kingdoms, and any man who hath seen any or the least of these hath seen God moving in his majesty and power" (D&C 88:45–47). [Allen]

LIKENING THE SCRIPTURES TO OUR LIVES

John 9:39 And Jesus said, For judgment I am come into this world, that they which see not might see; and that they which see might be made blind.

Application: Let us open our eyes to see the goodness and mercy of God and our Savior, Jesus Christ. Let us open our eyes to all our wonderful blessings. Let us open our eyes to see all the good that we can do.

2. JESUS IS THE GOOD SHEPHERD

THEME: The Lord loves and cares for His children even as a shepherd truly cares for his flock.

MOMENT OF TRUTH

The Savior is a master teacher who understands how to effect the transfer of truth from His bosom, where the scriptures reside (D&C 35:20), to the hearts and minds of believing listeners. Using the metaphor of the Good Shepherd—which echoed the anticipatory sayings of the prophets of old (Ps. 23:1–6; Isa. 40:11; Ezek. 34:11–12) and resonated with His contemporary and future disciples—He illustrated His love for His sheep in words of unsurpassed persuasion and power:

> The thief cometh not, but for to steal, and to kill, and to destroy: I am come that they might have life, and that they might have *it* more abundantly.
> I am the good shepherd: the good shepherd giveth his life for the sheep.
> But he that is an hireling, and not the shepherd, whose own the sheep are not, seeth the wolf coming, and leaveth the sheep, and fleeth: and the wolf catcheth them, and scattereth the sheep.
> The hireling fleeth, because he is an hireling, and careth not for the sheep.
> I am the good shepherd, and know my sheep, and am known of mine.
> As the Father knoweth me, even so know I the Father: and I lay down my life for the sheep. (John 10:10–15)

Even alluding to His "other sheep" in ancient America (John 10:16), the Savior continued to expound His mission and role as Good Shepherd and Redeemer. The Jewish leaders took offense at His doctrine, but He bore solemn witness of His divine Sonship and declared: "My sheep hear my voice, and I know them, and they follow me" (John 10:27). Furthermore, He proclaimed, "I and my Father are one" (John 10:30) and responded to charges of blasphemy—that He had testified that He was the Son of God—by appealing to the ancient scriptural declaration: "I have said, Ye are gods; and all of you are children of the most High" (Ps. 82:6). Why, therefore, should they take offense at Him for saying that He was the Son of God? After all, He was doing the works of His Father—and these works could be the pathway to their belief. But they believed Him not and sought to take His life, so He departed from their midst and resorted to the place where John the Baptist had first baptized. Here, many came to listen to Him and believed on Him, accepting Him as the Good Shepherd of the fold of God.

MODERN PROPHETS SPEAK

Thomas S. Monson:

> When Jesus of Nazareth personally walked the rockstrewn pathways of the Holy Land, He, as the good shepherd, showed all who would believe how they might follow that narrow way and enter that strait gate to life eternal. "Come, follow me," He invited. "I am the way." (*Be Your Best Self* [Salt Lake City: Deseret Book, 1979], 9)

ILLUSTRATIONS FOR OUR TIME

The Good Shepherd

The illustrative power of the word *shepherd* connotes a deep concern for the welfare of the flock both collectively and individually. We learn from Easton's *Illustrated Bible Dictionary* deeper insights as to how the Lord is truly the Good Shepherd:

> This word is used figuratively to represent the relation of rulers to their subjects and of God to his people (Ps. 23:1; 80:1; Isa. 40:11; 44:28; Jer. 25:34, 35; Nahum 3:18; John 10:11, 14; Heb. 13:20; 1 Pet. 2:25; 5:4).
>
> The duties of a shepherd in an unenclosed country like Palestine were very onerous. "In early morning he led forth the flock from the fold, marching at its head to the spot where they were to be pastured. Here he watched them all day, taking care that none of the sheep strayed, and if any for a time eluded his watch and wandered away from the rest, seeking diligently till he found and brought it back. In those lands sheep require to be supplied regularly with water, and the shepherd

for this purpose has to guide them either to some running stream or to wells dug in the wilderness and furnished with troughs. At night he brought the flock home to the fold, counting them as they passed under the rod at the door to assure himself that none were missing. Nor did his labours always end with sunset. Often he had to guard the fold through the dark hours from the attack of wild beasts, or the wily attempts of the prowling thief (see 1 Sam. 17:34)." (*Illustrated Bible Dictionary*, "Shepherd," [Grand Rapids, MI: Baker Book House, 1978])

This metaphor of the Good Shepherd is close to the one the Lord uses often in regard to a hen who gathereth her chicks. He said:

O ye people of these great cities which have fallen, who are descendants of Jacob, yea, who are of the house of Israel, how oft have I gathered you as a hen gathereth her chickens under her wings, and have nourished you.

And again, how oft would I have gathered you as a hen gathereth her chickens under her wings, yea, O ye people of the house of Israel, who have fallen; yea, O ye people of the house of Israel, ye that dwell at Jerusalem, as ye that have fallen; yea, how oft would I have gathered you as a hen gathereth her chickens, and ye would not. O ye house of Israel whom I have spared, how oft will I gather you as a hen gathereth her chickens under her wings, if ye will repent and return unto me with full purpose of heart. (3 Ne. 10:4–6)

If you have witnessed the concern of a hen as she scurries around almost frantically to protect her chicks, you can begin to see what great concern the Lord has for us. [Pinegar]

LIKENING THE SCRIPTURES TO OUR LIVES

Alma 5:38–40 Behold, I say unto you, that the good shepherd doth call you; yea, and in his own name he doth call you, which is the name of Christ; and if ye will not hearken unto the voice of the good shepherd, to the name by which ye are called, behold, ye are not the sheep of the good shepherd. And now if ye are not the sheep of the good shepherd, of what fold are ye? Behold, I say unto you, that the devil is your shepherd, and ye are of his fold; and now, who can deny this? Behold, I say unto you, whosoever denieth this is a liar and a child of the devil. For I say unto you that whatsoever is good cometh from God, and whatsoever is evil cometh from the devil.

Application: Let us take care always to hearken to the voice of the Lord, the Good Shepherd, lest we follow the adversary and become a child of the devil.

3. OUR ROLE AS SHEPHERDS FOR THE LORD

THEME: We as undershepherds of the Lord have the same purpose as the Lord Himself. We should have ultimate concern for all mankind in the spirit of love and service.

MOMENT OF TRUTH

In using the imagery of the shepherd and his flock to teach a lesson about the charity of redemption, the Savior was making a contrast between legitimate and divinely appointed service on the one hand and the self-interest of dangerous interlopers on the other: "Verily, verily, I say unto you, He that entereth not by the door into the sheepfold, but climbeth up some other way, the same is a thief and a robber. But he that entereth in by the door is the shepherd of the sheep. . . . The thief cometh not, but for to steal, and to kill, and to destroy: I am come that they might have life, and that they might have it more abundantly" (John 10:1–2, 10). The Savior's lesson was directed toward the ecclesiastical leaders of His day who were seeking to undermine and destroy His mission. At the same time, the Savior's lesson is applicable to all who follow in His footsteps as undershepherds, seeking to help Him secure the safety and well-being of the flock in the spirit of nurture and charity.

MODERN PROPHETS SPEAK

Russell M. Nelson:

> The Good Shepherd lovingly cares for all sheep of His fold, and we are His true undershepherds. Our privilege is to bear His love and to add our own love to friends and neighbors—feeding, tending, and nurturing them—as the Savior would have us do. By so doing, we evidence one of the godly characteristics of His restored Church upon the earth. (*Perfection Pending, and Other Favorite Discourses* [Salt Lake City: Deseret Book, 1998], 222)

ILLUSTRATIONS FOR OUR TIME

A Plea from a Prophet
Howard W. Hunter has admonished us to be faithful undershepherds. He said:

> Because of what the Master said about leaving the ninety-nine and going into the wilderness to seek the one that is lost, and because of the invitation of the First Presidency to those who have ceased activity or have been critical to "come back,"

we invite you to become involved in saving souls. Reach out to the less active and realize the joy that will come to you and those you help if you and they will take part in extending invitations to come back and feast at the table of the Lord.

The Lord, our Good Shepherd, expects us to be his undershepherds and recover those who are struggling or are lost. We can't tell you how to do it, but as you become involved and seek inspiration, success will result from efforts in your areas, regions, stakes, and wards. Some stakes have responded to previous pleadings and have had remarkable success. (Howard W. Hunter, *That We Might Have Joy* [Salt Lake City: Deseret Book, 1994], 85–86)

ENRICHMENT SECTION

"Feed My Sheep"

Most of us are familiar with the Savior's description of members of the Church and their leaders. True followers He called sheep, and priesthood leaders He called shepherds.

We remember his unforgettable example of a true shepherd's concern for His sheep: "If a man have an hundred sheep, and one of them be gone astray, doth he not leave the ninety and nine, . . . and seeketh that which is gone astray? And if it so be that he find it, . . . he rejoiceth more of that sheep, than of the ninety and nine which went not astray" (Matt. 18:12–13). . . .

The true shepherd was willing to give his life for the sheep. He would go in among the sheep and fight for their welfare. The hireling, on the other hand, valued his own personal safety above the sheep and would usually flee from the danger.

Jesus used this common illustration of His day to declare that He was the Good Shepherd, the True Shepherd. Because of His love for His brothers and sisters, He would willingly and voluntarily lay down His life for them (see John 10:17–18). Eventually the Good Shepherd did give His life for the sheep—for you and me—for us all.

Later, during His resurrected ministry, Jesus directed Peter, "Feed my lambs. . . . Feed my sheep. . . . Feed my sheep" (John 21:15–17). Three times this charge was repeated to the newly designated head shepherd. Do you think that Peter recalled the parable of the good shepherd? Do you think that Peter could remember what a good shepherd was to be, what he was to do? Do you think that he ever questioned his Lord's example as being too idealistic? It must have impressed Peter deeply, for tradition has it that he also willingly gave his life for the cause. . . .

Today our Lord repeats the same charge He gave Peter. He repeats it with the same emphasis, the same repetition: "Feed my lambs. . . . Feed my sheep. . . . Feed my sheep!" (*Come unto Christ* [Salt Lake City: Deseret Book, 1983], 63–65, 69)

LIKENING THE SCRIPTURES TO OUR LIVES

Ezekiel 34:2 Son of man, prophesy against the shepherds of Israel, prophesy, and say unto them, Thus saith the Lord God unto the shepherds; Woe be to the shepherds of Israel that do feed themselves! should not the shepherds feed the flocks?

Application: The Lord reminds us that, as shepherds of the flock, we have a duty to feed the flock. He gives us a warning that we must ever seek to feed His sheep, even as Peter was admonished (see John 21:15–17).

SUMMARY

King David, who reigned 28 generations before the mortal ministry of the Divine King (see Matt. 1:17), gave magnificent utterance to the concept of the Good Shepherd:

> The Lord is my shepherd; I shall not want.
> He maketh me to lie down in green pastures: he leadeth me beside the still waters.
> He restoreth my soul: he leadeth me in the paths of righteousness for his name's sake.
> Yea, though I walk through the valley of the shadow of death, I will fear no evil: for thou art with me; thy rod and thy staff they comfort me.
> Thou preparest a table before me in the presence of mine enemies: thou anointest my head with oil; my cup runneth over.
> Surely goodness and mercy shall follow me all the days of my life: and I will dwell in the house of the Lord for ever. (Ps. 23:1–6)

Likewise, Isaiah envisioned the compassion and nurturing mission of the Good Shepherd: "He shall feed his flock like a shepherd: he shall gather the lambs with his arm, and carry them in his bosom, and shall gently lead those that are with young" (Isa. 40:11). And Ezekiel, too, was inspired to invoke the spirit of shepherding when he witnessed: "For thus saith the Lord God; Behold, I, even I, will both search my sheep, and seek them out. As a shepherd seeketh out his flock in the day that he is among his sheep that are scattered; so will I seek out my sheep, and will deliver them out of all places where they have been scattered in the cloudy and dark day"(Ezek. 34:11–12).

All of the prophets of God were blessed to discern the ministering charity of the Redeemer—from Mosiah (Mos. 26:21) to Alma (Alma 5:60) to our present-day leaders.

The scriptures bear record of the power and goodness of Jesus as the Good Shepherd. The Spirit confirms His divine commission. We, as undershepherds of the Lord, have the singularly magnificent opportunity to help Him tend His flock and feed His sheep. May we do so with valor and faith, devotion and loyalty, so that the work of the Kingdom may go forth in glory and truth.

CHAPTER 17

"WHAT SHALL I DO *that* I MAY INHERIT ETERNAL LIFE"

Reading Assignment: Mark 10:17–30; 12:41–44; Luke 12:13–21; 14; 16.

Additional Reading: Matthew 6:19–21, 33; 19:16–30; Luke 18:18–30; 21:1–4; Jacob 2:18–19; D&C 6:6–7.

> *Eternal perfection is reserved for those who overcome all things and inherit the fulness of the Father in his heavenly mansions. Perfection consists in gaining eternal life—the kind of life that God lives.*
>
> —RUSSELL M. NELSON, "PERFECTION PENDING," *ENSIGN,* NOV. 1995, 87.

THEMES *for* LIVING

1. Trust in Things of Heaven, Rather Than Things of the World
2. Seek Treasures in Heaven, Rather Than Treasures on Earth
3. True Disciples Sacrifice All

INTRODUCTION

The battle for the souls of men has gone on since premortal times. Here on the earth, the war continues. Do we choose the world and its treasures, or do we seek the treasures of Heaven? If our love for God slackens and we seek the things of the world, we become subject to the devil. This has been the case since the time of Adam, as we learn in the Pearl of Great Price: "And Satan came among them, saying: I am also a son of God; and he commanded them, saying: Believe it not; and they believed it not, and they loved Satan more than God. And men began from that time forth to be carnal, sensual, and devilish" (Moses 5:13).

When we put anything ahead of the Lord, we put ourselves in jeopardy. The counsel of the Lord is clear, "Lay not up for yourselves treasure upon earth, where moth and rust doth corrupt, and where thieves break through and steal. But lay up for yourselves treasures in heaven, where neither moth nor rust doth corrupt, and where thieves do not break through nor steal. For where your treasure is, there will your heart be also" (JST, Matt. 6:19). As we become true disciples of Christ, our joy will be in the joy of the Lord. We will seek His will and His purposes, and aspire to build up His Kingdom by laying our all upon the altar of God.

1. TRUST IN THINGS OF HEAVEN, RATHER THAN THINGS OF THE WORLD

THEME: Things of the world have no exalting power, only the Lord and the things of His Kingdom can lead us to exaltation.

MOMENT OF TRUTH

In one of the Savior's most memorable sayings, He crystallized the stark contrast of opposing values in life: "No servant can serve two masters: for either he will hate the one, and love the other; or else he will hold to the one, and despise the other. Ye cannot serve God and mammon" (Luke 16:13). Several of the Lord's parables illustrate this point, showing how we can be in the world, but not of the world. An example is the parable of the unjust steward who was accused of wasting the goods of his lord (see Luke 16:1–8). The steward was called to give an accounting of his performance prior to being dismissed from his position. Acting strategically, in his own interest, the steward hastened to forgive a generous portion of the debts of the lord's debtors. In this way, the steward wanted to ingratiate himself with the debtors, that he might have a place to go after being termi-nated. His lord then commended the steward (Luke 16:8)—either for his shrewdness and street wisdom or perhaps for having forgiven the interest on the debts (which was unlaw-ful and would have had repercussions if it were discovered). Tsung-Ting Yang sheds light on the interpretation that the Savior then gave to His listeners:

> After telling the parable, Jesus explained some points that were important to Him.
> 1. *Those who are spiritually strong need to give proper attention to the temporal affairs in their lives.* "For the children of this world are in their generation wiser than the children of light" (Luke 16:8).

2. When possible the righteous should be friends, not enemies, with people in positions of authority or wealth, for someday those friends may assist the righteous and the kingdom of God. "Make to yourselves friends of the mammon of unrighteousness; that, when ye fail, they may receive you into everlasting habitations" (Luke 16:9; see D&C 82:22).

3. Those who wisely manage their temporal affairs are more likely to also wisely manage their spiritual affairs. "He that is faithful in that which is least is faithful also in much. . . . And if ye have not been faithful in that which is another man's, who shall give you that which is your own?" (Luke 16:10, 12; see D&C 51:19).

4. Obedience to God is much more important than making money. "Ye cannot serve God and mammon" (Luke 16:13; see D&C 56:16–17). . . .

From the parable of the unjust steward, we realize we must learn how to use properly the worldly things God has entrusted to our care. . . .

I no longer wonder why the Savior gave this parable. It reminds me of principles that continue to bless me and my family. I am thankful that the Lord's parables not only contain great spiritual concepts but also provide very practical advice for achieving financial success within the teachings of His glorious gospel. ("Parables of Jesus: The Unjust Steward," *Ensign,* July 2003, 29–31)

MODERN PROPHETS SPEAK

Spencer W. Kimball:

Secular knowledge, important as it may be, can never save a soul nor open the celestial kingdom nor create a world nor make a man a god, but it can be most helpful to that man who, placing first things first, has found the way to eternal life and who can now bring into play all knowledge to be his tool and servant. (*President Kimball Speaks Out* [Salt Lake City: Deseret Book, 1981], 92)

ILLUSTRATIONS FOR OUR TIME

Mammon—The Downfall of Countless Souls

I will cite the dominant characteristics of the rich that the scriptures give. Those who "hasten to be rich have an evil eye" and are not innocent (Prov. 28:20, 22). They soon fall into temptations and snares, into foolish and hurtful lusts, which "drown men in destruction and perdition" (1 Tim. 6:9). Trusting in "uncertain riches" (1 Tim. 6:17), people grow wise in their own conceit (Prov. 28:11) and wax proud (Alma 4:6). They lift up their hearts because of their riches (Ezek. 28:5), refusing to give heed to the word of God (Alma 45:24), becoming unfruitful (Matt. 13:22).

The rich pass over the deeds of the wicked and do not judge the needy's cause (Jer. 5:28). They despise the poor and drag them before the judgment seats (James 2:6). They set their hearts on riches and the vain things of the world, scorning and persecuting those who do not believe according to their will and pleasure (Alma 4:8). The rich defraud and condemn the just and suppose that they are better than they (Jacob 2:13; Mosiah 4:22). In brief, the love of money is the root of every kind of evil, causing men to "err from the faith" (1 Tim. 6:10). . . .

Jacob counseled the rich to think of their brethren like unto themselves, to be familiar with all and free with their substance—"that they may be rich like unto you" (Jacob 2:17). Before people seek for riches, he advised, they should seek for the kingdom of God, obtaining first a hope in Christ (Jacob 2:18–19). A hope in Christ means that as we devote our lives to God, we at some point receive a witness by the Holy Ghost that we have obtained a remission of our sins. We can justify pursuing riches, therefore, but only within a narrow compass: "for the intent to do good—to clothe the naked, and to feed the hungry, and to liberate the captive, and administer relief to the sick and the afflicted" (Jacob 2:19). In the scriptures, that constitutes the sole justification of pursuing riches. (*By Study and Also by Faith: Essays in Honor of Hugh W. Nibley on the Occasion of His Eightieth Birthday, 27 March 1990,* 2 vols., ed. John M. Lundquist and Stephen D. Ricks [Salt Lake City and Provo: Deseret Book, Foundation for Ancient Research and Mormon Studies, 1990], 2:382, 383–84)

LIKENING THE SCRIPTURES TO OUR LIVES

Mark 10:24–25 And the disciples were astonished at his words. But Jesus answereth again, and saith unto them, Children, how hard is it for them that trust in riches to enter into the kingdom of God! It is easier for a camel to go through the eye of a needle, than for a rich man to enter into the kingdom of God.

Application: Worldly things can get in the way of spiritual growth and righteousness. The love of money is truly the root of evil (1 Tim. 6:10; Morm. 8:37). The Lord exhorts us to be aware of the temptation and snare of placing our trust in worldly wealth rather than spiritual wealth.

2. SEEK TREASURES IN HEAVEN, RATHER THAN TREASURES ON EARTH

THEME: As we seek to do the will of God in all things—continually pondering how and whom we can bless, how and when we can express our gratitude to the Lord—we will harvest rich blessings of inner peace and store up heavenly treasures.

MOMENT OF TRUTH

The Savior was a consummate teacher, often supporting His theme by the skillful use of contrasts. For example, in the parable of Lazarus, He placed an infirm beggar at the doors of a haughty rich man who scarcely took note of the man's misery and desire to share at least the crumbs from the rich man's table. When both died, the homeless beggar was taken into the loving care of Abraham, whereas the rich man was consigned to hellfire. When the formerly rich man cried out to Abraham, requesting that Lazarus be sent to dip his finger in water and sooth his scorched tongue, Abraham reminded him that the tables had now been turned, that it was Lazarus's time to be comforted, and that "a great gulf" now separated the two camps, preventing passage (Luke 16:26). Then the tormented man requested that Lazarus at least be sent to warn his brethren of the dangers of torment. But Abraham pointed out that those still in the mortal sphere already have Moses and the prophets: "If they hear not Moses and the prophets, neither will they be persuaded, though one rose from the dead" (Luke 16:31).

The Savior's point is clear: Those who are caught up in the riches of the world, at the expense of spiritual wealth, cannot easily enter through the gates of heaven. As He explained to His disciples:

> Children, how hard is it for them that trust in riches to enter into the kingdom of God!
>
> It is easier for a camel to go through the eye of a needle, than for a rich man to enter into the kingdom of God.
>
> And they were astonished out of measure, saying among themselves, Who then can be saved?
>
> And Jesus looking upon them saith, With men it is impossible, but not with God: for with God all things are possible. (Mark 10:24–27)

This last statement of the Savior is rendered more accurately in the Joseph Smith Translation as follows: "With men that trust in riches, it is impossible; but not impossible with men who trust in God and leave all for my sake, for with such all these things are possible" (JST, Mark 10:26).

MODERN PROPHETS SPEAK

Dallin H. Oaks:

> The Savior and his Apostles gave many warnings against setting our hearts upon the treasures of this world.

Jesus taught that we should not lay up for ourselves "treasures upon earth, where moth and rust doth corrupt, and where thieves break through and steal: . . . For where your treasure is, there will your heart be also" (Matt. 6:19, 21). In other words, the treasures of our hearts—our priorities—should not be the destructible and temporary things of this world. . . . Those who preach the gospel of success and the theology of prosperity are suffering from "the deceitfulness of riches" and from supposing that "gain is godliness" (1 Tim. 6:5). The possession of wealth or the acquisition of significant income is not a mark of heavenly favor, and their absence is not evidence of heavenly disfavor. Riches can be among the blessings that follow right behavior—such as the payment of tithing (Mal. 3:9–12)—but riches can also be acquired through the luck of a prospector or as the fruits of dishonesty. . . . In the midst of prophetic utterances about his Second Coming, the Savior warned that we should not be so pre-occupied with the cares of this life that we are unprepared for that great day: "And take heed to yourselves, lest at any time your hearts be over-charged with surfeiting, and drunkenness, and cares of this life, and so that day come upon you unawares" (Luke 21:34). . . .

The Book of Mormon identifies the love of riches and the pride it engenders as the cause of the spiritual and temporal downfall of the people of God.

When Lehi's descendants had established themselves successfully in the New World, Jacob cautioned them against the spiritual dangers of riches: But wo unto the rich, who are rich as to the things of the world. For because they are rich they despise the poor, and they persecute the meek, and their hearts are upon their treasures; wherefore, their treasure is their God (2 Ne. 9:30). (*Pure in Heart* [Salt Lake City: Bookcraft, 1988], 74–77, 79)

ILLUSTRATIONS FOR OUR TIME

Money Does Not Exalt
Look and see what the love of money and the treasures of the earth have done to the people of the world. The evidence is everywhere. Let us be wise: Money and things cannot exalt—only by the grace of God and obedience to the commandments of God can we build up treasures in heaven. [Pinegar]

Royalty in Disguise
They were often very limited in their worldly wealth and temporal resources—poor by any standard of measurement—but these humble German families often took us in as missionaries and regaled us with the best they could afford. I remember one elderly sister who watched with delight as we consumed the small clump of beef she had meticulously divided between us. When we asked about her portion, she replied that she did not care for any. We knew that she had willingly sacrificed her part so that we

could have more. Like the widow at the treasury, she had given her all (Mark 12:41–44). We thanked her for her thoughtfulness, and we saw the joy of service reflected in her eyes. Another family was excited to offer us baked rabbit one day after they had caught the animal nearby in a thicket. It was delicious not so much because of our fondness for rabbit but because of the atmosphere of charity and generosity in which it was prepared and gifted to us. They had nothing else to offer but that rabbit and their loving kindness.

After all of these decades, I can still see that same family in my mind's eye when I met them unexpectedly at the Swiss temple many months later. They looked resplendent in their temple clothing, complete with the glow of happiness about their countenances. It occurred to me then, and still remains a valued conviction, that this family was royalty in disguise all along. In the House of the Lord, they had set aside the homely and simple everyday clothing of their poverty for the robes of spiritual abundance. They had appeared as what they were all along—sons and daughters of God endowed with the capacity to be royal servants of the Almighty. They were storing up treasures of a heavenly kind (Matt. 6:21). They were seeking first the kingdom of God—with the faith that all would work out on their mortal journey (Matt. 6:33). As the Savior said: "And behold, ye are the children of the prophets; and ye are of the house of Israel; and ye are of the covenant which the Father made with your fathers, saying unto Abraham: And in thy seed shall all the kindreds of the earth be blessed" (3 Ne. 20:25). [Allen]

LIKENING THE SCRIPTURES TO OUR LIVES

JST, Matthew 6:21 For where your treasure is, there will your heart be also.

Application: Remember that our thoughts precede our actions. If our goals are the things of the world, then these "things" become our gods and we deny the very God who gave us life. Our heart is the center of our being—our decision maker, our mind, and the affections of our soul. So if our heart is not in the right place, we can never be with the Lord.

3. TRUE DISCIPLES SACRIFICE ALL

THEME: True disciples of Jesus Christ follow the Savior, doing the things that He would have them do and investing all that they have to support the cause of building up the kingdom of God.

MOMENT OF TRUTH

The Savior of the world was Divinity incarnate. He took up a mortal tabernacle and lived among God's children in the meridian of time. What better authority to speak about the dichotomy of earthly and heavenly things than Jesus Christ, who was at once mortal and immortal? His abiding theme was the need to rise above worldly and transient entities and attain unto the eternal and everlasting. So often in His discourses, He would teach the principle of investing one's all in that which leads to immortality and eternal life rather than squandering one's loyalty by giving allegiance to the ephemeral and shallow things of the world. Jesus counseled the man who had hitherto been compliant with God's laws to go one further step and sell all that he had to provide resources for the poor and take up his cross and follow the Lord. But the man was sad, "for he had great possessions" (Mark 10:22).

On another occasion, the Savior expressed great satisfaction with the widow in penury who donated her pittance to the treasury, for "she of her want did cast in all that she had, even all her living" (Mark 12:44). Those who seek the Kingdom are disposed toward humility and meekness, not pride and station: "For whosoever exalteth himself shall be abased; and he that humbleth himself shall be exalted" (Luke 14:11). It is the poor and the beggars—those who are devoid of the trappings of luxury and extravagance—who are invited to the "Great Supper" of the Lord (Luke 14:16–24). Like the builder of a house or the king governing his armies, the aspiring disciple of Christ is to lay a solid foundation for action and calculate the cost of discipleship in advance, before taking up his cross: "So likewise, whosoever he be of you that forsaketh not all that he hath, he cannot be my disciple" (Luke 14:33).

MODERN PROPHETS SPEAK

Ezra Taft Benson:

> My good brethren of the Melchizedek Priesthood and Aaronic Priesthood, home teaching is an inspired program. It is the heart of caring, of loving, of reaching out to the one—both the active and the less active. It is priesthood compassionate service. It is how we express our faith in practical works. It is one of the tests of true discipleship. It is the heart of the activation effort of the Church. It is a calling that helps to fulfill the scriptural injunction "Out of small things proceedeth that which is great" (D&C 64:33). There is no greater Church calling than that of a home teacher. There is no greater Church service rendered to our Father in Heaven's children than the service rendered by a humble, dedicated, committed home teacher. (*TETB*, 225)

ILLUSTRATIONS FOR OUR TIME

Bruce R. McConkie teaches the meaning of true discipleship. He explains:

> "A true disciple, if called upon to do so, forsakes all—riches, home, friends, family even his own life—in the Master's Cause." (*Commentary*, 1:503) "And whoso is not

willing to lay down his life for my sake is not my disciple" (D&C 103:28). Are they even to hate their family members? "Not hate in the sense of intense aversion or abhorrence; such is contrary to the whole spirit and tenor of the gospel. Men are to love their enemies, to say nothing of their own flesh and blood. Rather, the sense and meaning of Jesus' present instruction is that true disciples have a duty toward God which takes precedence over any family or personal obligation" (*Commentary,* 1:503). . . .

Only those who make up their minds to do so—come what may come—have power to keep the commandments in times of trial and tribulation. To dramatize his teaching "that converts should count the cost *before* joining the Church; that they should come into the kingdom only if they are prepared to make the sacrifices required; that they should go the whole way in the gospel cause, or stay out entirely; that they 'not . . . follow him, unless' they are 'able to continue' in his word, to 'do the things' which he teaches and commands" (*Commentary,* 1:504). (Bruce R. McConkie, *The Mortal Messiah: From Bethlehem to Calvary,* 4 vols. [Salt Lake City: Deseret Book, 1979–1981], 3:240)

LIKENING THE SCRIPTURES TO OUR LIVES

JST, Luke 14:26 If any man come to me, and hate not his father, and mother, and wife, and children, and brethren, and sisters, or husband, yea and his own life also; or in other words, is afraid to lay down his life for my sake, he cannot be my disciple.

Application: Discipleship requires that we submit our will totally to the will of God. Our life is to be lived to prove ourselves worthy and for the good of others (this is the cause of the Lord)—to build up the kingdom of God (see JST, Matt. 6:38).

SUMMARY

The sacred counsel reflected in these records of the Savior's mortal ministry is clear: Trust in things of heaven rather than in things of the earth; seek treasures in heaven rather than treasures of the world; dedicate your all for the building up of the kingdom of God.

Wealth is a fundamental part of the gospel of Jesus Christ—wealth of the eternities. Jacob, brother of Nephi, expressed this doctrine as follows "But before ye seek for riches, seek ye for the kingdom of God. And in our day, the Lord has renewed the call for the Saints to keep their priorities focused on things pertaining to salvation: "Now, as you have asked, behold, I say unto you, keep my commandments, and seek to bring forth and establish the cause of Zion; Seek not for riches but for wisdom, and behold, the mysteries of God shall be unfolded unto you, and then shall you be made rich. Behold, he that hath eternal life is rich" (D&C 6:6–7).

CHAPTER 18

THE WORTH of SOULS—HELPING EVERYONE COME UNTO CHRIST

Reading Assignment: Luke 15; 17.

Additional Reading: Matthew 18:11–14; D&C 18:10–16; 58:42; Mosiah 26:30; Alma 26:11–16; 31:34–35.

> *I say to bishops throughout the world that with all you have to do—and we recognize that it is much—you cannot disregard the converts. Most of them do not need very much. As I have said before, they need a friend. They need something to do, a responsibility. They need nurturing with the good word of God. They come into the Church with enthusiasm for what they have found. We must immediately build on that enthusiasm. You have people in your wards who can be friends to every convert. They can listen to them, guide them, answer their questions, and be there to help in all circumstances and in all conditions. Brethren, this loss must stop. It is unnecessary. I am satisfied the Lord is not pleased with us. I invite you, every one of you, to make this a matter of priority in your administrative work. I invite every member to reach out in friendship and love for those who come into the Church as converts.*

—GORDON B. HINCKLEY, "SOME THOUGHTS ON TEMPLES, RETENTION OF CONVERTS, AND MISSIONARY SERVICE," *ENSIGN*, NOV. 1997, 51.

THEMES *for* LIVING

1. Great Is the Worth of Souls
2. Rejoicing in Heaven and Earth over a Repentant Soul
3. Gratitude for Blessings and Miracles in Our Lives
4. Let Us Increase Our Faith

INTRODUCTION

The work and glory of our Father in Heaven and His Son is to bring about our immortality and eternal life (see Moses 1:39). The central figure in the plan of salvation is our Lord Jesus Christ, who provides His infinite and eternal Atonement—the power that can save mankind. The Atonement is at the core of the gospel of Jesus Christ. The only way we can make the Atonement totally efficacious in our life is through repentance—even faith unto repentance (see Alma 34:15–17), with a covenant made through baptism and the bestowal of the Holy Ghost. All the prophets preach nothing but faith and repentance (see Mosiah 18:20; 18:7; 2 Ne. 26:27; Alma 7:14), baptism (see 3 Ne. 11, 15), and the gift of the Holy Ghost (see John 3:5; 2 Ne. 31:13; 2 Ne. 32:5; Alma 34:38; 3 Ne. 27:20). Repentance and obedience bring joy to the Lord (see D&C 18:13) and to all those who help in this process (see Alma 29:9–10). Only through the grace of God can a soul be saved, based on obedience to the principles and ordinances of the gospel and enduring to the end. This is what life is all about. Oh, how we should be filled with gratitude for the goodness of God and His tender mercies towards His children. As we increase our faith in Jesus Christ, we will be able to do all things whatsoever He commands us to do (see Ether 12).

1. GREAT IS THE WORTH OF SOULS

THEME: The worth of souls is great in the sight of the Lord, whose purpose it is to bring about the will of the Father in saving and blessing His children.

MOMENT OF TRUTH

The Savior desired to impart unto the people and their leaders an understanding of how much joy is felt in heaven when a wandering soul is recovered and returned to the fold. Thus He unfolded for them the parable of the lost sheep—which was so closely aligned with His theme of the Good Shepherd. The Lord personalized this tender story for His listeners:

> What man of you, having an hundred sheep, if he lose one of them, doth not leave
> the ninety and nine in the wilderness, and go after that which is lost, until he find it?
>   And when he hath found it, he layeth it on his shoulders, rejoicing. (Luke
> 15:4–5)

In this manner, the Lord invited His audience to step into the story and feel and sense the emotion of the narrative so that they could understand the message: "I say unto you, that likewise joy shall be in heaven over one sinner that repenteth, more than over ninety and nine just persons, which need no repentance" (Luke 15:7).

In a story with a parallel message, the Lord presented the parable of the lost piece of silver: "Either what woman having ten pieces of silver, if she lose one piece, doth not light a candle, and sweep the house, and seek diligently till she find it? And when she hath found it, she calleth her friends and her neighbours together, saying, Rejoice with me; for I have found the piece which I had lost. Likewise, I say unto you, there is joy in the presence of the angels of God over one sinner that repenteth" (Luke 15:8–10).

MODERN PROPHETS SPEAK

David O. McKay:

> There is an unchanging truth in an unchanging world which should be an anchor to the soul of every person in it: the sacredness of personality. The least child was sacred to Jesus. It is not the will of your Father in heaven that one of these little ones should perish. That simple truth in the world, what would it mean? "Inasmuch as ye have done it unto one of the least of these my brethren, ye have done it unto me." (Matt. 25:40) And in this modern day he said: "Remember the worth of souls is great." (D&C 18:10) A proper conception of this divine principle would change the attitude of the world to the benefit and happiness of all human beings. It would bring into active operation the Golden Rule: Do unto others as you would have others do unto you (see Matt. 7:12). (*Gospel Ideals: Selections from the Discourses of David O. McKay* [Salt Lake City: Improvement Era, 1953], 347)

ILLUSTRATIONS FOR OUR TIME

What Would Be of Most Worth?

The Whitmer brothers came to the Prophet Joseph seeking direction in their lives. Section 14 was given to David; John and Peter received sections 15 and 16, respectively. It is interesting to note that sections 15 and 16 are identical. John and Peter had similar desires to know what would be of most worth unto them (see sections 15 and

16 verse 4). The Lord through the Prophet Joseph said these magnificent words, which we can all apply to our lives, "And now, behold, I say unto you, that the thing which will be of the most worth unto you will be to declare repentance unto this people, that you may bring souls unto me, that you may rest with them in the kingdom of my Father" (D&C 16:6). Inviting all to come unto Christ is the objective of the Church and kingdom of God. This is fulfilled through the three-fold purpose of the Church as we proclaim the gospel, redeem the dead, and perfect the Saints. All of this has to do with saving souls—with blessing our brothers and sisters by inviting them to come unto Christ and persuading them to do good (see Jacob 1:7; Moro. 7:16).

The Lord has described this in the Doctrine and Covenants when He revealed to the Prophet Joseph the following:

> Remember the worth of souls is great in the sight of God;
>
> For, behold, the Lord your Redeemer suffered death in the flesh; wherefore he suffered the pain of all men, that all men might repent and come unto him.
>
> And he hath risen again from the dead, that he might bring all men unto him, on conditions of repentance.
>
> And how great is his joy in the soul that repenteth!
>
> Wherefore, you are called to cry repentance unto this people.
>
> And if it so be that you should labor all your days in crying repentance unto this people, and bring, save it be one soul unto me, how great shall be your joy with him in the kingdom of my Father!
>
> And now, if your joy will be great with one soul that you have brought unto me into the kingdom of my Father, how great will be your joy if you should bring many souls unto me! (D&C 18:10–16) [Pinegar]

The Parable of the Lost Sheep—Is It Fair?

When the pharisees and scribes ridiculed the Savior for consorting with publicans and sinners, He recounted for them the incomparable parable of the lost sheep (Luke 15:3–7). In the space of just a few words, the Savior unfolded the psychological transition that must have taken place within the soul of the shepherd—the transition from anguish to joy and from panic to relief—as he found again the wandering creature and entered into a celebratory phase of rejoicing with his friends and neighbors: "for I have found my sheep which was lost" (Luke 15:6). The Savior's message to His detractors was lucidly clear: "I say unto you, that likewise joy shall be in heaven over one sinner that repenteth, more than over ninety and nine just persons, which need no repentance" (Luke 15:7).

This story has reverberated down through the generations and still captures the imagination of anyone who is touched by the spirit of charity and responsibility for others: parents, teachers, leaders, and companions alike. But there is a hidden wrinkle that might just emerge for some. Did the shepherd not "leave the ninety and nine in the wilderness" (Luke 15:4) in order to search out the missing sheep? Were these others at that point not left alone for a time? And is there not to be joy in heaven in greater measure for the recovered soul than for the ninety and nine that were righteous? From the standpoint of the faithful and devout, could this appear to be somewhat unfair?

There was a time in my life when I reasoned in that way and wondered about the fairness of the parable—even while at the same time rejoicing in the good news surrounding the circumstances of the found sheep. And then, with growing maturity and experience in life, I came to realize the deeper spiritual fairness of the Savior's story. It is true that there is joy in heaven over the repentant soul greater than over the faithful and devout, because the Savior has confirmed it. However, according to the Lord's mathematics, there is not a jot or tittle of unfairness in the story. Why? Because the point of the story is not necessarily to equate ourselves with the ninety and nine, but with the one! Every one of us is lost—to a lesser or greater degree—at some point in our lives. Every one of us has need for continual repentance. Every one of us plays the part of the wandering sheep, the lost soul that needs to have the rescuing influence of the Good Shepherd and His loyal undershepherds.

Father Lehi taught Jacob and his other sons that "by the law no flesh is justified" (2 Ne. 2:5), for all fall short of keeping the commandments in perfect measure, and all depend on the "merits, and mercy, and grace of the Holy Messiah" (2 Ne. 2:8) to enjoy the blessings of the Atonement and savor the living waters of the gospel. Alma confirmed the same thing: "For it is expedient that an atonement should be made; for according to the great plan of the Eternal God there must be an atonement made, or else all mankind must unavoidably perish; yea, all are hardened; yea, all are fallen and are lost, and must perish except it be through the atonement which it is expedient should be made" (Alma 34:9). And to whom does the Atonement apply? To all. We are all lost sheep. "All we like sheep have gone astray; we have turned every one to his own way; and the Lord hath laid on him the iniquity of us all" (Isa. 53:6; compare Mosiah 14:6).

Let us therefore rejoice doubly at the outcome of the parable of the lost sheep, for it verily pertains to each one of us. Let us express gratitude daily for being the one who is found. Let us marvel that it is we over whom the angels in heaven celebrate in joy when we repent and return to the fold in faith and contrition. And let us remember, as well, to feel joy within ourselves in being at last found, lifted up upon the shoulders of the Good Shepherd, and returned to His eternal family. [Allen]

LIKENING THE SCRIPTURES TO OUR LIVES

Moses 1:39 For behold, this is my work and my glory—to bring to pass the immortality and eternal life of man.

Application: If we truly comprehend this scripture we can realize how much Heavenly Father and our Savior love us. Their work and glory is the salvation of mankind. We are of great worth. The Savior spoke of His joy when we repent (see D&C 18:13).

2. REJOICING IN HEAVEN AND EARTH OVER A REPENTANT SOUL

THEME: True joy has to do with souls coming to Christ in humility and obedience, thus receiving the immediate and eternal blessings of the redemption and Atonement.

MOMENT OF TRUTH

In the parable of the prodigal son—one of the Savior's most detailed and psychologically searching stories—we are presented with the contrasting perspectives of two sons in a man's household: a profligate and wayward young man who repented and returned home and an older brother who remained faithfully at home on the farm. Lessons had to be learned by both: the young son needed to learn self-discipline and wise stewardship; the older son needed to learn forgiveness and long-suffering. The father of the story embodied all these qualities, for he said to his workers: "For this my son was dead, and is alive again; he was lost, and is found" (Luke 15:24), and to his supercilious and somewhat jealous older son: "Son, thou art ever with me, and all that I have is thine. It was meet that we should make merry, and be glad: for this thy brother was dead, and is alive again; and was lost, and is found"(Luke 15:31–32). What greater symbolism could there be to explain the process of spiritual rebirth and regeneration—and the power of redemption and forgiveness that is germane to this process?

MODERN PROPHETS SPEAK

Bruce R. McConkie:

> It is because of their understanding of this doctrine of the worth of souls that our Lord's ministers go forth with all the energy and capacity they have to labor in the vineyard, pleading with men to repent and save their souls, that they may have eventual eternal joy in the Father's kingdom. (*DNTC*, 1965], 1:394)

ILLUSTRATIONS FOR OUR TIME

The Promise
Let me illustrate these points with an experience I had some years ago. It was about 1969 when a young girl named Susan came to see me. "Bishop you've got to take my name off the records of the Church."

I said, "Oh, Susan, what's wrong?"

"My brothers think I'm a dork for being here at BYU, and I can't stand the pressure when I go home and my parents are wondering what's gone wrong with me."

And then all of a sudden, the Lord stepped in and words came out of my mouth like this: "Susan, I promise you that if you stay faithful, your brothers will join the Church and your parents' hearts will soften." Now how could I say that? I couldn't. Only the Lord could.

She said, "Oh, I just don't know, Bishop. I just don't know."

I said, "Well, Susan, is the Book of Mormon true?"

"Of course it is, Bishop."

"Do you love the Savior and do you believe in Heavenly Father?"

"Yes, I do."

"Is the prophet the head of the Church today?"

"Of course."

"Is this the true Church?"

"Of course it is. But I just can't stand the pressure."

I said, "Susan, will you be willing to try? Because the Lord just gave you a promise."

She said, "I guess I can try." That year she moved out of the ward and I lost track of her.

Well, at BYU in 1972, I volunteered to teach another religion class, besides the Book of Mormon, before going to my dental office. It was the Gospel Principles and Practices class. There were about sixty students in the class, and life was going just merrily along, and on the last day to drop the class, this student came up to me and he said, "I've got to drop your class."

I asked, "How come?"

He said, "I'm on scholarship, and if I don't get a B or a B+, I could lose my scholarship; and I got a C+ on the test, and besides I'm not a Mormon."

I looked at his little information sheet I had him fill out before class. He'd checked "nonmember" so close to the "member" that I'd missed it.

I said, "Well, Jim, you mean you're just afraid you won't get a B?"

He said, "How can I? I'm not a member, and I just can't risk it."

I said, "Jim, I've got an idea. Do you normally study once a week for this class?"

He answered, "Yes."

I said, "Jim, I've got it. Would you mind studying with me Tuesday nights before Wednesday's class for an hour?"

He said, "Yes, but what will that do?"

I continued, "Well, Jim, you want a B, right? Do you know who makes out the grade?"

He answered, "You do."

I smiled. "That's right, Jim, I'm guaranteeing you a B or a B+. I'm going to teach you extra Tuesday nights. If you're in my house for an hour, well, I'll make up the test too. I'll even help you prepare for the test. Jim, I'm guaranteeing you this."

Jim said, "Well, that's a deal. I'm going to study with you."

This went on for a couple of weeks, and then one day he asked, "Hey, Brother Ed, could I bring my brother and my roommate up? I mean, we have banana splits and root beer floats and doughnuts every study night; we might as well have parties when you teach."

And so I said, "You bet, you bring them up."

So we went along for several more weeks, and then this one night they came up and they were kind of kidding around a lot, so I said, "You guys are sure having a hoot tonight. What's up around here?"

They looked at each other as if to say, *OK, who's going to tell him?* and then Jim finally said, "Brother Ed, we've been thinking, and we talked to our bishop, and we all want to be baptized, and will you baptize us and confirm us members of the Church next week?"

As I floated down from the ceiling, I said, "Yes, Jim. I will, I will, I will." Well, Jim was Susan's brother; Susan was at the baptism, and joy was felt by all.

Now you tell me that God our Father and Jesus Christ are not in charge of everything on this earth. How could those words come out of my mouth, "Your brothers will join the Church"? How, two years later, could one of those brothers be in my class? There were 20,000 students at BYU. Don't tell me that the Lord's hand isn't in all things that are good. All three boys served missions. All three were married in the temple. The roommate recently returned from presiding over the Switzerland Geneva Mission 2000–2003. [Pinegar]

LIKENING THE SCRIPTURES TO OUR LIVES

Alma 29:9–10 I know that which the Lord hath commanded me, and I glory in it. I do not glory of myself, but I glory in that which the Lord hath commanded me; yea, and this is my glory, that perhaps I may be an instrument in the hands of God to bring some soul to repentance; and this is my joy. And behold, when I see many of my brethren truly penitent, and coming to the Lord their God, then is my soul filled with joy; then do I remember what the Lord has done for me, yea, even that he hath heard my prayer; yea, then do I remember his merciful arm which he extended towards me.

Application: When we truly are converted, we have an overwhelming concern for the welfare of our fellowmen (see Mosiah 28:3). We should seek to bless everyone we contact by inviting and persuading them to come unto Christ. Prayerfully develop a plan to bless members as well as those who do not yet enjoy the blessings of the gospel of Jesus Christ.

3. GRATITUDE FOR BLESSINGS AND MIRACLES IN OUR LIVES

THEME: Showing gratitude for all things pleases God and fills us with joy and peace.

MOMENT OF TRUTH

On one occasion, as the Savior was passing through Samaria and Galilee, He entered into a village and observed ten lepers in the distance. What happened then has become an icon of the process of remembering to be grateful:

> And they lifted up their voices, and said, Jesus, Master, have mercy on us.
>
> And when he saw them, he said unto them, Go shew yourselves unto the priests. And it came to pass, that, as they went, they were cleansed.
>
> And one of them, when he saw that he was healed, turned back, and with a loud voice glorified God,
>
> And fell down on his face at his feet, giving him thanks: and he was a Samaritan.
>
> And Jesus answering said, Were there not ten cleansed? but where are the nine?
>
> There are not found that returned to give glory to God, save this stranger.
>
> And he said unto him, Arise, go thy way: thy faith hath made thee whole. (Luke 17:13–19)

MODERN PROPHETS SPEAK

Joseph F. Smith:

> The grateful man sees so much in the world to be thankful for, and with him the good outweighs the evil. Love overpowers jealousy, and light drives darkness out of his life. Pride destroys our gratitude and sets up selfishness in its place. How much happier we are in the presence of a grateful and loving soul, and how careful we should be to cultivate, through the medium of a prayerful life, a thankful attitude toward God and man! (*Gospel Doctrine: Selections from the Sermons and Writings of Joseph F. Smith,* comp. John A. Widtsoe [Salt Lake City: Deseret Book, 1939], 263)

ILLUSTRATIONS FOR OUR TIME

The Perspective of Gratitude
The grateful person has a refreshing way of looking at the world. Gratitude is the catalyst for growth and change. We heard a young man express with great sincerity his

gratitude for a certain blessing in his life. He came to an understanding and appreciation for that blessing, and his new state of mind, in turn, changed his life. The principle is clear. When you feel grateful, you will show it through service. And you will
be amazed how others will follow your example. That is the miracle of gratitude.
Certainly one of the hallmarks of a disciple of the Savior is a lifestyle that reflects gratitude and thanksgiving.

Howard W. Hunter gave this advice concerning the cardinal virtue of gratitude:

> How can we really pay the debt of gratitude we owe to our parents, brothers and
> sisters, teachers, and those who have served us in so many ways? How can we show
> appreciation for good homes, husbands and wives who are true and faithful, chil-
> dren who have the desire to live righteously and serve the Lord? How do we express
> thankfulness for our baptisms, for the privilege of partaking of the sacrament and
> renewing our covenants, for the priesthood we bear, for the light of the restored
> gospel, for the program of the Church devised to help us make progress toward exal-
> tation and eternal life?
>
> We pay our debt of gratitude by living in such a way as to bring credit to our
> parents and the name we bear, by doing good to others, by being of service, by being
> willing to share the light and knowledge we have received so that others will also have
> joy and happiness, by living the principles of the gospel in their fulness. Paul told us
> we should be filled with the Spirit, "giving thanks always for all things unto God and
> the Father in the name of our Lord Jesus Christ" (Eph. 5:20). (*THWH,* 93)

Gratitude

There is joy in cultivating gratitude on a grand scale, even for the smallest deeds of
goodness. Our Father in Heaven is grateful when we are gratefully living up to our
covenants and placing ourselves in the position of hearing His words: "Well done,
thou good and faithful servant: thou hast been faithful over a few things, I will make
thee ruler over many things: enter thou into the joy of thy lord" (Matt. 25:21).

Joseph Smith was an admirable exemplar of being grateful. On December 10,
1835, a number of brethren met to participate in a service project: chopping and
hauling a supply of wood to carry the Prophet's family through the winter. Joseph
Smith was deeply grateful for this Christian gesture. Note the scope of the blessing he
gives to these men:

> In the name of Jesus Christ I invoke the rich benediction of heaven to rest upon
> them and their families; and I ask my heavenly Father to preserve their health, and
> that of their wives and children, that they may have strength of body to perform
> their labors in their several occupations in life, and the use and activity of their

limbs, also powers of intellect and understanding hearts, that they may treasure up wisdom, understanding and intelligence above measure, and be preserved from plagues, pestilence, and famine, and from the power of the adversary, and the hands of evil-designing men, and have power over all their enemies, and the way be prepared for them that they may journey to the land of Zion, and be established on their inheritances, to enjoy undisturbed peace and happiness forever, and ultimately be crowned with everlasting life in the celestial Kingdom of God. (*HC* 2:328–29)

The Prophet remembers Leonard Rich, who had conceived the idea of the service project, with special favor: "And I shall ever remember him with much gratitude, for this testimony of benevolence and respect, and thank the great I AM for putting into his heart to do me this kindness" (329).

All of this for chopping and hauling firewood for a man of God! Similarly, our Father in Heaven bestows blessings upon our heads in infinite measure as compared with the modest contribution He asks of us. How grateful we should be for His loving-kindness. [Allen]

LIKENING THE SCRIPTURES TO OUR LIVES

Ephesians 5:20 Giving thanks always for all things unto God and the Father in the name of our Lord Jesus Christ.

Application: We should always give thanks to our Heavenly Father. Nothing offends God so much as not showing gratitude (see D&C 59:21), and this includes thankfulness for all things that we receive here upon the earth (see Alma 7:23).

4. LET US INCREASE OUR FAITH

THEME: We should seek to increase our faith in the Lord Jesus Christ, for it is through the power of faith that all will be accomplished for our salvation and the salvation of our families.

MOMENT OF TRUTH

When the Apostles said to the Savior one day, "Lord, increase our faith" (Luke 17:5), He drew their attention to a mustard seed: "If ye had faith as a grain of mustard seed, ye might say unto this sycamine tree, Be thou plucked up by the root, and be thou planted in the sea; and it should obey you" (Luke 17:6). At the same time, the Lord reminded them to cultivate unceasing devotion and to honor their duty willingly, humbly, and indefatigably: "When ye shall have done all those things which are commanded you, say, We are unprofitable servants: we have done that which was our duty to do" (Luke 17:10).

That is the essence of how to increase one's faith—a message delivered also by King Benjamin to his subjects in this manner:

> I say unto you, my brethren, that if you should render all the thanks and praise which your whole soul has power to possess, to that God who has created you, and has kept and preserved you, and has caused that ye should rejoice, and has granted that ye should live in peace one with another—
>
> I say unto you that if ye should serve him who has created you from the beginning, and is preserving you from day to day, by lending you breath, that ye may live and move and do according to your own will, and even supporting you from one moment to another—I say, if ye should serve him with all your whole souls yet ye would be unprofitable servants.
>
> And behold, all that he requires of you is to keep his commandments; and he has promised you that if ye would keep his commandments ye should prosper in the land; and he never doth vary from that which he hath said; therefore, if ye do keep his commandments he doth bless you and prosper you. (Mosiah 2:20–22)

MODERN PROPHETS SPEAK

Ezra Taft Benson:
> Now let me describe to you what faith in Jesus Christ means. Faith in Him is more than mere acknowledgment that He lives. It is more than professing belief. Faith in Jesus Christ consists of complete reliance on Him. As God, He has infinite power, intelligence, and love. There is no human problem beyond His capacity to solve. Because He descended below all things, He knows how to help us rise above our daily difficulties. (*TETB*, 66)

ILLUSTRATIONS FOR OUR TIME

Faith and Miracles
We sometimes forget the great power of faith. We fail to exercise it according to the will of God. This great example from the life of Wilford Woodruff reminds us that miracles only cease when we fail to exercise our faith. He records:

> December 3rd found my wife very low. I spent the day in taking care of her, and the following day I returned to Eaton to get some things for her. She seemed to be gradually sinking and in the evening her spirit apparently left her body, and she was dead.

The sisters gathered around her body, weeping, while I stood looking at her in sorrow. The spirit and power of God began to rest upon me until, for the first time during her sickness, faith filled my soul, although she lay before me as one dead.

I had some oil that was consecrated for my anointing while in Kirtland. I took it and consecrated it again before the Lord for anointing the sick. I then bowed down before the Lord and prayed for the life of my companion, and I anointed her body with the oil in the name of the Lord. I laid my hands upon her, and in the name of Jesus Christ I rebuked the power of death and the destroyer, and commanded the same to depart from her, and the spirit of life to enter her body.

Her spirit returned to her body, and from that hour she was made whole; and we all felt to praise the name of God, and to trust in Him and to keep His commandments.

While this operation was going on with me (as my wife related afterwards) her spirit left her body, and she saw it lying upon the bed, and the sisters weeping. She looked at them and at me, and upon her babe, and, while gazing upon this scene, two personages came into the room carrying a coffin and told her they had come for her body. One of these messengers informed her that she could have her choice: she might go to rest in the spirit world, or, on one condition she could have the privilege of returning to her tabernacle and continuing her labors upon the earth. The condition was, if she felt that she could stand by her husband, and with him pass through all the cares, trials, tribulation and afflictions of life which he would be called to pass through for the gospel's sake unto the end. When she looked at the situation of her husband and child she said: "Yes, I will do it!"

At the moment that decision was made the power of faith rested upon me, and when I administered unto her, her spirit entered her tabernacle, and she saw the messengers carry the coffin out at the door. (*Leaves from My Journal* [Salt Lake City: Juvenile Instructor's Office, 1882])

LIKENING THE SCRIPTURES TO OUR LIVES

Luke 17:5 And the apostles said unto the Lord, Increase our faith.

Application: If the Apostles of the Lord needed an increase in faith, oh, how much more do we need faith in our lives. If we search the scriptures (Rom. 10:17) and fast and pray (Hel. 3:35), our faith will increase.

SUMMARY

What transcendent lessons are to be gleaned from a prayerful study of the New Testament—that the worth of souls is great in the sight of God, that the heavens rejoice over a repentant soul, that we should continually express gratitude for blessings and miracles in our lives, and that we can bring immortality and eternal light in view as we increase our faith and honor our sacred covenants before the Lord. Let us, in turn, share such truths with others in the spirit of charity and service—especially those who are not yet in the fold or who may have strayed from the course at present—for great will be our joy with them in the hereafter. As Alma expressed in his supplication: "O Lord, wilt thou grant unto us that we may have success in bringing them again unto thee in Christ. Behold, O Lord, their souls are precious, and many of them are our brethren; therefore, give unto us, O Lord, power and wisdom that we may bring these, our brethren, again unto thee" (Alma 31:34–35; compare Mosiah 26:30–31; D&C 58:42–43). In the spirit of gratitude for the Lord's blessings, let us proclaim with Ammon: "Therefore, let us glory, yea, we will glory in the Lord; yea, we will rejoice, for our joy is full; yea, we will praise our God forever. Behold, who can glory too much in the Lord? Yea, who can say too much of his great power, and of his mercy, and of his long-suffering towards the children of men? Behold, I say unto you, I cannot say the smallest part which I feel" (Alma 26:16).

CHAPTER 19

"THY FAITH HATH SAVED THEE"

Reading Assignment: Luke 18:1–8, 35–43; 19:1–10; John 11.

Additional Reading: Mark 10:46–52; Luke 11:5–13; 2 Timothy 4:7; Colossians 3:12–14; Ether 3:3–13; D&C 101:81–93; Bible Dictionary, "Faith" (669–670).

Thank God for the life and ministry of the Master, Jesus the Christ, who broke the bonds of death, who is the light and life of the world, who set the pattern, who established the guidelines for all of us, and who proclaimed: "I am the resurrection, and the life: he that believeth in me, though he were dead, yet shall he live: And whosoever liveth and believeth in me shall never die" (John 11:25–26).

Yes, life is eternal. We live on and on after earth life, even though we ofttimes lose sight of that great basic truth. . . .

This is but a place of temporary duration. We are here to learn the first lesson toward exaltation—obedience to the Lord's gospel plan.

There is the ever-present expectancy of death, but in reality there is no death—no permanent parting. The resurrection is a reality. The scriptures are replete with evidence.

—Ezra Taft Benson, "Life is Eternal," *Ensign,* Aug. 1991, 2.

THEMES *for* LIVING

1. Always Pray in Faith Without Ceasing
2. Faith Leads to Life Eternal
3. Maintaining an Attitude of Kindness Toward Everyone

INTRODUCTION

Because of his great faith, the Brother of Jared could not be excluded from the presence of the premortal Savior, who declared unto him: "Behold, I am he who was prepared from the foundation of the world to redeem my people. Behold, I am Jesus Christ. I am the Father and the Son. In me shall all mankind have life, and that eternally, even they who shall believe on my name; and they shall become my sons and my daughters" (Ether 3:14). During His mortal ministry, the Savior continued to teach this consistent theme: faith unto eternal life for those who believe in Him and practice obedience, prayerful humility, and charity to all. He reached out in love as a hen gathers her chicks beneath her wings. He healed the sick and raised the dead to life. He was kind and gracious to all—even to His enemies. He left us a legacy of life-giving charity in action. We observe in the sacred scriptures of the New Testament the power of God at work to bring about the immortality and eternal life of man (Moses 1:39). Who is not touched by these accounts and stimulated to be a little kinder, to be a little more faithful and obedient, and to follow a little more closely in the Master's footsteps? Who is not reminded in his or her heart: "Ask, and it shall be given you; seek, and ye shall find; knock, and it shall be opened unto you. For every one that asketh receiveth; and he that seeketh findeth; and to him that knocketh it shall be opened" (Luke 11:9–10; compare Matt. 7:7–8).

1. ALWAYS PRAY IN FAITH WITHOUT CEASING

THEME: Our Father in Heaven hears our faithful supplications—even when some among our judges and magistrates turn a deaf ear. The Lord said, "Now, unto what shall I liken the children of Zion? I will liken them unto the parable of the woman and the unjust judge, for men ought always to pray and not to faint" (D&C 101:81).

MOMENT OF TRUTH

During the Savior's ministry, His followers learned the painful lesson that their freedom of religious choice and persuasion was often contravened by the actions and judgments of the authorities and rulers. To place such adversity into the eternal context and entreat the people to persist in their prayers unto the Most High, the Savior told His followers the parable of the unjust judge (Luke 18:1–8)—"to this end, that men ought always to pray, and not to faint" (Luke 18:1). Robert J. Matthews provides a succinct summary of the story:

> This parable was spoken to the disciples to teach them diligence and perseverance.
> It tells of a judge who has the power to help a poor widow but is not concerned for

her plight. After much importuning on her part, the judge responds because he is weary with her persistent pleas. The parable was restated in the Doctrine and Covenants (101:81–85) with application to the Saints in the 1830s seeking legal redress for loss of property by mob action in Missouri. (*Behold the Messiah* [Salt Lake City: Bookcraft, 1994], 178)

The Savior's message is summarized in His interpretation of the parable: "And shall not God avenge his own elect, which cry day and night unto him, though he bear long with them? I tell you that he will avenge them speedily. Nevertheless when the Son of man cometh, shall he find faith on the earth?" (Luke 18:7–8).

MODERN PROPHETS SPEAK

Jeffrey R. Holland:

> Many have wondered how one can pray without ceasing in a way that does not "multiply words." The key is that if our desire to communicate is great enough, we will be given what we should say. Furthermore, the Holy Ghost will intercede in our behalf, aiding in the communication of our hearts even if words seem to fail us. "The Spirit also helpeth our infirmities," Paul taught, "for we know not what we should pray for as we ought: but the Spirit itself maketh intercession for us with groanings which cannot be uttered." Urgency and desire coupled with divine promptings preclude any shallow multiplication of words in prayer. (*Christ and the New Covenant: The Messianic Message of the Book of Mormon* [Salt Lake City: Deseret Book, 1997], 280)

ILLUSTRATIONS FOR OUR TIME

Bruce R. McConkie has provided a rich source of understanding and enlightenment concerning the parable of the unjust judge. He explained:

> Prayers are answered and proper petitions granted whenever sufficient faith is exercised (3 Ne. 18:20; Moro. 7:26). Faith is the power which brings answers to prayers, and prayers are effective only when offered in faith. The mere recitation of words in prayers means little unless such are uttered with real intent and are accompanied by an honest, heartfelt, sincere desire and hope that the blessings sought shall be granted (Moro. 7:6–9). And faith itself—the power which brings answers to prayers—is increased through the spiritual communion that attends true prayer. . . .
>
> Accordingly, in this parable we find Jesus teaching the saints that when their cause is just, the Lord expects them to continue in importunate, determined, and persevering prayer—day after day, year after year, as long as they live. By such a course they strengthen their own faith and so attain the desired blessings. (*DNTC*, 1:542)

LIKENING THE SCRIPTURES TO OUR LIVES

Mosiah 26:39 And they did admonish their brethren; and they were also admonished, every one by the word of God, according to his sins, or to the sins which he had committed, being commanded of God to pray without ceasing, and to give thanks in all things.

Application: It is a commandment to pray without ceasing (see 1 Thess. 5:17–18), for we can do nothing that is good without God, for all good cometh of God (see Alma 5:40; Moro. 7:12–13, 22).

2. FAITH LEADS TO LIFE ETERNAL

THEME: Whether to be healed or raised from the dead—it is by faith, according to the will of God, that the power of God is manifested to His children here upon the earth.

MOMENT OF TRUTH

So munificent is the compassion of the Savior that the sheer number of miraculous healings brought about through His interventions becomes overwhelming. One can scarcely keep track of the number of blessings He bestowed to restore the blind to sight, the lame to mobility, and the deaf to hearing. Yet each event is a unique witness that stands out like a beacon in the night to attest to the glory and love of the Savior. On one occasion, the Savior and His disciples visited Jericho. On their way out of the city, accompanied by a large throng of people, they passed by a blind man, Bartimaeus by name, son of Timaeus, who was sitting at the side of the highway, begging. When Bartimaeus heard the noise of the entourage and learned that the Savior was there, he cried out, "Jesus, thou son of David, have mercy on me" (Mark 10:47), not heeding the attempts of the crowd to restrain him. When he was brought before the Savior, the following transpired: "And Jesus answered and said unto him, What wilt thou that I should do unto thee? The blind man said unto him, Lord, that I might receive my sight. And Jesus said unto him, Go thy way; thy faith hath made thee whole. And immediately he received his sight, and followed Jesus in the way" (Mark 10:51–52; compare the account in Luke 18:35–43).

As dramatic as this event was, the raising of Lazarus, as given in John 11, represents a light of even greater magnitude. Lazarus was the brother of Mary and Martha, hence close to the Savior's inner circle of followers. When the sisters summoned Jesus to Bethany, near Jerusalem, on behalf of their ailing brother, He was slow in responding, as if to foster increased faith in these people whom He loved (John 11:5). Lazarus passed away before the Savior was on scene, and Martha expressed her anguish that her brother might have been spared if divine attention had been accessible at his bedside more promptly. To this, the Savior responded with words that have become a glorious maxim of gospel truth: "I am the resurrection, and the life: he that believeth in me, though he were dead, yet shall he live: And whosoever liveth and believeth in me shall never die" (John 11:25–26).

When the Savior then asked Martha, "Believest thou this?" she confirmed her faith and sent for Mary, with whom the scene was repeated: anguish over the late arrival of the Master, and the Master's rising in majesty as the Giver and Preserver of life. It was a scene of ultimate contrasts: the inconsolable weeping of the bereaved, accompanied by the inner groanings and outer weeping of the Savior Himself, and then the majestic act of calling Lazarus forth from the grave, accompanied by the all-consuming joy and inexpressible rapture of the family of the faithful. A side note of great meaning is the wording of the prayer of Jesus prior to the enlivening of Lazarus: "And Jesus lifted up his eyes, and said, Father, I thank thee that thou hast heard me. And I knew that thou hearest me always: but because of the people which stand by I said it, that they may believe that thou hast sent me" (John 11:41–42). The entire episode was a witness of the power of God in blessing the lives of the people.

MODERN PROPHETS SPEAK

President Thomas S. Monson recounts the following story about the power of faith and love in the life of a young man:

> Some years ago there went to his eternal reward one of the kindest and most loved men to grace the earth. I speak of Louis C. Jacobsen. He ministered to those in need, he helped the immigrant to find employment, and he delivered more sermons at more funeral services than any other person I have known.
>
> One day while in a reflective mood, Louis Jacobsen told me of his boyhood. He was the son of a poor Danish widow. He was small in stature, not comely in appearance—easily the object of his classmates' thoughtless jokes. In Sunday School one Sabbath morning, the children made light of his patched trousers and his worn shirt. Too proud to cry, tiny Louis fled from the chapel, stopping at last, out of breath, to sit and rest on the curb that ran along Third West Street in Salt Lake City. Clear water flowed along the gutter next to the curb where Louis sat. From his pocket he took a piece of paper that contained the outlined Sunday School lesson and skillfully shaped a paper boat, which he launched on the flowing water. From his hurt boyish heart came the determined words, "I'll never go back."

Suddenly, through his tears Louis saw reflected in the water the image of a large and well-dressed man. Louis turned his face upward and recognized George Burbidge, the Sunday School superintendent. "May I sit down with you?" asked the kind leader. Louis nodded affirmatively. There on the gutter's curb sat a good Samaritan ministering to one who surely was in need. Several boats were formed and launched while the conversation continued. At last the leader stood and, with a boy's hand tightly clutching his, they returned to Sunday School. Later Louis himself presided over that same Sunday School. Throughout his long life of service, he never failed to acknowledge the traveler who rescued him along a Jericho Road. (Thomas S. Monson, *Be Your Best Self* [Salt Lake City: Deseret Book, 1979], 155–56)

LIKENING THE SCRIPTURES TO OUR LIVES

John 11:40–43 Jesus saith unto her, Said I not unto thee, that, if thou wouldest believe, thou shouldest see the glory of God? Then they took away the stone from the place where the dead was laid. And Jesus lifted up his eyes, and said, Father, I thank thee that thou hast heard me. And I knew that thou hearest me always: but because of the people which stand by I said it, that they may believe that thou hast sent me. And when he thus had spoken, he cried with a loud voice, Lazarus, come forth.

Application: The power of God is manifested to those who believe, showing that the Lord is truly in control of all things—thus increasing our faith and confidence in the power and goodness of God.

3. MAINTAINING AN ATTITUDE OF KINDNESS TOWARD EVERYONE

THEME: Treat everyone with kindness regardless of position, title, possessions, or appearance.

MOMENT OF TRUTH

The publicans—those who collected and dealt with tax revenues—were detested by the Jews and cut off from mainstream worship. Yet the publicans were often among those who most readily accepted the gospel of Jesus Christ. A good case in point is the story of Zacchaeus, the wealthy chief of the publicans in Jericho, as given in Luke 19:1–10. Because of his small stature, Zacchaeus could not catch sight of Jesus among the throng as He was passing through the city, so he mounted a sycamore tree to gain a clear perspective of the Savior. When Jesus observed him high in the tree, He bid him descend and informed him, much to his joy, that he was to host the Savior in his home that day. The observers took offense at this social connection, arguing that Jesus was consorting with a sinner. But Zacchaeus proved to be an accommodating host, for he gave a report to the Savior of his generous and honorable pattern of life and heard the comforting words: "This day is salvation come to this house, forsomuch as he also is a son of Abraham. For the Son of man is come to seek and to save that which was lost" (Luke 19:9–10). In a similar way, all of us are counseled to deal with our colleagues in kindly and gracious ways, for all are sons and daughters of God. If people importune us for charitable assistance, we should follow the example of the Lord and be generous in our giving (see Luke 11:5–13).

MODERN PROPHETS SPEAK

Joseph Smith:

> Nothing is so much calculated to lead people to forsake sin as to take them by the hand, and watch over them with tenderness. When persons manifest the least kindness and love to me, O what power it has over my mind, while the opposite course has a tendency to harrow up all the harsh feelings and depress the human mind. (*HC* 5:23–24)

Gordon B. Hinckley:

> Let us as Latter-day Saints cultivate a spirit of brotherhood in all of our associations. Let us be more charitable in our judgments, more sympathetic and understanding of those who err, more willing to forgive those who trespass against us. Let us not add to the measure of hatred that periodically sweeps across the world. Let us reach out in kindness to all men, even toward those who speak evil of us and who would, if they could, harm us. (*TGBH,* 661)

ILLUSTRATIONS FOR OUR TIME

"The Virtue of Kindness"

> When we are filled with kindness, we are not judgmental. The Savior taught, "Judge not, and ye shall not be judged: condemn not, and ye shall not be condemned: forgive, and ye shall be forgiven" (Luke 6:37). He also taught that "with what judgment ye judge, ye shall be judged: and with what measure ye mete, it shall be measured to you again" (Matt. 7:2).
>
> "But," you ask, "what if people are rude?"
>
> Love them.
>
> "If they are obnoxious?"

Love them.

"But what if they offend? Surely I must do something then?"

Love them.

"Wayward?"

The answer is the same. Be kind. Love them.

Why? In the scriptures Jude taught, "And of some have compassion, making a difference" (Jude 1:22).

Who can tell what far-reaching impact we can have if we are only kind?

My brothers and sisters, the gospel of Jesus Christ transcends mortality. Our work here is but a shadow of greater and unimaginable things to come.

The heavens opened to the Prophet Joseph Smith. He saw the living God and His Son, Jesus the Christ.

In our day, a prophet, President Gordon B. Hinckley, walks the earth and provides direction for our time.

As our Heavenly Father loves us, we also should love His children. (Joseph B. Wirthlin, "The Virtue of Kindness," *Ensign,* May 2005, 26)

LIKENING THE SCRIPTURES TO OUR LIVES

Colossians 3:12–14 Put on therefore, as the elect of God, holy and beloved, bowels of mercies, kindness, humbleness of mind, meekness, longsuffering; Forbearing one another, and forgiving one another, if any man have a quarrel against any: even as Christ forgave you, so also do ye. And above all these things put on charity, which is the bond of perfectness.

Application: The power of the pure love of Christ never fails, for when we have it, we will be kind, compassionate, forgiving, and nonjudgmental. Oh, that we might pray with all the energy of our hearts for this precious gift (see Moro. 7:48).

SUMMARY

This continuing chronicle of the Lord's mortal sojourn provides a refreshing repast of the bread of life and the quenching living waters of truth so essential to sustain us in our mortal journey. We learn that great blessings flow to us when we pray in faith without ceasing, for faith leads to eternal life (see Ether 3:14)—so long as we keep the commandments and maintain a pattern of charity and kindness toward all. Just as the Savior raised Lazarus from the dead, He can raise us up to a new life of spiritual enlightenment and righteousness. From the higher perspective, we can imagine the moment in time when we might stand before our Redeemer and say, with Paul, "I have fought a good fight, I have finished my course, I have kept the faith: Henceforth there is laid up for me a crown of righteousness, which the Lord, the righteous judge, shall give me at that day: and not to me only, but unto all them also that love his appearing" (2 Tim. 4:7–8).

CHAPTER 20

LET US STRENGTHEN OUR COMMITMENT *to* JESUS CHRIST *and* AVOID ALL HYPOCRISY

Reading Assignment: Matthew 21–23; John 12:1–8.

Additional Reading: Matthew 26:6–13; Mark 11–12; 14:3–9; Luke 11:37–51; 19:29–48; 20; John 12:12–18; Bible Dictionary, "Pharisees" (750); "Sadducees" (767); "Spikenard" (776); Joshua 24:15; 1 Nephi 3:7; Omni 1:26; D&C 4:1–2; 20:37.

> *This question may appear as a play on the words of the Lord when he said this is the true and living church. When I ask, "Am I a true and living member?" my question is, Am I deeply and fully dedicated to keeping the covenants I have made with the Lord? Am I totally committed to living the gospel and being a doer of the word and not a hearer only? Do I live my religion? Will I remain true? Do I stand firm against Satan's temptations? He is seeking to cause us to lose our way in a storm of derision and a tide of sophistry. We can have victory, however, by responding to that inner voice calling "Stand firm!"*

> —HOWARD W. HUNTER, *THAT WE MIGHT HAVE JOY* [SALT LAKE CITY: DESERET BOOK, 1994], 149.

THEMES *for* LIVING

1. A Symbol of Love and Devotion: Mary Anoints Jesus' Feet
2. Recognize and Accept Jesus as the Christ—The Triumphal Entry into Jerusalem
3. The Parables Teach Commitment to the Lord

4. The Savior Knows Our Hearts

5. How to Avoid the Sin of Hypocrisy

INTRODUCTION

Our commitment and loyalty to the Savior Jesus Christ will help us keep our covenants. Our stalwart devotion will cause us to have in our minds at all times and in all places the teachings and values of the gospel of Jesus Christ. We will act with no hypocrisy and have no guile. We will have the desire to take upon us the divine nature of Christ. We will seek to act and do as the Savior would have us do: "Verily, verily, I say unto you, He that believeth on me, the works that I do shall he do also; and greater works than these shall he do; because I go unto my Father. And whatsoever ye shall ask in my name, that will I do, that the Father may be glorified in the Son" (John 14:12–13).

1. A SYMBOL OF LOVE AND DEVOTION: MARY ANOINTS JESUS' FEET

THEME: The ideal of enduring service to the Lord is reflected throughout the scriptures and reinforced through many symbols of transcendent compassion—such as the anointing of the Savior's feet by Mary. Serving one another within the kingdom is a sign of our love and devotion to the Lord.

MOMENT OF TRUTH

Six days before the time of the Passover, Jesus came to Bethany to participate in a supper at the home of Martha and Mary. Lazarus, whom Jesus had restored to life, was also at the table with them. One can only imagine the feelings of reverence and gratitude in the hearts of the family members. While Martha served, Mary accomplished an act of love and humble thanks toward the Savior: "Then took Mary a pound of ointment of spikenard, very costly, and anointed the feet of Jesus, and wiped his feet with her hair: and the house was filled with the odour of the ointment" (John 12:3). Present also was Judas Iscariot, who objected to the use of such an expensive ointment, which, he maintained, could have been sold to generate revenue for the poor. The Savior's response is instructive: "Let her alone: against the day of my burying hath she kept this. For the poor always ye have with you; but me ye have not always" (John 12:7–8). In the contrast of the two perspectives lies a world of wisdom and insight.

MODERN PROPHETS SPEAK

Howard W. Hunter:

> James then very pointedly defines what he refers to as pure religion, as distinguished from forms of ritualistic worship and iron rules of practice as described by Paul. James said: "Pure religion and undefiled before God and the Father is this, To visit the fatherless and widows in their affliction, and to keep oneself unspotted from the world" (James 1:27). The wording is simple and unpretentious, yet the meaning is profound and has deep significance. The words "visit the fatherless and widows" are a reminder that we should have compassion for our neighbor, our fellowmen. This is the teaching of the Master in his frequent reference to love. The Lord said: "Thou shalt love thy neighbour as thyself" (Matt. 22:39). This is what James was expressing—a love for, and devotion to, God, by compassionate service to fellowmen. (*That We Might Have Joy* [Salt Lake City: Deseret Book, 1994], 160)

ILLUSTRATIONS FOR OUR TIME

Serving Others Is the Joy of Life

When you become a "service oriented" person, life's greatest blessing will come to you—happiness. It is the by-product of the expression of love. As we consider our lives and where we are and what we can do, let us always remember that service is multifaceted and gives one a variety of ways to assist and bless others. Make service your life, and life will serve you well. You will have a life filled with the joy of serving.

This was expressed beautifully by a student after we participated on one occasion as a class in a Christmas project. I thought that I would give them each a dollar so they could multiply their talents. A dollar was worth something in the 70s. "Let's raise some money, and we'll help some of the families that need a Christmas," I suggested. Well, the money was given, and the students went to work. Oh, the money multiplied. Several thousand dollars were raised. We selected a committee to go out and visit the families we had been given to help. The parents were so grateful. The committee went and delivered the wonderful gifts. I asked the chairperson to make a report. She recorded this in her little summary: "I felt so good—love is really serving others. As we did this for these families, my heart began to swell with joy. I just could not believe it—the feeling I felt. Serving and helping others is the joy of life. I'd heard service preached; I'd heard love preached; I'd heard things taught all my life; but I never truly understood it until I participated in this Christmas project. I will never forget the joy of serving others that sometimes cannot help themselves." [Pinegar]

Icon of Charity

The tender scene of Mary anointing the feet of Jesus and wiping them with her hair (John 12:7–8) has become an enduring symbol of charity and reverence. What other icons of charity prevail in our minds and hearts? Perhaps, most personally, the image of one's own mother rises in prominence as a living reminder of what charity and sacrifice truly mean.

One of the rare jewels in my library is a small maroon binder containing reminiscences about my mother. The collection was compiled by one of her thoughtful friends and coworkers in the Church and community. Mother passed away giving birth to my younger brother when I was ten, and these 47 letters from friends and associates, recounting stories about her remarkable character and charitable service, have preserved for her three children the priceless memory of this noble woman's exemplary accomplishments as viewed by those who knew her best. In the colorful panorama of fleeting recollections and vignettes is captured the essence of a life that reflected the spirit of joy, harmony, compassion, and pure friendship. The image thus restored has become for me an icon of charity that serves as an invitation to emulate the quality of service so central to a life centered on Christ.

One statement in the collection, written by a coworker on the Stake Primary and Sunday School Boards, summarizes with particular poignancy the essence of my mother's pattern of life: "Some people are satisfied if they are happy. Others are concerned with the happiness of friends and relatives. A few are anxious to find the stranger or lonely person and make them happy too. Your mother belonged to this last group."

Perhaps only one other icon of charity exceeds in radiance the image of motherhood, and that would be the image of the risen Lord, resplendent in His victory over death following the great and final atoning sacrifice on behalf of all mankind. "Behold, I am Jesus Christ, whom the prophets testified shall come into the world. And behold, I am the light and the life of the world; and I have drunk out of that bitter cup which the Father hath given me, and have glorified the Father in taking upon me the sins of the world, in the which I have suffered the will of the Father in all things from the beginning" (3 Ne. 11:10–11). The Savior is charity incarnate. Mothers are next in line—for they verily place their lives at risk in bringing forth life as part of Heavenly Father's plan. My own mother gave her life in this service on behalf of a choice new child. The last person she ever spoke to at the hospital that day wrote: "We were both at the hospital together where our babies were born. . . . That morning she had been so very sweet and kind to me by insisting that I sit down by her and she fixed my hair very nice. She came in my room after dinner and sat and we talked and laughed together for a long time. Then she was taken in to the case room, and soon a little new life was here on earth, but Amy had been called home."

Such was also the pattern of the Savior, but in universal scope, for He gave His life that all might live. Let us in gratitude follow the icon of charity down pathways leading to joy and eternal life. [Allen]

LIKENING THE SCRIPTURES TO OUR LIVES

Mosiah 21:35 They were desirous to be baptized as a witness and a testimony that they were willing to serve God with all their hearts.

Application: Let us always remember that we have made a covenant to serve God with all our hearts. This means we serve our fellowmen as well (see Mosiah 2:17).

2. RECOGNIZE AND ACCEPT JESUS AS THE CHRIST—THE TRIUMPHAL ENTRY INTO JERUSALEM

THEME: Recognizing our Savior is not enough. We must accept Him as our Savior, take His name upon us, and keep His commandments.

MOMENT OF TRUTH

Over five hundred years prior to the coming of the Lord in the meridian of time, the Prophet Zechariah proclaimed: "Rejoice greatly, O daughter of Zion; shout, O daughter of Jerusalem: behold, thy King cometh unto thee: he is just, and having salvation; lowly, and riding upon an ass, and upon a colt the foal of an ass" (Zech. 9:9). That same ass and her colt—envisioned by the prophet—were waiting in the village of Bethphage as the Savior approached with His disciples on the day of His entry into Jerusalem. The Savior sent two disciples to retrieve the animals, and, in fulfillment of the prophecy, He rode in triumph upon the animals amidst the exultation and praise of the multitude, who were strewing branches and clothing along the way in celebration of the entry, crying: "Hosanna to the Son of David: Blessed is he that cometh in the name of the Lord; Hosanna in the highest" (Matt. 21:9). All of Jerusalem was moved by the procession, saying: "Who is this? And the multitude said, This is Jesus the prophet of Nazareth of Galilee" (Matt. 21:11).

As we were preparing this "Moment of Truth," we asked ourselves the question: Was the Savior's entry into Jerusalem "triumphal" or was it "triumphant"? Each term implies something a little different, the first referring exclusively to the celebration of an actual victory, the latter, a more general term, referring to a triumph in any of its senses, such as a brilliant success or exultation (H. W. Fowler, *A Dictionary of Modern*

English Usage, 2nd ed. rev. [New York and Oxford: Oxford University Press, 1965], 649). In fact, we decided that the Savior's entry was *both.* It was a *triumphal* entry (the word we have used in the title to this section) because it represented an actual victory of the forces of divine truth over the calcified traditions of those who were not prepared for the higher law. Although the immediate fight was to be lost—with the Savior's imminent crucifixion and death—the long-term battle for the victory of life over death was soon to be celebrated—an authentic triumphal victory. At the same time, the Savior's entry into Jerusalem that day was also a *triumphant* entry because it foreshadowed the brilliant success of the next phase of the divine plan of salvation, a plan that evoked among the believers both joy and exultation, albeit on the way to Calvary. The Father knows all, and He knew that His Only Begotten Son would soon fulfill the divine will by bringing about the Atonement—the *triumphal* and *triumphant* victory of the forces of light and truth. With the Savior's entry into Jerusalem that day, the stage was set, and the inexorable outcomes of God's design were about to be realized.

MODERN PROPHETS SPEAK

Ezra Taft Benson:
> As members of The Church of Jesus Christ of Latter-day Saints, we need to place unreserved confidence in the Lord Jesus Christ, whom we accept as the Son of God. Until the world accepts Him as the Savior of mankind, lives His teachings, and looks to Him as the *Way,* the *Truth,* and the *Life* in all phases of our lives, we shall continue in our anxiety about the future and our ability to cope with the challenges that mortality brings to each of us. ("Jesus Christ: Our Savior and Redeemer," *Ensign,* Nov. 1983, 6)

ILLUSTRATIONS FOR OUR TIME

To receive all the blessings our Heavenly Father has for us depends upon our willingness to accept Jesus as the Christ, the Savior and Redeemer of all mankind, and follow Him in all things. In this connection, Joseph Fielding Smith taught the following:

> If it be true Christianity to accept Jesus Christ in person and in mission as divine; to revere Him as the Son of God, the crucified and risen Lord, through whom alone can mankind attain salvation; to accept His teachings as a guide, to adopt as a standard and observe as a law the ethical code He promulgated; to comply with the requirements prescribed by Him as essential to membership in His Church, namely, faith, repentance, baptism by immersion for the remission of sins, and the laying on of hands for the gift of the Holy Ghost,—if this be Christianity, then are we

Christians, and the Church of Jesus Christ of Latter-day Saints is a Christian Church. (*Life of Joseph F. Smith* [Salt Lake City: Deseret Book, 1969], 382–83)

LIKENING THE SCRIPTURES TO OUR LIVES

3 Nephi 5:26 And then shall they know their Redeemer, who is Jesus Christ, the Son of God; and then shall they be gathered in from the four quarters of the earth unto their own lands, from whence they have been dispersed; yea, as the Lord liveth so shall it be.

Application: Let us all come to know that Jesus is the Son of God, the Great Redeemer—and let every tongue confess that Jesus is the Christ (see Phil. 2:11).

3. THE PARABLES TEACH COMMITMENT TO THE LORD

THEME: The Lord has made clear what our work in life is to be: "Behold, this is your work, to keep my commandments, yea, with all your might, mind and strength" (D&C 11:20). Therefore, we are to do all in our power to strengthen our commitment to our covenants with the Lord.

MOMENT OF TRUTH

The chief priests of the temple came to the Savior while He was teaching and asked Him, "By what authority doest thou these things, and who gave thee this authority?" (Matt. 21:23). Discerning their deceitful and cunning strategy, the Savior responded that He would answer their question if they would first tell him whether the baptism of John the Baptist was from heaven or of men. Thus were the chief priests silenced, for if they were to answer "from heaven," then they could be held accountable for not believing John; but if they were to say "of men," the people would revolt, for they believed that John was a prophet. To seal His witness of the truth, the Savior then told a parable about two sons whose father wanted to send them into the vineyard to work. The first declined, "but afterward he repented, and went" (Matt. 21:29). The second agreed to go, but then neglected to do so. "Whether of them twain did the will of his father?" asked the Savior (Matt. 21:31). They responded (as logic demanded) that the first son did the will of the father. At that point, the Savior, having established the correctness of His position, could issue His call to repentance: "Verily I say unto you, That the publicans and the harlots go into the kingdom of God before you. For John came unto you in the way of righteousness, and ye believed him not: but the publicans and the harlots believed him: and ye, when ye had seen it, repented not afterward, that ye might believe him" (Matt. 21:31–32; compare also the fuller JST, rendering of this passage).

Using a parable with similar implications, the Savior then spoke to His detractors about a certain householder who left his vineyard in the hands of a husbandman and went to a distant country. The householder proved to be a master of malfeasance and insubordination, even stooping so low as to kill the householder's servants and his very son when they were dispatched to obtain an accounting of the business. When the Savior asked what the householder would do under such circumstances, the chief priests responded that he would destroy his enemies. Then came the Lord's bold message: "Did ye never read in the scriptures, The stone which the builders rejected, the same is become the head of the corner: this is the Lord's doing, and it is marvellous in our eyes? Therefore say I unto you, The kingdom of God shall be taken from you, and given to a nation bringing forth the fruits thereof. And whosoever shall fall on this stone shall be broken: but on whomsoever it shall fall, it will grind him to powder" (Matt. 21:42–44). Then the chief priests and Pharisees finally perceived that the Savior was speaking about them—but they dared not raise their hand against Him yet, for the people perceived Him to be a prophet of God.

MODERN PROPHETS SPEAK

W. Mack Lawrence:
> As I have pondered this and prayed about it, I have concluded that the problem lies in a lack of conversion and commitment: *conversion* to Christ, His gospel, and His Church; and, subsequently, *commitment* to the covenants and individual callings one may have received to serve and strengthen others. In this regard, it is of interest to consider Christ's words to Peter: When thou art converted, strengthen thy brethren (Luke 22:32). Thus, commitment seems to be an outgrowth or fruit of conversion. ("Conversion and Commitment," *Ensign,* May 1996, 74)

ILLUSTRATIONS FOR OUR TIME

The Doctrine of Remembering
We change no faster than we make and keep commitments. The Lord uses this principle as we enter into sacred covenants and receive life-saving ordinances that can bring us back into the presence of God—if we but keep the covenants. The Lord assists us in this process by having us renew our covenants weekly as we partake of the sacrament. This helps us to remember our Savior always and keep in mind continually all that He has done for us.

Spencer W. Kimball stated, "When you look in the dictionary for the most important word, do you know what it is? . . . 'Remember' is the word" ("Circles of Exaltation," [Address to religious educators, BYU, 28 June 1968], 8)

Remembering is a dynamic spiritual process of bringing key things to mind on a continual basis in order to cultivate "a godly walk and conversation" (D&C 20:69). To *remember* is to align oneself with the will of God in order to become, on a daily basis, more and more like Him. Thoughts lead to action; thus remembering in a faithful and obedient way leads to living in a faithful and obedient way. The power to remember becomes integral to keeping our commitments and promises to the Lord by keeping the commandments, thus qualifying to have His Spirit to be with us always. It is the Spirit that will help us keep our commitments to our covenants. [Pinegar]

LIKENING THE SCRIPTURES TO OUR LIVES

Alma 46:21 And it came to pass that when Moroni had proclaimed these words, behold, the people came running together with their armor girded about their loins, rending their garments in token, or as a covenant, that they would not forsake the Lord their God; or, in other words, if they should transgress the commandments of God, or fall into transgression, and be ashamed to take upon them the name of Christ, the Lord should rend them even as they had rent their garments.

Application: We, like the Nephites, should commit never to forsake the Lord. We should not be ashamed of the gospel of Jesus Christ (see Rom. 1:16). We should renew our covenants by partaking of the sacrament and remain steadfast to the end of our lives (see 2 Ne. 31:20; Mosiah 4:6).

4. THE SAVIOR KNOWS OUR HEARTS

THEME: The Savior knows our thoughts and the desires of our hearts. He cannot be deceived. We should live our lives in such a way that we would be pleased to have the Lord behold what we write upon the tablets of our hearts and minds day by day.

MOMENT OF TRUTH

As the Lord continued to teach the truth to the Jewish priests and leaders who were seeking to entrap Him, He told them the parable of the marriage feast. A king had organized the feast in honor of his son. When the invited guests, without exception, found reason not to attend, and even slew his servants, the king sent his armies forth to destroy the disloyal friends and then gathered instead other guests from the highways. One of the guests who turned up was banished to outer darkness, for he did not have on the prescribed wedding garment. The Savior concluded: "For many are called, but few are chosen" (Matt. 22:14). And the Joseph Smith Translation adds the words:

"wherefore all do not have on the wedding garment." The message was all too clear to the hypocritical listeners: though called to service, they were clearly not to be considered chosen on the basis of obedience and honoring the commandments.

Not deterred by the Lord's unassailable mastery of logic and reasoning, the Pharisees sought to entangle Him in a political quagmire with a no-win outcome. "Is it lawful to give tribute unto Caesar, or not?" they asked Him (Matt. 22:17). Then the Savior called their bluff in the majesty of divine discourse by displaying a coin with Caesar's image and proclaiming: "Render therefore unto Caesar the things which are Caesar's; and unto God the things that are God's" (Matt. 22:21). The Sadducees, likewise, were rendered speechless by the Lord's overpowering preachments concerning marriage (Matt. 22:23–33), as were the Pharisees when one of them, a lawyer, further questioned the Savior, "Master, which is the great commandment in the law?" (Matt. 22:36). He responded, "Thou shalt love the Lord thy God with all thy heart, and with all thy soul, and with all thy mind. This is the first and great commandment. And the second is like unto it, Thou shalt love thy neighbour as thyself" (Matt. 22:37–39). No matter how they tried to entrap Him, He skillfully slipped through their snares on the basis of His perfect knowledge of the scriptures and His inspired rhetoric. For that reason, no man from that day onward dared to ask Him any further questions (Matt. 22:46).

MODERN PROPHETS SPEAK

Dallin H. Oaks:

> The Savior told the Pharisees, "God knoweth your hearts" (Luke 16:15). Paul warned the Hebrews that God "is a discerner of the thoughts and intents of the heart," and that "all things are naked and opened unto the eyes of him with whom we have to do" (Heb. 4:12–13; see also 1 Cor. 4:5). Ammon taught his people that God "knows all the thoughts and intents of the heart; for by his hand were they all created from the beginning" (Alma 18:32; also see Mosiah 24:12; D&C 6:16). And Mormon wrote, "for none is acceptable before God, save the meek and lowly in heart" (Moro. 7:44).
>
> In this dispensation, the Lord has reaffirmed that God "is a discerner of the thoughts and intents of the heart" (D&C 33:1). . . .
>
> In other words, God knows who is pure in heart. He can and will judge us not only for our actions but also for our motives, desires, and attitudes. This reality is challenging, not surprising. (*Pure in Heart* [Salt Lake City: Bookcraft, 1988], 10–11)

ILLUSTRATIONS FOR OUR TIME

Richard L. Evans has reminded us of the goodness and power of God and how He truly knows our innermost desires and thoughts.

And over and over again I am comforted with this great, sustaining, strengthening thought, and I leave it with our young people, and with all of us, for such consideration as it may merit: Our Father in heaven knows us; he knows our hearts; he knows our thoughts. He understands us and loves us as his children, as we love our own children but with his infinitely greater capacity and wisdom and understanding. He knows the motives which move us to do the things we do or fail to do. He knows the influences by which we are sometimes swayed. He understands our missing a perfect performance. He knows our desires, our difficulties, our sorrows, our disappointments, our hopes, our objectives, our wants and our wishes. And he will help us, if we will take him into our confidence in our daily lives, if we will admit him into the counsel of our hearts, and approach him in prayer. He will help to sustain us in life against all adversity and difficulty and disappointment, against all uncertainty, against all the evils of the day. In the fulfilling of our worthy plans and purposes and our cherished hopes, he will help us. It is his declared purpose and intention to help us to immortality and eternal life. It is always comforting and sustaining to know that he understands us and that this is his declared purpose, if we will take him into our confidence and live to merit his companionship and direction, with this great saving, comforting, sustaining principle of repentance ever in mind. (CR, October 1952, 127)

LIKENING THE SCRIPTURES TO OUR LIVES

1 Kings 8:39 Then hear thou in heaven thy dwelling place, and forgive, and do, and give to every man according to his ways, whose heart thou knowest; (for thou, even thou only, knowest the hearts of all the children of men).

Application: The Lord knows our hearts. We are to be pure in our hearts. "Yea, and he looketh down upon all the children of men; and he knows all the thoughts and intents of the heart; for by his hand were they all created from the beginning" (Alma 18:32).

5. HOW TO AVOID THE SIN OF HYPOCRISY

THEME: The Lord condemns the sin of hypocrisy. It is well that we recognize the fact that we all—just as in the case of the sin of pride—are guilty of hypocrisy to one degree or another and should seek to purify ourselves.

MOMENT OF TRUTH

In an oration of acute boldness and candor (Matt. 23), the Savior pronounced woes upon the scribes and Pharisees for the hypocrisy of feigning righteousness but practicing greed and extortion, abusing the poor, and neglecting "the weightier matters of the law, judgment, mercy, and faith" (Matt. 23:23). He compared them to "whited sepulchres, which indeed appear beautiful outward, but are within full of dead men's bones, and of all uncleanness. Even so ye also outwardly appear righteous unto men, but within ye are full of hypocrisy and iniquity" (Matt. 23:27–28). Then in an expression of passion as well as compassion, the Savior declares: "O Jerusalem, Jerusalem, thou that killest the prophets, and stonest them which are sent unto thee, how often would I have gathered thy children together, even as a hen gathereth her chickens under her wings, and ye would not!" (Matt. 23:37).

MODERN PROPHETS SPEAK

David O. McKay:

> Thoughts are the seeds of acts and precede them. Mere compliance with the word of the Lord, without a corresponding inward desire, will avail but little. Indeed, such outward actions and pretending phrases may disclose hypocrisy, a sin that Jesus most vehemently condemned. (*Gospel Ideals: Selections from the Discourses of David O. McKay* [Salt Lake City: Improvement Era, 1958], 382)

ILLUSTRATIONS FOR OUR TIME

Understanding Hypocrisy

Hypocrisy is pretending to be something that you are not. It is being sanctimonious in judgment of others when you are guilty yourself. It is insincere and beguiling. It is using dishonesty to mislead when you know full well the truth. This flaw in the character of man is destructive to others and especially to one's self. It is a form of self-deception that undermines and destroys one's progress in becoming a person of moral integrity. Our egos are so important to our psyche that we can become hypocritical to protect ourselves. We can become excessively egocentric. How can we become aware of hypocrisy and then take the proper steps to eliminate it from our behavior?

We have all suffered from the sin of hypocrisy or the effects thereof at one time or another. It is important to avoid becoming habituated to it as a means to protect our egos. The damage to families and society is evident. Double standards of behavior have devastating results. Trust and confidence are destroyed. When trust is weakened, real communication closes. In an atmosphere of hypocrisy, we don't understand or appreciate one another, and the depth of our feelings toward one another is inevitably destroyed. It behooves us all to be true to ourselves and loving to our fellowmen and in so doing to defeat hypocrisy among us. We can be pure in both heart and deed as we eliminate hypocrisy from our lives and replace it with honor, sincerity, and integrity.

We can start by thinking good thoughts and remember to say only what is kind, true, and necessary.

LIKENING THE SCRIPTURES TO OUR LIVES

Matthew 23:28 Even so ye also outwardly appear righteous unto men, but within ye are full of hypocrisy and iniquity.

Application: Let us earnestly strive to purify our hearts so that our actions are acceptable to the Lord. Indeed we must cleanse the inner vessel (see Alma 60:23). Our motives must be pure.

SUMMARY

Just as the Savior knew the hearts and motivations of His contemporaries—the faithful as well as the deceitful—so does He know our hearts. Will He find in our hearts an enduring love of God and our fellowmen? Will He find there a commitment to follow Him in obedience and righteousness? Will He find there an absence of any vestige of hypocrisy or pride? Will He find in our hearts and spirits a disposition to choose the better part and exercise charity and service as a governing pattern for our lives, just as Joshua counseled: "choose you this day whom ye will serve; . . . but as for me and my house, we will serve the Lord" (Josh. 24:15)? Will the Lord find in our hearts a commitment to keep all of His commandments, as Nephi promised to do with such overarching faith and conviction (see 1 Ne. 3:7)? Will the Savior find in our hearts a hunger to come unto Him in all humility? "And now, my beloved brethren, I would that ye should come unto Christ, who is the Holy One of Israel, and partake of his salvation, and the power of his redemption. Yea, come unto him, and offer your whole souls as an offering unto him, and continue in fasting and praying, and endure to the end; and as the Lord liveth ye will be saved" (Omni 1:26). In short, will we rise as disciples of Christ and join His triumphal and triumphant procession of Saints engaged in a royal journey toward an eternal homeland, approved and worthy of all acceptation through our covenant worthiness?

CHAPTER 21

THE SECOND COMING

Reading Assignment: Joseph Smith—Matthew [Matthew 24].

Additional Reading: Mark 13; Luke 21:5–38; 1 John 4:16–18; D&C 6:34–36; 45:15–57; 46:7–8; 59:23; Isaiah 2:2–3; Daniel 2:44–45.

> *Faithfulness will prepare us for the Second Coming. If you are on a moving train of cars, as long as you sit still and occupy your seat that train will take you to the point you wish to go; but if you step off the cars it will be dangerous, and it may be a long time before another train will come along. It is the same with us—if we are living right, doing our work, we are going along, and if we are keeping our covenants, we are doing the work of God and accomplishing His purposes, and we will be prepared for the time when Jesus the Son of God will come in honor and glory, and will confer upon all those who prove faithful all the blessings that they anticipate, and a thousand times more.*

—Lorenzo Snow, The Teachings of Lorenzo Snow, Ed. Clyde J. Williams, 149.

THEMES *for* LIVING
1. The Certainty of Prophecy
2. Signs Preceding the Second Coming

INTRODUCTION

In the last days, there will be signs that indicate that the time is near for the Second Coming of the Lord Jesus Christ prior to the beginning of the millennium. We are living in the last days. We have a duty to warn people (see D&C 88:81) and to help them prepare for the Second Coming of the Lord (see D&C 1:12). Bruce R. McConkie lists 51 events or signs that will take place prior to or at the advent of the Second Coming, of which 43 have been completed or are in the process of being completed at this time (see *MD*, 645–63). Since no man knows the date and hour of His coming or the date and time that we may be called upon to leave this earthly existence, it seems that the question is: Are we doing all we can in our preparation to meet our Savior and our Heavenly Father? These are our days of probation here upon the earth and every day is precious—one more day to prepare to meet God.

1. THE CERTAINTY OF PROPHECY

THEME: The prophecies of the Lord will always be fulfilled: "What I the Lord have spoken, I have spoken, and I excuse not myself; and though the heavens and the earth pass away, my word shall not pass away, but shall all be fulfilled, whether by mine own voice or by the voice of my servants, it is the same" (D&C 1:38). Moreover: "Although the days will come, that heaven and earth shall pass away, yet my words shall not pass away; but all shall be fulfilled" (JS—M 1:35).

MOMENT OF TRUTH

The hour was fast approaching when the Savior would accomplish His atoning sacrifice. A feeling of urgency had entered into the hearts of His disciples, for He had prophesied to them that the great temple at Jerusalem was to be destroyed: "Verily I say unto you, there shall not be left here, upon this temple, one stone upon another that shall not be thrown down" (JS—M, 1:3). As He retreated to the Mount of Olives, some of His disciples came to Him—according to Mark it was Peter, James, John, and Andrew (Mark 13:3)—and sought His wisdom on the signs that would precede His Second Coming. He spoke to them of the impending persecution at the hands of apostates and false prophets, of the destruction of Jerusalem, and of the need to "stand in the holy place" and be watchful for the cataclysmic cleansing destruction at His return in glory. Enumerating many of the signs of the times leading to that awesome hour, He counseled them: "Therefore be ye also ready, for in such an hour as ye think not, the Son of Man cometh" (JS—M 1:48). Not even the angels of heaven know that hour (JS—M 1:40)—no, not even the Son (Mark 13:42)—but the Father alone. The Savior gave His disciples a parable as the consummation of His instruction on this subject—a parable with an interpretation than cannot be misunderstood: "For the Son of man is as a man taking a far journey, who left his house, and gave authority to his servants, and to every man his work, and commanded the porter to watch. Watch ye therefore: for ye know not when the master of the house cometh, at even, or at midnight, or at the cockcrowing, or in the morning: Lest coming suddenly he find you sleeping. And what I say unto you I say unto all, Watch" (Mark 13:34–37; compare also the modern revelation concerning these events given in D&C 45:15–57).

MODERN PROPHETS SPEAK

Ezra Taft Benson:

> When the Savior spoke of these signs and prophecies to His disciples in Jerusalem, they were apprehensive. He said to them, "Be not troubled, for, when all these things shall come to pass, ye may know that the promises which have been made unto you shall be fulfilled." (D&C 45:35) . . .
>
> We will live in the midst of economic, political, and spiritual instability. When these signs are observed—unmistakable evidences that His coming is nigh—we need not be troubled, but "stand . . . in holy places, and be not moved, until the day of the Lord come." (D&C 87:8)
>
> Holy men and women stand in holy places, and these holy places consist of our temples, our chapels, our homes, and the stakes of Zion, which are, as the Lord declares, "for a defense, and for a refuge from the storm, and from wrath when it shall be poured out without mixture upon the whole earth." (D&C 115:6) We must heed the Lord's counsel to the Saints of this dispensation: "Prepare yourselves for the great day of the Lord." (D&C 133:10) . . .
>
> Will we be among those who are faithful to the end? Will we endure? Are we prepared? Can we live in the world and not partake of the sins of the world? Will we "arise and shine forth," as the Lord has commanded? Will we be a light and a "standard" (*Come unto Christ* [Salt Lake City: Deseret Book, 1983], 114–115).

ILLUSTRATIONS FOR OUR TIME

C. Max Caldwell explains Section 45 of the Doctrine and Covenants as follows:

> When the Savior comes a second time, he will make at least three general appearances:
>
> 1. He will appear to the Saints or covenant members of his church (v. 45–46, 56–57). The Savior likened those faithful members to the five wise virgins who had taken the Holy Spirit to be their guide (cf. Matt. 25:1–13).

2. He will appear to the Jews at Jerusalem (v. 47–53). When the Jews are engaged in a battle for survival, the Savior will appear and intervene in their behalf and they will recognize him as their Messiah.

3. He will appear to the world (v. 74–75). This appearance will not be to a select group, but rather will be of such magnitude that the wicked will be destroyed, leaving only the righteous to enjoy the millennial reign of the Savior. The second coming of the Savior will coincide with the resurrection of faithful covenant members of his Church who shall be caught up to meet him when he comes in his glory (v. 45). And the heathen who lived without the law will be resurrected, and also "they that knew no law" (v. 54). (*Encyclopedia,* 413)

LIKENING THE SCRIPTURES TO OUR LIVES

Mormon 8:22–23 For the eternal purposes of the Lord shall roll on, until all his promises shall be fulfilled. Search the prophecies of Isaiah. Behold, I cannot write them. Yea, behold I say unto you, that those saints who have gone before me, who have possessed this land, shall cry, yea, even from the dust will they cry unto the Lord; and as the Lord liveth he will remember the covenant which he hath made with them.

Application: Let us humbly exercise our faith in the words of our prophets—both living and those who have been recorded in the Holy Scriptures—for their prophecies will be fulfilled (see D&C 1:38; Amos 3:7).

2. SIGNS PRECEDING THE SECOND COMING

THEME: Those who are ready and spiritually prepared will recognize and understand the signs that precede the Second Coming and will gather in holy places of refuge.

MOMENT OF TRUTH

The signs of the times, concerning the final hours of the earth's history prior to the Second Coming, constitute a call to action. These signs are more than mileposts along the way to a final and ultimate destruction of heaven and earth: they are rather signals and prompts that galvanize the faithful to a state of readiness, a state that will be characterized by peace, not fear. The Savior said, "Behold, I speak these things unto you for the elect's sake; and you also shall hear of wars, and rumors of wars; see that ye be not troubled, for all I have told you must come to pass; but the end is not yet" (JS—M 1:23). In our time, the Lord has said: "But if ye are prepared ye shall not fear" (D&C 38:30). Luke recorded this counsel from the Lord: "And take heed to yourselves, lest at any time your hearts be overcharged with surfeiting, and drunkenness, and cares of this life, and so that day come upon you unawares. For as a snare shall it come on all them that dwell on the face of the whole earth. Watch ye therefore, and pray always, that ye may be accounted worthy to escape all these things that shall come to pass, and to stand before the Son of man" (Luke 21:34–36). The ultimate refuge, in the face of these signs of the times, is the process of gathering to holy places (D&C 45:32; 87:8; 101:22).

MODERN PROPHETS SPEAK

Bruce R. McConkie:

> These are the last days; the signs of the times are now being shown forth on every hand; and the coming of the Lord is not far distant. In the early days of this final gospel dispensation, when his servants were just beginning to lay the foundations of his earthly kingdom, the Lord said: "The voice of the Lord is unto the ends of the earth, that all that will hear may hear: Prepare ye, prepare ye for that which is to come, for the Lord is nigh" (D&C 1:11–12). Prepare for the pestilence and plagues and sorrows of the last days. Prepare for the second coming of the Son of Man. Prepare to abide the day, to stand when he appeareth, and to live and reign with him on earth for a thousand years. Prepare for the new heaven and the new earth whereon dwelleth righteousness. Prepare to meet thy God. (*The Millennial Messiah: The Second Coming of the Son of Man* [Salt Lake City: Deseret Book, 1982], 570–71)

ILLUSTRATIONS FOR OUR TIME

The Prophet Joseph Smith spoke concerning the Second Coming as follows:

> I will prophesy that the signs of the coming of the Son of Man are already commenced. One pestilence will desolate after another. We shall soon have war and bloodshed. The moon will be turned into blood. I testify of these things, and that the coming of the Son of Man is nigh, even at your doors. If our souls and our bodies are not looking forth for the coming of the Son of Man; and after we are dead, if we are not looking forth, we shall be among those who are calling for the rocks to fall upon them. (*HC* 4:11)

> Judah must return, Jerusalem must be rebuilt, and the temple, and water come out from under the temple, and the waters of the Dead Sea be healed. It will take some time to rebuild the walls of the city and the temple, &c.; and all this must be done before the Son of Man will make His appearance. There will be wars and rumors of wars, signs in the heavens above and on the earth beneath, the sun turned into darkness and the moon to blood, earthquakes in divers places, the seas heaving beyond

their bounds; then will appear one grand sign of the Son of Man in heaven. But what will the world do? They will say it is a planet, a comet, &c. But the Son of Man will come as the sign of the coming of the Son of Man, which will be as the light of the morning cometh out of the east. (*HC* 5:336–37)

LIKENING THE SCRIPTURES TO OUR LIVES

D&C 34:6 To lift up your voice as with the sound of a trump, both long and loud, and cry repentance unto a crooked and perverse generation, preparing the way of the Lord for his second coming.

Application: As the dispensation of the fulness of times rolls forth, we have a duty to fulfill: warn all nations, kindreds, tongues, and peoples to repent and come unto Christ, for the end is nigh and no one knows the hour of His coming or when we will be called home to meet our Savior.

SUMMARY

The Savior made it clear: "Although, the days will come, that heaven and earth shall pass away; yet my words shall not pass away, but all shall be fulfilled" (JS—M 1:35). For us to have confidence in approaching the final days, we are to cultivate a life style that reflects charity and love: "And we have known and believed the love that God hath to us. God is love; and he that dwelleth in love dwelleth in God, and God in him. Herein is our love made perfect, that we may have boldness in the day of judgment: because as he is, so are we in this world" (1 Jn. 4:16–17). We are, moreover, to build upon the solid foundation of gospel principles: "Therefore, fear not, little flock; do good; let earth and hell combine against you, for if ye are built upon my rock, they cannot prevail. Behold, I do not condemn you; go your ways and sin no more; perform with soberness the work which I have commanded you. Look unto me in every thought; doubt not, fear not" (D&C 6:34–36; compare D&C 46:7–8). Finally, just as the wise virgins, we are to take the Holy Spirit for our guide (D&C 45:56–59) so that we might look forward to a resolution of all of our mortal challenges: "But learn that he who doeth the works of righteousness shall receive his reward, even peace in this world and eternal life in the world to come" (D&C 59:23).

CHAPTER 22

"INHERIT *the* KINGDOM PREPARED *for* YOU"

Reading Assignment: Matthew 25.

Additional Reading: Bible Dictionary, "Parables" (740–41).

We have been called to difficult tasks in a difficult age, but this could be for each of us a time of high adventure, of great learning, of great inner satisfaction. For the converging challenges posed by war, urbanization, dilution of doctrine, and domestic decay surely provide for us the modern equivalent of crossing the plains, enduring misunderstanding, establishing a kingdom throughout the world in the midst of adversity. I pray that we may do our part during the journey, and be with, and leading, the caravan of the Church as it enters the final chosen place—His presence.

—HAROLD B. LEE, *THBL,* 408.

THEMES *for* LIVING

1. Parable of the Ten Virgins
2. Parable of the Talents
3. Parable of the Sheep and the Goats

INTRODUCTION

The parables of the ten virgins, the talents, and the sheep and the goats all have special meanings as they relate to our preparation and diligence in keeping the commandments and becoming worthy of receiving promised blessings. These parables emphasize our worthiness to meet our Savior, our devotion and dedication to work hard with that which the Lord has given us, and then the judgment that will come upon the earth for all mankind—according to how well we have kept the commandments. As individuals, we do not know the hour when we will be called home; thus we do not know the timing of our first judgment—at death or at the time of the Second Coming of the Lord. It behooves us, therefore, to be ready by living righteously according to the whisperings of the Spirit, doing the very best we can in all things, and seeking to build up the kingdom of God—thus proving ourselves worthy to be on the Lord's side.

1. PARABLE OF THE TEN VIRGINS

THEME: The parable of the ten virgins teaches us to prepare diligently and be ready for the Second Coming of the Lord. We should live by the Spirit—thus having the needed oil in our lamps.

MOMENT OF TRUTH

On the eve of His atoning sacrifice, the Savior presented three parables representing a legacy of truth that He wished to leave behind concerning the kingdom of God—parables that taught the saving doctrines of being continually prepared, magnifying one's talents in worthy causes, and committing to a pattern of life that would please the Lord and enable Him to serve on our behalf as Holy Advocate with the Father on the day of judgment. In the first of these parables, concerning the five wise and five foolish virgins (Matt. 25:1–13), the Lord spoke of the coming of the bridegroom and how to prepare for that momentous event by honoring and keeping the prescribed counsel for righteous living. The righteous were admitted to the wedding, but the unrighteous were excluded, with the devastating dictum: "Verily I say unto you, I know you not" (Matt. 25:12). The moral of the parable is given in the Savior's final words: "Watch therefore, for ye know neither the day nor the hour wherein the Son of man cometh" (Matt. 25:13).

MODERN PROPHETS SPEAK

Howard W. Hunter:

Preparation for the Second Coming does not require a preoccupation with the future. Jesus taught his disciples to watch and pray; however, he taught them that prayerful watching does not require sleepless anxiety and preoccupation with the future, but rather the quiet, steady attention to present duties. (*THWH*, 201)

Bruce R. McConkie:

Salvation is a personal matter. It comes only to those who keep the commandments and whose souls are filled with the Holy Spirit of God. No man can keep the commandments for and on behalf of another; no one can gain the sanctifying power of the Holy Spirit in his life and give or sell that holy oil to another. Every man must light his own lamp with the oil of righteousness which he buys at the market of obedience. Few doctrines are more evil and wicked than the false doctrine of supererogation, which is, that the saints, by doing more than is necessary for their own salvation, build up an immense treasure of merit in heaven, which can be dispensed and assigned to others so they too can be saved.

All that one person can do for the salvation of another is to preach, teach, expound, and exhort; all that one man can do for his fellows is to teach them the truth and guide their feet into paths of virtue and rectitude. All that the five wise virgins can do for the foolish is to tell them how to gain oil for themselves. (*The Mortal Messiah: From Bethlehem to Calvary,* 4 vols. [Salt Lake City: Deseret Book, 1979–1981], 3: 468)

ILLUSTRATIONS FOR OUR TIME

Be Prepared

The precursor to success or failure can usually be found in preparation. There are many facets found in success, i.e. vision, desire, commitment, and a host of others. When the vision and desire are in place, preparation becomes the master. Preparation precedes power. If you are prepared, you will not suffer from anxiety—or as the Lord expressed it: "if ye are prepared ye shall not fear" (D&C 38:30). Confucius said, wisely, "A man who does not think and plan long ahead will find trouble right at his door." Preparation has a price. It takes time, effort, dedication, and often sacrifice in order to prepare well. Many want to be the best, be the champion, and win the prize—and a litany of other reasons to achieve could be listed. The hard fact is: How many want to prepare to be the best and thus to be the champion and win the prize? Preparation becomes the key to success along with the perseverance and dedication to see it through.

Ezra Taft Benson has admonished us to prepare well. He taught, "But the best preparation for eternal life is to be prepared at all times to die—fully prepared by a valiant fight for right" (*TETB,* 117).

Roy Doxey explains:

> During his mortal ministry, the Lord spoke concerning the preparedness of believers in the last days. The parable of the ten virgins, five of whom were prepared to meet the bridegroom while the remaining five were unprepared and rejected from entrance to the marriage feast, is closed with this application: "verily I say unto you, I know you not. Watch therefore, for ye know neither the day nor the hour wherein the Son of Man cometh (Matt. 25:12–13).
>
> Does this parable apply to the Latter-day Saints? Definitely so. Hear the words of the Lord to the Prophet Joseph Smith:
>
> And at that day, when I shall come in my glory, shall the parable be fulfilled which I spake concerning the ten virgins.
>
> For they that are wise and have received the truth, and have taken the Holy Spirit for their guide, and have not been deceived—verily I say unto you, they shall not be hewn down and cast into the fire, but shall abide the day.
>
> And the earth shall be given unto them for an inheritance; and they shall multiply and wax strong, and their children shall grow up without sin unto salvation.
>
> For the Lord shall be in their midst, and his glory shall be upon them, and he will be their king and their lawgiver (D&C 45:56–59).
>
> No one else upon the face of the earth meets the description given in these verses better than do the Latter-day Saints, for "—they have received the truth, and have taken the Holy Spirit for their guide, and have not been deceived" (45:57). (Roy W. Doxey, *The Doctrine and Covenants Speaks* [Salt Lake City: Deseret Book, 1964], 1:307)

LIKENING THE SCRIPTURES TO OUR LIVES

Matthew 25:9 But the wise answered, saying, Not so; lest there be not enough for us and you: but go ye rather to them that sell, and buy for yourselves.

Application: The implication here is not that they simply go out and "buy oil," but rather that the individual has to take steps for himself or herself to gain spiritual mastery and qualify for heavenly blessings. You cannot transfer to others your testimony of Jesus Christ or your life of righteous living. You can only guide, encourage, and set a good example.

2. PARABLE OF THE TALENTS

THEME: The parable of the talents teaches us to magnify our gifts from God.

MOMENT OF TRUTH

In the parable of the talents (Matt. 25:14–30), the Lord teaches that we have a solemn responsibility as stewards of God to account for the gifts and endowments that He bestows upon us for the purpose of building up His Kingdom and nurturing and guiding His children. To magnify our talents is to invoke the comforting confirmation of God's satisfaction with our service: "His lord said unto him, Well done, thou good and faithful servant: thou hast been faithful over a few things, I will make thee ruler over many things: enter thou into the joy of thy lord" (Mat. 25:21). To confine and bury our talents either slothfully or with trepidation is to invoke the severe judgments of God upon such people, who are counted as ungrateful and unprofitable in His cause: "For unto every one that hath shall be given, and he shall have abundance: but from him that hath not shall be taken away even that which he hath" (Matt. 25:29). As the Only Begotten Son of God, Jesus Christ served as consummate exemplar of one who perfectly magnified His calling as Redeemer and Advocate with the Father. He asks only that we do our part in following His example in all diligence and faith.

MODERN PROPHETS SPEAK

J. Reuben Clark:
> And I would like to add this as a sobering thought to myself and to you, each of you, and all of you: Remember the parable of the talents where the man who failed to improve the talent given him, had it taken from him? I ask you brethren, and myself, are we magnifying our Priesthood in such a way, are we living close enough to the Lord and in obedience to his commandments that we may exercise this power, or shall it be wholly or in part taken away from us? You would better think about it. It is worth thinking about. It is the greatest power that has been revealed to man.
>
> God grant that we may all so live that we shall not lose that power, but that always it shall be available to us. (*Behold the Lamb of God* [Salt Lake City: Deseret Book, 1991], 286)

ILLUSTRATIONS FOR OUR TIME

All of us have been given talents, opportunities, and callings here upon the earth— some with a limited time span and some with an eternal scope. The question that will be asked of each of us is this: "Did you improve upon your talents? Did you magnify your callings?" Each calling or role honorably fulfilled ultimately blesses someone's life; therefore, when we magnify our talent or calling, we build up, enlarge, and strengthen the people we serve through our calling. Blessing and serving our fellowmen is helping build up the kingdom of God (see JST, Matt. 6:38), in that we invite all to come unto Christ and strengthen those who have made covenants (see D&C 108:7). Each role and calling is important within the stewardship and framework in which we serve. Gordon B. Hinckley has stated, "We magnify our calling, we enlarge the potential of our priesthood when we reach out to those in distress and give strength to those who falter" ("Magnify Your Calling," *Ensign,* May 1989, 49; *TGBH,* 478). Let us therefore diligently seek to magnify our eternal roles and callings, thus qualifying ourselves to return to the presence of our Heavenly Father.

Howard W. Hunter taught this hope-filled truth: "The Lord never calls a man to any office in his Church but what he will by revelation help that man to magnify his calling" (*THWH,* 215). As we magnify our callings, we are building up the kingdom of God. The kingdom of God is composed of Heavenly Father's children—so by magnifying our callings, we are blessing our brothers and sisters. This is the greatest good. This is the purpose of every calling within the Church.

The Magnificent Spiral

When I was perhaps five or six years old, one of the leaders in the ward in the small Canadian town where my family was living at the time asked me to participate in an upcoming sacrament meeting program. The image of his walking up to me as I was playing on the lawn in front of our home is still vivid after all these years. After listening to his request, I pondered for a moment about the intimidation of having to appear before such a large congregation and said that I would prefer not to do it. The brother was very kind and gentle. He just thanked me for considering it and then went on his way.

That's when the lesson started. For the next few days, I recall having a feeling of constriction and shame within myself for having turned down the calling when it would have been relatively easy to comply. Not wanting to confess to my parents about my shortcoming, I kept the circumstances to myself (though they probably knew all about it). The most burdensome experience was having to sit through the sacrament meeting a few weeks later and watch as another boy performed very well the part that I should have taken. It made me feel rather small and inadequate. At the time, I did not understand that this feeling was diametrically opposite to what the prophet Jacob described when he talked about how to "magnify our office" (Jacob 1:19). Constriction, reduction, limitation, isolation, shrinking—the things I felt as a youngster at that time—these are antonyms for magnifying, radiating, expanding, enveloping, illuminating, blessing, unfolding—the feelings that attend the acceptance and fulfillment of one's service in the kingdom of God with devotion, enthusiasm, and a willing heart. As I later learned in life through an endless array of positive experiences on the errand of the Lord, the process is one of "magnifying." That is the essence of righteous service. It is part of applying and enlarging one's gifts for spiritual profit, as the Savior taught in the Parable of the Talents (Matt. 25:14–30).

To magnify means to make greater, to make more splendid. There are really three kinds of magnifying evidenced in the gospel. First, there is the process of magnifying an office by accepting it with humility, gratitude, soberness, and devotion—as Jacob exemplified when he spoke of "taking upon us the responsibility, answering the sins of the people upon our own heads if we did not teach them the word of God with all diligence" (Jacob 1:19; 2:2). A similar usage is reflected in the revelation given to Joseph Smith and Oliver Cowdery in July 1830: "Attend to thy calling and thou shalt have wherewith to magnify thine office, and to expound the scriptures, and continue in laying on of the hands and confirming the churches" (D&C 24:9). And again, as in this further revelation to Joseph Smith: "Keep these sayings, for they are true and faithful; and thou shalt magnify thine office, and push many people to Zion with songs of everlasting joy upon their heads" (D&C 66:11). Perhaps the most celebrated usage of this kind is found in the oath and covenant of the priesthood: "For whoso is faithful unto the obtaining these two priesthoods of which I have spoken, and the magnifying their callings are sanctified by the Spirit unto the renewing of their bodies" (D&C 84:33).

Second, the principal purpose of gospel service is to bring glory to God, to magnify Him and His Son and cause others to do the same: "Remember that thou magnify his work, which men behold" (Job 36:24). "O magnify the Lord with me, and let us exalt his name together" (Ps. 34:3). The psalmist said, "I will praise the name of God with a song, and will magnify him with thanksgiving" (Ps. 69:30). Nephi declared: "Wherefore, my soul delighteth to prophesy concerning him, for I have seen his day, and my heart doth magnify his holy name" (2 Ne. 25:13). Perhaps the most famous of such instances was uttered by the mother of the Redeemer: "And Mary said, my soul doth magnify the Lord, And my spirit hath rejoiced in God my Saviour" (Luke 1:46–47).

Third, gospel service causes people themselves to be magnified personally or rendered more splendid in the spiritual sense. "And the Lord said unto Joshua, This day will I begin to magnify thee in the sight of all Israel, that they may know that, as I was with Moses, so I will be with thee" (Josh. 3:7). Furthermore: "What is man that thou shouldest magnify him, and that thou shouldest set thine heart on him?" (Job 7:17).

There is a continual process implied with such references. We *magnify* our calling by *magnifying* the Lord and enlarging His holy name before the world; and thus we are, in turn, *magnified* through His blessings unto us. This triad of enlargement—this eternal circle of service—is a buoyant force, a lifting force. When the three stages are completed, the cycle starts again at a higher level. Thus we see emerging a *magnificent spiral* that carries us ever upward as we contribute to, and are nurtured by, the process of magnification. What a grand and magnanimous blessing it is to have part in such a program of enlargement and building as the kingdom of God expands and grows like the stone that was cut from the mountain without hands and rolls forth to fill the whole world (Dan. 2:34–35).

There are, of course, circumstances where it might be difficult or impossible to respond to a calling. At such times, the Lord, in His compassion, may judge the heart of those involved and see that they "cease not their diligence" and thus "require the work no more" of them, but "accept of their offerings" (D&C 124:49). And perhaps the Lord, in His loving kindness, will forgive a five- or six-year-old boy who did not yet have an inkling of the divine process of growth and development that comes when the Saints of God display a devoted heart and a willing mind (D&C 64:33–34) tuned to the mission of building up Zion for the glory of God. [Allen]

LIKENING THE SCRIPTURES TO OUR LIVES

Matthew 25:15 And unto one he gave five talents, to another two, and to another one; to every man according to his several ability; and straightway took his journey.

Application: Remember that the Lord has expectations for each of us according to that which we have been given. This is not a comparison test. It is a test of doing our very, very best with what the Lord has given us and then magnifying it with all our heart, might, mind, and soul. All can be exalted if they keep the commandments. High station or position does not exalt—only the grace of God after all we can do (see 2 Ne. 25:23).

3. PARABLE OF THE SHEEP AND THE GOATS

THEME: The parable of the sheep and the goats teaches us to follow our Shepherd, even Christ the Lord, that we may be found worthy to be on His right hand.

MOMENT OF TRUTH

What more penetrating discourse could there be than to hear the Savior explain the process of ultimate judgment—when the righteous will be gathered in joy on His right hand to reap "life eternal," and the wicked on His left, consigned to "everlasting punishment" (Matt. 25:46). The parable of the sheep and the goats (Matt. 25:31–46) is one of the final parables offered by the Savior on the eve of His crucifixion. At the core of the judgment process will be an inquiry into the charitable devotion of the Saints—whether they had remembered those in need: "And the King shall answer and say unto them, Verily I say unto you, Inasmuch as ye have done it unto one of the least of these my brethren, ye have done it unto me" (Matt. 25:40). These words were anticipated over 150 years prior to this, in the distant land of America, by King Benjamin, who taught his people—the "other sheep" of which the Savior spoke (John 10:16)—the following doctrine: "And behold, I tell you these things that ye may learn wisdom; that ye may learn that when ye are in the service of your fellow beings ye are only in the service of your God" (Mosiah 2:17).

MODERN PROPHETS SPEAK

Spencer W. Kimball:

> There will be a wise and just God to sit in judgment on all men. There could be a delay in judgment. The wicked may prosper for a time, the rebellious may seem to profit by their transgressions, but the time is coming when, at the bar of justice, all men will be judged, "every man according to their works" (Rev. 20:13). No one will "get by" with anything. On that day no one will escape the penalty of his deeds, no one will fail to receive the blessings he has earned. Again, the parable of the sheep and the goats gives us assurance that there will be total justice (see Matt. 25:31–46). (*The Miracle of Forgiveness* [Salt Lake City: Bookcraft, 1969], 305)

ILLUSTRATIONS FOR OUR TIME

The Sheep and the Goats

The Lord made it clear in the parable of the sheep and the goats that the difference between the two groups was in the way they served their fellowmen. We somehow have difficulty in showing Christlike love and serving others in the most elemental ways—a smile, a kind word, showing gratitude, honest praise that lifts and encourages, and the list goes on.

We have also been commanded to love one another even as our Savior has loved us (see John 13:34–35). He suffered and died for us and performed the infinite and eternal Atonement that through Him we might, if obedient, return to the presence of our Heavenly father.

We have now been charged to invite all to come unto Christ. We must preach the gospel to every nation, kindred, tongue, and people (see Morm. 9:22). We have been encouraged to warn our neighbor (see D&C 88:81). We have been asked to strengthen our brothers and sisters in all things (see D&C 108:7). We have been commanded to feed His sheep (see John 21:15–17). Indeed, we are to bear one another's burdens and stand as witnesses of Christ at all times and in all things (see Mosiah 18:8–9). We are to proclaim the gospel, perfect the Saints, and redeem the dead. Lest we forget, we can be perfected no faster than we do our vicarious temple service (see D&C 128:15).

These are the things the Lord's flock, even His sheep that He knows by name, are commanded and encouraged to do—and if we are obedient, we will indeed be on His right hand. Make a commitment to bless someone today. [Pinegar]

LIKENING THE SCRIPTURES TO OUR LIVES

Matthew 25:40, 45 And the King shall answer and say unto them, Verily I say unto you, Inasmuch as ye have done it unto one of the least of these my brethren, ye have done it unto me. . . . Then shall he answer them, saying, Verily I say unto you, Inasmuch as ye did it not to one of the least of these, ye did it not to me.

Application: Every act we perform on this earth is a reflection of our love, or the lack of love, for our Savior Jesus Christ and our Heavenly Father. When we love the Lord, we will keep the commandments (see John 14:15); alternately, if we love Satan more than God, we will become carnal, sensual, and devilish (see Moses 5:13). Thus are the sheep separated from the goats.

SUMMARY

In the parables of Jesus concerning ultimate truths of the Kingdom—parable of the ten virgins, parable of the talents, and parable of the sheep and the goats—we have some of the Savior's final counsel on matters of salvation prior to His crucifixion. These stories resonate in our hearts and minds as we continue to seek spiritual mastery in our lives by following in His footsteps. Are we filling our lamps of devotion with the oil of charity and obedience? Are we providing the Lord with an acceptable "return on investment" by magnifying and sharing with others the measure of light and truth we have been given? Are we living each day in such a way that we could be found worthy to take our places on the right hand of the Lord in the day of judgment? To be given these guidelines from the Savior is a gem of inestimable worth. How will we respond? Alma, in reflecting on the mysteries (higher truths) of the gospel, had this observation:

> It is given unto many to know the mysteries of God; nevertheless they are laid under
> a strict command that they shall not impart only according to the portion of his

word which he doth grant unto the children of men, according to the heed and diligence which they give unto him.

And therefore, he that will harden his heart, the same receiveth the lesser portion of the word; and he that will not harden his heart, to him is given the greater portion of the word, until it is given unto him to know the mysteries of God until he know them in full. (Alma 12:9–10)

May we resolve to live the gospel truths afforded us through these and other scriptures, that our joy might be full and our cup positioned to receive even greater manifestations of spiritual truth according to the benevolence and grace of the Lord.

CHAPTER 23

"LOVE ONE ANOTHER, AS I HAVE LOVED YOU"

Reading Assignment: Luke 22:1–38; John 13–15.

Additional Reading: Matthew 26:1–5, 14–35; Mark 14:1–2, 10–31; D&C 20:77, 79; 3 Nephi 18:5–12.

> *Love is one of the chief characteristics of Deity, and ought to be manifested by those who aspire to be the sons of God. A man filled with the love of God, is not content with blessing his family alone, but ranges through the whole world, anxious to bless the whole human race.*
>
> —JOSEPH SMITH, *HC,* 4:227.

THEMES *for* LIVING

1. The Sacrament
2. Love One Another
3. Jesus Is the Way, the Truth, the Life, and the True Vine

INTRODUCTION

The blessings we receive on this earth come from God our Father through and because of His Beloved Son Jesus Christ, our Lord and Savior. By partaking of the sacrament, we symbolically partake of His atoning sacrifice with all its accompanying blessings. We take His name upon us and covenant to remember Him always and keep His commandments and thus qualify for His spirit always to be with us. The commandments of God are designed to bring us happiness and joy and lead us to immortality and eternal life—the work and glory of God. As we begin to acquire the divine nature of Christ, we will be full of charity, we will love one another, and we will treat others even as we would treat our Master Jesus Christ. We look to our Savior for all things. He is the way, the truth, the light, and life of the world—even the true vine that gives us sustenance and strength. He is our rock and foundation upon which we must build (see Hel. 5:12). His gospel of redemption is the power to draw us to Him and is the foundation of His Church (see 3 Ne. 27:8–15). He is the light that we look to and hold up (see 3 Ne. 12:15; 15:12–16; 18:24). He is the strength through which we can do all things (see Alma 20:4).

1. THE SACRAMENT

THEME: Remember to make the sacrament a meaningful and covenant-renewing experience.

MOMENT OF TRUTH

It is a matter of tender poignancy that the Savior instituted the sacrament during the celebration of the Passover—with its unleavened bread and attendant offering of the sacrificial lamb—for it was on this particular occasion that He Himself was shortly to become the sacrificial Lamb of God—not in commemoration of the sparing of the Israelites at the time of Egyptian bondage, but rather in the glory of the redemptive act of saving all mankind through the plan of salvation. The Savior sent Peter and John to prepare the Passover supper, telling them to go in quest of a man bearing a pitcher of water within the city who would guide them to a place where they could gather in privacy. At the appointed hour, the Savior and His Apostles celebrated the last of their suppers: "And he took bread, and gave thanks, and brake it, and gave unto them, saying, This is my body which is given for you: this do in remembrance of me. Likewise also the cup after supper, saying, This cup is the new testament in my blood, which is shed for you" (Luke 22:19–20; compare Matt. 26:26–28; Mark 14:22–24). On that occasion, the Savior announced the disconcerting news that one among them would betray Him: "But, behold, the hand of him that betrayeth me is with me on the table" (Luke 22:21). In the wake of that devastating revelation, there was a discussion within the circle of who might be the greatest among them. The Savior provided the key: he who *serves* is the chief—a reference to His divine role as atoning servant for all mankind, being the Exemplar in whose footsteps all should follow. As reported by John, the Savior washed the feet of the disciples following the supper (John 13:4–10). When Peter proclaimed his unshakable allegiance to the Master, he heard the troubling prophecy that even he would deny the Savior three times before the crowing of the cock (see Luke 22:34). Thereafter the Savior retired to the Mount of Olives. His hour had come.

MODERN PROPHETS SPEAK

George Albert Smith:

> Partaking of the sacrament increases our spiritual strength. I feel that a comprehension of the sacredness of the sacrament of the Lord's Supper is important to the members of the Church. We partake of physical food—that is, we partake of bread and water etc., to nourish the physical body. It is just as necessary that we partake of the emblems of the body and blood of our risen Lord to increase our spiritual strength. It is observed that men and women who go from year to year without partaking of the Lord's Supper gradually lose the Spirit of our Heavenly Father; they forfeit its companionship where they have had opportunity to participate in that blessing, but have failed to take advantage of it. The sacrament is of great importance. The Lord himself ordained that we partake of these emblems. There are many people who believe it is necessary to be baptized, and to have other ordinances of the gospel performed in their behalf, and yet they become indifferent and careless regarding the sacrament of the Lord's Supper. It was regarded of such importance by our Father in Heaven that, through his Beloved Son, and the Apostles and prophets, as recorded in the scriptures, the Saints were admonished to partake of it regularly. (*The Teachings of George Albert Smith,* ed. Robert McIntosh and Susan McIntosh, 95)

ILLUSTRATIONS FOR OUR TIME

Thomas S. Monson tells a tender story of the significance of the sacrament in one's life and the blessings afforded through the welfare program. He relates:

> My introduction to the welfare program came when I was a deacon at twelve years of age. The bishop asked that I take the sacrament to a bedfast brother who longed for this blessing. The morning was sunny, and I didn't mind missing my Sunday School class to walk the three-quarters of a mile distance from the chapel, down the street, across the railroad tracks to the modest residence. I knocked at the kitchen door and heard a feeble voice say, "Come in."

I entered the kitchen, then moved to the bedside of Brother Edward Wright. When I uncovered the sacrament, he asked if I would place a piece of bread in his shaking hand and press the cup of water to his trembling lips. His gratitude overwhelmed me. The Spirit of the Lord came over me. I stood on sacred ground. . . .

I left that humble home and skipped back to the chapel—the same chapel where, ten years later, I would be sustained as the bishop, presiding over a membership that, more than any other in the Church, needed the welfare program. (*Inspiring Experiences That Build Faith: From the Life and Ministry of Thomas S. Monson* [Salt Lake City: Deseret Book, 1994], 188)

LIKENING THE SCRIPTURES TO OUR LIVES

D&C 20:77 O God, the Eternal Father, we ask thee in the name of thy Son, Jesus Christ, to bless and sanctify this bread to the souls of all those who partake of it, that they may eat in remembrance of the body of thy Son, and witness unto thee, O God, the Eternal Father, that they are willing to take upon them the name of thy Son, and always remember him and keep his commandments which he has given them; that they may always have his Spirit to be with them. Amen.

Application: The sacramental prayer reminds us of the blessings we receive if we remember our Savior and His suffering, take His name upon us, and keep His commandments so that we may always have His Spirit to be with us. Remember, let us keep the commandments and renew all our covenants that we have entered into—baptismal, priesthood, and temple.

2. LOVE ONE ANOTHER

THEME: Loving one another is a commandment—the motive for every righteous act and the source of true joy.

MOMENT OF TRUTH

During the last hours with His Apostles before His crucifixion, the Savior taught them lessons of magnificence concerning the doctrines of the kingdom. In a display of gracious humility, He washed the feet of His anointed successors. At first, Peter objected: "Thou shalt never wash my feet. Jesus answered him, If I wash thee not, thou hast no part with me. Simon Peter saith unto him, Lord, not my feet only, but also my hands and my head" (John 13:8–9). The Lord assured him: "He that is washed needeth not save to wash his feet, but is clean every whit: and ye are clean, but not all" (John 13:10), a reference in this latter phrase to Judas, who would betray the Lord. In contrast to the vile deceit of Judas, the Lord expounded a doctrine of mutual loyalty and charity: "If I then, your Lord and Master, have washed your feet; ye also ought to wash one another's feet. For I have given you an example, that ye should do as I have done to you. Verily, verily, I say unto you, The servant is not greater than his lord; neither he that is sent greater than he that sent him. If ye know these things, happy are ye if ye do them" (John 13:14–17).

Then the Lord pronounced a commandment superseding all others as a demonstration of fidelity to the divine cause: "A new commandment I give unto you, That ye love one another; as I have loved you, that ye also love one another. By this shall all men know that ye are my disciples, if ye have love one to another" (John 13:34–35). Furthermore: "If ye love me, keep my commandments" (John 14:15). And: "If a man love me, he will keep my words: and my Father will love him, and we will come unto him, and make our abode with him" (John 14:23). The Savior promised to send them the Comforter: "Peace I leave with you, my peace I give unto you: not as the world giveth, give I unto you. Let not your heart by troubled, neither let it be afraid" (John 14:27). Finally: "This is my commandment, That ye love one another, as I have loved you. Greater love hath no man than this, that a man lay down his life for his friends" (John 15:12–13).

MODERN PROPHETS SPEAK

Gordon B. Hinckley:

> The Savior spoke prophetically of that sacrifice and of the love that culminated in his redemptive sacrifice when he declared, "Greater love hath no man than this, that a man lay down his life for his friends" (John 15:13).
>
> To all of us who would be his disciples, he has given the great commandment, "A new commandment I give unto you, That ye love one another; as I have loved you, that ye also love one another" (John 13:34).
>
> If the world is to be improved, the process of love must make a change in the hearts of mankind. It can do so when we look beyond self to give our love to God and others, and do so with all our heart, with all our soul, and with all our mind. (*Faith: The Essence of True Religion* [Salt Lake City: Deseret Book, 1989], 48–49)

ILLUSTRATIONS FOR OUR TIME

Elaine L. Jack, former general president of the Relief Society of the Church, shares the following thoughts and tender examples about love:

> To summarize—these have been my suggestions for increasing love:

1. Share your best times with your family. Work and play together. Put family before business and friends and other pressures.

2. Talk about the gospel daily. Study scriptures and live gospel values.

3. Express love to your Heavenly Father, to your family, to your friends, every day. . . .

If the troubles in the world stem from lack of genuine love for one another, the simple yet profound commandments given by the Savior are the answer. The greatest commandments deal with relationships: "Love one another, as I have loved you" (John 15:12). Our loving interaction with others—with family, friends, business associates—will heal the world. Such interactions call for more understanding among us and increased ability to communicate. We all can strive to improve our sensitivity in relationships. Love begins in families, families in all their dimensions. The bottom line is that we care about each other and are willing to show it. (*LDS Women's Treasury: Insights and Inspiration for Today's Woman* [Salt Lake City: Deseret Book, 1997], 314)

LIKENING THE SCRIPTURES TO OUR LIVES

John 13:34–35 A new commandment I give unto you, That ye love one another; as I have loved you, that ye also love one another. By this shall all men know that ye are my disciples, if ye have love one to another.

Application: True feelings and expressions of love are the hallmark of true disciples of Christ. Remember that love can be demonstrated as the ultimate concern for another person. It is love that brings about righteous service.

3. JESUS IS THE WAY, THE TRUTH, THE LIFE, AND THE TRUE VINE

T<small>HEME</small>: Jesus Christ is our foundation and the only way by which we can return to our Heavenly Father.

MOMENT OF TRUTH

In His final moments with the Apostles, the Savior—ever a master at image and symbol to enhance the power of His instruction—likened Himself to the vine of God: "I am the true vine, and my Father is the husbandman. . . . I am the vine, ye are the branches: He that abideth in me, and I in him, the same bringeth forth much fruit: for without me ye can do nothing" (John 15:1, 5). The spiritual essence of this organic symbol is clear: "Herein is my Father glorified, that ye bear much fruit; so shall ye be my disciples" (John 15:8). The fruit of which He spoke reflects the qualities of pure love and sacrifice—"Greater love hath no man than this, that a man lay down his life for his friends" (John 15:13); obedience, authority from God—"Ye have not chosen me, but I have chosen you, and ordained you, that ye should go and bring forth fruit," (John 15:16); humble service, and the guidance of the Comforter as divine witness of truth (see John 15:26).

MODERN PROPHETS SPEAK

Ezra Taft Benson:

> Do you recall the passage in the fourteenth chapter of the Gospel according to John where Jesus is tenderly saying his farewell to his disciples after the Last Supper? He tells them that he goes to prepare a place for them in his Father's house; that where he is, they also may be. And "Thomas saith to him, Lord, we know not whither thou goest; and how can we know the way?
>
> "Jesus saith unto him, I am the way, the truth, and the life: no man cometh unto the Father, but by me" (John 14:5–6).
>
> The road lies before us. It is clearly marked. The means to travel it are richly provided. We must follow the path set for us by the Son of God in all that we desire, think, and do. (*So Shall Ye Reap*, comp. Reed A. Benson, 169)

ILLUSTRATIONS FOR OUR TIME

The True Vine

When we all take time to reflect upon our own lives, we can see our dependence upon our Savior Jesus Christ. He is the way, the truth, the light, and life of the world. He is the Vine that gives us all the strength to carry on. Stop and think: He preserves our very lives and lends us breath (see Mosiah 2:21). He strengthens us against temptations of every kind and succors us in all our afflictions (see Alma 7:11–12). He atoned for our sins because He loves us (see 2 Ne. 26:24). He has set the perfect example for us (see 3 Ne. 27:27). He has given us the way back to the Father by showing us how to keep His commandments and endure to the end (see 2 Ne. 31:20). As we come to understand and appreciate these wonderful truths, we will be filled with gratitude and, indeed, we will change. We will truly seek our Savior and His ways in all that we do. Our motto would simply become, "Do as Jesus would do." Nephi prayed for strength to burst his bonds and the Lord blessed him (see 1 Ne. 17:17). Yes, through prayer we can call upon Father in the name of Jesus Christ and we will be shown the way by the Spirit—even when we don't know what to do (see 1 Ne. 4:6). We can receive everlasting truths through fasting and prayer (see Alma 5:46). Remember that only in and through Christ can salvation be received (see Mosiah 3:17).

Howard W. Hunter has illustrated the power of prayer and how we can be strengthened and shown the way by the Spirit. He said, "Living members give heed to the Spirit, which quickens the inner life. They constantly seek its direction. They pray for strength and overcome difficulties. Their hearts are not set upon the things of this world but upon the infinite. Spiritual renewal is not sacrificed for physical gratification. Living members put Christ first in their lives, knowing from what source their lives and progress come" (*That We Might Have Joy* [Salt Lake City: Deseret Book, 1994], 151). [Pinegar]

The Branches of the Lord
In His final set of instruction to His disciples, the Savior invoked a splendid image to explain the relationships between Deity and mankind:

> I am the true vine, and my Father is the husbandman.
>
> Every branch in me that beareth not fruit he taketh away: and every branch that beareth fruit, he purgeth it, that it may bring forth more fruit. . . .
>
> Abide in me, and I in you. As the branch cannot bear fruit of itself, except it abide in the vine; no more can ye, except ye abide in me.
>
> I am the vine, ye are the branches: He that abideth in me, and I in him, the same bringeth forth much fruit: for without me ye can do nothing.
>
> If a man abide not in me, he is cast forth as a branch, and is withered; and men gather them, and cast them into the fire, and they are burned. . . .
>
> Herein is my Father glorified, that ye bear much fruit; so shall ye be my disciples" (John 15:1–2, 4–6, 8).

What kind of "branch" is herein implied? I thought it might be of interest to gospel students to learn how the scriptures themselves answer this question. A survey of the relevant scriptural references to such "branches of the Lord" and similar imagery yields an interesting array of revealed wisdom that can be used to put together an ideal portrait of what is expected by the Lord in this regard. Here is a summary of the results of this survey, organized according the acronym B-R-A-N-C-H-E-S, for ease of reference:

B—Beautiful. In the scriptures, the image of the Lord's "branches" takes on the characteristic of *beauty:* "In that day shall the branch of the Lord be beautiful and glorious, and the fruit of the earth shall be excellent and comely for them that are escaped of Israel" (Isa. 4:2; compare 2 Ne. 14:2). The word "beauty" in such references can generally be applied to the priesthood truths and powers that devolve upon the Saints through the grace and beneficence of God.

R—Righteous. The branches of the Lord reflect an enduring commitment to keep the commandments and obey the word of the Lord. *Righteousness* is therefore a further quality of these branches: "Thy people also shall be all righteous: they shall inherit the land for ever, the branch of my planting, the work of my hands, that I may be glorified" (Isa. 60:21).

A—Abundant. As the Lord states in His instructions to the disciples concerning the vine and its branches, the people of God are fruitful, that is, *abundant,* in producing a high and pure yield unto the Lord. We would expect to see such abundance by virtue of the fact that the branches are connected to the vine, the divine source. This imagery is consistent with that used elsewhere in the scriptures. When Jacob bestowed his patriarchal blessing upon his son Joseph, he spoke the inspired words: "Joseph is a fruitful bough, even a fruitful bough by a well; whose branches run over the wall" (Gen. 49:22; compare 1 Ne. 10:12–14; 15:12).

N—Name of the Lord. All branches of the Lord operate in His name and reflect His identity. In fact, the word "Branch" is specifically one of the names of the Lord, as confirmed by the following passages: "And there shall come forth a rod out of the stem of Jesse, and a Branch shall grow out of his roots" (Isa. 11:1). Who is this "Branch"? It is the Savior, Jesus Christ (see Isa. 11:2–10).

C—Covenant-centered. The branches of the Lord are related to each other and integrated together into a sacred charitable network by virtue of their joint participation in the covenant commission of God. Under the Abrahamic covenant, the children of Abraham are appointed servants to the entire world to convey to all peoples the truths concerning the plan of salvation and the saving ordinances of the priesthood (Abr. 2:9–11). The magnificent and astoundingly complex allegory of the olive tree prepared by the prophet Zenos, as reported by Jacob (Jacob 5), is constructed around covenant principles. The grafting in of the tame and/or wild olive branches in diverse, and multiple venues within the vineyard of the Lord surely has reference to the upbuilding of the kingdom of God through the expansive missionary work of the Lord. He moves His peoples—His "branches"—around and about His vineyard from time to time to optimize and maximize the yield of faithful and obedient Saints. No fewer than 37 verses in Jacob 5 have references to branches (compare the multiple passages in the D&C that refer to ecclesiastical branches: examples—D&C 10:60, 20:65–66; 72:23).

H—Holy. A further quality of the branches of the Lord is *holiness,* as explained by Paul: "For if the firstfruit be holy, the lump is also holy: and if the root be holy, so are the branches" (Rom. 11:16).

E—Exalted as an Ensign. In addition, the branches of the Lord are to be *exalted* in stature and location: "Thus saith the Lord God; I will also take of the highest branch of the high cedar, and will set it; I will crop off from the top of his young twigs a tender one, and will plant it upon an high mountain and eminent: In the mountain of the height of Israel will I plant it: and it shall bring forth boughs, and bear fruit, and be a goodly cedar: and under it shall dwell all fowl of every wing; in the shadow of the branches thereof shall they dwell" (Ezek. 17:22–23). Such branches are in fact an ensign of God unto the world.

S—Saved. Finally, the branches of the Lord consist of people who, as they honor their covenant vows and endure to the end, are saved in the kingdom of God. Jacob makes this point clear: "And how merciful is our God unto us, for he remembereth the house of Israel, both roots and branches; and he stretches forth his hands unto them all the day long; and they are a stiffnecked and a gainsaying people; but as many as will not harden their hearts shall be saved in the kingdom of God" (Jacob 6: 4).

The Savior said, "I am the vine, ye are the branches" (John 15:5). Alma provided a joyful summary of this grand process of spiritual growth and productivity: "That they might not be hardened against the word, that they might not be unbelieving, and go on to destruction, but that they might receive the word with joy, and as a branch be grafted into the true vine, that they might enter into the rest of the Lord their God" (Alma 16:17). [Allen]

LIKENING THE SCRIPTURES TO OUR LIVES

John 14:6 Jesus saith unto him, I am the way, the truth, and the life: no man cometh unto the Father, but by me.

Application: Let us never forget that our Savior Jesus Christ is the only way back to the presence of our Heavenly Father. His infinite and eternal Atonement, the blessings of His gospel, the power of His priesthood with its accompanying covenants and ordinances, and His teachings and doctrines will bring us happiness and joy.

SUMMARY

From the account of the Savior's final instructions to His disciples, we derive spiritual sustenance of enormous significance: the vital importance of the sacrament in ensuring that we remember and observe all the principles of salvation, the governing role of active love in building up of the kingdom of God, and the expediency of accepting and following the Savior as the true vine of the Father. In regard to the sacrament, the Savior reemphasized His will to the ancient American Saints following His resurrection: "And this shall ye always observe to do, even as I have done, . . . And I give unto you a commandment that ye shall do these things. And if ye shall always do these things blessed are ye, for ye are built upon my rock" (3 Ne. 18:6, 12).

CHAPTER 24

"THIS IS LIFE ETERNAL"

Reading Assignment: John 16–17.

Additional Reading: John 14:16–31; 15:26–27; 1 Corinthians 12:3; Galatians 5:22–23; Philippians 1:27; Mosiah 18:21; 3 Nephi 19:19–36; 4 Nephi 1:15–17; D&C 6:15; 11:13; 35:2; 38:24–27; Bible Dictionary, "Comforter" (648); "Holy Ghost" (704).

> *In His great, moving prayer in the Garden before His betrayal, Christ pleaded with His Father concerning the Apostles, whom He loved, saying:*
>
> *"Neither pray I for these alone, but for them also which shall believe on me through their word;*
>
> *"That they all may be one; as thou, Father, art in me, and I in thee, that they also may be one in us" (John 17:20–21).*
>
> *It is that perfect unity between the Father, the Son, and the Holy Ghost that binds these three into the oneness of the divine Godhead.*
>
> *Miracle of miracles and wonder of wonders, they are interested in us, and we are the substance of their great concern. They are available to each of us. We approach the Father through the Son. He is our intercessor at the throne of God. How marvelous it is that we may so speak to the Father in the name of the Son.*
>
> —GORDON B. HINCKLEY, "THE FATHER, SON, AND HOLY GHOST," *ENSIGN,* NOV. 1986, 51.

THEMES *for* LIVING

1. The Gift of the Holy Ghost
2. Prophecies of the Death and Resurrection of the Lord Jesus Christ
3. The Great Intercessory Prayer—Knowing God and Jesus Christ

INTRODUCTION

The purpose of Heavenly Father's magnificent plan of salvation is to enable His children to be happy and enter into a state of never-ending joy (see Mosiah 2:41). This gift—even eternal life—is the greatest of all the gifts of God (see D&C 14:7), given to us if we will but choose to obey and keep His commandments. It is made possible through the grace of God, which entails the infinite and eternal Atonement and resurrection of our beloved Savior Jesus Christ, performed on our behalf so that we might be saved, after all we can do (see 2 Ne. 25:23). We have been given a most priceless companion from our Heavenly Father to help us in this quest for happiness (see Alma 27:18)—even the Holy Ghost, the third member of the Godhead (see 2 Ne. 32:12). We must humbly plead for the Spirit in all of our undertakings (see 3 Ne. 19:9), and then it will show us all things to do (see 2 Ne. 32:5).

1. THE GIFT OF THE HOLY GHOST

THEME: The Holy Ghost comforts, teaches, testifies, enlightens our mind, leads us to do good, to walk humbly, to do justly, and to judge righteously; it shows us all things to do and brings us love, peace, gentleness, goodness, and a whole host of other righteous feelings, qualities, and blessings. (See John 14:26; 15:26; 16:13–14; D&C 11:12–13; 2 Ne. 32:5; Gal. 5:22–23). We are to seek the Holy Ghost and then obey its promptings.

MOMENT OF TRUTH

The Apostles were consumed with the anguish of having to experience the imminent loss of the Good Shepherd from their midst. How were they to be consoled? It was slight comfort, perhaps, given the dramatic urgency of the moment, that they heard prophetic words from the Master about their own inevitable persecution and martyrdom for the cause. The Savior could discern their agony: "But because I have said these things unto you, sorrow hath filled your heart" (John 16:6). Therefore, He had for them a special gift in store:

> It is expedient for you that I go away: for if I go not away, the Comforter will not come unto you; but if I depart, I will send him unto you.

And when he is come, he will reprove the world of sin, and of righteousness, and of judgment:

Of sin, because they believe not on me;

Of righteousness, because I go to my Father, and ye see me no more;

Of judgment, because the prince of this world is judged.

I have yet many things to say unto you, but ye cannot bear them now.

Howbeit when he, the Spirit of truth, is come, he will guide you into all truth: for he shall not speak of himself; but whatsoever he shall hear, *that* shall he speak: and he will shew you things to come.

He shall glorify me: for he shall receive of mine, and shall shew *it* unto you. (John 16:7–14)

This glorious promise concerning the Comforter must have instilled in the hearts of the disciples a warming glow of hope in anticipation of such a marvelous future manifestation. The Savior added this promise, which has applicability for all those of faith who likewise become bereaved: "Verily, verily, I say unto you, That ye shall weep and lament, but the world shall rejoice: and ye shall be sorrowful, but your sorrow shall be turned into joy. . . . I will see you again, and your heart shall rejoice, and your joy no man taketh from you" (John 16:20, 22). All of this is rendered true, as the Savior confirmed, because of the love that the Father has for His own (John 16:27), a love which engenders peace and comfort: "These things I have spoken unto you, that in me ye might have peace. In the world ye shall have tribulation: but be of good cheer; I have overcome the world" (John 16:33).

MODERN PROPHETS SPEAK

Harold B. Lee:

> Eternal blessings can come by yielding to the Holy Ghost. I am aware of the fact that for us to gain a testimony and, yes, beyond that, a knowledge, and finally the privilege of dwelling in the presence of God the Father and His Son, which will be that eternal life spoken of, I am made aware that that can only be had because of our yielding obedience to the Spirit of the Holy Ghost, which is given to the baptized members of the Church, in which light we shall walk forward until we shall have accomplished all things and shall be numbered among the faithful, with those who shall inherit celestial glory. (*THBL,* 99–100)

ILLUSTRATIONS FOR OUR TIME

A Lesson in Spirituality

The Prophet Joseph Smith lived by the spirit of revelation. He made decisions by it, he learned by it, and he taught by it. Because of this spirit, which is the gift of the Holy

Ghost, the Prophet could unlock the closed doors of biblical knowledge and could obtain "the true meaning and intention" of even the most vague and "mysterious passages" (JS—H 1:74). He learned how to recognize the voice of the Spirit and thus to get revelation when it was needed. Although such an ability is a gift, it is also an attainment and requires energy, experience, and practice, even for a prophet. . . .

Translating by the spirit of revelation as the Prophet searched the scriptures is both a lesson and an invitation to all of us. Although none of us is commissioned by the Lord to make another translation of the Bible, yet it is plain to see that light, inspiration, and revelation come to those who pursue it for the right reasons through searching the scriptures. We have before us in the history of the Church several examples showing this principle at work. It was reading James 1:5 that caused the Prophet to seek for additional information that led to the First Vision in 1820; it was reading the newly translated account from the Book of Mormon that led Joseph and Oliver to inquire about baptism, which resulted in John the Baptist conferring the Aaronic Priesthood upon them in 1829; and it was President Joseph F. Smith's pondering over the meaning, after having read 1 Pet. 3 and 4, that parted the veil and gave him a view of how the gospel is preached in the world of departed spirits (see D&C 138:1–11). . . .

Such experiences are patterns that show us there is understanding and new knowledge to be gained when we search, pray, ponder, and meditate upon the holy scriptures and hear the voice of the Lord through his Spirit. In this way we come to know not only the doctrines of the gospel and the will of the Lord as revealed in ancient time but also the application to us individually in our own time. (Robert J. Matthews, *Selected Writings of Robert J. Matthews:* Gospel Scholars Series, 301–3)

LIKENING THE SCRIPTURES TO OUR LIVES

John 14:26 But the Comforter, which is the Holy Ghost, whom the Father will send in my name, he shall teach you all things, and bring all things to your remembrance, whatsoever I have said unto you.

Application: We are instructed to seek the blessings of the Holy Ghost (see 3 Ne. 19:9) as we keep the commandments (see D&C 20:77, 79).

2. PROPHECIES OF THE DEATH AND RESURRECTION OF THE LORD JESUS CHRIST

THEME: Down through the ages, the prophets of God—including the Savior Himself—have foretold of His death and ultimate resurrection.

MOMENT OF TRUTH

This moment of the imminent consummation of the atoning sacrifice of the Redeemer was not an isolated moment in time, not a moment devoid of anchor and context in the flow of human and eternal affairs; rather, this moment was—along with the Creation and the Fall—the most connected moment in all of history. Every individual assigned from before the foundations of the world to participate in the mortal experience on earth was and is connected to this very moment. Every word of every prophet in all dispensations was connected to this hallowed moment that would bring the fulfillment of the will of the Father and His immortal designs for the salvation, immortality, and eternal life of man. Every breath of life and every heartbeat in the panorama of human existence was connected to this sacred moment, because out of this moment would flow the power and light of life for all of God's creations. How raptly focused must have been the view of the legions of heaven on this moment in time as the curtains were drawn inexorably back in anticipation of this preordained event so absolutely essential to the salvation of mankind. The Savior was about to do the will of the Father and bring under His feet all enemies of God's supernal plan of salvation, including death. It is therefore wise to recall and remember in our hearts the continual process of foretelling and prophesying that presaged this event—from Adam to Noah, from Abraham to Moses, from Isaiah to Malachi, from Lehi to Samuel the Lamanite and all the rest of God's servants—all pointing to this holy and singularly significant moment.

MODERN PROPHETS SPEAK

Bruce R. McConkie:

> Around his crucifixion, death, and resurrection many ancient prophecies are centered. Isaiah, David, Nephi, Nephi the son of Helaman, and Samuel the Lamanite, for instance, speak pointedly of the fact that God himself, having come into mortality, would die (Ps. 16:10; Isa. 26:19–21; 53:9; Acts 13:35; 1 Ne. 10:11; 11:32–34; Hela. 8:19–20; 14). That this death should result from crucifixion was forerevealed by Isaiah, Nephi, Jacob the brother of Nephi, and Enoch, among others (Isa. 22:21–25; 1 Ne. 11:32–34; 19:10–13; 2 Ne. 10:3; Moses 7:55). And the glorious resurrection of our Lord was spoken of on many occasions (Isa. 25:8–9; 26:19–21; Hela. 14). (*MD*, 490)

ILLUSTRATIONS FOR OUR TIME

Seeing into the Future

We know from the Holy Scriptures that the Lord is omniscient—relative to the past, present, and future. He taught Moses: "And I have a work for thee, Moses, my son;

and thou art in the similitude of mine Only Begotten; and mine Only Begotten is and shall be the Savior, for he is full of grace and truth; but there is no God beside me, and all things are present with me, for I know them all" (Moses 1:6). The Lord also revealed through Joseph Smith His nature in this regard: "Thus saith the Lord your God, even Jesus Christ, the Great I Am, Alpha and Omega, the beginning and the end, the same which looked upon the wide expanse of eternity, and all the seraphic hosts of heaven, before the world was made; The same which knoweth all things, for all things are present before mine eyes;" (D&C 38:1–2).

Because all things are "present" before the Lord, He was able to inspire His prophets to peer into the future and envision His condescension and atoning sacrifice with unmistakable clarity. To Isaiah, He vouchsafed through the Spirit these immortal words: "For unto us a child is born, unto us a son is given: and the government shall be upon his shoulder: and his name shall be called Wonderful, Counsellor, The mighty God, The everlasting Father, The Prince of Peace" (Isa. 9:6). Countless are the prophetic pronouncements of the Savior's mission in mortality spoken under inspiration by all the prophets of God prior to His coming.

As we consider the miraculous sequence of prophecies leading up to the coming of our Lord and Savior in the meridian of time, we are strengthened in our conviction that the word of the Lord "shall all be fulfilled" (D&C 1:38). He has blessed us with a vast inventory of wisdom in the sacred canon concerning the principles and details of His plan for the immortality and eternal life of man. All of this will transpire in the due time of the Lord. [Allen]

LIKENING THE SCRIPTURES TO OUR LIVES

Helaman 14:15–17 For behold, he surely must die that salvation may come; yea, it behooveth him and becometh expedient that he dieth, to bring to pass the resurrection of the dead, that thereby men may be brought into the presence of the Lord. Yea, behold, this death bringeth to pass the resurrection, and redeemeth all mankind from the first death—that spiritual death; for all mankind, by the fall of Adam being cut off from the presence of the Lord, are considered as dead, both as to things temporal and to things spiritual. But behold, the resurrection of Christ redeemeth mankind, yea, even all mankind, and bringeth them back into the presence of the Lord.

Application: The Saints of the past, prior to the advent of our Savior, lived with the hope of the coming of our Savior, His sacrifice, and His resurrection to the newness of life. This glorious news, even the good news of the gospel of Jesus Christ, is what gives us hope as well—that the Lord and Savior died that we might live through the power of the resurrection. For this we should be filled with overwhelming gratitude for our Savior and for the grace and goodness of Heavenly Father.

3. THE GREAT INTERCESSORY PRAYER—KNOWING GOD AND JESUS CHRIST

THEME: We belong to the Lord and to the Father in unity and purpose. The great intercessory prayer given by the Lord is filled with doctrine, compassion, and concern for His disciples and all believers.

MOMENT OF TRUTH

The pathway of life, leading homeward to God, is beset with contrasting and alternating shadows and light. Along that pathway we sometimes encounter experiences of unfathomable darkness and oppression; at other times, by contrast, our hearts and minds are filled with overpowering spiritual illumination that fills the soul with unspeakable joy. Such was the case in the transitional period of time between the Savior's last discourses to His disciples, including His extraordinary intercessory prayer to the Father—characterized by the transcendent light of divine truth and glory strong enough to overshadow sorrow—and the bleakness of the sinister betrayal by one of the Twelve into whom Satan had entered (John 13:27). The great intercessory prayer of the Redeemer, given on the eve of the betrayal, is a pinnacle of light and hope shining in the blackness of ignorance and vile oppression at the hands of evil men. The theme of that prayer—"And this is life eternal, that they might know thee the only true God, and Jesus Christ, whom thou hast sent" (John 17:3)—is echoed over and over again in the revolving and interlocking references by the Lord to glory, joy, unity, sanctification, truth, testimony, and love. What a marvelous example of a selfless and compassionate prayer is this—given by the Savior specifically "that they might have my joy fulfilled in themselves" (John 17:13).

MODERN PROPHETS SPEAK

James E. Faust:

> As the hour of the Savior's death and Resurrection drew near, He offered His great Intercessory Prayer. After commending His Apostles to the Father and praying for them, He then prayed for all those who would believe on Him through their word, and pleaded with the Father for all of us. He prayed that we could all be one as He is one with the Father and that the world would believe that He was sent by the Father.
>
> No more poignant prayer was ever uttered than that given by the Savior in the Garden of Gethsemane. He withdrew from His Apostles, knelt, and prayed, "Father, if thou be willing, remove this cup from me: nevertheless not my will, but thine, be done." An important element of all of our prayers might well be to follow the pat-

tern of that prayer in Gethsemane: "not my will, but thine, be done." By this, then, we acknowledge our devotion and submission to the overriding purposes of the Lord in our lives. As He said, "If ye abide in me, and my words abide in you, ye shall ask what ye will, and it shall be done unto you." What a glorious day it will be for each of us when we pray with confidence that "if we ask anything according to his will, he heareth us." (James E. Faust, "The Lifeline of Prayer," *Ensign,* May 2002, 61–62)

ILLUSTRATIONS FOR OUR TIME

The Great Intercessory Prayer

The power of prayer, the compassion of Christ, and the supernal doctrines of God are expressed and taught in this transcending time in the Garden of Gethsemane. Our Savior knew of the impending suffering and sacrifice that would bring about the infinite and eternal Atonement that all mankind might gain immortality and eternal life. He is our Advocate and prays not only for His Apostles but for all who would come unto Him. Christ had been given power over all things and specified the conditions to gain eternal life by knowing God the Father and Jesus Christ our Savior. The Lord revealed to the Prophet Joseph a key to knowing our Heavenly Father and our Savior: "And again, verily I say unto you that it is your privilege, and a promise I give unto you that have been ordained unto this ministry, that inasmuch as you strip yourselves from jealousies and fears, and humble yourselves before me, for ye are not sufficiently humble, the veil shall be rent and you shall see me and know that I am—not with the carnal neither natural mind, but with the spiritual" (D&C 67:10). We come to know Deity by the power of the Holy Ghost, who is a witness of the Father and the Son (see 2 Ne. 31:18; 3 Ne. 28:11). Knowing God and Jesus Christ is imperative—but it is also recorded that They must know us (see Matt. 7:21–23; 3 Ne. 14:21–23), else we are cast off. Christ expresses His obedience to the will of the Father, indicating that He had glorified the Father even as we are asked to glorify the Father through our good works (see 3 Ne. 12:16). He speaks of His beloved Apostles whom the Father had given Him, having previously prayed to Him for direction (see Luke 6:12). The Apostles had been easily entreated and had believed His words and that He had been sent by the Father. Christ's joy and glory were in the Twelve and His followers. At this time, He prayed not for the world but for His disciples and followers, that they might have eternal life (see D&C 45:5). He prayed as well for their "oneness," even as Christ and the Father are one, for we must be "one" in order to be His (see D&C 38:27). The Savior speaks more of this oneness in verses 21–23. The worth of souls surely is what matters to our Heavenly Father and Savior (see D&C 18:13; Moses 1:39). He expanded on this counsel to the Nephites as He prayed that we avoid evil and the tempter's snare (see 3 Ne. 18:18; Hel. 3:29). He prayed for our sanctification through

His Word, who is Christ (see Rev. 19:13), the light, life, and truth (see Alma 38:9; Ether 4:12).

Through the grace of God, we can become sanctified in Christ, made clean and pure by the power of the Holy Ghost (see 3 Ne. 27:19–20; Moro. 10:32–33). This sanctification comes through the Atonement of Christ as we receive the principles and ordinances of the gospel of Jesus Christ. Sanctification is more than just doing, it is "becoming," which is within the soul—even a change, a mighty change, receiving a heart yielding to the enticings of the Spirit and unto God. Then the one being sanctified is prepared, made holy, consecrated, and set apart for sacred service. The Lord then commends us that we might be sent into the world so that others might hear the everlasting gospel. As the Lord concludes His great prayer, He seeks for the companionship of His beloved Apostles in His glorified state. The Savior then reminds all of us of the love Heavenly Father has for His Beloved Son and seeks for that love to be within the Twelve. We can possess this love as a gift from God as we pray with all the energy of our hearts (see Moro. 7:48), for surely God the Father has demonstrated His love for us by giving us His Only Begotten Son (see John 3:16). [Pinegar]

LIKENING THE SCRIPTURES TO OUR LIVES

John 17:20 Neither pray I for these alone, but for them also which shall believe on me through their word.

Application: We, like Christ, should pray for all mankind, and especially for those who know not God (see Alma 6:6). In service and devotion we should go every step of the way with a prayer in our hearts (see 3 Ne. 20:1).

SUMMARY

On the eve of His departure from mortality, the Savior announced the coming bestowal of the gift of the Holy Spirit upon His followers—God's gift of comfort, light, confirmation, and divine remembrance for the faithful. As He prepared for the hour of the Atonement—an event prophesied and foretold by all of God's prophets from the beginning of time—the Savior offered one of the greatest of all prayers ever sent up from the vales of the earth to the courts of heaven—the great intercessory prayer. This sacred prayer memorialized the key to eternal life—knowing God and Jesus Christ, and then acting in faith and unity to follow the commandments in strict obedience to the will of the Father. We learn in that prayer the ultimate motivation of the Redeemer in completing His work: "And for their sakes I sanctify myself, that they also might be sanctified through the truth" (John 17:19).

CHAPTER 25

"NOT MY WILL, BUT THINE, BE DONE"

Reading Assignment: Matthew 26:36–46; Mark 14:32–42; Luke 22:39–46.

Additional Reading: 1 Nephi 10:21; 2 Nephi 2:5–8; 9:5–8; Mosiah 3:7–9; 16:6–9; Alma 7:11–14; 34:8–16; 42:1–31; D&C 19:15–24; Moses 6:48; Articles of Faith 1:3; Bible Dictionary, "Atonement" (617); "Gethsemane" (680).

The central fact, the crucial foundation, the chief doctrine, and the greatest expression of divine love in the eternal plan of salvation—truly a "plan of happiness," as Alma called it—is the Atonement of the Lord Jesus Christ. Much goes before it and much comes after, but without that pivotal act, that moment of triumph whereby we are made free from the spiritual bondage of sin and the physical chains of the grave, both of which are undeniable deaths, there would be no meaning to the plan of life, and certainly no ultimate happiness in it or after it. . . .

In the words of Moroni, "By Adam came the fall of man. And because of the fall of man came Jesus Christ . . . ; and because of Jesus Christ came the redemption of man. And because of the redemption of man, . . . they are brought back into the presence of the Lord."

—Jeffrey R. Holland, *Christ and the New Covenant: The Messianic Message of the Book of Mormon* [Salt Lake City: Deseret Book, 1997], 197.

THEMES *for* LIVING

1. The Savior Suffered to Take Our Sins and Infirmities upon Himself
2. The Atonement of Jesus Christ—Our Only Hope

INTRODUCTION

Understanding the Atonement of Christ and its relationship to our eternal existence is the greatest knowledge we can have in support of our quest to return to God, our Eternal Father. Thomas S. Monson has stated: "The greatest single lesson we can learn is that when God speaks and a man obeys, that man will always be right" ("Peace in Our Savior," *Ensign,* June 2005, 4). God's words are centered around the power of the Atonement to save lives and guide the faithful back home again. The Atonement is the center of the gospel of Jesus Christ. When we diligently apply its principles to our lives through the covenant process, we become liberated from the fallen state we are in. We become free through Christ by obedience. Yet it is by the grace of God that we are saved, after all we can do (2 Ne. 25:23).

It is such knowledge that will motivate us and cause us to change. This is why the Book of Mormon was given to us as another witness and testament that Jesus is the Christ, the Anointed One. The Lord said,

> Behold I have given unto you my gospel, and this is the gospel which I have given unto you—that I came into the world to do the will of my Father, because my Father sent me.
>
> And my Father sent me that I might be lifted up upon the cross; and after that I had been lifted up upon the cross, that I might draw all men unto me, that as I have been lifted up by men even so should men be lifted up by the Father, to stand before me, to be Judged of their works, whether they be good or whether they be evil—
>
> And for this cause have I been lifted up; therefore, according to the power of the Father I will draw all men unto me, that they may be judged according to their works. (3 Ne. 27:13–15)

The reality of the Atonement demonstrates the tender mercy and the goodness of God, who gave His Only Begotten Son for the salvation of mankind. It is through the atoning sacrifice of our Savior that He is able to nurture us in all our infirmities and afflictions as described by Alma:

> And he shall go forth, suffering pains and afflictions and temptations of every kind; and this that the word might be fulfilled which saith he will take upon him the pains and the sicknesses of his people.
>
> And he will take upon him death, that he may loose the bands of death which bind his people; and he will take upon him their infirmities, that his bowels may be filled with mercy, according to the flesh, that he may know according to the flesh how to succor his people according to their infirmities. (Alma 7:11–12)

1. THE SAVIOR SUFFERED TO TAKE OUR SINS AND INFIRMITIES UPON HIMSELF

THEME: Our Savior suffered willingly in Gethsemane, even to the sweating of blood from every pore, for the sins, infirmities, and afflictions of all mankind, granting us the blessings of eternity if we but come unto Him.

MOMENT OF TRUTH

Across the brook Kedron (or Kidron), near the Mount of Olives, lies a garden called Gethsemane ("Oil Press"). The Savior went to this place with His disciples on the night of His betrayal. He said to them, "Sit ye here, while I go and pray yonder" (Matt. 26:36). Taking Peter, James, and John with Him, He then repaired to a place not far away—"about a stone's cast" (Luke 22:41)—to deal with His feelings of heaviness, for He was "sorrowful, even unto death" (Matt. 26:38). He instructed the three, "tarry ye here, and watch with me" (Matt. 26:38), and then went farther and fell on His face and spoke the hauntingly memorable words: "O my Father, if it be possible, let this cup pass from me: nevertheless not as I will, but as thou wilt" (Matt. 26:39). Upon His return, He found the Apostles sleeping and said to Peter, "What, could ye not watch with me one hour? Watch and pray, that ye enter not into temptation: the spirit indeed is willing, but the flesh is weak" (Matt. 26:40). The Savior then went and repeated His prayer, not once, but twice more. Luke gives this account of the circumstances of the extraordinary event: "And there appeared an angel unto him from heaven, strengthening him. And being in an agony he prayed more earnestly: and his sweat was as it were great drops of blood falling down to the ground. And when he rose up from prayer, and was come to his disciples, he found them sleeping for sorrow" (Luke 22:43–45). The Savior's final words to His slumbering Apostles in the garden of agony were compassionate and resigned: "Sleep on now, and take your rest: behold, the hour is at hand, and the Son of man is betrayed into the hands of sinners. Rise, let us be going: behold, he is at hand that doth betray me" (Matt. 26:45–46).

MODERN PROPHETS SPEAK

M. Russell Ballard:

> Thankfully, Jesus Christ courageously fulfilled this sacrifice in ancient Jerusalem. There in the quiet isolation of the Garden of Gethsemane, He knelt among the gnarled olive trees, and in some incredible way that none of us can fully comprehend, the Savior took upon Himself the sins of the world. Even though His life was pure and free of sin, He paid the ultimate penalty for sin yours, mine, and everyone who has ever lived. His mental, emotional, and spiritual anguish were so great they

caused Him to bleed from every pore (see Luke 22:44; D&C 19:18). And yet Jesus suffered willingly so that we might all have the opportunity to be washed clean—through having faith in Him, repenting of our sins, being baptized by proper priesthood authority, receiving the purifying gift of the Holy Ghost by confirmation, and accepting all other essential ordinances. Without the Atonement of the Lord, none of these blessings would be available to us, and we could not become worthy and prepared to return to dwell in the presence of God. ("The Atonement and the Value of One Soul," *Ensign,* May 2004, 85)

ILLUSTRATIONS FOR OUR TIME

S. Kent Brown describes Gethsemane:

The name Gethsemane (derived from Hebrew "oil press") is mentioned twice in the Bible, both in the New Testament (Matt. 26:36; Mark 14:32); in each case, it is called a "place" (Greek *chorion,* "piece of land") to which Jesus Christ and his apostles retired after their last supper together. The fourth gospel calls the area "a garden" (John 18:1). For Latter-day Saints, Gethsemane was the scene of Jesus' greatest agony, even surpassing that which he suffered on the cross, an understanding supported by Mark's description of Jesus' experience (Mark 14:33–39). . . .

Modern LDS leaders have emphasized that Jesus' most challenging experience came in Gethsemane. Speaking in a general conference of the Church in 1982, Marion G. Romney, a member of the First Presidency, observed that Jesus suffered "the pains of all men, which he did, principally, in Gethsemane, the scene of his great agony" (*Ensign,* May 1982, 6). Church President Ezra Taft Benson wrote that "it was in Gethsemane that Jesus took on Himself the sins of the world, in Gethsemane that His pain was equivalent to the cumulative burden of all men, in Gethsemane that He descended below all things so that all could repent and come to Him" (Benson, 7).

While tradition locates Gethsemane on the lower slopes of the Mount of Olives, the exact spot remains unknown. Luke associates it with the Mount of Olives (Luke 22:39), and John notes that it lay across the Kidron brook (John 18:1), which flows from the north along Jerusalem's east side. The particular use of "place" (Greek *topos*) to describe the spot in the gospels of Luke and John suggests that the location was bound up with Jesus' destiny and consequently possesses a sacred character (Luke 22:40; John 18:2). It was a spot that Jesus and his disciples customarily visited (Luke 22:39), which allowed Judas and the others to find him on the night of his arrest (John 18:2). (*Encyclopedia,* 542–43)

LIKENING THE SCRIPTURES TO OUR LIVES

D&C 19:16–20 For behold, I, God, have suffered these things for all, that they might not suffer if they would repent; But if they would not repent they must suffer even as I; Which suffering caused myself, even God, the greatest of all, to tremble because of pain, and to bleed at every pore, and to suffer both body and spirit—and would that I might not drink the bitter cup, and shrink—Nevertheless, glory be to the Father, and I partook and finished my preparations unto the children of men. Wherefore, I command you again to repent, lest I humble you with my almighty power; and that you confess your sins, lest you suffer these punishments of which I have spoken, of which in the smallest, yea, even in the least degree you have tasted at the time I withdrew my Spirit.

Application: The Lord has suffered and paid the universal debt for all mankind's sins in order to satisfy the demands of justice. This blessing can be ours if we choose to repent and come unto Him; if not, we must suffer even as He did.

2. THE ATONEMENT OF JESUS CHRIST— OUR ONLY HOPE

THEME: We can be saved only through the grace of God and the infinite and eternal Atonement of our Savior Jesus Christ.

MOMENT OF TRUTH

The scene in the Garden of Gethsemane was at the vortex of all the flow of history, both human and divine. This was a moment in time unlike any other. It was a moment of infinite agony and redeeming charity, sorrow "unto death" (Matt. 26:38) and Atonement unto life, suffering unspeakable and triumph immeasurable—the ultimate result of eternal design and heavenly will. What did this moment mean to humankind? It meant the victory of life over death; the hope of liberty over the reality of everlasting spiritual imprisonment; the possibility of eternal joy in the presence of God over the horror of a never-ending night of separation from one's heavenly roots and home. This was the moment when faith for all of God's children was raised to a higher power—"this being the intent of this last sacrifice, to bring about the bowels of mercy, which overpowereth justice, and bringeth about means unto men that they may have faith unto repentance" (Alma 34:15). This moment in time was motivated by love, empowered by grace, sustained by courage, and accomplished by the inexorable will of God unto the saving of all mankind. Only one other moment in time ranks significantly with this one—and that is the moment in which each individual will decide, in faith and hope, to accept the Atonement of the Redeemer in all devotion and valor, taking upon himself or herself the name of Jesus Christ, thereafter to live in a state of humble and grateful compliance with all the commandments of God. Such a moment of commitment in the life of each individual honors and validates that moment of infinite reach—that long moment of excruciating suffering and transcendent compassion—when the Savior gave His all for our happiness and joy.

MODERN PROPHETS SPEAK

Gordon B. Hinckley:

> Everything depended on Him—His atoning sacrifice. That was the key. That was the keystone in the arch of the great plan which the Father had brought forth for the eternal life of His sons and daughters. Terrible as it was to face it, and burdensome as it was to realize it, He faced it, He accomplished it, and it was a marvelous and wonderful thing. It is beyond our comprehension, I believe. Nevertheless, we glimpse it in small part and must learn to appreciate it more and more and more. (*TGBH*, 30)

ILLUSTRATIONS FOR OUR TIMES

"Balm of Gilead"

In the well-known hymn "Did You Think to Pray?" the final verse asks the searching questions, "When sore trials came upon you,/Did you think to pray?/When your soul was full of sorrow,/Balm of Gilead did you borrow/At the gates of day?" I remember, as a young bishop many years ago, being approached by a new convert to the Church, a young father, who took me aside after a meeting and, in hushed tones, almost in the manner of supplication, asked me to explain to him the meaning of the phrase "balm of Gilead." His reverential attitude and quiet humility suggested that he felt it was time to be introduced to yet another of the grand mysteries of the Gospel. Smiling, I explained that balm of Gilead was a traditional natural remedy from the Holy Land that had healing effects and was widely used by the Israelites. As such it is an image for the healing essence of the atonement. He seemed almost relieved at the simplicity of the principle and went his way with a smile on his face.

Balm of Gilead is an apt metaphor for a gospel principle. Because forgiveness is the essence of the divine nature, the Savior readily extends His loving-kindness to all mankind and rescues them from ultimate temporal death, and through their faith and obedience, from the spiritual death that inevitably would come through universal weakness. The balm of the Atonement, like the balm of Gilead in the temporal sphere, is the healing power of salvation proclaimed from the foundation of the earth as the answer to the spiritual quest of mankind. Upon the administration of the Atonement, there will be no remaining ailment, no enduring injury—for its renewing curative power is eternal, coming from the Son of Righteousness, with "healing in his wings" (3 Nephi 25:2). [Allen]

LIKENING THE SCRIPTURES TO OUR LIVES

Jacob 7:12 And this is not all—it has been made manifest unto me, for I have heard and seen; and it also has been made manifest unto me by the power of the Holy Ghost; wherefore, I know if there should be no Atonement made all mankind must be lost.

Application: We are totally dependent upon our Savior for all our blessings and nurturing (see Alma 7:11–12). We would be subject to the devil had there been no Atonement (see 2 Ne. 9:8–10), and lest we forget, we are saved by our Lord's grace after all we can do (see 2 Ne. 25:23). Let us truly never forget our need for the Savior's Atonement as we strive to gain eternal life.

SUMMARY

The third Article of Faith states: "We believe that through the Atonement of Christ, all mankind may be saved, by obedience to the laws and ordinances of the Gospel." From the record of the Holy Scriptures for this chapter, we have seen that the Savior suffered to take our sins and infirmities upon Himself. The Atonement of Jesus Christ is our only hope for salvation, immortality, and eternal life. No individual can gain these blessings through perfect compliance with the laws and commandments of God, for no one who has ever lived upon the earth, or who will ever live upon the earth, is perfect—save only the Savior. Therefore, there must of necessity be a way to make up the difference—a divine plan to satisfy the demands of justice through an infinite sacrifice of mercy and compassion. Lehi taught this truth with crystal clarity:

> And men are instructed sufficiently that they know good from evil. And the law is given unto men. And by the law no flesh is justified; or, by the law men are cut off.
>
> Yea, by the temporal law they were cut off; and also, by the spiritual law they perish from that which is good, and become miserable forever.
>
> Wherefore, redemption cometh in and through the Holy Messiah; for he is full of grace and truth. Behold, he offereth himself a sacrifice for sin, to answer the ends of the law, unto all those who have a broken heart and a contrite spirit; and unto none else can the ends of the law be answered.
>
> Wherefore, how great the importance to make these things known unto the inhabitants of the earth, that they may know that there is no flesh that can dwell in

the presence of God, save it be through the merits, and mercy, and grace of the Holy Messiah, who layeth down his life according to the flesh, and taketh it again by the power of the Spirit, that he may bring to pass the resurrection of the dead, being the first that should rise. (2 Ne. 2:5–8; compare 2 Ne. 9:5–8; Mosiah 3:7–9)

Without the intervention of the Redeemer, all would have been consigned to a state of everlasting oblivion and damnation. Abinadi proclaimed before the court of the evil King Noah: "And now if Christ had not come into the world, speaking of things to come as though they had already come, there could have been no redemption. And if Christ had not risen from the dead, or have broken the bands of death that the grave should have no victory, and that death should have no sting, there could have been no resurrection. But there is a resurrection, therefore the grave hath no victory, and the sting of death is swallowed up in Christ. He is the light and the life of the world; yea, a light that is endless, that can never be darkened; yea, and also a life which is endless, that there can be no more death" (Mosiah 16:6–9; compare Alma 7:11–14; 34:8–16; 42:1–31; Moses 6:48).

What do we need to do to merit the magnificent blessing of the Atonement? The Savior taught in our day the key to this redemptive power: "Learn of me, and listen to my words; walk in the meekness of my Spirit, and you shall have peace in me. I am Jesus Christ; I came by the will of the Father, and I do his will" (D&C 19:23–24). In this context, our assignment for mortality is abundantly precise and clear: "Behold, this is your work, to keep my commandments, yea, with all your might, mind and strength" (D&C 11:20).

CHAPTER 26

"TO THIS END WAS I BORN"

Reading Assignment: Matthew 26:47 to 27:66; Mark 14:43 to 15:39; Luke 22:47 to 23:56; John 18–19.

Additional Reading: Isa. 53; Mark 15:39–47; John 3:16; 15:13; 1 Nephi 11:32–33; 19:7–10; 2 Nephi 9:21–22; Bible Dictionary, "Crucifixion" (651).

> *If some are feeling the "scars . . . that have come to you in places where you ought not have gone," to them is extended the special peace and promise available through the atoning sacrifice of the Lord Jesus Christ. His love and the restored gospel principles and ordinances that make that love available to us with all their cleansing and healing power are freely given. The power of these principles and ordinances, including complete and redeeming repentance, are fully realized only in this, the true and living church of the true and living God. We should all "come unto Christ" for the fullness of soul and symbol and sacrament he offers us.*
>
> —JEFFREY R. HOLLAND AND PATRICIA T. HOLLAND, *ON EARTH AS IT IS IN HEAVEN,* 197.

THEMES for LIVING

1. Strength in the Face of Oppression: The Betrayal, Arrest, and Accusations of Blasphemy Against the Savior
2. Test of Loyalty: Peter Denies Jesus
3. Ultimate Challenge: The Trial and Sentencing of Jesus
4. "Father, Forgive Them"—Jesus Is Scourged and Crucified

INTRODUCTION

It is our deepest obligation never to forget the love that the Lord Jesus Christ has for us as His brothers and sisters. Nephi described His love with these words: "He doeth not anything save it be for the benefit of the world; for he loveth the world, even that he layeth down his own life that he may draw all men unto him. Wherefore, he commandeth none that they shall not partake of his salvation"(see 2 Ne. 26:24). King Benjamin taught how Christ is our Father, as He has spiritually begotten us: "And now, because of the covenant which ye have made ye shall be called the children of Christ, his sons, and his daughters; for behold, this day he hath spiritually begotten you; for ye say that your hearts are changed through faith on his name; therefore, ye are born of him and have become his sons and his daughters" (Mosiah 5:7).

When we recognize what He went through to be an offering for our sins, and when we try to understand and appreciate His infinite Atonement, our love for and devotion toward our Savior will increase. We should become like the people of King Benjamin when they came to understand that Jesus was the Christ and Redeemer of the world and their personal Savior. They expressed their feelings in this way: "And they all cried with one voice, saying: Yea, we believe all the words which thou hast spoken unto us; and also, we know of their surety and truth, because of the Spirit of the Lord Omnipotent, which has wrought a mighty change in us, or in our hearts, that we have no more disposition to do evil, but to do good continually" (Mosiah 5:2).

1. STRENGTH IN THE FACE OF OPPRESSION: THE BETRAYAL, ARREST, AND ACCUSATIONS OF BLASPHEMY AGAINST THE SAVIOR

THEME: Appreciating what the Lord Jesus Christ went through prior to His crucifixion will help us to understand the nobility, compassion, and willing acquiescence of the Savior in giving His life for all mankind.

MOMENT OF TRUTH

Contemplate the resolve and patience of the Savior in conducting the affairs of the Twelve Apostles knowing that Judas, the betrayer, was a member of that very quorum. The sinister act of conspiring with the authorities to take the Savior into captivity had been perceived by prophetic insight centuries before it happened: "And I said unto them, If ye think good, give me my price; and if not, forbear. So they weighed for my price thirty pieces of silver. And the Lord said unto me, Cast it unto the potter: a goodly price that I was prised at of them. And I took the thirty pieces of silver, and cast them to the potter in the house of the Lord" (Zech. 11:12–13). Because of greed, Judas sold the Savior into the hands of the envious and evil authorities who then adduced false evidence against Him and attempted to ensnare Him in sinister sophistries. Said Caiaphas, the High Priest: "I adjure thee by the living God, that thou tell us whether thou be the Christ, the Son of God" (Matt. 26:63), to which the Savior responded, "Thou hast said: nevertheless I say unto you, Hereafter shall ye see the Son of man sitting on the right hand of power, and coming in the clouds of heaven" (v. 64). "Then the high priest rent his clothes, saying, He hath spoken blasphemy; what further need have we of witnesses? behold, now ye have heard his blasphemy. What think ye? They answered and said, He is guilty of death" (Matt. 26:65–66). Thus unfolded the unjust and evil proceeding against the Lord—resulting in His conveyance before Pilate and the ensuing death sentence to appease the mob.

MODERN PROPHETS SPEAK

Joseph Smith:

> From apostates the faithful have received the severest persecutions. Judas was rebuked and immediately betrayed his Lord into the hands of His enemies, because Satan entered into him. . . . What nearer friend on earth, or in heaven, had Judas than the Savior? And his first object was to destroy Him. (*HC* 2:23)

ILLUSTRATIONS FOR OUR TIME

There is nothing quite so difficult as to be doing good and yet be criticized, demeaned, or victimized for your actions. Such was the case for our Beloved Savior Jesus Christ. The Lord knew His anointed status as the Savior of the world when He said, "To this end was I born" (John 18:37). The irony of it all was that He was sacrificing His life for the very people who sought to take it away. In the act of betrayal, Judas broke his trust, was unfaithful to his Savior, and disclosed by a kiss the Son of God to the band of the officers of the Jews who took Him to Annas (John 18:13).

We learn from the oft-told story concerning Karl G. Maesar what it means to never betray a trust. It is recorded:

> But of greater value even than the technical training was the inspiration of that great educator, Karl G. Maeser. From him the students learned of the real purpose of life, the value of achievement, the meaning of service. From him they learned that great man's interpretation of life, of character, of success. From him they received many valuable suggestions as to the place they might fill in the great drama of life. "Whatever you are, don't be a scrub," he would say in his characteristic, earnest style.

And he used often to say, "Let me tell you what I mean by giving my word of honor. If I were to be locked in a prison with walls twenty feet thick, there would be a chance that I might escape. But should you place me in the center of this room and draw a circle around me with a piece of chalk, and I should give you my word of honor that I would stay inside that circle, do you think I would step over that line? No! Never! I would die first." (Claude Richards, *J. Golden Kimball: The Story of a Unique Personality* [Salt Lake City: Deseret News Press, 1934], 38)

LIKENING THE SCRIPTURES TO OUR LIVES

1 Peter 3:16–17 Having a good conscience; that, whereas they speak evil of you, as of evildoers, they may be ashamed that falsely accuse your good conversation in Christ. For it is better, if the will of God be so, that ye suffer for well doing, than for evil doing.

Application: The pure love of Christ motivates us to return good for evil, to pray for those who despitefully use us, and to show mercy and forgiveness to everyone.

2. TEST OF LOYALTY: PETER DENIES JESUS

THEME: Loyalty to a righteous cause is a divine virtue. We can learn from Peter's denial of the Savior the enormous cost of failing to invoke and maintain one's standard of loyalty and steadfastness.

MOMENT OF TRUTH

The predicted denial of the Christ by Peter, the supreme deputy of the Lord, is one of the most wrenching abdications of leadership in holy writ. And at the same time, it is one of the most compelling reminders of humanness, with its ongoing quest for transcendence and the unfolding of nascent perfectibility. When the cock crowed, following Peter's three-fold denial—a jolting confirmation of the Savior's prophecy (Luke 22:34, 61; John 13:38)—this otherwise stalwart and often impulsive fisherman went through a transformation of monumental proportions, eventually emerging from this seminal period of the Savior's Atonement and resurrection fully prepared to receive the guidance of the Holy Ghost and rise to the pinnacle of loyalty and valor as the Lord's chief representative on earth. Though Peter "wept bitterly" over his performance that day (Matt. 26:75; Luke 22:62; compare Mark 14:72), yet would he come to know the triumph of standing firm in defense of the truth—even unto the sealing of his testimony with his life.

MODERN PROPHETS SPEAK

Gordon B. Hinckley:

> Now, may I go back to Peter, who denied and wept. Recognizing his error, repenting of his weakness, he turned about and became a mighty voice in bearing witness of the risen Lord. He, the senior apostle, dedicated the remainder of his life to testifying of the mission, the death, and the resurrection of Jesus Christ, the living Son of the living God. He preached the moving sermon on the day of Pentecost when the multitude were touched in their hearts by the power of the Holy Ghost. In the authority of the priesthood received from his Master, he, with John, healed the lame man, the miracle that brought on persecution. He fearlessly spoke for his brethren when they were arraigned before the Sanhedrin. His was the vision that led to carrying the gospel to the Gentiles (see Acts 2–4, 10).
>
> He suffered chains and prison and a terrible martyr's death as a witness of Him who had called him from his nets to become a fisher of men (see Matt. 4:19). He remained faithful and true to the great and compelling trust given when the resurrected Lord in his final instructions to the eleven apostles charged them to go "and teach all nations, baptizing them in the name of the Father, and of the Son, and of the Holy Ghost" (Matt. 28:19). And he it was who, with James and John, came back to earth in this dispensation to restore the holy priesthood, under which divine authority the Church of Jesus Christ was organized in these latter days and under which same authority it now functions. These mighty works and many more unmentioned were done by Peter, who once had denied and sorrowed and then rose above that remorse to carry forward the work of the Savior following his ascension and to participate in the restoration of that work in this dispensation. (*Be Thou an Example* [Salt Lake City: Deseret Book, 1981], 63)

ILLUSTRATIONS FOR OUR TIME

Lest we forget a great truth—the power of the Holy Ghost to empower us to testify and do good—Marion G. Romney has taught us clearly concerning the Holy Ghost. He said:

> This great source of pure knowledge, wisdom, light, and intelligence is, of course, the Holy Ghost who the Savior said would lead men into all truth. To understand and appreciate this great gift it must be experienced. But I bear you witness that it is real and will work a miracle in your understanding. You will remember that without it Peter denied Jesus on the night of his great trial. Possessing it, Peter and John defied their captors, (although those captors had the power to put them to death and

in a sense had the disposition to do so) with this declaration: "whether it be right in the sight of God to hearken unto you more than unto God, judge ye. "For we cannot but speak the things which we have seen and heard" (Acts 4:19–20). While one enjoys this gift his belief in Jesus Christ is secure. (Marion G. Romney, CR, April 1959, 11)

And thus we learn that without the Holy Ghost we cannot testify, teach, bless, or strengthen others.

LIKENING THE SCRIPTURES TO OUR LIVES

John 15:26 But when the Comforter is come, whom I will send unto you from the Father, even the Spirit of truth, which proceedeth from the Father, he shall testify of me.

Application: Let us remember that we need to have the Spirit to know truth, be edified (see D&C 50:17–22), and testify of all truth (see Moro. 10:4–5).

3. ULTIMATE CHALLENGE: THE TRIAL AND SENTENCING OF JESUS

THEME: The Redeemer was perfect and without blame, yet He suffered unspeakable abuse, and did so willingly for the sake of all mankind. Understanding the details and circumstances concerning the trial and sentencing of Jesus helps us to view His compassion and sacrifice in the light of the eternal gospel.

MOMENT OF TRUTH

Morning had come, the dawning of a day of infamy—and triumph. In the brightness of the sunlight over Jerusalem, the City of David, the turncoat Judas repented of his egregious deed and, seeking relief from his monumental burden, returned the blood money to the sponsors of terror and ended his own life (Matt. 27:5). At the trial before Pilate, silence prevailed, for the Savior, knowing that His hour had come, answered none of the illegal charges leveled against him by conspiring men. What was Pilate to do when caught between his conscience and the wrath of the multitude? He knew in his heart that this man was innocent (and a dream of his wife that day confirmed his inklings—see Matt. 27:19), yet he was placed under enormous pressure by the bloodthirsty priests and elders. "When Pilate saw that he could prevail nothing, but that rather a tumult was made, he took water, and washed his hands before the multitude, saying, I am innocent of the blood of this just person: see ye to it. Then answered all the people, and said, His blood be on us, and on our children" (Matt. 27:24–25). Thus the Savior was sentenced to be crucified—subjected to unspeakable mockery and abuse and then robbed of His life—all for being who He was, the Son of God. (Compare also the accounts in Mark 15:1–14; Luke 23:1–26; and John 18:28–40)

In Walter Chandler's excellent book [*Trial of Jesus from a Lawyer's Standpoint*], the record of fact in the case and the Hebrew criminal law bearing thereon are exhaustively considered. Then follows an elaborate "Brief," in which the following points are set forth in order.

> *Point 1: The arrest of Jesus was illegal.* . . .
>
> *Point 2: The private examination of Jesus before Annas or Caiaphas was illegal.* . . .
>
> *Point 3: The indictment against Jesus was, in form, illegal.* . . .
>
> *Point 4: The proceedings of the Sanhedrin against Jesus were illegal because they were conducted at night.* . . .
>
> *Point 5: The proceedings of the Sanhedrin against Jesus were illegal because the court convened before the offering of the morning sacrifice.* . . .
>
> *Point 6: The proceedings against Jesus were illegal because they were conducted on the day preceding a Jewish Sabbath; also on the first day of unleavened bread and the eve of the Passover.* . . .
>
> *Point 7: The trial of Jesus was illegal because it was concluded within one day.* . . .
>
> *Point 8: The sentence of condemnation pronounced against Jesus by the Sanhedrin was illegal because it was founded upon His uncorroborated confession.* . . .
>
> *Point 9: The condemnation of Jesus was illegal because the verdict of the Sanhedrin was unanimous.* . . .
>
> *Point 10: The proceedings against Jesus were illegal in that: (1) The sentence of condemnation was pronounced in a place forbidden by law: (2) The high priest rent his clothes: (3) The balloting was irregular.* . . .
>
> *Point 11: The members of the Great Sanhedrin were legally disqualified to try Jesus.* . . .
>
> *Point 12: The condemnation of Jesus was illegal because the merits of the defense were not considered.* . . . (Walter M. Chandler, *Trial of Jesus from a Lawyer's Standpoint* [Buffalo, NY: William S. Hein & Co., 1983], quoted in *JC*, 599–600)

MODERN PROPHETS SPEAK

Neal A. Maxwell:

> Jesus . . . told the original Twelve to be of good cheer when, on the surface, there was nothing to be cheerful about (John 16:33). The indescribable agonies of

Gethsemane were imminent. Judas's betrayal lay immediately ahead. Likewise, Jesus' arrest and arraignment. The Twelve would be scattered like sheep. Jesus' unjust and mocking trial and His terrible scourging were but hours away. The shrill and disappointing cry of the mob—to release Barabbas instead of Jesus—would soon echo in the air. Then would come the final, awful moments on Calvary!

Therefore, how could Jesus expect the Twelve to be of good cheer? Because, the Savior said, *"In the world ye shall have tribulation: but be of good cheer; I have overcome the world"* (John 16:33; italics added).

Because Christ had overcome the world, the Atonement was about to be accomplished! Death would be irrevocably defeated! Satan would have failed to stop the unfolding plan of salvation! All mankind would be given—through the grace of God—immortality! Additionally, for those who would earn it, there would be the richness of eternal life! These were among the resplendent realities and the fundamental facts which justified the Twelve's being of good cheer—not their grim, temporary circumstances! The precious perspectives of the gospel give to us this gospel of gladness! ("Be of Good Cheer," *Ensign,* Nov. 1982, 66)

ILLUSTRATIONS FOR OUR TIME

Overcoming Adversity

We are counseled to rise above adversity and tribulation with grace and thanksgiving. Like so many of God's prophets, the Prophet Joseph Smith was intimately acquainted with adversity and grief—so much so that in the midst of overwhelming suffering, he pleaded one day in anguish to the Master for redress on behalf of the embattled and persecuted Saints. March 20, 1839, is the date the Prophet gives to the first of two inspired epistles written from Liberty Jail in Missouri that would serve later as the basis for Sections 121, 122, and 123 of the Doctrine and Covenants. The Prophet and several colleagues had been held there under conditions of extraordinary deprivation since November 30, 1838. In stark contrast to the squalid environment in which they were confined, Section 121 affords the most sublime language in holy writ concerning the effectual operation of the priesthood of God. Section 122 is the source of unsurpassed inspiration in transcending adversity. Section 123 is an impassioned plea for the Saints to fulfill their duty to God and to their suffering families by bringing to light the facts around the injustices being heaped upon them. The coming forth of these treasures of wisdom, revealed from the womb of adversity, is a lasting memorial to the process of how the blessings of God flow "after much tribulation" (D&C 58:4).

No being who has ever lived has had greater familiarity with adversity than the Savior. He knew all too well the indignity and injustice that evil and conspiring forces can heap upon the innocent. He knew the pain of coming under false and vilifying accusations. He knew the anguish of separation from loved ones. He knew pain without measure. All of this experience became an inseparable ingredient of His atoning sacrifice. Thus He could counsel the Prophet of the Restoration from firsthand understanding:

> If the billowing surge conspire against thee; if fierce winds become thine enemy; if the heavens gather blackness, and all the elements combine to hedge up the way; and above all, if the very jaws of hell shall gape open the mouth wide after thee, know thou, my son, that all these things shall give thee experience, and shall be for thy good.
>
> The Son of Man hath descended below them all. Art thou greater than he?
>
> Therefore, hold on thy way, and the priesthood shall remain with thee; for their bounds are set, they cannot pass. Thy days are known, and thy years shall not be numbered less; therefore, fear not what man can do, for God shall be with you forever and ever. (D&C 122:7–9)

The account of the Savior's illegal trial and impious condemnation—leading to insufferable torture and death—is the archetypal representation of life's adversity, echoed countless times in the careers of the Lord's prophets and the travails of His Saints from time immemorial. And yet there is light aflame in the annals of such suffering—the light of transcendent courage and unassailable will toward accomplishing enduring good. In the example of the Savior and His servants we can find an anchor for our souls as we strive to overcome the tribulations of life and rise to ever higher levels of sanctification—through grace, "after all we can do" (2 Ne. 25:23). In this our goal is clear: We are to persist in faith "till we all come in the unity of the faith, and of the knowledge of the Son of God, unto a perfect man, unto the measure of the stature of the fulness of Christ" (Eph. 4:13). [Allen]

LIKENING THE SCRIPTURES TO OUR LIVES

John 18:37 Pilate therefore said unto him, Art thou a king then? Jesus answered, Thou sayest that I am a king. To this end was I born, and for this cause came I into the world, that I should bear witness unto the truth. Every one that is of the truth heareth my voice.

Application: The Lord's sacrifice and Atonement bear witness of the Father's plan. If we are His sheep, we will always hear His voice (see John 10:27).

4. "FATHER, FORGIVE THEM"—JESUS IS SCOURGED AND CRUCIFIED

THEME: The Savior died for us. Knowing this and following His example is the key to our faith and salvation.

MOMENT OF TRUTH

The accounts of the Savior's crucifixion (Matt. 27:26–66; Mark 15:15–47; Luke 23:27–56; John 19:13–42) resonate with unforgettable views: the intense suffering of our Lord; His forgiving mercy vis-à-vis the soldiers ("Father, forgive them; for they know not what they do"—Luke 23:34); His consciousness of having to complete His divine mission alone ("And at the ninth hour Jesus cried with a loud voice, saying, Eloi, Eloi, lama sabachthani? which is, being interpreted, My God, my God, why hast thou forsaken me?"—Mark 15:34); and His tender concern for His mother ("Behold thy mother!" John 19:27). When all was done, the Savior "bowed his head, and gave up the ghost" (John 19:30). The Atonement was complete, and the Redeemer had fulfilled the will of the Father: "Though he were a Son, yet learned he obedience by the things which he suffered; And being made perfect, he became the author of eternal salvation unto all them that obey him;" (Heb. 5:8–9).

MODERN PROPHETS SPEAK

Bruce R. McConkie:

> Our Lord's sufferings—the pain, torture, crown of thorns, scourging, and final crucifixion—which he endured between the night of the Last Supper and his death on the cross are collectively spoken of as the Passion of Christ (Acts 1:3). The sectarian world falsely suppose that the climax of his torture and suffering was on the cross (Matt. 27:26–50; Mark 15:1–38; Luke 23:1–46; John 18; 19:1–18)—a view which they keep ever before them by the constant use of the cross as a religious symbol. The fact is that intense and severe as the suffering was on the cross, yet the great pains were endured in the Garden of Gethsemane (Matt. 26:36–46; Mark 14:32–42; Luke 22:39–46; John 18:1). It was there that he trembled because of pain, bled at every pore, and suffered both in body and in spirit, and would that he "might not drink the bitter cup" (D&C 19:15–19; Mosiah 3:7). It was there he underwent his greatest suffering for men, taking upon himself, as he did, their sins on conditions of repentance (D&C 18:10–15). (*MD*, 555)

ILLUSTRATIONS FOR OUR TIME

Statements by the Savior while on the Cross

1. "Father, forgive them; for they know not what they do." (Luke 23:34) The Prophet Joseph makes clear the reference is to the soldiers (see the Joseph Smith Translation): "Then said Jesus, Father, forgive them; for they know not what they do. (Meaning the soldiers who crucified him,) and they parted his raiment and cast lots." (JST, Luke 23:35)

> Now, as we draw the curtain on 150 years of our history, it becomes us as a grateful people to reach out with a spirit of forgiveness and an attitude of love and compassion toward those we have felt may have wronged us.
>
> We have need of this. The whole world has need of it. It is of the very essence of the gospel of Jesus Christ. He taught it. He exemplified it as none other has exemplified it. In the time of his agony on the cross of Calvary, with vile and hateful accusers before him, they who had brought him to this terrible crucifixion, he cried out, "Father, forgive them; for they know not what they do" (Luke 23:34). None of us is called on to forgive so generously, but each of us is under a divinely spoken obligation to reach out with pardon and mercy. (Gordon B. Hinckley, *Be Thou an Example* [Salt Lake City: Deseret Book, 1981], 47–48)

2. "Verily I say unto thee, To day shalt thou be with me in paradise." (Luke 23:43)

> After the death of Jesus on the cross, during the three days while his body lay in the tomb, "quickened by the spirit . . . he went and preached (the gospel) unto the spirits in prison . . . that they might be judged according to men in the flesh, but live according to God in the Spirit" (I Peter 3:18–20; 4:6). In so doing he kept his promise to the thief on the cross, "Today shalt thou be with me in paradise" (Luke 23:43). He spoke of paradise as the place of departed spirits where the spirits of all who die must await the day of resurrection. To those who are righteous it is a place of peace and happiness but to those who are unrighteous it is a state of fearful anxiety for the judgments of God upon them." (Harold B. Lee, *Decisions for Successful Living* [Salt Lake City: Deseret Book, 1973], 118–119)

3. "When Jesus therefore saw his mother, and the disciple standing by, whom he loved, he saith unto his mother, Woman, behold thy son! Then saith he to the disciple, Behold thy mother! And from that hour that disciple took her unto his own home" (John 19:26–27). John the beloved then became responsible for the welfare of Mary the mother of Jesus Christ. It is to be noted that the usage of the word woman is different in biblical times as described by M. Eastman: "The word 'woman,' as used in Matt. 15:28, John 2:4, and 20:13, 15, implies tenderness and courtesy and not disrespect. Only where revelation is known has woman her due place of honour assigned to her." (*Illustrated Bible Dictionary*, "Woman," [Grand Rapids, MI: Baker Book House, 1978])

4. "And about the ninth hour Jesus cried with a loud voice, saying, Eli, Eli, lama sabachthani? that is to say, My God, my God, why hast thou forsaken me?" (Matt 27:46; compare Mark 15:34)

> The third Article of Faith states: "We believe that through the Atonement of Christ, all mankind may be saved, by obedience to the laws and ordinances of the Gospel." Christ's atoning act transcends the concept of time, affecting limitless numbers of souls for all eternity. It does so because of his choice and his preparation to be obedient to divine law.
>
> Not even for God's Son could divine law be broken. This plaintive plea was spoken at the time of his Atonement: "And he said, Abba, Father, all things are possible unto thee; take away this cup from me: nevertheless not what I will, but what thou wilt." (Mark 14:36) Later he cried out, "Eloi, Eloi, lama sabachthani? which is, being interpreted, My God, my God, why hast thou forsaken me?" (Mark 15:34).
>
> Through the love that he bore for his Son, God let the full weight of the Atonement bear down on the Savior, that the victory over death might be his and his alone. (Russell M. Nelson, *The Power within Us* [Salt Lake City: Deseret Book, 1988], 57)

5. "After this, Jesus knowing that all things were now accomplished, that the scripture might be fulfilled, saith, I thirst." (John 19:28)

> After these words comes the Psalmic declaration: "They gave me also gall for my meat; and in my thirst they gave me vinegar to drink" (Ps. 69:21). Their fulfillment is noted by Matthew in these words: "They gave him vinegar to drink mingled with gall: and when he had tasted thereof, he would not drink. And they crucified him." Also: After Jesus had, as they supposed, called for Elias, the account says: "And straightway one of them ran, and took a spunge, and filled it with vinegar, and put it on a reed, and gave him to drink" (Matt. 27:34–35, 47–48). John's account of this same occurrence ties the act at the crucifixion in with David's prediction by recounting: "Jesus knowing that all things were now accomplished, that the scripture might be fulfilled, saith, I thirst." It is as though advisedly and with deliberation, though he was in agony beyond compare, yet he consciously continued to the last moment of mortal life, with the avowed purpose of fulfilling all of the Messianic utterances concerning his mortal Messiahship. "Now there was set a vessel full of vinegar," John's account continues, "and they filled a spunge with vinegar, and put it upon hyssop, and put it to his mouth. When Jesus therefore had received the vinegar, he said, It is finished: and he bowed his head, and gave up the ghost" (John 19:28–30). (Bruce R. McConkie, *The Promised Messiah: The First Coming of Christ* [Salt Lake City: Deseret Book, 1981], 533–34)

6. "When Jesus therefore had received the vinegar, he said, It is finished: and he bowed his head, and gave up the ghost." (John 19:30)

> "It is finished." He had meekly and submissively done—perfectly and gloriously—that which He had been sent forth to do. This utterance also tells us of His obedience, His persistence, and His endurance, for in the Joseph Smith Translation we read, "Father, it is finished, thy will is done."
>
> The Savior's supernal service gave Him true and full joy as He gladly attested when, following His resurrection, He visited the lost sheep in the Americas, taught and blessed them, and, weeping twice, said, "And now behold, my joy is full." Therein we see a "finished" Soul who was perfected in His love and obedience, perfected in His capacity to render service. . . .
>
> There will be another time when He will once again use those same special three words: "It is finished; it is finished." Then in full spiritual celebration of the end of the world, the Lamb of God, who has overcome and who has trodden the winepress alone, will signify the finale of that remarkable achievement—at the center of which achievement is His marvelous love of all and His submissiveness, which brought about the Atonement for all. (Neal A. Maxwell, *Even As I Am* [Salt Lake City: Deseret Book, 1982], 19–20)

7. "And when Jesus had cried with a loud voice, he said, Father, into thy hands I commend my spirit: and having said thus, he gave up the ghost." (Luke 23:46)

> Out of the darkness and horror of Calvary came the voice of the Lamb, saying, "Father, into thy hands I commend my spirit" (Luke 23:46). And the dark was no longer dark, for He was with His Father. He had come from God and to God He had returned. So also those who walk with God in this earthly pilgrimage know from blessed experience that He will not abandon His children who trust in Him. In the night of death His presence will be "better than a light and safer than a known way." (Thomas S. Monson, *Be Your Best Self* [Salt Lake City: Deseret Book, 1979], 5)

LIKENING THE SCRIPTURES TO OUR LIVES

1 Nephi 19:9 And the world, because of their iniquity, shall judge him to be a thing of naught; wherefore they scourge him, and he suffereth it; and they smite him, and he suffereth it. Yea, they spit upon him, and he suffereth it, because of his loving kindness and his long-suffering towards the children of men.

Application: The motive for the work of God the Father is love (see John 3:16). The Savior has the identical motive and design (see 2 Ne. 26:24). All that has been done, or will yet be done, is for the benefit of all mankind, thus bringing to pass much righteousness. Our task in life is to come to realize and feel the love the Father and Son have for us and then show Christlike love to our fellowmen with acts of loving kindness.

SUMMARY

In these pages of scripture, we see reflected the supreme qualities of the divine nature: the Savior's unwavering strength in the face of betrayal, arraignment, judgment, and execution; His forgiving spirit while hanging in the most exquisite pain on the cross; His inextinguishable love for His earthly mother and for all of God's children; and His unflinching determination to do the will of the Father. We see also in Peter's denial the vestige of mortal humanness that would persist in all of us—were in not for the blessings of the Spirit and the mighty change of heart that enables us to move forward in the strength of the Lord. When Pilate asked Jesus, "Art thou a king then?" the Savior answered, "Thou sayest that I am a king. To this end was I born, and for this cause came I into the world, that I should bear witness unto the truth. Every one that is of the truth heareth my voice." Then as Pilate consigned the Savior into the hands of His enemies, he spoke the haunting words: "What is truth?" (John 18:37–38). We can answer that question with certainty by looking ahead to the consummating episode in the life of the Redeemer—the triumphal resurrection that was to signify the ultimate victory over death.

CHAPTER 27

THE RESURRECTION *of the* LORD JESUS CHRIST

Reading Assignment: Matthew 28; Luke 24; John 20–21.

Additional Reading: Mark 16; Bible Dictionary, "Resurrection" (761).

> *I thank the Lord for the assurance that has come to us of the immortality of the soul. We have walked around old churchyards where are buried the dead who died long ago. Someday they will rise in the resurrection, with a renewal of body and spirit under the plan of the Almighty, made possible by the Atonement of the Lord Jesus Christ. What a wonderful thing that is! We do not need to feel dour. We ought to rejoice.*
>
> —GORDON B. HINCKLEY, *TGBH*, 553–54.

THEMES *for* LIVING

1. Witnesses of the Resurrected Lord
2. Gratitude for the Resurrection

INTRODUCTION

The culmination of the Atonement was the glorious resurrection of the Lord Jesus Christ. Knowing of the power of the Resurrection through the Lord Jesus Christ gives us hope to carry on in life's deepest hours of trial, tribulation, and even death—for we will all live again. We can have hope to come forth in the morning of the First Resurrection if we keep our covenants (see D&C 76:64–65). Many in the Savior's day witnessed the reality of His Resurrection, and the confirming testimony from the Prophet Joseph and Sidney Rigdon in this dispensation echoes in our hearts: "And now, after the many testimonies which have been given of him, this is the testimony, last of all, which we give of him: That he lives! For we saw him, even on the right hand of God; and we heard the voice bearing record that he is the Only Begotten of the Father—That by him, and through him, and of him, the worlds are and were created, and the inhabitants thereof are begotten sons and daughters unto God" (D&C 76:22–24).

1. WITNESSES OF THE RESURRECTED LORD

THEME: To behold and know the Lord—whether in person as special witnesses or through the spiritual eye as confirmed by the Holy Ghost—is the essence of eternal life. Many saw the resurrected Lord shortly after His coming forth from the sepulcher. These witnesses included Mary Magdalene and other women, plus a number of the disciples and the eleven Apostles.

MOMENT OF TRUTH

On the Mount of Transfiguration, the Savior had charged Peter, James, and John to retain these experiences within themselves, privately, "till the Son of man were risen from the dead" (Mark 9:10). This they did, not fully understanding what "rising from the dead should mean" (Mark 9:11). The unprecedented events that transpired three days following the crucifixion of our Lord provided them with the answer, for the resurrection of the Savior came as a literal fulfillment of the word of God. To the incredulous Jewish leaders also, the Savior had conveyed advance word of His coming Resurrection. "What sign shewest thou unto us, seeing that thou doest these things?" asked the authorities in regard to the Savior's ministry. "Jesus answered and said unto them, Destroy this temple, and in three days I will raise it up" (John 2:18–19). Raise it up He did—the most transcendent event to occur since the Creation itself and the ensuing fall of man. Through the supernal gift of the Resurrection, the Lord ensured the immortality of all who came to this mortal sphere—and the eternal life and exaltation of all who follow His teachings and endure to the end.

 Word of the Lord's rising on the first day of the week spread rapidly—to the unspeakable joy of His followers and to the disbelief or disdain of most others. When the chief priests learned of the empty tomb, they bribed the soldiers of the watch to say that Jesus' disciples had stolen away his body (Matt. 28:11–15). But the disciples knew better—beginning with Mary Magdalene and her sisterly companions (she being the first to witness the risen Lord—Matt. 28:1–10; Mark 16:1–11; Luke 24:1–10), then to the two disciples on the road to Emmaus (one being Cleopas, the other most likely Luke—Mark 16:12–13; Luke 24:13–32), then to the disciples and Apostles that same evening in the upper room in Jerusalem and also the following week (John 20:19–31), and finally to the Apostles on the seashore of the sea of Galilee (John 21:1–24) and on a mount in that vicinity (Matt. 28:16–20; Mark 16:15–18). In all, the Savior made numerous appearances during his forty-day, post-resurrection ministry. In his summary of such appearances, Paul mentions: "After that, he was seen of above five hundred brethren at once; of whom the greater part remain unto this present, but some are fallen asleep" (1 Cor. 15:6). In addition, the resurrected Savior ministered to several thousands of Saints in ancient America (see 3 Ne. 11). The roster of these favored witnesses is large. The evidence of the reality of the resurrection on that sacred Sunday is overwhelming. The purpose for such a detailed accounting is manifest: "And many other signs truly did Jesus in the presence of his disciples, which are not written in this book: But these are written, that ye might believe that Jesus is the Christ, the Son of God; and that believing ye might have life through his name" (John 20:30–31).

MODERN PROPHETS SPEAK

James E. Faust:

> The resurrection of Jesus is one of the greatest messages of all Christianity. It is a divine gift of the Atonement for all mankind. The idea that one who has died can live again was so unprecedented, so foreign to all human experience, that even the Apostles, who had been told it would happen, could hardly believe it. . . . Latter-day Saints have additional witnesses of the reality of the resurrection of Jesus Christ and of the certainty of life after death. One of these witnesses is the Book of Mormon, a record containing the ministry of the resurrected Christ upon the American continent after his death and resurrection in Jerusalem. (*In the Strength of the Lord: The Life and Teachings of James E. Faust*, 405)

ILLUSTRATIONS FOR OUR TIME

The Prophet Joseph Smith's Vision of the Resurrection
For all of us who know of the Savior and His gospel, the resurrection is a transcendent reality. Because of the grace and love of the Savior, all will rise again to immortality. "For as in Adam all die, even so in Christ shall all be made alive" (1 Cor. 15:22).

Through His atoning sacrifice, all the obedient and faithful—without exception—can enjoy the fruits of eternal life and exaltation. How can we bring the practical reality of the resurrection into our minds? The words of the Prophet Joseph Smith may serve this very purpose.

On the occasion of the death of Lorenzo D. Barnes at Bradford, England, on December 20, 1842—the first elder to die on a foreign mission—the Prophet Joseph made the following remarkable commentary concerning the resurrection (as recorded by Willard Richards and Wilford Woodruff):

> The expectation of seeing my friends in the morning of the resurrection cheers my soul and makes me bear up against the evils of life. It is like their taking a long journey, and on their return we meet them with increased joy.
>
> God has revealed His Son from the heavens and the doctrine of the resurrection also; and we have a knowledge that those we bury here God will bring up again, clothed upon and quickened by the Spirit of the great God; and what mattereth it whether we lay them down, or we lay down with them, when we can keep them no longer? Let these truths sink down in our hearts, that we may even here begin to enjoy that which shall be in full hereafter. (*HC,* 5:362)

As we prayerfully internalize the extraordinary scriptural accounts of the Resurrection of the Lord (Matt. 28; Mark 16; Luke 24; John 20–21) and contemplate the record of His post-resurrection visit to the Saints in America (3 Ne. 11), we should be filled anew with a desire to serve Him in reverent gratitude and share the good news of the gospel with our friends and colleagues everywhere. Setting the example, James E. Faust has said:

> In my capacity as a special witness, I set my seal and testimony upon these events and upon the divine calling of Jesus as our Lord, Savior, and Redeemer. I testify that He lives, that He loves us, and that this is His holy work. I testify that His are the words of eternal life. I testify that through this Church His work and His glory—to bring about the immortality and eternal life of the faithful and the obedient—is being accomplished. (James E. Faust, "A Testimony of Christ," *Ensign,* Mar. 2005, 7)

LIKENING THE SCRIPTURES TO OUR LIVES

Luke 14:14 And thou shalt be blessed; for they cannot recompense thee: for thou shalt be recompensed at the resurrection of the just.

Application: We are given our ultimate blessings from the Lord after we are resurrected. We are restored in the resurrection (see Alma 41:4) according to the degree of glory we obtain through the grace of God, after all we can do (see 2 Ne. 25:23).

2. GRATITUDE FOR THE RESURRECTION

THEME: Gratitude for the resurrection—being the catalyst that moves us to righteous action—will motivate us to keep the commandments and be filled with hope to carry us through this earthly journey in obedient compliance with gospel principles.

MOMENT OF TRUTH

From the written word—and the confirming whisperings of the Spirit—we have the hope and assurance that the resurrection is a reality for all mankind. This doctrine is given to us so "that ye might believe that Jesus is the Christ, the Son of God; and that believing ye might have life through his name" (John 20:30–31). The extraordinary news of the resurrection should instill in us feelings of peace (John 20:19, 21, 26), gladness (John 20:20; Matt. 28:8), charity (John 21:15–17), inspiration (Luke 24:32), joy and wonder (Luke 24:41, 52), understanding (Luke 24:45), reverence (Matt. 28:17), and praise for God (Luke 24:53). All these responses of eyewitnesses are recorded in the New Testament account. Moreover, the overwhelming impact of the visit of the resurrected Christ to the Saints in ancient America was such that the people cried out with one accord: "Hosanna! Blessed be the name of the Most High God! And they did fall down at the feet of Jesus, and did worship him" (3 Ne. 11:17). Gratitude is perhaps the most appropriate response we can have to the assurance of the resurrection—reverent gratitude demonstrated through humble obedience to the principles and ordinances of the gospel of Jesus Christ, who made all of this possible.

MODERN PROPHETS SPEAK

Neal A. Maxwell:

> The gift of immortality to all mankind through the reality of the Resurrection is so powerful a promise that our rejoicing in these great and generous gifts should drown out any sorrow, assuage any grief, conquer any mood, dissolve any despair, and tame any tragedy. Those who now see life as pointless will one day point with adoration to the performance of the Man of Galilee in those crowded moments of time known as Gethsemane and Calvary. Those who presently say life is meaningless will yet applaud the Atonement which saves us from meaninglessness. Christ's victory over death ended the human predicament. Now there are only personal predicaments,

and from these too we may be rescued by following the teachings of him who rescued us from general extinction. (*The Neal A. Maxwell Quote Book*, 286–87)

ILLUSTRATIONS FOR OUR TIME

Joseph Fielding Smith counsels us on the need to be grateful for the Savior's atoning sacrifice and the Resurrection:

> Is it possible to think of any fate that would be as terrible as to be denied the resurrection, our spirits becoming subject to Satan forever? How grateful to our Redeemer every soul should be to think that Jesus so loved the world that he was willing to suffer and redeem every soul from death and give us the resurrection of the dead. Surely every member of The Church of Jesus Christ should be willing to show gratitude by obedience to the Savior's commandments.
>
> No mortal can fully realize the price that he paid. No mortal could have stood the anguish and suffering of such a sacrifice. It was a sacrifice that a God had to endure. It is an insignificant price we are asked to pay, and we should be willing to pay it in the spirit of thanksgiving, love, and obedience to every divine command. As he loves us, so we should love him, showing our deep gratitude in obedience and in humble prayer. (*AGQ*, 4:62–63)

LIKENING THE SCRIPTURES TO OUR LIVES

3 Nephi 27:13–14 Behold I have given unto you my gospel, and this is the gospel which I have given unto you—that I came into the world to do the will of my Father, because my Father sent me. And my Father sent me that I might be lifted up upon the cross; and after that I had been lifted up upon the cross; that I might draw all men unto me, that as I have been lifted up by men even so should men be lifted up by the Father, to stand before me, to be judged of their works, whether they be good or whether they be evil.

Application: The plan of salvation teaches us about the essential place of the Fall and the Atonement (see Alma 11:40). When we realize what our situation would be without our Savior's infinite Atonement, we are drawn to Him. We become filled with gratitude, love, and a desire to live a life worthy of exaltation.

SUMMARY

When we understand and appreciate the blessing and power of the resurrection, we will be motivated to righteousness. Let us never forget what our fate might have been in the absence of the Atonement (see 2 Ne. 9:8–9). If we remember these things, we will be filled with gratitude, which will become a catalyst for obedience and valor in our lives. We will live worthy of coming forth in the morning of the First Resurrection. We will become "just"—with all the accompanying blessings (see D&C 76:69). We will be made perfect in Christ and become joint heirs with Him (see Rom. 8:17). Let us take a lesson from Thomas, who at first doubted the verity of the resurrection until the very moment where the Lord had him touch the marks on His hands and His sides: "And Thomas answered and said unto him, My Lord and my God. Jesus saith unto him, Thomas, because thou hast seen me, thou hast believed: blessed are they that have not seen, and yet have believed" (John 20:28–29). Belief leads to obedience; obedience leads to sanctification; sanctification leads to exaltation. All will be resurrected; those who are faithful and endure to the end will participate in the resurrection of glory, even the glory of the celestial kingdom.

CHAPTER 28

"WE ARE WITNESSES"

Reading Assignment: Acts 1–5.

Additional Reading: Matthew 28:16–20; Mark 16:19–20; Luke 24:49–53; Joseph Smith—History 1:1:21–25.

> *It is a covenant obligation of all who are baptized into the Church of Jesus Christ to "stand as witnesses of God at all times, and in all things, and in all places" (Mosiah 18:9). Once warned, "it becometh every man to warn his neighbor" (D&C 88:81). The messengers who deliver the warning will be present at the day of judgment as witnesses (D&C 75:21; 2 Ne. 33:11; Moro. 10:34). The essence of missionary work is for each member of the Church to become a voice of warning to those who have not been warned (see DS 1:307–311).*
>
> —Neil J. Flinders, *Encyclopedia of Mormonism,* ed. Daniel H. Ludlow (New York: Macmillan, 1992), 3:1539.

THEMES *for* LIVING

1. The Heavenly Commission—The Savior's Final Instructions Prior to His Ascension
2. The Ultimate Confirming Witness—Gift of the Holy Ghost
3. Healing Power of God—Apostolic Miracles
4. Boldness in Preaching Jesus the Christ

INTRODUCTION

The resurrected Savior spent forty days teaching His beloved disciples the doctrines of the kingdom before His Ascension. Following the day of Pentecost on which they were endowed with the Holy Ghost, the Apostles moved forward in their commission to build up the kingdom and teach all nations the gospel truth, and many people were brought into the fold. The Apostles, having been endowed from on high, taught the people, blessed the converts, and healed the sick and afflicted. They were courageous as they bore solemn witness that Jesus was and is the Christ, the Savior and Redeemer of the world.

1. THE HEAVENLY COMMISSION— THE SAVIOR'S FINAL INSTRUCTIONS PRIOR TO HIS ASCENSION

THEME: We should feast on every word of the Lord and fulfill the commission to carry the gospel to all the world. The resurrected Lord laid the foundation for missionary work as He taught His disciples concerning the kingdom of God prior to His ascension into Heaven.

MOMENT OF TRUTH

The Savior announced to His Apostles at the end of His post-resurrection ministry: "All power is given unto me in heaven and in earth" (Matt. 28:18), whereupon He gave to them the universal commission: "Go ye therefore, and teach all nations, baptizing them in the name of the Father, and of the Son, and of the Holy Ghost: Teaching them to observe all things whatsoever I have commanded you: and lo, I am with you always, even unto the end of the world. Amen" (Matt. 28:19–20; compare Mark 16:15–18; Luke 24:46–50; John 21:15–25). This evangelical commission included the elements of going forth, teaching, baptizing, cultivating obedience, and, in accordance with the dictum to Peter to "feed my sheep" (see John 21:15–17), serving the people with godlike charity. To do these things with power and authenticity, the Apostles needed two things: (1) the Savior to be with them continually (as He promised them), and (2) the endowment of the Holy Ghost: "But ye shall receive power, after that the Holy Ghost is come upon you: and ye shall be witnesses unto me both in Jerusalem, and in all Judaea, and in Samaria, and unto the uttermost part of the earth" (Acts 1:8). These were the last recorded words of the Savior prior to His Ascension.

MODERN PROPHETS SPEAK

Ezra Taft Benson:

> After our Lord's literal physical resurrection, but before His ascension into heaven, He commanded the apostles to "teach all nations" His gospel (see Matt. 28:19). He further exhorted them to be "witnesses . . . in Jerusalem, and in all Judea, and in Samaria, and unto the uttermost part of the earth" (Acts 1:8). Obedient to that command, the apostles took the gospel throughout the world. The gospel message, once confined to Palestine, became a worldwide message. From its centers in Jerusalem, and later Antioch of Syria, Christianity spread to foreign frontiers with a harvest of converts. As expressed by Jesus in the parable, the mustard seed became as a tree with its branches extending into various parts of the earth. Because of its rapid growth, the church became noticeable. Persecutions followed, first by the Jews and then by the Roman government. Some of the leaders of the church were martyred, including James, Peter, and Paul. Disaffection spread among the members in the infant church. Since valiance to the cause meant certain death, some chose apostasy. Eventually, the apostles were killed, leaving no legal administrators on the earth to regulate the affairs of the kingdom, to settle doctrinal disputes, or to pass on the authority they held. (*This Nation Shall Endure,* 114–15)

ILLUSTRATIONS FOR OUR TIME

Points to Ponder Concerning the Kingdom of God

Let us ask ourselves the questions: Are our priorities aligned with building up the kingdom of God? What is entailed in building up the Kingdom? What is the composition of the kingdom of God?

When we answer these questions, we will come to realize that souls are precious and that people are what really count. Unless our actions bless the lives of our brothers and sisters, we may want to reevaluate our lives. Remember that the work and glory of our Heavenly Father and Savior are the immortality and eternal life of all of us (see Moses 1:39). Everything the Father and Son do is motivated by love for us (see John 3:16; 2 Ne. 26:24). Now we better understand why the Lord asked Peter if he loved Him—because only perfect, Christlike love will ensure that we care for and feed the Lord's flock. The result is that more people come unto Christ and the kingdom of God is built up to the glory of God. [Pinegar]

LIKENING THE SCRIPTURES TO OUR LIVES

Acts 1:3 To whom also he shewed himself alive after his passion by many infallible proofs, being seen of them forty days, and speaking of the things pertaining to the kingdom of God.

Application: The kingdom of God on the earth is indeed The Church of Jesus Christ, whether it be among the former-day Saints or now in the latter days. The essence of this scripture is to show that the Lord instructed His Apostles on the establishment of His Church and kingdom here upon the earth. It is His Church and bears His name; therefore, it reflects His priesthood, His gospel, and His doctrine. We can have every confidence in following His anointed leaders, for they are led by our Savior Jesus Christ.

2. THE ULTIMATE CONFIRMING WITNESS— GIFT OF THE HOLY GHOST

THEME: The gift of the Holy Ghost is given to bless Heavenly Father's children as they teach, preach, and bear witness of the Savior Jesus Christ. This consummate power was bestowed upon the Apostles on the Day of Pentecost to carry on the work established by Jesus Christ and to enable them to bear the gospel to all the world.

MOMENT OF TRUTH

The Feast of Pentecost—a name deriving from the Greek word for "fifty"—was held fifty days after the Feast of Passover. During that span of time, the harvest of corn was gathered in. The Old Testament account refers to "the feast of harvest, the firstfruits of thy labours, which thou hast sown in the field: and the feast of ingathering, which is in the end of the year, when thou hast gathered in thy labours out of the field" (Ex. 23:16). Originally, Pentecost was celebrated on a single day, but the time was extended in later generations. It was on the Day of Pentecost—the day of harvest—that the magnificent harvest of spiritual blessings occurred following the Atonement and Resurrection of the Savior. This harvest was conveyed through the promised bestowal of the Holy Ghost upon the successor leadership of the Church. The scriptures describe this milestone event as follows: "And suddenly there came a sound from heaven as of a rushing mighty wind, and it filled all the house where they were sitting. And there appeared unto them cloven tongues like as of fire, and it sat upon each of them. And they were all filled with the Holy Ghost, and began to speak with other tongues, as the Spirit gave them utterance" (Acts 2:2–4).

The multitudes assembled from many lands on that occasion were astonished to hear the truth expressed in their own native tongues. Peter stood with boldness and preached of Christ and His doctrine, inspiring the audience to ask what they should do. Peter responded with the classic missionary exhortation: "Repent, and be baptized every one of you in the name of Jesus Christ for the remission of sins, and ye shall receive the gift of the Holy Ghost. For the promise is unto you, and to your children, and to all that are afar off, even as many as the Lord our God shall call" (Acts

2:38–39). As a result of this extraordinary convocation, some 3,000 souls were added to the fold, with others following them: "And the Lord added to the church daily such as should be saved" (Acts 2:47).

MODERN PROPHETS SPEAK

J. Reuben Clark Jr.:

> The conferring and reception of the Holy Ghost, which bears record of the Father and the Son must be again provided for. The Holy Ghost was promised to the Apostles by the Savior in the Passover chamber (John 14), but he explained that "if I go not away, the Comforter will not come unto you" (*Ibid.,* 16:7). Just before his ascension, Jesus again promised them the Holy Ghost, which was to come to them, "not many days hence" (Acts 1:5). On the day of Pentecost, the Holy Ghost came with a sound like the "rushing mighty wind," and "appeared unto them cloven tongues like as of fire, and it sat upon each of them," and miraculous manifestations followed (*Ibid.,* 2:1 ff).
>
> As to how necessary the power of the Holy Ghost is, may be gathered from the following scriptures which speak of his functions. Discoursing on the Comforter to his Apostles in the Passover chamber Jesus said:
>
> But the Comforter, which is the Holy Ghost, whom the Father will send in my name, he shall teach you all things, and bring all things to your remembrance, whatsoever I have said unto you. . . .
>
> But when the Comforter is come, whom I will send unto you from the Father, even the Spirit of truth, which proceedeth from the Father, he shall testify of me (John 14:26, 15:26). (*Behold the Lamb of God* [Salt Lake City: Deseret Book, 1991], 86–87)

ILLUSTRATIONS FOR OUR TIME

The Holy Ghost—Precious Gift for Us in Mortality

The Holy Ghost is the greatest gift we receive from our Heavenly Father to help us in our sojourn here upon the earth. We should seek the Spirit in mighty prayer (see 3 Ne. 19:9). The Holy Ghost comforts, testifies, sanctifies, and acts as the constant companion of those who have received this gift and live worthy of it. The Holy Ghost will show us all things to do (see 2 Ne. 32:5). To live worthy of this blessing, we must repent and be baptized, receive the Holy Ghost by the laying on of hands, and then keep the commandments (see D&C 20:77, 79). The Holy Ghost becomes prominent in our lives as we increase our faith (see 1 Ne. 10:17), show abundant love, purify ourselves (see D&C 76:116), and become obedient (see Moro. 4:3; 5:2). We lose the

Spirit through wickedness and unbelief (see Morm. 1:14), as it will not dwell in unholy temples (see Hel. 4:24). It is by the Spirit that all things are brought to our remembrance and we are thus able to testify and teach (see John 14:26; 15:26).

The Prophet Joseph possessed an old New Testament written in Latin, Hebrew, German, and Greek. He seemed to prefer the German translation, but he went on to say, "I thank God that I have got this old book; but I thank him more for the gift of the Holy Ghost. I have got the oldest book in the world; but I have got the oldest book in my heart, even the gift of the Holy Ghost" (Joseph Smith, *Discourses of the Prophet Joseph Smith,* comp. Alma P. Burton [Salt Lake City: Deseret Book, 1977], 343–44).

The Spirit is the key to understanding and righteousness. With the help of the Spirit, we can live a life patterned after our Savior Jesus Christ. [Pinegar]

LIKENING THE SCRIPTURES TO OUR LIVES

Acts 1:8 But ye shall receive power, after that the Holy Ghost is come upon you: and ye shall be witnesses unto me both in Jerusalem, and in all Judaea, and in Samaria, and unto the uttermost part of the earth.

Application: It is by the power of the Holy Ghost that we teach and preach the gospel (see 2 Ne. 33:1; D&C 42:14; 50:17–22). The Holy Ghost bears witness of the Father and the Son (see 2 Ne. 31:18; 3 Ne. 28:11).

3. HEALING POWER OF GOD— APOSTOLIC MIRACLES

THEME: It is in, through, and by Jesus Christ that the Father accomplishes His eternal gospel plan here upon the earth. It is by the same power that we accomplish our work in building up the kingdom of God in the name of Jesus Christ.

MOMENT OF TRUTH

Peter and his associates had been witness to miracle after miracle performed at the hands of the Master, including extraordinary healings. They had been schooled on the power of the priesthood invested and applied for the blessing of the faithful. It was now their moment to rise in majesty following the munificent tutelage of the Master Teacher and assume the leadership of the kingdom as His representatives on the earth. On their way to the temple, Peter and John passed near a man begging for his keep, having come into the world lame and crippled. When he saw the two Apostles, he beckoned to them for help. The well-known account never fails to kindle the flame of wonder at the power of faith and the benevolence of God:

> And Peter, fastening his eyes upon him with John, said, Look on us.
>
> And he gave heed unto them, expecting to receive something of them.
>
> Then Peter said, Silver and gold have I none; but such as I have give I thee: In the name of Jesus Christ of Nazareth rise up and walk.
>
> And he took him by the right hand, and lifted *him* up: and immediately his feet and ancle bones received strength.
>
> And he leaping up stood, and walked, and entered with them into the temple, walking, and leaping, and praising God. (Acts 3:4–8)

The people who witnessed this miracle were astonished beyond measure. Peter took the occasion to render praise unto the Lord and bear witness of His divine calling. Whereas the crippled man had been liberated from his physical infirmities, Peter now called upon the people to be liberated from the shackles of their sins through the power of the Atonement. This doctrine he expressed in the famous words that anticipate the restoration of the gospel in latter days, when the Redeemer would again return: "Repent ye therefore, and be converted, that your sins may be blotted out, when the times of refreshing shall come from the presence of the Lord; And he shall send Jesus Christ, which before was preached unto you: Whom the heaven must receive until the times of restitution of all things, which God hath spoken by the mouth of all his holy prophets since the world began" (Acts 3:19–21).

MODERN PROPHETS SPEAK

Bruce R. McConkie:

> Peter did not ask the Lord to heal the cripple; he did not pray to God to pour out his grace and healing virtue upon the lame man. Instead—acting in the Lord's name and by virtue of a delegation of priestly authority already received—he himself commanded the miracle to occur. Peter was the Lord's servant, his representative and agent; he stood in the place and stead of Christ, doing what the Master would have done if personally present. The illustration here seen of the relationship of Master and servant, of Principal and agent, of the Lord and his representative, is the same as is involved in the ordinance of administration to the sick (see Jas. 5:12–20). (*DNTC,* 2:46)

On the day of Pentecost three thousand new converts were baptized, and thereafter "the Lord added to the church daily such as should be saved" (Acts 2:41–47). After

Peter and John healed the man lame from birth, five thousand men came into the fold, for "all men glorified God for that which was done" (Acts 4:1–22). And following the taking of Ananias and Sapphira the record says, "Believers were the more added to the Lord, multitudes both of men and women" (Acts 5:1–16). (*DNTC*, 2:61–62)

ILLUSTRATIONS FOR OUR TIME

Gifts from God

"And all these gifts come from God, for the benefit of the children of God" (D&C 46:26). Through the goodness of God, we receive the gifts of the Spirit, and they are many (see Moro. 10:7–18; D&C 46:8–26). The power exhibited by the early Apostles included the gift of healing, which they did in the name of Jesus Christ: "And again, to some it is given to have faith to be healed; And to others it is given to have faith to heal" (D&C 46:19–20). Today, in this dispensation, as in days past, this gift and blessing is evident. Wilford Woodruff records such a happening in the *Journal of Discourses:*

> Mary Pitt . . . was something like the lame man who lay at the gate of the Temple called "Beautiful" at Jerusalem—she had not been able to walk a step for fourteen years, and confined to her bed nearly half that time. She had no strength in her feet and ankles and could only move about a little with a crutch or holding on to a chair. She wished to be baptized. Brother Pitt [Mary's brother] and myself took her in our arms, and carried her into the water and I baptized her. When she came out of the water I confirmed her. She said she wanted to be healed and she believed she had faith enough to be healed. I had had experience enough in this Church to know that it required a good deal of faith to heal a person who had not walked a step for fourteen years. I told her that according to her faith it should be unto her. It so happened that on the day after she was baptized, Brother Richards and President Brigham Young came down to see me. We met at Brother Kington's. Sister Mary Pitt was there also. I told President Young what Sister Pitt wished, and that she believed she had faith enough to be healed. We prayed for her and laid hands upon her. Brother Young was mouth, and commanded her to be made whole. She laid down her crutch and never used it after, and the next day she walked three miles. (*JD,* 15:344)

LIKENING THE SCRIPTURES TO OUR LIVES

Acts 3:6 Then Peter said, Silver and gold have I none; but such as I have give I thee: In the name of Jesus Christ of Nazareth rise up and walk.

Application: When inspired by the Holy Ghost, we can use the priesthood and act according to the will of God. Just as Peter did, those who bear this holy priesthood can, under the direction of the Holy Ghost, perform miracles according to their faith (see Ether 12:16).

4. BOLDNESS IN PREACHING JESUS THE CHRIST

THEME: The Apostles set a glorious example of faith and courage as they sought to obey God and preach of the Lord Jesus Christ.

MOMENT OF TRUTH

When the priests and elders confronted Peter, demanding by what power or name He had healed the crippled man near the temple, it was the chief Apostle's turn to step forward fearlessly:

> Then Peter, filled with the Holy Ghost, said unto them, Ye rulers of the people, and elders of Israel,
>
> If we this day be examined of the good deed done to the impotent man, by what means he is made whole;
>
> Be it known unto you all, and to all the people of Israel, that by the name of Jesus Christ of Nazareth, whom ye crucified, whom God raised from the dead, even by him doth this man stand here before you whole.
>
> This is the stone which was set at nought of you builders, which is become the head of the corner.
>
> Neither is there salvation in any other: for there is none other name under heaven given among men, whereby we must be saved. (Acts 4:8–12)

When the elders commanded Peter and his colleagues to refrain from any ministry in the name of Christ, they steadfastly refused to comply and continued apace with their proselyting work: "And with great power gave the apostles witness of the resurrection of the Lord Jesus: and great grace was upon them all" (Acts 4:33). Not even imprisonment could dissuade them from honoring the call issued to them by the Savior, for the angel of the Lord liberated them and commanded them to continue preaching the gospel in the temple (Acts 5:19–20).

In response to threats from the authorities, Peter—the same one who had thrice denied the Savior on the eve of the crucifixion—now unflinchingly and courageously declared: "We ought to obey God rather than men. The God of our fathers raised up Jesus, whom ye slew and hanged on a tree. Him hath God exalted with his right hand to be a Prince and a Saviour, for to give repentance to Israel, and forgiveness of sins. And we are his witnesses of these things; and so is also the Holy Ghost, whom God hath given to them that obey him" (Acts 5:29–32). At this point, it took the counsel of the Pharisee Gamaliel to dissuade his colleagues from executing the Apostles, saying, with more truth than he realized: "Let them alone: for if this counsel or this work be of men, it will come to naught: But if it be of God, ye cannot overthrow it" (Acts 5:38–39).

MODERN PROPHETS SPEAK

Gordon B. Hinckley:

> We must strengthen ourselves and our people to get our teachers to speak out of their hearts rather than out of their books, to communicate their love for the Lord and this precious work, and somehow it will catch fire in the hearts of those they teach. (*TGBH,* 619–20)

ILLUSTRATIONS FOR OUR TIME

Preach My Gospel

There is little activity in building the kingdom of God to surpass in excitement and enthusiasm the initiatives for preparing up-and-coming young missionaries for full-time service in the mission fields of the Church. My wife and I have the privilege of serving as directors for the Young Missionary Training Program of our stake, which involves meeting most Sunday afternoons with several dozen young men and women who are eager to learn the principles and practices outlined in the Church's new training manual *Preach My Gospel.* As the participants in the group receive mission calls and embark on the Lord's errand, we can envision them going forth applying with valor the principles outlined in Doctrine and Covenants Section 4—principles such as faith, virtue, knowledge, temperance, patience, brotherly kindness, godliness, charity, humility, and diligence. These future missionaries are especially keen to develop the courage needed to proclaim the gospel with boldness and conviction, as the scriptures direct:

> Yea, verily, verily, I say unto you, that the field is white already to harvest; wherefore, thrust in your sickles, and reap with all your might, mind, and strength.
>
> Open your mouths and they shall be filled, and you shall become even as Nephi of old, who journeyed from Jerusalem in the wilderness.
>
> Yea, open your mouths and spare not, and you shall be laden with sheaves upon your backs, for lo, I am with you.

> Yea, open your mouths and they shall be filled, saying: Repent, repent, and prepare ye the way of the Lord, and make his paths straight; for the kingdom of heaven is at hand. (D&C 33:7–10)

We rejoice in learning from time to time how these young missionaries lift up their voices "as with the sound of a trump, declaring my word like unto angels of God" (D&C 42:6). Recently the stake president took us aside and shared a report he had just received from one of our outbound missionaries who had just arrived in the mission field. This young man had not postponed thrusting "in his sickle with his might" (D&C 4:4): He had found the courage to give his first missionary discussion while on the airplane and had distributed three passalong cards at that time. His enthusiasm for preaching the gospel was boundless.

Richard G. Scott reported the success the Church is having with *Preach My Gospel:*

> Missionaries are not alone in benefiting from *Preach My Gospel:*
> • One mission president's wife studied and pondered every word in *Preach My Gospel,* including every scriptural reference. She then did something she had lacked the courage to do—she invited a close relative to study and ponder the Book of Mormon. That individual accepted her invitation and has been greatly benefited.
> • Another family uses *Preach My Gospel* to help prepare their children for missions. They reported: "Our 17-year-old was the first to get an assignment. As expected, he looked for the shortest segment in the book. His lesson, however, was a 20-minute heartfelt expression of the principles, complete with scriptures and testimony." . . .
> Much good has been accomplished in the brief seven months since *Preach My Gospel* was introduced, but the best is yet to come as we all become more proficient in the use of this extraordinary missionary tool. (Richard G. Scott, "The Power of *Preach My Gospel,*" *Ensign,* May 2005, 31)

By following the Spirit as we open our mouths—boldly yet humbly—we can truly serve as willing and effective servants of the Lord in helping to build the kingdom of God. Just as the Apostles of old who followed the Savior's commission to carry the gospel to all peoples, we can venture forth—each member a missionary—to share the truths of the Restoration, for "it is necessary and expedient in me that you should open your mouths in proclaiming my gospel, the things of the kingdom, expounding the mysteries thereof out of the scriptures, according to that portion of Spirit and power which shall be given unto you, even as I will" (D&C 71:1). [Allen]

LIKENING THE SCRIPTURES TO OUR LIVES

Acts 5:29 Then Peter and the other apostles answered and said, We ought to obey God rather than men.

Application: We should always seek to obey God as Peter and the Apostles did. They were full of the Spirit and feared no man. The Lord will give us strength to do all things that He would have us do.

SUMMARY

The "times of restitution of all things" about which Peter spoke following the ascension of Christ (Acts 3:21) are *now*. The restoration of the gospel has been accomplished in our day, involving, among other heavenly messengers, "Peter, and James, and John, whom I have sent unto you, by whom I have ordained you and confirmed you to be apostles, and especial witnesses of my name, and bear the keys of your ministry and of the same things which I revealed unto them" (D&C 27:12). The same commission given by the Savior to His former Apostles has devolved, by modern-day revelation, upon us. Through the ultimate confirming witness of the Holy Ghost and the application of spiritual gifts bestowed upon the faithful, we can accomplish miracles by proclaiming the gospel with conviction and boldness and building up the kingdom of God in all of its glory.

CHAPTER 29

THE GROWTH *of the* CHURCH

Reading Assignment: Acts 6–9.

Additional Reading: Acts 22:1–16; 26:1–5, 9–18; 1 Corinthians 12:12–31, Ephesians 4:11–16, D&C 64:33–34; 107:99.

> *Within the Church there is a constant need for unity, for if we are not one, we are not his (see D&C 38:27). We are truly dependent on each other, "and the eye cannot say unto the hand, I have no need of thee: nor again the head to the feet, I have no need of you" (1 Cor. 12:21). Nor can the North Americans say to the Asians, nor the Europeans to the islanders of the sea, "I have no need of thee." No, in this church we have need of every member. We pray, as did Paul when he wrote to the church in Corinth, "that there should be no schism in the body; but that the members should have the same care one for another. And whether one member suffer, all the members suffer with it; or one member be honoured, all the members rejoice with it" (1 Cor. 12:25–26). . . .*
>
> *It is unity and oneness that has thus far enabled us to bear our testimony around the globe, bringing forward tens of thousands of missionaries to do their part. More must be done. It is unity that has thus far enabled the Church, its wards and stakes, branches and districts, and members, to construct temples and chapels, undertake welfare projects, seek after the dead, watch over the Church, and build faith. More must be done. These great purposes of the Lord could not have been achieved with dissension or jealousy or selfishness. Our ideas may not always be quite like those who preside in authority over us, but this is the Lord's church, and he will bless each of us as we cast off pride, pray for strength, and contribute to the good of the whole.*
>
> —Howard W. Hunter, *That We Might Have Joy* [Salt Lake City: Deseret Book, 1994], 49–50.

THEMES *for* LIVING

1. Additional Leaders for an Expanding Church
2. Stand for Truth and Righteousness—Sacrifice All
3. Conversion—Receiving the Word of God by the Spirit

INTRODUCTION

The kingdom of God on the earth is The Church of Jesus Christ of Latter-day Saints. As the Church grows, it requires many leaders and servants to build it up (see JST, Matt. 6:38). We are organized after the manner of the Church during the dispensation of our Savior Jesus Christ. The Church organization fits the growth as well as the geography of the Church according to the directions of the Lord. The Apostle Paul describes and compares the Church to one body in Christ. We are all one in Christ. We are symbiotic—organized according to a relationship of mutual support and benefit—and should practice unity and work together synergistically. We need each other and the Lord needs us to build up His Kingdom (see 1 Cor. 12:12–31).

1. ADDITIONAL LEADERS FOR AN EXPANDING CHURCH

THEME: As the kingdom of God expands, the Lord provides an augmented and broadened organization to accomplish divine purposes and ensure beneficial services. In the days of Peter and his colleagues, seven special representatives, including Stephen, were called to assist in the work of building up the kingdom of God. We are all needed to build up the kingdom of God.

MOMENT OF TRUTH

The commission of the Savior to His Apostles was "Go ye therefore, and teach all nations, baptizing them in the name of the Father, and of the Son, and of the Holy Ghost" (Matt. 28:19). As the circle of adherents in the growing Kingdom expanded, there was a concomitant expansion in the need to provide services to the flock, especially for groups such as the widows. As a result, the Apostles called for additional workers to assist in the cause: "Wherefore, brethren, look ye out among you seven men of honest report, full of the Holy Ghost and wisdom, whom we may appoint over this business" (Acts 6:3). The seven who were commissioned for the administration of services were these: Stephen ("a man full of faith and of the Holy Ghost"— Acts 6:5), Philip, Prochorus, Nicanor, Timon, Parmenas, and Nicolas. In this way, the first expansion in Church leadership was accomplished, allowing the Apostles to continue with their special calling for "the ministry of the word" (Acts 6:4).

MODERN PROPHETS SPEAK

Gordon B. Hinckley:

> Whether it be teaching a class, whether it be serving as a home teacher, whether it be serving as a Church officer, whether it be working as a missionary, serving in the temple or any such thing, it deserves our best effort. There is nothing unimportant about any call in this Church. Every call is important. When we all do our duty working together, the whole Church moves forward in an orderly and wonderful fashion. (*TGBH,* 66)

ILLUSTRATIONS FOR OUR TIME

Unity in Temporal and Spiritual Matters
Having all things in common was the goal when Christ established the Church in the old world (see Acts 2:44) as well as in the western hemisphere (see 3 Ne. 26:19; 4 Ne. 1:3). In this dispensation, the prophet Joseph, in order to help establish Zion, revealed the law of consecration as practiced in the united order (see D&C 49:20; 51:3; 78:5; 105:5).

James E. Talmage explains the unity and devotion of the earlier Saints at the time of Christ to be united by having all things in common:

> No condition recorded of the early apostolic ministry expresses more forcefully the unity and devotion of the Church in those days than does the fact of the members establishing a system of common ownership of property (Acts 2:44, 46; 4:32–37; 6:1–4). One result of this community of interest in temporal things was a marked unity in spiritual matters; they "were of one heart and of one soul." Lacking nothing, they lived in contentment and godliness. Over thirty centuries earlier the people of Enoch had rejoiced in a similar condition of oneness, and their attainments in spiritual excellence were so effective that "the Lord came and dwelt with his people; . . . And the Lord called his people Zion, because they were of one heart and one mind, and dwelt in righteousness; and there was no poor among them" (Moses 7:16–18). The Nephite disciples grew in holiness, as "they had all things common among them, every man dealing justly, one with another" (3 Ne. 26:19; see also 4 Ne. 1:2–3). A system of unity in material affairs has been revealed to the Church in this current dispensation, (D&C 82:17, 18; 51:10–13, 18; 104:70–77), to the blessings of which the people may attain as they learn to replace selfish concern by altruism, and individual advantage by devotion to the general welfare." (*JC,* 667)

LIKENING THE SCRIPTURES TO OUR LIVES

Acts 6:3 Wherefore, brethren, look ye out among you seven men of honest report, full of the Holy Ghost and wisdom, whom we may appoint over this business.

Application: The business to which these seven were primarily assigned was ministering to the widows and their needs. However, every person is needed to build up the Kingdom within his or her sphere of responsibility and influence.

2. STAND FOR TRUTH AND RIGHTEOUSNESS—SACRIFICE ALL

THEME: Stephen—whose courage and principles led to his martyrdom in the name of Christian values—is an inspiring example of standing up for truth, even if it means giving one's life in sacrifice.

MOMENT OF TRUTH

The callous and sinister conspiracy among certain of the priests and elders to thwart the mission of the Savior was quickly extended to His followers in the faith. In the case of Stephen, one of the newly called group of seven administrators and assistants to the Twelve, the leaders of the synagogue advanced charges of blasphemy, which they supported through the testimony of false witnesses. As Stephen was brought before the council to answer to these charges of subverting the ways of Moses, a miraculous transformation in his appearance took place: "And all that sat in the council, looking stedfastly on him, saw his face as it had been the face of an angel" (Acts 6:15). It was in this transfigured state that Stephen delivered his inspired and powerful discourse on the history of God's dealings with the covenant people of Abraham, including the service of Moses in bringing about the deliverance from Egypt and prophesying of a future leader of the people: "A prophet shall the Lord your God raise up unto you of your brethren, like unto me; him shall ye hear" (Acts 7:37; compare Deut. 18:15). Who was this prophet? It was Jesus Christ, declared Stephen to his detractors, "the Just One; of whom ye have been now the betrayers and murderers" (Acts. 7:52). To this direct and bold accusation, the priests and elders responded by casting Stephen out of the city and stoning him to death (Acts 7:58). One of the participants in this egregious act was the young Saul of Tarsus.

Meanwhile, Philip, an associate of Stephen among the seven assistants, went down to Samaria, preaching Christ and performing mighty miracles (Acts 8:5–8). Soon thereafter, an angel of the Lord spoke to him and commanded him to go south from

Jerusalem toward Gaza, where he encountered an emissary from the court of Queen Candace of Ethiopia. This eunuch was traveling in his chariot studying the section in the writings of Isaiah which reads in the King James version as follows: "He was oppressed, and he was afflicted, yet he opened not his mouth: he is brought as a lamb to the slaughter, and as a sheep before her shearers is dumb, so he openeth not his mouth. He was taken from prison and from judgment: and who shall declare his generation? for he was cut off out of the land of the living: for the transgression of my people was he stricken" (Isa. 53:7–8). When the eunuch inquired of Philip what this passage meant, Philip unfolded to him with great persuasion the mission of the Savior. As a result, when they presently came to a body of water, the eunuch asked to be baptized. "And Philip said, If thou believest with all thine heart, thou mayest. And he answered and said, I believe that Jesus Christ is the Son of God. And he commanded the chariot to stand still: and they went down both into the water, both Philip and the eunuch; and he baptized him. And when they were come up out of the water, the Spirit of the Lord caught away Philip, that the eunuch saw him no more: and he went on his way rejoicing" (Acts 8:37–39).

MODERN PROPHETS SPEAK

Gordon B. Hinckley:

> Oh, how we need in this day and time men and women who will stand up for decency and truth and honesty and virtue and law and order and all of the other good qualities on which our society is founded. . . .
>
> The problem with most of us is that we are afraid. We want to do the right thing, but we are troubled by fears and we sit back and the world drifts about us.
>
> I confess to you that by nature I was a very timid boy. When I left to go on a mission my great father said, "I want to give you only one verse of scripture." I think this has become, perhaps, the greatest help of my life, these words of the Lord to the ruler of the synagogue whose daughter was reported dead. And the Lord turned to the ruler of the synagogue and said: "Be not afraid, only believe." (Mark 5:36)
>
> "Be not afraid, only believe." I commend to you these wonderful words of the Lord as you think of your responsibilities and opportunities. (*TGBH*, 128–129)

ILLUSTRATIONS FOR OUR TIME

Armor of God

It is our lot to be vigilant and watchful in standing on principle and guarding the truths of the gospel. Think of the courage and conviction of the Lord's Apostles in carrying on the work of the ministry with boldness and spiritual leadership following the cru-cifixion, resurrection, and ascension of the Savior. Think of the fearless witness of Stephen—one of the seven newly called assistants to the Twelve—when he answered the council's charges of blasphemy and willingly gave his life to seal his testimony. These valiant heroes of truth were acting to secure and protect the work of building up the kingdom of God. They were continuing the work of so many prophets and leaders from earlier dispensations.

One example of stalwart vigilance from the Old Testament is Nehemiah, who con-tributed much toward the consolidation of covenant society by leading the movement to restore the protective walls of Jerusalem after the Babylonian conquest. An influential "cupbearer" at the court of King Artaxerxes of Persia (465–425 B.C.; see Neh. 1:11), Nehemiah was moved by the accounts of the sufferings of his compatriots at Jerusalem and launched a major campaign to come to their assistance for the purpose of restoring the security of the city. For twelve years, he labored as governor—against daunting odds and life-threatening plots by enemy forces—to complete the walls of the city: "They which builded on the wall, and they that bare burdens, with those that laded, every one with one of his hands wrought in the work, and with the other hand held a weapon" (Neh. 4:17). Thus Nehemiah, like his contemporary Ezra, has left us a stirring example of restoration, rebuilding, fortifying, strengthening, renewing—all to the glory of God and the service of establishing His kingdom upon the earth.

The story of Nehemiah's leadership in organizing the Israelites to rebuild the walls of Jerusalem, often under threat of attack from enemy forces round about, reminds me of an incident from modern Church history that occurred on January 8, 1834, in Kirtland, Ohio. On that day, guards were stationed to protect the Kirtland temple as a result of persecution by detractors and the threat of violence at the hands of the gathering mob. Some workmen were seen armed with a hammer in one hand and a rifle in the other. Joseph Smith records in his journal: "On the morning of the 8th of January, about 1 o'clock, the inhabitants of Kirtland were alarmed by the firing of about thirteen rounds of cannon, by the mob, on the hill about half a mile northwest of the village" (*HC,* 2:2). However, with the coming of dawn, it was determined that the temple was not damaged. Of this period, Heber C. Kimball writes in the *Times and Seasons:* "And we had to guard ourselves night after night, and for weeks were not permitted to take off our clothes, and were obliged to lay with our fire locks [rifles] in our arms" (*HC,* 2:2). Do we ponder often enough upon the sacrifices and trials of our forebears and upon their vigilance in securing for us the blessings that we enjoy so abundantly today? Are we prepared to stand up for righteous principles and guard the things of God with our lives as they did?

In the days of Nehemiah, as in the days of the Kirtland Saints, the righteous were constrained to carry on their labors with a tool in one hand and a weapon in the other. And so it is today—and at all times during the experience of mortality. The prudent and wise never venture forth in their pursuits without first providing themselves with divine armor. As Paul stated it: "Put on the whole armour of God, that ye may be able to stand against the wiles of the devil" (Eph. 6:11). And in our day, the Lord has counseled:

> Wherefore, lift up your hearts and rejoice, and gird up your loins, and take upon you my whole armor, that ye may be able to withstand the evil day, having done all, that ye may be able to stand.
>
> Stand, therefore, having your loins girt about with truth, having on the breastplate of righteousness, and your feet shod with the preparation of the gospel of peace, which I have sent mine angels to commit unto you;
>
> Taking the shield of faith wherewith ye shall be able to quench all the fiery darts of the wicked;
>
> And take the helmet of salvation, and the sword of my Spirit, which I will pour out upon you, and my word which I reveal unto you, and be agreed as touching all things whatsoever ye ask of me, and be faithful until I come, and ye shall be caught up, that where I am ye shall be also. (D&C 27:15–18)

These weapons of godly armament—truth, righteousness, preparations of the gospel of peace (as in the scriptures), faith, salvation, and the Spirit—are more than pleasant images. They are real, potent, and highly effective defenses when used in the Lord's way—meaning as a collective group: "take upon you my *whole* armor," He said (D&C 27:15; emphasis added). When we venture into the world to complete our labors, we wisely leave no part of our being exposed to worldly onslaughts and temptations, but instead fight our battles like the stripling warriors, "as if with the strength of God" (Alma 56:56). [Allen]

LIKENING THE SCRIPTURES TO OUR LIVES

Acts 7:60 And he [Stephen] kneeled down, and cried with a loud voice, Lord, lay not this sin to their charge. And when he had said this, he fell asleep.

Application: The righteousness of Stephen was exhibited by his willingness to forgive and not lay this sin upon them. Indeed, the attitude of mercy and forgiveness comes back to all who truly act in this manner (see Matt. 5:7; Luke 6:13). It should be our goal to show mercy and forgiveness, which is the ultimate display of charity.

3. CONVERSION—RECEIVING THE WORD OF GOD BY THE SPIRIT

THEME: When God speaks, man is to respond. The miraculous calling and conversion of Saul of Tarsus as an emissary and Apostle of the Lord to the world is an unforgettable instance of the Lord's intervention on behalf of His program for spreading the gospel to the world. Though our own personal conversion story may not be as dramatic, it is certain that every authentic conversion is miraculous, because it necessarily involves the intercession of the Holy Spirit, "for no man can say that Jesus is the Lord, but by the Holy Ghost" (1 Cor. 12:3). Thus each person who experiences the "mighty change of heart" is to respond forthrightly and with full dedication to the Lord, as the Spirit might direct.

MOMENT OF TRUTH

Saul of Tarsus, who participated in the stoning of Stephen, is characterized in the scriptural account as one "breathing out threatenings and slaughter against the disciples of the Lord" (Acts 9:1). In his own words, he recalled: "And I persecuted this way unto the death, binding and delivering into prisons both men and women" (Acts 22:4). Before Agrippa, Saul confessed: "And many of the saints did I shut up in prison, having received authority from the chief priests; and when they were put to death, I gave my voice against them" (Acts 26:10). Saul was clearly no friend to the Saints of his day, using his influence, knowledge, and strategy in every way possible to contravene the work of the kingdom. But the Lord knew his soul and his potential—that he was destined to be a mighty tool for carrying the gospel message to many nations with authority and great spiritual power. Thus as he was journeying one day to Damascus to continue his campaign against the Christians, he experienced a most unexpected encounter:

> At midday, O king, I saw in the way a light from heaven, above the brightness of the sun, shining round about me and them which journeyed with me.
>
> And when we were all fallen to the earth, I heard a voice speaking unto me, and saying in the Hebrew tongue, Saul, Saul, why persecutest thou me? it is hard for thee to kick against the pricks.
>
> And I said, Who art thou, Lord? And he said, I am Jesus whom thou persecutest.
>
> But rise, and stand upon thy feet: for I have appeared unto thee for this purpose, to make thee a minister and a witness both of these things which thou hast seen, and of those things in the which I will appear unto thee. (Acts 26:13–16)

In this manner Saul went through a dramatic and miraculous conversion—emerging from the experience as Paul, an Apostle of the Lord who performed extraordinary missionary labors to build the kingdom of God.

In a similar manner, a century and half earlier on the distant American continent, Alma, son of the High Priest Alma, experienced a dramatic intervention by an angel of the Lord sent to call him and his colleagues to repentance for their concerted efforts to destroy the Church of God (Mosiah 27:11–16). From this life-changing event, the young Alma went forward with a commission to become one of the greatest of the Lord's prophets in effecting a mighty change for good in the hearts of the people.

MODERN PROPHETS SPEAK

Ezra Taft Benson:

> When we have undergone this mighty change, which is brought about only through faith in Jesus Christ and through the operation of the Spirit upon us, it is as though we have become a new person. Thus the change is likened to a new birth. Thousands of you within the sound of my voice have experienced this change. You have forsaken lives of sin, sometimes deep and offensive sin, and through applying the blood of Christ in your lives, have become clean. You have no more disposition to return to your old ways. You are in reality a new person. This is what is meant by a change of heart ("A Mighty Change of Heart," address prepared [but not delivered], 1986). (*TETB*, 470)

ILLUSTRATION FOR OUR TIME

The Conversion of Saul

James E. Talmage describes the conversion of Saul and his work as he completed the marvelous transition from enemy of God to emissary of truth:

> The sudden change of heart by which an ardent persecutor of the saints was so transformed as to become a true disciple, is to the average mind a miracle. Saul of Tarsus was a devoted student and observer of the law, a strict Pharisee. We find no intimation that he ever met or saw Jesus during the Lord's life in the flesh; and his contact with the Christian movement appears to have been brought about through disputation with Stephen. In determining what he would call right and what wrong the young enthusiast was guided too much by mind and too little by heart. His learning, which should have been his servant, was instead his master. He was a leading spirit in the cruel persecution of the first converts to Christianity; yet none can doubt his belief that even in such he was rendering service to Jehovah (compare John 16:2).

His unusual energy and superb ability were misdirected. As soon as he realized the error of his course, he turned about, without counting risk, cost, or the certainty of persecution and probable martyrdom. His repentance was as genuine as had been his persecuting zeal. All through his ministry he was tortured by the past (Acts 22:4, 19, 20; 1 Cor. 15:9; 2 Cor. 12:7; Gal. 1:13); yet he found a measure of relief in the knowledge that he had acted in good conscience (Acts 26:9–11). It was "hard for him to kick against the pricks" (revised version "goad," Acts 9:5; 26:14) of tradition, training, and education; yet he hesitated not. He was a chosen instrument for the work of the Lord (Acts 9:15); and promptly he responded to the Master's will. Whatever of error Saul of Tarsus had committed through youthful zeal, Paul the apostle gave his all—his time, talent, and life—to expiate. He was preeminently the Lord's apostle to the Gentiles; and this opening of the doors to others than Jews was the main contention between himself and Stephen. In accordance with the divine and fateful purpose, Paul was called to do the work, in opposition to which he had been a participant in the martyrdom of Stephen. At the Lord's word of direction Paul was ready to preach Christ to the Gentiles; only by a miracle could the Jewish exclusiveness of Peter and the Church generally be overcome (Acts 10; and 11:1–18). (*JC*, 667–68)

LIKENING THE SCRIPTURES TO OUR LIVES

Acts 9:6 And he trembling and astonished said, Lord, what wilt thou have me to do? And the Lord said unto him, Arise, and go into the city, and it shall be told thee what thou must do.

Application: Paul had a revelation from the Lord and he responded with these clarion words, "Lord, what wilt thou have me do?" He had been called to repentance. The key to repentance and conversion is turning one's will over to the Lord. When we are truly converted, we have a desire to do good continually (see Mosiah 5:2), we strengthen our brothers and sisters (see Luke 22:32), we have a concern for the welfare of our brothers and sisters (see Enos 1:9, 11; Mosiah 28:3), and we truly seek to do the will of the Lord.

SUMMARY

From these passages preserved in the Acts of the Apostles, we are witness to the blessings of the Lord in watching over His infant Church. We are encouraged to see that He guided the Apostles from the very beginning to expand the circle of leadership appropriately for the good of the flock as the Church and kingdom grew. We are stirred by the courage and conviction of such as Peter and Stephen in standing for truth and righteousness—even if it should require the ultimate sacrifice. We are moved by the dramatic and miraculous conversion of Saul of Tarsus through the personal intervention of the resurrected Lord. As we ponder and consider these accounts, we are prompted to apply them to our own lives. What are we doing to ease the burdens of those in need, including the widows and fatherless? How do we perform our duties in the strength of the Lord when our values come under attack from outward forces of darkness? How valiant are we in remembering the promptings of the Spirit that came to us during the process of our own conversion—the mighty change of heart that brings us beyond the threshold of worldliness and into the light of the gospel? We all have an important role to play. Just as the Apostle Paul taught, we need each other and the Lord needs us to build up His Kingdom (see 1 Cor. 12:12–31).

CHAPTER 30

"GOD IS NO RESPECTER *of* PERSONS"

Reading Assignment: Acts 10–14; 15:1–35.

Additional Reading: Romans 2:9–11; 2 Nephi 26:33; Bible Dictionary, "Circumcision" (646); "Cornelius" (650).

> *The most important prophet in any age is the living prophet. The prophets who have gone before have left to us their precious teachings which will be used for the instruction and comfort of mankind. But, it is the living prophet who helps us by his teachings, example, and direction to meet and to solve the problems of today, our day. To follow the living prophet, the interpreter of the past, is the essence of wisdom. The very strength of the Church lies in the doctrine of continuous revelation through a living prophet.*
>
> —JOHN A. WIDTSOE, *EVIDENCES AND RECONCILIATIONS* [SALT LAKE CITY: IMPROVEMENT ERA], 352.

THEMES *for* LIVING

1. The Gospel to Be Preached to All People
2. The Lord's Servants Are Blessed in Their Work
3. The Law of Moses Was Fulfilled in Christ

INTRODUCTION

The gospel of Jesus Christ was and is intended for all of God's children. We have been commanded to take the gospel to all the earth (see Mark 16:15; Morm. 9:22; D&C

39:15). The Lord has made it clear that we are to invite all to come unto Him: "and he doeth nothing save it be plain unto the children of men; and he inviteth them all to come unto him and partake of his goodness; and he denieth none that come unto him, black and white, bond and free, male and female; and he remembereth the heathen; and all are alike unto God, both Jew and Gentile" (2 Ne. 26:33). The Lord's servants have been blessed and are continually being blessed as they carry the message of Christ to all the world.

Since the beginning of time, the Lord has made known His gospel to His prophets through revelation. Continuous revelation is an eternal verity as it relates to the kingdom of God here upon the earth. We cannot operate the Lord's Church without His direction: "And I do this that I may prove unto many that I am the same yesterday, today, and forever; and that I speak forth my words according to mine own pleasure. And because that I have spoken one word ye need not suppose that I cannot speak another; for my work is not yet finished; neither shall it be until the end of man, neither from that time henceforth and forever" (2 Ne. 29:9). We see that the Lord will indeed reveal to mankind all that is necessary for our salvation and exaltation. The doctrine is clear: "We believe all that God has revealed, all that He does now reveal, and we believe that He will yet reveal many great and important things pertaining to the Kingdom of God" (A of F 1:9).

In addition, we know that the Holy Ghost reveals the truth to God's chosen servants and that the gifts of the Spirit are given to the faithful in rich abundance: "And I would exhort you, my beloved brethren, that ye remember that he is the same yesterday, today, and forever, and that all these gifts of which I have spoken, which are spiritual, never will be done away, even as long as the world shall stand, only according to the unbelief of the children of men" (Moro. 10:19). We learn that God's dealings with mankind are just and true and that He seeks our welfare above all else. Indeed, He is the same yesterday, today, and forever.

1. THE GOSPEL TO BE PREACHED TO ALL PEOPLE

THEME: God is no respecter of persons (see Acts 10:34; compare Rom. 2:9–11). Just as Peter received the revelation to deliver the gospel of Jesus Christ to the Gentiles, in a similar way, continuing with this commission, we are to preach the truth in all quarters of the earth, bringing souls unto Christ from all nations, kindreds, tongues, and peoples.

MOMENT OF TRUTH

Caesarea was an important Palestinian seaport community located about sixty miles northwest of Jerusalem on the main coastal road leading southward toward Egypt. The centurion Cornelius, of Gentile extraction, lived in Caesarea: "A devout man, and one that feared God with all his house, which gave much alms to the people, and prayed to God always" (Acts 10:2). An angel of the Lord appeared to Cornelius and bade him send to Joppa, a seaport to the north, to obtain counsel from Peter, who was staying there with Simon, the tanner. While the servants of Cornelius were underway, Peter received a manifestation from the Lord revealing to him that the time had come to preach the gospel of Jesus Christ to the Gentiles (see Acts 10:9–16). Thus Peter, moved upon by the Spirit, went with the servants of Cornelius and certain others from Joppa to Caesarea and met with the Gentile assemblage. The Apostle declared: "Of a truth I perceive that God is no respecter of persons: But in every nation he that feareth him, and worketh righteousness, is accepted with him" (Acts 10:34–35). As Peter proclaimed the gospel of Jesus Christ, the Holy Ghost fell on the audience of believers—an astounding extension of God's blessings to His non-Jewish flock (Acts 10:44)—and Peter commanded them to be baptized.

Subsequently, at Jerusalem, the disciples contended with Peter over this development, but he set their hearts at rest in recounting the events at Caesarea and the manifestation of the Holy Ghost: "Then remembered I the word of the Lord, how that he said, John indeed baptized with water; but ye shall be baptized with the Holy Ghost. Forasmuch then as God gave them the like gift as he did unto us, who believed on the Lord Jesus Christ; what was I, that I could withstand God? When they heard these things, they held their peace, and glorified God, saying, Then hath God also to the Gentiles granted repentance unto life" (Acts 11:16–18).

Paul and Barnabas, as well, extended their missionary labors to the Gentiles, declaring to the Jewish people who were not receptive of their word:

> It was necessary that the word of God should first have been spoken to you: but seeing ye put it from you, and judge yourselves unworthy of everlasting life, lo, we turn to the Gentiles.
>
> For so hath the Lord commanded us, *saying*, I have set thee to be a light of the Gentiles, that thou shouldest be for salvation unto the ends of the earth.
>
> And when the Gentiles heard this, they were glad, and glorified the word of the Lord: and as many as were ordained to eternal life believed.
>
> And the word of the Lord was published throughout all the region. (Acts 13:46–49)

MODERN PROPHETS SPEAK

Spencer W. Kimball:

> Now is the moment in the timetable of the Lord to carry the gospel farther than it has ever been carried before—farther geographically, and farther in density of coverage. Many a person in this world is crying, knowingly and unknowingly, "Come

over . . . and help us." He might be your neighbor. She might be your friend. He might be a relative. She might be someone you met only yesterday. But we have what they need. Let us take new courage from our studies and pray, as did Peter, "And now, Lord, grant unto thy servants, that with all boldness they may speak thy word." (Acts 4:29) (*TSWK,* 546)

ILLUSTRATIONS FOR OUR TIME

A Church for All Mankind

It was my honor and privilege to make the acquaintance of a remarkable black man a few years ago who had become a student of the restored gospel. He and his family had operated a well-known business not far from the Oakland Temple for many years, and he had often gazed upon the transcendent beauty of the temple and wondered about its purpose and place in the religious life of its patrons. He even had a member of the Church in his employ, but the gentleman had never raised with him the theme of latter-day theology. It was later my opportunity to be among a series of priesthood brethren who shared their testimony with this good man and participated in missionary discussions with him. Having come from a family line with a long and distinguished history of pastors and churchmen, his faith was remarkably strong. At one point, he was diagnosed with cancer, but told the doctors that his "Physician in Heaven" would watch out for him, and he miraculously survived the ordeal.

One of his heroes was Joseph Johnson of Ghana, Africa, who was touched by the spirit of the Joseph Smith story long before he had the opportunity to receive the missionary discussions, and long before the Official Declaration of 30 September 1978, making the priesthood available to all worthy male members of the Church without regard to race or color. Brother Johnson waited faithfully and patiently for the time when he could receive all the blessings of the restored gospel. "I used to walk 50 miles a day [teaching others about the truth] and wasn't bothered about it. Whenever I walked, I reflected on the early missionaries, and I gained strength because it seemed as if I was following in the footsteps of the pioneers. Their example inspired me—the way some died in the snow and the way they toiled to bring the truth. They were great people" (*Ensign,* Dec. 1999, 47). Brother Johnson's dream of being baptized a member of the Church was realized in 1978, and he continued to help build up the kingdom of God in that part of the world, serving subsequently as a patriarch in the Cape Coast Ghana Stake of the Church.

His admirer, my black friend referred to above, has the dream that he too can serve as an instrument in furthering the work of the gospel among his ancestral forebears who are seeking for the truth. The gospel of Jesus Christ is a universal gospel intended for all mankind. The blessings of Covenant Israel are open to all who believe and come into the fold of Christ. "For he doeth that which is good among the children of men; and he doeth nothing save it be plain unto the children of men; and he inviteth them all to come unto him and partake of his goodness; and he denieth none that come unto him, black and white, bond and free, male and female; and he remembereth the heathen; and all are alike unto God, both Jew and Gentile" (2 Ne. 26:33). [Allen]

LIKENING THE SCRIPTURES TO OUR LIVES

Acts 10:34–35 Then Peter opened his mouth, and said, Of a truth I perceive that God is no respecter of persons: But in every nation he that feareth him, and worketh righteousness, is accepted with him.

Application: All mankind are the children of God and all are alike unto Him. Whoever will come unto Him through His Son Jesus Christ will be accepted by Him. All can become the sons and daughters of Christ (see Mosiah 5:7).

2. THE LORD'S SERVANTS ARE BLESSED IN THEIR WORK

THEME: The Lord will bless and support His servants as they teach and preach His word.

MOMENT OF TRUTH

When Herod slew James, the brother of John, the Lord exacted judgment by ending the life of this evil king (see Acts 12:2, 23), thus permitting the ministry of the gospel to continue. Peter, who had been imprisoned by Herod pending execution, was liberated through the intervention of the angel of the Lord, much to the astonishment and delight of the disciples. Meanwhile, Paul and Barnabas were commissioned of the Holy Ghost to perform their missionary labors:

> As they [the disciples] ministered to the Lord, and fasted, the Holy Ghost said, Separate me Barnabas and Saul for the work whereunto I have called them.
>
> And when they had fasted and prayed, and laid their hands on them, they sent them away. (Acts 13:2–3)

Paul and Barnabas carried on their missions with honor and dignity in places such as Antioch. Elsewhere, they encountered much tribulation at the hands of envious and doubting authorities, Paul even being stoned for his pronouncements (see Acts 14:19)—though he was soon thereafter restored to health and continued to preach Christ Jesus throughout the region: "Confirming the souls of the disciples, and exhorting them to continue in the faith, and that we must through much tribulation enter into the kingdom of God. And when they had ordained them elders in every church, and had prayed with fasting, they commended them to the Lord, on whom they believed" (Acts 14:22–23). We see that the hand of the Lord was outstretched to prosper and bless the work of His chosen servants. In due time, Paul determined to revisit the cities where he had conducted his ministry among the Saints—"and see how they do" (Acts 15:36). With Silas, a new companion, he departed, "confirming the churches" (Acts 15:42).

MODERN PROPHETS SPEAK

M. Russell Ballard:

> Through the years I have watched countless missionaries come and go, and I have seen extraordinary things happen in their lives and in the lives of their families as a result. The work they are called to do is hard and sometimes discouraging. But because they have the assurance that they are on God's errand, they are able to valiantly serve Him. I often suggest to those who want to know if the Church is true that they spend a few hours working with our missionaries. It doesn't take long to learn that no one can do all of the things a missionary does every day without knowing beyond any question that what they are doing is right and true.
>
> The Lord does bless His missionaries just as surely as they bless the lives of those they teach and baptize. Difficult languages are learned with astonishing speed and skill. Financially strapped families back home find unforeseen means to support their missionaries. Weaknesses become strengths, challenges become opportunities, trials become triumphs, and adversity becomes an adventure in the service of the Lord—another fruit of gospel living. (*Our Search for Happiness: An Invitation to Understand The Church of Jesus Christ of the Latter-day Saints* [Salt Lake City: Deseret Book, 1993], 108)

ILLUSTRATION FOR OUR TIME

The Protecting Hand of the Lord
Derin Head Rodriguez tells of the protecting hand of the Lord in El Salvador:

> In 1980 Elder Amado was called to be president of the Guatemala City Mission, one of the two missions in the country. One day toward the end of his missionary

assignment, which generally lasts three years, he and Sister Amado had to go to Mexico City on Church business. Unable to get a direct flight, they made reservations for a flight that made a stop in El Salvador, which borders on Guatemala. As they flew over that troubled country, both had strong feelings that it was time to reopen the El Salvador Mission, which had been closed for about three years because of political instability. Similar feelings on the way home caused them to begin to talk, fast, and pray about the matter. In the summer of 1982, Elder Amado was asked to reopen missionary work in El Salvador and to serve as president there, in addition to presiding over his current mission. With the help of ten elders, Salvadorans who were serving in the Guatemala City Mission, he reopened the mission, to the delight of the 25,000 or so Latter-day Saints there.

"I will always remember the feelings of the members and missionaries in El Salvador and the way the Lord protected us," he recalls. "It didn't matter how much conflict there was in that country, the spirit of the Lord guided us to avoid problems with the government, guerrillas, bombs, and everything. The Lord kept us out of danger." He served as mission president in El Salvador for one year, and a total of four years in Guatemala." (Derin Head Rodriguez, *From Every Nation: Faith-promoting Personal Stories of General Authorities from Around the World* [Salt Lake City: Deseret Book, 1990], 214–15)

Evacuation from Germany

In August 1939, Hitler began to mass troops along the border of Poland. War was about to begin in Europe. The Church sent out word for all missionaries to leave immediately. Those in eastern Germany were to head to Denmark; those in the western and southern parts of Germany were to escape to Holland.

The nation was in chaos. Trains were being taken over for troops, and telephone lines were jammed. Missionaries were soon on their own, with little chance to communicate with mission leaders . . . Elder Joseph Fielding Smith of the Quorum of the Twelve had been touring the missions of Europe with his wife at the time. They had managed to get out of Germany to Holland before the border closed and then, amazingly, had gotten a flight to Copenhagen. Elder Smith wanted to be there as the missionaries arrived. He spent the next several weeks arranging for their passage out of Europe. Each day, during the wait, he met with them and taught them principles of the gospel. This turned out to be one of the great experiences of most of these young missionaries' lives. Elder Smith later bore powerful testimony that he knew the Lord had protected His missionaries and led them safely home. (Dean Hughes and Tom Hughes, *We'll Bring the World His Truth: Missionary Adventures from Around the World* [Salt Lake City: Deseret Book, 1995], 49, 52)

LIKENING THE SCRIPTURES TO OUR LIVES

D&C 84:88 And whoso receiveth you, there I will be also, for I will go before your face. I will be on your right hand and on your left, and my Spirit shall be in your hearts, and mine angels round about you, to bear you up.

Application: Let us always remember that this is the Lord's work. He is in charge and will assist us as we seek to do His will. He will be there to support and sustain us in the work—even giving us through the Spirit the words to say (see D&C 84:85; 100:5–6). We can serve, trusting in the Lord that He will open for us the way and provide strength to preach His word.

3. THE LAW OF MOSES WAS FULFILLED IN CHRIST

THEME: The Law of Moses was fulfilled through the atoning mission of the Savior. The provisions of the Law of Moses, which pointed toward the coming Savior, were superseded by the gospel as taught by the Master. Thus circumcision, which was a token of the covenant from former times, was no longer required of new converts.

MOMENT OF TRUTH

A faction of the religious community in Antioch advocated the position that circumcision, in accordance with the Law of Moses, was essential to salvation. Paul and Barnabas were dispatched to Jerusalem to obtain counsel on this matter from the Brethren. Amidst considerable disputation, Peter, the chief Apostle, arose and made known his opinion:

> Men and brethren, ye know how that a good while ago God made choice among us, that the Gentiles by my mouth should hear the word of the gospel, and believe.
>
> And God, which knoweth the hearts, bare them witness, giving them the Holy Ghost, even as he did unto us;
>
> And put no difference between us and them, purifying their hearts by faith.
>
> Now therefore why tempt ye God, to put a yoke upon the neck of the disciples, which neither our fathers nor we were able to bear?
>
> But we believe that through the grace of the Lord Jesus Christ we shall be saved, even as they. (Acts 15:7–11)

James answered by blending his testimony with that of Peter in confirming the wisdom of suspending the requirement for circumcision, asking the Gentile converts instead to hold to the faith and avoid any entanglement in sin, among other things (see Acts 15:20). This word was dispatched to Antioch, causing the new converts to rejoice "for the consolation" (Acts 15:31). In this, the Apostles did well, for the resurrected Savior Himself stated to the Saints in far-off America—His "other sheep" (John 10:16)—that the Law of Moses was fulfilled in Him and had an end: "And as many as have received me, to them have I given to become the sons of God; and even so will I to as many as shall believe on my name, for behold, by me redemption cometh, and in me is the law of Moses fulfilled. I am the light and the life of the world. I am Alpha and Omega, the beginning and the end" (3 Ne. 9:17–18). And further: "For behold, the covenant which I have made with my people is not all fulfilled; but the law which was given unto Moses hath an end in me" (3 Ne. 15:8; compare 3 Ne. 15:4; Ether 12:11; D&C 4:3).

MODERN PROPHETS SPEAK

George Q. Cannon:

> "The Lord's Day" (Rev. 1:10) is the day on which He rose from the dead and on which His disciples at that period assembled to worship and break bread in His name. That was the "first day of the week" (John 20:1; Acts 20:7), as they counted time. This custom was observed in the primitive Christian Church, and the Seventh Day was also observed by the Jewish disciples for a time. But Paul and other leading Elders of the Church set themselves against the observance of the rites and rules of the Mosaic law and proclaimed the liberty of the Gospel, the law having been fulfilled in Christ. He chided those who were sticklers for special days as required by the law but himself observed the Lord's Day—the first day of the week. (*Gospel Truth: Discourses and Writings of President George Q. Cannon,* ed. Jerreld L. Newquist [Salt Lake City: Deseret Book, 1987], 391)

ILLUSTRATIONS FOR OUR TIME

The Relationship of the Gospel of Jesus Christ to the Law of Moses

As we look back through the chronicles of God's dealings with His peoples over time, we are confirmed in our witness that His divine purposes are being fulfilled with precision. The Church is founded upon the gospel of Jesus Christ and is centered in Him, as are all things. The gospel was given to Moses, but due to the rebellious nature of the Israelites, they were also given a law of carnal commandments, which was a lesser law, a schoolmaster to point them toward Christ and prepare them to come unto Him. Thus the Law of Moses was given to the Israelites. Moses gave the people many gospel truths, but due to their stiffneckedness and transgressions, they were still required to keep the performances of the Law of Moses (see Gal. 3:19). We learn of this process from the clear teachings of the Nephites:

> For we labor diligently to write, to persuade our children, and also our brethren, to believe in Christ, and to be reconciled to God; for we know that it is by grace that we are saved, after all we can do.
>
> And, notwithstanding we believe in Christ, we keep the law of Moses, and look forward with steadfastness unto Christ, until the law shall be fulfilled.
>
> For, for this end was the law given; wherefore the law hath become dead unto us, and we are made alive in Christ because of our faith; yet we keep the law because of the commandments." (2 Ne. 25:23–25)

Then, when the Lord came, He fulfilled the law, as stated clearly in 3 Nephi:

> Behold, I say unto you that the law is fulfilled that was given unto Moses.
>
> Behold, I am he that gave the law, and I am he who covenanted with my people Israel; therefore, the law in me is fulfilled, for I have come to fulfil the law; therefore it hath an end.
>
> Behold, I do not destroy the prophets, for as many as have not been fulfilled in me, verily I say unto you, shall all be fulfilled.
>
> And because I said unto you that old things have passed away, I do not destroy that which hath been spoken concerning things which are to come.
>
> For behold, the covenant which I have made with my people is not all fulfilled; but the law which was given unto Moses hath an end in me.
>
> Behold, I am the law, and the light. Look unto me, and endure to the end, and ye shall live; for unto him that endureth to the end will I give eternal life." (3 Ne. 15:4–9) [Pinegar]

LIKENING THE SCRIPTURES TO OUR LIVES

Galatians 3:24 Wherefore the law was our schoolmaster to bring us unto Christ, that we might be justified by faith.

Application: The entire purpose of the Law of Moses was to help the people look forward to and come to know Jesus as the Messiah and Savior of the world. Likewise, all that the Lord has given us today through His word, ordinances, and covenants is to help us come to know our Heavenly Father and our Savior Jesus Christ and to keep the commandments.

SUMMARY

The commission of the Savior to His Apostles, "Go ye unto all the world, and preach the gospel to every creature" (Mark 16:15), was now beginning to be fulfilled. The seeds of universal missionary work—an essential and sacred service under the provisions and promises of the Abrahamic covenant—were starting to germinate and sprout in the meridian of time. The Lord blessed His servants as they began the process of carrying the gospel message to the countries and cultures beyond the borders of Palestine. The truths of the gospel of Jesus Christ were beginning to light the skies over the Gentile nations as the Apostles of the Lord and their associates gave their all, sometimes at great peril, to declare the doctrines of the kingdom to many lands. The "Schoolmaster" had completed its work; the Law of Moses was fulfilled in Christ. The fulness of the gospel was dawning upon the world. From those extraordinary beginnings—which were to be all too short-lived because of unbounded pride and apostasy—the Lord was to continue the design of heaven by bringing about the Restoration in the latter days, that "marvellous work and a wonder" (Isa. 29:14) whose purpose it was to extend the blessings of God to countless millions awaiting the truth. It is our honor and privilege to carry on this work as servants of the Almighty.

CHAPTER 31

"AND SO WERE *the* CHURCHES ESTABLISHED *in* *the* FAITH"

Reading Assignment: Acts 15:36–18:22; 1 and 2 Thessalonians.

Additional Reading: 1 Corinthians 2:4–5, 10–13; 2 Corinthians 4:5; D&C 4:1–7, 38:41; 88:81; 121:12–14; Bible Dictionary, "Pauline Epistles; Epistles to the Thessalonians" (743).

> *The Saints need to share the gospel with their neighbors. It is my firm conviction, my brethren and sisters, that unless we stir ourselves more than we are doing, that when we go to the other side of the veil, we will meet there men and women who have been our neighbors, and associates, and lived among us, that will condemn us because we have been so inconsiderate of them in not telling them of the truth of the gospel of our Lord. When a man is sick, if he is our neighbor, we minister to him gladly; if there is a death in his family, we try to comfort him. But year in and year out we allow him to walk in paths that will destroy his opportunity for eternal life; we pass him by, as if he were a thing of naught.*

—George Albert Smith, *The Teachings of George Albert Smith*, ed. Robert McIntosh and Susan McIntosh [Salt Lake City: Bookcraft, 1996], 151–52.

THEMES *for* LIVING

1. Preach the Gospel—Duty of the Saints
2. Testify of Truth—The Spirit Is the Key
3. Counsel from the Prophets

INTRODUCTION

Since the beginning of time, and throughout all dispensations, the message from God—whether in the canonized scriptures or through the counsel of living prophets—has been to proclaim the gospel, to teach and preach the plan of redemption through Jesus Christ the Savior and Redeemer of the world. This is especially true today for this is the last time that the vineyard will be pruned: "And the Lord of the vineyard said unto them: Go to, and labor in the vineyard, with your might. For behold, this is the last time that I shall nourish my vineyard; for the end is nigh at hand, and the season speedily cometh; and if ye labor with your might with me ye shall have joy in the fruit which I shall lay up unto myself against the time which will soon come" (Jacob 5:71).

Joseph F. Smith received revelation reminding us that we were prepared from premortal times to come forth to labor in the vineyard: "Even before they were born, they, with many others, received their first lessons in the world of spirits and were prepared to come forth in the due time of the Lord to labor in his vineyard for the salvation of the souls of men" (D&C 138:56).

We preach here during our sojourn on the earth, and when we depart, we continue to preach the gospel in the spirit world, as the vision recounted by President Smith confirms: "I beheld that the faithful elders of this dispensation, when they depart from mortal life, continue their labors in the preaching of the gospel of repentance and redemption, through the sacrifice of the Only Begotten Son of God, among those who are in darkness and under the bondage of sin in the great world of the spirits of the dead" (D&C 138:57).

Yes, our joy and glory should be like that of Alma: "I know that which the Lord hath commanded me, and I glory in it. I do not glory of myself, but I glory in that which the Lord hath commanded me; yea, and this is my glory, that perhaps I may be an instrument in the hands of God to bring some soul to repentance; and this is my joy" (Alma 29:9). That is why Alma labored unceasingly, that he might help others to partake of the joy of which he did partake (see Alma 36:24). For that reason, full-time proselyting missionaries, when they return from their service to the Lord, are frequently heard to say: "It was the happiest two years of my life." "It was the best two years of my life." "I never realized I could feel so much joy for other people."

Love for others is at the core of all missionary endeavor. The sons of Mosiah displayed that kind of charitable concern on behalf of those whom they feared might be cast off: "Now they were desirous that salvation should be declared to every creature, for they could not bear that any human soul should perish; yea, even the very thoughts that any soul should endure endless torment did cause them to quake and tremble" (Mosiah 28:3). It is evident that we have a duty that can generate for us a consuming joy when we seek to bless others by helping them come unto Christ.

1. PREACH THE GOSPEL—DUTY OF THE SAINTS

THEME: Paul, Silas, and Timothy preached the gospel throughout Macedonia and Greece. Likewise, it is our responsibility and privilege to take the gospel to our neighbors and to all peoples of the earth.

MOMENT OF TRUTH

As Paul and his associates labored in the vineyard of the Lord, they witnessed how the Lord dispensed the fruit of the gospel to the faithful Saints in abundance: "And so were the churches established in the faith, and increased in number daily" (Acts 16:5). The Holy Ghost directed them away from certain areas, but toward others, such as Macedonia (see Acts 16:6–10). In Philippi, a city in Macedonia, Paul brought Lydia and her family into the Church but came under condemnation from the authorities for casting a devil from a woman sorcerer (and thus curtailing the commercial revenues that her sponsors were bringing in). Paul and Silas were beaten and cast into prison, where they were able to convert the jailor, who asked them: "What must I do to be saved?" (Acts 16:30). Their response: "Believe on the Lord Jesus Christ, and thou shalt be saved, and thy house" (v. 31), whereupon the prisoners were authorized to go free and the jailor and his household were baptized into the Church. Paul and Silas then continued their missionary labors in Thessalonica, capital of Macedonia, where some believed their message and others reviled against them in envy. Thence they went to Berea where the people received them more willingly: "These were more noble than those in Thessalonica, in that they received the word with all readiness of mind, and searched the scriptures daily, whether those things were so" (Acts 17:11). Paul then journeyed to Athens, where he had his famous encounter with the local intelligentsia on Mars Hill.

Later, in Corinth, Paul had some success among the Jewish people—"and many of the Corinthians hearing believed, and were baptized" (Acts 18:8); however, most rejected him, so he turned chiefly to the Gentiles from that time on (see Acts 18:6), journeying to such additional places as Ephesus.

MODERN PROPHETS SPEAK

Ezra Taft Benson:

> Early in this dispensation the Savior placed on the Church the responsibility to share the gospel. On November 1, 1831, He said: "The voice of warning shall be unto all people, by the mouths of my disciples, whom I have chosen in these last days. And they shall go forth and none shall stay them, for I the Lord have commanded them" (D&C 1:4–5). . . .

More recently, we have received this counsel from Spencer W. Kimball:

"We are still just scratching the surface of the needs of our Father's other children who dwell upon the earth. Many still hunger and thirst after truth and are kept from it only 'because they know not where to find it.' (Doctrine and Covenants 123:12) There are still more places to go than there are full-time missionaries and organized missions to serve them. There are still millions more being born, living, and dying, than are hearing testimonies borne to them by the servants of the Lord.

"All of this means, quite frankly, brethren, that we cannot share the gospel with every nation, kindred, tongue, and people with [our present number of] missionaries (as wonderful as they are), but we must have several million more to help them. We must, therefore, involve the members of the Church more effectively in missionary work. Member-missionary work is the key to the future growth of the Church, and it is one of the great keys to the individual growth of our members. . . ."

Membership in the Lord's church is a gift and a blessing that the Lord has given us in mortality, and He expects us to share that blessing with those who do not have it. (*Come unto Christ* [Salt Lake City: Deseret Book, 1983], 89–91)

ILLUSTRATIONS FOR OUR TIME

Overcoming Fear

I'll never forget when I served as a mission president in the MTC. The last meeting before the missionaries would go out, I would speak about being bold, obedient, full of love, and courageous in opening their mouths. "Do not be afraid. The worth of souls is great. You have a mighty role in the kingdom." Well, some of them were still afraid. I would challenge them to have a defining experience of opening their mouths on their way to their mission.

This sweet young sister wrote me a letter after she'd been out two weeks, and this is how it went: "Dear President, after your talk Sunday night, I was so nervous, I didn't know what to do. I knew I'd be leaving Wednesday and I was going to have to open my mouth. And I thought, *I can't do it, I can't do it.* So, I fasted and I prayed and I left Wednesday on the plane, and to my joy I had a window seat and my companion sat next to me. So I said, 'Oh dear I won't be able to talk to anybody on the plane,' and so I was relieved. But then, I got into the airport and I sat down, and here was a man sitting across from me. He was old and different looking, and I didn't know what to do. All I could remember was your voice telling us, 'Open your mouths; it will be filled, I promise you.' Well, I girded up my loins and I opened my mouth and said, 'Hi, where you headed?' From that little beginning began an hour conversation. Pretty soon, we became friends. And after a bit I said, 'If you knew there was another book written about Jesus Christ, would you be interested in reading that? The Book of Mormon?'

"He said, 'Oh, I have a Book of Mormon.' I committed him right there to read the book, and then he told me, 'My daughter is taking the discussions too.'

"And then I said, 'Is it OK if I have the missionaries come by and see you?' He said, 'That will just be fine.' Oh, President, it's so easy to open your mouth. The Lord will fill it. There's nothing to it."

I read that letter every time to departing missionaries because it helped them realize that we can all do it. All of us, member missionaries and full-time proselyting missionaries, can open our mouths and they will be filled. The Lord will help us all. We simply need to do it—open our mouths.

M. Russell Ballard, an Apostle of the Lord Jesus Christ, came to the McKay Building at the UVSC campus and spoke. Eight thousand people were there. He said, "Set a date to find someone to share the gospel with. Set a date and then pray that the Lord will provide you with someone who wants to hear the gospel. You members go out and find people, and the missionaries will teach them."

Now, for missionaries to get members to do this, we need a relationship of trust with those members. We need to present them a message about the worth of souls and how important members are in the conversion process—how important it is to friendship and fellowship investigators and new converts. You've got to make sure that the members are converted to doing this.

Well, Elder Ballard converted many members on this point. One brother found a boy by the name of Ty McDonald, and he was baptized; and I thought, *Well, I'm a member too. I've got to find somebody,* so I set a date. And I remember a name came into my mind; he was the one. So I came back from that fireside that week, and I said to my missionary preparation class, "You know, I know just the person, and I've got the date, but I don't know where he is. He was here at UVSC, but he's gone. I haven't seen him for a year." I said, "Jeff is his name. Do any of you know someone by that name?"

What was the mathematical probability of that happening? A boy in the class raised his hand and he said, "Oh, Jeff? I know him. He's a nonmember. He lives with my best friend down at BYU."

I said, "Can you give me his phone number?"

He said, "Of course."

That week, I got Jeff's phone number and called him. "Jeff, this is Brother Ed."

"Brother Ed, my friend." We were friends because I taught him as a nonmember at the institute and he had the discussions, but then he moved. So I had to find him again.

I said, "Jeff, I want to talk to you. Would you be so kind and friendly as to come and see me?" Jeff came out to my office. We visited three times. I challenged him, and he was baptized. On January 12, 1997, I baptized Jeff at BYU and spoke at his baptism.

What if Elder Ballard hadn't spoken? What if I hadn't opened my mouth in class and said, "Who knows Jeff?" And lo and behold, what did the Lord do? He arranged for somebody to be in class that day, someone who knew where Jeff lived and knew his roommate. And oh, by the way, to make it a little easier for me, He made sure he had his phone number so I could call him. [Pinegar]

LIKENING THE SCRIPTURES TO OUR LIVES

D&C 88:81 Behold, I sent you out to testify and warn the people, and it becometh every man who hath been warned to warn his neighbor.

Application: It is our duty to open our mouths. We must witness and testify by example and precept that all might have the opportunity to come unto Christ. Make a plan, set a date, distribute passalong cards, place copies of the Book of Mormon with a promise to read, and prepare people to receive the gospel of Jesus Christ. Remember that many are kept from the truth because they know not where to find it (see D&C 123:12).

2. TESTIFY OF TRUTH—THE SPIRIT IS THE KEY

THEME: Paul stood courageously on Mars Hill and preached to the Greek philosophers. In the same spirit, we must be willing to open our mouths and testify of the truthfulness of the gospel.

MOMENT OF TRUTH

When Paul journeyed to Athens, he perceived the idolatry that formed the fiber of that culture and spoke to the local philosophers on Mars Hill concerning the inscription he had seen, dedicated "To the Unknown God" (Acts 17:23). Paul contrasted that vague superstition to the clarity and verity of the gospel of Jesus Christ:

> For in him we live, and move, and have our being; as certain also of your own poets have said, For we are also his offspring.
>
> Forasmuch then as we are the offspring of God, we ought not to think that the Godhead is like unto gold, or silver, or stone, graven by art and man's device.
>
> And the times of this ignorance God winked at; but now commandeth all men every where to repent:
>
> Because he hath appointed a day, in the which he will judge the world in righteousness by that man whom he hath ordained; whereof he hath given assurance unto all men, in that he hath raised him from the dead. (Acts 17:28–31)

In response, the Athenians mocked Paul and, for the most part, rejected his gospel message. Some few, however, believed his witness and were touched by the truths he taught. Clearly, it is imperative that we stand up for truth and deliver our witness in the strength of the Lord. Not all will respond, but the honest at heart will be moved by the Spirit to come forward and join the flock.

MODERN PROPHETS SPEAK

Brigham Young:

> Let every one get a knowledge for himself that this work is true. We do not want you to say that it is true until you know that it is; and if you know it, that knowledge is as good to you as though the Lord came down and told you. (*Discourses,* 429)

ILLUSTRATIONS FOR OUR TIME

The Lord's Promise

I will never forget those two sisters. It was a dark, dark night in the heart of London. So dark that they were nervous. A man came up by them at the bus stop, a large, dark man, and they were nervous. And then they said they remembered what President Pinegar said, "Don't fear, the Lord is before your face; He's on your right hand; he's on your left hand; His Spirit is in your heart; His angels round about you" (see D&C 84:88). So these two sister missionaries spoke. "Excuse me, sir, would you be so kind and friendly as to answer a few questions that might bring you happiness?"

And he said, "Well, I'd be glad to, young ladies." And he did. He was from the Solomon Islands. He was in England for four weeks. He heard the message, and, since the sisters cannot teach a man alone, they went to the church to find others. Later, this man, Peter, said, "I want to meet your president." So I went with them on a discussion. Peter is an elect man of God, just like we learn in the Doctrine and Covenants—that the elect shall hear his voice and know that it's true (see D&C 29:7). These two sisters taught him. We arranged for a baptism. Peter spoke at his own baptism. It was the greatest talk I have ever heard at a baptism.

It was as though he were already a bishop and had been in the Church all of his life. I thought, *Who is this man?* They took him to church on Sunday, where he was interviewed and ordained to the office of a priest. He then left for the Solomon Islands, which was in one of the Australian missions at the time. I called the Australian mission president and informed him of the baptism of Peter, who lived in the Solomon Islands. He said, "That's great. That's part of our mission. I think we have one member there on that island. We'll see what we can do."

Time went by, and Elder Sonnenberg of the Quorum of the Seventy, who was the president of the Australian area, and Elder Faust, then a member of the Twelve, went on a visit to the Solomon Islands to see what they could do to start the branches there. Peter greeted them at the airport. "I am Peter, and this is my son. I am a priest in The Church of Jesus Christ of Latter-day Saints. How can I help you build up the Church here?" Where would Peter be if those two magnificent sisters had not opened their mouths? If we allow one person to walk by and not open our mouth, we deprive them at that time of the opportunity for exaltation. This isn't a business; this is a matter of spiritual life and death. I am grateful that those faithful sisters opened their mouths so that they could be the instruments in the hands of the Lord to bless that great brother. They were bold like Paul of old. They stood for truth and righteousness and relied upon the Lord. [Pinegar]

LIKENING THE SCRIPTURES TO OUR LIVES

Mosiah 18:9 Yea, and are willing to mourn with those that mourn; yea, and comfort those that stand in need of comfort, and to stand as witnesses of God at all times and in all things, and in all places that ye may be in, even until death, that ye may be redeemed of God, and be numbered with those of the first resurrection, that ye may have eternal life.

Application: We are duty bound to open our mouths and witness of the truthfulness of the gospel of Jesus Christ. We, as Saints of the Lord Jesus Christ, are to live our lives in such a way that we will draw people to the Lord (see 3 Ne. 12:15–16).

3. COUNSEL FROM THE PROPHETS

THEME: Paul gave inspired counsel to the Saints in Thessalonica. We should follow the counsel of our prophets—past and present—especially those living prophets whom the Lord has placed in our midst.

MOMENT OF TRUTH

As he fulfilled his commission to preach the gospel, Paul was careful not to neglect the well-being and nurture of the convert Saints who came into the fold. While in Athens, for example, Paul sent two glorious epistles to the Thessalonians, exhorting them to be true to the faith and honor their covenants. Examples from these exhortations:

> Rejoice evermore.
> Pray without ceasing.
> In every thing give thanks: for this is the will of God in Christ Jesus concerning you.

Quench not the Spirit.

Despise not prophesyings.

Prove all things; hold fast that which is good. (1 Thes. 5:16–21)

And this famous line: "But ye, brethren, be not weary in well doing" (2 Thes. 3:13)—which anticipates the word of the Lord in the latter days: "Wherefore, be not weary in well-doing, for ye are laying the foundation of a great work. And out of small things proceedeth that which is great" (D&C 64:33).

MODERN PROPHETS SPEAK

Russell M. Nelson:

> Gratefully we thank God for a prophet to guide us in these latter days. But many turn a deaf ear to the teachings of the living prophets, oblivious to their prophetic position. They do so at great risk, for scriptures contain this warning:
>
> "A prophet shall the Lord your God raise up unto you . . . ; him shall ye hear in all things whatsoever he shall say unto you. . . .
>
> "Every soul, which will not hear that prophet, shall be destroyed from among the people."
>
> President J. Reuben Clark, Jr., said, "We do not lack a prophet; what we lack is a listening ear." Words of the Lord are taught by His disciples. Wise members listen to learn from Church leaders. (*Perfection Pending, and Other Favorite Discourses* [Salt Lake City: Deseret Book, 1998], 48)

ILLUSTRATIONS FOR OUR TIME

Simple Truth

My wife was so pleased to accompany her friend to the stand where Ezra Taft Benson, then President of the Quorum of the Twelve, was receiving visitors. He had just spoken to a special gathering of Saints in the Washington, D.C., area, and my wife wanted her friend to meet him. This young woman had just that day—in the same stake center—been baptized a member of the Church, after many months of learning the gospel and being fellowshipped by my wife. So we stood in line waiting for our turn to meet Elder Benson. When we finally reached the place where the Apostle was standing, we greeted him, and then my wife introduced her friend as a new convert. He held the friend's hand and looked her straight in the eye. With a spirit of great kindness, but also soberness and firmness, he said to her, "The gospel is true. If you live it, you will be happy. If you don't, you won't." What a rare blessing for a new convert to hear a personal witness from an Apostle of the Lord and receive such direct and penetrating counsel.

My wife and I have spoken of this incident many times since, and the words echo in our minds and hearts as advice that all can benefit from: "If you live it, you will be happy. If you don't, you won't." And so it is. In many different variations and expressions the prophets have always conveyed the same message from the Lord: "I give unto you directions how you may act before me, that it may turn to you for your salvation. I, the Lord, am bound when ye do what I say; but when ye do not what I say, ye have no promise" (D&C 82:9–10). [Allen]

LIKENING THE SCRIPTURES TO OUR LIVES

Matthew 10:40 He that receiveth you receiveth me, and he that receiveth me receiveth him that sent me.

Application: When we receive the prophets and their direction, we receive our Savior and our Heavenly Father. If we are true and faithful we can receive all that the Father has (see D&C 84:36–38).

SUMMARY

What a stimulating and inspiring experience it is to trace the footsteps of the Lord's indefatigable and devoted witnesses during the early years of the Church of Jesus Christ in the meridian of time. From the exemplary service of Paul and his colleagues, we are confirmed in our commitment to carry the gospel message to all peoples and to testify through the Spirit that Jesus is the Christ. Let us follow the counsel of our prophets—both past and present—in cultivating a "godly walk and conversation" (D&C 20:69) and honoring our covenant obligations with an eye single to the glory of God.

CHAPTER 32

"LIVE *in* *the* SPIRIT"

Reading Assignment: Acts 18:23 to 20:38; Galatians.

Additional Reading: Moroni 8:25–26; 10:3–5; D&C 6:22–23; Bible Dictionary, "Holy Ghost" (p, 704); "Pauline Epistles; Epistle to the Galatians" (744–745).

> *Make up your minds to live by the Spirit. Make up your minds to live humbly and in such a way that you will always have the spirit of the Lord to be your friend, to make suggestions to you from time to time as shall be needed under the peculiar circumstances in which you may be placed. . . . I do desire, and it is something that you should desire, to have that humility, and that meekness, and that simplicity, to enjoy the spirit of reve-lation. It is your privilege, every one of you, to have enough of the spirit of revelation to know exactly what is proper for you to do. It is your privilege to know when men speak by the spirit of God and whether the counsel they give is proper or not.*
>
> —LORENZO SNOW, *THE TEACHINGS OF LORENZO SNOW,* ED. CLYDE J. WILLIAMS, 114.

THEMES *for* LIVING

1. The Holy Ghost—The Lord's Magnificent Gift Following Conversion and Baptism
2. Teaching the Saints—A Divine Mandate
3. Chastening by the Spirit—A Manifestation of Love

INTRODUCTION

When we enjoy the companionship and blessings of the Holy Spirit, we will be comforted in all things and be inspired to do good. We become self-mastered in the sense that we are spiritually directed in our lives, rather than carnally-minded. Our spirit, by the power of the Holy Ghost, directs our lives—our flesh is governed by the spirit. In this state, we can be shown all things to do (see 2 Ne. 32:5). We have begun the process of sanctification as we yield to the enticings of the Holy Spirit (see Mosiah 3:19). We seek the will of Heavenly Father. We yield our hearts to the Lord. We have an eye single to His glory and feel motivated to bless and serve our fellowman. The blessings of spirituality received from the Holy Spirit are many and varied—enumerated as the gifts of the Spirit (see Moro. 10:7–19; D&C 46:8–31), the fruits of the Spirit (see Gal. 5:22–23), trust in the Spirit, which leads one to do good (see D&C 11:12–13), and a multiplicity of other blessings of the Spirit. Jacob said it best: "Remember, to be carnally-minded is death, and to be spiritually-minded is life eternal" (2 Ne. 9:39).

1. THE HOLY GHOST—THE LORD'S MAGNIFICENT GIFT FOLLOWING CONVERSION AND BAPTISM

THEME: The gift and blessings of the Holy Ghost are given to those who come unto Christ as they are converted and baptized. The Holy Ghost can give direction to our lives. We should continually seek the promptings of the Spirit in our lives.

MOMENT OF TRUTH

As Paul returned to Ephesus, capital of the Roman province of Asia, on his third missionary journey, he inquired of the disciples there whether they had received the Holy Ghost since their conversion. The record shows that the following then transpired:

And they said unto him, We have not so much as heard whether there be any Holy Ghost.

And he said unto them, Unto what then were ye baptized? And they said, Unto John's baptism.

Then said Paul, John verily baptized with the baptism of repentance, saying unto the people, that they should believe on him which should come after him, that is, on Christ Jesus.

When they heard this, they were baptized in the name of the Lord Jesus.

And when Paul had laid his hands upon them, the Holy Ghost came on them; and they spake with tongues, and prophesied. (Acts 19:2–6)

The influence of Paul the Apostle during his somewhat lengthy sojourn in that region, teaching the gospel to the people, was significant. As the scripture says: "And this continued by the space of two years; so that all they which dwelt in Asia heard the word of the Lord Jesus, both Jews and Greeks" (Acts 19:10). We read that "the name of the Lord Jesus was magnified" (Acts 19:17) and "mightily grew the word of God and prevailed" (Acts 19:20). Paul continued his ministry with devotion and power, even raising a young man from the dead (see Acts 20:9) and teaching faith, repentance, and selfless service in the name of Jesus Christ.

MODERN PROPHETS SPEAK

Joseph B. Wirthlin:
> By choosing the light of the Lord, knowledge and truth, and the light of love in our lives, we will be qualified to live by the light of the Spirit. If we cultivate a heart that is constantly in tune with the Spirit of the Lord, our lives will be enriched. We will be able to make good decisions, and we will be comforted in times of trial and adversity.
>
> We could compare learning to live by the Spirit with the way a pianist prepares for a concert. A pianist cannot cram his knowledge of music and his playing skill into one week or even one month of solid practice to prepare for a concert. But he prepares himself through consistent, diligent practice, day by day over a long period of time. Our spiritual preparation requires the same kind of effort, "line upon line, precept upon precept, here a little and there a little" (2 Ne. 28:30).
>
> As we choose to live by the light of the Spirit, the greatest example on how to prepare ourselves spiritually is the pattern set forth by our Lord and Savior Jesus Christ. (*Finding Peace in Our Lives*, 75)

ILLUSTRATIONS FOR OUR TIME

Perils of Not Obeying the Voice of the Spirit
> I will now give an example from my own experience of the result of not obeying the voice of the Spirit.
>
> Some years since I had part of my family living in Randolph, Rich County. I was there on a visit, with my team in the month of December.
>
> One Monday morning my monitor, the Spirit watching over me, said: "Take your team and go home to Salt Lake City."
>
> When I named it to my family who were at Randolph they urged me strongly to stop longer.

Through their persuasion I stayed until Saturday morning, with the Spirit continually prompting me to go home. I then began to feel ashamed to think that I had not obeyed the whisperings of the Spirit to me before.

I took my team and started early on Saturday morning. When I arrived at Woodruff, the Bishop urged me to stop until Monday and he would go with me.

I told him, "No, I have tarried too long already."

I drove on sprightly, and when within fifteen miles of Wasatch, a furious storm overtook me, the wind blowing heavily in my face.

In fifteen minutes I could not see any road whatever, and knew not how or where to guide my horses.

I left my lines loosely on my animals, went inside my wagon, tied down my cover, and committed my life and guidance into the hands of the Lord, trusting to my horses to find the way, as they had twice before passed over that road.

I prayed to the Lord to forgive my sin in not obeying the voice of the Spirit to me, and implored Him to preserve my life.

My horses brought me onto the Wasatch station at 9 o'clock in the evening, with the hubs of my wagon dragging in the snow.

I got my horses under cover, and had to remain there until next Monday night, with the snow six feet deep on the level, and still snowing.

It was with great difficulty at last that I saved the lives of my horses by getting them into a box car and taking them to Ogden; while, if I had obeyed the revelation of the Spirit of God to me, I should have traveled to Salt Lake City over a good road without any storm.

As I have received the good and the evil, the fruits of obedience and disobedience, I think I am justified in exhorting all my young friends to always obey the whisperings of the Spirit of God, and they will always be safe. (Wilford Woodruff, *Leaves from My Journal* [Salt Lake City: Juvenile Instructor's Office, 1882], 90–91)

LIKENING THE SCRIPTURES TO OUR LIVES

John 14:26 But the Comforter, which is the Holy Ghost, whom the Father will send in my name, he shall teach you all things, and bring all things to your remembrance, whatsoever I have said unto you.

Application: The Spirit will console and encourage us in our times of need. The Spirit will lead us to do good, walk humbly, do justly, judge righteously, and will enlighten our souls (see D&C 11:12–13) and give us the wonderful feelings of love, peace, joy, and faith (see Gal 5:22–23).

2. TEACHING THE SAINTS—A DIVINE MANDATE

THEME: One of the major responsibilities of our prophet leaders is teaching and preaching the word of God. They testify of Christ, teach the doctrines and principles of the gospel, and encourage us to live righteously. We, too, should take seriously our obligations to share the gospel with others and give counsel and encouragement at every opportunity.

MOMENT OF TRUTH

Paul was a consummate teacher and counselor, full of charity and imbued with the Spirit of the Lord, ever committed to speaking the truths of saving grace and obedience to the Lord's commandments—"Testifying both to the Jews, and also to the Greeks, repentance toward God, and faith toward our Lord Jesus Christ" (Acts 20:21). As such, Paul provides a sterling model for us to follow in learning how to fulfill our callings to teach the gospel with courage and forthrightness to our families, associates, and all students of truth. "For I have not shunned," he says, "to declare unto you all the counsel of God" (Acts 20:27).

Here is a sampling of the wisdom from the mouth or pen of the Apostle Paul—both words of warning as well as words of edification:

- On the coming apostasy: "Take heed therefore unto yourselves, and to all the flock, over the which the Holy Ghost hath made you overseers, to feed the church of God, which he hath purchased with his own blood. For I know this, that after my departing shall grievous wolves enter in among you, not sparing the flock" (Acts 20:28–29).
- On charitable service: "I have shewed you all things, how that so labouring ye ought to support the weak, and to remember the words of the Lord Jesus, how he said, It is more blessed to give than to receive" (Acts 20:35).
- On remembering our covenants: "And the scripture, foreseeing that God would justify the heathen through faith, preached before the gospel unto Abraham, saying, In thee shall all nations be blessed. So then they which be of faith are blessed with faithful Abraham" (Gal. 3:8–9).
- On the divine heritage of the seed of Abraham: "Wherefore the law was our schoolmaster to bring us unto Christ, that we might be justified by faith. But after that faith is come, we are no longer under a schoolmaster. For ye are all the children of God by faith in Christ Jesus. For as many of you as have been baptized into Christ have put on Christ. There is neither Jew nor Greek, there is neither bond nor free, there is neither male nor female: for ye are all one in Christ Jesus. And if ye be

Christ's, then are ye Abraham's seed, and heirs according to the promise" (Gal. 3:24–29).

- On the need to live by the Spirit: "For all the law is fulfilled in one word, even in this; Thou shalt love thy neighbour as thyself. But if ye bite and devour one another, take heed that ye be not consumed one of another. This I say then, Walk in the Spirit, and ye shall not fulfil the lust of the flesh. . . . But the fruit of the Spirit is love, joy, peace, longsuffering, gentleness, goodness, faith, Meekness, temperance: against such there is no law. . . . If we live in the Spirit, let us also walk in the Spirit" (Gal. 5:14–16, 22–23, 25).

- On the consequences of our behavior: "Be not deceived; God is not mocked: for whatsoever a man soweth, that shall he also reap. For he that soweth to his flesh shall of the flesh reap corruption; but he that soweth to the Spirit shall of the Spirit reap life everlasting. And let us not be weary in well doing: for in due season we shall reap, if we faint not. As we have therefore opportunity, let us do good unto all men, especially unto them who are of the household of faith" (Gal. 6:7–10).

MODERN PROPHETS SPEAK

Joseph Smith:

When asked how he governed so many people, the Prophet Joseph Smith said, "I teach them correct principles, and they govern themselves." (*TSWK,* 191–92)

ILLUSTRATIONS FOR OUR TIME

"That All Might Be Profited"

Who shall be counselors in the Church and kingdom of God? Everyone! We all teach continually—through word and deed. It seems to be the design of the Almighty that we should depend upon one another and benefit from mutual assurances and the sharing of our spiritual gifts and talents. It is not only from our bishops and other Church leaders that we receive valuable counsel, but also from the myriad "angels on earth" who comprise our circle of friends and "fellowcitizens with the Saints" (Eph. 2:19).

On one occasion where I was serving in a stake presidency, a young man came to me to complain that various leaders in his ward were giving him conflicting advice when he asked them for help on a challenging marital situation. He felt that the Relief Society president had the most valuable counsel to give and was troubled that the bishop hadn't come up with any better solutions himself. I assured him, first of all, that it was the individual's responsibility to consider prayerfully all options and then make the decision based on correct principles. Next, I reminded him that each one of his mentors would look at his situation with a different level of empathy and understanding, viewed from a unique set of personal experiences—and thus diversity of opinion is inevitable. But my main point can best be understood through the following excerpt of the letter I wrote to him a few days later:

> A bishop is the common judge in Israel, which means that he must decide on matters of serious moral consequence and must issue temple recommends as well as monitor progress of priesthood brethren as to their advancement. The bishop is also the presiding high priest in the ward and is responsible for receiving the funds contributed. The bishop is nearly always a loving and concerned man, is frequently a radiant and warm individual, and is typically an effective counselor. He is almost never the single and ultimate font of wisdom for all members of his ward in all matters and at all times. . . . It seems to me that the Lord intended His Church to be a community of mutual support and mutual trust. There is a natural tendency for us to look to the leaders for guidance and direction; surely this is proper. However, the Church—if I understand 1 Corinthians 12 and D&C 46 correctly—is a complete network of resources where even the humblest and least visible member is of value and worth. In fact, it might be from the most unlikely source that inspiration might flow to one in need (not just from the bishop or Relief Society president). The reason that not all have all gifts is, it seems to me, so that we might have a need to depend on one another, 'that all may be profited thereby' (D&C 46:12). [Allen]

Teaching by the Spirit Is the Power to Influence Others to Do Good.
There is an ancient Greek saying: "If a teacher influences but one, his influence never stops." How true that is. In life we are constantly learning and teaching. We are continually bombarded with information that we have to sift through. Is it true? Will it help? The questions go on. In teaching we must be sure it is true. We must be sure it will help. Never take the haughty or cynical view toward students in the sense that you can test them or try them or trick them; rather, take the view of "How can I help them and strengthen them to be all they can be?" "How can I help strengthen their faith in Jesus Christ?" Yes, teaching is a power for good. Let each of us seek to be a good teacher. Above all, let us strive to emulate the greatest teacher who ever lived, our Master Jesus Christ, who said, "Learn of me, and listen to my words; walk in the meekness of my Spirit, and you shall have peace in me" (D&C 19:23). [Pinegar]

LIKENING THE SCRIPTURES TO OUR LIVES

Mosiah 23:14 And also trust no one to be your teacher nor your minister, except he be a man of God, walking in his ways and keeping his commandments.

Application: What a blessing to be led by living prophets whom we can trust and follow in all things. Remember, they will never lead us astray. We will have the word of God through our prophet (see D&C 21:4–6; 1:38; Amos 3:7; Acts 3:21; Eph. 4:11; Jacob 1:19), and we should listen and obey.

3. CHASTENING BY THE SPIRIT— A MANIFESTATION OF LOVE

THEME: The Lord chastens those whom He loves. As they speak for the Lord, the prophets warn, exhort, chasten, and in general continually call upon us and all people to repent.

MOMENT OF TRUTH

It is certain that Paul visited the Galatian churches on his second (see Acts 16:6) and third (see Acts 18:23) missionary journeys. While continuing his travels, probably across Macedonia, he received the troubling news that many of the Galatian Saints were abandoning the gospel plan and returning to the restrictive practices of their traditional Jewish religion. He therefore wrote his epistle to turn their hearts back to Jesus Christ. In this frank but loving call to repentance, Paul reminded the Galatians that the Law of Moses was but a schoolmaster pointing to the Atonement and triumph of the Savior (see Gal. 3:24), and that the doctrine of faith superseded the preparatory gospel and led to a fulfillment of the promises given under the Abrahamic covenant: "And if ye be Christ's, then are ye Abraham's seed, and heirs according to the promise" (Gal. 3:29). Paul exhorted the people to cultivate the fruits of the Spirit (see Acts 5:22–24) and abide in Christ: "From henceforth let no man trouble me: for I bear in my body the marks of the Lord Jesus. Brethren, the grace of our Lord Jesus Christ be with your spirit" (Gal. 6:17–18). Through this magnificent apostolic chastening, we can savor the loving disposition of a servant of God led by the Spirit to bring wayward souls back to the mainstream of gospel living.

MODERN PROPHETS SPEAK

Harold B. Lee:

> Sometimes we need chastening. It's an interesting thing that sometimes it takes calamity to drive us together. It's a terrifying thing to think that that's necessary, but the Lord said through one of His prophets that sometimes we have to have the chastening hand of the Almighty before we will wake up and humble ourselves to do the thing that He has asked us to do (see Helaman 12:3–6). In talking about

the conditions that would come, He warned the people that death and destruction and all sorts of difficulties would have to come before people would listen, before they would obey, and He removes His hand and lets these things occur, or our people would not repent and come unto the Lord. (*THBL,* 191)

ILLUSTRATIONS FOR OUR TIME

Here are some points to ponder concerning the law of chastening: Do we accept the counsel from our living prophets? Are we awakened to our wrongdoing only through external pressures? Do we learn from the scriptures and the word of God, or must we be compelled to be humble? Are we grateful for chastening, or do we become angered against those who correct us?

Throughout every dispensation, the Lord has continually warned and chastened His people because they would not hearken to His word or His prophets. We learn from Hebrews eternal truths regarding the principle and power of chastening:

> For whom the Lord loveth he chasteneth, and scourgeth every son whom he receiveth.
>
> For they verily for a few days chastened us after their own pleasure; but he for our profit, that we might be partakers of his holiness.
>
> Now no chastening for the present seemeth to be joyous, but grievous: nevertheless afterward it yieldeth the peaceable fruit of righteousness unto them which are exercised thereby. (Heb. 12:6, 10–11)

The Prophet Joseph learned the love of the Lord as He chastened the Saints regarding the building of the Kirtland Temple:

> Verily, thus saith the Lord unto you whom I love, and whom I love I also chasten that their sins may be forgiven, for with the chastisement I prepare a way for their deliverance in all things out of temptation, and I have loved you—
>
> Wherefore, ye must needs be chastened and stand rebuked before my face;
>
> For ye have sinned against me a very grievous sin, in that ye have not considered the great commandment in all things, that I have given unto you concerning the building of mine house. (D&C 95:1–3)

A transcending truth is taught in these verses, for it is in chastening that the Lord prepares a way for us to repent and be delivered from our sins. This is why chastening is one of the highest yet most difficult expressions of love. We see clearly the methodology of the power of influence and chastening as taught by the Lord:

No power or influence can or ought to be maintained by virtue of the priesthood, only by persuasion, by long-suffering, by gentleness and meekness, and by love unfeigned;

By kindness, and pure knowledge, which shall greatly enlarge the soul without hypocrisy, and without guile—

Reproving betimes with sharpness, when moved upon by the Holy Ghost; and then showing forth afterwards an increase of love toward him whom thou hast reproved, lest he esteem thee to be his enemy;

That he may know that thy faithfulness is stronger than the cords of death. (D&C 121:41–44)

We learn that we correct or chasten only as moved upon by the power of the Holy Ghost. The prophets and those called of God teach and preach by that very spirit. [Pinegar]

LIKENING THE SCRIPTURES TO OUR LIVES

Helaman 12:3 And thus we see that except the Lord doth chasten his people with many afflictions, yea, except he doth visit them with death and with terror, and with famine and with all manner of pestilence, they will not remember him.

Application: It would seem that we are never grateful to walk until we can't. So often we forget to be thankful for our health until we are sick. Too often we seem ungrateful for our blessings until we lose them. Let us learn from this scripture always to remember the goodness of God and hearken to His words, so that we can be blessed as we walk uprightly before Him.

SUMMARY

The gospel of Jesus Christ is anchored in eternal principles and is revisited and reinforced in every dispensation of time under the guidance of the Lord's anointed. To walk the pathways of gospel service with Paul is to experience a lofty review of these truths as presented by a master teacher and one of the Savior's most devoted servants. We are edified once again to see reconfirmed in the ministry of Paul the promise and bestowal of the Holy Ghost—the Lord's magnificent gift following conversion and baptism. We are inspired through Paul's exhortations to strengthen our own resolve to be effective and charitable guides to our fellow Saints. And we are reminded to be receptive of chastening from the Almighty, who acts always out of love and compassion for His children. A choice summary of these ideas and principles is given by Mormon in an epistle to his son Moroni:

And the first fruits of repentance is baptism; and baptism cometh by faith unto the fulfilling the commandments; and the fulfilling the commandments bringeth remission of sins;

And the remission of sins bringeth meekness, and lowliness of heart; and because of meekness and lowliness of heart cometh the visitation of the Holy Ghost, which Comforter filleth with hope and perfect love, which love endureth by diligence unto prayer, until the end shall come, when all the saints shall dwell with God. (Moro. 8:25–26; compare Moro. 10:3–5; D&C 6:22–23)

CHAPTER 33

"YE ARE THE TEMPLE *of* GOD"

Reading Assignment: 1 Corinthians 1–6.

Additional Reading: 1 Corinthians 7–10; Galatians 5:16; Mosiah 18:21–22; 3 Nephi 11:29–30; 12:27–30; D&C 42:22; 46:33; Bible Dictionary, "Pauline Epistles; Epistles to the Corinthians" (743–44).

> *We do not need a new moral standard in our modern society. The laws of God have not been abrogated. They were not given to one generation to be laid aside by another. Their disregard can result only in trouble, misery, and insecurity as witness the fruits of the erosion of morality among us. Their application is the way of life and peace and progress.*
>
> —GORDON B. HINCKLEY, *TGBH,* 377–78.

THEMES *for* LIVING

1. Seek Unity—Avoid Contention
2. Trust in the Spirit—Not in Man or the World
3. Be Morally Clean

INTRODUCTION

Blessings of the Lord are poured out upon His children as they become unified in all things, live by the Spirit, and keep themselves clean from the sins of immorality.

The Lord has counseled us to be one:

> Neither pray I for these alone, but for them also which shall believe on me through their word;
>
> That they all may be one; as thou, Father, art in me, and I in thee, that they also may be one in us: that the world may believe that thou hast sent me.
>
> And the glory which thou gavest me I have given them; that they may be one, even as we are one:
>
> I in them, and thou in me, that they may be made perfect in one; and that the world may know that thou hast sent me, and hast loved them, as thou hast loved me." (John 17:20–23)

Indeed the purpose of unity is being of one mind, one purpose, and one action—that the work of the Lord might go forward in blessing our brothers and sisters. In unity, we are not only strengthened and blessed with the Spirit to direct us in all things, but there will be no contention to separate us. The Lord has warned us, "I say unto you, be one; and if ye are not one ye are not mine" (D&C 38:27).

When we are one with the Lord, we partake of His goodness. We live by the Spirit and seek to do as Christ would do. We seek to have the image of Christ in our countenance (see Alma 5:14). We strive to be like the people of Enoch (see Moses 7:16–21). Righteous living is a result of being one with the Lord, for we begin to possess charity, thus becoming like Him (see Moro. 7:48). There would be no contention or strife if we would begin to live like the people described in the Book of Mormon:

> And it came to pass that there was no contention in the land, because of the love of God which did dwell in the hearts of the people.
>
> And there were no envyings, nor strifes, nor tumults, nor whoredoms, nor lyings, nor murders, nor any manner of lasciviousness; and surely there could not be a happier people among all the people who had been created by the hand of God.
>
> There were no robbers, nor murderers, neither were there Lamanites, nor any manner of -ites; but they were in one, the children of Christ, and heirs to the kingdom of God. (4 Ne. 1:15–17)

And thus we would see the blessings of the love of God in our lives. We would not seek to encumber ourselves with the vanities of the world, but would anchor ourselves in heavenly things. We would enjoy the blessings of the Spirit and keep ourselves clean and pure before the Lord.

1. SEEK UNITY—AVOID CONTENTION

THEME: Unity with the Lord and with our fellow beings is essential to peace and happiness. The Lord is the author of salvation and the protector of harmony; but the devil is the source of contention.

MOMENT OF TRUTH

The first of the two extant epistles of Paul to the Saints at Corinth—a major commercial seaport in southern Greece—was written (like 2 Corinthians, Galatians, and Romans) between A.D. 55 and 56. Paul begins his exhortations in 1 Corinthians with an impassioned plea to root out all contention and establish unity of purpose and spirit: "Now I beseech you, brethren, by the name of our Lord Jesus Christ, that ye all speak the same thing, and that there be no divisions among you; but that ye be perfectly joined together in the same mind and in the same judgment" (1 Cor. 1:10). Paul cuts to the quick by adducing evidence of the carnality still operating within the community of Saints at Corinth:

> For ye are yet carnal: for whereas there is among you envying, and strife, and divisions, are ye not carnal, and walk as men?
>
> For while one saith, I am of Paul; and another, I am of Apollos; are ye not carnal?
>
> Who then is Paul, and who is Apollos, but ministers by whom ye believed, even as the Lord gave to every man?
>
> I have planted, Apollos watered; but God gave the increase.
>
> So then neither is he that planteth any thing, neither he that watereth; but God that giveth the increase. (1 Cor. 3:3–7)

Though many have labored to lay the foundation of the Church and kingdom of God, it is incumbent upon all who continue the work to maintain singleness of purpose and harmony within the family of God according to the central, unifying power and influence of the Savior: "For other foundation can no man lay than that is laid, which is Jesus Christ" (1 Cor. 3:11). The fruit of unity in the body of Christ is the unfathomable reward of being heirs to all things heavenly: "Therefore let no man glory in men. For all things are yours; Whether Paul, or Apollos, or Cephas, or the world, or life, or death, or things present, or things to come; all are yours; And ye are Christ's; and Christ is God's" (1 Cor. 3:21–23).

MODERN PROPHETS SPEAK

Marvin J. Ashton:

> We need to be reminded that contention is a striving against one another, especially in controversy or argument. It is to struggle, fight, battle, quarrel, or dispute. Contention never was and never will be an ally of progress. Our loyalty will never be measured by our participation in controversy. Some misunderstand the realm, scope, and dangers of contention. Too many of us are inclined to declare, "Who, me? I am not contentious, and I'll fight anyone who says I am." There are still those among us who would rather lose a friend than an argument. How important it is to know how to disagree without being disagreeable. It behooves all of us to be in the position to involve ourselves in factual discussions and meaningful study, but never in bitter arguments and contention.
>
> No home or heart exists that cannot be hurt through contention. It is sad when children are raised in a contentious home. It is just as sad when an organization has contention as one of the planks of its platform, declared or unannounced. Generally speaking, people who come from noncontentious households find themselves repulsed by those who would make it part of their daily diet.
>
> The family as an institution today is beset on all sides. Conflicts within the family are critical and often damaging. Contention puts heavy strain on stability, strength, peace, and unity in the home. There is certainly not time for contention in building a strong family. ("No Time for Contention," *Ensign,* May 1978, 8)

ILLUSTRATIONS FOR OUR TIME

Marvin J. Ashton teaches us clearly about ways to avoid contention by acquiring a spirit of calmness and patience. He entitles his topic, "The Gift to Calm":

> What a majestic gift it is to be able to calm others! We thank God for those who are calm instead of contentious. "He that hath the spirit of contention is not of me, but is of the devil, who is the father of contention, and he stirreth up the hearts of men to contend with anger, one with another" (3 Ne. 11:29). . . .
>
> "Cease to contend one with another; cease to speak evil one of another" (D&C 136:23). Argument and debate must be supplanted by calm discussion, study, listening, and negotiation. The gospel teaches harmony, unity, and agreement. It must be presented in love, and with glad tidings, by those who are calm. We should learn to talk together, listen together, pray together, decide together, and avoid all forms of possible contention. We must learn to curb anger. Satan knows that when contention begins, orderly progress is thwarted.

There has never been a time when it is more important for us as members of The Church of Jesus Christ of Latter-day Saints to take a stand, remain firm in our convictions, and conduct ourselves with calm assurance under all circumstances. We must not be manipulated or enraged by those who subtly foster contention over issues of the day. . . .

Those with the gift of being calm make lasting peace possible. (Marvin J. Ashton, *The Measure of Our Hearts* [Salt Lake City: Deseret Book, 1991], 20)

LIKENING THE SCRIPTURES TO OUR LIVES

3 Nephi 11:29–30 For verily, verily I say unto you, he that hath the spirit of contention is not of me, but is of the devil, who is the father of contention, and he stirreth up the hearts of men to contend with anger, one with another. Behold, this is not my doctrine, to stir up the hearts of men with anger, one against another; but this is my doctrine, that such things should be done away.

Application: Let us never forget that contention is of the devil. It is essential that we learn to be civil and full of charity in all our dealings, thus enjoying the Spirit of the Lord and the resultant fruits of the Spirit: peace, love, and joy (see Gal. 5:22–23).

2. TRUST IN THE SPIRIT— NOT IN MAN OR THE WORLD

THEME: The message of God down through the ages has been to trust in the Spirit and never in the arm of flesh, for one is of God and the other is of the world. The Lord builds upon the small and the weak things of the world and makes of them a mighty monument to spirituality.

MOMENT OF TRUTH

Continuing his exhortations, Paul adjures the Corinthians to anchor their testimonies and faith in eternal principles, rather than worldly things: "And my speech and my preaching was not with enticing words of man's wisdom, but in demonstration of the Spirit and of power: That your faith should not stand in the wisdom of men, but in the power of God" (1 Cor. 2:5). Placing trust in God opens up the vista of grand blessings of a spiritual nature: "But as it is written, Eye hath not seen, nor ear heard, neither have entered into the heart of man, the things which God hath prepared for them that love him. But God hath revealed them unto us by his Spirit: for the Spirit searcheth all things, yea, the deep things of God. . . . Now we have received, not the spirit of the world, but the spirit which is of God; that we might know the things that are freely given to us of God" (1 Cor. 2:9–10, 12; compare Isa. 64:4; D&C 76:10). The key to wisdom is an enduring commitment to spiritual growth; by seeking after and cultivating the gifts and blessings of the Spirit, one transcends the learning of the world, which is transitory and ephemeral, and discerns the uplifting and transforming patterns of godliness.

> But the natural man receiveth not the things of the Spirit of God: for they are fool-
> ishness unto him: neither can he know them, because they are spiritually discerned.
>   But he that is spiritual judgeth all things, yet he himself is judged of no man.
>   For who hath known the mind of the Lord, that he may instruct him? But we
> have the mind of Christ. (1 Cor. 2:14–16)

Such wisdom is available to all who believe and obey. Thus even the weak can rise in majesty to confound the best wisdom the world can bring to bear: "But God hath chosen the foolish things of the world to confound the wise; and God hath chosen the weak things of the world to confound the things which are mighty; And base things of the world, and things which are despised, hath God chosen, yea, and things which are not, to bring to nought things that are" (1 Cor. 1:27–28).

MODERN PROPHETS SPEAK

Neal A. Maxwell:
> Just how God will use the simple and the weak to acclaim the gospel and to thresh
> the world by the power of His spirit is not completely clear. But let us make no mis-
> take, there will be some rather dramatic things happen. The Lord said, "The weak
> things of the world shall come forth and break down the mighty and strong ones, that
> man should not counsel his fellow man, neither trust in the arm of flesh" (D&C
> 1:19). The Lord has said further that He will "call upon the weak things of the world,
> those who are unlearned and despised, to thrash the nations by the power of [His]
> Spirit" (D&C 35:13). To do such things will take steadfastness and hopefulness on
> our part. It will be no picnic at the park. (*Wherefore, Ye Must Press Forward*, 66)

ILLUSTRATIONS FOR OUR TIME

Prepared in All Things
In his writings to the Corinthian Saints, the Apostle Paul provides a cogent reminder of the need to cultivate wisdom of the spiritual kind by placing one's trust in the Lord and the principles of salvation and exaltation, rather than in worldly things (see espe-

cially 1 Cor. 2:5, 9–12, 14–16, 27–28). At the same time, the Lord has counseled us to expand our understanding of the secular disciplines in order to be prepared as missionaries to communicate sacred truths to the world:

> And I give unto you a commandment that you shall teach one another the doctrine of the kingdom. Teach ye diligently and my grace shall attend you, that you may be instructed more perfectly in theory, in principle, in doctrine, in the law of the gospel, in all things that pertain unto the kingdom of God, that are expedient for you to understand;
>
> Of things both in heaven and in the earth, and under the earth; things which have been, things which are, things which must shortly come to pass; things which are at home, things which are abroad; the wars and the perplexities of the nations, and the judgments which are on the land; and a knowledge also of countries and of kingdoms—
>
> That ye may be prepared in all things when I shall send you again to magnify the calling whereunto I have called you, and the mission with which I have commissioned you. (D&C 88:78–80)

The need to make heavenly wisdom predominant in our lives while at the same time cultivating a knowledge of earthly things in sufficient scope to communicate effectively with others is a principle of delicate balance and wise prudence. Years ago, as a graduate student at The Johns Hopkins University in Baltimore, I was searching through the library card index files one day and happened to come upon a number of entries under the authorship of James E. Talmage. It was a startling reminder of the range of knowledge that encompasses the human condition. Elder Talmage (1862–1933) did advanced work at Johns Hopkins in geology and related fields, going on later to serve as president of the University of Utah from 1894 to 1897. He was called as a member of the Quorum of the Twelve Apostles in 1911. While rising to pre-eminence in secular knowledge, he became a celebrated exponent of sacred knowledge as well, authoring such perennial classics as *Articles of Faith* (1899), *The House of the Lord* (1912), and *Jesus the Christ* (1915).

The example of Elder Talmage and his commitment to worthwhile teaching and learning of all kinds is a salient illustration of the Lord's commandment to be prepared in all things and seek a breadth of knowledge as a fundamental means of preparation in building up the kingdom of God on earth. While the quest for knowledge is to be broad and all encompassing, the central goal for God's servants is to serve as well-prepared instruments in advancing the cause of the gospel and its saving principles.

This preeminence of gospel knowledge over secular knowledge was illustrated by Theodore Burton, under whom I served as a missionary in Germany many years ago.

He would on occasion speak of his career as a chemistry professor of note, drawing attention to his numerous honors and publications in that field. However, he would emphasize that his purpose in saying that was not to boast, but rather to provide evidence that he had been blessed with a searching and inquiring mind, well-trained to detect error and falsehood. Then he would bear fervent testimony of the truth of the gospel and the restored Church, saying that if the rationale of logic and meaning attached to the Church and its teachings were in any way suspect, he would have long ago detected such discontinuities and exposed them as misguided. However, such was not the case, he would emphasize, reporting that the gospel was not only logically true, but confirmed in its spiritual veracity through the power of the Holy Ghost. Thus President Burton used his secular accomplishments as an adjunct to the higher or more important knowledge that comes through divine revelation. [Allen]

LIKENING THE SCRIPTURES TO OUR LIVES

D&C 11:12–14 And now, verily, verily, I say unto thee, put your trust in that Spirit which leadeth to do good—yea, to do justly, to walk humbly, to judge righteously; and this is my Spirit. Verily, verily, I say unto you, I will impart unto you of my Spirit, which shall enlighten your mind, which shall fill your soul with joy; And then shall ye know, or by this shall you know, all things whatsoever you desire of me, which are pertaining unto things of righteousness, in faith believing in me that you shall receive.

Application: The blessings of living worthy of and trusting in the Spirit are enumerable. We can enjoy the Spirit as we increase our faith (see 1 Ne. 10:17), show abundant love (see D&C 76:116), and keep the commandments (see D&C 20:77, 79). Let us remind ourselves to follow the Spirit, for it will lead us even when we know not what to do (see 1 Ne. 4:6). We can recognize the Spirit by the fruits of the Spirit (see Gal. 5:22–23). Always trust in the Lord and lean not to your own understanding (see Prov. 3:5–6).

3. BE MORALLY CLEAN

THEME: Purity and cleanliness of mind and body are absolutely essential to qualify for the Spirit in one's life. Sexual permissiveness and transgressions have devastating effects upon the mind and spirit of individuals and families.

MOMENT OF TRUTH

In a famous statement, Paul uses an effective metaphor to generate in his audience a renewed commitment to be morally clean and holy: "Know ye not that ye are the temple of God, and that the Spirit of God dwelleth in you? If any man defile the temple of God, him shall God destroy; for the temple of God is holy, which temple ye are" (1 Cor. 3:16–17). Later on in his epistle, Paul reemphasizes this same principle with these words: "What? know ye not that your body is the temple of the Holy Ghost which is in you, which ye have of God, and ye are not your own? For ye are bought with a price: therefore glorify God in your body, and in your spirit, which are God's" (1 Cor. 6:19–20). Then in a subsequent detailed exposition (chapter 7), Paul extols self-discipline and temperance regarding issues of morality and answers questions about marriage among those who are called on missions.

MODERN PROPHETS SPEAK

Gordon B. Hinckley:

> Be clean. "Be ye clean that bear the vessels of the Lord" (D&C 133:5). That is His injunction to us, young or old. Be clean. "Let virtue garnish thy thoughts unceasingly." Those great words written in the cold and the misery of Liberty Jail come as a great clarion call to us in this day when there is so much of filth and rot and sleaze and trash being peddled. . . . Be clean in thought and word and deed. Then comes the promise: "Then shall thy confidence wax strong in the presence of God; and the doctrine of the priesthood shall distil upon thy soul as the dews from heaven. The Holy Ghost shall be thy constant companion, and thy scepter an unchanging scepter of righteousness and truth; and thy dominion shall be an everlasting dominion, and without compulsory means it shall flow unto thee forever and ever" (D&C 121:45–46). I do not know of another promise anywhere of the magnitude and beauty and wonder of that divinely given promise. (*TGBH,* 49)

ILLUSTRATIONS FOR OUR TIME

"If Only I Had Known Five Minutes Before"
As told by Jayne Ann Payne

> We will never forget that sweet young girl of sixteen who came to live with us one summer for the remaining months of her unwed pregnancy. My husband is an attorney and was handling the adoption of her baby. She hadn't wanted to marry the boy who was the father of her unborn child. She had been beguiled and had partaken of the bitter fruit.
>
> In September she gave birth to a beautiful little boy, and the day she was to leave the hospital, Dean and I had to go to Salt Lake City. We stopped at the hospital long enough to meet the couple who were adopting the baby. Under hospital rules, this young mother, sixteen years old, had to take her beautiful nine-pound boy

from the arms of the nurse and hand him over to my husband, who then stepped outside the room and gave the baby to the adopting parents. It tore me apart to watch her and to see that young couple leave with her baby.

She said to me, "Sister Payne, he lied to me when he said nobody would get hurt, and that because we loved each other, anything we did was alright. He didn't really love me. That is why I didn't marry him, because he wasn't worthy to be the father of my little boy. It's all a great big lie, and I don't want to live a lie!

"Oh, if only I had known five minutes before I was immoral how I would feel five minutes after I gave my baby away!"

For this girl not to have thought ahead about the consequences of her actions and not to have realized that lust is the mere image of love is indeed heartbreaking. It is so important to keep in tune, keep in touch, to receive the Spirit each and every day. We never know what is going to happen; and if we make the commitment in our private rooms, by the side of our beds, to our Father in heaven, of what we want to be in life—what we will do and what we won't do—and then ask for his help in keeping our commitments, he will help us in public and private. (Leon R. Hartshorn, comp., *Remarkable Stories from the Lives of Latter-day Saint Women,* 2 vols. [Salt Lake City: Deseret Book, 1973], 2:203–4)

LIKENING THE SCRIPTURES TO OUR LIVES

1 Corinthians 3:16–17 Know ye not that ye are the temple of God, and that the Spirit of God dwelleth in you? If any man defile the temple of God, him shall God destroy; for the temple of God is holy, which temple ye are.

Application: Recognizing that we are the divine offspring of God should give us self-esteem. Knowing who we really are empowers us to realize that we must be clean and pure in order to enjoy the Spirit in our lives (see 1 Cor. 6:19; Mosiah 2:37; Hela. 4:24).

SUMMARY

The First Epistle of Paul the Apostle to the Corinthians makes a compelling case for embracing three of the major themes of gospel life: seek unity and avoid contention, trust in the Spirit of the Lord rather than in man and worldly endeavors, and be morally clean. These universal themes are echoed in other scriptures as well. Alma the Elder taught the Saints who congregated at the Waters of Mormon the same doctrine: "And he commanded them that there should be no contention one with another, but that they should look forward with one eye, having one faith and one baptism, having their hearts knit together in unity and in love one towards another. And thus he commanded them to preach. And thus they became the children of God" (Mosiah 18:21–22). Like Paul, Isaiah reminded us to set our sights on heavenly wisdom:

> Seek ye the Lord while he may be found, call ye upon him while he is near:
>
> Let the wicked forsake his way, and the unrighteous man his thoughts: and let him return unto the Lord, and he will have mercy upon him; and to our God, for he will abundantly pardon.
>
> For my thoughts are not your thoughts, neither are your ways my ways, saith the Lord.
>
> For as the heavens are higher than the earth, so are my ways higher than your ways, and my thoughts than your thoughts. (Isa. 55:6–9; compare D&C 38:5)

And in our day, the Lord has renewed the vital commandment to be holy and morally clean: "And ye must practise virtue and holiness before me continually" (D&C 46:33; compare D&C 42:22–24).

The consequence of honoring and keeping these commandments is to be favored of the Lord and blessed with sacred spiritual wealth—wealth so overwhelming and glorious that only the spiritual senses can behold its magnificent scope and reality (1 Cor. 2:9–16; Isa. 64:4).

CHAPTER 34

KEEP *the* COVENANTS AND ORDINANCES *of the* GOSPEL

Reading Assignment: 1 Corinthians 11–16.

Additional Reading: James 1:17; 3 Nephi 18:1–14; 29:5–6; Moroni 7:44–48; 10:8–18; D&C 46:1–26; 76:50–119; 88:27–32, 95–102.

> *The Savior compared the kingdom, in other words the Church, to ten virgins, five of whom were wise and five of whom were foolish; and so we must not get the understanding that because we are members of the Church it is all well with us, and our salvation is secure, that is, our exaltation is secure. It is not so.*
>
> *We must continue to the end; we must obey the commandments. We must keep the ordinances. We must receive covenants, sealings, the sealing power, and privileges which are obtained in the temple of the Lord, and then live in accordance with them. That we must do.*

—JOSEPH FIELDING SMITH, *DS,* 2:15

THEMES *for* LIVING

1. A Sacred Relationship—Husband and Wife Together and with the Lord
2. The Sacrament
3. Spiritual Gifts
4. Resurrection and the Degrees of Glory

INTRODUCTION

There is power given to us by the Lord as we keep the covenants and ordinances of the gospel of Jesus Christ. We honor our covenants and ordinances by keeping the commandments and we renew our commitments in partaking of the sacrament. The Lord "doth immediately bless" us (see Mosiah 2:24), in that we can always have His Spirit to guide, direct, and comfort us in our lives—as well as the appropriate gifts necessary to bless and serve our fellowmen. The key to having good relationships within the family, and particularly between husband and wife, is to live the doctrines of the gospel. When we come to understand and appreciate any doctrine, principle, ordinance, or covenant, our attitude and behavior change. This is especially evident within the family unit. It is also observed in every walk of life in our interactions and relationships with our fellowmen. The Sermon on the Mount and at the Temple as recorded in Matthew 5–7 and 3 Nephi 12–14 literally comprise the celestial laws for living. The relationships and camaraderie we have here upon the earth will go with us into the eternities (see D&C 130:2). It is to this state of happiness and never-ending joy that we aspire as we look forward to eternal life with our Heavenly Father, Savior, and with our loved ones, knowing that all blessings are predicated upon our obedience (see Mosiah 2:41; D&C 130:20).

1. A SACRED RELATIONSHIP— HUSBAND AND WIFE TOGETHER AND WITH THE LORD

THEME: Fostering and cultivating an edifying covenant relationship with your spouse and with the Lord will lead to greater happiness and joy in this life and eternal blessings in the life to come.

MOMENT OF TRUTH

The Apostle Paul includes in his epistle to the Corinthians (1 Corinthians) solemn advice concerning the sacred relationship that should exist between man and wife— and between them and the Lord. Paul's oft-cited statement in this regard is the following: "Nevertheless neither is the man without the woman, neither the woman without the man, in the Lord" (1 Cor. 11:11). In his discourse, Paul discusses a number of customs and practices that contribute to the preservation and cultivation of harmonious and righteous interdependence of husband and wife within the framework of covenant fidelity and honor. Then, as now, the importance of this holy relationship is key to progress along the pathway to perfection.

MODERN PROPHETS SPEAK

Gordon B. Hinckley:

> The most important decision of life is the decision concerning your companion. Choose prayerfully. And when you are married, be fiercely loyal one to another. Selfishness is the great destroyer of happy family life. I have this one suggestion to offer. If you will make your first concern the comfort, the well-being, and the happiness of your companion, sublimating any personal concern to that loftier goal, you will be happy, and your marriage will go on through eternity. (*TGBH*, 328–29)

ILLUSTRATIONS FOR OUR TIME

Bruce C. Hafen and Marie K. Hafen explain the joy of the eternal family relationships so integral to the doctrine of eternal life:

> The loving attachments of marriage and family life often develop so naturally and so deeply that it may surprise us to learn that in modern revelation the Lord has actually commanded us to love our spouses: "*Thou shalt* love thy wife with all thy heart, and shalt cleave unto her and none else" (D&C 42:22). And more broadly, "*Thou shalt* live together in love, insomuch that thou shalt weep for the loss of them that die" (D&C 42:45).
>
> Further, no individual, woman or man, has access to the highest degree of celestial life alone: "Neither is the man without the woman, neither the woman without the man, in the Lord" (1 Cor. 11:11). To obtain exaltation, we must receive the priesthood ordinance of eternal marriage (see D&C 131:1–3). And one of exaltation's further blessings is the promise that parents sealed in the new and everlasting covenant of marriage will be joined in those eternal bonds by their worthy children.
>
> Our children anticipate the fulfillment of this promise when they sing that through Heavenly Father's plan, "families can be together forever." President Ezra Taft Benson has spoken of this joyful anticipation in describing heavenly reunions for families where there are "no empty chairs." Thus, if we keep our covenants, we may look forward with assurance to that day: "When the Savior shall appear we shall see him as he is. We shall see that he is a man like ourselves. And that same sociality which exists among us here will exist among us there, only it will be coupled with eternal glory" (D&C 130:1–2). The ongoing enjoyment of prized relationships—"that same sociality which exists among us here"—is fundamental to our very definition of eternal life. (*The Belonging Heart: The Atonement and Relationships with God and Family* [Salt Lake City: Deseret Book, 1994], 18–19)

LIKENING THE SCRIPTURES TO OUR LIVES

Ephesians 5:25 Husbands, love your wives, even as Christ also loved the church, and gave himself for it.

Application: Love begets love. Love is that ultimate concern that brings about righteous service. Everything the Lord has ever done for us has been motivated by His love for us (see 2 Ne. 26:24). Let us love and serve each other.

2. THE SACRAMENT

THEME: To understand and appreciate the sacrament is to savor and continually renew covenant promises so that the Spirit can have a defining place in our lives.

MOMENT OF TRUTH

Paul reminds the Corinthian Saints that the sacrament is an ordinance established personally by the Savior by way of commandment:

> And when he had given thanks, he brake it, and said, Take, eat: this is my body, which is broken for you: this do in remembrance of me.
>
> After the same manner also he took the cup, when he had supped, saying, This cup is the new testament in my blood: this do ye, as oft as ye drink it, in remembrance of me.
>
> For as often as ye eat this bread, and drink this cup, ye do shew the Lord's death till he come. (1 Cor. 11:24–26)

Paul entreats his audience that they should partake of the sacrament worthily:

> But let a man examine himself, and so let him eat of that bread, and drink of that cup.
>
> For he that eateth and drinketh unworthily, eateth and drinketh damnation to himself, not discerning the Lord's body. (1 Cor. 11:28–29)

MODERN PROPHETS SPEAK

Gordon B. Hinckley:
> The sacrament and the partaking of these emblems is the very heart of our sabbath worship. It includes a renewal of covenants with God. It carries with it a promise of His Holy Spirit to be with us. It is a blessing without peer to be enjoyed by all and

made possible by the authority given to worthy young men. (*TGBH,* 561)

ILLUSTRATIONS FOR OUR TIME

George Albert Smith illuminates for us the significance of the sacrament:

> Partaking of the sacrament increases our spiritual strength. I feel that a comprehension of the sacredness of the sacrament of the Lord's Supper is important to the members of the Church. We partake of physical food—that is, we partake of bread and water etc., to nourish the physical body. It is just as necessary that we partake of the emblems of the body and blood of our risen Lord to increase our spiritual strength. It is observed that men and women who go from year to year without partaking of the Lord's Supper gradually lose the Spirit of our Heavenly Father; they forfeit its companionship where they have had opportunity to participate in that blessing, but have failed to take advantage of it. The sacrament is of great importance. The Lord himself ordained that we partake of these emblems. There are many people who believe it is necessary to be baptized, and to have other ordinances of the gospel performed in their behalf, and yet they become indifferent and careless regarding the sacrament of the Lord's Supper. It was regarded of such importance by our Father in Heaven that, through his Beloved Son, and the Apostles and prophets, as recorded in the scriptures, the Saints were admonished to partake of it regularly. (George Albert Smith, *The Teachings of George Albert Smith* [Salt Lake City: Bookcraft, 1998], ed. Robert McIntosh and Susan McIntosh, 95)

LIKENING THE SCRIPTURES TO OUR LIVES

D&C 20:77 O God, the Eternal Father, we ask thee in the name of thy Son, Jesus Christ, to bless and sanctify this bread to the souls of all those who partake of it, that they may eat in remembrance of the body of thy Son, and witness unto thee, O God, the Eternal Father, that they are willing to take upon them the name of thy Son, and always remember him and keep his commandments which he has given them; that they may always have his Spirit to be with them. Amen.

Application: The sacramental prayers extend great promises as we renew our covenants and partake of the emblems with a truly broken heart and contrite spirit. The commitment to our covenants will bring the Spirit into our lives, along with untold blessings from heaven. Remember that the Spirit is the key to following Christ and living a Christlike life. It is important to renew all our covenants—baptism, priesthood, and temple-related—and promise to keep all the commandments.

3. SPIRITUAL GIFTS

THEME: To recognize the importance of seeking and cultivating the gifts of the Spirit is to imbue our lives with untold blessings from heaven.

MOMENT OF TRUTH

In the First Epistle to the Corinthians, Paul includes in chapter 12 a magnificent treatment of the gifts of the Spirit—one that has become (along with Moro. 10 and D&C 46) a staple in scriptural discourse on this important theme. The most fundamental gift of the Spirit, as Paul announces at the beginning of his explanation, is the gift of testimony granted by the Spirit: "Wherefore I give you to understand, that no man speaking by the Spirit of God calleth Jesus accursed: and that no man can say that Jesus is the Lord, but by the Holy Ghost" (1 Cor. 12:3). He then proceeds to outline the "diversities of gifts" as given by the same Spirit (v. 5–11), with the reminder that all of these various gifts, given severally to the members of the Church, contribute to the unity and oneness of the body of Christ, and that all members are important in contributing their respective roles and talents for the building up of the kingdom of God (v. 12–30).

Therefore, we should "covet earnestly the best gifts" (v. 31). Fundamental to the operation of all of the gifts of the Spirit is charity. Paul's succinct and elegant statement concerning charity (1 Cor. 13) is among the most celebrated and articulate of expressions on this divine quality. He concludes: "And now abideth faith, hope, charity, these three; but the greatest of these is charity" (1 Cor. 13:13; compare Moro. 7:43–48). In 1 Corinthians 14, Paul encourages the Saints to seek after the best spiritual gifts as a means of edification and unfolding the spiritual enlightenment of the community of God: "Even so ye, forasmuch as ye are zealous of spiritual gifts, seek that ye may excel to the edifying of the church" (1 Cor. 14:12).

MODERN PROPHETS SPEAK

Marion G. Romney:

> I can think of no aid to parents in the training of children equal to the guidance of the Holy Spirit. Among his gifts are faith, discernment, knowledge, judgment, and wisdom. The fruits of the Holy Spirit include virtue, diligence, humility, hope, patience, kindness, charity, love, composure, peace, Godliness, and joy. . . .
>
> How is one to come by these precious gifts and fruits? The Lord has said, "the Spirit shall be given unto you by the prayer of faith" (D&C 42:14).
>
> Seek the guidance of the Holy Spirit. Seek it by faith and by prayer, by study, and by righteous living. Learn what the scriptures and the teachings of the Prophet

Joseph Smith say about it. Develop a desire for it. Live worthy of it and cultivate its companionship. Take it for your guide. If you do so, your rewards will be eternal; for when the Savior comes in his glory and the parable of the ten virgins is fulfilled—"they that are wise and have received the truth, and have taken the Holy Spirit for their guide, and have not been deceived . . . shall not be hewn down and cast into the fire, but shall abide the day" (D&C 45:57). (Marion G. Romney, *Learning for the Eternities* [Salt Lake City: Deseret Book, 1977], 125–26)

ILLUSTRATIONS FOR OUR TIME

The Antidote for Envy

The young man was shy and reserved. He did not comfortably blend into the sometimes competitive and outspoken assertiveness of his peers. But he had some unique qualities that were already shining through. He told me on one occasion that he felt envious of the others who found it so easy to take initiative in social settings. That was my opportunity as the Young Men's president to remind him of the gifts and talents that he had been given—different from those of his colleagues. There were remarkable things he could do that they could not so easily do—and these gifts from God would enable him in his life to render valuable service. Over the years, I have watched that young man grow into a more self-confident and mature individual who derives much satisfaction and joy in the accomplishments and contributions that relate to his unique talents.

It is the blending together of the several gifts in the congregations of the Saints in the spirit of service that can remove from all of us the feelings of being out of place or lonely, for there are contributions that we can make that may be unique and indispensable. Paul said it this way: "Now therefore ye are no more strangers and foreigners, but fellowcitizens with the saints, and of the household of God . . . In whom ye also are builded together for an habitation of God through the Spirit" (Eph. 2:19, 22). And elsewhere, he said:

> And the eye cannot say unto the hand, I have no need of thee: nor again the head to the feet, I have no need of you.
>
> Nay, much more those members of the body, which seem to be more feeble, are necessary:
>
> And those members of the body, which we think to be less honourable, upon these we bestow more abundant honour; and our uncomely parts have more abundant comeliness.
>
> For our comely parts have no need: but God hath tempered the body together, having given more abundant honour to that part which lacked:

> That there should be no schism in the body; but that the members should have the same care one for another.
>
> And whether one member suffer, all the members suffer with it; or one member be honoured, all the members rejoice with it.
>
> Now ye are the body of Christ, and members in particular. (1 Cor. 12:21–27)

I believe the plainest antidote to envy and jealousy is to focus on those gifts and talents we are given and cultivate them for the building up of the kingdom. The Lord counsels: "And again, verily I say unto you, I would that ye should always remember, and always retain in your minds what those gifts are, that are given unto the church. For all have not every gift given unto them; for there are many gifts, and to every man is given a gift by the Spirit of God" (D&C 46:10–11). Since the Lord gives to everyone at least one of these spiritual gifts, we can gratefully cultivate our gift "for the benefit of the children of God" (v. 26) and "give thanks unto God in the Spirit for whatsoever blessing ye are blessed with" (v. 32). This being the case, there is no room in our hearts and minds for envy and jealousy, and we can instead "practice virtue and holiness" before the Lord continually (v. 33). [Allen]

LIKENING THE SCRIPTURES TO OUR LIVES

D&C 46:8–9 Wherefore, beware lest ye are deceived; and that ye may not be deceived seek ye earnestly the best gifts, always remembering for what they are given; For verily I say unto you, they are given for the benefit of those who love me and keep all my commandments, and him that seeketh so to do; that all may be benefited that seek or that ask of me, that ask and not for a sign that they may consume it upon their lusts.

Application: The purpose of God in bestowing the gifts of the Spirit is to benefit His children. Let us therefore seek the Spirit and the associated spiritual gifts so that we might be an instrument in the hands of God to bless others.

4. RESURRECTION AND THE DEGREES OF GLORY

THEME: Understanding the reality of the resurrection and the nature of the degrees of glory that are obtainable by the children of God according to their faithfulness and through the grace of God are key elements in the plan of happiness.

MOMENT OF TRUTH

Evidence of the resurrection of the Lord is summarized by Paul in 1 Corinthians 15:1–8, including his own personal confirmation deriving from his encounter with the risen Lord on the road to Damascus: "And last of all he was seen of me also, as of one born out of due time" (v. 8). Paul's meekness and humility in bearing personal witness show forth his admirable qualities: "For I am the least of the apostles, that am not meet to be called an apostle, because I persecuted the church of God. But by the grace of God I am what I am: and his grace which was bestowed upon me was not in vain; but I laboured more abundantly than they all: yet not I, but the grace of God which was with me" (1 Cor. 15:9–10).

How to confirm and verify the Resurrection then becomes Paul's agenda. The logic is irrefutable: "If in this life only we have hope in Christ, we are of all men most miserable" (1 Cor. 15:19). But such is not the case: "For as in Adam all die, even so in Christ shall all be made alive" (1 Cor. 15:22). In addition, there is the vicarious work for the dead, which depends wholly on the verity and reality of the Resurrection: "Else what shall they do which are baptized for the dead, if the dead rise not at all? why are they then baptized for the dead?" (1 Cor. 15:29). This last statement is considered cryptic by all sectarian commentators who are not apprised of the blessings of temple work carried on in the Church and kingdom of God. Paul concludes his treatise on the Resurrection by talking of the three degrees of glory to which resurrected beings can be assigned (1 Cor. 15:40–41—comparable, symbolically, to the relative glory of the sun, moon, and stars). Paul then exhorts the Saints to remember the extraordinary and blessed outcome of the Savior's Atonement and Resurrection:

> O death, where is thy sting? O grave, where is thy victory?
>
> The sting of death is sin; and the strength of sin is the law.
>
> But thanks be to God, which giveth us the victory through our Lord Jesus Christ.
>
> Therefore, my beloved brethren, be ye stedfast, unmoveable, always abounding in the work of the Lord, forasmuch as ye know that your labour is not in vain in the Lord. (1 Cor. 15:55–58)

MODERN PROPHETS SPEAK

Ezra Taft Benson:

> May prayer increase your faith in God—and your trust and love—so that whatever of trials and desolation life may hold for you, you may say with Job: "I know that my redeemer liveth."
>
> Be not ashamed to believe and proclaim that God lives, that he is the Father of our spirits; that Jesus is the Christ, the Redeemer of the world; that the resurrection is a reality; that we lived as spirits before mortal birth and will live again as immortal beings through the eternities to come. Blessed are you if you have a testimony of these things. These great spiritual truths have seen systems come and go,

and so it will be in the future. These truths will, if you are wise, take precedence in your lives "over all contrary theories, dogmas, hypotheses or relative-truths from whatever source or by whomsoever" advocated. (*So Shall Ye Reap* [Salt Lake City: Deseret Book, 1960], comp. Reed A. Benson, 176.)

ILLUSTRATIONS FOR OUR TIME

The Vision of the Resurrection

No doctrine in the sacred canon of eternal principles captures the imagination with more compelling urgency than the Resurrection. This word derives from the Latin term "resurgere," meaning "to rise again." Mortals, without exception, understand the process whereby the miraculous human frame is gradually transformed through the passage of time into an increasingly frail and weathered state, tempered by the elements and reduced to a fraction of the original vigor and vitality. Some, from birth, or through trauma, find this process of reduction suddenly imposed upon them or accelerated beyond measure. We know the process all too intimately: strength is diminished; wrinkles abound; infirmities arise.

Is it any wonder that the hope of the resurrection—bringing about the vanquishing of the process of human withering and aging and the eventual triumph over death—should engender in those who believe—or want to believe—an attitude of peaceful anticipation and a future-oriented vision of a glorious state of betterment that awaits all mortals? Faith in the verity of the resurrection brings a transformed view of things as they are and as they will be. Those who hope for the fruits of Christ's atoning sacrifice, with its promise of the resurrection, can see things in a different light. In the place of challenging handicaps, they see wholeness and liberation; in the place of degenerative illness, they see relief and vitality; in the place of separation from loved ones, they see union and conviviality.

Where can you find the vision of the resurrection at work in our daily lives? Consider this: Why is it that when you see an older couple walking together with hands clasped, the two partners are invariably smiling? That is the vision of the resurrection. These two, wizened perhaps and shuffling a bit, look at each other with refreshing love. The wrinkles, so visible to others, are invisible to them. Each sees the other as the fair and attractive person he or she first knew—and as the glorious and restored person he or she will accompany on celestial walks in the resurrected state, just as always.

Why is it when a group of widows take a newly widowed sister into their circle of friendship, they look upon her with eyes of understanding and nurture? Having been schooled in the academy of loneliness, they have learned how to apply the antidote of sociality and service as they await a reunion with loved ones some day in the future.

That is the vision of the resurrection. That is the higher perspective of life that instills hope and generates momentum toward a future sociality coupled with eternal glory (see D&C 130:2).

Why is it that the temples of the Lord are havens of peace and security amidst a world of turmoil and ephemerality? Is it not because the perspective taught in the House of the Lord transcends the earthly vale of tears and lifts one's spirit to a state of wholeness and completion, a state of bringing all the elements together in an ultimate and permanent bonding through which process alone complete joy and happiness are possible? "The elements are eternal," says the scripture, "and spirit and element, inseparably connected, receive a fulness of joy" (D&C 93:33; 138:17). That is the vision of the resurrection, made possible through the Atonement of the Savior.

On December 20, 1842, the Prophet Joseph Smith shared with his associates his view of the resurrection, imparted to him in a vision from the Almighty: "So plain was the vision, that I actually saw men, before they had ascended from the tomb, as though they were getting up slowly. They took each other by the hand and said to each other, 'My father, my son, my mother, my daughter, my brother, my sister.' And when the voice calls for the dead to arise, suppose I am laid by the side of my father, what would be the first joy of my heart? To meet my father, my mother, my brother, my sister; and when they are by my side, I embrace them and they me" (*HC* 5:362).

I recall visiting a nursing home some years ago to render charitable service to the elderly patients there. One woman, unable to speak, was clutching a small photograph in her hands. She beckoned me to look, and I saw there a mother and daughter in close and affectionate embrace. Clearly this frail woman was reliving with joy her youthful memories at the side of a loving mother. Perhaps her smile confirmed that she was also peering into the future and beholding the time when these two would once more be together in a sphere of peace and rest. That is the vision of the resurrection. Thank God for that doctrine and that hope, planted into our hearts and confirmed by the Spirit.

The Savior performed mighty miracles when He walked the earth—healing the infirm, causing the blind to see and the deaf to hear, even raising people from the grave. At times, we look back upon those choice accounts and wish that He were here among us today to perform those same deeds of love: making our children whole, returning departed loved ones to our side, causing disease and malady to retreat behind the heavenly triumph of wellness and restoration. The truth of the matter is that the Savior is here today, and He will perform the desired miracles on our behalf—in His own due time. "Zion shall be redeemed in mine own due time" (D&C 136:18), said the Lord. That redemption also includes the resurrection, which will bring with it as many miracles as there are people to experience it. When we are operating within the Lord's time frame, then we are always on schedule, and with patience we will find that "His own due time" will be soon enough. Meanwhile, as we wait with faith, facing adversity and trial, we can take to heart that "all these things shall give thee experience, and shall be for thy good" (D&C 122:7).

The Apostle Paul taught the Corinthians the vision of the resurrection:

> But now is Christ risen from the dead, and become the firstfruits of them that slept.
>
> For since by man came death, by man came also the resurrection of the dead.
>
> For as in Adam all die, even so in Christ shall all be made alive.
>
> But every man in his own order: Christ the firstfruits; afterward they that are Christ's at his coming.
>
> Then cometh the end, when he shall have delivered up the kingdom to God, even the Father; when he shall have put down all rule and all authority and power.
>
> For he must reign, till he hath put all enemies under his feet.
>
> The last enemy that shall be destroyed is death. . . .
>
> O death, where is thy sting? O grave, where is thy victory? . . .
>
> But thanks be to God, which giveth us the victory through our Lord Jesus Christ.
>
> Therefore, my beloved brethren, be ye stedfast, unmoveable, always abounding in the work of the Lord, forasmuch as ye know that your labour is not in vain in the Lord. (1 Cor. 15:20–26, 55, 57–58)

And so it is that we go through life one day at a time—remembering the blessed promise of the resurrection, hoping in faith for a time when we will rise again and enter into the rest of God as whole and reclaimed beings at last, "which rest is the fullness of his glory" (D&C 84:24). That is the vision of the resurrection. [Allen]

LIKENING THE SCRIPTURES TO OUR LIVES

D&C 76:69 These are they who are just men made perfect through Jesus the mediator of the new covenant, who wrought out this perfect atonement through the shedding of his own blood.

Application: Entering the celestial glory requires the infinite and eternal Atonement by our Savior. A knowledge of the possibility of inheriting such a glory should fill us with gratitude. Likewise required of us is that we live a life that qualifies us as a "just" person. The just shall live by faith in Jesus Christ (see Hab. 2:5; Rom. 1:17; Gal. 3:12; Heb. 10:38). Faith is the foundation of all righteousness. The oil of the lamp is our personal righteousness. To liken this scripture to our lives we must truly increase and exercise our faith in Jesus Christ and thus obtain the celestial glory.

SUMMARY

It is a refreshing thing, amidst the cares and travails of daily life, to step into the circle of students being taught by the Apostle Paul and learn from him noble and edifying truths: the sacred relationship of husband and wife working interdependently beneath the canopy of heaven, the beauty and magnificence of the sacrament as a means to renew holy covenants, the breathtaking power of spiritual gifts as instruments of service in building the kingdom of God, and the hope and reality of the resurrection as the gateway to future degrees of glory. May we apply these doctrines and principles in our lives with devotion and thanksgiving, ever mindful of our obligations to obey all of God's commandments and follow in the footsteps of His Only Begotten Son.

CHAPTER 35

"BE YE RECONCILED *to* GOD"

Reading Assignment: 2 Corinthians.

Additional Reading: Bible Dictionary, "Pauline Epistles; Epistle to the Corinthians, Analysis of 2 Corinthians" (744).

> *Only through the Atonement can we return to God. The simple essence of all you need to know about the Atonement is to be found in the teachings of the great prophet Nephi when he said, "We labor diligently to write, to persuade our children, and also our brethren, to believe in Christ, and to be reconciled to God; for we know that it is by grace that we are saved, after all we can do" (2 Ne. 25:23).*
>
> *Don't you let anyone try to persuade you to any other doctrine than that. Except for the atoning power, the redeeming power, of the Master, redeeming the world from the Fall, bringing us back into relationship with one of the Godhead, the Holy Ghost—were it not for His sacrifice for us, none of us would be worthy to enter into His presence, except we were bathed in His blood through repentance of all our sins and our faithfulness to the end (see 3 Ne. 27:19). That [is] the pure doctrine of the scriptures.*
>
> —HAROLD B. LEE, *THBL*, 7–8.

THEMES *for* LIVING

1. Overcoming Trials and Tribulations
2. Forgiving Others
3. Godly Sorrow for Sin
4. Becoming Reconciled to God

INTRODUCTION

In his Second Epistle to the Corinthians, Paul expounds on a variety of different topics and doctrines. In this chapter, we will emphasize the themes of trials and tribulations, forgiving others, the process of repentance—in particular, experiencing godly sorrow and learning how we must be reconciled to God through the Atonement of Jesus Christ. Opposition in all things is an eternal verity (see 2 Ne. 2:11). Likewise, temptation is necessary that we might exercise our moral agency: "And it must needs be that the devil should tempt the children of men, or they could not be agents unto themselves; for if they never should have bitter they could not know the sweet" (D&C 29:39). Forgiving and showing mercy to others is required of us as we come to acquire the attribute of charity in our lives. Surely we obtain mercy and forgiveness as we show mercy and forgiveness to others (see Matt. 5:7; Luke 6:37; 2 Cor. 2:10). True repentance requires godly sorrow, not sorrow for being caught or exposed, but a broken heart and contrite spirit of the soul. The Atonement of Christ and the process of repentance are essential in the process of becoming reconciled to God (see 2 Cor. 5:17–20; Rom. 5:8–12; Jacob 4:11). Through reconciliation we are restored to a state where we can become worthy of the presence of God.

1. OVERCOMING TRIALS AND TRIBULATIONS

THEME: Enduring persecution for the Lord's sake will bring eternal rewards. Dealing with the daily trials and tribulations of life will bring humility and dependence upon the Lord. This is the process that helps us understand the purpose of opposition in all things, the moral agency of man, and our total dependence upon the Lord. It is through this process that we grow and become more Christlike.

MOMENT OF TRUTH

Paul offers to the Saints at Corinth encouragement in the face of daunting opposition and adversity. Being no stranger to persecution and suffering himself (see 2 Cor. 11:23–33), he was in a position of considerable authority to speak upon this subject, and in doing so, confirmed for his audience the doctrine of consolation:

> Blessed be God, even the Father of our Lord Jesus Christ, the Father of mercies, and the God of all comfort;
>
> Who comforteth us in all our tribulation, that we may be able to comfort them which are in any trouble, by the comfort wherewith we ourselves are comforted of God.

> For as the sufferings of Christ abound in us, so our consolation also aboundeth by Christ.
>
> And whether we be afflicted, it is for your consolation and salvation, which is effectual in the enduring of the same sufferings which we also suffer: or whether we be comforted, it is for your consolation and salvation.
>
> And our hope of you is stedfast, knowing, that as ye are partakers of the sufferings, so shall ye be also of the consolation. (2 Cor. 1:3–7)

Paul then rejoices with the Saints concerning the grace of God, which has enabled them to cultivate righteous patterns of living and to support one another continually: "For our rejoicing is this, the testimony of our conscience, that in simplicity and godly sincerity, not with fleshly wisdom, but by the grace of God, we have had our conversation in the world, and more abundantly to you-ward" (2 Cor. 1:12). Though the burdens may seem heavy in this world, they are nevertheless light in the context of the bliss of the eternal rewards awaiting the faithful: "For our light affliction, which is but for a moment, worketh for us a far more exceeding and eternal weight of glory" (2 Cor. 4:17).

MODERN PROPHETS SPEAK

Harold B. Lee:

> Overcoming adversity makes one strong. The overcoming of obstacles and the solution of problems involve the expenditure of energy that builds character, that increases the capacity of the individual. It was said by Benjamin Franklin "that to be thrown on one's own resources is to be cast in the very lap of fortune, for our faculties undergo a development and a display of energy of which they were previously unsusceptible." Remember it is the pursuit of easy things that makes men weak. Our ancestors became a strong, virile people because they braved dangers, overcame and triumphed in the face of seeming impossibilities. (*THBL,* 193)

> Trials may test our obedience. I believe that sometimes we have to go through testing and trial in order to have purged out from us that which would be in disobedience. (*THBL,* 193)

ILLUSTRATIONS FOR OUR TIME

Some classic vignettes about those who have overcome adversity:

> Cripple him, and you have a Sir Walter Scott. Lock him in a prison cell, and you have a John Bunyan. Bury him in the snows of Valley Forge, and you have a George

Washington. Land him in poverty, and you have an Abraham Lincoln. Subject him to bitter religious strife, and you have a Disraeli. Strike him with Infantile Paralysis, and you have a Franklin D. Roosevelt, the only President of the United States to be elected to four terms of office. Burn him so severely in a schoolhouse fire that the doctors say he will never walk, and you have a Glenn Cunningham, who set a world record in 1934 for running the mile in 4 minutes, 6.7 seconds.

Deafen a genius composer who continues to compose some of the world's most beautiful music, and you have a Beethoven. Drag him more dead than alive out of a rice paddy in Vietnam, and you have a Rocky Blaier, that beautiful running back for the Pittsburgh Steelers. Have him or her born black in a society filled with racial discrimination, and you have a Booker T. Washington, Harriet Tubman, or Martin Luther King Jr. Have him born of parents who survived a Nazi concentration camp, paralyze him from the waist down at the age of four, and you have an Itzhak Perlman, the incomparable violinist. Call him "retarded" and write him off as "uneducatable," and you have an Albert Einstein.

After losing both his legs in an airplane crash, let an RAF fighter pilot fly, and you have World War II ace, Douglas Bader, who was captured by the Germans three times and escaped three times on two artificial limbs. Label him too stupid to learn, and you have a Thomas Edison. Label him a hopeless alcoholic, and you have a Bill Wilson, the founder of Alcoholics Anonymous. Tell her she is too old to start painting at 80, and you have a Grandma Moses. Blind him at age 44, and you have a John Milton, who 10 years later, wrote Paradise Lost. Call him dull and hopeless and flunk him in the 6th grade, and you have a Winston Churchill.

Tell a young boy who loved to draw and sketch that he had no talent, and you have a Walt Disney. Rate him mediocre in chemistry, and you have a Louis Pasteur. Take a crippled child whose only home was an orphanage, and you have a Louis E. West, who became the first chief executive of the Boy Scouts of America. Spit on him, humiliate him, betray his trust, say one thing and do another. Mistrust those whom he loves. Mock him. Make him carry a heavy wooden cross, and then crucify him—and he forgives you and calls you a friend. [Anonymous]

LIKENING THE SCRIPTURES TO OUR LIVES

D&C 121:7–8 My son, peace be unto thy soul; thine adversity and thine afflictions shall be but a small moment; And then, if thou endure it well, God shall exalt thee on high; thou shalt triumph over all thy foes.

Application: Through adversity we are tested; through trials and tribulation we grow and develop. It requires faith and trust in the Lord.

2. FORGIVING OTHERS

THEME: Forgiving others is a commandment. Desiring to forgive and practicing forgiveness are truly Christlike attributes.

MOMENT OF TRUTH

Among the doctrines covered by Paul in 2 Corinthians is the commandment that the Saints should forgive others in a Christlike manner, lest Satan should gain power over them:

> Wherefore I beseech you that ye would confirm your love toward him [an offender].
>
> For to this end also did I write, that I might know the proof of you, whether ye be obedient in all things.
>
> To whom ye forgive any thing, I forgive also: for if I forgave any thing, to whom I forgave it, for your sakes forgave I it in the person of Christ;
>
> Lest Satan should get an advantage of us: for we are not ignorant of his devices.
> (2 Cor. 2:8–11)

In teaching this way, Paul was confirming the doctrine of the Savior: "For if ye forgive men their trespasses, your heavenly Father will also forgive you: But if ye forgive not men their trespasses, neither will your Father forgive your trespasses" (Matt. 6:14–15). And from modern-day revelation, we have further substantiation of this doctrine: "Wherefore, I say unto you, that ye ought to forgive one another; for he that forgiveth not his brother his trespasses standeth condemned before the Lord; for there remaineth in him the greater sin. I, the Lord, will forgive whom I will forgive, but of you it is required to forgive all men" (D&C 64:9–10).

MODERN PROPHETS SPEAK

Joseph Smith:
> Meekly persuade and urge everyone to forgive one another all their trespasses, offenses and sins, that they may work out their own salvation with fear and trembling. Brethren, bear and forbear one with another, for so the Lord does with us. Pray for your enemies in the Church and curse not your foes without: for vengeance is mine, saith the Lord, and I will repay. To every ordained member, and to all, we say, be merciful and you shall find mercy. (*HC*, 2:229–30)

ILLUSTRATIONS FOR OUR TIME

Unconditional Forgiveness

Many have experienced in life the feeling of being condemned by others unjustly or accused of unkind motives that they have never harbored. The Prophet Joseph Smith was repeatedly subjected to the most vile derision and persecution without cause or provocation. His response was consistent. He forgave. He fought for the right and defended the Church and its doctrines indefatigably in the face of the most outrageous lies and malicious attacks. He fought valiantly and forcefully, but he forgave, nonetheless.

Consider his behavior toward those who inflicted serious bodily harm upon him on March 24, 1832. At that time, he and his family were staying at the home of John Johnson in Hiram, Ohio. Suddenly, a mob of some two dozen drunken men tore Joseph from the side of his ailing son, eleven-month-old Joseph Murdock Smith (one of two adopted twins), dragged him from the house, stripped him of his clothes, beat him brutally, and tarred and feathered him. All during that night, friends and family removed the skin-searing tar from his body, taking up large areas of skin in the process. Sidney Rigdon had been dragged feet-first from his home, sustaining a concussion as his head thumped down the steps and along the frozen ground. He was beaten and left comatose in the snow. Young Joseph Murdock, already suffering with measles, contracted pneumonia from the exposure that night and died a few days later. On the morning of Sunday, March 25, the day after the brutal attack, Joseph delivered a sermon before the gathering of Saints. What was his theme? Forgiveness. A number of individuals were baptized that afternoon. Three of the mobsters present at the Prophet's sermon on forgiveness were converted and joined the Church (see *HC* 1:261–65).

It was a remarkable instance of unconditional forgiveness and a lasting memorial to the Prophet's understanding and embracing of the Lord's injunction to cultivate a forgiving heart and practice forgiveness every day: "Ye have heard that it hath been said, Thou shalt love thy neighbor, and hate thine enemy. But I say unto you, Love your enemies, bless them that curse you, do good to them that hate you, and pray for them which despitefully use you, and persecute you; That ye may be the children of your Father which is in heaven" (Matt. 5:43–45). It is clear that children of God should exemplify the epitome of unconditional forgiveness. [Allen]

LIKENING THE SCRIPTURES TO OUR LIVES

D&C 64:8–10 My disciples, in days of old, sought occasion against one another and forgave not one another in their hearts; and for this evil they were afflicted and sorely chastened. Wherefore, I say unto you, that ye ought to forgive one another; for he that forgiveth not his brother his trespasses standeth condemned before the Lord; for there remaineth in him the greater sin. I, the Lord, will forgive whom I will forgive, but of you it is required to forgive all men.

Application: The act of forgiving surely entails the greatest amount of charity in one's heart. Yet in this act is brought about the greatest good in one's life—for the person who forgives can look forward to forgiveness in greater measure. Surely having a forgiving heart is the attribute of godliness.

3. GODLY SORROW FOR SIN

THEME: Godly sorrow works by the Spirit. Our hearts are broken and our spirits are contrite. We recognize our offense against God and against those whom we have wronged. We confess and forsake and seek to restore that which was taken or lost. This is why the phrase "godly sorrow worketh repentance to salvation" accurately defines true repentance (2 Cor. 7:10).

MOMENT OF TRUTH

The Apostle Paul, whose epistles rank among the most magnificent statements of doctrine in all of the scriptures, makes a compelling contrast at one point between lip service and the spiritual imprint of the touch of the Master upon the soul: "Ye are our epistle written in our hearts, known and read of all men: Forasmuch as ye are manifestly declared to be the epistle of Christ ministered by us, written not with ink, but with the Spirit of the living God; not in tables of stone, but in fleshy tables of the heart" (2 Cor. 3:3). This image recalls the similar words of Jeremiah, spoken many hundreds of years prior to the ministry of Paul, around the time Lehi left Jerusalem with his family: "But this shall be the covenant that I will make with the house of Israel; After those days, saith the Lord, I will put my law in their inward parts, and write it in their hearts; and will be their God, and they shall be my people" (Jer. 31:33).

A key element in this new kind of covenant, written upon the heart, is penitence and sincere sorrow for sin. Paul's celebrated words capture the essence of the genuinely broken heart and contrite spirit:

> Now I rejoice, not that ye were made sorry, but that ye sorrowed to repentance: for ye were made sorry after a godly manner, that ye might receive damage by us in nothing.
>
> For godly sorrow worketh repentance to salvation not to be repented of: but the sorrow of the world worketh death.
>
> For behold this selfsame thing, that ye sorrowed after a godly sort, what carefulness it wrought in you, yea, what clearing of yourselves, yea, what indignation, yea, what fear, yea, what vehement desire, yea, what zeal, yea, what revenge! In all things ye have approved yourselves to be clear in this matter. (2 Cor. 7:9–11)

It is this godly sorrow for sin, with the resulting repentance and renewal of the spirit through the Atonement of Christ, that transforms individuals into liberated sons and daughters of God—those who find their "sufficiency" in God: "Not that we are sufficient of ourselves to think any thing as of ourselves; but our sufficiency is of God; Who also hath made us able ministers of the new testament; not of the letter, but of the spirit: for the letter killeth, but the spirit giveth life. . . . Now the Lord is that Spirit: and where the Spirit of the Lord is, there is liberty" (2 Cor. 3:5–6, 17).

MODERN PROPHETS SPEAK

James E. Faust:

> The price of discipleship is to forsake evil transgression and enjoy what President Kimball has called "the miracle of forgiveness." It is never too late. But there can be no remission of sin without a godly sorrow being abundantly manifested in the mind, in the heart, and in the actions of the offender. A major step toward purging oneself of wrongdoing is for the transgressor to confess the transgression to the common judge in Israel, who is the inspired bishop or branch president of the offender. While forgiveness comes only from the Lord, confession is necessary, among other reasons, to eliminate the deceit inherent in wrongdoing. (*To Reach Even unto You*, 115)

ILLUSTRATIONS FOR OUR TIME

Here are some points to ponder on godly sorrow: What is the essence of godly sorrow? Have we ever felt godly sorrow? Why is godly sorrow so important in our lives? Do we need to have godly sorrow in order to repent?

The key to having godly sorrow lies in yielding our hearts to the Spirit. King Benjamin taught us well concerning the natural man, one who is an enemy to God and who will not repent:

> For the natural man is an enemy to God, and has been from the fall of Adam, and will be, forever and ever, unless he yields to the enticings of the Holy Spirit, and putteth off the natural man and becometh a saint through the Atonement of Christ the Lord, and becometh as a child, submissive, meek, humble, patient, full of love, willing to submit to all things which the Lord seeth fit to inflict upon him, even as a child doth submit to his father. (Mosiah 3:19)

We learn also in this verse that the only way to overcome the natural man—one who also loves Satan more than God and becomes carnal, sensual, and devilish (see Moses 5:13)—is to yield to the enticings of the Holy Spirit and thus become a Saint.

This is all made possible through the Atonement of Jesus Christ. We then become innocent, like a child, because our guilt is swept away through faith on Jesus Christ and by practicing the principle of repentance (see Enos 1:6–8). Note the words "submissive, meek, humble, patient, and full of love." When we are in this state, we are willing to offer our sacrifice before the Lord, which is part of the process of repentance. And what is that sacrifice? "And ye shall offer for a sacrifice unto me a broken heart and a contrite spirit. And whoso cometh unto me with a broken heart and a contrite spirit, him will I baptize with fire and with the Holy Ghost" (3 Ne 9:20). Godly sorrow is necessary if we are to become purified, justified, and sanctified through the Lord Jesus Christ . . . because we are willing to repent. [Pinegar]

LIKENING THE SCRIPTURES TO OUR LIVES

2 Corinthians 7:10 For godly sorrow worketh repentance to salvation not to be repented of: but the sorrow of the world worketh death.

Application: Only through godly sorrow can we fully repent and be forgiven of our sins.

4. BECOMING RECONCILED TO GOD

THEME: Becoming reconciled through repentance and the Atonement of Jesus Christ is the essence of spiritual regeneration.

MOMENT OF TRUTH

Reconciliation to the Father through the intercession of the Son is the essence of our hope in Christ. Paul teaches this doctrine with clarity and eloquence in 2 Corinthians:

> Therefore if any man be in Christ, he is a new creature: old things are passed away; behold, all things are become new.
>
> And all things are of God, who hath reconciled us to himself by Jesus Christ, and hath given to us the ministry of reconciliation;
>
> To wit, that God was in Christ, reconciling the world unto himself, not imputing their trespasses unto them; and hath committed unto us the word of reconciliation.
>
> Now then we are ambassadors for Christ, as though God did beseech you by us: we pray you in Christ's stead, be ye reconciled to God.
>
> For he hath made him to be sin for us, who knew no sin; that we might be made the righteousness of God in him. (2 Cor. 5:17–21)

The emissaries of the Lord—chief among whom was Paul in regard to conveying the gospel to the Gentiles—are most assuredly bearers of "the word of reconciliation," as he called it, for the message of the gospel is centered in the Atonement, which is based on divine intercession, love, and advocacy. "My grace is sufficient for thee, for my strength is made perfect in weakness" (2 Cor. 12:9) is how Paul—sensitive to his own weaknesses—quoted the consoling words of the Lord. Then Paul concludes his epistle with this apostolic blessing and admonition: "Finally, brethren, farewell. Be perfect, be of good comfort, be of one mind, live in peace; and the God of love and peace shall be with you" (2 Cor. 13:11).

MODERN PROPHETS SPEAK

Bruce R. McConkie:

> In pleading with men to believe in Christ and be reconciled to God so as to gain a remission of their sins, Nephi said: "we talk of Christ, we rejoice in Christ, we preach of Christ, we prophesy of Christ, . . . [for] the right way is to believe in Christ, and deny him not; and Christ is the Holy One of Israel; wherefore ye must bow down before him, and worship him with all your might, mind, and strength, and your whole soul; and if ye do this ye shall in nowise be cast out" (2 Ne. 25:26, 29). (CR, October 1970, 127)

ILLUSTRATIONS FOR OUR TIME

Here are some questions to ponder regarding the doctrine of reconciliation: What does it mean to be reconciled to God? What do we have to do to be reconciled? Bruce R. McConkie answers these provoking questions. He has said:

> Through the Lord's atoning sacrifice, reconciliation between God and man is possible (Jac. 4:11). In other words, man is ransomed from a state of sin and spiritual darkness and restored to one of harmony and unity with Deity. To those who by faith had become new creatures of the Holy Ghost, Paul wrote: God "hath reconciled us to himself by Jesus Christ, and hath given to us the ministry of reconciliation; To wit, that God was in Christ, reconciling the world unto himself, not imputing their trespasses unto them; and hath committed unto us the word of reconciliation. Now then we are ambassadors for Christ, as though God did beseech you by us: we pray you in Christ's stead, be ye reconciled to God" (2 Cor. 5:17–20; Rom. 5:8–12; 11:15; Heb. 2:17). Jacob gave similar counsel: "Reconcile yourselves to the will of God, and not to the will of the devil and the flesh; and remember, after ye are reconciled unto God, that it is only in and through the grace of God that ye are saved" (2 Ne. 10:24; 25:23; 33:9). (*MD,* 620)

It behooves us to partake of the goodness of God through the Atonement of our Savior Jesus Christ, become reconciled to God and help others do likewise. [Pinegar]

The Divine Reconciliation
A pall of gray hung over the streets of Washington, D.C., on that November morning in 1963 as Jackie Kennedy and her two little ones, dressed in solemn black, made their way down the east steps of the Capitol. My wife and I watched in silence along with tens of thousands of other mourning onlookers. The endless, plaintive roll of the drums accompanied the caisson through the rain-drenched streets of the city as it bore the body of the fallen president to its resting place at Arlington Cemetery. In our mortal experience, few events rival the profound grief that attends the unexpected loss of a national hero—a president, a king, a queen, a worldly leader of stature. And herein lies a lesson.

The most important event in all of the history of mankind took place when the King of Heaven gave His life for us and then took it up again through the Resurrection. From the foundations of the world, His death and Easter rising from the grave enabled and empowered God's children to transcend the temporal death with ultimate immortal renewal and, through faith and obedience, achieve salvation and eternal life. No earthly king could do what the Heavenly King did for us. No earthly king could merit our allegiance to that degree of gratitude where we sing praises to the very preserver of life and spiritual vitality. He testified to the ancient Americans at the time of His post-resurrection visit to Bountiful: "Behold, I am Jesus Christ, whom the prophets testified shall come into the world. And behold, I am the light and the life of the world; and I have drunk out of that bitter cup which the Father hath given me, and have glorified the Father in taking upon me the sins of the world, in the which I have suffered the will of the Father in all things from the beginning" (3 Ne. 11:10–11).

It was this immortal sacrifice that enabled and empowered the divine intercession between God and man that is at the heart of the gospel of Jesus Christ. It was this eternal Atonement that made a reconciliation with Deity a reality, allowing mankind, through obedience, to be reborn of the water and of the Spirit. As Paul declared: "Therefore if any man be in Christ, he is a new creature: old things are passed away; behold, all things are become new. And all things are of God, who hath reconciled us to himself by Jesus Christ, and hath given to us the ministry of reconciliation" (2 Cor. 5:17–18). [Allen]

LIKENING THE SCRIPTURES TO OUR LIVES

2 Nephi 10:24 Wherefore, my beloved brethren, reconcile yourselves to the will of God, and not to the will of the devil and the flesh; and remember, after ye are reconciled unto God, that it is only in and through the grace of God that ye are saved.

2 Nephi 25:23 For we labor diligently to write, to persuade our children, and also our brethren, to believe in Christ, and to be reconciled to God; for we know that it is by grace that we are saved, after all we can do.

2 Corinthians 5:18 And all things are of God, who hath reconciled us to himself by Jesus Christ, and hath given to us the ministry of reconciliation.

Application: We, through Christ and the merciful plan of our Heavenly Father, can be reconciled to God. In turn, we should help others to come unto Christ and thus be reconciled to God. This should be our work and glory.

SUMMARY

What a blessing it is to be able to open the pages of 2 Corinthians and savor the bread of life, served up by a master teacher in a banquet of timeless spiritual doctrine. We learn that we can overcome all trials and tribulations through the strength of the Lord. Is that not a relevant principle for our times as well as for the Corinthian Saints of old? We learn that forgiveness is the essence of the divine character of the Savior. Does that not still apply to each of us in modern times? We learn what it means to display godly sorrow for our sins, so that we can become reconciled to God through the intercession of the Only Begotten. What a timeless message that is!

CHAPTER 36

"BELOVED *of* GOD,
CALLED TO BE SAINTS"

Reading Assignment: Romans.

Additional Reading: Bible Dictionary, "Grace" (697); "Saint" (767); "Pauline Epistles: Romans" (745).

> *Furthermore, even though the world worsens and coarsens, we can, notwithstanding, pro-*
> *ceed with our Lord-given task of putting off the natural man and becoming saint-like.*
> *Simultaneously, though we feel weak, our help is much needed by those hundreds of thou-*
> *sands of converts coming into the Church who will be undertaking the very same "mighty*
> *change" in their hearts and lives.*
>
>   *As together we become less spotted by the world and more pure, achieving this con-*
> *dition in a time of gross immorality and corruption, then we can become worthy of being*
> *called "true believers in Christ."*
>
> —NEAL A. MAXWELL, *NOTWITHSTANDING MY WEAKNESS* [SALT LAKE CITY: DESERET
> BOOK, 1981], 2.

THEMES *for* LIVING
1. Justified by Faith in Jesus Christ
2. Joint-heirs with Christ
3. Becoming a Saint—Living a Saintly Life

INTRODUCTION

We become "Saints" as we enter into the covenant of baptism and receive the Holy Ghost. We change because we are converted to Jesus Christ and His gospel. We take upon us the name of Jesus Christ, and because of this, we should think and act differently. We become a Saint as described by King Benjamin: "he yields to the enticings of the Holy Spirit, and putteth off the natural man and becometh a saint through the Atonement of Christ the Lord, and becometh as a child, submissive, meek, humble, patient, full of love, willing to submit to all things which the Lord seeth fit to inflict upon him, even as a child doth submit to his father" (Mosiah 3:19). This is a process of becoming, not an event. We become holy and without blemish, even unspotted from the world, as we apply the Atonement to our lives through faith unto repentance (see Alma 34:15–17). This requires great faith, the foundation of all righteousness, to make the mighty change and be born again. By so doing, we will be rewarded to become joint-heirs with Christ. We must press forward steadfastly as described by Nephi:

And now, my beloved brethren, after ye have gotten into this strait and narrow path, I would ask if all is done? Behold, I say unto you, Nay; for ye have not come thus far save it were by the word of Christ with unshaken faith in him, relying wholly upon the merits of him who is mighty to save.

Wherefore, ye must press forward with a steadfastness in Christ, having a perfect brightness of hope, and a love of God and of all men. Wherefore, if ye shall press forward, feasting upon the word of Christ, and endure to the end, behold, thus saith the Father: Ye shall have eternal life.

And now, behold, my beloved brethren, this is the way; and there is none other way nor name given under heaven whereby man can be saved in the kingdom of God. And now, behold, this is the doctrine of Christ, and the only and true doctrine of the Father, and of the Son, and of the Holy Ghost, which is one God, without end. Amen. (2 Ne. 31:19–21)

1. JUSTIFIED BY FAITH IN JESUS CHRIST

THEME: We stand approved before the Lord, justified through the Atonement and by the Holy Ghost, as we exercise our faith in Jesus Christ and bring forth good works, confirming our devotion and commitment to the cause of building up the kingdom of God.

MOMENT OF TRUTH

Paul wrote his Epistle to the Romans in the time frame A.D. 55 to A.D. 57, toward the end of his stay in Corinth, as referred to in Acts 20:3. In part, the epistle was intended to prepare the Saints at Rome for a planned visit by Paul and, in part, to summarize and explicate certain key doctrines of truth that were being accepted and adopted by the new converts. Among these was the doctrine of justification through faith in Jesus Christ (see Rom. 3:10–25). At the basis of this doctrine is the fact that all people, by virtue of their mortal estate, fall short of perfection and absolute compliance with the laws of God: "As it is written, There is none righteous, no, not one: There is none that understandeth, there is none that seeketh after God. They are all gone out of the way, they are together become unprofitable; there is none that doeth good, no, not one. . . . Therefore by the deeds of the law there shall no flesh be justified in his sight: for by the law is the knowledge of sin" (Rom. 3:10–12, 20; compare Rom. 7:14–25). Against the bleakness of this awful verity shines forth the glory of the Atonement of the Lamb of God to bring about a reconciliation through grace: "For all have sinned, and come short of the glory of God; Being justified freely by his grace through the redemption that is in Christ Jesus: Whom God hath set forth to be a propitiation through faith in his blood, to declare his righteousness for the remission of sins that are past, through the forbearance of God" (Rom. 3:23–25).

Those who, through faith, accept the Lord and follow His counsel—and are thus justified before God—are counseled by Paul not to lapse into a state of self-satisfied boasting, for the gift comes of God, not of ourselves and not of our own doing in the absence of heavenly intervention: "Therefore we conclude that a man is justified by faith without the deeds of the law" (Rom. 3:28).

Many hundreds of years before the ministry of Paul, the prophet Lehi counseled Jacob and his other sons on this same doctrine, speaking in terms that cannot be misunderstood:

And men are instructed sufficiently that they know good from evil. And the law is given unto men. And by the law no flesh is justified; or, by the law men are cut off. Yea, by the temporal law they were cut off; and also, by the spiritual law they perish from that which is good, and become miserable forever.

Wherefore, redemption cometh in and through the Holy Messiah; for he is full of grace and truth.

Behold, he offereth himself a sacrifice for sin, to answer the ends of the law, unto all those who have a broken heart and a contrite spirit; and unto none else can the ends of the law be answered.

Wherefore, how great the importance to make these things known unto the inhabitants of the earth, that they may know that there is no flesh that can dwell in the presence of God, save it be through the merits, and mercy, and grace of the Holy Messiah, who layeth down his life according to the flesh, and taketh it again by the power of the Spirit, that he may bring to pass the resurrection of the dead, being the first that should rise. (2 Ne. 2:5–8)

Like Lehi, Paul emphasizes the obligations that justification brings upon the believer to act in patience and love:

> Therefore being justified by faith, we have peace with God through our Lord Jesus Christ:
>
> By whom also we have access by faith into this grace wherein we stand, and rejoice in hope of the glory of God.
>
> And not only *so,* but we glory in tribulations also: knowing that tribulation worketh patience;
>
> And patience, experience; and experience, hope:
>
> And hope maketh not ashamed; because the love of God is shed abroad in our hearts by the Holy Ghost which is given unto us. (Rom. 5:1–5)

It is for this reason—justification through the Atonement made effectual on the basis of faith—that Paul extols the magnificence of the gospel of Jesus Christ, saying: "For I am not ashamed of the gospel of Christ: for it is the power of God unto salvation to every one that believeth; to the Jew first, and also to the Greek. For therein is the righteousness of God revealed from faith to faith: as it is written, The just shall live by faith" (Rom. 1:16–17).

MODERN PROPHETS SPEAK

Bruce R. McConkie:

> What then is the law of justification? It is simply this: "All covenants, contracts, bonds, obligations, oaths, vows, performances, connections, associations, or expectations" (D&C 132:7), in which men must abide to be saved and exalted, must be entered into and performed in righteousness so that the Holy Spirit can justify the candidate for salvation in what has been done (1 Ne. 16:2; Jac. 2:13–14; Alma 41:15; D&C 98; 132:1, 62). *An act that is justified by the Spirit is one that is sealed by the Holy Spirit of Promise, or in other words, ratified and approved by the Holy Ghost.* This law of justification is the provision the Lord has placed in the gospel to assure that no unrighteous performance will be binding on earth and in heaven, and that no person will add to his position or glory in the hereafter by gaining an unearned blessing.
>
> As with all other doctrines of salvation, justification is available because of the atoning sacrifice of Christ, but it becomes operative in the life of an individual only on conditions of personal righteousness. As Paul taught, men are not justified by the works of the Mosaic law alone any more than men are saved by those works alone. The grace of God, manifest through the infinite and eternal Atonement wrought by

his Son, makes justification a living reality for those who seek righteousness (Isa. 53:11; Mosiah 14:11). (*MD*, 408)

ILLUSTRATIONS FOR OUR TIME

Here are several points to ponder on the subject of justification: What is justification by faith? How do we increase in our faith? What is the relationship between our faith and the Lord's infinite Atonement? What role does the Holy Ghost play in our being justified?

When our faith is exercised as the moving cause of all action, it gives us power to do all things. The most important thing we can do with our faith, as it relates to our individual exaltation, is to repent. Repentance is our part of the reconciliatory process acting on the goodness and grace of God in providing the Atonement of our Beloved Savior Jesus Christ. We can increase our faith as we hear the word of God through the words of those inspired by the Holy Ghost (see Rom. 10:14–17; D&C 68:3–7) and as we search the scriptures (see Rom. 10:17). Our faith will also increase as we fast and pray for this precious gift (see Hel. 3:35). Our faith, which moves us to repentance, is our link to the atoning sacrifice of our Savior. Paul reminds us that with faith we are doers of the word: "For not the hearers of the law are just before God, but the doers of the law shall be justified" (Rom. 2:13). The Holy Ghost can then put His seal upon this action, "For by the water ye keep the commandment; by the Spirit ye are justified, and by the blood ye are sanctified" (Moses 6:60). [Pinegar]

LIKENING THE SCRIPTURES TO OUR LIVES

2 Nephi 25:23 For we labor diligently to write, to persuade our children, and also our brethren, to believe in Christ, and to be reconciled to God; for we know that it is by grace that we are saved, after all we can do.

Application: We must never forget that it is only through the Atonement that repentance is made possible to provide us an escape from our fallen state. Gratitude for the goodness of God should move us to obedience and righteousness.

2. JOINT-HEIRS WITH CHRIST

THEME: We can become joint-heirs with the Lord Jesus Christ by honoring and filling the requirements of our covenant bond with God.

MOMENT OF TRUTH

Paul confirmed for the Roman Saints the transcendent symbolism of baptism as a representation of the death and resurrection of the Lord, He willingly submersing Himself in the vault of death and then coming forth again as the curator of all life and the firstfruits of the Resurrection:

> What shall we say then? Shall we continue in sin, that grace may abound?
>
> God forbid. How shall we, that are dead to sin, live any longer therein?
>
> Know ye not, that so many of us as were baptized into Jesus Christ were baptized into his death?
>
> Therefore we are buried with him by baptism into death: that like as Christ was raised up from the dead by the glory of the Father, even so we also should walk in newness of life.
>
> For if we have been planted together in the likeness of his death, we shall be also in the likeness of his resurrection:
>
> Knowing this, that our old man is crucified with him, that the body of sin might be destroyed, that henceforth we should not serve sin.
>
> For he that is dead is freed from sin. (Rom. 6:1–7; compare D&C 76:50–52)

The process of coming into the fold of Christ and participating in the Abrahamic covenant (either through lineage or through adoption—Rom. 8:23) brings with it extraordinary blessings, including becoming joint-heirs with Christ:

> For as many as are led by the Spirit of God, they are the sons of God.
>
> For ye have not received the spirit of bondage again to fear; but ye have received the Spirit of adoption, whereby we cry, Abba, Father.
>
> The Spirit itself beareth witness with our spirit, that we are the children of God:
>
> And if children, then heirs; heirs of God, and joint-heirs with Christ; if so be that we suffer with him, that we may be also glorified together.
>
> For I reckon that the sufferings of this present time are not worthy to be compared with the glory which shall be revealed in us. . . .
>
> And not only they, but ourselves also, which have the firstfruits of the Spirit, even we ourselves groan within ourselves, waiting for the adoption, to wit, the redemption of our body.
>
> For we are saved by hope. (Rom. 8:14–18, 23–24)

As joint-heirs of Christ, we can look forward in faith and hope—beyond the veil of tears and tribulation that all too often defines our mortal existence—to an eternal reward of glory in the hereafter with Father and Son:

And we know that all things work together for good to them that love God, to them who are the called according to his purpose. . . .

For I am persuaded, that neither death, nor life, nor angels, nor principalities, nor powers, nor things present, nor things to come,

Nor height, nor depth, nor any other creature, shall be able to separate us from the love of God, which is in Christ Jesus our Lord. (Rom. 8:28, 38–39)

MODERN PROPHETS SPEAK

Bruce R. McConkie:

A joint-heir is one who inherits equally with all other heirs including the Chief Heir who is the Son. Each joint-heir has an equal and an undivided portion of the whole of everything. If one knows all things, so do all others. If one has all power, so do all those who inherit jointly with him. If the universe belongs to one, so it does equally to the total of all upon whom the joint inheritances are bestowed.

Joint-heirs are possessors of all things (D&C 50:26–28). All things are theirs for they have exaltation (D&C 76:50–60). They are made "equal" with their Lord (D&C 88:107). They gain all power both in heaven and on earth and receive the fulness of the Father, and all knowledge and truth are theirs (D&C 93:15–30). They are gods (D&C 132:20). Celestial marriage is the gate to this high state of exaltation (*DS, 2:24, 35–39;* D&C 131:1–4; 132). (*MD,* 395)

ILLUSTRATIONS FOR OUR TIME

All That My Father Hath

In his Epistle to the Romans, the Apostle Paul expounds the glorious doctrine of joint-heirship with God: "The Spirit itself beareth witness with our spirit, that we are the children of God: And if children, then heirs; heirs of God, and joint-heirs with Christ; if so be that we suffer with him, that we may be also glorified together" (Rom. 8:16–17). In similar terms, according to the oath and covenant of the priesthood, those who honor and magnify their priesthood stand to receive blessings of unspeakable magnitude: "And he that receiveth my Father receiveth my Father's kingdom; therefore all that my Father hath shall be given unto him" (D&C 84:38). To receive all that the Father has is a promise of overpowering scope and reach. How can we fathom such a blessing?

I can recall as a young boy having the opportunity to accompany my father on numerous fishing trips in the Canadian Rockies, not far from where we lived. On one occasion, he invited an underprivileged youth from the neighborhood to come with us—a boy who had few such opportunities. The lad was excited, and we were happy to have him join us. The highway toward the mountains happened to pass by a large

ranch that the Church owned and operated at that time as part of the welfare program. As we were passing by the ranch, my father spoke up and said to the boy,
"There is your ranch."

"What do you mean?" asked the boy in wonderment over the abundance and
beauty of the property.

"That is part of the Church," my father said, "and since you belong to the
Church, that is your ranch also."

The boy's eyes opened wide and he started to smile. "That is *my* ranch, too?"

"Yes," confirmed my father, with words to this effect: "God has promised us that
if we are faithful, everything He has will be ours. And that means you, too."

I could see a look of peace come over the boy's face as he contemplated the privilege of belonging to the kingdom of God where such blessings are reserved for the
righteous. And I confess, too, that I felt a keen sense of pride in sharing ownership of
God's creation and kingdom. My father had discerned a teaching moment and took
advantage of it in a quiet and effective way that has echoed in my heart ever since.

To this day, I still think of that occasion when I read scriptures such as the following: "He that spared not his own Son, but delivered him up for us all, how shall
he not with him also freely give us all things?" (Rom. 8:32). Against the promise of so
much spiritual wealth, it should be an easy thing to throw off the tentacles of worldly
entanglements and avoid the snares of materialistic excess. As John the Revelator
stated: "He that overcometh shall inherit all things; and I will be his God, and he shall
be my son" (Rev. 21:7). [Allen]

LIKENING THE SCRIPTURES TO OUR LIVES

Romans 8:16–17 The Spirit itself beareth witness with our spirit, that we are the children of God: And if children, then heirs; heirs of God, and joint-heirs with Christ; if
so be that we suffer with him, that we may be also glorified together.

Application: As the divine spirit children of God the Eternal Father, we have the right
of being heirs, provided we fulfill in obedience all things that the Lord requires of us.
When we do all these things and partake of all the covenants and ordinances regarding
exaltation, we can receive all that the Father has (see D&C 84:38).

3. BECOMING A SAINT— LIVING A SAINTLY LIFE

THEME: The task and test of mortality, following the reception of the lifesaving
covenants and ordinances, is to live a saintly and Christlike life.

MOMENT OF TRUTH

Paul concludes the doctrinal aspects of his epistle to the Romans with an exhortation to live a righteous life (see Rom. 12–15). A desirable and godlike quality of life reflects a commitment to do the following: apply the several gifts of the Spirit for the good of the community of Christ (see Rom. 12:6–8); "Abhor that which is evil; cleave to that which is good" (Rom. 12:9); cultivate brotherly love, industry, hope, patience, charity, forgiveness, and humility (see Rom. 12:9–20); "Be not overcome of evil, but overcome evil with good" (Rom. 12:21); sustain the anointed leaders of the Church (see Rom. 13:6); keep the commandments—sufficiently encapsulated in the enjoinder "Thou shalt love thy neighbour as thyself" (Rom. 13:9); "cast off the works of darkness" and "put on the armour of light" (Rom. 13:12); and avoid the unrighteous judgment of others (see Rom. 14:1–11), but rather fellowship the Saints in the spirit of love and harmony:

> Now the God of patience and consolation grant you to be likeminded one toward another according to Christ Jesus:
>
> That ye may with one mind and one mouth glorify God, even the Father of our Lord Jesus Christ.
>
> Wherefore receive ye one another, as Christ also received us to the glory of God. (Rom. 15:5–7)

MODERN PROPHETS SPEAK

Howard W. Hunter:

> Following the Savior will bring unmeasured blessings. We sense that our people everywhere are striving more diligently to live Christlike lives, which is our charge. Following the Savior will bring us unmeasured blessings, protection, and opportunities. The doctrines that the Savior taught contain the answers to our problems, both personally and collectively. No message is more needed in the world. Individuals and nations can find peace and prosperity by hearkening to the words of the Master. Of this I bear solemn witness. (*THWH*, 45)

ILLUSTRATIONS FOR OUR TIME

"The Savior: An Example for Everyone"

> While some may think otherwise, the Savior never added a footnote to his life or to his of teachings that said, "By the way, everything that I have done and everything that I have said is relevant to only 48 percent of the population; the other 52 percent will have to look some place else to find the way, the truth, and the light,

because what I have said and what I have done are not relevant to women." Instead, he came to teach all people, both men and women, the kind of life our Father in heaven would have us lead.

Yet often, sometimes without even realizing it, we women hear certain of the Savior's teachings and we think that while it is a beautiful message, it doesn't apply to us, or at least not very forcefully. I would even guess that nearly every woman has at some time, in some way, excused herself from really responding to the admonitions of the Savior, simply because she is a woman. What a tragedy it is to think that the one perfect life that was ever lived, the one infallible example that we have, the one teacher we have as to what to do with our earth life, is somehow not fully for us. . . .

To know that we are daughters of our Father in heaven should give us a tremendous sense of joy but also a tremendous sense of responsibility. I hope we can say to ourselves, "I am the daughter of my Father in heaven. As his daughter, I know that I am important because I am me. I know I am capable of great growth, capable of significant service. I will not cancel myself in any way by yielding to false influences that tell me that I am a shallow being or a being of lesser worth or lesser ability. I know that the Savior's examples and teachings were to all people. I will please my Father in heaven by taking his daughters seriously." (Karen Lynn Davidson, "The Savior: An Example for Everyone," in *Woman to Woman: Selected Talks from the BYU Women's Conferences* [Salt Lake City: Deseret Book, 1986], 102–3, 113)

LIKENING THE SCRIPTURES TO OUR LIVES

Romans 12:1–2 I beseech you therefore, brethren, by the mercies of God, that ye present your bodies a living sacrifice, holy, acceptable unto God, which is your reasonable service. And be not conformed to this world: but be ye transformed by the renewing of your mind, that ye may prove what is that good, and acceptable, and perfect, will of God.

Application: Our goal is to do all we can to conform our mind to the will of God. As we do this, our lives will be patterned after our Savior Jesus Christ—we will have charity, and when He appears, we will be like Him (see Moro. 7:48).

SUMMARY

We are privileged to sit at the feet of Paul the Apostle and bask in the light of truth, confirming our faith in the gospel of Jesus Christ according to the words of this devoted and magnanimous Apostle. As such, we participate in the faith-building process that Paul recommended to the Roman Saints:

How then shall they call on him in whom they have not believed? and how shall they believe in him of whom they have not heard? and how shall they hear without a preacher?

And how shall they preach, except they be sent? as it is written, How beautiful are the feet of them that preach the gospel of peace, and bring glad tidings of good things!

But they have not all obeyed the gospel. For Esaias [Isaiah] saith, Lord, who hath believed our report?

So then faith cometh by hearing, and hearing by the word of God. (Rom. 10:14–17)

As we read the epistles of Paul, we hear the word of God spoken to us. The word of God through Paul to the Romans embraces the doctrines of justification through faith in Jesus Christ, becoming joint-heirs with the Savior, and being perfected in righteousness by living a saintly and Christlike life. In this we are confirmed in our faith: "And we know that all things work together for good to them that love God, to them who are the called according to his purpose" (Rom. 8:28).

CHAPTER 37

JESUS CHRIST: "THE AUTHOR and FINISHER of OUR FAITH"

Reading Assignment: Hebrews.

Additional Reading: Bible Dictionary, "Pauline Epistles: Epistle to the Hebrews" (746–47).

> *Christ is the Author of Salvation. This means that he made salvation available to all men in that he worked out the infinite and eternal atonement. Paul's statement that Christ is "the author of eternal salvation unto all them that obey him" (Heb. 5:9), as the marginal reading shows, means that he is the "cause" thereof; that is, salvation is possible because of his atoning sacrifice; without this sacrifice there would be no salvation. Paul's other statement that Christ is "the author and finisher of our faith" (Heb. 12:2), also according to the marginal reading, means that he is the "leader" in the cause of salvation.*
>
> —BRUCE R. MCCONKIE, *MD*, 66.

THEMES for LIVING
1. Jesus Christ Is Our Savior and Redeemer
2. The Melchizedek Priesthood
3. The Gospel of Jesus Christ—The New Covenant with the Children of God
4. Exercise Faith in Jesus Christ

INTRODUCTION

Jesus Christ is our only hope of salvation and eternal life. He was the Creator, the promised Messiah, the Only Begotten Son of God in the flesh, and the Anointed One who would atone for all mankind, who through obedience to His commandments, can return to the presence of our Heavenly Father. Paul reminds us of our total dependence upon our Savior Jesus Christ: "Looking unto Jesus the author and finisher of our faith; who for the joy that was set before him endured the cross, despising the shame, and is set down at the right hand of the throne of God" (Heb. 12:2). Through Jesus Christ, as the "author of eternal salvation unto all them that obey him" (Heb. 5:9), we can enter into God's rest. In bringing forth the new and higher covenant of salvation, the Lord restored the Melchizedek Priesthood (see Heb. 7:11). The Law of Moses was fulfilled, and the gospel of Jesus Christ, with its new covenant, was established in the dispensation of the meridian of time. By exercising faith in Jesus Christ and entering into the higher law of grace and reconciliation, one could, by keeping the commandments, inherit the kingdom of God.

1. JESUS CHRIST IS OUR SAVIOR AND REDEEMER

THEME: Jesus Christ is the Only Begotten Son of God the Father in the flesh. He is the Creator of all things and the only name under heaven by which we can be saved.

MOMENT OF TRUTH

Sometime shortly after A.D. 60, at the end of his third mission, Paul wrote the Epistle to the Hebrews—intended for the Jewish members of the Church—to confirm the doctrines and practices of the higher gospel law of Jesus Christ that had superseded the law of Moses. Many generations of tradition regarding the former ways of worship and religious practice were, for some, apparently, difficult to abandon. They had given themselves over to being "zealous of the law" (Acts 21:20) and needed redirection and refocusing on the truth that the work of Moses was a preparatory work pointing to the ministry and Atonement of the Savior. Paul provided in Hebrews an elegant and carefully crafted discourse on the mission of the Savior, incorporating numerous references from the Old Testament to substantiate the fact that the atoning sacrifice and the institution of the higher law was the fulfillment of centuries of prophetic anticipation.

    The brief opening chapter of Hebrews is a superb and moving portrait of the Savior that begins:

God, who at sundry times and in divers manners spake in time past unto the fathers
by the prophets,

Hath in these last days spoken unto us by his Son, whom he hath appointed
heir of all things, by whom also he made the worlds;

Who being the brightness of his glory, and the express image of his person, and
upholding all things by the word of his power, when he had by himself purged our
sins, sat down on the right hand of the Majesty on high. (Heb. 1:1–3)

The sublime language of this portrayal, which is extended and expanded in the
subsequent chapters of Hebrews, stimulates readers to ask themselves the questions:
"If I were asked to provide a characterization of the Savior from the depths of my
heart, how would I render my feelings? How would I express my innermost convictions of the divinity and everlasting power of this magnificent Being?" Paul's language
and treatment of this sacred subject provide a splendid model for us to follow.

Some analysts have thought the literary style of Hebrews to be somewhat different from that used in the other epistles of Paul; however, the Bible Dictionary
points out that "the ideas are certainly Paul's" (746). His authoritative leadership
helped to stabilize the community of Saints in his day, uphold the doctrines and truths
of the higher law, and testify through the Spirit of the verity of Christ's atoning mission—all in ways that still touch the hearts of believers and resound to the glory of
God and the Son.

MODERN PROPHETS SPEAK

Gordon B. Hinckley:

With certitude I give you my witness of the truth. I know that God our Eternal
Father lives. I know that Jesus is the Christ, the Savior and Redeemer of mankind,
the author of our salvation. (*Faith: The Essence of True Religion* [Salt Lake City:
Deseret Book, 1989], 6)

Thomas S. Monson:

His laws were not inscribed upon stone, but upon human hearts. I speak of the Master
Teacher, even Jesus Christ, the Son of God, the Savior and Redeemer of all mankind.
(*Conference Classics*, 3 vols. [Salt Lake City: Deseret Book, 1981–1984], 2:38)

[Jesus Christ] is a teacher of truth—but He is more than a teacher. He is the Exemplar
of the perfect life—but He is more than an exemplar. He is the Great Physician—but
He is more than a physician. He is the literal Savior of the world, the Son of God, the
Prince of Peace, the Holy One of Israel, even the risen Lord. ("Your Personal
Influence," *Ensign,* May 2004, 23)

James E. Faust:

> Mine is the certain knowledge that Jesus is our divine Savior, Redeemer, and the Son of God the Father. I know of his reality by a sure perception so sacred I cannot give utterance to it. (*Finding Light in a Dark World* [Salt Lake City: Deseret Book, 1995], 38)

ENRICHMENT SECTION

Let us remember that the purpose of our Savior is to assist us in doing all we can to bring about our immortality and eternal life. Our purpose is to center our lives on our Savior Jesus Christ and His gospel plan. As we live the gospel and receive the sacred ordinances of the temple, we come to know our Savior and can receive the blessings of exaltation. We hope and pray for all mankind to come unto Christ, that they may partake of His goodness and eventually return to our heavenly home in the celestial kingdom, blessed with the presence of both Father and Son.

Here are some ideas to help us understand and apply the principles and doctrines concerning how to know, accept, love, and follow Christ:

1. Know and Accept That Jesus Is the Christ—the Savior and Redeemer of the World.

- Search the scriptures, for they testify of Christ—The word of God testifies of Christ (see John 5:39). As we learn of Christ through His words, we shall enjoy His peace (see D&C 19:23). The prophets and the scriptures speak of God and Christ (see Alma 30:44). The Book of Mormon is to convince the world that Jesus is the Christ (see title page of the Book of Mormon).
- Seek revelation from God—We can know that Jesus is the Christ by the power of revelation (see Matt. 16:17). The Holy Ghost will give us this knowledge (see 1 Cor. 12:3). Through our prayers, we can learn the truth of all things (see Moro. 10:5).
- Do the will of God and you will know of the truthfulness of the doctrine of Christ—When we live the doctrine of Christ, we will know the Author (see John 7:17).
- All things testify of God and Christ—The magnificent creation speaks of God (see Alma 30:44).

2. Love Our Savior Jesus Christ.

- Remember the goodness of our Savior at all times—Everything the Lord has done for us, including the infinite Atonement, is because He loves us (see 2 Ne. 26:24). We should love Him because He first loved us (see 1 Jn. 4:19). Does this not fill our hearts with gratitude?

- Remember that He succors us in all things—The Savior suffered so He would be able to help us according to the flesh (see Alma 7:11–12). The Savior blesses us in all things. We truly are indebted to Him for our very lives (see Mosiah 2:21). Surely this should inspire us to keep the commandments (see Mosiah 2:22), because when we love Him we will keep His commandments (see John 14:15).

3. Follow Our Savior Jesus Christ.

- In accepting the principles of the gospel of Jesus Christ we "come unto Him"— Through faith, repentance, baptism, and receiving the Holy Ghost, we take upon ourselves the name of Jesus Christ. We become His sons and daughters (see Mosiah 5:7). These are the first steps in following our Savior. As we endure to the end, we can be perfected and enter into our exaltation (see 3 Ne. 12:48; Moro. 10:32).
- We live by the word of God—We live by every word of our Lord and Savior (see D&C 84:43–46), and the Word will tell us all things that we should do (see 2 Ne. 32:3).
- We seek to build up the kingdom of God—As members of the Church, we seek to magnify our callings (see JST, Matt. 6:38) by bringing souls unto Christ (see Alma 29:9–10; Alma 36:24), strengthening our brothers and sisters (see D&C 108:7), and entering into our temple covenants for our eternal blessing and that of our forebears through vicarious service (see D&C 128:15).

ILLUSTRATIONS FOR OUR TIME

"That Was Christ"

I was attending the celebrated Passion Play at Oberammergau in southern Germany in 1960, along with a number of other missionaries. It was interesting to walk the streets of this quaint and beautiful village and observe the townsfolk, virtually all of whom participated on stage during the performances. Every man, woman, and child looked as though they had just stepped out of a period of time millennia old. At one point, we entered the bookstore near the theater to purchase a copy of the text for the performance next day. As we were considering our purchase, we noticed a distinguished gentleman enter the store. He had a pleasant countenance, with a prepossessing smile, a well-trimmed beard, and long, neat tresses. Everyone in the store fell silent at his approach. He made a purchase and then left. Noting our puzzled looks, the saleswoman leaned over and whispered to us in hushed tones, "Das war der Christus" ("That was Christ"). It gave us a chill to think that we had come so close to "Christus"—even though in this case he was only an actor, albeit one who commanded great respect in the village, even reverence.

Then we pondered the lesson flowing out of this brief encounter: "Beloved, now are we the sons of God, and it doth not yet appear what we shall be: but we know that, when he shall appear, we shall be like him; for we shall see him as he is" (1 Jn. 3:2). There will come a time, for all mankind, when the encounter with the Son of God will be literal—for the faithful and obedient, a moment of glory and peace; for the disobedient and non-valiant, a moment of profound remorse. And when we see Him, we will also see the Father, for Christ is "the brightness of his glory, and the express image of his person" (Heb 1:3). As we are created in the image of God and His Son, we are reminded to honor this heritage and rise spiritually to meet the awesome potential that is within us. [Allen]

LIKENING THE SCRIPTURES TO OUR LIVES

Matthew 16:15–17 He saith unto them, But whom say ye that I am? And Simon Peter answered and said, Thou art the Christ, the Son of the living God. And Jesus answered and said unto him, Blessed art thou, Simon Barjona: for flesh and blood hath not revealed it unto thee, but my Father which is in heaven.

Application: We, like Peter, must all come to know by revelation that Jesus is the Christ. We must have a witness by the power of the Holy Ghost that Jesus is the Christ (see John 15:26; 1 Cor. 12:3; 2 Ne. 31:18; 3 Ne. 16:6; D&C 46:3). As we study, pray, and live His word, we will come to know that Jesus is the Christ by the power of the Holy Ghost.

2. THE MELCHIZEDEK PRIESTHOOD

THEME: The Holy Melchizedek Priesthood is always restored with its power and keys in each dispensation of time. The Melchizedek Priesthood is the power to act for God and administers the lifesaving covenants and ordinances of the gospel in the kingdom of God here upon the earth.

MOMENT OF TRUTH

In chapter three of his Epistle to the Hebrews, Paul invites his audience to consider the sacred office and calling of Jesus Christ:

> Wherefore, holy brethren, partakers of the heavenly calling, consider the Apostle and High Priest of our profession, Christ Jesus;
> Who was faithful to him that appointed him, as also Moses was faithful in all his house.

> For this man was counted worthy of more glory than Moses, inasmuch as he
> who hath builded the house hath more honour than the house.
>
> For every house is builded by some man; but he that built all things is God.
> (Heb. 3:1–4)

Paul then cites the words of the Lord to the ancient Israelites whereby He excluded the adults among them from entering into the promised land because they had "provoked" Him through disobedience (see Num. 14:21–23; compare Jacob 1:7–8; Alma 12:36), then applies this doctrine to his own audience: "For we are made partakers of Christ, if we hold the beginning of our confidence stedfast unto the end; While it is said, To day if ye will hear his voice, harden not your hearts, as in the provocation" (Heb. 3:14–15). Enjoining the Jewish Saints to exercise faith in the Savior, Paul goes on to confirm the divine calling of Jesus: "And no man taketh this honour unto himself, but he that is called of God, as was Aaron. So also Christ glorified not himself to be made an high priest; but he that said unto him, Thou art my Son, to day have I begotten thee. As he saith also in another place, Thou art a priest for ever after the order of Melchisedec" (Heb. 5:4–6). As such, Jesus became the author of salvation for mankind: "Though he were a Son, yet learned he obedience by the things which he suffered; And being made perfect, he became the author of eternal salvation unto all them that obey him" (Heb. 5:8–9).

As High Priest after the order of Melchizedek, and author of eternal salvation, the Savior administers the unfolding majesty of the kingdom of God through the power and authority of the Melchizedek Priesthood, which transcends the office and function of the Levitical or Aaronic Priesthood: "And it is yet far more evident: for that after the similitude of Melchisedec there ariseth another priest, Who is made, not after the law of a carnal commandment, but after the power of an endless life. For he testifieth, Thou art a priest for ever after the order of Melchisedec. . . . For the law made nothing perfect, but the bringing in of a better hope did; by the which we draw nigh unto God" (Heb. 7:15–17, 19). It is through the power and authority of the higher priesthood that the new covenant of the gospel plan is put into effect (see Heb. 8).

MODERN PROPHETS SPEAK

Bruce R. McConkie:

> What, then, is the doctrine of the priesthood? And how shall we live as the servants of the Lord?
>
> This doctrine is that God our Father is a glorified, a perfected, and an exalted being who has all might, all power, and all dominion, who knows all things and is infinite in all his attributes, and who lives in the family unit.

It is that our Eternal Father enjoys this high status of glory and perfection and power because his faith is perfect and his priesthood is unlimited.

It is that priesthood is the very name of the power of God, and that if we are to become like him, we must receive and exercise his priesthood or power as he exercises it.

It is that he has given us an endowment of heavenly power here on earth, which is after the order of his Son and which, because it is the power of God, is of necessity without beginning of days or end of years.

It is that we can enter an order of the priesthood named the new and everlasting covenant of marriage (see D&C 131:2), named also the patriarchal order, because of which order we can create for ourselves eternal family units of our own, patterned after the family of God our Heavenly Father.

It is that we have power, by faith, to govern and control all things, both temporal and spiritual; to work miracles and perfect lives; to stand in the presence of God and be like him because we have gained his faith, his perfections, and his power, or in other words the fulness of his priesthood.

This, then, is the doctrine of the priesthood, than which there neither is nor can be anything greater. This is the power we can gain through faith and righteousness.

Truly, there is power in the priesthood—power to do all things! ("The Doctrine of the Priesthood," *Ensign,* May 1982, 33–34)

AUTHORS' NOTE

Our Savior is referred to as being a High Priest forever after the order of Melchizedek. In this context, let us not forget the following scriptural explanation:

There are, in the church, two priesthoods, namely, the Melchizedek and Aaronic, including the Levitical Priesthood.

Why the first is called the Melchizedek Priesthood is because Melchizedek was such a great high priest.

Before his day it was called the Holy Priesthood, after the Order of the Son of God.

But out of respect or reverence to the name of the Supreme Being, to avoid the too frequent repetition of his name, they, the church, in ancient days, called that priesthood after Melchizedek, or the Melchizedek Priesthood.

All other authorities or offices in the church are appendages to this priesthood." (D&C 107:1–5; emphasis added)

LIKENING THE SCRIPTURES TO OUR LIVES

D&C 84:19–21 And this greater priesthood administereth the gospel and holdeth the key of the mysteries of the kingdom, even the key of the knowledge of God. Therefore, in the ordinances thereof, the power of godliness is manifest. And without the ordinances thereof, and the authority of the priesthood, the power of godliness is not manifest unto men in the flesh.

Application: The Melchizedek Priesthood allows mankind the privilege of receiving the gospel, understanding the mysteries of God (the doctrines and truths that bring joy and eternal life; see D&C 42:61), and receiving the ordinances of salvation: baptism, the reception of the Holy Ghost, and all of our temple blessings, which ordinances manifest the power of godliness and the keys to the knowledge of God. In such a context, one can surely see the goodness of God in allowing His children the privilege of exercising His power and authority here upon the earth. These verses of scripture should inspire reverence for the priesthood and induce one never to defile it but rather live worthy at all times to exercise it.

3. THE GOSPEL OF JESUS CHRIST— THE NEW COVENANT WITH THE CHILDREN OF GOD

THEME: The fulness of the gospel was restored in the dispensation of the Lord Jesus Christ and became the new covenant by which mankind should live. Through the Restoration in the latter days, this sacred covenant privilege is once again available to all who will receive it in obedience to the Lord's commandments.

MOMENT OF TRUTH

Paul, with his superb command of the law and the prophets of the Old Testament, invokes for his audience the precise references to energize them around a spiritual commitment to Jesus Christ as "the mediator of a better covenant, which was established upon better promises" (Heb. 8:6). Citing Jeremiah, Paul characterizes the new covenant as follows:

> Behold, the days come, saith the Lord, when I will make a new covenant with the house of Israel and with the house of Judah:
>
> Not according to the covenant that I made with their fathers in the day when I took them by the hand to lead them out of the land of Egypt; because they continued not in my covenant, and I regarded them not, saith the Lord.

> For this is the covenant that I will make with the house of Israel after those days, saith the Lord; I will put my laws into their mind, and write them in their hearts: and I will be to them a God, and they shall be to me a people. (Heb. 8:8–10; compare Jer. 31:31–33)

Under this new covenant, the ceremonial sacrifice of animals as under the Mosaic law—instituted to prefigure the Atonement of the Savior—is fulfilled through and superseded by the divine sacrifice of the Son of God:

> But Christ being come an high priest of good things to come, by a greater and more perfect tabernacle, not made with hands, that is to say, not of this building;
>
> Neither by the blood of goats and calves, but by his own blood he entered in once into the holy place, having obtained eternal redemption for us. . . .
>
> And for this cause he is the mediator of the new testament, that by means of death, for the redemption of the transgressions that were under the first testament, they which are called might receive the promise of eternal inheritance.
>
> For where a testament is, there must also of necessity be the death of the testator. . . .
>
> And almost all things are by the law purged with blood; and without shedding of blood is no remission. (Heb. 9:11–12, 15–16, 22)

Paul then concludes this aspect of his epistle with an admonition to honor and partake of the new covenant:

> This is the covenant that I will make with them after those days, saith the Lord, I will put my laws into their hearts, and in their minds will I write them;
>
> And their sins and iniquities will I remember no more.
>
> Now where remission of these is, there is no more offering for sin.
>
> Having therefore, brethren, boldness to enter into the holiest by the blood of Jesus,
>
> By a new and living way, which he hath consecrated for us, through the veil, that is to say, his flesh;
>
> And having an high priest over the house of God;
>
> Let us draw near with a true heart in full assurance of faith, having our hearts sprinkled from an evil conscience, and our bodies washed with pure water.
>
> Let us hold fast the profession of our faith without wavering. (Heb. 10:16–23)

MODERN PROPHETS SPEAK

Gordon B. Hinckley:

> I want to thank you for living the gospel, for doing what is right, for keeping the commandments and living in faith. I want to thank you for the goodness of your lives. You are the kind of people who keep the Church going. You pay your tithing and your fast offerings, you observe the Word of Wisdom. You try to do the right thing. You have family home evening. You try to help one another. You read the scriptures. You are my kind of people—good people, faithful people. Thank you for being the kind of people you are.
>
> I encourage you to go forward and live the gospel and love the gospel. Make it a part of your lives—this great and glorious thing which has come to us through the providence of the Almighty. Live the gospel. Love the gospel. Read the scriptures. You won't get a testimony of the Book of Mormon unless you read the Book of Mormon. You won't get a testimony of the Doctrine and Covenants unless you read the Doctrine and Covenants. Faith comes of drinking at the fountain of eternal truth. (*TGBH,* 245)

ILLUSTRATIONS FOR OUR TIME

Children of the Covenant

Russell M. Nelson provides this illustration of the covenant blessings of the gospel of Jesus Christ:

> Years ago as a young medical student I saw many patients afflicted with diseases that are now preventable. Today it is possible to immunize individuals against conditions that once were disabling—even deadly. One medical method by which acquired immunity is conferred is inoculation. The term *inoculate* is fascinating. It comes from two Latin roots: *in,* meaning "within"; and *oculus,* meaning "an eye." The verb to *inoculate,* therefore, literally means "to put an eye within"—to monitor against harm.
>
> An affliction like polio can cripple or destroy the body. An affliction like sin can cripple or destroy the spirit. The ravages of polio can now be prevented by immunization, but the ravages of sin require other means of prevention. Doctors cannot immunize against iniquity. Spiritual protection comes only from the Lord—and in his own way. Jesus chooses not to inoculate, but to indoctrinate. His method employs no vaccine; it utilizes the teaching of divine doctrine—a governing "eye within"—to protect the eternal spirits of his children. . . .
>
> A giant step toward spiritual immunity is taken when we understand the expression "children of the covenant." To what covenant did the Savior refer? "The covenant which he made with Abraham" [3 Ne. 20:27]. The Lord added, "I will

remember the covenant which I have made with my people; and I have covenanted with them that I would gather them together *in mine own due time*" [3 Ne. 20:29; emphasis added. See also 1 Pet. 5:6; 3 Ne. 5:25; Morm. 5:12; D&C 93:19]. . . .

Indeed, the Lord has not forgotten us. And to ensure that we do not forget him, children of the covenant receive his doctrine and claim it by covenant. Brigham Young said: "All Latter-day Saints enter the new and everlasting covenant when they enter this Church. . . . They enter the new and everlasting covenant to sustain the kingdom of God and no other kingdom." [*Discourses,* 160] (Russell M. Nelson, "Children of the Covenant," *Ensign,* May 1995, 32–33)

LIKENING THE SCRIPTURES TO OUR LIVES

D&C 76:40–42 And this is the gospel, the glad tidings, which the voice out of the heavens bore record unto us—That he came into the world, even Jesus, to be crucified for the world, and to bear the sins of the world, and to sanctify the world, and to cleanse it from all unrighteousness; That through him all might be saved whom the Father had put into his power and made by him.

Application: The gospel is centered in the Atonement of the Lord Jesus Christ. It is only through our Savior that all mankind can be saved by obedience to the principles and ordinances of the gospel.

4. EXERCISE FAITH IN JESUS CHRIST

THEME: By exercising faith in the Lord Jesus Christ, we have a belief and hope of things not seen which are true (see Heb. 11:1; Alma 32:21), we are moved to action (see James 2:18), and we have power to do all things according to the will of God (see Heb. 11; Ether 12).

MOMENT OF TRUTH

The Epistle to the Hebrews is remarkable in its breadth of wisdom, grasp of preceding scripture, and compass of doctrine and principle. Almost every sentence and phrase is replete with insight and depth of understanding. The fabric of this composition is singularly marked by precision of detail and economy of expression—all measured and designed to bring about a logical acceptance of the mission and ministry of the Savior and a commitment to live by the precepts of His gospel plan. It is thus amazing that Paul, after having covered with masterful skill the doctrines of the divine Atonement, the function and operation of the Melchizedek Priesthood, and the gospel of the new covenant with the children of God, now gives to us in addition one of the most beautiful and edifying expositions of faith in all of the holy scriptures. "Now faith is the substance of things hoped for, the evidence of things not seen," he begins (Heb. 11:1), continuing then with a comprehensive summary of events from Israelite history that illustrate and testify of the power of faith—the fundamental and defining principle of the gospel.

His concluding exhortations on faith contain this spiritual jewel:

> Wherefore seeing we also are compassed about with so great a cloud of witnesses, let us lay aside every weight, and the sin which doth so easily beset us, and let us run with patience the race that is set before us,
>
> Looking unto Jesus the author and finisher of our faith; who for the joy that was set before him endured the cross, despising the shame, and is set down at the right hand of the throne of God. (Heb. 12:1–2)

Paul then admonishes his audience that they should remember to:

- endure in faith the inevitable process of chastening ("For whom the Lord loveth he chasteneth"—Heb. 12:6),
- provide charitable service to the needy ("Wherefore lift up the hands which hang down, and the feeble knees"—Heb. 12:12),
- take their place among "the general assembly and church of the firstborn" (Heb. 12:23), and
- go on to perfection in the Lord ("Make you perfect in every good work to do his will, working in you that which is wellpleasing in his sight, through Jesus Christ; to whom be glory for ever and ever"—Heb. 13:21).

MODERN PROPHETS SPEAK

Ezra Taft Benson:
> Now let me describe to you what faith in Jesus Christ means. Faith in Him is more than mere acknowledgment that He lives. It is more than professing belief. Faith in Jesus Christ consists of complete reliance on Him. As God, He has infinite power, intelligence, and love. There is no human problem beyond His capacity to solve. Because He descended below all things, He knows how to help us rise above our daily difficulties. (*TETB*, 66)

ILLUSTRATIONS FOR OUR TIME

Faith of a Child
Our children have had outstanding teachers in the Church. One such teacher was Carol Pearce, who has since passed away. She was wonderful in every way. She prepared

well. She was their friend at all times and not just in her Primary class. She truly loved and cared for her students—they were her friends. They loved her and had faith as only a child can have in what she taught them. One day she gave a lesson concerning how one could live with Heavenly Father and have eternal life by exercising faith in Jesus Christ. She inspired them and encouraged them to go home and ask their parents to help them increase in their faith, keep all the commandments, and gain eternal life. She said, "I know that someday you are going to live with Heavenly Father."

Not knowing of the lesson or the request for her students to talk to their parents, I was surprised when my son Brett, about six to seven years of age, said, "Dad I would like to visit with you after dinner." I was shocked and surprised at the request and his eagerness for a visit. I felt like I was in trouble and hadn't done something I was supposed to have done. Following dinner, we went down to his bedroom and he related the lesson Sister Pearce had given and said, "Dad, I really want to be good. I want to live with Heavenly Father. I want to be good. Will you help me make a list of some things I need to do?" I was overjoyed at the desire of my magnificent son, whom I love with all my heart, so young and yet so full of faith and with a desire to be good. We sat there enjoying the fruits of the Spirit, having a desire to do good, and felt great joy. We made a plan.

A righteous teacher, a faith-inspiring teacher, a faithful son receptive of the word—thus faith in Jesus Christ was taught and strengthened. [Pinegar]

LIKENING THE SCRIPTURES TO OUR LIVES

Hebrews 11:6 But without faith it is impossible to please him: for he that cometh to God must believe that he is, and that he is a rewarder of them that diligently seek him.

Application: As children of God, our desires are to please Him and do His will. Recognizing this fact makes having and exercising faith in God and the Lord Jesus Christ paramount in our lives.

SUMMARY

When the resurrected Savior appeared unto Saul of Tarsus as he journeyed on the road to Damascus (Acts 9), He enlisted a true warrior into the ranks of the spiritual leadership of the Church. As Paul the Apostle, this intrepid emissary carried the gospel to the Gentiles and confirmed and strengthened the Jewish Christians as well. The Epistle to the Hebrews is a masterpiece of doctrinal wisdom, covering the key topics of the mission and Atonement of Jesus Christ as Savior and Redeemer, the purpose and operation of the Melchizedek Priesthood, the nature and supernal scope of the new covenant between the Father and His children, and the essential role of faith in the grand design of the gospel plan. Let us be grateful that these inspired words of Paul have been preserved to serve as a guide and beacon in our day, reinforcing and confirming the principles of truth again bestowed upon mankind through the latter-day Restoration, and witnessing that "Jesus Christ is the same yesterday, and to day, and for ever" (Heb. 13:8).

CHAPTER 38

WITNESS *and* TESTIFY *of* JESUS CHRIST

Reading Assignment: Acts 21–28.

Additional Reading: Bible Dictionary: "Acts of the Apostles" (603–4); review the maps of Paul's missionary journeys (18–22).

> *No man can be a minister of Jesus Christ except he has the testimony of Jesus; and this is the spirit of prophecy. Whenever salvation has been administered, it has been by testimony.*
>
> —JOSEPH SMITH, *HC* 3:389–90.

THEMES *for* LIVING

1. Missionary Labors Amidst Persecution
2. Be Valiant When Unjustly Accused
3. Bear Testimony with Courage
4. Adversity and Opposition Are Always with Us

INTRODUCTION

We may face all types of adversity as we bear witness of Jesus Christ and testify to the truthfulness of the gospel. Let us press forward with faith despite the apathy, indifference, worldliness, overweening secular knowledge, nefarious ways, prideful attitudes and behaviors, lasciviousness, greed, and all manner of persecution we encounter in others. We are to share our testimonies regardless of the opposition and apparent hard-heartedness of others. Mormon described it this way to his son Moroni: "And now, my beloved son, notwithstanding their hardness, let us labor diligently; for if we should cease to labor, we should be brought under condemnation; for we have a labor to perform whilst in this tabernacle of clay, that we may conquer the enemy of all righteousness, and rest our souls in the kingdom of God" (Moro. 9:6). We can go forward, knowing that the Lord will bless us as we open our mouths (see D&C 33:8–11; 84:85–88; 100:5–6). The Holy Ghost empowers our testimony, for truth without testimony is hollow.

1. MISSIONARY LABORS AMIDST PERSECUTION

THEME: We are to follow the Lord's commandment to labor as missionaries of the gospel: "Therefore, O ye that embark in the service of God, see that ye serve him with all your heart, might, mind and strength, that ye may stand blameless before God at the last day" (D&C 4:2). For we have been commanded: "thou art called . . . to proclaim mine everlasting gospel unto the inhabitants thereof, in the midst of persecution and wickedness" (D&C 99:1).

MOMENT OF TRUTH

The second half of the Acts of the Apostles (chapters 21–28) recounts the travails and courage of Paul while serving as a missionary for the Lord. En route back to Jerusalem at one point, he encounters adamant resistance from colleagues, who fear that he will face dire persecution if he returns. His courage, however, prevails: "What mean ye to weep and to break mine heart? for I am ready not to be bound only, but also to die at Jerusalem for the name of the Lord Jesus. And when he would not be persuaded, we ceased, saying, The will of the Lord be done" (Acts 21:13–14). At Jerusalem he does, indeed, experience severe mistreatment and imprisonment from the Jewish leaders, who accuse him unjustly of undermining the law of Moses and degrading their traditional religious practices. It is their determination to see him executed. However, his case is heard before governmental authorities at ascending levels of power—from the chief captain of the military to Felix (procurator of Judaea), thence to Festus (successor procurator), next to King Agrippa at Caesarea, and thereafter with an eventual referral to Caesar at Rome. As a Roman citizen, Paul was accorded at least some sense of dignity in his lengthy process of defense and stood forth valiantly in declaring the truth about the gospel of Jesus Christ in spite of the most cruel persecution from his detractors.

MODERN PROPHETS SPEAK

Joseph Smith:

> Our missionaries are going forth to different nations, and in Germany, Palestine, New Holland, Australia, the East Indies, and other places, the Standard of Truth has been erected; no unhallowed hand can stop the work from progressing; persecutions may rage, mobs may combine, armies may assemble, calumny may defame, but the truth of God will go forth boldly, nobly, and independent, till it has penetrated every continent, visited every clime, swept every country, and sounded in every ear, till the purposes of God shall be accomplished, and the Great Jehovah shall say the work is done. (*HC,* 4:540)

ILLUSTRATIONS FOR OUR TIME

Observing Our Covenants by Sacrifice

The statement by Paul's associates "The will of the Lord be done" is truly the motto for all missionary work. In the face of all adversity, privation, and hardship, the Lord's errand moves forward: "And they shall go forth and none shall stay them, for I the Lord have commanded them" (D&C 5:1).

We are therefore to follow the example of devotion and sacrifice set by those who follow in the Lord's footsteps: "Verily I say unto you, all among them who know their hearts are honest, and are broken, and their sprits contrite, and are willing to observe their covenants by sacrifice—yea, every sacrifice which I, the Lord, shall command—they are accepted of me" (D&C 97:8).

One of the most celebrated farewells in the annals of missionary work during the Restoration period took place on September 14, 1839. On this day, amidst a severe malaria epidemic in the region, Brigham Young left his home in Montrose, Iowa, for his apostolic mission to Great Britain. "His health was very poor; he was unable to go thirty rods to the river without assistance. After he had crossed the ferry he got Brother Israel Barlow to carry him on his horse behind him to Heber C. Kimball's where he remained sick until the 18th. He left his wife sick with a babe only ten days old, and all his children sick, unable to wait upon each other" (*HC,* 4:9). On the 18th, the two Apostles, both still sick, left the Kimball household in Nauvoo, all ailing except four-year-old Heber Parley. " 'It seemed to me,' he [Brother Kimball] remarked afterwards in relating the circumstances, 'as though my very inmost parts would melt within me at the thought of leaving my family in such a condition, as it were, almost in the arms of death. I felt as though I could scarcely endure it.' 'Hold up!' said he to the teamster, who had just started, 'Brother Brigham, this is pretty tough, but let us rise and give them a cheer!' Brigham, with much difficulty, rose to his feet, and joined

Elder Kimball in swinging his hat and shouting, 'Hurrah, hurrah, hurrah, for Israel!' The two sisters, hearing the cheer came to the door—Sister [Vilate] Kimball with much difficulty [Mary Ann Young having come to the Kimball household to help nurse her husband]—and waved a farewell; and the two apostles continued their journey, without purse, without scrip, for England" (*HC,* 4:10).

Beneath the banner of such extraordinary devotion in the commission of service to the Lord, we can do no less than rise in courage to observe our covenants by sacrifice. [Allen]

LIKENING THE SCRIPTURES TO OUR LIVES

2 Timothy 3:11 Persecutions, afflictions, which came unto me at Antioch, at Iconium, at Lystra; what persecutions I endured: but out of them all the Lord delivered me.

Application: Inspired by the example of Paul and all of God's servants past and present, we are never to forget that the Lord will deliver us from our persecutions. The Prophet Joseph Smith learned, then taught us, well that in and through persecutions we grow (see D&C 121:7–8; 122:5–8).

2. BE VALIANT WHEN UNJUSTLY ACCUSED

THEME: Many have been unjustly accused in regard to preaching the gospel. Many have been unjustly accused in everyday life. How do we rely on the Lord and deal with being unjustly accused?

MOMENT OF TRUTH

While in the hands of the chief captain of the military, having been falsely accused by Jewish leaders of sedition, blasphemy, and the attempt to overthrow the Jewish religious structure, Paul stood his ground and depended upon the Lord to carry him through the crisis. In the midst of the bleakness of his confinement, Paul was again visited by the Lord: "And the night following the Lord stood by him, and said, Be of good cheer, Paul: for as thou hast testified of me in Jerusalem, so must thou bear witness also at Rome" (Acts 23:11). Later, Paul was involved in a tragic shipwreck while en route to Rome—an event that he had predicted by inspiration, warning the incredulous sailors and assuring them that there would be no loss of life if they went forward (see Acts 27:22). He survived the disaster to continue his labors in Rome, just as the Lord had promised him: "Be it known therefore unto you," he said to the Jews in Rome during his status of confinement at the behest of the authorities there, "that the salvation of God is sent unto the Gentiles, and that they will hear it. And when he had said these words, the Jews departed, and had great reasoning among themselves. And Paul dwelt two whole years in his own hired house, and received all that came in unto him, Preaching the kingdom of God, and teaching those things which concern the Lord Jesus Christ, with all confidence, no man forbidding him" (Acts 28:28–31).

MODERN PROPHETS SPEAK

Neal A. Maxwell:

> Did Joseph experience the same anxieties in carrying out his mission as did other prophets? Indeed! Joseph could understand with what feelings a weary and beset Paul wrote:
>
> "For, when we were come into Macedonia, our flesh had no rest, but we were troubled on every side; without were fightings, within were fears" (2 Cor. 7:5; see also 2 Cor. 4:8).
>
> Was Joseph unjustly accused as were other prophets? Yes! Even unto this very day fragments of fact are flung at his memory. Paul was accused of being mad and deranged (see Acts 26:24). Even Jesus himself was accused of being a winebibber, of being possessed of a devil, and of being mad (see Matt. 11:19; John 10:20).
>
> Yet, in the midst of all these things, as promised, Joseph loved the work to which he had been called. And he loved his associates! In giving individual assignments to the Twelve, we see his love and humor tenderly intertwined. ("Joseph, the Seer," in *The Prophet and His Work: Essays from General Authorities on Joseph Smith and the Restoration* [Salt Lake City: Deseret Book, 1996], 46)

ILLUSTRATIONS FOR OUR TIME

Miscommunication and False Accusations Can Be Resolved Through Charity

Consider the exchange of correspondence between Moroni, head of the armies, and Pahoran, governor in Zarahemla, during a period of intense conflict between the Nephites and the Lamanite and a serious internal insurrection:

Moroni's Letter to Pahoran:

> And now behold, I say unto you, I fear exceedingly that the judgments of God will come upon this people, because of their exceeding slothfulness, yea, even the slothfulness of our government, and their exceedingly great neglect towards their brethren, yea, towards those who have been slain. . . .
>
> But why should I say much concerning this matter? For we know not but what ye yourselves are seeking for authority. We know not but what ye are also traitors to

your country. Or is it that ye have neglected us because ye are in the heart of our country and ye are surrounded by security, that ye do not cause food to be sent unto us, and also men to strengthen our armies? Have ye forgotten the commandments of the Lord your God? Yea, have ye forgotten the captivity of our fathers? Have ye forgotten the many times we have been delivered out of the hands of our enemies? Or do ye suppose that the Lord will still deliver us, while we sit upon our thrones and do not make use of the means which the Lord has provided for us? Yea, will ye sit in idleness while ye are surrounded with thousands of those, yea, and tens of thousands, who do also sit in idleness, while there are thousands round about in the borders of the land who are falling by the sword, yea, wounded and bleeding? Do ye suppose that God will look upon you as guiltless while ye sit still and behold these things? Behold I say unto you, Nay. Now I would that ye should remember that God has said that the inward vessel shall be cleansed first, and then shall the outer vessel be cleansed also. (Alma 60:14,18–23)

Pahoran's Letter to Moroni:

I, Pahoran, who am the chief governor of this land, do send these words unto Moroni, the chief captain over the army. Behold, I say unto you, Moroni, that I do not joy in your great afflictions, yea, it grieves my soul. . . .

And now, in your epistle you have censured me, but it mattereth not; I am not angry, but do rejoice in the greatness of your heart. I, Pahoran, do not seek for power, save only to retain my judgment-seat that I may preserve the rights and the liberty of my people. My soul standeth fast in that liberty in the which God hath made us free. . . .

Gather together whatsoever force ye can upon your march hither, and we will go speedily against those dissenters, in the strength of our God according to the faith which is in us (Alma 61:2, 9, 17). . . .

And now it came to pass that when Moroni had received this epistle his heart did take courage, and was filled with exceedingly great joy because of the faithfulness of Pahoran, that he was not also a traitor to the freedom and cause of his country. (Alma 62:1)

LIKENING THE SCRIPTURES TO OUR LIVES

D&C 122:6–9 If thou art accused with all manner of false accusations; if thine enemies fall upon thee; . . . And if thou shouldst be cast into the pit, or into the hands of murderers, and the sentence of death passed upon thee; if thou be cast into the deep; if the billowing surge conspire against thee; if fierce winds become thine enemy; if the heavens gather blackness, and all the elements combine to hedge up the way;

and above all, if the very jaws of hell shall gape open the mouth wide after thee, know thou, my son, that all these things shall give thee experience, and shall be for thy good. The Son of Man hath descended below them all. Art thou greater than he? Therefore, hold on thy way, and the priesthood shall remain with thee; for their bounds are set, they cannot pass. Thy days are known, and thy years shall not be numbered less; therefore, fear not what man can do, for God shall be with you forever and ever.

Application: We face all manner of trials, tribulations, false accusations, and afflictions here upon the earth. If we focus on the goodness of God and recognize that Christ has suffered for all things, then these earthly experiences can be for our good. Let us remember that God will be with us in all things forever and ever.

3. BEAR TESTIMONY WITH COURAGE

THEME: We should stand as witness at all times, and all places, and in all things (see Mosiah 18:8–9). We should bear our testimony of Jesus Christ and His Kingdom when and wherever we can, by word and by deed.

MOMENT OF TRUTH

While in military confinement, Paul was called upon to face those who had pressed unjust and unholy accusations against him. He rose in majesty and recounted his extraordinary vision in which the resurrected Lord commanded him to cease persecuting the followers of Christ and called him into the service of the ministry (see Acts 22:3–10). Subsequently, as Paul explained, a devout man by the name of Ananias, one who had been called by the Lord to take the bewildered Paul under his care, confirmed the divine commission: "For thou shalt be his witness unto all men of what thou hast seen and heard" (Acts 22:15). Paul later recounted the same testimony before King Agrippa at Caesarea with such persuasive power that the king uttered the now famous words: "Almost thou persuadest me to be a Christian" (Acts 26:28). Paul's example of intrepid courage and unshakable testimony before vicious and unrelenting enemies is a model for us all to follow.

MODERN PROPHETS SPEAK

Spencer W. Kimball:

> Bearing earnest testimony is basic to missionary success. We have something which no one else can have. The pope in Rome might be a good man. Some ministers and some priests may be righteous. Some might be as devoted and as sincere as we are.

But there can be none except in our church, of course, who have this controlling thing, the testimony of the truth, and that is the thing that brings people into the kingdom. It is not our logic. Some may be more adept than others, some may have more natural endowments and greater talents than others, and some may be able to give a better lesson. But that is not the controlling factor, though it helps. It is tremendously important that we do everything in our power to present it well, but the testimony is the sealing element. (*TSWK*, 569)

ILLUSTRATIONS FOR OUR TIME

Acquiring That Special Witness
Harold B. Lee:

> I shall never forget my feelings of loneliness the Saturday night after I was told by the President of the Church that I was to be sustained the next day as a member of the Quorum of the Twelve Apostles. That was a sleepless night. There ran through my mind all the petty things of my life, the nonsense, the foolishness of youth. I could have told you about those against whom I had any grievances and who had any grievance against me. And before I was to be accepted the next day, I knew that I must stand before the Lord and witness before him that I would love and forgive every soul that walked the earth and in return I would ask Him to forgive me that I might be worthy of that position. . . .

> The following day I went to the temple where I was ushered into the room where the Council of the Twelve meet with the First Presidency each week in an upper room. . . .

> And then one of the brethren, who arranged for Sunday evening radio programs, said, "Now you know that after having been ordained, you are a special witness to the mission of the Lord Jesus Christ. We want you to give the Easter talk next Sunday night." The assignment was to bear testimony of the mission of the Lord concerning His resurrection, His life, and His ministry, so I went to a room in the Church Office Building where I could be alone, and I read the Gospels, particularly those that had to do with the closing days and weeks and months of the life of Jesus. And as I read, I realized that I was having a new experience.

> It wasn't any longer just a story; it seemed as though I was actually seeing the events about which I was reading, and when I gave my talk and closed with my testimony, I said, "I am now the least of all my brethren and want to witness to you that I know, as I have never known before this call came, that Jesus is the Savior of this world. He lives and He died for us." Why did I know? Because there had come a witness, that special kind of a witness, that may have been the more sure word of prophecy that one must have if he is to be a special witness. (quoted in Jack M.

Lyon, Jay A. Parry, and Linda R. Gundry, eds., *Best-Loved Stories of the LDS People*
[Salt Lake City: Deseret Book, 1999], 2:388–89)

LIKENING THE SCRIPTURES TO OUR LIVES

2 Timothy 1:8 Be not thou therefore ashamed of the testimony of our Lord, nor of me his prisoner: but be thou partaker of the afflictions of the gospel according to the power of God.

Application: Let us be courageous and bold in bearing testimony of Jesus Christ—and we shall be blessed.

4. ADVERSITY AND OPPOSITION ARE ALWAYS WITH US

THEME: Adversity and opposition are constant in our lives (see D&C 29:39; 2 Ne. 2:11). This is part of the test of mortality (see Abr. 3:25). We can transcend these challenges in the strength of the Lord (see Alma 20:4).

MOMENT OF TRUTH

The experiences of Paul and his colleagues in the leadership of the newly established kingdom of God upon the earth provide evidence that adversity and persecution follow the believers, just as the Savior had predicted: "Remember the word that I said unto you, The servant is not greater than his lord. If they have persecuted me, they will also persecute you" (John 15:20). And further: "These things have I spoken unto you, that ye should not be offended. They shall put you out of the synagogues: yea, the time cometh, that whosoever killeth you will think that he doeth God service. And these things will they do unto you, because they have not known the Father, nor me" (John 16:1–3). Only in the strength of the Lord and through the guidance of the Spirit can we hope to overcome the daunting challenges placed in the pathway of light by the servants of darkness. The solution is given by the Lord: "Be faithful unto the end, and lo, I am with you. These words are not of man nor of men, but of me, even Jesus Christ, your Redeemer, by the will of the Father" (D&C 31:13; compare Matt. 28:20; John 13:33; D&C 33:9; 34:11; 100:12; 105:41; 108:8).

MODERN PROPHETS SPEAK

Howard W. Hunter:

> We will all have some adversity in our lives. I think we can be reasonably sure of that. Some of it will have the potential to be violent and damaging and destructive. Some of it may even strain our faith in a loving God who has the power to administer relief in our behalf.
>
> To those anxieties I think the Father of us all would say, "Why are ye so fearful? How is it that ye have no faith?" And of course that has to be faith for the whole journey, the entire experience, the fullness of our life, not simply around the bits and pieces and tempestuous moments. (*THWH*, 83)

> *We have a promise of divine assistance in times of need.* All of us face times in our lives when we need heavenly help in a special and urgent way. We all have moments when we are overwhelmed by circumstances or confused by the counsel we get from others, and we feel a great need to receive spiritual guidance, a great need to find the right path and do the right thing. In the scriptural preface to this latter-day dispensation, the Lord promised that if we would be humble in such times of need and turn to him for aid, we would "be made strong, and [be] blessed from on high, and receive knowledge from time to time" (D&C 1:28). That help is ours if we will but seek it, trust in it, and follow what King Benjamin, in the Book of Mormon, called "the enticings of the Holy Spirit" (Mosiah 3:19).
>
> Perhaps no promise in life is more reassuring than that promise of divine assistance and spiritual guidance in times of need. It is a gift freely given from heaven, a gift that we need from our earliest youth through the very latest days of our lives. (*THWH*, 85)

ILLUSTRATIONS FOR OUR TIME

Though we can experience severe trials and adversity, it is refreshing to look at the lighter side when faced with situations that can engender anger and frustration. President Hinckley relates a humorous story of adversity and concludes with positive and hopeful advice. He relates:

> I know something of the frustrations of life in general. I have had my head bumped and my shins barked. On some of these occasions when I have needed a laugh I have turned to a letter which . . . was first published in the Manchester, England, *Guardian* and later reprinted in the *Deseret News*.
>
> A hurricane had hit the West Indies, and a bricklayer was sent to repair the damage. He wrote to the home office as follows, and I hope you can get this delightful picture:

"Respected Sirs:

"When I got to the building I found that the hurricane had knocked some bricks off the top. So I rigged up a beam with a pulley at the top of the building and hoisted up a couple of barrels full of bricks. When I had fixed the building, there was a lot of bricks left over. I hoisted the barrel back up again and secured the line at the bottom, and then went up and filled the barrel with the extra bricks. Then I went to the bottom and cast off the line. Unfortunately the barrel of bricks was heavier than I was, and before I knew what was happening the barrel started down, jerking me off the ground. I decided to hang on, and halfway up I met the barrel coming down and received a severe blow on the shoulder. I then continued to the top, banging my head against the beam and getting my finger jammed in the pulley. When the barrel hit the ground it bursted its bottom, allowing all the bricks to spill out. I was now heavier than the barrel and so started down again at high speed. Halfway down, I met the barrel coming up and received severe injuries to my shins. When I hit the ground I landed on the bricks, getting several painful cuts from the sharp edges. At this point I must have lost my presence of mind because I let go of the line. The barrel then came down, giving me another heavy blow on the head and putting me in hospital. I respectfully request sick leave."

Life is like that—ups and downs, a bump on the head, and a crack on the shins. It was ever thus. Hamlet went about crying, "To be or not to be," but that didn't solve any of his problems. There is something of a tendency among us to think that everything must be lovely and rosy and beautiful without realizing that even adversity has some sweet uses. ("God Shall Give unto You Knowledge by His Holy Spirit," *BYU Speeches of the Year,* September 25, 1973, 105–6) (*TGBH,* 6)

If as a people we will build and sustain one another, the Lord will bless us with the strength to weather every storm and continue to move forward through every adversity ("Five Million Members—A Milestone and Not a Summit," *Ensign,* May 1982, 46). (*TGBH,* 7)

LIKENING THE SCRIPTURES TO OUR LIVES

D&C 136:31 My people must be tried in all things, that they may be prepared to receive the glory that I have for them, even the glory of Zion; and he that will not bear chastisement is not worthy of my kingdom.

Application: Heavenly Father knows what is best for us (see Prov. 3:5–6). We become perfected through the process of sacrifice, enduring to the end, and learning to submit to all things that the Father should inflict upon us (see Mosiah 3:19). Let us cultivate an attitude of hope and faith and go forward trusting in the goodness of God.

SUMMARY

Under the provisions and promise of the Abrahamic covenant, we are all enlisted in God's service with the obligation to carry the gospel of Jesus Christ to the four corners of the world. That task is often fraught with peril as well as inconvenience, danger as well as sacrifice, and persecution as well as a heavy investment of time and energy. But the rewards and joys are infinitely greater than the burdens. Paul's labors illustrate that missionary work proceeds despite persecution, that we are to stand valiantly upon principle when unjustly accused, and that we are to bear testimony of Jesus Christ and His gospel plan with courage and devotion—all with the promise that we can transcend the inevitable adversity and opposition in life in the strength of the Lord and through the guidance of His Spirit. We can say with Paul: "Having therefore obtained help of God, I continue unto this day, witnessing both to small and great, saying none other things than those which the prophets and Moses did say should come: That Christ should suffer, and that he should be the first that should rise from the dead, and should shew light unto the people, and to the Gentiles" (Acts 26:22–23).

To this we can add our witness of the Restoration of the Church and kingdom of God in the latter days, including the coming forth of the Book of Mormon as another testament of Jesus Christ, and the availability of all the priesthood keys and ordinances leading to salvation, immortality, and eternal life. With so great a message, how can we shrink from the divine commission to be honorable in keeping our covenants and going forth, just as Paul, in our circles of friendship and assigned spheres of activity, to preach the gospel of Jesus Christ?

CHAPTER 39

"FOR THE PERFECTING *of the* SAINTS"

Reading Assignment: Ephesians.

Additional Reading: John 17:11; Mosiah 18:21–22; D&C 27:15–18; 38:25–27; Bible Dictionary, "Dispensations" (657–58); "Pauline Epistles, Epistle to the Ephesians" (746).

> *We live in the dispensation of the fulness of times. That is to say, we live in the dispensation of the fulness of dispensations. We have received all of the "keys, and powers, and glories," possessed by them of old. Angelic ministrants have come from those Biblical dispensations which had distinctive keys and powers—"all declaring their dispensation, their rights, their keys, their honors, their majesty and glory, and the power of their priesthood" (D&C 128:18–21).*
>
> *"In the dispensation of the fulness of times," as Paul promised, the Lord will "gather together in one all things in Christ, both which are in heaven, and which are on earth" (Eph. 1:10). All of the rivers of the past have or will flow into the ocean of the present; already all of the keys and powers have fallen to our lot; in due course all of the doctrines and truths will be manifest to us.*
>
> —BRUCE R. MCCONKIE, "THIS FINAL GLORIOUS GOSPEL DISPENSATION," *ENSIGN*, APR. 1980, 22.

THEMES *for* LIVING

1. The Dispensation of the Fulness of Times
2. Jesus Christ Is the Chief Cornerstone
3. Unity of the Family—Husband and Wife, Parents and Children
4. Put on the Armor of God

INTRODUCTION

The purpose of the dispensation of the fulness of times is to restore the fulness of the gospel, all the priesthood power, authority, and keys pertaining to the salvation, exaltation, and perfection of mankind, so that, "he might gather together in one all things in Christ, both which are in heaven, and which are on earth; even in him" (Eph 1:10; see also D&C 27:13). This is indeed that restitution of all things spoken of by Peter (see Acts 3:21). Everything pertaining to the plan of salvation and happiness will be brought together in and through the Lord Jesus Christ—all things that have been revealed and will yet be revealed between earth and heaven will be one under the direction and power of the Lord Jesus Christ as the chief cornerstone. He is our rock upon which we build both individually and as a church. He is our foundation (see Hel. 5:12). Our Savior has surely shown us the way, for He is the light and life of the world.

Through His holy prophets, He has revealed His teachings that can and will preserve the most sacred unit of the Church, even the family. The relationships between husband and wife are made clear. They must be one in purpose, cause, and action. The husband should love his wife even as Christ has loved the Church; hence the wife would cooperatively accept his leadership within the family in righteousness, even as we submit to the leadership of Christ in the Church and our lives. As fathers and mothers lead with love and righteousness, their children will be more likely to obey and honor their parents. As families, we can prepare for the vicissitudes of life by putting on the armor of God, which can and will protect us from the adversary.

1. THE DISPENSATION OF THE FULNESS OF TIMES

THEME: The dispensation of the fulness of times began with the Prophet Joseph Smith when he received all the priesthood power, authority, and keys—along with the restitution of all things—for the salvation of all mankind (see Acts 3:21).

MOMENT OF TRUTH

Paul's epistle to the Ephesians was written in the time frame A.D. 60 to A.D. 62, similar to Philippians, Colossians, Philemon, and Hebrews. These epistles were written from Rome during Paul's confinement there at the behest of the Roman authorities. Ephesus (located near the western coast of what is now modern-day Turkey) was the capital city of the Roman province of Asia and a major commercial center, connecting trade from east to west. Paul visited Ephesus toward the end of his second missionary journey (see Acts 18:19) and then returned during his third missionary journey, residing there for a period of some two years (see Acts 19). Missionary service in the city, which included some quarter million inhabitants in New Testament times, was productive, and a goodly circle of followers of Christ was established there. Paul was forced to leave the city under pressure from the silversmith industry, which provided silver shrines in honor of Artemis or Diana, whose temple—regarded as one of the seven wonders of the ancient world—was located within the city. The growing Christian circle—for which artifacts for idols were anathema—was compromising the silversmiths' trade, so they rose up against the Church and its expansion.

Paul's extraordinary epistle to the Ephesians is, among other things, a noteworthy exposition of the nature, organization, and future destiny of the Church and kingdom of God. Paul, naturally grounded in the details of the recent establishment of the Church under the personal and immediate leadership of the Redeemer and Lord, Jesus Christ, was also a man of keen retrospective vision (having intimate familiarity with covenant history and the canon of scripture leading back to Adam). He was also a person of forward-reaching spiritual vision concerning the unfolding of the kingdom of God, even unto the ends of the earth. As such, he was well versed in the prophetic view of the Restoration of the gospel in the latter days, as confirmed by his words to the Ephesians:

> Having made known unto us the mystery of his will, according to his good pleasure which he hath purposed in himself:
>
> That in the dispensation of the fulness of times he might gather together in one all things in Christ, both which are in heaven, and which are on earth; even in him:
>
> In whom also we have obtained an inheritance, being predestinated according to the purpose of him who worketh all things after the counsel of his own will:
>
> That we should be to the praise of his glory, who first trusted in Christ. (Eph. 1:9–12)

Peter had made a similar statement shortly after the ascension of the Lord, an indication that the Apostles and Church leaders had been fully apprised of the future restoration of the gospel:

> Repent ye therefore, and be converted, that your sins may be blotted out, when the times of refreshing shall come from the presence of the Lord;
>
> And he shall send Jesus Christ, which before was preached unto you:

Whom the heaven must receive until the times of restitution of all things, which God hath spoken by the mouth of all his holy prophets since the world began. (Acts 3:19–21)

In the same context of understanding the mysteries and ways of God through the Spirit, Paul invoked the blessings of the Lord upon the Saints at Ephesus, praying "That the God of our Lord Jesus Christ, the Father of glory, may give unto you the spirit of wisdom and revelation in the knowledge of him: The eyes of your understanding being enlightened; that ye may know what is the hope of his calling, and what the riches of the glory of his inheritance in the saints" (Eph. 1:17–18).

MODERN PROPHETS SPEAK

Joseph Fielding Smith:

> There are other matters of great interest in relation to the keys of the priesthood, which may not be clearly understood by some. The Lord has revealed that in the present dispensation—the Dispensation of the Fulness of Times—all things from the beginning are to be revealed and the keys of each dispensation restored. This has been "spoken of by the mouth of all his holy prophets since the world began." (Acts 3:21; Eph. 1:10) In fulfilment of this prediction, the prophets holding keys, from Adam to Peter, James, and John, each came to the Prophet Joseph Smith and Oliver Cowdery and restored their keys. We do not have the detailed report of each of these restorations, but we do have the general statement that such was done. (D&C 128:19–21) (*AGQ,* 2:41)

ILLUSTRATIONS FOR OUR TIME

LeGrand Richards ponders the vital importance of the Restoration in the dispensation of the fulness of times:

> Now the church was established by the Savior with the calling of the Twelve in his day, but the holy prophets foresaw that it would not remain upon the earth, but that there would come a latter day when the Lord would finish his work.
>
> The apostle Paul said that the Lord had revealed the mystery of his will to him, "That in the dispensation of the fulness of times [and we live in that dispensation] he might gather together in one all things in Christ, both which are in heaven, and which are on earth; even in him." (Eph. 1:10) Now we have that message and that is why the people of the world can't adequately and properly find their way back into the presence of the Lord unless they are willing to heed the message that we have. . . .
>
> Our message to the world today is the restoration of the gospel. Paul said, "But though we, or an angel from heaven, preach any other gospel unto you than that

which we have preached unto you, let him be accursed." (Gal. 1:8) Now that is quite a statement, but Paul was not at all backward in indicating what he thought of those who didn't teach the truth that had come to them through the Savior and his teachings. . . .

Great was the day when the Church was organized in the days of the Savior, but it is more glorious when the final or finishing touches are added. Of course, we couldn't have that without the great redemption work that he wrought. But Paul saw "that in the dispensation of the fulness of times he might gather together in one all things in Christ, both which are in heaven, and which are on earth." (Eph. 1:10) We are the only church in the world that has that and that is the finishing touch. We are in the dispensation of the fulness of times. ("One Lord, One Faith, One Baptism," *Ensign,* May 1975, 95)

LIKENING THE SCRIPTURES TO OUR LIVES

Ephesians 1:10 That in the dispensation of the fulness of times he might gather together in one all things in Christ, both which are in heaven, and which are on earth; even in him.

Application: We should feel grateful to live in a day when all the blessings of the Lord are available to us and our progenitors who have gone before. We have a responsibility to strengthen others (see D&C 108:7), proclaim the gospel (see D&C 1:23), and redeem the dead (see D&C 128:15).

2. JESUS CHRIST IS THE CHIEF CORNERSTONE

THEME: It is necessary for us to build our life upon the gospel, doctrines, and Atonement of the Lord Jesus Christ—which is a sure foundation. It is through Him that we are blessed in all things.

MOMENT OF TRUTH

In the spirit of charity and friendship, Paul reaches out to the Gentile converts in the city of Ephesus and assures them of their full-fledged citizenship in the kingdom of God—just like the Jewish converts of Israelite lineage:

Now therefore ye are no more strangers and foreigners, but fellowcitizens with the saints, and of the household of God;

And are built upon the foundation of the apostles and prophets, Jesus Christ himself being the chief corner stone;

In whom all the building fitly framed together groweth unto an holy temple in the Lord:

In whom ye also are builded together for an habitation of God through the Spirit. (Eph. 2:19–22)

Paul encapsulates the doctrine of adoption into the fold of Christ in this verse: "That the Gentiles should be fellowheirs, and of the same body, and partakers of his promise in Christ by the gospel" (Eph. 3:6). With Christ as the "chief corner stone" of the Church, all are welcome before Him as believers and followers of the principles of salvation and exaltation. Paul invokes this wonderful apostolic blessing upon the people:

For this cause I bow my knees unto the Father of our Lord Jesus Christ,

Of whom the whole family in heaven and earth is named,

That he would grant you, according to the riches of his glory, to be strengthened with might by his Spirit in the inner man;

That Christ may dwell in your hearts by faith; that ye, being rooted and grounded in love,

May be able to comprehend with all saints what is the breadth, and length, and depth, and height;

And to know the love of Christ, which passeth knowledge, that ye might be filled with all the fulness of God. (Eph. 3:14–19)

Expanding his discourse about the organization of the Church, Paul moves outward from the chief cornerstone of Christ to encompass all the offices and helps of the kingdom of God:

And he gave some, apostles; and some, prophets; and some, evangelists; and some, pastors and teachers;

For the perfecting of the saints, for the work of the ministry, for the edifying of the body of Christ:

Till we all come in the unity of the faith, and of the knowledge of the Son of God, unto a perfect man, unto the measure of the stature of the fulness of Christ:

That we henceforth be no more children, tossed to and fro, and carried about with every wind of doctrine, by the sleight of men, and cunning craftiness, whereby they lie in wait to deceive;

But speaking the truth in love, may grow up into him in all things, which is the head, even Christ:

From whom the whole body fitly joined together and compacted by that which every joint supplieth, according to the effectual working in the measure of every part, maketh increase of the body unto the edifying of itself in love. (Eph. 4:11–16)

Every missionary of the Lord today is familiar with these words and freely uses them in bearing testimony about the grace and love of God in providing for us an organization designed to maximize the blessings to the Saints and open up for them a pathway to salvation, exaltation, and eternal life according to the designs of the Father and the Son.

MODERN PROPHETS SPEAK

Harold B. Lee:

> The Master's church was an orderly, organized body "built upon the foundation of the apostles and prophets, Jesus Christ himself being the chief corner stone" (Eph. 2:20). This organization with teachers, helps, and a complete government (see 1 Cor. 12:28) was "for the perfecting of the saints, for the work of the ministry, for the edifying of the body of Christ" (Eph. 4:12). The officers in the true church had to have divine authority from authorized ordinances and not just "assumed" authority. The Lord told His apostles: "Ye have not chosen me, but I have chosen you, and ordained you, that ye should go and bring forth fruit . . ." (John 15:16) and to the chiefest of the apostles He gave the "keys" of the kingdom of God, or in other words, the keys of authority to the Church of Jesus Christ, that whatsoever would be bound in earth should be bound in heaven. (*Stand Ye in Holy Places* [Salt Lake City: Deseret Book, 1976], 314–15)

ILLUSTRATIONS FOR OUR TIME

Lively Stones

On the occasion of the completion and dedication of the Mount Timpanogos Temple in American Fork, Utah, in 1996, the local stake leaders provided the youth with a memento of the grandeur and spiritual wonder of this beautiful House of the Lord. The memento was a small rectangular piece of Sierra white granite used in the construction of the building. The objective was for the young people to place this polished stone in a visible place somewhere among their belongings to remind them of the spiritual values of the gospel and the temple.

The image of a stone, symbolizing spiritual vitality and divine leadership, is used pervasively throughout the scriptures. The central icon in such metaphorical discourse is the Savior, whom Paul identified as "the chief corner stone" of God's program of salvation and exaltation (Eph. 2:19). The Psalmist declared: "I will praise thee: for thou hast heard me, and art become my salvation. The stone which the builders refused is become the head stone of the corner" (Ps. 118:21–22; compare Matt. 21:42; Mark 12:10; Luke 20:17; Acts 4:11; 1 Pet. 2:7).

Radiating from the central motif of the chief cornerstone of God's Kingdom are connecting links to other "stones" that play essential roles in furthering the cause of Zion. Among these are the prophets, seers, and revelators whose office is anchored in the principle of continuous revelation through the Spirit of God. To Peter, the Lord declared: "And I say also unto thee, That thou art Peter, and upon this rock I will build my church; and the gates of hell shall not prevail against it. And I will give unto thee the keys of the kingdom of heaven: and whatsoever thou shalt bind on earth shall be bound in heaven: and whatsoever thou shalt loose on earth shall be loosed in heaven" (Matt. 16:18–19). The Lord was counseling His chief Apostle in the context of an interesting linguistic word play: The name Peter is related to the Greek word "petros," meaning small rock, while at the same time the Greek word "petra" refers to bedrock, in the sense that Christ is "the stone of Israel" (D&C 50:44; see also John 1:42; 1 Cor. 3:11; 10:4; D&C 128:10).

Thus the Apostles and prophets are associate stones in the edifice of the kingdom of God, operating as they do through the foundational principle of divine revelation. Yet at the same time all of the members of the Church are in fact also "stones" in this monumental organization of God's kingdom. Peter admonished the people to come unto Christ, "as unto a living stone, disallowed indeed of men, but chosen of God, and precious, Ye also, as lively stones, are built up a spiritual house, an holy priesthood, to offer up spiritual sacrifices, acceptable to God by Jesus Christ. . . . But ye are a chosen generation, a royal priesthood, an holy nation, a peculiar people; that ye should shew forth the praises of him who hath called you out of darkness into his marvellous light" (1 Pet. 2:4–5, 9).

As "lively stones" in the structure of God's kingdom, we are to reflect in our daily living the truths and saving principles of the gospel. We are not to have hearts of stone—Zechariah referred to such recalcitrant and hardened hearts as "an adamant stone" (Zech. 7:12)—but rather hearts that are softened and contrite, willing to do the will of the Father and honor the teachings of the "chief corner stone," even Jesus Christ. As "lively stones," we are to have hearts ready to be touched and transformed by the Master's hand, just as the sixteen stones gathered by the Brother of Jared were touched by the Lord and transformed into luminous objects that radiated light to guide the Jaredites' journey toward the promised land (see Ether 3:6).

Paul reminded us that we are ourselves in fact a temple structure: "Know ye not that ye are the temple of God, and that the Spirit of God dwelleth in you?" (1 Cor. 3:16). As the community of Christ, we, severally and unitedly, form the greater temple of God's Kingdom—each supplying a stone—a "lively stone"—as an essential building unit for the spiritual construction, "In whom all the building fitly framed together groweth unto an holy temple in the Lord" (Eph. 2:21).

This growing and expanding kingdom can likewise be likened unto a stone, the stone that Daniel foresaw being "cut out of the mountain without hands" (Dan. 2:45) and rolling forth until it had become "a great mountain, and filled the whole earth" (Dan. 2:35; compare D&C 65:2; 109:72). We are part of that great stone, being as we are commissioned of God to fulfill the provisions and promises of the Abrahamic covenant to build and expand His kingdom without limits and to bless and edify the lives of all who will believe and come unto Christ with broken hearts and contrite spirits. In fact, the word "edify" itself means to build up a house, deriving as it does from a Greek term based on two smaller Greek words, "oikos" (house) and "demo" (to build). Thus we are to "edify" or build up a temple unto the Lord, which temple is the kingdom of God. As Paul taught: "Even so ye, forasmuch as ye are zealous of spiritual gifts, seek that ye may excel to the edifying of the church" (1 Cor. 14:12).

When the stake leadership associated with the Timpanogos Temple in Utah provided the youth in the area with a memento "stone" of Sierra white marble to keep their minds focused on spiritual things, they were, in fact, anticipating a marvelous gift that the Lord has promised to bestow upon His faithful and valiant servants:

> This earth, in its sanctified and immortal state, will be made like unto crystal and will be a Urim and Thummim to the inhabitants who dwell thereon, whereby all things pertaining to an inferior kingdom, or all kingdoms of a lower order, will be manifest to those who dwell on it; and this earth will be Christ's.
>
> Then the white stone mentioned in Revelation 2:17, will become a Urim and Thummim to each individual who receives one, whereby things pertaining to a higher order of kingdoms will be made known;
>
> And a white stone is given to each of those who come into the celestial kingdom, whereon is a new name written, which no man knoweth save he that receiveth it. The new name is the key word. (D&C 130:9–11)

At that future time of unspeakable glory and blessings, each individual will be, as it were, a seer, being illuminated with the light of truth in consummate measure and knowing the beginning from the end through an endowment of grace and love from the Father and the Son. Should we not therefore, day by day, strive, in our present imperfect state, to be "lively stones" of faith and valor, being shaped and prepared for a future integration into the body and temple of Christ as worthy servants, fitting harmoniously into the greater kingdom of our Father in Heaven? [Allen]

LIKENING THE SCRIPTURES TO OUR LIVES

Helaman 5:12 And now, my sons, remember, remember that it is upon the rock of our Redeemer, who is Christ, the Son of God, that ye must build your foundation; that when the devil shall send forth his mighty winds, yea, his shafts in the whirlwind, yea, when all his hail and his mighty storm shall beat upon you, it shall have no power over you to drag you down to the gulf of misery and endless wo, because of the rock upon which ye are built, which is a sure foundation, a foundation whereon if men build they cannot fall.

Application: Everything we do should be built upon the values and standards of the gospel of Jesus Christ. Even so, we must remember that we can do nothing without the grace of God and Atonement of Jesus Christ. It is through the gospel of Jesus Christ that we exercise our faith, repent, take upon us His name, and covenant to keep His commandments through baptism. Because of Him, the Father did in fact give us the blessing of the Holy Ghost in our lives. As we build our lives upon the foundation of our Savior Jesus Christ, we will be able to endure to the end.

3. UNITY OF THE FAMILY—HUSBAND AND WIFE, PARENTS AND CHILDREN

THEME: The family is the basic unit of the Church. It is the Lord's plan to strengthen His children in and through the family unit (see D&C 68:25–28). A family can be united in all things if they have values based upon the gospel of Jesus Christ. When they agree and build upon these values, they will have unity in the family.

MOMENT OF TRUTH

Paul's instructions to the Ephesian Saints includes warm and salient counsel for husbands and wives:

> Wives, submit yourselves unto your own husbands, as unto the Lord.
> For the husband is the head of the wife, even as Christ is the head of the church: and he is the saviour of the body.
> Therefore as the church is subject unto Christ, so let the wives be to their own husbands in every thing.
> Husbands, love your wives, even as Christ also loved the church, and gave himself for it. (Eph. 5:22–25)

Children are admonished to be obedient and to honor their parents—"which is the first commandment with promise" (Eph. 6:2), extending to them the assurance that things will go well with them and that they might live long in the land. Thus Paul reaches out to ensure the sanctity and well-being of the families within the Church and kingdom of God, just as our prophets and leaders do for us today (see *The Family: A Proclamation to the World,* 1995).

MODERN PROPHETS SPEAK

Gordon B. Hinckley:

> We are a church which bears testimony of the importance of the family—the father, the mother, the children—and of the fact that we are all children of God our Eternal Father. Parents who bring children into the world have a responsibility to love those children, to nurture them and care for them, to teach them those values which would bless their lives so that they will grow to become good citizens. If there is less trouble in the homes, there will be less trouble in the nations. I want to emphasize that which is already familiar to you, and that is the importance of binding our families together with love and kindness, with appreciation and respect, and with teaching the ways of the Lord so that your children will grow in righteousness and avoid the tragedies which are overcoming so many families across the world. (*TGBH*, 208)

ILLUSTRATIONS FOR OUR TIME

An Antarctic Insight

Admiral Byrd was alone at Ross Barrier in the midst of a terrible Antarctic storm. The temperature was 72 degrees below zero. The stove in his makeshift shelter was faulty—and carbon monoxide threatened his life. He did, however, survive and lived to write his book, *Alone.*

While keeping his lonely vigil in that far part of our universe, he meditated much and penned these profound words:

> At the end only two things really matter to a man, regardless of who he is, and they are the affection and understanding of his family.
>
> Anything and everything else he creates are insubstantial; they are ships given over to the mercy of the winds and tides of prejudice. But the family is an everlasting anchorage, a quiet harbor where a man's ship can be left to swing in the moorings of pride and loyalty.

LIKENING THE SCRIPTURES TO OUR LIVES

Ephesians 5:25 Husbands, love your wives, even as Christ also loved the church, and gave himself for it;

Application: Love is the motivation behind every righteous act (see John 3:16; 2 Ne. 26:24). We as husbands and wives should do all in our power to love, serve, and help each other so as to enjoy the blessings of earth life and exaltation in the celestial kingdom.

Colossians 3:20 Children, obey your parents in all things: for this is well pleasing unto the Lord.

Application: Parents are to lead and teach (see D&C 68:25–28). Children are to learn and obey. These roles need to be understood and appreciated so that all family members will be respectful of one another.

4. PUT ON THE ARMOR OF GOD

THEME: We have been counseled by prophets to put on the "armor of God." It is our protection from the adversary. It is our responsibility to prepare ourselves and our families by taking upon ourselves the protection that the Lord will provide for us as we yield to His loving enticings from the written word, His living prophets, and the Holy Spirit.

MOMENT OF TRUTH

Paul's concluding words in the Epistle to the Ephesians is the admonition to "take unto you the whole armour of God" (Eph. 6:13) in order to remain valiant and well protected from the incursions of evil influences. These well-known verses (Eph. 6:14–18) outline a defense strategy of unlimited power—since it defines our trust in the Lord as the source of our spiritual vitality.

LIKENING THE SCRIPTURES TO OUR LIVES

D&C 27:15–18 Wherefore, lift up your hearts and rejoice, and gird up your loins, and take upon you my whole armor, that ye may be able to withstand the evil day, having done all, that ye may be able to stand. Stand, therefore, having your loins girt about with truth, having on the breastplate of righteousness, and your feet shod with the preparation of the gospel of peace, which I have sent mine angels to commit unto you; Taking the shield of faith wherewith ye shall be able to quench all the fiery darts of the wicked; And take the helmet of salvation, and the sword of my Spirit, which I will pour out upon you, and my word which I reveal unto you, and be agreed as touching all things whatsoever ye ask of me, and be faithful until I come, and ye shall be caught up, that where I am ye shall be also. Amen.

Application: Let us faithfully don the armor of God to protect ourselves from the adversary. Note that the main areas protected are the loins, heart, feet, and head, all of which are vulnerable to the temptations of the world. Thus, putting on the whole armor is vital to our spiritual protection and success, because spiritual injury to any of these areas weakens all the others. It takes time and effort—but it is the only way in which we can shield ourselves from the devil and all the powers of darkness.

SUMMARY

The message of the Spirit, through Paul the Apostle, is that the Lord, in His infinite wisdom, grace, and mercy, has given to us a divinely ordained and authorized organization "for the perfecting of the saints, for the work of the ministry, for the edifying of the body of Christ" (Eph. 4:12). That which was established by the Savior in the meridian of time has been restored in this, the dispensation of the fulness of times, with Christ Himself as the chief cornerstone, and key offices of the Melchizedek Priesthood—including the living Apostles and prophets—in presiding capacity over the unfolding of the work. Within the kingdom of God, the family is the central unit, to be sustained by an abundance of love always protected by the armor of God in its supernal commission to provide the seedbed for the raising up of the children of God. These are the lessons that Paul taught the Saints at Ephesus, and, by extension, all subsequent sons and daughters of God.

CHAPTER 40

"I CAN DO ALL THINGS THROUGH CHRIST"

Reading Assignment: Philippians; Colossians; Philemon.

Additional Reading: Bible Dictionary, "Pauline Epistles: Epistle to the Philippians; Colossians; Philemon" (745–46).

> *None of us has attained perfection or the zenith of spiritual growth that is possible in mortality. Every person can and must make spiritual progress. The gospel of Jesus Christ is the divine plan for that spiritual growth eternally. It is more than a code of ethics. It is more than an ideal social order. It is more than positive thinking about self-improvement and determination. The gospel is the saving power of the Lord Jesus Christ with his priesthood and sustenance and with the Holy Spirit. With faith in the Lord Jesus Christ and obedience to his gospel, a step at a time improving as we go, pleading for strength, improving our attitudes and our ambitions, we will find ourselves successfully in the fold of the Good Shepherd. That will require discipline and training and exertion and strength. But as the Apostle Paul said, "I can do all things through Christ which strengtheneth me" (Philip. 4:13).*
>
> *A modern-day revelation makes this promise: "Put your trust in that Spirit which leadeth to do good—yea, to do justly, to walk humbly, to judge righteously; and this is my Spirit. Verily, verily, I say unto you, I will impart unto you of my Spirit, which shall enlighten your mind, which shall fill your soul with joy; and then shall ye know, or by this shall you know, all things whatsoever you desire of me, which are pertaining unto things of righteousness, in faith believing in me that ye shall receive" (D&C 11:12–14).*
>
> —Howard W. Hunter, *That We Might Have Joy* [Salt Lake City: Deseret Book, 1994], 184–85.

THEMES *for* LIVING

1. Saints Should Always Follow Christ
2. Redemption Comes Only Through Jesus Christ
3. Responsibilities of the Saints as the Elect of God

INTRODUCTION

Jesus, the perfect example, set a pattern of submissiveness to the will of Heavenly Father. He was meek and humble in all things that He suffered. This is how we too should follow Him, as He described, "And he that sent me is with me: the Father hath not left me alone; for I do always those things that please him" (John 8:29). We should seek to please our Heavenly Father and our Savior by keeping the commandments. The Lord counseled us to "be even as He is" (see 3 Ne. 27:27). Let us remember that our hope is in Christ because of His redeeming power. This insight should continually remind us of our responsibilities as faithful Saints. Those who are filled with charity, the pure love of Christ, become the elect of God (see Col. 3:12–15; 2 Pet. 1:3–12; Moro. 7:48). All of the attributes of charity are evident in the lives of the faithful Saints.

1. SAINTS SHOULD ALWAYS FOLLOW CHRIST

THEME: The example has been set and the admonition of our Savior has been given: "Come and follow me" (Matt. 19:21). Let us remember that we cannot serve both mammon and God (see Matt. 6:24).

MOMENT OF TRUTH

Paul's Epistles to the Philippians, the Colossians, and Philemon were written (like Ephesians and Hebrews) in the time frame A.D. 60 to A.D. 62. As previously noted, all of these epistles were written from Rome during Paul's confinement there under the direction of the Roman authorities. Philippi was a city in Macedonia (now part of northern Greece) that had been named in honor of the father of Alexander the Great. Paul had visited the city as part of his missionary service (see Acts 16:12–40; 20:6; Philip. 1:1; 1 Thess. 2:2). Colosse was a town in Phrygia (located in what is now Turkey) close to the commercial highway from Ephesus to the Euphrates. Philemon was a native of Colosse, and he was one of Paul's converts to the faith.

In these writings we see reflected the apostolic counsel to follow the Savior in all that we do. Here are some representative examples:

- On being unified in Christ:

  For unto you it is given in the behalf of Christ, not only to believe on him, but also to suffer for his sake (Philip. 1:27–29).

  Fulfil ye my joy, that ye be likeminded, having the same love, being of one accord, of one mind (Philip. 2:2).

- On being steadfast in the Lord:

  Therefore, my brethren dearly beloved and longed for, my joy and crown, so stand fast in the Lord, my dearly beloved (Philip. 4:1).

- On rejoicing in the Lord of Peace in the spirit of thanksgiving:

  Rejoice in the Lord alway: and again I say, Rejoice.

  Let your moderation be known unto all men. The Lord is at hand.

  Be careful for nothing; but in every thing by prayer and supplication with thanksgiving let your requests be made known unto God.

  And the peace of God, which passeth all understanding, shall keep your hearts and minds through Christ Jesus (Philip. 4:4–7).

- On being worthy as "saints in light":

  That ye might walk worthy of the Lord unto all pleasing, being fruitful in every good work, and increasing in the knowledge of God;

  Strengthened with all might, according to his glorious power, unto all patience and longsuffering with joyfulness;

  Giving thanks unto the Father, which hath made us meet to be partakers of the inheritance of the saints in light (Col. 1:10–12).

MODERN PROPHETS SPEAK

Joseph B. Wirthlin:

What [the Savior] declared in the meridian of time stands as unassailably true today as it was nearly two thousand years ago when he proclaimed, "I am the way, the truth, and the life" (John 14:6). In the Book of Mormon, Jacob powerfully exhorts us to come unto Christ and to follow the Lord's straight course: "O then, my beloved brethren, come unto the Lord, the Holy One, Remember that his paths are righteous. Behold, the way for man is narrow, but it lieth in a straight course before him, and the keeper of the gate is the Holy One of Israel; and he employeth no servant there; and there is none other way save it be by the gate; for he cannot be deceived, for the Lord God is his name" (2 Ne. 9:41).

Jacob's elder brother, Nephi, queried, "Can we follow Jesus save we shall be willing to keep the commandments?" (2 Ne. 31:10). The resounding response is found in the Redeemer's own words: "If ye love me, keep my commandments" (John 14:15), "for the works which ye have seen me do that shall ye also do" (3 Ne. 27:21).

To follow Christ, we must obey his commandments. (*Finding Peace in Our Lives* [Salt Lake City: Deseret Book, 1995], 231)

ILLUSTRATIONS FOR OUR TIME

Keeping the commandments is the only way to truly follow our Savior Jesus Christ. Joseph B. Wirthlin explains:

> With all my heart I echo the Savior's admonition that we choose to hear and heed the word of God. . . .
>
> We must keep *all* the commandments. We cannot approach the gospel as we would a buffet or smorgasbord, choosing here a little and there a little. We must sit down to the whole feast and live the Lord's loving commandments in their fullness. . . .
>
> The righteous King Benjamin, who loved his people dearly, gathered his people together near the end of his righteous life to share with them the deepest feelings of his heart. After reviewing the basic beliefs and commandments of the gospel of Christ with them, he offered this simple but powerful exhortation: "And now, if you *believe* all these things see that ye *do* them" (Mosiah 4:10; emphasis added). . . .
>
> No more powerful invitation to follow the Savior can be found in scripture than Moroni's valedictory admonition: "Come unto Christ, and be perfected in him, and deny yourselves of all ungodliness" (Moro. 10:32). May we follow Christ to a rich, full, abundant life of peace and joy. When we are heavy laden, his promise of soul-refreshing rest is sure (see Matt. 11:28–29). And may we follow him to life eternal, to dwell forever with him and with our Father who is in heaven. (Joseph B. Wirthlin, *Finding Peace in Our Lives* [Salt Lake City: Deseret Book, 1995], 232–34)

LIKENING THE SCRIPTURES TO OUR LIVES

2 Nephi 31:10 And he said unto the children of men: Follow thou me. Wherefore, my beloved brethren, can we follow Jesus save we shall be willing to keep the commandments of the Father?

Application: Following Christ means keeping all of His commandments. If we love Him, we will keep His commandments (see John 14:15).

2. REDEMPTION COMES ONLY THROUGH JESUS CHRIST

THEME: A constant theme and reminder throughout all scripture is that we are redeemed by the atoning blood of our Savior Jesus Christ. There is no other name given by which we can be saved and exalted (see Mosiah 3:17; 5:8).

MOMENT OF TRUTH

In Paul's writings under consideration in this chapter, we see confirmed the Apostle's unshakeable faith in the atoning mission of the Savior as the only source for eternal salvation and exaltation. Here are some representative examples:

- On the mission of the exalted Son, Creator, and Lord of all:
  Let this mind be in you, which was also in Christ Jesus:

  Who, being in the form of God, thought it not robbery to be equal with God:

  But made himself of no reputation, and took upon him the form of a servant, and was made in the likeness of men:

  And being found in fashion as a man, he humbled himself, and became obedient unto death, even the death of the cross.

  Wherefore God also hath highly exalted him, and given him a name which is above every name:

  That at the name of Jesus every knee should bow, of things in heaven, and things in earth, and things under the earth;

  And that every tongue should confess that Jesus Christ is Lord, to the glory of God the Father (Philip. 2:5–11).

- On the Savior, Master of Life and spiritual transformation:
  For our conversation is in heaven; from whence also we look for the Saviour, the Lord Jesus Christ:

  Who shall change our vile body, that it may be fashioned like unto his glorious body, according to the working whereby he is able even to subdue all things unto himself (Philip. 3:20–21).

- On the Redeemer, Firstborn of God and eternal Head of the Kingdom:
  Who hath delivered us from the power of darkness, and hath translated us into the kingdom of his dear Son:

  In whom we have redemption through his blood, even the forgiveness of sins:

  Who is the image of the invisible God, the firstborn of every creature:

  For by him were all things created, that are in heaven, and that are in earth, visible and invisible, whether they be thrones, or dominions, or principalities, or powers: all things were created by him, and for him:

And he is before all things, and by him all things consist.

And he is the head of the body, the church: who is the beginning, the firstborn from the dead; that in all things he might have the preeminence.

For it pleased the Father that in him should all fulness dwell;

And, having made peace through the blood of his cross, by him to reconcile all things unto himself; by him, I say, whether they be things in earth, or things in heaven. (Col. 1:13–20)

MODERN PROPHETS SPEAK

Bruce R. McConkie:

As Paul journeyed to Jerusalem to face bonds and chains for the testimony of Jesus, he charged the Ephesian elders, whose faces he would not again see in mortality, "to feed the church of God, which he hath purchased with his own blood" (Acts 20:17–28). To both the Colossians and the Ephesians he wrote that the saints have "redemption through his blood, even the forgiveness of sins" (Col. 1:14. See also Eph. 1:7). To the Romans he testified that the law of justification itself is operative because of "his blood" (Rom. 5:9), and that we are thereby "justified freely by his grace through the redemption that is in Christ Jesus: Whom God hath set forth to be a propitiation through faith in his blood." That is to say, "remission of sins" comes to those who have "faith in his blood"; it is to them that the effects of his pro-pitiatory sacrifice are given (Rom. 3:24–25). To the Hebrews, whose practice it then was to shed the blood of animals in blood sacrifices, Paul taught that all Mosaic sac-rifices were in fact similitudes of the coming sacrifice of the Messiah. He showed them that under both the old and the new covenants sins are purged only "with blood," and that "without shedding of blood is no remission." His witness was that "the blood of Christ, who . . . offered himself without spot to God," was the only thing that would purge men from "dead works" and evil deeds and enable them "to serve the living God" and gain salvation in his kingdom (Heb. 9). (*The Promised Messiah: The First Coming of Christ* [Salt Lake City: Deseret Book, 1981], 254)

ILLUSTRATIONS FOR OUR TIME

John Taylor expounds upon the doctrine of redemption through the Atonement of the Lord Jesus Christ:

One great and very striking statement is here made by the Lord himself, to the effect that it behooved Christ to suffer, and the question at once presents itself before us, why did it behoove him? Or why was it necessary that he should suffer? For it would seem from his language, through his sufferings, death, Atonement, and resurrection, "that repentance and remission of sins" could be preached among all nations, and that consequently if he had not atoned for the sins of the world, repentance and remission of sins could not have been preached to the nations. A very important principle is here enunciated, one in which the interests of the whole human family throughout all the world are involved. That principle is the offering up of the Son of God as a sacrifice, an Atonement, and a propitiation for our sins. . . .

If it were not for the Atonement of Jesus Christ, the sacrifice he made, all the human family would have to lie in the grave throughout eternity without any hope. But God having provided, through the Atonement of the Lord Jesus Christ, the medium whereby we can be restored to the bosom and presence of the Father, to participate with him among the Gods in the eternal worlds—he having provided for that, has also provided for the resurrection. He proclaimed himself the resurrection and the life. Said he, "I am the resurrection, and the life: he that believeth in me, though he were dead, yet shall he live" (John 11:25). By and by the tombs will be opened and the dead will hear the voice of the Son of God, and they shall come forth, they who have done good to the resurrection of the just, and they who have done evil to the resurrection of the unjust. (John Taylor, *The Gospel Kingdom: Selections from the Writings and Discourses of John Taylor,* selected, arranged, and edited, with an introduction by G. Homer Durham [Salt Lake City: Improvement Era, 1941], 117–18)

LIKENING THE SCRIPTURES TO OUR LIVES

Colossians 1:12–14 Giving thanks unto the Father, which hath made us meet to be partakers of the inheritance of the saints in light: Who hath delivered us from the power of darkness, and hath translated us into the kingdom of his dear Son: In whom we have redemption through his blood, even the forgiveness of sins.

Application: Gratitude should be felt and expressed for the goodness of God and the suffering of our Savior, that we might have deliverance from our sins if we but repent.

3. RESPONSIBILITIES OF THE SAINTS AS THE ELECT OF GOD

THEME: As Saints with the honor and promise of being the elect of God, we should be rooted in Christ and honorably take upon us His name, seeking to emulate Him in all that we do.

MOMENT OF TRUTH

Paul exhorts the Saints at Philippi and Colosse to honor their covenant obligations as Saints of the Most High by living a life reflecting the highest principles of the gospel. Here is a sampling of his timeless counsel:

- On working out our salvation within the context of the Atonement:
  Wherefore, my beloved, as ye have always obeyed, not as in my presence only, but now much more in my absence, work out your own salvation with fear and trembling.

  For it is God which worketh in you both to will and to do of his good pleasure.(Philip. 2:12–13).
- On cultivating Christian virtues:
  Finally, brethren, whatsoever things are true, whatsoever things are honest, whatsoever things are just, whatsoever things are pure, whatsoever things are lovely, whatsoever things are of good report; if there be any virtue, and if there be any praise, think on these things.

  Those things, which ye have both learned, and received, and heard, and seen in me, do: and the God of peace shall be with you.

  But I rejoiced in the Lord greatly, that now at the last your care of me hath flourished again; wherein ye were also careful, but ye lacked opportunity.

  Not that I speak in respect of want: for I have learned, in whatsoever state I am, therewith to be content.

  I know both how to be abased, and I know how to abound: every where and in all things I am instructed both to be full and to be hungry, both to abound and to suffer need.

  I can do all things through Christ which strengtheneth me (Philip. 4:8–13).
- On walking after the pattern of Jesus Christ:
  As ye have therefore received Christ Jesus the Lord, so walk ye in him:

  Rooted and built up in him, and stablished in the faith, as ye have been taught, abounding therein with thanksgiving.

  Beware lest any man spoil you through philosophy and vain deceit, after the tradition of men, after the rudiments of the world, and not after Christ.

  For in him dwelleth all the fulness of the Godhead bodily.

  And ye are complete in him, which is the head of all principality and power:

  In whom also ye are circumcised with the circumcision made without hands, in putting off the body of the sins of the flesh by the circumcision of Christ:

  Buried with him in baptism, wherein also ye are risen with him through the faith of the operation of God, who hath raised him from the dead (Col. 2:6–12).
- On setting our priorities on heavenly things:
  Set your affection on things above, not on things on the earth (Col. 3:2).

- On cultivating a life abounding in charity:

  Put on therefore, as the elect of God, holy and beloved, bowels of mercies, kindness, humbleness of mind, meekness, longsuffering;

  Forbearing one another, and forgiving one another, if any man have a quarrel against any: even as Christ forgave you, so also do ye.

  And above all these things put on charity, which is the bond of perfectness.

  And let the peace of God rule in your hearts, to the which also ye are called in one body; and be ye thankful.

  Let the word of Christ dwell in you richly in all wisdom; teaching and admonishing one another in psalms and hymns and spiritual songs, singing with grace in your hearts to the Lord.

  And whatsoever ye do in word or deed, do all in the name of the Lord Jesus, giving thanks to God and the Father by him (Col. 3:12–17; compare D&C 121:41–46).

- On preserving unity and love in the family:

  Wives, submit yourselves unto your own husbands, as it is fit in the Lord.

  Husbands, love your wives, and be not bitter against them.

  Children, obey your parents in all things: for this is well pleasing unto the Lord.

  Fathers, provoke not your children to anger, lest they be discouraged (Col. 3:18–21).

- On forgiving others:

  Not now as a servant, but above a servant, a brother beloved, specially to me, but how much more unto thee, both in the flesh, and in the Lord?

  If thou [Philemon] count me therefore a partner, receive him [Onesimus, the slave] as myself.

  If he hath wronged thee, or oweth thee ought, put that on mine account (Philem. 1:16–18).

MODERN PROPHETS SPEAK

Bruce R. McConkie:

Election is akin to and synonymous with calling, and in a general sense the elect comprise the whole house of Israel (Isa. 45:4; 65:9). Jesus and Paul and Peter speak of the elect as the saints, as the faithful believers, as those who love the Lord and are seeking righteousness (Matt. 24:22; Mark 13:20; Luke 18:7; Col. 3:12; 2 Tim. 2:10; Titus 1:1). And the Lord in our day has promised to gather and save his elect (D&C 29:7; 33:6; 35:20). Paul speaks of the elect along with the called, setting forth that they are foreordained to be like Christ, that their conduct here is justified, and that they shall be glorified hereafter (Rom. 8:28–30). Peter specifies that their high status is "according to the foreknowledge of God the Father" (1 Pet. 1:2), and Isaiah assures us that great blessings shall flow to them during the Millennial Era (Isa. 65:22). (*DNTC*, 3:329–30)

ILLUSTRATIONS FOR OUR TIME

The Spiritually-Centered Life

In his celebrated epistles, the Apostle Paul enjoined the Saints of his day to stand true to the principles of salvation by means of which they enjoyed a place of enduring peace and joy as the elect of God within the fold of the Church.

This brings to mind an experience from my own past. Several years after the completion of the Washington D.C. Temple, I invited two good nonmember friends and university colleagues to drive down with me to the Visitors Center at the temple for a tour. One was a young sociology professor and the other was a Catholic priest who taught courses in comparative religion. They listened and observed carefully. Following the tour, my Catholic friend made a significant statement, which I recorded in my journal. He noted, in general, that many clergy have two religions, one that they "carry in their pocket" and one that they present in public. "Often there is a considerable gap between the two," he said, inferring that they might be more "religious" outwardly than inwardly. "With the Mormons, it is different," he observed. "The gap in their case seems to be rather small." With this compliment, he was articulating his own perspective that members of the Church typically live by their convictions, and since they seem to accomplish much practical good, they must therefore, he believed, have a strong, genuine faith. He was right. Such is indeed the case with Latter-day Saints who abide by the teachings of the Master and strive to make their lives consistently centered in spiritual paths—both outwardly as well as inwardly. They fulfill the harvest from the good seed about which Jesus spoke: "But that on the good ground are they, which in an honest and good heart, having heard the word, keep it, and bring forth fruit with patience" (Luke 8:15). [Allen]

LIKENING THE SCRIPTURES TO OUR LIVES

Colossians 3:12–14 Put on therefore, as the elect of God, holy and beloved, bowels of mercies, kindness, humbleness of mind, meekness, longsuffering; Forbearing one another, and forgiving one another, if any man have a quarrel against any: even as Christ forgave you, so also do ye. And above all these things put on charity, which is the bond of perfectness.

Application: If we are the elect of God, we should seek to obtain faith, virtue, knowledge, temperance, patience, brotherly kindness, godliness, and charity in all humility and diligence (see D&C 4:6). We are to live the celestial law (see Matt. 5–7; 3 Ne. 12–14). We are to seek to become like Him (see Moro. 7:48).

SUMMARY

Paul's timeless and universal counsel is a refreshing review of our gospel obligations to follow the Savior in all that we do, to remember that the name of Christ is the only name under which salvation and exaltation can be obtained, and to perform with full devotion our obligations and responsibilities as the Saints and the elect of God. Paul's injunction to "work out your own salvation with fear and trembling" (Philip. 2:12)—under the aegis and power of the Atonement—is reminiscent of what Amulek had taught nearly a century previous: "And now, my beloved brethren, I desire that ye should remember these things, and that ye should work out your salvation with fear before God, and that ye should no more deny the coming of Christ" (Alma 34:37; compare Morm. 9:27). Nephi, as well, had taught the primacy of the redemption of grace, which alone can assure salvation, after we have performed to our maximum ability the works of righteousness essential to please God: "For we labor diligently to write, to persuade our children, and also our brethren, to believe in Christ, and to be reconciled to God; for we know that it is by grace that we are saved, after all we can do" (2 Ne. 25:23). Through these and every other word of God we find the sustenance and strength needed for our transformation from the old to the new, from the proud and self-centered to the humble and receptive, and from drifting and lost to the secure and reclaimed of the Lord.

CHAPTER 41

UNDERSTANDING *and* APPLYING *the* DOCTRINES *of* CHRIST

Reading Assignment: 1 and 2 Timothy; Titus.

Additional Reading: Bible Dictionary, "Pauline Epistles; 1 and 2 Timothy" (747–48); "Titus" (785–86).

> You have seen [the gospel] change the lives of people, you've seen them change their habits and their thinking and their living. You know what it does for families; just think what it would be if all people of the world would have this same understanding, what a great change would come to the human family here upon the earth. We would live in peace and in plenty, and there would be happiness for all people who live. . . . Peace will never come to the world nor will men ever learn to live together in peace and harmony except by the principles of the restored gospel of Jesus Christ. He came into the world with the message of peace, but people have never learned to live the principles.
>
> —HOWARD W. HUNTER, *THWH*, 265.

THEMES *for* LIVING

1. The Key to Change—Applying Gospel Knowledge and True Doctrine
2. Power of Example
3. Seek Righteousness and Deny Yourselves of All Ungodliness

INTRODUCTION

Gospel knowledge has to do with eternal truths given by God to man—the knowledge that can save. When we gain a clear understanding of the doctrines, principles, concepts, and covenants pertaining to the gospel and the kingdom of God, we have knowledge of the truth. We are enlightened. We increase in our intelligence, for we have acquired light and truth. This pure knowledge comes by the power of the Holy Ghost. "And by the power of the Holy Ghost ye may know the truth of all things" (Moro. 10:5). We should seek this knowledge that we might understand the things of God and the nature of God. Let us remember that gaining this knowledge is part of taking upon ourselves the divine nature of Jesus Christ (see 2 Pet.1:3–12). When we live according to these eternal truths, we will know God and Jesus Christ (see John 17:3).

When the Savior visited the Saints in ancient America following His resurrection, He provided His disciples with the consummate counsel for the unending process of self-perfection and covenant service: "Therefore, what manner of men ought ye to be? Verily I say unto you, even as I am" (3 Ne. 27:27). His example is the pinnacle of the "godly walk and conversation" (D&C 20:69) we are striving to acquire and practice, the ultimate righteousness.

Righteousness is that state of being in which one is blameless, full of faith, seeking the will of the Father with an eye single to His glory, full of good works, being exactly, immediately, and courageously obedient to the laws and commandments of the Lord. We seek to be righteous—that is our compass and our charge. Righteousness is the oil of our lamp. Righteousness is happiness (see 2 Ne. 2:13). The Prophet Joseph put into perspective the design of our existence, which brings the priority of righteousness to the forefront in obtaining happiness. He said, "Happiness is the object and design of our existence; and will be the end thereof, if we pursue the path that leads to it; and this path is virtue, uprightness, faithfulness, holiness, and keeping all the commandments of God" (Joseph Smith, *HC* 5:134–35).

1. THE KEY TO CHANGE—APPLYING GOSPEL KNOWLEDGE AND TRUE DOCTRINE

THEME: People can change when they are taught true doctrine, consisting of knowledge of God and His ways. When their heart is touched with appreciation and gratitude for such knowledge, they change their attitude and behavior and conform to the teachings of the gospel of Jesus Christ.

MOMENT OF TRUTH

Paul's epistles to Titus and Timothy (First and Second Timothy) date from the period A.D. 64–65. They are the last of the extant writings of this choice Apostle of the Lord. The First Epistle to Timothy was written, following Paul's first imprisonment, as a means to counsel this trusted younger associate in his ministerial duties at Ephesus. The Second Epistle to Timothy dates from the period of Paul's second imprisonment, prior to his martyrdom. Titus and Timothy were among the most devoted associates of the Apostle Paul in his missionary and pastoral labors.

Paul's counsel to Timothy and Titus incorporates eternal principles of spiritual leadership in building the kingdom of God. We see that the essence of his message is expressed early on: "Now the end of the commandment is charity out of a pure heart, and of a good conscience, and of faith unfeigned" (1 Tim. 1:5). At the center of focus is the Savior: "For there is one God, and one mediator between God and men, the man Christ Jesus" (1 Tim. 2:5). The Church has a divine inner core, for it is indeed "the church of the living God, the pillar and ground of the truth. And without controversy great is the mystery of godliness: God was manifest in the flesh, justified in the Spirit, seen of angels, preached unto the Gentiles, believed on in the world, received up into glory" (1 Tim. 3:15–16). For that reason, meticulous care should be given to matters of governance, counseled Paul: "Lay hands suddenly on no man, neither be partaker of other men's sins: keep thyself pure" (1 Tim. 5:22). Such purity is aligned with the spiritual gifts of leadership, as Paul confirms:

> Wherefore I put thee in remembrance that thou stir up the gift of God, which is in thee by the putting on of my hands.
>
> For God hath not given us the spirit of fear; but of power, and of love, and of a sound mind.
>
> Be not thou therefore ashamed of the testimony of our Lord, nor of me his prisoner: but be thou partaker of the afflictions of the gospel according to the power of God;
>
> Who hath saved us, and called us with an holy calling, not according to our works, but according to his own purpose and grace, which was given us in Christ Jesus before the world began,
>
> But is now made manifest by the appearing of our Saviour Jesus Christ, who hath abolished death, and hath brought life and immortality to light through the gospel. (2 Tim. 1:6–10)

Through obedience to the principles of salvation, those who serve the Saints have divine assurances of God's intervening help: "Nevertheless the foundation of God standeth sure, having this seal, The Lord knoweth them that are his. And, Let every one that nameth the name of Christ depart from iniquity" (2 Tim. 2:19). Specifically, Paul admonishes Timothy to set his mind and heart on the word of God as the channel of divine counsel: "And that from a child thou hast known the holy scriptures, which are able to make thee wise unto salvation through faith which is in Christ Jesus. All scripture is given by inspiration of God, and is profitable for doctrine, for reproof, for correction, for instruction in righteousness: That the man of God may be perfect, throughly furnished unto all good works" (2 Tim. 3:15–17). Above all, as Paul reminds Titus, one should depend on the Spirit for guidance in all spiritual matters: "Not by works of righteousness which we have done, but according to his mercy he saved us, by the washing of regeneration, and renewing of the Holy Ghost; Which he shed on us abundantly through Jesus Christ our Saviour; That being justified by his grace, we should be made heirs according to the hope of eternal life" (Titus 3:5–7).

MODERN PROPHETS SPEAK

Gordon B. Hinckley:

> As we talk of reading, I should like to add a word concerning that which we absorb not only out of the processes of the mind, but something further which comes by the power of the Spirit. Remember this promise given by revelation: "God shall give unto you knowledge by his Holy Spirit, yea, by the unspeakable gift of the Holy Ghost." (D&C 121:26) (*TGBH,* 299)

ILLUSTRATIONS FOR OUR TIME

"For Their Sakes"

Every faithful laborer in the Kingdom is moved by a sacred ensign, and that is Christ Jesus, and Him crucified and raised up as the "author of eternal salvation unto all them that obey him" (Heb. 5:9). This is the ensign that is sustained and glorified throughout the Holy Scriptures in myriad variations around that central theme. From time to time, each person called on the errand of the Lord—and that includes all of us as Saints in the Church and kingdom of God—will be touched by this or that scriptural passage as a particularly keen reminder of the essence of the gospel of Jesus Christ. For me, over the years, one special statement of the Savior during His intercessory prayer just prior to the crucifixion has become a resonating beacon of grandeur and inspiration. He said, "And for their sakes I sanctify myself, that they also might be sanctified through the truth" (John 17:19). "For their sakes" He did all of this, meaning "for *our* sakes"—as "children of the prophets" and "children of the covenant" (3 Ne. 20:25–26). What a grand and humbling insight—an echo, in fact, of what the Lord revealed to Moses: "For behold, this is my work and my glory—to bring to pass the immortality and eternal life of man" (Moses 1:39).

Toward the end of his ministry as the Lord's great missionary to both Jew and Gentile, the Apostle Paul made a statement very similar to that of the Savior in His intercessory prayer. Paul wrote to his young associate, Timothy: "Therefore I endure all things for the elect's sakes, that they may also obtain the salvation which is in Christ Jesus with eternal glory" (2 Tim. 2:10). In doing so, Paul showed that he had adopted the theme of the Savior's all-encompassing design of sacrifice and redemption and applied it as a governing principle to his own ministry. We can do no less. Where the Savior said, "Here am I, send me" (Abr. 3:27), we are to say the same in response to the call to serve, just as Isaiah did, word for word (see Isa. 6:8).

We are called to prepare ourselves in order to strengthen our brethren and sisters and guide our families toward heavenly goals. Despite the challenges thrown up in our way by dissenting voices and worldly influences that would intrude and degrade, we can keep ourselves pure and remember what the Lord said: "And for their sakes I sanctify myself, that they also might be sanctified through the truth" (John 17:19). We can do no less, even though the sacrifice will test our very souls, as Peter confirmed: "But and if ye suffer for righteousness' sake, happy are ye: and be not afraid of their terror, neither be troubled" (1 Pet. 3:14; compare Isa. 45:4; D&C 84:48). By committing our whole being to the Lord and honoring our sacred covenants to render charitable service toward His children continually—doing it "for their sakes"—we can be blessed to view in our mind's eye the future moment in time when our journey will be done, when we will have given our best, and be able to say, with Paul: "I have fought a good fight, I have finished my course, I have kept the faith" (2 Tim. 4:7). [Allen]

LIKENING THE SCRIPTURES TO OUR LIVES

1 Timothy 4:5–6 For it is sanctified by the word of God and prayer. If thou put the brethren in remembrance of these things, thou shalt be a good minister of Jesus Christ, nourished up in the words of faith and of good doctrine, whereunto thou hast attained.

Application: We can become an instrument in the hands of God as we treasure up His words (see D&C 84:85) and seek to live by every word that proceeds from the mouth of God (see D&C 84:43–46).

2. POWER OF EXAMPLE

THEME: The power of a righteous example can change lives forever. Without showing a good example in our lives, we ensure that our words may be in vain.

MOMENT OF TRUTH

In his exhortations to Timothy, Paul places a crown of honor on the power of example. No matter what our role or our position, no matter what our age or our presence, we can invest our spirituality in the service of others with the assurance that the Lord will guide our footsteps for the good of the community of Saints:

> Let no man despise thy youth; but be thou an example of the believers, in word, in conversation, in charity, in spirit, in faith, in purity.
>
> Till I come, give attendance to reading, to exhortation, to doctrine.
>
> Neglect not the gift that is in thee, which was given thee by prophecy, with the laying on of the hands of the presbytery.
>
> Meditate upon these things; give thyself wholly to them; that thy profiting may appear to all.
>
> Take heed unto thyself, and unto the doctrine; continue in them: for in doing this thou shalt both save thyself, and them that hear thee. (1 Tim. 4:12–16)

Above all, gentleness and meekness will engender good followership unto repentance and faith in the Lord: "And the servant of the Lord must not strive; but be gentle unto all men, apt to teach, patient, In meekness instructing those that oppose themselves; if God peradventure will give them repentance to the acknowledging of the truth" (2 Tim. 2:24–25).

MODERN PROPHETS SPEAK

Ezra Taft Benson:

> If we are to pattern our lives in accordance with the divine example set for us by the Savior, we must attain to that stature by releasing and developing our capacities to the fullest through devoted service. Only in this way may we become worthy examples of the kingdom of God on earth and merit consideration for membership in the kingdom of God in heaven. (*TETB*, 330)

ILLUSTRATIONS FOR OUR TIME

Gordon B. Hinckley relates the following powerful example of a military veteran:

> Not long after that I talked with another young man also recently returned from the war. He too had walked the jungle patrols, his heart pounding with fear. But reluctantly he admitted that the greatest fear he had was the fear of ridicule.
>
> The men of his company laughed at him, taunted him, plastered him with a nickname that troubled him. They told him they were going to force him to do

some of the things they reveled in. Then on one occasion when the going was rough, he faced them and quietly said, "Look, I know you think I'm a square. I don't consider myself any better than any of the rest of you. But I grew up in a different way. I grew up in a religious home and a religious town. I went to church on Sundays. We prayed together as a family. I was taught to stay away from these things. It's just that I believe differently. With me it's a matter of religion, and it's kind of a way of respecting my mother and my dad. All of you together might force me toward a compromising situation, but that wouldn't change me, and you wouldn't feel right after you'd done it."

One by one they turned silently away. But during the next few days each came to ask his pardon, and from his example others gained the strength and the will to change their own lives. He taught the gospel to two of them and brought them into the Church. (*TGBH,* 181)

"Like Father, Like Son"
In my life, I have been affected tremendously by the power of example, just as you have. For good or ill, example is always there. I'll never forget the day when I took my two youngest sons, ages eight and six, to look at new cars. We casually walked through the car lot. As we passed a car, I kicked the tire as we all sometimes do. I looked back to check my sons to see if they were close to me. I watched in awe as each son walked by the car and kicked the tires just like their dad. It hit me with such impact—*I must be a good example for my children. They will do what I do.* I'd best consider my ways and choose always to be a good example in all things. Take the time to be an example at all times and in all places. [Pinegar]

LIKENING THE SCRIPTURES TO OUR LIVES

1 Timothy 4:12 Let no man despise thy youth; but be thou an example of the believers, in word, in conversation, in charity, in spirit, in faith, in purity.

Application: Being a good example requires the involvement of your entire being— your demeanor, your dress, your words, your countenance, and all that you radiate. The question might be asked, "What message are you sending today?"

3. SEEK RIGHTEOUSNESS AND DENY YOURSELVES OF ALL UNGODLINESS

THEME: Seek to be righteous in all things and deny yourself of all ungodliness—for that is the pathway to happiness, salvation, and exaltation.

MOMENT OF TRUTH

From their chief mentor and guide, Paul the Apostle, Timothy and Titus received inspiring counsel on how to use God-given agency wisely and how to instruct their followers to do the same. Here is the famous passage on worldly wealth that Paul wrote to Timothy:

> But godliness with contentment is great gain.
>
> For we brought nothing into this world, and it is certain we can carry nothing out.
>
> And having food and raiment let us be therewith content.
>
> But they that will be rich fall into temptation and a snare, and into many foolish and hurtful lusts, which drown men in destruction and perdition.
>
> For the love of money is the root of all evil: which while some coveted after, they have erred from the faith, and pierced themselves through with many sorrows.
>
> But thou, O man of God, flee these things; and follow after righteousness, godliness, faith, love, patience, meekness.
>
> Fight the good fight of faith, lay hold on eternal life, whereunto thou art also called, and hast professed a good profession before many witnesses. (1 Tim. 6:6–12)

Paul counseled Timothy to teach through righteous conduct, separating himself from worldly entanglements: "Thou therefore, my son, be strong in the grace that is in Christ Jesus. And the things that thou hast heard of me among many witnesses, the same commit thou to faithful men, who shall be able to teach others also. Thou therefore endure hardness, as a good soldier of Jesus Christ. No man that warreth entangleth himself with the affairs of this life; that he may please him who hath chosen him to be a soldier" (2 Tim. 2:1–4). This is particularly pertinent advice, given Paul's dire prediction concerning the impending apostasy:

> This know also, that in the last days perilous times shall come.
>
> For men shall be lovers of their own selves, covetous, boasters, proud, blasphemers, disobedient to parents, unthankful, unholy,
>
> Without natural affection, trucebreakers, false accusers, incontinent, fierce, despisers of those that are good,
>
> Traitors, heady, highminded, lovers of pleasures more than lovers of God;
>
> Having a form of godliness, but denying the power thereof: from such turn away.
>
> For of this sort are they which creep into houses, and lead captive silly women laden with sins, led away with divers lusts,

Ever learning, and never able to come to the knowledge of the truth. (2 Tim. 3:1–7)

In contrast to such devious patterns, Paul reminded Titus of the necessity of remaining pure and avoiding the pollutions of disbelief: "Unto the pure all things are pure: but unto them that are defiled and unbelieving is nothing pure; but even their mind and conscience is defiled" (Titus 1:15).

MODERN PROPHETS SPEAK

Marion G. Romney:

> The Lord's statement that the cause of the world's distress is failure to seek him "to establish his righteousness" is verily true, notwithstanding the fact that it is generally rejected on the ground that it is an oversimplification. When men reject God, they set themselves adrift on the sea of life without guiding star, compass, or rudder; they have no concept of their origin or of their destiny; they are without a standard by which to distinguish good from evil; they recognize neither the Spirit of Christ, which would enlighten them through the world, nor the power of the devil, which is dragging them down. (*Learning for the Eternities* [Salt Lake City: Deseret Book, 1977], 2)

ILLUSTRATIONS FOR OUR TIME

Russell M. Nelson explains what it means to hunger and thirst after righteousness:

> I was with Elder Mark E. Petersen in the Holy Land in October 1983, during his last mortal journey. Elder Petersen was not well. Evidences of his consuming malignancy were painfully real to him, yet he derived strength from the Savior he served. Following a night of intense suffering, exacerbated by pangs of his progressive inability to eat or to drink, Elder Petersen addressed throngs assembled at the Mount of the Beatitudes to hear his discourse on the Sermon on the Mount. After he recited "Blessed are they which do hunger and thirst after righteousness," he departed from the biblical text and pleaded this question: "Do you know what it is to be really hungry? Do you know what it is to really be thirsty? Do you desire righteousness as you would desire food under extreme conditions or drink under extreme conditions? [The Savior] expects us to literally hunger and thirst after righteousness and seek it with all our hearts!"
>
> I was one of the few present on that occasion who knew how hungry and thirsty Elder Petersen really was. His encroaching cancer had deprived him of relief from physical hunger and thirst, so he understood that doctrine. He withstood the trial.

He thanked the Lord, who lent him power to preach his last major sermon at the sacred site where Jesus himself had preached. (*The Power Within Us* [Salt Lake City: Deseret Book, 1988], 21)

LIKENING THE SCRIPTURES TO OUR LIVES

1 Timothy 6:10–11 For the love of money is the root of all evil: which while some coveted after, they have erred from the faith, and pierced themselves through with many sorrows. But thou, O man of God, flee these things; and follow after righteousness, godliness, faith, love, patience, meekness.

Application: When we love anything other than God, we will be of the world—and the love of money will envelope us in all manner of evil. When we love God, we will follow after righteousness in all things. We do this as we seek to build up the kingdom of God and His righteousness (see JST, Matt. 6:38).

SUMMARY

The power of the gospel is to bring about a spiritual transformation in our hearts and minds, lifting us upward toward our divine potential as sons and daughters of God. The key for going through this "mighty change of heart," about which King Benjamin taught and concerning which Alma spoke so eloquently (Mosiah 5:2; Alma 5:14), is to apply gospel knowledge and true doctrine to our lives consistently. Paul confirmed this sacred strategy in his epistles and demonstrated its efficacy through his exemplary life. Moreover, those who experience the blessings of the Lord's Atonement in their lives have the obligation to share the gospel with others (as Paul and his colleagues did) by serving as honorable examples and by setting their priorities according to heavenly standards, denying themselves of all ungodliness (see Titus 2:12; Moro. 10:32). In doing so, we align our efforts with those of Paul and all other devoted servants of God and increase the chances of our being able to say, as did Paul at the end of his mortal journey: "For I am now ready to be offered, and the time of my departure is at hand. I have fought a good fight, I have finished my course, I have kept the faith" (2 Tim. 4:6–7; compare 2 Tim. 3:11–12).

CHAPTER 42

"PURE RELIGION"

Reading Assignment: James.

Additional Reading: Bible Dictionary, "James" (709); "James, Epistle of" (709–10).

We can let the events that surround us determine our actions—or we can personally take charge and rule our lives, using as guidelines the principles of pure religion. Pure religion is learning the gospel of Jesus Christ and then putting it into action. Nothing will ever be of real benefit to us until it is incorporated into our own lives.

It seems to me there has never been a period in history when it has been more important for us to be engaged in pure religion as taught by the Savior. This religion is not to retaliate, or to exchange in kind, evil actions or unkind statements. Pure religion encompasses the ability to cherish, to build up, and to turn the other cheek in place of destroying and tearing down. Blessed are they who strive to serve the Lord without wasting time faulting Him or those who serve Him.

—MARVIN J. ASHTON, *BE OF GOOD* CHEER [SALT LAKE CITY: DESERET BOOK, 1987], 10.

THEMES *for* LIVING
1. Endure Affliction Patiently
2. Pray to God in Faith
3. Self-Control—Be "Slow to Wrath"
4. "Showing Our Faith by Our Works"

INTRODUCTION

In his general epistle, James outlines a series of key doctrines leading to salvation and happiness, including prayer, patience, kindness, moderation in speech, and faith through good works. The virtue of patience is of primary importance in becoming like our Savior Jesus Christ. Patience is part of His divine nature. To emulate His example of patience is of great importance in enduring affliction, achieving spiritual success, and in dealing with people in productive and helpful ways. This does not mean that we are permissive, easily manipulated, or readily taken advantage of. Rather, patience truly signifies a level of maturity that ennobles one's character. Patience, like perseverance, is a governing virtue of success—success in all facets of life. This can be exhibited as we pray in faith and willingly accept the answer from Heavenly Father. The prayer of faith is heard and will be answered (see James 1:5–6).

As we gain strength from the Lord, we can become spiritually-minded and even Spirit-directed in all things and thus gain self-mastery. We have the power, through the Spirit, to control our lives. This can be demonstrated as we begin to act as Christ would act and do as He would do. We would show our faith in Jesus Christ by our works. We would be doers of the word (James 1:22).

1. ENDURE AFFLICTION PATIENTLY

THEME: We should seek to endure our afflictions cheerfully and patiently.

MOMENT OF TRUTH

The authorship of the General Epistle of James is usually attributed to James, brother of the Savior (Gal. 1:19). This James (one of several in the New Testament) was an important Church leader in Jerusalem. His short epistle reflects the grace and conviction of a true believer and is written in an aphoristic style reminiscent of the Proverbs and much of Psalmic writing. A good example of such style is James's maxim about the importance of showing forth patience as servants of God: "Knowing this, that the trying of your faith worketh patience. But let patience have her perfect work, that ye may be perfect and entire, wanting nothing" (James 1:3–4).

MODERN PROPHETS SPEAK

Neal A. Maxwell:

> To "endure well" to the end is actually enduring well to the very beginning. Meanwhile, this life is the second estate over the prospects of which we once shouted

for joy (Job 38:7), even though there may be brief moments when we might wonder what all that shouting was about.

But here we are in the midst of "all these things," including those things which the tutoring Lord "seeth fit to inflict upon us" (Mosiah 3:19; 1 Pet. 4:19). Can we be like a group of ancient American Saints who experienced some special stress and strain? They carried some unusual burdens, but the scriptures say "they did submit cheerfully and with patience to all the will of the Lord" (Mosiah 24:15). Our capacity to love and to endure well are bound together by patience. (*Not My Will, But Thine* [Salt Lake City: Bookcraft, 1998], 113)

ILLUSTRATIONS FOR OUR TIME

Spencer W. Kimball explains to us the power of affliction and pain as a mighty teacher to our souls:

And Elder James E. Talmage wrote: "No pang that is suffered by man or woman upon the earth will be without its compensating effect . . . if it be met with patience."

On the other hand, these things can crush us with their mighty impact if we yield to weakness, complaining, and criticism.

No pain that we suffer, no trial that we experience is wasted. It ministers to our education, to the development of such qualities as patience, faith, fortitude and humility. All that we suffer and all that we endure, especially when we endure it patiently, builds up our characters, purifies our hearts, expands our souls, and makes us more tender and charitable, more worthy to be called the children of God . . . and it is through sorrow and suffering, toil and tribulation, that we gain the education that we come here to acquire and which will make us more like our Father and Mother in heaven. . . .

The power of the priesthood is limitless but God has wisely placed upon each of us certain limitations. I may develop priesthood power as I perfect my life, yet I am grateful that even through the priesthood I cannot heal all the sick. I might heal people who should die. I might relieve people of suffering who should suffer. I fear I would frustrate the purposes of God. (Spencer W. Kimball, *Faith Precedes the Miracle* [Salt Lake City: Deseret Book, 1972], 98–99)

LIKENING THE SCRIPTURES TO OUR LIVES

D&C 24:8 Be patient in afflictions, for thou shalt have many; but endure them, for, lo, I am with thee, even unto the end of thy days.

Application: Let us remember that in all our afflictions the Lord is with us and will bear us up. Let us be cheerful in enduring patiently our afflictions (James 5:10–11).

2. PRAY TO GOD IN FAITH

THEME: We should pray with real intent, exercising our deepest faith in the Lord Jesus Christ, in whose name we pray.

MOMENT OF TRUTH

A classic statement on prayer, one that energized the young Joseph Smith to inquire of the Lord in his quest for truth, is found in this passage from James: "If any of you lack wisdom, let him ask of God, that giveth to all men liberally, and upbraideth not; and it shall be given him. But let him ask in faith, nothing wavering. For he that wavereth is like a wave of the sea driven with the wind and tossed. For let not that man think that he shall receive any thing of the Lord" (James 1:5–7). James later warns his audience not to neglect the proper spiritual framework when they pray: "Ye ask, and receive not, because ye ask amiss, that ye may consume it upon your lusts" (James 4:3). His counsel is to ask in charity and purity: "Confess your faults one to another, and pray one for another, that ye may be healed. The effectual fervent prayer of a righteous man availeth much" (James 5:16).

MODERN PROPHETS SPEAK

Harold B. Lee:
> And if we pray in real sincerity and faith, there will come back to us the answer to that prayerful inquiry. The answer has come oft repeated, time and time again, that all that we do should be done "with an eye single to the glory of God." What is the glory of God? The Lord told Moses, ". . . this is my work and my glory—to bring to pass the immortality and eternal life of man" (Moses 1:39). (*Stand Ye in Holy Places* [Salt Lake City: Deseret Book, 1974], 102)

ILLUSTRATIONS FOR OUR TIME

Thomas S. Monson counsels us well in illustrating for us the need for and power of prayer in our lives:

> Jacob, the brother of Nephi, declared: "Look unto God with firmness of mind, and pray unto him with exceeding faith." (Jacob 3:1)

This divinely inspired counsel comes to us today as crystal clear water to a parched earth. We live in troubled times. Doctors' offices throughout the land are filled with individuals who are beset with emotional problems as well as physical distress. Our divorce courts are doing a land-office business because people have unsolved problems. Personnel workers and grievance committees in modern industry work long hours in an effort to assist people with their problems. . . .

A prominent American judge was asked what we, as citizens of the countries of the world, could do to reduce crime and disobedience to law and to bring peace and contentment into our lives and into our nations. He thoughtfully replied, "I would suggest a return to the old-fashioned practice of family prayer."

As a people, aren't we grateful that family prayer is not an out-of-date practice with us? There is not a more beautiful sight in all this world than to see a family praying together. There is real meaning behind the oft-quoted adage: "The family that prays together stays together."

The Lord directed that we have family prayer when He said: "Pray in your families unto the Father, always in my name, that your wives and your children may be blessed" (3 Ne. 18:21). . . .

As we offer unto God our family prayers and our personal prayers, let us do so with faith and trust in Him. If we have been slow to hearken to the counsel to pray always, there is no finer hour to begin than now. Those who feel that prayer might denote a physical weakness should remember that individuals never stand taller than when they are upon their knees. (*Live the Good Life* [Salt Lake City: Deseret Book, 1988], 125–27)

LIKENING THE SCRIPTURES TO OUR LIVES

Jacob 3:1 But behold, I, Jacob, would speak unto you that are pure in heart. Look unto God with firmness of mind, and pray unto him with exceeding faith, and he will console you in your afflictions, and he will plead your cause, and send down justice upon those who seek your destruction.

Application: As we purify our hearts through righteousness and exercise our faith, we can call down the powers of Heaven and the Lord will bless us in all our afflictions. This is a promise from the Lord. Gratitude should fill our souls and we can have peace as only the Lord can give.

3. SELF-CONTROL—BE "SLOW TO WRATH"

THEME: Self-mastery, with all its accompanying blessings, can help us to have self-control in all situations. We become Spirit-directed rather than yielding to the pressures of the moment. We edify others rather than displaying the attributes of one without self-control, including anger.

MOMENT OF TRUTH

Among the teachings included in James is the admonition to avoid contention and verbal abuse: "Behold also the ships, which though they be so great, and are driven of fierce winds, yet are they turned about with a very small helm, whithersoever the governor listeth. Even so the tongue is a little member, and boasteth great things. Behold, how great a matter a little fire kindleth!" (James 3:4–5). Rather than kindle this kind of destructive fire, James encourages us to seek after the peaceable fire of the Spirit: "But the wisdom that is from above is first pure, then peaceable, gentle, and easy to be intreated, full of mercy and good fruits, without partiality, and without hypocrisy. And the fruit of righteousness is sown in peace of them that make peace"(James 3:17–18). Humility is the divine quality we should strive to cultivate: "But he giveth more grace. Wherefore he saith, God resisteth the proud, but giveth grace unto the humble. Submit yourselves therefore to God. Resist the devil, and he will flee from you. Draw nigh to God, and he will draw nigh to you. Cleanse your hands, ye sinners; and purify your hearts, ye double minded" (James 4:6–8).

MODERN PROPHETS SPEAK

Ezra Taft Benson:

> There is something higher than intellect. There is something higher than excellence. It is dedication to principle. It is self-mastery, self-control. It is living what one really believes in his heart. (*TETB*, 445)
>
> An attribute described by Peter as being part of the divine nature is temperance. A priesthood holder is temperate. This means he is restrained in his emotions and verbal expressions. He does things in moderation and is not given to overindulgence. In a word, he has self-control. He is the master of his emotions, not the other way around.
>
> A priesthood holder who would curse his wife, abuse her with words or actions, or do the same to one of his own children is guilty of grievous sin. "Can ye be angry, and not sin?" asked the Apostle Paul (JST, Eph. 4:26).
>
> If a man does not control his temper, it is a sad admission that he is not in control of his thoughts. He then becomes a victim of his own passions and emotions, which leads him to actions that are totally unfit for civilized behavior, let alone behavior for a priesthood holder. . . .
>
> A patient man is understanding of others' faults. (*TETB*, 446)

ILLUSTRATIONS FOR OUR TIME

Those Refs

I played ball all my life. I loved athletics. I enjoyed the thrill of competition. There was one problem: the men in the striped shirts—the referees. They were the judge, the jury, and often the ones who decided the outcome of the game. We as spectators become the observers who yell and scream for our team—and at the man with the whistle. After my playing days, I became a true "fan"—you know, the one who protects the home team by yelling at those "refs."

As my children grew up, they too became athletes—state champions, all-state honors, all-American honors—and I was their personal protector, so I continued to scream at the referees. It often embarrassed the children. I would be good for a while, and then I would get upset and lose my self-control . . . not really bad, never shouting obscenities, mind you, just riding the referees, telling them to do better. This was and is wrong. It showed a lack of dignity, manners, and true compassion and love for my fellowmen. I was wrong. I needed to change. I needed to gain self-control.

I set a goal. I would exercise good sportsmanship and compassion for all—especially at ball games. My desire was strong. My plan was to pray before each game to be a "good sport" and be dignified at all times. My children and my wife couldn't believe it. I became a true gentleman. I had gained self-control. I was so pleased.

One day, I attended a basketball game of our youngest daughter, Tricia, and I was doing just fine until the referee made a horrible mistake, at least in my eyes, and I yelled out, "Come on, ref, get in the game." My older daughter, Traci, said, "Dad, did you forget to pray?" I dropped my head, realizing that I had forgotten. I left the game, found a quiet place outside, and said a little prayer. I returned to the game, and sure enough, I became a true gentleman, dignified in every way. So here's what one does to gain self-control: set a goal, make a plan, get the support of family and friends, and support from above . . . and you can gain self-control. [Pinegar]

LIKENING THE SCRIPTURES TO OUR LIVES

James 1:19 Wherefore, my beloved brethren, let every man be swift to hear, slow to speak, slow to wrath.

Application: Listen . . . don't judge. Be patient . . . don't react. Think . . . before you speak. Never yell or scream . . . unless the house is burning down or life is in danger. Remember . . . charity never faileth.

4. "SHOWING OUR FAITH BY OUR WORKS"

THEME: True faith is always exhibited with action and power. Faith is the moving cause of all action and the power to do all things.

MOMENT OF TRUTH

James preaches a most practical kind of religion—one that reflects compassion for one's fellows, translated into action and follow-through:

> But be ye doers of the word, and not hearers only, deceiving your own selves.
>
> For if any be a hearer of the word, and not a doer, he is like unto a man beholding his natural face in a glass:
>
> For he beholdeth himself, and goeth his way, and straightway forgetteth what manner of man he was.
>
> But whoso looketh into the perfect law of liberty, and continueth therein, he being not a forgetful hearer, but a doer of the work, this man shall be blessed in his deed. (James 1:22–25)

For James, the measure of religion comes in the record of one's charitable deeds performed in righteousness, as reflected in this celebrated passage: "Pure religion and undefiled before God and the Father is this, To visit the fatherless and widows in their affliction, and to keep himself unspotted from the world" (James 1:27).

Above all, good works can be taken as a measure of one's faith:

> Yea, a man may say, Thou hast faith, and I have works: shew me thy faith without thy works, and I will shew thee my faith by my works.
>
> Thou believest that there is one God; thou doest well: the devils also believe, and tremble.
>
> But wilt thou know, O vain man, that faith without works is dead?
>
> Was not Abraham our father justified by works, when he had offered Isaac his son upon the altar?
>
> Seest thou how faith wrought with his works, and by works was faith made perfect? (James 2:18–22)

What kinds of good works are singled out? Among others, ministering to the needs of the sick ("Is any sick among you? let him call for the elders of the church; and let them pray over him, anointing him with oil in the name of the Lord: And the prayer of faith shall save the sick, and the Lord shall raise him up; and if he have committed sins, they shall be forgiven him" James 5:14–15), and bringing the gospel into the lives of God's children ("Brethren, if any of you do err from the truth, and one convert him; Let him know, that he which converteth the sinner from the error of his way shall save a soul from death, and shall hide a multitude of sins" James 5:19–20).

MODERN PROPHETS SPEAK

Spencer W. Kimball:

> Faith is the power behind good works. The exercising of faith is a willingness to accept without total regular proof and to move forward and perform works. "Faith without works is dead" (James 2:26), and a dead faith will not lead one to move forward to adjust a life or to serve valiantly. A real faith pushes one forward to constructive and beneficial acts as though he knew in absoluteness. The Prophet Alma gave the near perfect address on faith in the thirty-second chapter of Alma. He gives us: "Faith is not to have a perfect knowledge of things; therefore if ye have faith ye hope for things which are not seen, which are true" (Alma 32:21). (*TSWK*, 71–72)

ILLUSTRATIONS FOR OUR TIME

Looking Forward in Faith

James wrote in his general epistle to the twelve tribes: "But be ye doers of the word, and not hearers only, deceiving your own selves. . . . But whoso looketh into the perfect law of liberty, and continueth therein, he being not a forgetful hearer, but a doer of the work, this man shall be blessed in his deed" (James 1:22, 25). The Church and kingdom of God is the ideal and indispensable venue for learning and practicing this doctrine. Every Sunday, for instance, members of the Church have the singular opportunity to participate in the sacrament, a blessing and an opportunity of exceptional depth and reverence. As I watch those young men each week bear the vessels of the Lord with such humility and care, I am constantly reminded of the compassion of the Lord in allowing His young sons the sacred privilege of becoming His service representatives on earth, valiant future leaders in training. Alma taught that priesthood callings unto the Saints were of very ancient date, being initiated in the premortal existence "according to the foreknowledge of God, on account of their exceeding faith and good works" (Alma 13:3). That being the case, we can view these stalwart, young Aaronic Priesthood brethren as fulfilling a destiny of the most extraordinary kind, being part of the elite corps of priesthood servants called "after the order of the Son, the Only Begotten of the Father" (Alma 13:9).

Alma explained that being called after the order of the Son imparts to the recipients a unique perspective, i.e., one that is forward-looking and future-centered: "Now these ordinances were given after this manner, that thereby the people might look forward on the Son of God, it being a type of his order, or it being his order, and this that they might look forward to him for a remission of their sins, that they might enter into the rest of the Lord" (Alma 13:16). What a marvelous blessing for these young men participating in the sacrament and other priesthood duties to be called after the order of Christ and thus have placed upon them this forward-viewing template of righteousness. Thus the priesthood that has been conferred upon them allows them, by its very nature (being named after the order of the Son), to look forward with hope and joy to a continual remission of their sins according to the laws of faith and repentance. Through this ordination, they can view through the eye of faith their ultimate state of becoming the literal sons of God, who will one day receive a reward of glory and immortality in keeping with Alma's admonition: "Having faith on the Lord; having a hope that ye shall receive eternal life; having the love of God always in your hearts, that ye may be lifted up at the last day and enter into his rest" (Alma 13:29).

By the same token, the Lord allows all of us—men, women, and children—to look forward with hope to the blessings of a future domicile in the mansions of heaven as part of the eternal family of God. The pathway toward that supernal goal is illuminated with the light of faith in Jesus and marked with the milestones of service to family, community, and those seeking the truth. As James declared: "Yea, a man may say, Thou hast faith, and I have works: shew me thy faith without thy works, and I will shew thee my faith by my works" (James 2:18). In just that same way, the vision of any believer who practices a practical faith—faith unto good works—extends forward into the future of his or her spiritual possibilities, the ultimate goal of which is our reunion with our Father in Heaven and His Only Begotten Son. [Allen]

LIKENING THE SCRIPTURES TO OUR LIVES

James 2:22–26 Seest thou how faith wrought with his works, and by works was faith made perfect? And the scripture was fulfilled which saith, Abraham believed God, and it was imputed unto him for righteousness: and he was called the Friend of God. Ye see then how that by works a man is justified, and not by faith only. Likewise also was not Rahab the harlot justified by works, when she had received the messengers, and had sent them out another way? For as the body without the spirit is dead, so faith without works is dead also.

Application: Our works personify our faith. If one has little or no faith in Jesus Christ, there will be lack of good works. Let us remember that faith is the seedbed for good works and the precursor of all righteousness.

SUMMARY

James reminds us, in the spirit of grace and devotion, to endure affliction with patience, to pray to God in faith, to exercise temperance and self-control, and to continually show forth our faith to the Lord through the performance of worthy and charitable service. Above all, we are to endure to the end in valor and righteousness: "Behold, we count them happy which endure. Ye have heard of the patience of Job, and have seen the end of the Lord; that the Lord is very pitiful, and of tender mercy" (James 5:11). That we may endure in patience and honor is our goal under the guidance of the Spirit and through the blessings of perfecting grace.

CHAPTER 43

"A CHOSEN GENERATION"

Reading Assignment: 1 and 2 Peter; Jude.

Additional Reading: Bible Dictionary, "Peter, Epistles of" (749–750); "Jude, Epistle of" (719); 1 John 3:2–3; 3 Nephi 12:48; D&C 122:7–8.

> *We have one Lord, one faith, one baptism. In fulfillment of the words of Peter, we are "a chosen generation, a royal priesthood, an holy nation, a peculiar people; that [we] should shew forth the praises of him who hath called [us] out of darkness into his marvellous light" (1 Pet. 2:9). . . .*
>
> *No matter where we are, no matter our circumstances, we all can be faithful Latter-day Saints. We can pray and worship the Lord in the privacy of our own closet. We can sing anthems of praise to the Almighty even when we are alone. We can study the scriptures. We can live the gospel. We can pay our tithes and offerings though the amount be ever so small. We can walk in faith. We can strive to live lives patterned after the life of our Master.*
>
> —GORDON B. HINCKLEY, "WELCOME TO CONFERENCE," *ENSIGN*, NOV. 1998, 4–5.

THEMES *for* LIVING

1. A Chosen Generation of Faith and Holiness
2. Follow the Savior's Example
3. Partake of the Divine Nature of Christ
4. Resist False Teachers—Stand for Truth

INTRODUCTION

We are a chosen people, a holy nation, a peculiar people with a responsibility to praise and extol the virtues and atoning sacrifice of the Lord Jesus Christ by letting our light shine to all mankind. Once we come to the knowledge of the Lord, we have a duty to follow Him in obedience by honoring His precepts and example. We should go forward in righteousness, living His teachings, regardless of the trials and tribulations that we face. The process of our development in becoming like the Lord—taking upon ourselves His divine nature—is described as adding to one's faith the qualities of virtue, knowledge, temperance, patience, brotherly kindness, godliness, and charity—accomplished with all humility and diligence (see 2 Pet. 1:3–12; D& C 4:6). We then can have our calling and election made sure (see 2 Pet. 1:10), so that when the Lord appears, we will be like Him (see Moro. 7:48). Once we come to the knowledge of the truth and live by the Spirit, we will have the ability to discern truth and error, being better able to resist false teachers and their false doctrines.

1. A CHOSEN GENERATION OF FAITH AND HOLINESS

THEME: We have a duty, as a chosen generation and as God's "peculiar" people, to live lives of faith and holiness.

MOMENT OF TRUTH

The Apostle Peter wrote the first of his two extant epistles around A.D. 64, probably from Rome, in the wake of the persecutions of Christians under Nero's tenure. The first epistle is addressed (as also the second, presumably) to the Saints in "Pontus, Galatia, Cappadocia, Asia, and Bithynia" (1 Pet. 1:1), located in what is now Asia Minor. The agenda is to provide fortification and encouragement to those under intense pressure to deny the Lord and disavow their covenants. The message of Peter in his epistles is infused with a stirring spirit of courage and is composed of mighty threads of doctrine woven into a fabric of unsurpassed doctrinal power. According to the Prophet Joseph Smith, "Peter penned the most sublime language of any of the apostles" (*HC*, 5:392).

Peter reminds the Saints of their noble heritage and encourages them to rise to their grand potential: "That the trial of your faith, being much more precious than of gold that perisheth, though it be tried with fire, might be found unto praise and honour and glory at the appearing of Jesus Christ: Whom having not seen, ye love; in whom, though now ye see him not, yet believing, ye rejoice with joy unspeakable and full of glory: Receiving the end of your faith, even the salvation of your souls" (1 Pet. 1:7–9).

He lifts their vision to a realization of who they truly are: "But ye are a chosen generation, a royal priesthood, an holy nation, a peculiar people; that ye should shew forth the praises of him who hath called you out of darkness into his marvellous light: Which in time past were not a people, but are now the people of God: which had not obtained mercy, but now have obtained mercy" (1 Pet. 2:9–10).

No longer isolated and strangers, the Saints are an integral part of the kingdom of God, with a heavenly commission to stand for truth and right:

> If so be ye have tasted that the Lord is gracious.
>
> To whom coming, as unto a living stone, disallowed indeed of men, but chosen of God, and precious,
>
> Ye also, as lively stones, are built up a spiritual house, an holy priesthood, to offer up spiritual sacrifices, acceptable to God by Jesus Christ.
>
> Wherefore also it is contained in the scripture, Behold, I lay in Sion a chief corner stone, elect, precious: and he that believeth on him shall not be confounded.
>
> Unto you therefore which believe he is precious: but unto them which be disobedient, the stone which the builders disallowed, the same is made the head of the corner. (1 Pet. 2:3–7)

As such, these Saints are to honor their allegiance to God and the Son while serving their fellows in charity and remaining productive citizens in the jurisdictions of their domicile: "Honour all men. Love the brotherhood. Fear God. Honour the king" (1 Pet. 2:17).

MODERN PROPHETS SPEAK

Russell M. Nelson:

> Peter used uplifting terms in a prophecy regarding our day. He identified members of the Church as "a chosen generation, a royal priesthood, an holy nation, a *peculiar* people." We recognize the adjectives *chosen, royal,* and *holy* as complimentary. But what about the term *peculiar?*
>
> A modern dictionary defines *peculiar* as "unusual," "eccentric," or "strange." What kind of compliment is that?
>
> But the term *peculiar* as used in the scriptures means something quite different. In the Old Testament, the Hebrew term from which *peculiar* was translated is *segullah,* which means "valued property," or "treasure." In the New Testament, the Greek term from which *peculiar* was translated is *peripoiesis,* which means "possession," or "an obtaining."

With that understanding, we can see that the scriptural term *peculiar* signifies "valued treasure," "made" or "selected by God." Thus, for us to be identified by servants of the Lord as His *peculiar* people is a compliment of the highest order. (*Perfection Pending, and Other Favorite Discourses* [Salt Lake City: Deseret Book, 1998], 192–93)

ILLUSTRATIONS FOR OUR TIME

Gordon B. Hinckley instructs us on being "A Chosen Generation":

> I was asked by an interviewer, "What do we have to offer the people of the Philippines?" We have happiness to offer to the people of the Philippines. Sin never was happiness. Transgression never was happiness. Evil never was happiness. Good means happiness. Brotherhood means happiness. Service to one another means happiness. What was it that Peter wrote concerning us of this generation? He said, "Ye are a chosen generation, a royal priesthood, an holy nation, a peculiar people; that ye should shew forth the praises of him who hath brought you out of darkness into his marvelous light" (1 Pet. 2:9). "A chosen generation." This is the greatest generation in the history of the world. How wonderful to be born at this time in the history of the earth. I hope you young people are grateful that this is the season of your lives. And for every one of you, this is the time when the God of heaven has moved in fulfillment of His ancient promise that He would usher in the fulness of the gospel in the Dispensation of the Fulness of Times. "A chosen generation." You're not just here by chance. You are here under the design of God. "An holy nation." I don't think that speaks of a particular nation—the Philippines, the United States, or anything of that kind—it speaks of a vast congregation of those who accept the gospel of Jesus Christ and try to live its teachings. (*TGBH,* 719–20)

LIKENING THE SCRIPTURES TO OUR LIVES

1 Peter 2:9 But ye are a chosen generation, a royal priesthood, an holy nation, a peculiar people; that ye should shew forth the praises of him who hath called you out of darkness into his marvellous light.

Application: We have been ransomed by the Lord. We are His people. We have a responsibility to teach by precept and example the Lord Jesus Christ. He has brought us into the light of His gospel; therefore, we should seek to bring others into the light of the Lord.

2. FOLLOW THE SAVIOR'S EXAMPLE

THEME: We should follow our Savior's example in all things—especially as we endure trials, tribulations, and all manner of persecution for the sake of the gospel.

MOMENT OF TRUTH

Peter, himself no stranger to suffering and persecution, was motivated by a fervent desire to strengthen his fellowcitizens in the household of God as they encountered the inevitable campaign of retribution and torment from their detractors. The highest model to be emulated, he confirmed, is the Savior: "That the trial of your faith, being much more precious than of gold that perisheth, though it be tried with fire, might be found unto praise and honour and glory at the appearing of Jesus Christ: Whom having not seen, ye love; in whom, though now ye see him not, yet believing, ye rejoice with joy unspeakable and full of glory: Receiving the end of your faith, even the salvation of your souls" (1 Pet. 1:7–9). In the midst of persecution, the Saints are to treat one another with a full measure of kindness and support, according to the word of truth:

> Seeing ye have purified your souls in obeying the truth through the Spirit unto unfeigned love of the brethren, see that ye love one another with a pure heart fervently:
>
> Being born again, not of corruptible seed, but of incorruptible, by the word of God, which liveth and abideth for ever.
>
> For all flesh is as grass, and all the glory of man as the flower of grass. The grass withereth, and the flower thereof falleth away:
>
> But the word of the Lord endureth for ever. And this is the word which by the gospel is preached unto you. (1 Pet. 1:22–25)

As Christ, though perfect, suffered beyond all comprehension for all mankind, so must we endure in patience the burdens placed upon us:

> For even hereunto were ye called: because Christ also suffered for us, leaving us an example, that ye should follow his steps:
>
> Who did no sin, neither was guile found in his mouth:
>
> Who, when he was reviled, reviled not again; when he suffered, he threatened not; but committed himself to him that judgeth righteously:
>
> Who his own self bare our sins in his own body on the tree, that we, being dead to sins, should live unto righteousness: by whose stripes ye were healed.

ED J. PINEGAR AND RICHARD J. ALLEN

For ye were as sheep going astray; but are now returned unto the Shepherd and Bishop of your souls. (1 Pet. 2:21–25)

Why should we fear men when so great blessings and rewards await those who faithfully honor their covenants with the Lord, for He extends His arm of mercy unto all, even the departed spirits in prison:

> And who is he that will harm you, if ye be followers of that which is good?
>
> But and if ye suffer for righteousness' sake, happy are ye: and be not afraid of their terror, neither be troubled;
>
> But sanctify the Lord God in your hearts: and be ready always to give an answer to every man that asketh you a reason of the hope that is in you with meekness and fear:
>
> Having a good conscience; that, whereas they speak evil of you, as of evildoers, they may be ashamed that falsely accuse your good conversation in Christ.
>
> For it is better, if the will of God be so, that ye suffer for well doing, than for evil doing.
>
> For Christ also hath once suffered for sins, the just for the unjust, that he might bring us to God, being put to death in the flesh, but quickened by the Spirit:
>
> By which also he went and preached unto the spirits in prison;
>
> Which sometime were disobedient, when once the longsuffering of God waited in the days of Noah, while the ark was a preparing, wherein few, that is, eight souls were saved by water. (1 Pet. 3:13–20; compare 1 Pet. 4:6)

Thus in patience families should live in harmony and love (see 1 Pet. 3:7–8), feeding the flock of God (see 1 Pet. 5:2–3) and rejoicing in the Lord: "inasmuch as ye are partakers of Christ's sufferings; that, when his glory shall be revealed, ye may be glad also with exceeding joy. If ye be reproached for the name of Christ, happy are ye; for the spirit of glory and of God resteth upon you" (1 Pet. 4:13–14).

MODERN PROPHETS SPEAK

Ezra Taft Benson:

> The only measure of true greatness is how close a man can become like Jesus. That man is greatest who is most like Christ, and those who love Him most will be most like Him. How, then, does a man imitate God, follow His steps, and walk as He walked, which we are commanded to do? (see 3 Ne. 27:27; 1 Pet. 2:21; 1 Jn. 2:6). We must study the life of Christ, learn His commandments, and do them. God has promised that to follow this course will lead a man to an abundant life, a fulness of joy, and the peace and rest for which those who are heavy burdened long. (*TETB*, 327–28)

ILLUSTRATIONS FOR OUR TIME

Here are some points to ponder concerning the lessons taught by the Savior: What are some of the wonderful examples Christ set for us? How do we incorporate those examples into our lives? How can we remember to do as Jesus would do?

Knowing is not enough. We are to cultivate the desire to follow Christ in all things. We are to develop a careful and specific plan to become as He is—not just be satisfied with an attitude of casually wanting to be better. Life is full of events that take our mind away from the Lord and our time away from things that matter most. True discipleship takes a concentrated effort . . . we must remember.

The word *remember* or a form of the word occurs frequently throughout the scriptures (occurring in over 110 verses in the Book of Mormon and Doctrine and Covenants alone). We have made covenants with our Heavenly Father and promised to follow our Savior. It seems as though the power to do good and be good is tied to our ability to remember. The ability to keep sacred things in our minds is part of our covenants—to remember, to bear in mind, to keep in our mind, to recall and retain, and to think back upon these things, that we might remember the goodness of God and keep the commandments. To remember is more than just recalling the thought periodically. It means to always have the principles, doctrines, and covenants in our mind. In remembering, we should think, ponder, and meditate upon the things of the Lord—and in particular our covenants. This is a key point in living the gospel. "For as he thinketh in his heart, so is he" (Prov. 23:7).

The process of thinking or mental exertion is the beginning point in gaining the vision, which leads to a desire to live the gospel, which in turn leads to actions that bring our visions and desires to fruition. This is how the process works:

- A "thought" (perceived or received) is an idea, a consideration, a reflection, a deliberation, a concept, an aspiration, a meditation, a pondering about something. When this "thought" is . . .
- Dwelled upon—that is: brought to reside in your mind and to be continually present, such that you are engrossed in it and linger on it, this, in turn . . .
- Creates a desire—a want, a need, a penchant for, a wish, a willingness, a longing, an appetite, a passion or craving for something. When this is . . .
- Encouraged—which is to urge, help, inspire, promote, support, motivate, stimulate, strengthen, and to reassure, then it . . .
- Results in Action—which is to perform, execute, give effort, and to exert oneself. You actually do something. Your attitude has changed, and you now behave in a new way. You are a result of your "thoughts," which, if righteous and principle-centered, always lead to . . .

- Benefits and positive consequences—the desirable outcomes of wise and prudent thinking and action.

The catalyst for the transition from thoughts to desire is enhanced as we understand the gospel, appreciate the Lord's blessings, feel gratitude for His atoning sacrifice, and have an overwhelming desire to follow our Savior Jesus Christ. The question, at that point, is one of initiative and self-mastery: Now that we understand the principle, will we remember? Will we follow Jesus Christ in all things?

LIKENING THE SCRIPTURES TO OUR LIVES

1 Peter 2:21–23 For even hereunto were ye called: because Christ also suffered for us, leaving us an example, that ye should follow his steps: Who did no sin, neither was guile found in his mouth: Who, when he was reviled, reviled not again; when he suffered, he threatened not; but committed himself to him that judgeth righteously.

Application: As we seek to become like Christ, let us remember to learn to grow even as He did through the things which He suffered (see Heb. 5:8–9).

3. PARTAKE OF THE DIVINE NATURE OF CHRIST

THEME: The process of becoming like Christ is to acquire charity and inculcate charitable patterns of action in our lives.

MOMENT OF TRUTH

The Second Epistle of Peter contains the celebrated passage in which the Chief Apostle outlines the specific qualities of character that are associated with the divine nature of Christ, which we are commanded to acquire in our inward personalities through earnest and continual striving: "But let it be the hidden man of the heart, in that which is not corruptible, even the ornament of a meek and quiet spirit, which is in the sight of God of great price" (1 Pet. 3:4). Here is Peter's oft-quoted passage:

> According as his divine power hath given unto us all things that pertain unto life and godliness, through the knowledge of him that hath called us to glory and virtue:
>
> Whereby are given unto us exceeding great and precious promises: that by these ye might be partakers of the divine nature, having escaped the corruption that is in the world through lust.
>
> And beside this, giving all diligence, add to your faith virtue; and to virtue knowledge;

And to knowledge temperance; and to temperance patience; and to patience godliness;

And to godliness brotherly kindness; and to brotherly kindness charity.

For if these things be in you, and abound, they make you that ye shall neither be barren nor unfruitful in the knowledge of our Lord Jesus Christ.

But he that lacketh these things is blind, and cannot see afar off, and hath forgotten that he was purged from his old sins.

Wherefore the rather, brethren, give diligence to make your calling and election sure: for if ye do these things, ye shall never fall:

For so an entrance shall be ministered unto you abundantly into the everlasting kingdom of our Lord and Saviour Jesus Christ. (2 Pet. 1:3–11)

MODERN PROPHETS SPEAK

Joseph Smith:

The other Comforter spoken of is a subject of great interest, and perhaps understood by few of this generation. After a person has faith in Christ, repents of his sins, and is baptized for the remission of his sins and receives the Holy Ghost, (by the laying on of hands), which is the first Comforter, then let him continue to humble himself before God, hungering and thirsting after righteousness, and living by every word of God, and the Lord will soon say unto him, Son, thou shalt be exalted. When the Lord has thoroughly proved him, and finds that the man is determined to serve Him at all hazards, then the man will find his calling and his election made sure, then it will be his privilege to receive the other Comforter, which the Lord hath promised the Saints, as is recorded in the testimony of St. John, in the 14th chapter, from the 12th to the 27th verses. (*HC*, 3:379, 380)

ENRICHMENT SECTION

The Divine Nature of Christ.

The fourth section of the Doctrine and Covenants contains instructions for becoming loyal and productive servants of the Lord (see especially v. 6; compare 2 Pet. 1:5–6). Let us discuss each of these key objectives briefly:

Faith

The Prophet Joseph Smith, in the Lectures on Faith, describes the three degrees of faith. The first degree is the substance of things hoped for (see *Lectures on Faith* 1:7–8). Of the second degree, the Prophet Joseph said, "Faith is the moving cause of all action in intelligent beings" (*Lectures on Faith* 1:12). The third degree of faith is the principle and source of power (see *Lectures on Faith* 1:15). When all three degrees are applied, faith is exercised to its fullest. The Prophet went on to say: "Faith, then, is the first great governing principle which has power, dominion, and authority over all things; by it they exist, by it they are upheld, by it they are changed or by it they remain agreeable to the will of God" (*Lectures on Faith,* 1:24).

Virtue
Virtue has a double meaning. It refers to power (see Mark 5:30) as well as a moral goodness and uprightness in keeping the commandments.

Knowledge
Gospel knowledge has to do with eternal truths given by God to man—this is the pure knowledge that can save. This pure knowledge comes by the power of the Holy Ghost. "And by the power of the Holy Ghost ye may know the truth of all things"(Moro. 10:5).

Temperance (Self-control)
The trial and test in life is making the body subject to the spirit and in following the principles of the gospel rather than responding only to appetite and emotion. James E. Faust made clear our responsibility as disciples of the Savior: "Self-discipline and self-control are consistent and permanent characteristics of the followers of Jesus" (*To Reach Even unto You* [Salt Lake City: Deseret Book, 1980], 114).

Patience
The virtue of patience is of primary importance in becoming like our Savior Jesus Christ. Everyone appreciates the patient person. Being patient does not mean that we are permissive, easily manipulated, or readily taken advantage of. Rather, patience truly signifies a level of maturity that ennobles one's character. Patience is an integral part of charity (Moro. 7:44–45).

Brotherly Kindness
Kindness requires a character based on gospel principles. It becomes an outward expression of our love of God—a manifestation of a pure heart and genuine concern for others.

Godliness
Godliness implies those qualities associated with our Heavenly Father and our Savior Jesus Christ. We are devout in our worship of God and seek to be Christlike in our everyday behavior—we seek to do as He would do. Godliness has within it the qualities and virtues of God. This should be our goal—in every thing we do and in every thing we say.

Charity
Charity is the pure love of Christ. His pure love motivated His great sacrifice—the eternal, infinite, vicarious Atonement. When we possess that love, we act in our lives according to the principles of the Atonement.

Humility
Humility is a cardinal virtue of growth, the beginning virtue of exaltation. When we acknowledge and understand our relationship to and dependence upon God, we begin to become humble. We will have a broken heart and a contrite spirit. Humility causes one to relate to God in gratitude and love.

Diligence
Diligence is the scriptural term for effort or work. Every blessing we receive is predicated upon obedience to the principle on which it is based. In short, we must be diligent in all things (see D&C 75:29). Through diligence on our part and the grace of God we can enjoy the blessings of the Lord.

ILLUSTRATIONS FOR OUR TIME

The Emissary of Humility
The avuncular, silver-haired gentleman of kindly disposition who was assigned to visit me from the high council was among the least prideful persons I have ever known. He would come to our Johns Hopkins University student-housing apartment from time to time, always with a gentle spirit, always with an uplifting thought for the young new bishop and his wife. His quiet and humble demeanor belied his influential station in the highest leadership circles in Washington, D.C., for Rosel H. Hyde was at the time the Chairman of the Federal Communications Commission. But you would not know it from his modest deportment. I can still see his pleasant smile as he graced our sparse apartment with his presence, truly a servant of the Lord. The specifics of his messages have long since left my memory, but the image of him as an emissary of humility and meekness remains forever. He was an exponent of the principle that the Lord taught to His latter-day leaders: "Be thou humble; and the Lord thy God shall lead thee by the hand, and give thee answer to thy prayers" (D&C 112:10). Truly—like so many of the Lord's faithful servants—he reflected the qualities of humility and charity that Peter included among those essential traits associated with the divine nature of Christ (see 2 Pet. 1:4–8). [Allen]

LIKENING THE SCRIPTURES TO OUR LIVES

2 Peter 1:10 Wherefore the rather, brethren, give diligence to make your calling and election sure: for if ye do these things, ye shall never fall.

Application: Let us remember to prioritize our lives and diligently seek to acquire the divine nature of Jesus Christ—especially the quality of charity. We can do this as we become humble and, with all diligence, add to our faith the qualities of virtue, knowledge, temperance, patience, brotherly kindness, godliness, and, ultimately, charity.

4. RESIST FALSE TEACHERS—STAND FOR TRUTH

THEME: We should be aware that there are false teachers promulgating false doctrine all around us in various forms of delivery, i.e., constricted secular teaching, misguided sectarian preachers, and the polluted condition and values of some of the media groups, including certain aspects of the internet. By being aware of this, we can take steps to fortify ourselves against the evils of the day.

MOMENT OF TRUTH

Peter was fully apprised of the coming general apostasy (see Matt. 24:24). Because of this, he was determined to provide a spiritual shield for his audience, which included, at the forefront, the holy scriptures: "We have also a more sure word of prophecy; whereunto ye do well that ye take heed, as unto a light that shineth in a dark place, until the day dawn, and the day star arise in your hearts: Knowing this first, that no prophecy of the scripture is of any private interpretation. For the prophecy came not in old time by the will of man: but holy men of God spake as they were moved by the Holy Ghost" (2 Pet. 1:19–21). Through the power of the Holy Ghost, the Saints can deflect the encroachments of evil forces in the world and remain steadfast in the grace of the Lord: "Ye therefore, beloved, seeing ye know these things before, beware lest ye also, being led away with the error of the wicked, fall from your own stedfastness. But grow in grace, and in the knowledge of our Lord and Saviour Jesus Christ. To him be glory both now and for ever" (2 Pet. 3:17–18; compare 2 Pet. 2:1–4).

Jude, the brother of James, also contributed an epistle warning the members of the Church to resist the defectors among the Christian ranks who were allowing the incursion of pagan practices that could destroy the faith. He writes, "Beloved, when I gave all diligence to write unto you of the common salvation, it was needful for me to write unto you, and exhort you that ye should earnestly contend for the faith which was once delivered unto the saints" (Jude 1:3). Since this faith was under attack from evil forces, the Saints are reminded to be on guard: "Keep yourselves in the love of God, looking for the mercy of our Lord Jesus Christ unto eternal life" (Jude 1:21).

MODERN PROPHETS SPEAK

Neal A. Maxwell:

> Many so-called Christians will end up denying, as Peter prophesied, "the Lord that bought them" (2 Pet. 2:1). Denying the divinity of Jesus will be accompanied by denials of the reality of Lucifer. Equivocating ecclesiastics will play to the galleries because many of their constituents "will not endure sound doctrine . . . and shall be turned unto fables" (2 Tim. 4:3–4). Many nonbelievers will follow such popular leaders, and it will be by such followers that "the way of truth shall be evil spoken of" (2 Pet. 2:2).

> No attacks on the Church will be more bitter or more persistent than those made in the Salt Lake Valley. No taunts will be more shrill than those of apostates and excommunicants. In that valley and in the state of Utah, Church members will be accused of the "crime" of being a majority! Some clever defectors will imitate their model, Satan, and will try to take others over the side with them. Elsewhere, you will encounter the same sort of snobbery that gave rise to "can any good thing come out of Nazareth?" (*Wherefore, Ye Must Press Forward* [Salt Lake City: Deseret Book, 1977], 79–80)

ILLUSTRATIONS FOR OUR TIME

Joseph Fielding Smith has given us sound counsel to resist the world and avoid falling away in these the latter-days:

> Because of the love of the things of the world and the enticing influence of the powers of darkness, we (meaning Christian people generally) have departed from the strait path which leads to life and which our Lord has said few men find because they love darkness rather than light, their deeds being evil. We have permitted the philosophies of men, which deny the divinity of Jesus Christ and mock at the sacred ordinances of the gospel, to enter into our schools, and businesses, and our homes, thus weakening our faith and our reverence for our Creator, We have forgotten that man was created in the image of God, that the scriptures declare that we are his off-spring, and that we are commanded to seek first the kingdom of God and his right-eousness. . . .

> Unless we are on our guard we are in constant danger. This people who are under solemn covenants to keep the commandments of the Lord are threatened by the sins and worldly abominations of this generation, and many among us are liable

to be led astray, unless we keep a careful vigil and hedge them about by every means at our command. We have been called out from the world into the kingdom of God, and while we are yet in the world, we are not of the world in the sense that we are under any necessity to partake of their evil customs, and fashions, their follies, false doctrines and theories, which are in conflict with the spirit of truth. . . .

The man who receives the light of truth and then turns away, loses the light which he had, and if he continues in that course, eventually he will be bound by the chains of spiritual darkness. Darkness will take the place of truth, as the truth becomes gradually dimmed, until he has lost knowledge of spiritual things. He who walks in the light of truth receives more truth until he is glorified in divine truth-the truth that saves. (*DS*, 3:294)

LIKENING THE SCRIPTURES TO OUR LIVES

2 Peter 3:17 Ye therefore, beloved, seeing ye know these things before, beware lest ye also, being led away with the error of the wicked, fall from your own stedfastness.

Application: We know the truth. Let us therefore be on guard continually to escape the temptations and snares of the devil, which at times seem innocuous, yet stealthily deploy the shackles that can lead us carefully down to hell (see 2 Ne. 28:21). No one is immune—it can happen to the very best. Let us press forward with a steadfastness in Christ.

SUMMARY

As a chosen generation of faith and holiness, we are to follow the Savior's example in all we do and, eschewing all false doctrine and preachments, strive to partake of the divine nature of Christ. Faith, virtue, knowledge, temperance, patience, godliness, brotherly kindness, charity, accompanied by humility and diligence—these are the divine attributes that make up the heart of a just and faithful servant of the Lord, one prepared in all things to follow the will of God and rise triumphant as a loyal and devoted disciple of Christ.

CHAPTER 44

"GOD IS LOVE"

Reading Assignment: 1, 2, and 3 John.

Additional Reading: Bible Dictionary: "John, Epistles of" (714); Moroni 7:48; D&C 45:3–5.

Love! The crowning glory of all the attributes of God! We may revel in this attribute. "He that loveth not, knoweth not God; for God is Love!" "God is Love, and he that dwelleth in love dwelleth in God, and God in him." "Every one that loveth is born of God." "In this was manifested the Love of God towards us, because that God sent his only begotten Son into the world, that we might live through him. Herein is love, not that we loved God, but that he loved us, and sent his son to be the propitiation for our sins." "God so loved the world that he gave his only begotten Son, that whosoever believeth in him should not perish, but have everlasting life." More perfect evidence than this of love, even God cannot give.

—B. H. ROBERTS, *SEVENTY'S COURSE IN THEOLOGY* [OREM, UT: GRANDIN BOOK CO., 1994], 4:75.

THEMES *for* LIVING

1. Heavenly Father Loves Us
2. The Savior Jesus Christ Loves Us
3. Showing Our Love for Heavenly Father, Our Savior Jesus Christ, and Our Fellowmen

INTRODUCTION

Our Heavenly Father and our Savior Jesus Christ love us. We are the spirit children of God, the Eternal Father (see Acts 17:29). We become the children of Christ—since He spiritually begat us—as we accept His gospel (see Mosiah 5:7). The love of the Father is evident: "For God so loved the world, that he gave his only begotten Son, that whosoever believeth in him should not perish, but have everlasting life" (John 3:16). The Savior's love is likewise expressed: "He [Christ] doeth not anything save it be for the benefit of the world; for he loveth the world, even that he layeth down his own life that he may draw all men unto him. Wherefore, he commandeth none that they shall not partake of his salvation" (2 Ne 26:24). Everything Heavenly Father and our Savior do is for the purpose of bringing to pass our immortality and eternal life (see Moses 1:39). Our gratitude for this great outpouring of love from our Heavenly Father and our Savior can be manifested in many ways: by keeping the commandments (see John 14:15), by doing good unto others (see Matt. 25:40), and by reverently worshipping Heavenly Father in the name of His Beloved Son, Jesus Christ. Our Heavenly Father and His Son have great joy over the soul who repents (see D&C 18:13). There is likewise great joy among our earthly fathers when we are obedient and committed to living the gospel: "I have no greater joy than to hear that my children walk in truth" (3 Jn. 1:4).

Love is indeed the motive of every righteous act. The directive is clear: "A new commandment I give unto you, That ye love one another; as I have loved you, that ye also love one another. By this shall all men know that ye are my disciples, if ye have love one to another" (John 13:34–35). As we contemplate all the commandments and the counsel of the prophets, we see that these words are encapsulated in the two great commandments: "Thou shalt love the Lord thy God with all thy heart, and with all thy soul, and with all thy mind. This is the first and great commandment. And the second is like unto it, Thou shalt love thy neighbour as thyself. On these two commandments hang all the law and the prophets" (Matt. 22:37–40).

1. HEAVENLY FATHER LOVES US

THEME: Our Heavenly Father's love for us is manifested in all things.

MOMENT OF TRUTH

John is not mentioned in the three epistles that bear his name; however, the style of these epistles is similar to that of the Gospel of John, and the epistles have therefore been attributed to him. It is assumed that the epistles postdate the writing of the

Gospel. The first of the epistles is a memorable and moving statement about the love of God for all mankind and the need for us to love one another in that same spirit. "Beloved, let us love one another: for love is of God; and every one that loveth is born of God, and knoweth God. He that loveth not knoweth not God; for God is love" (1 Jn. 4:7–8). We are also warned about a general apostasy and encouraged to stay faithful to the Lord and His cause (see 1 Jn. 2:18–19; 2 Jn. 1:7–8).

MODERN PROPHETS SPEAK

Neal A. Maxwell:

> Thus we see that Father's love is expressed in many profound and significant ways. No wonder He is described as "merciful and gracious" (D&C 76:5). No wonder the Apostle John told us God so loved the world that He gave us His Son to lead us to eternal life (John 3:16). The Book of Mormon declares that God loves the world and does nothing save it be "for the benefit of the world" (2 Ne. 26:24). Even when we come to truly love Him, the fact is that He loved us first! (1 Jn. 4:19). (*Men and Women of Christ* [Salt Lake City: Bookcraft, 1991], 126)

ILLUSTRATIONS FOR OUR TIME

Knowing God

Here are some points to ponder concerning knowing our Heavenly Father and His Son: Do we know our Heavenly Father? Life eternal is to know Heavenly Father and His Beloved Son. What can we do to know them better?

It is important to know the character of God so that we are not only willing to worship Him but eager to show reverence and obedience to His commands—that we might please Him in all that we do. It is imperative that we understand the following: Our Heavenly Father loves us. We are His children. He is all-powerful (see Ether 3:4). He is all-knowing (see 2 Ne. 9:20). He is in and through all things (see D&C 88:41). The Doctrine and Covenants teaches us: "By these things we know that there is a God in heaven, who is infinite and eternal, from everlasting to everlasting the same unchangeable God, the framer of heaven and earth, and all things which are in them" (D&C 20:17). Heavenly Father is not only unchangeable in His role and dealings with His children, but He is no respecter of persons (see Moro. 8:18; D&C 38:16). His work and His glory are the immortality and eternal life of all of His children (see Moses 1:39). Having a relationship with God is what life is all about. "And this is life eternal, that they might know thee the only true God, and Jesus Christ, whom thou hast sent" (John 17:3). As we come to know our Heavenly Father and our Savior, we increase in humility, because we know that we are totally dependent upon Him for all things. We will seek the will of God and be forever grateful for all things. We will come to know Heavenly Father as we seek Him in mighty prayer, and He will give according to our needs and faith (see D&C 67:10). [Pinegar]

LIKENING THE SCRIPTURES TO OUR LIVES

1 Nephi 11:25 And it came to pass that I beheld that the rod of iron, which my father had seen, was the word of God, which led to the fountain of living waters, or to the tree of life; which waters are a representation of the love of God; and I also beheld that the tree of life was a representation of the love of God.

Application: Heavenly Father loves us and seeks only that we might come and partake of that love as we hold to the iron rod, the word of God. That love is expressed in His grace and mercy in that He gave His only begotten Son for our eternal salvation (see John 3:16).

2. THE SAVIOR JESUS CHRIST LOVES US

THEME: The love of our Savior Jesus Christ is manifested in all things.

MOMENT OF TRUTH

John bears witness in his epistles that the Savior loves us, as confirmed by His willingness to do the will of the Father: "In this was manifested the love of God toward us, because that God sent his only begotten Son into the world, that we might live through him. Herein is love, not that we loved God, but that he loved us, and sent his Son to be the propitiation for our sins" (1 Jn. 4:9–10; compare 1 Jn. 2:1–3). And further: "Behold, what manner of love the Father hath bestowed upon us, that we should be called the sons of God: therefore the world knoweth us not, because it knew him not. Beloved, now are we the sons of God, and it doth not yet appear what we shall be: but we know that, when he shall appear, we shall be like him; for we shall see him as he is. And every man that hath this hope in him purifieth himself, even as he is pure" (1 Jn. 3:1–3).

MODERN PROPHETS SPEAK

Neal A. Maxwell:

> By casting one's cares upon the Lord and by knowing He loves us—even when we
> cannot understand the meaning of all things that are happening about us or to us—

we permit the Lord to strengthen us, to give us courage and perseverance. (*We Talk of Christ, We Rejoice in Christ* [Salt Lake City: Deseret Book, 1984], 159)

ILLUSTRATIONS FOR OUR TIME

How Do You Know the Savior Loves You?

Knowing that the Savior loves you personally is the key to happiness. How can you know beyond any doubt that He—the Redeemer of all mankind—loves *you?* There are three ways that never fail: reading and pondering the scriptures, listening to the Spirit, and discerning love at work in the world.

I have often marveled at the accounts in the scriptures where the Savior—the Creator of all Creation under the leadership of our Father in Heaven—addressed individuals by name. To Moses on the mount the Lord said, "Behold, I am the Lord God Almighty, and Endless is my name . . . and I have a work for thee, Moses, my son" (Moses 1:3, 6). Clearly the relationship between the Savior and His children is meant to be personal and real. As the First Vision burst upon the world in 1820, the truth of this kind of relationship was confirmed once again. In the words of the young prophet Joseph: "When the light rested upon me I saw two Personages, whose brightness and glory defy all description, standing above me in the air. One of them spake unto me, calling me *by name* and said, pointing to the other—This is My Beloved Son. Hear Him!" (JS—H 1:17; emphasis added). To be called by name by Deity is to know that a relationship with the divine is personal in nature. This same mutual friendship of the Shepherd and His sheep is repeated again and again in the scriptures: "Behold, thou art Oliver. . . . Behold, I am Jesus Christ" (D&C 6:20, 21). "Behold thou art Hyrum. . . . Behold, I am Jesus Christ" (D&C 11:23, 28). "Behold, I am Jesus Christ. . . . And behold, thou art David" (D&C 14:9, 11).

It is a miracle to contemplate that the Savior loves us so much that He calls us by name and seeks to cultivate with each of us a personal relationship. It is a miracle that He includes us in the same pronouncement along with His own sacred name. And yet His name is our name, for we are to be known as His sheep, and we are to respond to His voice calling us. It is a measure of His generosity that He shares ownership of the Church with us, for it is both the Church of Jesus Christ, as well as The Church of Jesus Christ of *Latter-day Saints*. The scripture says, "And he numbereth his sheep, and they know him; and there shall be one fold and one shepherd; and he shall feed his sheep, and in him they shall find pasture" (1 Ne. 22:25). Nephi taught that we should apply the scriptures to ourselves (see 1 Ne. 19:23–24). With that authority, we can extend the personal love of the Savior to His chosen servants as recorded in the scriptures by knowing that this love is also applied to ourselves. "For God so loved the world, that he gave his only begotten Son, that whosoever believeth in him should not perish, but have everlasting life" (John 3:16).

The second way to know that the Savior loves us is to listen to the Spirit. When our personal prayers are answered in personal ways through the whisperings of the Spirit of the Lord, we can know in our hearts that He loves us and knows us personally. To Oliver Cowdery, the Lord said, "Verily, verily, I say unto you, if you desire a further witness, cast your mind upon the night that you cried unto me in your heart, that you might know concerning the truth of these things. Did I not speak peace to your mind concerning the matter? What greater witness can you have than from God? And now, behold, you have received a witness; for if I have told you things which no man knoweth have you not received a witness?" (D&C 6:22–24). Similarly, we can ask the Lord in faith, nothing doubting, and receive a personal witness of the truth of all things, including confirmation that we are loved by the Savior, our Redeemer. When we consider the kindness of the Savior in imparting truth and guidance to us individually through the avenue of a patriarchal blessing—truly a personal revelation from the Lord—we have further evidence through the Spirit of heavenly affection and love.

Finally, let us discern and appreciate the endless acts of charitable service being imparted all around us by the Lord's flock. One day I asked my wife the question, "How do you know the Savior loves you?" and she responded without hesitation: "Because there is so much love in the world imparted by God's children one to one another." And so it is. We are "children of the prophets" and "children of the covenant," to use the Lord's expression (see 3 Ne. 20:25–26). As such, we partake of the divine nature through obedience and humility and thus have the innate potential of showing love to others. This love, displayed for all with eyes to see and hearts to feel, is evidence of the love of the Savior for us. It cannot be denied, for we are His children.

Amulek taught: "And thus he shall bring salvation to all those who shall believe on his name; this being the intent of this last sacrifice, to bring about the bowels of mercy, which overpowereth justice, and bringeth about means unto men that they may have faith unto repentance" (Alma 34:15). By reading and pondering the scriptures, listening to the whisperings of the Spirit, and discerning and participating in acts of charity in our everyday lives, we can know of the love of our Savior. We can increase our faith. We can respond in gratitude to the love and compassion shown by the Redeemer through His Atonement by our act of love to further the cause of building up the kingdom of God. [Allen]

LIKENING THE SCRIPTURES TO OUR LIVES

D&C 45:5 Wherefore, Father, spare these my brethren that believe on my name, that they may come unto me and have everlasting life.

Application: Our Savior Jesus Christ is ever advocating our cause, because He loves us. As we remember Him and feel that we are filled with His love for us, we should have an overwhelming desire to serve Him and bless our brothers and sisters.

3. SHOWING OUR LOVE FOR HEAVENLY FATHER, OUR SAVIOR JESUS CHRIST, AND OUR FELLOWMEN

THEME: There are many ways that we can manifest our love for our Heavenly Father, our Savior Jesus Christ, and our fellowmen.

MOMENT OF TRUTH

John's epistles validate and expound on the Savior's commandment that we should love one another (John 13:34; 15:12, 17). Here are some examples:

> Beloved, let us love one another: for love is of God; and every one that loveth is born of God, and knoweth God. (1 Jn. 4:7)

> And we have known and believed the love that God hath to us. God is love; and he that dwelleth in love dwelleth in God, and God in him.
>
> Herein is our love made perfect, that we may have boldness in the day of judgment: because as he is, so are we in this world.
>
> There is no fear in love; but perfect love casteth out fear: because fear hath torment. He that feareth is not made perfect in love.
>
> We love him, because he first loved us. (1 Jn. 4:16–19)

> By this we know that we love the children of God, when we love God, and keep his commandments. (1 Jn. 5:2)

It is this spirit of love—manifested universally through the Father and the Son—that should resonate within us: "And he that keepeth his commandments dwelleth in him, and he in him. And hereby we know that he abideth in us, by the Spirit which he hath given us" (1 Jn. 3:24). By serving others in love, and helping them to come unto the Lord in faith, we can experience the profound joy of the gospel: "I have no greater joy than to hear that my children walk in truth" (3 Jn. 1:4).

MODERN PROPHETS SPEAK

Gordon B. Hinckley:

> This must be the foundation of our instruction: love of God and love for and service
> to others—neighbors, family, and all with whom we have association. That which
> we teach must be constantly gauged against these two standards established by the
> Lord. If we shall do so, this work will continue to roll forward. (*TGBH*, 316–17)

ILLUSTRATIONS FOR OUR TIME

"The Power of Love"

I was teaching high school in 1966. We were covering the subject of love and
expressing love. The students all seemed to be anxiously engaged in the conversation of the day. I got the idea of asking for a volunteer to do a special homework
assignment. I stopped the class and said, "Who will do me a favor?" The hands all
flew up. A young boy near the back of the room named Dennis seemed quite anxious. I called him up to the front and I said, "Dennis, do you really want to do this
favor for me?"

He said, "Sure!"

I said to him, "This is really hard."

He said, "I can do it. That's no problem. I can do it."

I said, "Well, this is really going to take some effort."

He said, "I can do it!"

I said, "Are you sure you can do it?"

In exasperation he said, "I'll do it. Just what do you want me to do?"

I said. "This is it. When you go home tonight, you call out for your mother. When
your mother comes to you, you take her in your arms and give her a big embrace. Yes,
Dennis, a big kiss. And then you whisper in her ear, 'Oh, Mom, I love you.'"

He stopped, looked at me, and said, "No way! No way can I do that."

I said, "Dennis, do you love your mother?"

"Of course I do."

I said, "Then why won't you do it?"

He replied, "You just don't do things like that."

I said, "Dennis, if you love her, you should tell her."

"No way!"

Well, Dennis and I were pretty good friends, and so I said to him, "Dennis, I
think I can hear a chicken clucking in this class." The class all started to laugh, and
Dennis felt uneasy. "In fact, Dennis, I think there's a yellow stripe coming right up
your back." Now everyone was laughing—even Dennis.

We played around for a minute, and finally he relented and said, "Okay, okay, I'll do it. Just let me go back to my seat." So Dennis went back to his seat. The class period ended, and life went on.

The next day, as I was greeting the members of the class as they came in, I said, "Dennis, how did it go last night?"

He looked at me and said, "Oh, it was wonderful!"

I said, "Can you tell me about it?"

He said, "Can I tell the whole class?"

So, after the introductory remarks to the class, I said, "We have a special report today from Dennis."

Dennis came up in front—the big junior in high school, but something was different. His lips began to quiver, and his eyes began to fill up with tears, then he blurted out, "Oh, you guys, it was the greatest day of my life. My mom cried for two hours. I can't believe it." They all laughed. Then he said, "You don't realize what we've done to our parents. We've locked them out of our lives. They've done everything for us, and we treat them like dirt. We should be ashamed. They're starved for our love just like we're starved for their love. But you've gotta say it. You've gotta tell 'em." Well, the class was just on fire. And he said, "You've all gotta go home and do it just like I did."

At that moment in class, silent commitments were made, and needless to say, they went home and did it.

A couple of weeks went by, and we had Parents' Night. In our class, we had all of the parents sit in the chairs of their children. I stood up in front and told them how we were discussing different things in class. One parent said, "What do you do in this class?" I attempted to explain again. She said, "No, you don't understand. My son's nice to me now. He even told me he loved me. And the only thing I can think of that's been different in his life lately is this class." Other hands came up. "Yes, that happened to me too." Well, the class was on fire. The parents suddenly felt so good about their children.

When I responded, I merely said, "Oh, it's just their goodness. You've just learned how good your children really are." Well, lives were changed by that experience of Dennis. He made a difference in all those young people's lives, for he had set an example and challenged them. They took the challenge, made the commitment, and families were blessed. Parents were happy, families were happy, and life was beautiful. Yes, the power of love, expressed, can make all the difference in the world. [Pinegar]

LIKENING THE SCRIPTURES TO OUR LIVES

John 14:15 If ye love me, keep my commandments.

Application: Our love for our Heavenly Father and our Savior is expressed by keeping the commandments.

1 John 4:11 Beloved, if God so loved us, we ought also to love one another.

Application: We reflect the love of God for us as we love one another.

SUMMARY

John's message is simple, pristine, and deeply moving as a testimony from one of the Lord's chosen Apostles, one who knew Him intimately throughout His ministry. It is the message of love. He confirms that Heavenly Father loves us, that the Savior Jesus Christ loves us, and that we should magnify our callings by loving one another in the same spirit. We have the sacred promise from heaven: "And this is the promise that he hath promised us, even eternal life" (1 Jn. 2:25). What we know, through the grace and infinite love of the Father, Son, and Holy Ghost, is the essence of life eternal: "And we know that the Son of God is come, and hath given us an understanding, that we may know him that is true, and we are in him that is true, even in his Son Jesus Christ. This is the true God, and eternal life" (1 Jn. 5:20). As beneficiaries of eternal life, through faith and obedience, we are to serve one another, not just in word, but in practical, everyday ways: "My little children, let us not love in word, neither in tongue; but in deed and in truth" (1 Jn. 3:18). Like John, who went on to even greater service in the kingdom of God in the days of the Restoration (see D&C 7; 27:12; 61:14; 77:1–15; 88:141; 3 Ne. 28:6), we can also move forward, in love, to assist in the great purposes of our Father in Heaven to bless the lives of His children everywhere.

CHAPTER 45

"HE THAT OVERCOMETH SHALL INHERIT ALL THINGS"

Reading Assignment: Revelation 1–3;12.

Additional Reading: Revelation 21:7; Bible Dictionary, "Revelations of John" (762–63).

In seeking to rivet upon the hearts of the Saints the eternal importance of keeping the commandments and of thereby overcoming the world, the scriptures use words and imagery of an incomparable nature. For instance:

"To him that overcometh will I give to eat of the tree of life, which is in the midst of the paradise of God" (Rev. 2:7). That is, he shall find peace and joy in paradise and then shall come forth to an inheritance of eternal life, which is the greatest of all the gifts of God (D&C 14:7). . . .

Again: "He that overcometh, the same shall be clothed in white raiment; and I will not blot out his name out of the book of life, but I will confess his name before my Father, and before his angels" (Rev. 3:5). Who is there among us who does not desire to keep his name forever in the Lamb's book of life and to hear the Lord Jesus confess it before his Father's throne? So shall it be with all those who overcome the world.

Again: "Him that overcometh will I make a pillar in the temple of my God, and he shall go no more out: and I will write upon him the name of my God" (Rev. 3:12). That is, he shall have exaltation and godhood. As Deity now is, he shall become. He shall have eternal life. . . .

And finally: "He that overcometh shall inherit all things; and I will be his God, and he shall be my son" (Rev. 21:7). Again, it is eternal life which is his. He shall be saved. As we quoted from the Prophet: "Salvation consists in the glory, authority, majesty, power and dominion which Jehovah possesses and in nothing else; and no being can possess it but himself or one like him" (N. B. Lundwall, comp., A Compilation Containing the Lectures on Faith . . . *[Salt Lake City: Bookcraft, n.d.], 63–64). He is our prototype. As he was in the world but not of the world, so must we be.*

—BRUCE R. MCCONKIE, SERMONS AND WRITINGS OF BRUCE R. MCCONKIE [SALT LAKE CITY: BOOKCRAFT, 1998], 366–67.

THEMES *for* LIVING

1. The Symbolic Vision of the Triumph of Good
2. Blessings Promised to Those Who Overcome
3. The Glory of the Atonement of Jesus Christ

INTRODUCTION

Although the symbolism used in the book of Revelation is sometimes challenging to understand and apply to one's life, the predominant theme that pervades the book is crystal clear, i.e., the ultimate triumph of God's plan for the salvation, eternal life, and immortality of mankind. The Prophet Joseph Smith sought answers to many questions concerning the symbolism of this profound vision (see D&C 77). The message that is paramount in the portion of the book of Revelation included with this chapter is the continual testing and trial of mortals and their capacity—through the blessings of God—to overcome all things and enjoy the promised gift of eternal life. Perceiving our tests and trials from a higher perspective invariably leads to greater understanding and frequently to the discovery of ultimate solutions. Let us remember that opposition in all things is essential for our growth. Without opposition, we could not understand or appreciate joy in contrast to sorrow or righteousness in contrast to wickedness. Without opposition, everything would be "a compound in one" (see 2 Ne. 2:11)—devoid of vitality and bereft of the opportunity for eternal progression. It is requisite that Satan tempt us: "And it must needs be that the devil should tempt the children of men, or they could not be agents unto themselves; for if they never should have bitter they could not know the sweet" (D&C 29:39). The Lord has not left us alone. He will strengthen and support us in all things through the power of His Atonement (see Alma 7:11).

1. THE SYMBOLIC VISION OF THE TRIUMPH OF GOOD

THEME: Guided by the visionary symbols in the revelation imparted to John the Divine, we can discern and appreciate the underlying spiritual theme of these extraordinary scriptural passages—God will prevail over all the forces of evil.

MOMENT OF TRUTH

In general, Revelation can be divided into two main parts: chapters 1–3 dealing with the Lord's counsel to seven of the churches in what is called Asia (i.e., Asia Minor) and the remainder of the book dealing with future events, including the Restoration, Second Coming, and Millennium. The work was written down by John the Divine (or John the Beloved, as he was called) while in exile on the Isle of Patmos. The Lord imparted to him the revelation from which he derived the record: "I was in the Spirit on the Lord's day, and heard behind me a great voice, as of a trumpet, Saying, I am Alpha and Omega, the first and the last: and, What thou seest, write in a book, and send it unto the seven churches which are in Asia; unto Ephesus, and unto Smyrna, and unto Pergamos, and unto Thyatira, and unto Sardis, and unto Philadelphia, and unto Laodicea" (Rev. 1:10–11).

The Book of Revelation is also known as the Apocalypse, deriving from a Greek word meaning to make known or uncover. Just as in the case of all of God's prophets, John makes known the visions of the Almighty imparted to him as a message unto the Church and the world. Rich in symbolic imagery, this book of scripture engages the imagination of the readers, galvanizing them into an exercise of spiritual inquiry concerning the themes and principles of action imbedded in the narrative.

Gerald N. Lund explains some symbols relating to the seven branches of the church:

> The candlestick is not a source of light but a holder of the light. Since the Church of Jesus Christ is not the actual source of truth but merely holds up Jesus Christ—the true light of the world—for all to see, the candlestick provides a beautiful representation of the church (Rev. 1:12–13, 20; cf. 3 Ne. 18:24). . . . In several places in the opening chapters, reference is made to "seven Spirits" (Rev. 1:4; 3:1; 4:5) and seven angels or "angels of the seven churches," each of which is then identified with a particular group of Saints (see Rev. 1:20; 2:1, 8, 12, 18; 3:1). As is, this makes it sound as though the seven spirits and the seven angels are different things. But the Prophet changed or explained all references to the seven spirits and the seven angels to show that the seven spirits and the seven angels both refer to the leaders of the

seven churches (see JST, for all of the above verses). John, who at this time is the leader of the Church, is writing to seven branches of the Church in Asia. The JST, makes it clear that he specifically addresses the leaders (the bishops or branch presidents, as it were) of each of these branches.

Also the JST makes it clear that the seven spirits (now servants) are the receivers, not the source, of the vision (see JST, Rev. 1:4).

Finally, the Prophet added to the concept of Christ's second coming that he would come clothed in "the glory of his Father" and be accompanied by "ten thousand of his saints" (JST, Rev. 1:7). Perhaps here is a good time to note that in Greek the largest named number was ten thousand, which is the word "myriad." Often it is used symbolically to express uncountable numbers." (Gerald N. Lund, *Selected Writings of Gerald N. Lund:* Gospel Scholars Series, 69, 88)

Donald W. Parry, Jay A. Parry, and Tina M. Peterson explain the symbolism of the sword used throughout the scriptures to convey the essence of the word of God. They say, concerning the phrase "mouth like a sharp sword" (Isa. 49:2), the following: "This term refers to the power of the message brought by God's servant. It is an expression common in revelation (Heb. 4:12; Rev. 1:16; D&C 6:2, for example). Nephi spoke of the truth cutting people "to the very center" (1 Ne. 16:2)." (Donald W. Parry, Jay A. Parry, and Tina M. Peterson, *Understanding Isaiah,* 425)

MODERN PROPHETS SPEAK

Bruce R. McConkie:

Candlesticks carry light; they do not create it. Their function is to make it available, not to bring it into being. So by using seven candlesticks to portray the seven churches to whom John is now to give counsel, the Lord is showing that his congregations on earth are to carry his light to the world. Christ is the Light of the world (John 8:12). "Hold up your light that it may shine unto the world. Behold I am the light which ye shall hold up—that which ye have seen me do" (3 Ne. 18:24; Matt. 5:14–16). So was it also in ancient Israel, when Moses made "a candlestick of pure gold," which held seven candles, for use in the tabernacle (temple) (Ex. 25:31–40). (*DNTC,* 3:442)

ILLUSTRATIONS FOR OUR TIME

Emblems of Glory

Why is it that the Holy Scriptures so frequently use symbols, metaphors, emblems, allegories, and parables to articulate the truths of the gospel? Is it not for the reason that these forms of expression tend to catch the imagination with more power, stimulate more effectively our engagement with the concepts and doctrines at hand, and effect a more complete transfer of truth from the prophetic source to the reader and listener? We should not be surprised that the visions imparted by the Lord to His servants are rich in visual imagery—imagery that invites us to "see" and "behold" (as in the sequence of supernal views granted unto Nephi—see 1 Nephi 11–14—or in the transcendent panoramas reported by Isaiah or in the visions described by John on the Isle of Patmos).

The Lord, in His mercy and kindness, makes frequent use of images that relate to our everyday life: the sacramental emblems (bread of life, living water), baptism (related to the process of birth and bringing forth a new life), relationships and organizational issues (branches, the true vine, etc.), and the process of erecting and building things unto God (temple of God, mountain of the Lord's house, etc.). The Lord is a consummate storyteller, often using parables that draw us instinctively into situations where we can rehearse the drama of life and come to understand the blessings of keeping the commandments and applying the teachings of the gospel in practical ways.

We respond to pictures because our unconscious seems to make abundant use of internal imagery (shapes, forms, constructs) in solving problems and putting together creative structures that add value to our lives. It seems to be human nature for us to strive to complete incomplete pictures and shapes that live within us, waiting to emerge as whole entities. We seem to solve problems and fashion our productive lives out of the guiding imagery that is cultivated within our minds and hearts. We tend to think in scenes and depictions. We strive to build shapes and views that are complete and elegant, reflecting the harmony of the universe and the glory of the Creator. Could it be that the Lord intends to grant to all of us "greater views" such as those given to the people of King Benjamin: "And we, ourselves, also, through the infinite goodness of God, and the manifestations of his Spirit, have great views of that which is to come; and were it expedient, we could prophesy of all things. And it is the faith which we have had on the things which our king has spoken unto us that has brought us to this great knowledge, whereby we do rejoice with such exceedingly great joy" (Mosiah 5:3–4). Through the blessings of the Spirit, we are able to view the big picture, behold the design of the heavens, perceive the pathway to salvation, and discern the guiding hand of the Lord in all things. These are the emblems of glory that give meaning to our lives and remind us of our divine parentage.

Certainly the Lord imparts to his prophets these "greater views" of the truth of all things—present, past, and future—which the prophets then pass on to us in the measure expedient for our salvation. Where John the Revelator speaks of candlesticks (the communities or congregations of the Saints), stars or angels (the servant leaders themselves), the emerging woman of glory (the church of God), and her delivered offspring (the priesthood governance power of the kingdom), or angels flying through the midst of heaven (the Restoration), we can rest assured that these images (see Rev. 1–3, 12, 14) are imparted to nourish and sustain our prayerful pondering of the doctrines of Christ in preparing ourselves for more faithful and devoted service to the cause. Let us be thankful the scriptures speak in symbols and parabolic imagery, for these emblems of glory are signs that our Father in Heaven is in charge of completing His design for our immortality and eternal life and granting us a glimpse of the blessings of eternity, which are to be perceived only through the Spirit of God opening up the inner eyes of the believers. [Allen]

LIKENING THE SCRIPTURES TO OUR LIVES

Revelation 1:20 The mystery of the seven stars which thou sawest in my right hand, and the seven golden candlesticks. The seven stars are the angels of the seven churches: and the seven candlesticks which thou sawest are the seven churches.

Application: Let us remember that the units (branches/wards/stakes) of the church (candlesticks) convey the light of the Lord and that the leaders/servants (angels) serve the people of the units. They hold up the light: "Therefore, hold up your light that it may shine unto the world. Behold I am the light which ye shall hold up—that which ye have seen me do. Behold ye see that I have prayed unto the Father, and ye all have witnessed" (3 Ne 18:24).

2. BLESSINGS PROMISED TO THOSE WHO OVERCOME

THEME: To rise above our mortal temptations and challenges—strengthened and supported by the Lord through His Spirit—qualifies us for the blessings of heaven. In Revelation, the word of the Lord is given to the seven branches, instructing them concerning their strengths and weaknesses and confirming the promised blessings when they overcome their temptations, trials, and tribulations and prevail through righteousness.

MOMENT OF TRUTH

John is shown the circumstances (both good and bad) prevailing at seven of the churches of the kingdom and is given the promises of the Lord unto the faithful. Among the righteous patterns of living recognized by the Lord in regard to various of the seven churches are patience, resisting wickedness and perversion, charitable service, overcoming adversity and tribulation, honoring the name of the Lord, keeping His word, faith, and purity.

On the other hand, the Lord is displeased with such lapses as a return to the former (preconversion) ways of life, seeking after earthly honors more than the things of God (as did Balaam of old—Rev. 2:14), immorality (as in the case of the sect of the Nicolaitans—Rev. 2:15), idolatry, lacking a firm commitment to righteousness ("So then because thou art lukewarm, and neither cold nor hot, I will spue thee out of my mouth"—Rev. 3:16), self-satisfaction, and pride. In such cases the Lord commands the people to repent of their evil ways and return to righteousness.

To those who are faithful, the Lord gives glorious promises, including the following:

> To him that overcometh will I give to eat of the tree of life, which is in the midst of the paradise of God. (Rev. 2:7; to the church at Ephesus; compare 1 Ne. 11:21–22 on the love of God)

> He that overcometh shall not be hurt of the second death. (Rev. 2:11; to the church at Smyrna; compare Alma 12:16 and Helaman 14:18 on the second death)

> To him that overcometh will I give to eat of the hidden manna, and will give him a white stone, and in the stone a new name written, which no man knoweth saving he that receiveth it. (Rev. 2:17; to the church at Pergamos; compare John 6:35, 49–51 on the bread of life; compare D&C 130:10–11 on a personal Urim and Thummim promised to the faithful)

> And he that overcometh, and keepeth my works unto the end, to him will I give power over the nations: And he shall rule them with a rod of iron; as the vessels of a potter shall they be broken to shivers: even as I received of my Father. And I will give him the morning star [i.e., Christ]. (Rev. 2:26–28; to the church at Thyatira; compare Rev. 22:16)

> He that overcometh, the same shall be clothed in white raiment [a reference to the blessings of the temple]; and I will not blot out his name out of the book of life, but I will confess his name before my Father, and before his angels. (Rev. 3:5; to the church at Sardis; compare D&C 128:7 on the book of life; see also Rev. 21:10, 23–27; Alma 5:58; D&C 88:2)

> Him that overcometh will I make a pillar in the temple of my God, and he shall go no more out: and I will write upon him the name of my God, and the name of the city of my God, which is new Jerusalem, which cometh down out of heaven from

my God: and I will write upon him my new name. (Rev. 3:12; to the church at Philadelphia)

Behold, I stand at the door, and knock: if any man hear my voice, and open the door, I will come in to him, and will sup with him, and he with me. To him that overcometh will I grant to sit with me in my throne, even as I also overcame, and am set down with my Father in his throne. (Rev. 3:20–21; to the church of the Laodiceans)

All of these promised blessings, though given to separate churches (or congregations), apply universally, as the Lord repeatedly confirms in each case: "He that hath an ear, let him hear what the Spirit saith unto the churches" (Rev. 3:22).

MODERN PROPHETS SPEAK

Lorenzo Snow:

> Man can inherit all God possesses. "He that overcometh shall inherit all things" [Rev. 21:7]. What an expression is that? Who believes it? If a father were to say to his son, "My son, be faithful, and follow my counsels, and when you become of age you shall inherit all that I possess," it would mean something, would it not? If the father told the truth, that son would have something to encourage him to be faithful. Did Jesus want to deceive us when He made use of this expression? I will assure you that there is no deception in the language. He meant precisely what He said. (*The Teachings of Lorenzo Snow,* ed. Clyde J. Williams [Salt Lake City: Bookcraft, 1984], 6–7)

ILLUSTRATIONS FOR OUR TIME

Overcoming All Things Through Self-Mastery—In the Strength of the Lord "When the Bell Rings"

> May I tell a story to illustrate the point that a man must respond to his better self if he is going to be a worthy holder of the priesthood.
> The story is told that the Arabians, when they are training their horses, put them to a final test of character and stamina. It is said that the finest of the Arabian horses which are kept for breeding stock are trained from the time they are colts to respond to a bell which rings intermittently at the tent of the master. Wherever they are and whatever they are doing, they must run to the tent of the master when the bell rings. Their mothers were taught it before them, and they respond, and the colts, running beside the mother, habitually as time goes on respond to the bell and know that it is the call of duty. When the colts are three years old, they are placed

in a pole corral that they can see through. They are left there three days and nights without food or water. At the end of the third day hay and grain and water are placed just outside the corral.

You can imagine the eagerness of the young colts as they look through the bars at the food and water. When the gate is opened the young colts rush out, and just as they are about to reach the food and water, the bell rings. Only those of them that have stamina enough to respond to the bell and resist the urge of appetite are kept for the breeding stock of the future.

Brethren, as we go forward, we become increasingly aware of the fact that there is a bell which rings very frequently throughout life. Sometimes men become unresponsive or hard of hearing and disregard the bell to their own sorrow. You young men are going to hear it many times between now and the time you are our age. We plead with you to resist the call of appetite and passion and hearken to the bell which is your conscience. If you are tempted to do wrong, there will always be something within you saying, "Don't do it." Hearken and respond to that bell, and you will be worthy of the confidence that the President of the Church has in you, worthy to take over the responsibilities now held by your fathers, your brothers, your leaders. (Hugh B. Brown, CR, April 1963, 91)

LIKENING THE SCRIPTURES TO OUR LIVES

D&C 75:16 And he who is faithful shall overcome all things, and shall be lifted up at the last day.

Application: Once we have proved ourselves worthy, regarding our earthly test, we will be lifted up. Let us remember that every day is a test that has a significant bearing on our eternal life. The promised reward from our Heavenly Father is to be a recipient of all things (see D&C 84:38).

3. THE GLORY OF THE ATONEMENT OF JESUS CHRIST

THEME: Through the power of the Lord, and by virtue of His infinite and eternal Atonement, we can overcome all things in the war with Satan. As to ourselves, we are nothing; yet armed with faith and the testimony of our Beloved Savior Jesus Christ, and going forward in His strength, we can do all things (see Alma 26:11–12).

MOMENT OF TRUTH

He who is in charge of the affairs of heaven and earth, according to the book of Revelation, is Jesus Christ:

> Who is the faithful witness, and the first begotten of the dead, and the prince of the kings of the earth. Unto him that loved us, and washed us from our sins in his own blood,
>
> And hath made us kings and priests unto God and his Father; to him be glory and dominion for ever and ever. Amen.
>
> Behold, he cometh with clouds; and every eye shall see him, and they also which pierced him: and all kindreds of the earth shall wail because of him. Even so, Amen. (Rev. 1:5–7)

John records the transcendent appearance of the resurrected Lord, whom he beholds at the beginning of the vision:

> And in the midst of the seven candlesticks was one like unto the Son of man, clothed with a garment down to the foot, and girt about the paps with a golden girdle.
>
> His head and his hairs were white like wool, as white as snow; and his eyes were as a flame of fire;
>
> And his feet like unto fine brass, as if they burned in a furnace; and his voice as the sound of many waters. (Rev. 1:13–15; compare the consistent description in D&C 110:1–4)

It is to this Messiah and Redeemer that we owe the blessing of being able to overcome sin and darkness through the majesty of His Atonement. He is the same who prevailed against the rebellious spirits in heaven and caused them to be cast down—including the great dragon or Satan (see Rev. 12:3–9)—through the power of God's plan of salvation: "And they overcame him by the blood of the Lamb, and by the word of their testimony; and they loved not their lives unto the death. Therefore rejoice, ye heavens, and ye that dwell in them" (Rev. 12:11–12).

John was also privileged to see in his vision a womanly figure, clothed with sun, moon, and stars, who brought forth a man child "to rule all nations with a rod of iron" (Rev. 12:5; compare v.1–2, 14–17)—a symbolic representation of the Church and kingdom of God empowered with the authority of priesthood governance to bless all mankind. "And the dragon prevailed not against Michael, neither the child, nor the woman which was the church of God, who had been delivered of her pains, and brought forth the kingdom of our God and his Christ" (JST, Rev. 12:7). Through the Atonement of Christ, the Church and Kingdom are destined to prevail over the satanic forces of evil bent on destroying the work and glory of God. That is the pervasive theme of the Book of Revelation.

MODERN PROPHETS SPEAK

Bruce R. McConkie:

> This life is a continuation of the war in heaven. In it Satan makes war with the saints, "which keep the commandments of God, and have the testimony of Jesus" (Rev. 12:17). Those saints who overcome the world thereby triumph over Satan and gain the victory. Of King Mosiah, for instance, the Book of Mormon account records, after he had "gone the way of all the earth," that he had "warred a good warfare, walking uprightly before God" (Alma 1:1). (*DNTC*, 3:116)

ILLUSTRATIONS FOR OUR TIME

Triumph of Truth and Right

Here are some points to ponder concerning our quest for victory over adversity and the forces of evil: How do we overcome adversity? How do we resist the temptations, wiles, and snares of the devil? How do we on a daily basis overcome the world?

Let us keep in mind the following strategies for spiritual growth and success:

- Faith in Jesus Christ—Heavenly Father has given each of us talents, gifts, and abilities that we can utilize to overcome adversity and serve others in love. As we exercise our faith in Jesus Christ, we will receive the strength to overcome our challenges (see 1 Ne. 7:17).
- The word of God—There is power in the word (see Alma 31:5). It will tell us all things that we should do (see 2 Ne. 32:3).
- Charity—The pure love of Christ embodies the motivation as well as the power to overcome temptation.
- Humility—Humility will give us strength in the Lord (see Ether 12:27).
- Obedience—Righteousness begets righteousness and yields not to temptation (see Alma 11:23). Keeping the commandments through obedience will allow us to have the Spirit—and we will not sin when we are acting under the influence of the Holy Ghost.
- Follow the Spirit—If we seek the Spirit in all things, we will not be led away into sin. The Spirit will lead us (see 1 Ne. 4:6), comfort us (see Moro. 8:26), give us gifts for doing all things (see Moro. 10 and D&C 46), show us all things to do (see 2 Ne. 32:5), and give us truths to live by (see Moro. 10:5). When we yield to the enticings of the Holy Spirit, we will put off the natural man (which is carnal, sensual, devilish, and unrepentant) and become a Saint with more power to resist temptation (see Mosiah 3:19).

- Prayer—The scriptures teach us clearly that if we but ask, the Lord will help us (see James 1:5–6; Mosiah 27:14; Alma 13:28).
- Hope—When we are full of hope, knowing that in the end all things shall work together for our good, we can endure and transcend adversity (see D&C 122:7).
- Patience—As we exercise patience, time will become our ally. The process of overcoming was never meant to be easy or a quick fix but rather a process of becoming (see D&C 24:8).
- People—Family, friends, associates, and/or even caring strangers are there to lend support (see D&C 108:7).

Consider the following temptations and antidotes:

1. Pride—Pride degrades our relationship with Heavenly Father and short circuits our dependence upon Him. It separates us from Him. It is the damning attribute that at all costs we should avoid. Not only does pride make us vulnerable to temptation, it contains sin within itself.

Antidote: Humility—Humility is the antithesis of pride. It is the beginning virtue of exaltation.

2. Selfishness—The predominant concern for oneself alone, with little or no concern for others, is characteristic of selfishness. It can destroy marriages and families.

Antidote: Love—Love is the ultimate concern that brings about righteous service. Love is the righteous motive for all good deeds.

3. Greed—Greed or avarice is an insatiable desire for gain. The greedy always want more, and especially more than others. This often leads to dishonest practices to gain more.

Antidote: Charity—When we truly love our fellowmen, we will have only the desire for all to succeed. The love of Christ—or charity—surely is the answer to greed. The United Order was a way in which people would have all things in common—no one would have "more" than his neighbor. This initiative failed because people were greedy and selfish, not grounded in the virtue of charity.

4. Lust—Lust is also an insatiable desire commonly associated with sexual relations. This temptation carries many destructive consequences when contemplated or—worse—acted out. Many souls and families are lost because of this transgression.

Antidote: Spiritual conversion—Understanding key doctrines and principles will help us in overcoming lust, namely, the worth of souls, our divine nature, the fact that we are temples of the Most High God, charity, self-mastery, to mention a few. When these are internalized, we will have the desire to protect and bless another person and never destroy that person's virtue—or our own.

5. Jealousy, Envy, Gossip—These evil tendencies that lead to sin are a result of resentment toward others for their achievements, qualities, and/or possessions. We often tear others down to aggrandize ourselves or raise ourselves higher in the eyes of others. This usually happens when we are low in our own self-esteem, self-image, self-worth, or self-confidence.

Antidote: Love for others—Love for our fellowmen and understanding the divine nature of our fellows can overcome jealousy, envy, and gossiping. Isn't it interesting, as we engage in this exercise of studying how to overcome temptation, to realize how much power love has. We begin to understand Matt. 22:36–40—love *does* fulfill all the law and the prophets.

6. Apathy—When we fail to care about life or when we feel indifferent, we are apathetic. Apathy leads us into many temptations and sins—we think that important things just don't matter. This is a major tool of the devil. Apathy often follows discouragement.

Antidote: Love—If apathy is failing to care, then ultimate caring will overcome apathy. Love is caring. Love is the opposite of apathy.

7. Ignorance—The lack of knowledge of gospel truths leaves us in a state of ignorance. We cannot be saved in ignorance (see D&C 131:6). If understanding and appreciating true doctrines and principles can change us for the better, so likewise the lack of it will change us for the worse. Where there is no standard, the desires and appetites of the flesh usually rule.

Antidote: Truth—Gospel knowledge and the word of God can give us life-saving truths that can and will lead us to salvation if we but learn and obey. The word of God has power (see Alma 31:5).

8. Precepts of Men—The moral conduct and values of mankind have deteriorated to such a point that the standards and behavior of society are not to be trusted. We should not put our trust in the arm of flesh (see 2 Ne. 4:34).

Antidote: Word of God—Gospel knowledge from the scriptures and the living prophets will give us a standard and value system based upon the Lord Jesus Christ that is a sure foundation (see Hel. 5:12). Understanding the doctrines, principles, and covenants in the gospel of Jesus Christ will not only give a standard for righteous behavior but will help us live the teachings of our Savior.

9. Fear of Man—Peer pressure and the fear of condemnation by another person often tempt us and lead us to sin. Such was the case with Martin Harris and the lost 116 pages of the Book of Mormon manuscript (see D&C 3:7). We likewise often are not at our best when seeking to "fit in" with the crowd—and in this we do err.

Antidote: Fear of God—Let us learn to reverence and respect the consequences of an offended God more than man. When we reverence our Heavenly Father, we will be exactly, immediately, and courageously obedient. We will seek to please God rather than man. When we love God, we will keep the commandments (see John 14:15).

10. Anger—Anger provokes and tempts us into irrational behavior. We are aroused to wrath and even rage. We behave in a totally un-Christlike manner. From abuse to road rage, anger leaves a trail of victims for which the sinner must pay.

Antidote: Prayer—The presence of anger in a person is a character flaw. We can improve our character through prayer (see Moro. 7:48; Hel. 3:35). We can pray for strength to overcome temptation (see 3 Ne. 18:18). We can search the scriptures and receive strength and courage to move forward. When we truly love another person, we will never strike out in anger, wreaking havoc or causing physical harm.

11. Hypocrisy—When we attempt to act by false pretense, we are hypocrites. The Lord condemned hypocrisy as a very grievous sin (see Matt. 6:2–5, 16; 7:5; 23).

Antidote: Belief in our divine nature—Like anger, hypocrisy is a character flaw. We seek to raise ourselves in the eyes of others. We were born with self-esteem—we are the divine children of God the Father. When we believe this, we value the worth of others as well as ourselves. We will not seek to put others down in an attempt to elevate ourselves. We will seek not to judge (see 3 Ne. 14:1). Let us seek to "become" like Christ and not just be a member of the Church in name or solely for social reasons.

12. Vanity—When we are preoccupied with our appearance and achievements, we suffer from vanity. Self-aggrandizement reeks of pride. We care more about ourselves than our fellowmen. We seek to appear better than others.

Antidote: Love—Love of fellowmen, recognizing your true worth, and humility—all these will help overcome vanity. There is also a great joy in honestly praising others. You really feel joy when you help others feel better.

13. Unbelief—When we fail to accept gospel truths or suffer from a lack of conviction, we are in a state of unbelief. This creates a major problem in our values and standards by which we should live—hence we are easily tempted and swayed by the sophistry of man. The Book of Mormon taught clearly how unbelief led the people astray (see 1 Ne. 12:22–23 and many additional references on this subject).

Antidote: A softened heart—Let us cultivate an easily entreated soul, a willingness to ask, and a genuine desire to be a seeker of truth. Yielding our heart and spirit to the Lord will surely help us begin to believe in the things of God.

LIKENING THE SCRIPTURES TO OUR LIVES

Revelation 12:11 And they overcame him by the blood of the Lamb, and by the word of their testimony; and they loved not their lives unto the death.

Application: We overcome adversity, deal with temptation, and are strengthened in our hour of need through the goodness, grace, and power of the Lord and the efficacy of His atoning sacrifice on our behalf. This is because we exercise our faith in Jesus Christ and bear testimony of Him. Even in death through martyrdom for the sake of Christ we would still emerge as having overcome all things and thus enjoy the presence of God.

SUMMARY

Unto John was given the keys of writing the account of the history of God's dealings in the final phase of the earth's history. The same apocalyptic vision was granted to Nephi and to other prophets, but Nephi was commanded not to write them down, in deference to the commission given unto John (see 1 Ne. 14:18–30). Therefore, the Book of Revelation is the decreed statement concerning the state of affairs in John's day and embracing the key prophecies concerning the consummation of the earth's history down through the Restoration and the millennial reign. The message of John's witness is clear, for he presented a symbolic vision of the triumph of good over evil, the blessings promised to those who overcome through faith and obedience, and the surpassing glory and power of the infinite Atonement of Jesus Christ. By reading and pondering the words of the Book of Revelation, we can renew our conviction that God's plan of salvation will prevail over all contravening forces, and that by honoring our covenants we can look forward to participating in the grand event of the Second Coming: "For behold, he cometh in the clouds with ten thousands of his saints in the kingdom, clothed with the glory of his Father. And every eye shall see him; and they who pierced him, and all kindreds of the earth shall wail because of him" (JST, Rev. 1:7).

CHAPTER 46

THE SAVIOR WILL REIGN
TRIUMPHANT: LIVE *with*
HOPE *in* *the* LORD

Reading Assignment: Revelation 5–6; 19–22.

Additional Reading: Revelation 4, 7; D&C 77; Bible Dictionary, "Revelations of John" (762–763).

During the Millennium the Lord shall reign personally upon the earth, and through him his Father shall reign in the hearts of men. . . . Before the Lord comes there shall be such anger, hate and enmity among and between nations as has never before been known, and out of it shall come the most devastating wars of history. "The Lord reigneth; let the people tremble" (Ps. 99:1). . . . The first resurrection when the faithful saints shall rise in glorious immortality. "For the day cometh that the Lord shall utter his voice out of heaven; the heavens shall shake and the earth shall tremble, and the trump of God shall sound both long and loud, and shall say to the sleeping nations: Ye saints arise and live; ye sinners stay and sleep until I shall call again" (D&C 43:18). See Rev. 20:4–6. . . . The righteous dead, the prophets, the saints of God, those both "small and great" who have kept his commandments shall come forth from their graves when the Lord comes; their resurrection shall be a judgment for they shall have celestial bodies; and ever thereafter shall they live and reign as kings and priests (Rev. 20:4–6; D&C 29:12–13). . . . When the Lord comes the wicked shall be destroyed. "For I will reveal myself from heaven," he says, "with power and great glory, with all the hosts thereof, and dwell in righteousness with men on earth a thousand years, and the wicked shall not stand" (D&C 29:11). "And every corruptible thing, both of man, or of the beasts of the field, or of the fowls of the heavens, or of the fish of the sea, that dwells upon all the face of the earth, shall be consumed" (D&C 101:24). See Rev. 6:12–17; 2 Pet. 3:10–18.

—Bruce R. McConkie, *DNTC,* 3:512–13.

THEMES *for* LIVING

1. Overcoming Satan, the Enemy of All Righteousness
2. The Millennium—The Lord Reigns and Satan Is Bound
3. The Last Judgment—The Righteous Will Dwell with God

INTRODUCTION

Our Father in Heaven, omniscient and omnipotent, knows the future. We can only peer dimly into the future with hope and a measure of happiness as we rely on the Lord and His mercy and grace. We know that the plan of happiness cannot be frustrated by the devil. If we but keep the commandments, we have been promised everlasting life in the presence of Heavenly Father. Beginning in the premortal spirit world, Lucifer made war against the children of God, and that war continues here upon the earth and will continue until the ushering in of the millennial reign. At that moment, Satan will be bound and we shall enjoy a measure of peace. When the millennial era ends, Satan will be loosed for a season, and the last great battle for the souls of all mankind will begin—the great battle between Israel and Gog and Magog (the leaders of the rebellious forces). The Lord will destroy those who fight against Israel (see Rev. 20:7–9; D&C 88:111–116), then the end will come and all shall be judged out of the books (see Rev. 20:12). The righteous shall dwell with God. Pain and sorrow as we know it will pass away, and the righteous shall inherit all things. This knowledge should motivate us to seek and serve God, keep the commandments, and bless our fellowmen.

1. OVERCOMING SATAN, THE ENEMY OF ALL RIGHTEOUSNESS

Theme: Satan has been at war with the righteous since the war in heaven. The battle between good and evil continues today. He seeks to destroy the souls of the children of God, but his design will be frustrated through the inevitable triumph of God's plan of salvation.

MOMENT OF TRUTH

Unto John was granted the privilege and commission to view the magnificence of the celestial realm (Rev. 4–5) in which all creation worshipped the Lord: "Saying with a loud voice, Worthy is the Lamb that was slain to receive power, and riches, and wisdom, and strength, and honour, and glory, and blessing. And every creature which is in heaven, and on the earth, and under the earth, and such as are in the sea, and all that are in them, heard I saying, Blessing, and honour, and glory, and power, be unto him that sitteth upon the throne, and unto the Lamb for ever and ever" (Rev. 5:12–13). The Lord Almighty is depicted as having all power over all the unfolding epochs of mortal history from the beginning to the end—as archived in the book with the seven seals: "We are to understand," explained the Prophet Joseph Smith, "that it [the book] contains the revealed will, mysteries, and the works of God; the hidden things of his economy concerning this earth during the seven thousand years of its continuance, or its temporal existence" (D&C 77:6). John recorded what transpired as each of the seven seals was opened by the Lord, revealing the events relating to each succeeding period of a thousand years (see Rev. chapter 6), leading to the period of the Restoration, associated with the sixth seal when the Saints who overcome all things through the Lord are enabled to serve Him forever in peace and light: "Therefore are they before the throne of God, and serve him day and night in his temple: and he that sitteth on the throne shall dwell among them. They shall hunger no more, neither thirst any more; neither shall the sun light on them, nor any heat. For the Lamb which is in the midst of the throne shall feed them, and shall lead them unto living fountains of waters: and God shall wipe away all tears from their eyes" (Rev. 7:15–17).

In contrast to this vista of rapture and bliss, we are also shown by John the raging evil of Satan and his hordes during the period of the seventh seal, prior to the Second Coming, as they amass in battle to destroy the agency of man and thwart the design of God and the Lamb to bring to pass the immortality and eternal life of mankind (see Rev. 8–9, 11–13, 16–18). The fuming and insidious machinations of Satan in the last days are but an intensified reflection of his rebellion in the premortal realm, when a third of the hosts of heaven were cast down: "And the great dragon was cast out, that old serpent, called the Devil, and Satan, which deceiveth the whole world: he was cast out into the earth, and his angels were cast out with him" (Rev. 12:9). But as the chronicle of John unfolds, we are to see that evil will ultimately be trumped by the power and glory of God and the Son, and that Satan and his minions will again be cast out—this time forever. Thus the theme of Revelation—that God is ever in control of the design of "the salvation of man" (D&C 77:12)—shines through these pages to illuminate the panorama of the destined triumph of goodness and truth over hatred and evil.

Harold B. Lee describes the devil and his ways to destroy the souls of mankind:

> He plans to destroy the agency of man. That was the issue in the contest which
> resulted in his expulsion with the third of the hosts of heaven. Moses declared that
> he is here "to destroy the agency of man" (Moses 4:3). . . .
> Satan's second purpose is to possess the bodies of Adam and his posterity. . . .
>
>   The third purpose of Satan, which is described carefully and accurately in the
> scriptures, was to make captive the souls of men (see Alma 34:35; 2 Ne. 26:22)
> (*THBL*, 37–38)

> Don't have any mistaken ideas about the devil. We sometimes rule out the possibility
> of evil and the power of the devil taking possession of a man's body or a woman's
> body and turning one from saint to sinner or from a normal person into a demon.
> You cannot tell me that there isn't such a thing as a devil possessing the body of a
> person who allows himself to take a course that makes that possible. If you forget
> everything else I have said today, please remember, young people, that the prince of
> this world, Satan, is going to try to trap every one of you. That is his program. He
> is trying to destroy our agency. If he can get you going along the path of taking a
> smoke, taking a drink, listening to sensuous music, or accepting in any degree an
> invitation that leads downward, he will take you to the bottom of the canyon on that
> road of sin to a place where no sunlight can be seen. But even in the deep canyon
> of sin there can come the refining process of repentance that can take you back to
> the sunlight of forgiveness. It may be a long, tortuous climb—slow and painful.
> (*THBL*, 40–41)

MODERN PROPHETS SPEAK

Wilford Woodruff:

> This arch enemy of God and man, called the devil, the "Son of the Morning," who
> dwells here on the earth, is a personage of great power; he has great influence and
> knowledge. He understands that if this kingdom, which he rebelled against in heaven,
> prevails on the earth, there will be no dominion here for him. He has great influ-
> ence over the children of men; he labors continually to destroy the works of God in
> heaven, and he had to be cast out. He is here, mighty among the children of men.
> There is a vast number of fallen spirits, cast out with him, here on the earth. They
> do not die and disappear; they have not bodies only as they enter the tabernacles of
> men. They have not organized bodies, and are not to be seen with the sight of the
> eye. But there are many evil spirits amongst us, and they labor to overthrow the
> church and kingdom of God. There never was a prophet in any age of the world but

what the devil was continually at his elbow. This was the case with Jesus himself. The devil followed him continually trying to draw him from his purposes and to prevent him carrying out the great word of God. . . .

This same character was with the disciples as well as with their master. He is with the Latter-day Saints; and he or his emissaries are with all men trying to lead them astray. He rules in the hearts of the inhabitants of the earth. They are governed and guided by him far more than by the power of God. This is strange, still it is true. See the wickedness in the world. See the abominations with which the earth is deluged, causing it to groan under the burden. Where does this evil come from? From the works of the devil. Everything that leads to good is from God, while everything that leads to evil is from the devil. Here are the two powers. (*The Discourses of Wilford Woodruff*, ed. G. Homer Durham [Salt Lake City: Bookcraft, 1969], 237–39)

ILLUSTRATIONS FOR OUR TIME

An Opposition in All Things

The Book of Revelation, written by John the Beloved at the Lord's command, is a compelling mixture of opposites juxtaposed in stark contradistinction: evil and good, death and life, destruction and renewal, tyranny and liberation, condemnation and sanctification—all unfolding before our eyes in a panoramic vision with one central theme: God is in control of the destiny of mankind to bring to pass the ultimate triumph of His plan of redemption and salvation. We are not shocked by the chiaroscuro of this narrative with its intertwining shades of abysmal dark and celestial light because our mortal life experience reflects a parallel blending of opposites. In the midst of the most edifying and transporting spiritual events that we are blessed to experience, we are all too often surprised by the sudden and unexpected incursions of worldly debasement. Around each corner, it seems, the forces of evil lie in wait to deceive and detract—all the more so since the time is short and Satan and his followers know that they must act in all haste to further their sinister designs before it is too late. Our lives are thus punctuated with temptations galore, the enticements of worldly entanglements, the constant beckoning of that which is carnal and degrading. Only through a definitive commitment to that which is holy and sacred can we hope to invite into our lives the overwhelming illumination of the Holy Spirit, which alone can open the way through the valley of mortal shadows toward the light of celestial glory. The revelations of the Lord through His prophets—including John's extraordinary chronicle—are the sure milestones along way to perfection.

Many years ago, I had an experience that brought home to me the fact that "it must needs be, that there is an opposition in all things" (2 Ne. 2:11). It was at a time when there were relatively few operating temples in the world. A small group of Latter-day Saints, of which I was a participant, had visited an institution on the outskirts of Basel, Switzerland, where an art exposition on biblical themes was being shown. We found the display characterized (to quote from my journal) by "bright greens and yellows and hideous satanic characters and forms." The effect of these bizarre configurations combined with the strange asymmetrical structures of the edifice in which they were housed to produce a most constricting and unsettling feeling in us, and several members of our group became physically ill and had to leave the site.

What happened next has become an enduring memory in my archive of cherished insights. The journal continues: "We ourselves didn't realize what an impression it [the art exposition and gallery] had made on us until we approached several hours later a small town just outside of Bern and saw through the trees the spire of an unusual edifice. The contrast between what we had experienced before and now the Swiss Temple was so great that it really opened our eyes. Truly this magnificent building nestled among the trees overlooking the white Alps on the horizon is a testimony of the order of heaven. What perfect symmetry and grace! We felt immediately a spirit of peace and serenity as we viewed the temple and read the inscription 'Holiness to the Lord.' How grateful we were to be members of His Church and possess the knowledge of His gospel!"

The peace and quiet within these walls is truly spiritually refreshing. The endowment of truth there dispensed quenches the thirst to learn the principles of the eternities: "But unto him that keepeth my commandments I will give the mysteries of my kingdom, and the same shall be in him a well of living water, springing up unto everlasting life" (D&C 63:23). At the end of the Book of Revelation, John uses similar language in quoting the Savior: "I Jesus have sent mine angel to testify unto you these things in the churches. I am the root and the offspring of David, and the bright and morning star. And the Spirit and the bride say, Come. And let him that heareth say, Come. And let him that is athirst come. And whosoever will, let him take the water of life freely" (Rev. 22:16–17). In light of this comforting doctrine, we can savor the precious experiences of life—such as the contrast we felt in Switzerland that day between the dark and the light—for they generate tranquility and joy: "And all thy children shall be taught of the Lord; and great shall be the peace of thy children" (3 Ne. 22:13). [Allen]

LIKENING THE SCRIPTURES TO OUR LIVES

2 Nephi 28:19–22 For the kingdom of the devil must shake, and they which belong to it must needs be stirred up unto repentance, or the devil will grasp them with his everlasting chains, and they be stirred up to anger, and perish; For behold, at that day shall he rage in the hearts of the children of men, and stir them up to anger against that which is good. And others will he pacify, and lull them away into carnal security, that they will say: All is well in Zion; yea, Zion prospereth, all is well—and thus the devil cheateth their souls, and leadeth them away carefully down to hell. And behold, others he flattereth away, and telleth them there is no hell; and he saith unto them: I am no devil, for there is none—and thus he whispereth in their ears, until he grasps them with his awful chains, from whence there is no deliverance.

Application: This is war. The devil is real and he seeks to destroy us. We must prepare for and resist the temptations of the devil by putting on the armor of God (see Eph. 6:11–17; D&C 27:15–18), holding to the iron rod (see 1 Ne. 15:24; Hel. 3:29), and praying for strength, protection, and deliverance (see Alma 13:28–30; 3 Ne. 18:18).

2. THE MILLENNIUM—THE LORD REIGNS AND SATAN IS BOUND

THEME: Wickedness and tribulation will be rampant prior to the Second Coming, which will usher in the millennial reign of our Savior Jesus Christ. At that point, Satan will be bound for a thousand years. At the end of the millennium, Satan will be loosed for a little season before he and his hordes are banished forever.

MOMENT OF TRUTH

John viewed the events associated with the Restoration of the gospel of Jesus Christ in the last days through angelic ministrations: "And I saw another angel fly in the midst of heaven, having the everlasting gospel to preach unto them that dwell on the earth, and to every nation, and kindred, and tongue, and people, Saying with a loud voice, Fear God, and give glory to him; for the hour of his judgment is come: and worship him that made heaven, and earth, and the sea, and the fountains of waters" (Rev. 14:6–7). Following the Restoration, and at the dawning of the millennial reign of the Savior, Satan will be bound: "And I saw an angel come down from heaven, having the key of the bottomless pit and a great chain in his hand. And he laid hold on the dragon, that old serpent, which is the Devil, and Satan, and bound him a thousand years, And cast him into the bottomless pit, and shut him up, and set a seal upon him, that he should deceive the nations no more, till the thousand years should be fulfilled: and after that he must be loosed a little season" (Rev. 20:1–3).

At the end of the thousand-year period, Satan will again be allowed to rage for a season and gather his armies of evil about the city of God: "And they went up on the breadth of the earth, and compassed the camp of the saints about, and the beloved city: and fire came down from God out of heaven, and devoured them. And the devil that deceived them was cast into the lake of fire and brimstone, where the beast and the false prophet are, and shall be tormented day and night for ever and ever" (Rev. 20:9–10). Until that day, the Saints of God are to toil in service to the cause of light and truth, keeping themselves unspotted and free of the stain of evil as they magnify their callings to build up the kingdom of God in the last days.

MODERN PROPHETS SPEAK

Gordon B. Hinckley:

> Certainly there is no point in speculating concerning the day and the hour. Let us rather live each day so that if the Lord does come while we yet are upon the earth we shall be worthy of that change which will occur as in the twinkling of an eye and under which we shall be changed from mortal to immortal beings. And if we should die before he comes, then—if our lives have conformed to his teachings—we shall arise in that resurrection morning and be partakers of the marvelous experiences designed for those who shall live and work with the Savior in that promised Millennium. We need not fear the day of his coming; the very purpose of the Church is to provide the incentive and the opportunity for us to conduct our lives in such a way that those who are members of the kingdom of God will become members of the kingdom of heaven when he establishes that kingdom on the earth. (*TGBH,* 576)

LIKENING THE SCRIPTURES TO OUR LIVES

D&C 29:11 For I will reveal myself from heaven with power and great glory, with all the hosts thereof, and dwell in righteousness with men on earth a thousand years, and the wicked shall not stand.

Application: To be with the Savior and partake of His glory during the millennial reign should be incentive enough to live a righteous life. The blessings and joy of serving others in the great work of the temples that will be accomplished during this period of time should fill our souls with joy (see D&C 18:10–16). Remember: every soul is precious.

3. THE LAST JUDGMENT—THE RIGHTEOUS WILL DWELL WITH GOD

THEME: At the final and last judgment, we will be judged out of the books (see Rev. 20:12). If we prove ourselves worthy, becoming just men and women and obtaining a state of righteousness, we will dwell with God forever.

MOMENT OF TRUTH

John's vision of the last days is consummated in the account of the final judgment: "And I saw the dead, small and great, stand before God; and the books were opened: and another book was opened, which is the book of life: and the dead were judged out of those things which were written in the books, according to their works" (Rev. 20:12). Those who were not written in the book of life were "cast into the lake of fire" (v. 15). The glorious blessings enjoyed by those found to be righteous surpass all understanding:

> And I heard a great voice out of heaven saying, Behold, the tabernacle of God is with men, and he will dwell with them, and they shall be his people, and God himself shall be with them, and be their God.
>
> And God shall wipe away all tears from their eyes; and there shall be no more death, neither sorrow, nor crying, neither shall there be any more pain: for the former things are passed away.
>
> And he that sat upon the throne said, Behold, I make all things new. And he said unto me, Write: for these words are true and faithful.
>
> And he said unto me, It is done. I am Alpha and Omega, the beginning and the end. I will give unto him that is athirst of the fountain of the water of life freely.
>
> He that overcometh shall inherit all things; and I will be his God, and he shall be my son. (Rev. 21:3–7)

John ends his account of the revelation granted to him by outlining the promises that await the faithful and valiant of the Lord's children, promises that are beyond comprehension for their glory and the supernal joy they bring:

> And they shall see his face; and his name shall be in their foreheads.
>
> And there shall be no night there; and they need no candle, neither light of the sun; for the Lord God giveth them light: and they shall reign for ever and ever.
>
> And he said unto me, These sayings are faithful and true: and the Lord God of the holy prophets sent his angel to shew unto his servants the things which must shortly be done.
>
> Behold, I come quickly: blessed is he that keepeth the sayings of the prophecy of this book. . . .
>
> And, behold, I come quickly; and my reward is with me, to give every man according as his work shall be.
>
> I am Alpha and Omega, the beginning and the end, the first and the last.
>
> Blessed are they that do his commandments, that they may have right to the tree of life, and may enter in through the gates into the city. . . .

And the Spirit and the bride say, Come. And let him that heareth say, Come. And let him that is athirst come. And whosoever will, let him take the water of life freely. (Rev. 22:4–7, 12–14, 17)

MODERN PROPHETS SPEAK

Neal A. Maxwell:

> Part of the basis for demonstrating the perfection of God's justice and mercy will thus be the cumulative record which we ourselves will have made (see Alma 41:7). Out of this we can be justly judged, a judgment that will include our compliance with outward gospel ordinances with all their respective covenants. (*Lord, Increase Our Faith* [Salt Lake City: Bookcraft, 1994], 75)

ILLUSTRATIONS FOR OUR TIME

Preparing for the Second Coming

As we will be judged by the standards of the gospel of Jesus Christ, here are several points to ponder concerning our preparation for the Second Coming: How are we doing in that regard? Do our deeds reflect a life patterned after the Lord Jesus Christ? Are our works works of righteousness? Do we pass the test of Alma chapter 5? Are our thoughts pure? What are the desires of our hearts?

We should take the time to evaluate our lives. Let us all set some goals and make some plans on how we intend to keep the commandments, live a Christlike life, and serve our fellowmen. Let us commit ourselves to take seriously the thirteenth Article of Faith: "We believe in being honest, true, chaste, benevolent, virtuous, and in doing good to all men; indeed, we may say that we follow the admonition of Paul—We believe all things, we hope all things, we have endured many things, and hope to be able to endure all things. If there is anything virtuous, lovely, or of good report or praiseworthy, we seek after these things" [Pinegar]

LIKENING THE SCRIPTURES TO OUR LIVES

Alma 41:3 And it is requisite with the justice of God that men should be judged according to their works; and if their works were good in this life, and the desires of their hearts were good, that they should also, at the last day, be restored unto that which is good.

Application: Let us remember that we will be judged out of the books—by the standards of the gospel in relation to our recorded deeds. We also will be judged according to the desires of our hearts. We are a result of our thoughts and desires. We do eventually act upon them and they become our "works." If we are good, the doctrine of restoration is clear: we receive good for being good (see Alma 41:3–15).

SUMMARY

The Lord's work is to "bring to pass the immortality and eternal life of man" (Moses 1:39). The vast design of God's plan of salvation is revealed in grandeur in the Revelation of John, serving as it does as a kind of epilogue and summation of all the declarations of God's holy prophets down through time. Our role within this heavenly design is clear: "Behold, this is your work, to keep my commandments, yea, with all your might, mind and strength" (D&C 11:20). How well we perform our labors in faith and obedience will determine the outcomes of our mortal experience. Our task is to overcome Satan, the enemy of all righteousness, and prepare for the coming of the millennial reign where the Lord will rule in glory and power and Satan will be bound. By virtue of the last and final judgment, each individual will come to know his or her ultimate resting place, either among those of a lesser glory or of outer darkness, or among those who will dwell in celestial precincts with the Father and the Son forever and ever. Through the strength of the Lord we can prevail and rise in majesty as the "children of the prophets" and the "children of the covenant" (3 Ne. 20:25–26), redeemed through the grace and mercy of the Lord to live with Him in everlasting peace and rest—"which rest is the fulness of his glory" (D&C 84:24).

THEMES FOR LIVING INDEX

ABOUT THE AUTHORS

ED J. PINEGAR is a retired dentist and long-time teacher of early-morning seminary and religion classes at Brigham young University. He taught at the Joseph Smith Academy and has served as a mission president in England and at the Missionary Training Center in Provo, Utah. He has been a bishop twice and a stake president and is a temple sealer. Ed and his wife, Patricia, are the parents of eight children and reside in Orem, Utah.

RICHARD ALLEN is a husband, father, teacher, and writer. He has served on several high councils, in several stake presidencies, and as a bishop. Richard's teaching assignments in the Church have included service as a full-time missionary, instructor in various priesthood quorums, gospel doctrine teacher, and stake institute director. He has served as a faculty member at both Brigham Young University and The Johns Hopkins University. Richard has coauthored many articles, manuals, and books and has served on a number of national educational boards. He and his wife, Carol Lynn Hansen Allen, have four children and five grandchildren.